Following the Fairways

Robert Wade **THE FINAL HAZARD** *Rosenstiel's*

Front Cover: **Craig Campbell** **DOWN THE MIDDLE** *De Montfort Art*

Back Cover: **Craig Campbell** **AN EAGLE PUTT** *De Montfort Art*

KENSINGTON WEST PRODUCTIONS
LONDON
ENGLAND

ACKNOWLEDGEMENTS

There have been all manner of hands that have guided the production of this, our updated, revised and considerably expanded sixth edition of Following the Fairways.

The company acknowledges the kind and generous advice of many golf professionals, secretaries and enthusiasts from all parts of Great Britain and Ireland. It is only by constant updating that a guide of this type maintains its value.

In our endeavour to illustrate the book, we have been kindly assisted by the Burlington Gallery, Rosenstiel's and other passionate collectors of golfing memorabilia. The colour work is all credited and we are most grateful to all our featured artists for kindly allowing us permission to use their works.

We greatly appreciate the assistance of the many people who helped us in selecting hotels, restaurants and pubs around the country. We are confident that you will relish savouring some of our suggestions, but do please let us know if you come across one that you can recommend.

As publisher, I would also like to thank the staff at Kensington West Productions for their hard work, dedication and enormous enthusiasm for the task which enabled us to meet our tight schedules. The company is greatly indebted to a legion of typists who put together all the facts, figures and fairways collated in this book.

I would like to thank Peter Alliss for penning our foreword, his dulcet tones are renowned and respected throughout the golfing world. It is a great bonus to have such a passionate enthusiast for the game add his sentiments to this work which has lovingly been compiled, written and of course researched!

Finally, I would like to thank Nick Edmund who is author of all the golf editorial, for his tremendous efforts in providing such distinguished copy and I thank all those companies who have helped with the production for their accomplished work.

Julian West

Kensington West Productions Ltd
338 Old York Road, Wandsworth, London, SW18 1SS
Tel : 081 877 9394, Fax: 081 870 4270

Editor
Nick Edmund

Consultant Editors
Janet Blair, Nova Jayne Heath, David MacLaren

Hotel Editors
Giles Appleton, Sally Conner, Jacqui Hawthorn

Cartography
Camilla Charnock, Craig Semple

Typesetting
Bookman Ltd., 2C Merrywood Road, Bristol
Wandsworth Typesetting Ltd., 205a St Johns Hill, London

Origination
Trinity Graphics (Hong Kong)

Printing
Nordica Printing Co. Ltd. (Hong Kong)

FOREWORD

Golf is really an extraordinary pedestrian, some say, fuddy duddy game. But then any game when analysed to the enth degree has a modicom of nonsense. Grown people cavorting about in such a way...tut..tut..tut! But, at least even if the golf is poor it does take us to so many beautiful places. 'Following the Fairways', is a beautifully constructed book, which has page after page of interesting information, stories and, if not exactly encyclopedic, it's one that should have a place in any travelling golfer's library. Places to go and things to see in great abundance.

There are so many corners of Britain and Ireland where the hand of publicity has not really touched but 'Following the Fairways' has discovered. Many people think I have played on almost every golf course in the UK but I doubt I've played on 10% and I'm always finding new gems – Thorpeness was my latest discovery in Suffolk and I've still to play Aldeburgh but that is a pleasure I hope only delayed!

So whether it be Suffolk, Cornwall, Scotland, along the Solway Firth, Wales or Ireland, gems abound, I only wish I could put the clock back 30 years and do it all over again, armed of course with this magic manuscript! Oh golf – you are indeed a strange and wondrous thing; please never grow old!

Peter Alliss

Frank Paton **ROYAL AND ANCIENT** *Rosenstiel's*

3

INTRODUCTION

Welcome to Following the Fairways 1993. This is the 6th edition of a year book first published in October 1986. The book's content and structure has changed considerably over the years: for one thing it has almost doubled in size! Probably the main reason for the increased pagination is the inclusion of a greater number of featured 'Championship Courses'. In the first edition, 'Following the Fairways 1987', 52 courses were so highlighted; in Following the Fairways 1993 we have finally reached 100. Perhaps the other major change since 1986/87 has been the addition of Irish golf courses: Following the Fairways 1987 was a purely British affair – now almost a quarter of the book is devoted to a study of golf in the Emerald Isle.

Although the content of Following the Fairways may have changed considerably in the past six years, the underlying philosophy behind the book has not. Following the Fairways seeks to guide the golfer (and his or her non golfing partner) in a leisurely and colourful way around the golf courses of Great Britain and Ireland, recommending the finest 18 holes – links, parkland, cliff top and heathland, and the finest 19th holes – places to eat, drink and sleep, along the way.

Naturally we have to be fairly selective with our 19th hole suggestions, however on the golfing front we are able to·be both selective and comprehensive. For easy reference the book is divided into 30 'golfing areas' each with its own attractive, hand drawn map. Every golf course within the area is included in a detailed directory section which we term **'Complete Golf'**. For each club there is a telephone number, address, course yardages, together with approximate green fees, visitor policy and location guide. Some 2,000 golf clubs are listed. Over 700 of these golf courses, and perhaps twice as many nearby hotels, inns and restaurants are recommended and highlighted in the main body of the golf area text – this is the '**Choice Golf**' section. This is supplemented by '**Gourmet Golf**', a wide and varied selection of more modest establishments – mostly – where comfortable accommodation can be found at reasonable prices.

Many of the leading golf courses of Great Britain and Ireland are given special attention, each having an entire page of text with an accompanying course plan. This is the aforementioned '**Championship Golf**' collection and within the 100 are all the great courses of Britain and Ireland from Sunningdale to St Andrews and from Turnberry to Ballybunion and Woodhall Spa. All details relating to these entries are carefully revised each year. In addition to the 'greats' many lesser known but beautifully situated courses are also featured in this section – places which we believe no holidaying golfer would want to miss – for instance Bamburgh Castle in Northumberland, Machrihanish on the Mull of Kintyre, Connemara in Co. Galway and the spectacular Isle of Purbeck course in Dorset. Overall we think it is a well balanced 100 – so 'balanced' in fact that it comprises exactly 50 links courses, and 50 inland or non links types.

★　★　★　★

It is interesting, and many might say alarming, to see how green fees have risen since Following the Fairways was first published. The increase hasn't been limited to the bigger clubs, rather it is across the board and in every area of Great Britain and Ireland. In a six year period green fees have risen by an average of almost 300 per cent. (At some famous courses the fees have actually risen more than four fold.) As it is also becoming increasingly difficult to arrange a weekend visit to a golf course unless accompanied by a member from that club (never mind the handicap certificate), let's all hope that included in the plethora of new courses planned for the next few years we have a larger number of good quality, inexpensive 'pay and play' venues.

★　★　★　★

Returning to Following the Fairways 1993, we very much hope that you enjoy our ever growing collection of golfing art. If only to be different, we have chosen to illustrate the main body of the text with pictures rather than photographs. The work reproduced ranges from some of the earliest golfing classics to specially commissioned fine art (prints of which incidentally, are available from the publishers of this book). As well as exploring the finest courses of Great Britain and Ireland, Following the Fairways 1993 also includes, for the first time, a ranking table of our top courses (something that is certain to be contentious!) and a 'Golf Club of the Year' award.

On a personal note, as editor I would like to thank everyone who has helped me compile the golf text and I am, of course, very grateful to Peter Alliss for penning such an excellent Foreword to this edition. Finally I would like to thank my wife, Teresa, for continuing to put up with my golfing wanderlust and wish you, the reader, a successful 1993 as you Follow the Fairways enjoying this wonderful game.

Nick Edmund
Editor
July, 1992

KILLARNEY
FOLLOWING THE FAIRWAYS GOLF CLUB OF THE YEAR

In a seriously religious country there can surely be no greater compliment for a place than for it to be known as 'Heaven's Reflex'. Killarney is where the hills and mountains of Co. Kerry slip into the clear blue waters of the lakes of Co. Kerry. It is quite simply shatteringly beautiful. In golfing terms Killarney has long been known as 'The Gleneagles of Ireland'. 'Only a man devoid of soul could apply his mind to playing championship golf at Killarney' observed the late Henry Longhurst.

Yet despite all the compliments – and to some extent because of them – as little as five years ago the first-time visitor to Killarney Golf and Fishing Club might have left just a shade disappointed. Very good golf yes, but golf worthy of the surroundings? The two 18 hole courses, Mahony's Point and the Killeen had several outstanding holes, especially perhaps the closing sequence of Mahony's Point, but neither the overall quality of the golfing challenge nor the condition of the courses would have scored ten out of ten. But since the late 1980s the golf has been worthy of the surroundings and the Killarney Golf and Fishing Club has undergone a seachange.

Firstly, there is the magnificent new clubhouse – possibly the best, certainly the best appointed in all Ireland. Looking back from the 1st and 3rd greens of the Killeen Course this splendidly designed building appears to be almost floating in Lough Leane. Secondly, there is the extraordinary transformation of the Killeen Course from something of a gentle 'holiday course' into a beautifully sculptured, genuine Championship test – one good enough to host the Carroll's Irish Open in 1991 and 1992, victory in each instance going to the world's best golfer, Nick Faldo.

For these two reasons alone Killarney might merit our inaugural Following the Fairways Golf Club of the Year Award. But there are other reasons. In 1996 the Mahony's Point Course is due to stage the Curtis Cup and the plan is to upgrade the 18 holes so that it is once again the equal of the Killeen: a truly mouth watering prospect. There are also plans to build a third course at Killarney. The Club receives visitors from many countries of Europe and America and I dare say that the green fee income amounts to a considerable sum! But it is refreshing to see a Club ploughing back so much of the profits into enhancing and extending the quality of the golf and the accompanying 19th hole facilities. The visiting fees at Killarney are in fact very reasonable, which leads us to the visitor-friendly aspect: no Club could be more welcoming than Killarney; here is where the Irish greeting 'Cead Mile Failte' (a hundred thousand welcomes) is genuinely apparent and maybe that it is the best reason of all for choosing Killarney as our Golf Club of the Year.

Nick Jones   *'What a lovely place to die!'*

CONTENTS

*F. Hopkins   **THE TEE SHOT AT WESTWARD HO!***
Burlington Gallery

Following the Fairways
Choice Golf

Inverness

GRAMPIAN & HIGHLAND Aberdeen

TAYSIDE & CENTRAL

Perth Dundee

FIFE

Edinburgh

Glasgow LOTHIAN

STRATHCLYDE DUMFRIES GALLOWAY
& BORDERS

Newcastle-Upon-Tyne

Carlisle

CUMBRIA & THE
NORTH EAST

Belfast

N·IRELAND ISLE OF MAN YORKSHIRE & HUMBERSIDE

NORTHWEST
IRELAND DUBLIN & THE LANCASHIRE & York
NORTH Dublin THE ISLE OF MAN Leeds Hull
SOUTHWEST EAST Manchester
IRELAND SOUTH EAST Liverpool Sheffield LINCOLNSHIRE,
IRELAND NOTTINGHAMSHIRE
ANGLESEY CHESHIRE, & DERBYSHIRE
Cork NORTH WALES
STAFFORDSHIRE Leicester Norwich
& SHROPSHIRE
Birmingham EAST EAST ANGLIA
&
GLOUCESTERSHIRE, WEST MIDLANDS
SOUTH & MID HEREFORD BUCKS HERTS, BEDS & ESSEX
WALES & WORCS OXON
Swansea & GTR LONDON
Cardiff Bristol BERKSHIRE & London
SOMERSET SURREY KENT
AVON, DORSET HAMPSHIRE
& WILTS & CHANNEL
DEVON Southampton ISLES SUSSEX
Exeter Portsmouth
ISLE OF WIGHT
CORNWALL Plymouth
Penzance
CHANNEL ISLES

CONTENTS

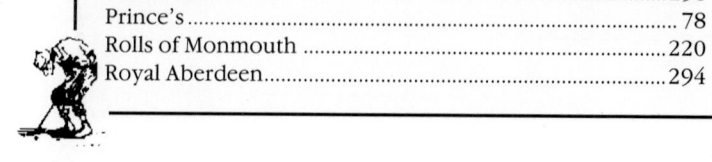

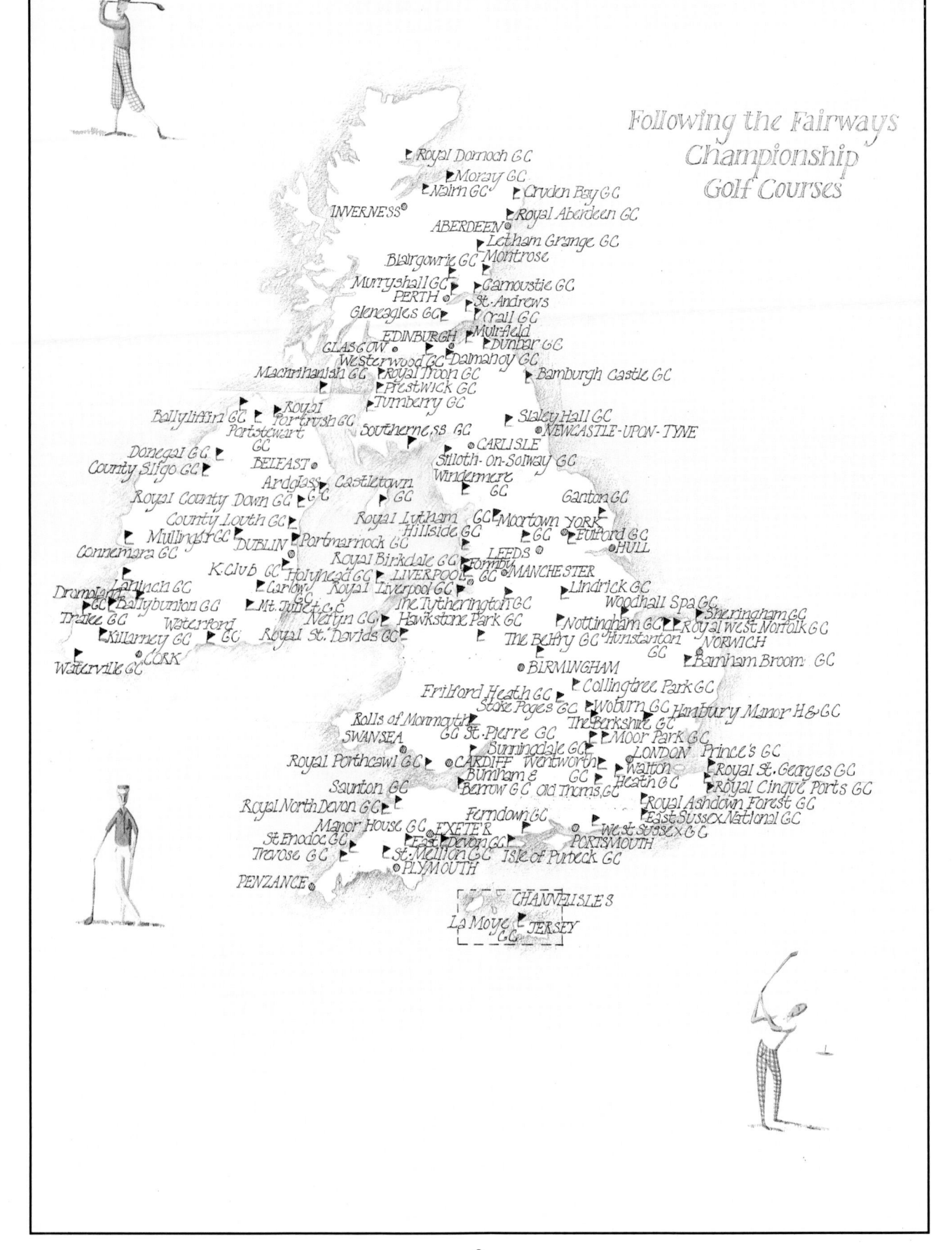

Following the Fairways
Championship
Golf Courses

Royal Dornoch G.C.
Moray G.C.
Nairn G.C. Cruden Bay G.C.
INVERNESS Royal Aberdeen G.C.
ABERDEEN Letham Grange G.C.
Blairgowrie G.C. Montrose
Murrayshall G.C. Carnoustie G.C.
PERTH St. Andrews
Gleneagles G.C. Crail G.C.
EDINBURGH Muirfield
GLASGOW Dunbar G.C.
Westerwood G.C. Dalmahoy G.C.
Machrihanish G.C. Royal Troon G.C. Bamburgh Castle G.C.
Prestwick G.C.
Turnberry G.C.
Royal Slaley Hall G.C.
Ballyliffin G.C. Portrush G.C. NEWCASTLE-UPON-TYNE
Portstewart Southerness G.C.
GC CARLISLE
Donegal G.C. Silloth-On-Solway G.C.
County Sligo G.C. BELFAST Windermere
Ardglass Castletown GC Ganton G.C.
Royal County Down G.C. GC GC
County Louth G.C. Royal Lytham GC Moortown YORK
Mullingar G.C. Hillside GC GC Fulford G.C.
Connemara G.C. DUBLIN Portmarnock G.C. LEEDS HULL
K. Club G.C. Holyhead G.C. Royal Birkdale G.C. Formby Lindrick G.C.
Dromoland La Hinch G.C. Carlow Royal Liverpool G.C. GC MANCHESTER
GC Ballybunion G.C. Mt. Juliet C.C. The Tytherington G.C. Woodhall Spa G.C. Sheringham G.C.
Tralee G.C. Nefyn G.C. Hawkstone Park G.C. Nottingham G.C. Royal West Norfolk G.C.
Killarney G.C. Waterford Royal St. Davids G.C. The Belfry G.C. Hunstanton NORWICH
Waterville G.C. CORK GC GC Barnham Broom G.C.
BIRMINGHAM
Frilford Heath G.C. Collingtree Park G.C.
Stoke Poges G.C. Woburn G.C. Hanbury Manor H&GC
Rolls of Monmouth The Berkshire G.C.
SWANSEA GC St. Pierre G.C. Moor Park G.C.
Sunningdale G.C. LONDON Prince's G.C.
Royal Porthcawl G.C. CARDIFF Wentworth Walton Royal St. Georges G.C.
Burnham & GC Heath G.C. Royal Cinque Ports G.C.
Saunton G.C. Barrow G.C. Old Thorns G.C. Royal Ashdown Forest G.C.
Royal North Devon G.C. Ferndown G.C. East Sussex National G.C.
Manor House G.C. EXETER West Sussex G.C.
St. Enodoc G.C. East Devon G.C. PORTSMOUTH
Trevose G.C. St. Mellion G.C. Isle of Purbeck G.C.
PENZANCE PLYMOUTH
CHANNEL ISLES
La Moye JERSEY
G.C.

9

OUR GREATEST GOLF COURSES
A PERSONAL VIEW BY THE EDITOR NICK EDMUND

To play the two finest links courses in the British Isles an Englishman must first cross the Irish Sea and if he, or she, wishes to play the best inland course then a trip to the heart of Lincolnshire must be arranged. Well, that's my opinion, and I've probably lost all my golfing friends from Scotland and Surrey!

The idea of ranking courses is not an original one; currently the most authoritative list for Great Britain and Ireland is the one published biennially by Golf World magazine. However if there is novelty in the Following the Fairways' listings it is that in addition to offering a 'Top 20' I have also tried to separate the best links courses from the best inland or non-links type courses: comparing the Old Course at St Andrews with the Nicklaus Course at St Mellion is surely a bit like trying to contrast a Rembrandt with a Picasso (and Sunningdale is a Monet, I hear you say). Before briefly discussing the first Following the Fairways rankings I should state what criteria were used when passing judgement on the relative merits of the courses:

A) The degree of challenge (test, quality of terrain) and variety offered.
B) The natural beauty of the situation and the sense of exhilaration when playing.
C) The feeling of 'occasion' experienced when playing – a mixture of history, tradition and reputation (which may be modern).
D) That difficult-to-define 'overall enjoyment' factor – perhaps a combination of A, B and C.
E) The general and normal condition of the course.

THE 'TOP 20'

I have probably exposed myself to criticism and argument on two main counts:

i) The precedence given to Irish courses – the top 2 positions; 4 in the top 10 and 7 in the top 20, and
ii) The inclusion of two 'golfing babes', namely East Sussex National (West) and Mount Juliet. How can courses which opened for play as recently as 1990 and 1991 respectively be considered top 20 material so quickly?

Golf World's ranking has traditionally included all 7 Open Championship courses in its top 20 and places Muirfield and Royal Birkdale at numbers 1 and 2 (positions 3 and 5 in the Following the Fairways list). Obviously I cannot climb inside the minds of the distinguished panel of voters but I suspect that it places a slightly greater emphasis on the element of history and tradition (our criterion C) than I have, while I am probably swayed a little more by the natural beauty/exhilaration factor (our criterion B). I dare say that it is not merely coincidental that if I were asked to name the course I considered the most beautifully situated in the British Isles it would be Royal Co. Down and the course that makes the pulse race faster than all others I would say Ballybunion. Not many I presume will quibble with Portmarnock and Portrush being in there, but Lahinch and Rosses Point? Well, in my view (and I had better mention that I haven't a single drop of Irish blood in me!) Lahinch is the supreme (or best) example of a classically natural links which winds its way through towering dunes and Rosses Point (Co. Sligo) has quite

the most stunning 360 degree backdrop.

And what of East Sussex National and the even newer Jack Nicklaus designed course at Mount Juliet in deepest Co. Kilkenny? To adopt the words of John Major, 'if you're good enough, you're old enough!' Both are maturing remarkably quickly and offer a truly magnificent 'modern' challenge, indeed in the case of East Sussex, two magnificent challenges, for in fact it is the East Course at East Sussex which will probably stage the 1993 European Open and is arguably the more testing of its two championship courses; however on account of its great variety and charm, I prefer the West.

THE TOP 40 LINKS COURSES

It is in the ranking of links courses that my predilection for Irish courses appears most marked. The inclusion of Tralee, The Island, Donegal, Ballyliffin and Portstewart may surprise many and of course it has meant that several fine Scottish courses have not made the Following the Fairways' 'Top 40' – this time at least!

Among those Scottish courses which just missed out were Gullane, Dunbar, North Berwick, Elie, Crail and four 'Ms' – Machrihanish, Murcar, Montrose and Moray. English traditionalists could also argue that St Annes Old Links, Westward Ho! and Prince's are worthy of inclusion and that Lytham, Hoylake, Brancaster and Deal (all 'Royal Clubs') merit higher rankings. And what about such classic 'holiday gems' as St Enodoc, Trevose, Bamburgh Castle and Holyhead (all featured in Following the Fairways)? Of course the problem with any 'Top 40' listing is that there should be at least 60 courses included within it!

THE TOP 40 INLAND/NON-LINKS COURSES

Two things should be noted with this list: firstly, it includes four courses – East Devon, Isle of Purbeck, Nefyn and Sheringham – which are not strictly 'inland courses', being laid out on cliffs overlooking the sea; however they are definitely not 'links' courses either and in terms of terrain have essentially, or predominantly inland characteristics. Secondly, I have rationed Golf Clubs to a 'one course inclusion' rule, hence Sunningdale, Wentworth, Gleneagles, East Sussex, The Berkshire, and perhaps one or two others who might feel that their 'second course' is worthy of a top 40 ranking will have to make do with one entry only!

THE FUTURE

It is our intention that the Following the Fairways' rankings will be regularly revised. On the next occasion it may be that English newcomers Hanbury Manor, Wisley and Bowood will make their way into the 'top 40'; Scotland's Loch Lomond too perhaps? And maybe from Ireland the recently opened layouts at St Margaret's and Slieve Russell will deserve to be included. The above mentioned are all inland courses and as for a bit of crystal ball gazing on the links front I fear I must once again return to the Emerald Isle (is there any undeveloped linksland left in Britain?) where great things are taking shape amidst the dunes of Belmullet (Co. Mayo) and at Brittas Bay, south of Dublin.

OUR GREATEST GOLF COURSES
A PERSONAL VIEW BY THE EDITOR NICK EDMUND

THE LEADING 20 COURSES IN GREAT BRITAIN AND IRELAND

1. **BALLYBUNION (OLD)**
2. **ROYAL CO. DOWN (NEWCASTLE)**
3. **MUIRFIELD**
4. **WOODHALL SPA**
5. **ROYAL BIRKDALE**
6. **PORTMARNOCK**
7. **ST ANDREWS (OLD)**
8. **SUNNINGDALE (OLD)**
9. **ROYAL PORTRUSH (DUNLUCE)**
10. **EAST SUSSEX NATIONAL (WEST)**
11. **ROYAL DORNOCH**
12. **HILLSIDE**
13. **TURNBERRY (AILSA)**
14. **GLENEAGLES (KINGS)**
15. **GANTON**
16. **MOUNT JULIET**
17. **LAHINCH**
18. **WENTWORTH (WEST)**
19. **WEST SUSSEX (PULBOROUGH)**
20. **CO. SLIGO (ROSSES POINT)**

TOP 40 LINKS COURSES

1. **Ballybunion**, Co. Kerry, Ireland
2. **Royal Co. Down**, Newcastle, Co. Down, N. Ireland
3. **Muirfield**, Gullane, Lothian, Scotland
4. **Royal Birkdale**, Southport, Merseyside, England
5. **Portmarnock**, Co. Dublin, Ireland
6. **St Andrews**, Fife, Scotland
7. **Royal Portrush**, Co. Antrim, N. Ireland
8. **Royal Dornoch**, Highland, Scotland
9. **Hillside**, Southport, Merseyside, England
10. **Turnberry**, Ayrshire, Scotland
11. **Lahinch**, Co. Clare, Ireland
12. **Co. Sligo**, Rosses Point, Co. Sligo, Ireland
13. **Carnoustie**, Tayside, Scotland
14. **Formby**, Merseyside, England
15. **Royal Porthcawl**, Mid Glamorgan, Wales
16. **Saunton**, Devon, England
17. **Waterville**, Co. Kerry, Ireland
18. **Co. Louth**, Baltray, Co. Louth, Ireland
19. **Royal St Georges**, Sandwich, Kent, England
20. **Royal Troon**, Ayrshire, Scotland
21. **Cruden Bay**, Grampian, Scotland
22. **Ballyliffin**, Co. Donegal, Ireland
23. **Nairn**, Highland, Scotland
24. **Rye**, East Sussex, England
25. **Tralee**, Co. Kerry, Ireland
26. **The Island**, Donabate, Co. Dublin, Ireland
27. **Royal Lytham**, Lancashire, England
28. **Southerness**, Dumfries & Scotland
29. **Royal Liverpool**, Hoylake, Cheshire, England
30. **Royal Aberdeen**, Grampian, Scotland
31. **Donegal**, Murvagh, Co. Donegal, Ireland
32. **Burnham and Berrow**, Somerset, England
33. **Western Gailes**, Ayrshire, Scotland
34. **Royal St Davids**, Harlech, Gwynedd, Wales
35. **Hunstanton**, Norfolk, England
36. **Portstewart**, Co. Londonderry, N. Ireland
37. **Silloth on Solway**, Cumbria, England
38. **Royal West Norfolk**, Brancaster, Norfolk, England
39. **Prestwick**, Ayrshire, Scotland
40. **Royal Cinque Ports**, Deal, Kent, England

TOP 40 INLAND/NON LINKS COURSES

1. **Woodhall Spa**, Lincolnshire, England
2. **Sunningdale**, Berkshire/Surrey, England
3. **East Sussex National**, Uckfield, E. Sussex, England
4. **Gleneagles**, Auchterarder, Perthshire, Scotland
5. **Ganton**, North Yorkshire, England
6. **Mount Juliet**, Thomastown, Co. Kilkenny, Ireland
7. **Wentworth**, Surrey, England
8. **West Sussex**, Pulborough, W. Sussex, England
9. **Killarney**, Co. Kerry, Ireland
10. **Walton Heath**, Tadworth, Surrey, England
11. **St Mellion**, Saltash, Cornwall, England
12. **Notts**, Hollinwell, Notts, England
13. **The Berkshire**, Ascot, Berkshire, England
14. **Woburn**, Bucks, England
15. **The K Club**, Straffan, Co. Kildare, Ireland
16. **Blairgowrie**, Rosemount, Perthshire, Scotland
17. **Lindrick**, South Yorkshire, England
18. **Carlow**, Co. Carlow, Ireland
19. **Slaley Hall**, Northumberland, England
20. **Royal Ashdown Forest**, Forest Row, E. Sussex, England
21. **Little Aston**, Sutton Coldfield, W. Midlands, England
22. **St George's Hill**, Weybridge, Surrey, England
23. **Frilford Heath**, Oxfordshire, England
24. **Swinley Forest**, Ascot, Berkshire, England
25. **The Belfry**, Sutton Coldfield, W. Midlands, England
26. **Moortown**, Leeds, West Yorkshire, England
27. **East Devon**, Budleigh Salterton, Devon, England
28. **Malone**, Belfast, N. Ireland
29. **Crowborough Beacon**, East Sussex, England
30. **Isle of Purbeck**, Swanage, Dorset, England
31. **Stoke Poges**, Bucks, England
32. **Alwoodley**, Leeds, West Yorkshire, England
33. **Nefyn & District**, Gwynedd, Wales
34. **Ferndown**, Dorset, England
35. **Letham Grange**, Tayside, Scotland
36. **Woking**, Surrey, England
37. **Mullingar**, Co. Westmeath, Ireland
38. **Collingtree Park**, Northants, England
39. **Dalmahoy**, Edinburgh, Lothian, Scotland
40. **Sheringham**, Norfolk, England

W.E.B   BUDLEIGH SALTERTON   Burlington Gallery

CORNWALL

MORWENSTOW
Bude & North Cornwall GC
BUDE
CRACKINGTON HAVEN

Launceston GC
LAUNCESTON

PORT ISAAC
St. Enodoc GC
Trevose G & GC   ROCK
ST. MERRYN   PADSTOW   ST. KEW

WADEBRIDGE

St. Mellion G & GC

ST. MAWGAN   BODMIN   ST MELLION

Newquay GC   SALTASH

NEWQUAY   Loswithiel G.C

Perranporth GC   CARLYON   GOLANT   Looe GC   TIDEFORD   Whitsand Bay
BAY   TALLAND   Hotel & GC
BY LOOE   EAST LOOE

MOUNT HAWKE   Truro   FOWEY   POLPERRO
Tehidy Park G.C   GC   St Austell GC   Carlyon Bay Hotel & G.C
ST. IVES   TRURO   TREGONWY
GARBIS BAY   West Cornwall   PHILLEIGH
G.C   MYLOR BRIDGE
PENZANCE   Budock Vean   ST. MAWES
Hotel & GC   FALMOUTH
Falmouth GC
LANDS END   HELFORD
MANACCAN
Mullion GC   MULLION

LIZARD POINT

G. Wallace   LINKS GOLF   Burlington Gallery

CORNWALL
CHOICE GOLF

'Brandy for the Parson, Baccy for the Clerk' – Cornwall is the land of the smuggler's cove. It is also the land of King Arthur and the Knights of the Round Table – a land of legends. To cross the Tamar is to enter foreign soil: for centuries the Cornish Celts had more in common with the Welsh and the French Bretons than the ever-invading Anglo Saxons. Well, the Anglo-Saxons still invade but nowadays in a more peaceful manner: 'grockles' they are called in Cornwall and they come in search of sun, sand and sea (not to mention holiday home!) But there is also a fairly recent addition, a sub-species commonly known as the 'golfing-grockle' who comes to Cornwall to seek out some of the finest golfing country in the Kingdom.

If one commences an imaginary tour by crossing the Tamar at Plymouth, **St Mellion** Golf and Country Club (0579) 50101 has surely to be the first port of call. It is one of the few places in Britain where one might bump into Jack Nicklaus. St Mellion, where there are two fine courses, one of which was designed by the great man, is featured later in this chapter. Not far away in Saltash, a new course has recently opened called **China Fleet**, apparently the Navy (British – not Oriental) is the guiding force behind it.

Heading westwards **Looe** Golf Club (formerly, Looe Bin Down) is situated on high ground to the north of Looe, near Widegates. An 18 hole moorland course it lies somewhat at the mercy of the elements and can get exceptionally windy. Not too far away at Portwinkle the **Whitsand Bay Hotel** (0503) 30276 is an ideal place to break a journey with its own 18 hole golf course stretching out along the cliffs and looking down over Whitsand Bay.

The area around Looe abounds with good hotels and restaurants with seafood not surprisingly a speciality. In Fowey, two restaurants to consider are The Food For Thought (072 683) 2221 and Cordon Bleu. Another hotel where the visitor can enjoy a little extra walking – on the cliffs as well as on the fairways is at Talland-on-Looe, The Talland Bay Hotel (0503) 72667. The Kitchen (0503) 72780 is an excellent restaurant in Polperro and finally, in Golant, The Cormorant Hotel (072 683) 3426 enjoys a glorious setting.

We'll now, if you'll pardon the expression, leave the Looe area and, still heading in a clock-wise direction set sail for St Austell where we find a twin attraction for golfers: the redoubtable **Carlyon Bay** and the **St Austell Golf Club**. The St Austell course is situated on the western edge of the town off the A390. Rather shorter than Carlyon Bay but with an ample spread of gorse and numerous bunkers, it possesses plenty of challenges and attractions of its own.

Carlyon Bay is surely one of Britain's best loved Hotel courses. Not a Turnberry or a Gleneagles perhaps, but very pleasing with several challenging holes and views over a number of beaches – one of which is frequented by naturists! St Austell is a pleasant place to spend a day or two and golfers of course may decide to stay at Carlyon Bay Hotel itself (0726) 812304. Obviously convenient and four-star comfort as well. As a first rate alternative though, Boscundle Manor (0726) 813557 at Tregrehan is highly recommended. The food alone is worth a trip. Heading northwards will bring one to the recently opened **Lostwithiel** Golf and Country Club (0208) 873550, where fine golf and agreeable accommodation are the order of the day.

Falmouth – a glorious harbour and seagulls aplenty. More good golf awaits. Like St Austell, there are two sets of fairways on which to exercise the swing (and maybe burn off all these extra calories we've accumulated!). They are to be found at the **Falmouth** Golf Club, south west of the town (fine cliff-top views over Falmouth Bay) and at **Budock Vean Hotel**. This latter course has only nine holes but plenty of variety and is exceptionally well-kept.

For hotels, Budock Vean (0326) 250288 takes pride of place but others to note include The Crill House (0326) 211880 and The Hotel St Michael's (0326) 312707. The opening words of The Wind in the Willows were written at The Greenbank (0326) 312440, clearly an inspiring place, while The Penmere Manor (0326) 211411 also has much to commend it. Three final thoughts for places to stay in this area are The Idle Rocks (0326) 270771 at St Mawes on the Roseland peninsula, The Rising Sun, also in St Mawes and the Meudon Hotel (0326) 250541 back in Falmouth.

Still heading down the coast, the course at **Mullion** is one of the short but sweet brigade. Situated seven miles south of Helston, it can lay claim to being the most southerly on the British mainland. Nestling around the cliff edges overlooking some particularly inviting sands and with distant views towards St Michael's Mount, Mullion typifies the charm of Cornish holiday golf. With the spectacular scenery of the Lizzard area, it's another good spot to spend a few days. In Mullion, or perhaps more precisely, Mullion Cove, Henscath House (0326) 240537 is perfect for the golf course. There is also a strong mention for The Riverside (032 623) 443 where there is some good accommodation and first rate cuisine.

Penzance is another place where people may wish to base themselves – golfers especially now that the 18 hole **Cape Cornwall** Golf and Country Club has been opened at nearby St. Just.

The **West Cornwall** Golf Club lies just beyond St Ives at Lelant. A beautiful and very natural old-fashioned type of links it was laid out a hundred years ago by the then Vicar of Lelant. Like St Enodoc, it is a genuine links course – sand dunes and plenty of sea breezes! – and quite short. Jim Barnes, who won both the Open and US Open was born in Lelant village.

In St Ives, two hotels to note are the Treganna Castle (0736) 795254 and The Garrack (0736) 796199 – ideal for the nearby cliffs and beaches as well as the golf course. Slightly further afield at Carbis Bay, The Boskerris Hotel (0736) 795295 is particularly friendly.

Passing numerous derelict tin and copper mines the inland course at **Tehidy Park** is soon reached. Located midway between Camborne and Portreath it presents a considerable contrast to the golf at Lelant: here we are amidst the pine trees, rhododendrons and bluebells – hopefully not right amidst them! Getting back to the coast, **Perranporth** and **Newquay** look closer on the map than they are by road. Both are links type courses with outstanding sea views. Not far away at St Mawgan a new 9 hole course, **Treloy**, has recently opened.

In Newquay, where the crash of the Atlantic waves offers a surfers paradise there are several welcoming establishments.

CORNWALL
CHOICE GOLF

The Atlantic Hotel (0637) 872244 is an ideal holiday base, as is The Hotel Bristol (0637) 875181. A less expensive but still superb option is The Priory Lodge Hotel (0637) 874111. Connoisseurs of the public house might care to visit The Falcon at St. Mawgan. Golfers at Tehidy might note the Tregarthan Country Cottage at Mount Hawke – quite small but friendly and good value.

Further along the coast lie two marvellous golfing challenges – **St Enodoc** at Rock and **Trevose** at Constantine Bay. They are often considered as a pair although in fact they are quite different in appearance. Trevose is the longer course but much more open and it doesn't possess the massive sandhills that are the feature of St Enodoc's links. Both are featured ahead.

The most convenient places for the golfing gourmet to stay are, at Trevose, the splendid Treglos Hotel (0841) 520727 and for St Enodoc, The St Enodoc Hotel (0208) 863394 in Rock and the St Morritz Hotel (0208) 862242 near Wadebridge. An early start can also be made from Crackington Manor (0840) 3397 at Crackington Haven and from The Castle Rock Hotel at Port Isaac (0208) 880300. This delightful fishing village also houses the 17th Century Port Gaverne Inn (0208) 880244 – tremendous food and a charming atmosphere.

Our coastal tour ends appropriately at Bude – a pleasant and unassuming seaside resort with a very good golf links, **Bude and North Cornwall** situated almost in the town centre and renowned for its rolling fairways and excellent greens. The town has an impressive array of hotels. The Burn Court Hotel (0288) 352872 is as comfortable as any and has the advantage of overlooking the golf course. One other popular spot for golfers in town is The Camelot (0288) 352361. In Morwenstow, a fine old pub The Bush is well worth visiting if only for the breathtaking clifftop views.

The golf course at Tehidy was mentioned on our coastal tour, but two other inland courses merit attention: the first is **Truro**, a shortish parkland course, close to the lovely cathedral and the second is at **Launceston** one of the best parkland courses in the county.

The White Hart coaching inn is an admirable base to explore the countryside around Launceston, however, the golf course itself is where some of the best views can be enjoyed. Located on high ground, to the west stretches Bodmin Moor – bogs and mystery and to the east, Dartmoor, bogs and even more mystery.

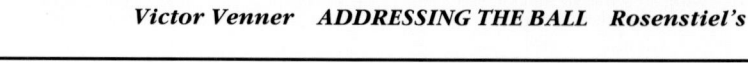

Victor Venner ADDRESSING THE BALL Rosenstiel's

LOSTWITHIEL HOTEL, GOLF AND COUNTRY CLUB

In an idyllic setting among the wooded hills which look down on the beautiful valley of the river Fowey, Lostwithiel Hotel, Golf and Country Club is unique.

A hotel of great charm and character, Lostwithiel offers outstanding service and comfort in a memorable setting in the heart of Cornwall. Old Cornish buildings, mellowed stone, beamed ceilings - these are all part of the rural tranquillity that awaits guests.

The spacious and individually designed bedrooms each have colour TV, direct dial telephone, tea and coffee making facilities and luxurious bathrooms. Imaginative and interesting menus emphasise fresh local produce and the wine list is impressive.

All guests have Golf and Leisure Club membership during their stay, with excellent facilities which include two all-weather tennis courts, and a superb indoor heated swimming pool. Keen anglers can enjoy excellent trout and salmon fishing. The hotel grounds sweep down to the banks of the river Fowey.

The variety of leisure facilities makes for very successful corporate days. In addition to well equipped conference rooms and banqueting facilities, activities can include golf, fishing, swimming, tennis, clay pigeon shooting, even hot air ballooning.

The 18 hole golf course is one of the most interesting and varied in Cornwall. Designed to take full advantage of the natural features of the landscape, it combines two very distinctive areas of hillside and valley. All along the challenging and interesting front nine there are magnificent views down the valley while the back nine with its lakes and streams go through leafy parkland, flanked by the waters of the Fowey. Exceptional all year round practice facilities include a foodlit driving range with undercover and grass bays, two-tier putting green and practice bunkers. What more could you ask for?

For those of you who don't know Cornwall, you will discover that Lostwithiel is a perfect base for discovering its breathtakingly beautiful coastline, quiet inland villages, ancient towns and historic houses. You can explore the haunting landscape of Bodmin, Llanhydrock House in its fascinating Edwardian timewarp or the catherdral city of Truro.

Lostwithiel Hotel, Golf and Country Club
Lower Polscoe
Lostwithiel
Cornwall Pl2 0HQ
Tel: (0208) 873550
Fax: (0208) 873479

15

ST MELLION
CHAMPIONSHIP GOLF

I wonder what the golfing critics would have said if a few years ago, someone had suggested that **Jack Nicklaus** would one day be designing a Championship course in Cornwall? 'Go tell it to the pixies', I should imagine. Well, in Cornwall myths, legends and fairy tales have a habit of turning out to be true.

St. Mellion is the brainchild of farming brothers **Martin** and **Hermon Bond**. What made these charming people turn from profitable pig breeding and potato farming to golf course building remains something of a mystery; what is certain, however, is that their success has been nothing short of phenomenal.

The St. Mellion story really has two parts to it. Act One commenced in the mid 1970's when the Bonds first decided to create a golf course. In short, their idea met with resounding triumph and a first class Championship course was constructed. Within a few years, tournament golf came to Cornwall (T.V. cameras and all) for the first time. Ambition swelled and Act Two was conceived: 'Let's build the best course in Europe' (well, why not!) An additional two hundred acres of adjoining woodland was purchased from the Duchy of Cornwall and an approach was made to the great man himself, Jack Nicklaus. Negotiations followed and Nicklaus came over to inspect the new land. His initial thought was that the land was far too hilly and narrow – an impossible task. But of course, like the Bond brothers, Jack could never resist a challenge....

Plans were drawn up and at least on paper the object was a simple one, to build, in Jack's words, 'Potentially the world's greatest galleried golf course'. Let us just say that the construction team put in a few good hours! The end result is now ready for all the world to see. Some have described it as an 'Augusta in Cornwall'; others reckon it to be the toughest course in Britain. Perhaps the best idea is to go and judge for yourself – you'll be made most welcome.

The Director of Golf at St. Mellion is the very helpful **Mr. David Webb**. He can be contacted by telephone on **(0579) 50101.** Any written correspondence should be addressed to **The Golf Director, St. Mellion Golf and Country Club, St. Mellion, Saltash, Cornwall, PL12 6SD**. While there is an under-standable wish to play the **Nicklaus Course**, we shouldn't forget that there are two fine courses at St. Mellion. When the Nicklaus course was being built, certain changes to the old Championship course (now known as the **'Old Course'**) were

necessary. However, it remains a worthy test of golf and is certainly a long way from your average 'holiday course'. Visitors (with handicaps) are welcome to play either course between Mondays and Fridays, and teeing times can be booked through **the starter** on **(0579) 51182**. The green fee to play a round over the Nicklaus Course was £42 in 1992. On the Old Course, the cost of a game was £22. Reduced rates are available for junior golfers and groups. The professional at St. Mellion is **Tony Moore**.

Although it nestles deep in the Cornish countryside, St. Mellion is easily accessible from all directions. Travelling from afar most will come via Plymouth which is situated eight miles to the south east. Plymouth is linked to Exeter by the A38 and Exeter in turn to Bristol by the M5. On reaching Plymouth the A38 should be followed towards Liskeard and the turning for St. Mellion is clearly signposted.

It is difficult to say which are the best holes on the Nicklaus Course; a few, however, do stand out and they exude the Nicklaus approach. The **3rd** is an excellent hole – miss the fairway to the right and you can be facing a desperate uphill shot over a huge ravine to a heavily protected green. On the **5th**, the drive is across a lake and thereafter the fairway sweeps around to the left towards the green which has a stream running in front of it. And so it goes on, but note especially the par three **11th** and par five **12th** which have been likened to Augusta's 12th and 13th. For all the comparisons with Augusta and Jack's best courses in America, the golfer only has to lift his eyes and look around to be reminded where he is. The surrounding scenery is unmistakably Cornish: the rolling green fields, the babbling brook with its kingfisher and the gnarled trees that huddle around many of the greens and look as if they've endured a million English winters.

In May 1990, **Benson and Hedges** brought their prestigious International Open tournament to the Nicklaus Course and victory that year fittingly went to one of the world's leading players, **Jose-Maria Olazabal**. The Spaniard was succeeded as champion by **Bernhard Langer** and in 1992 it was the turn of the southern hemisphere with Australian **Peter Senior** defeating Zimbabwean **Tony Johnstone** in a play-off. What of the Bond brothers – ambitions fulfilled? In 1992 they released plans for the next phase of the St Mellion dream which included the building of a luxury five star hotel and a third 18 hole course. Better tell the pixies to raise the curtains on Act Three.

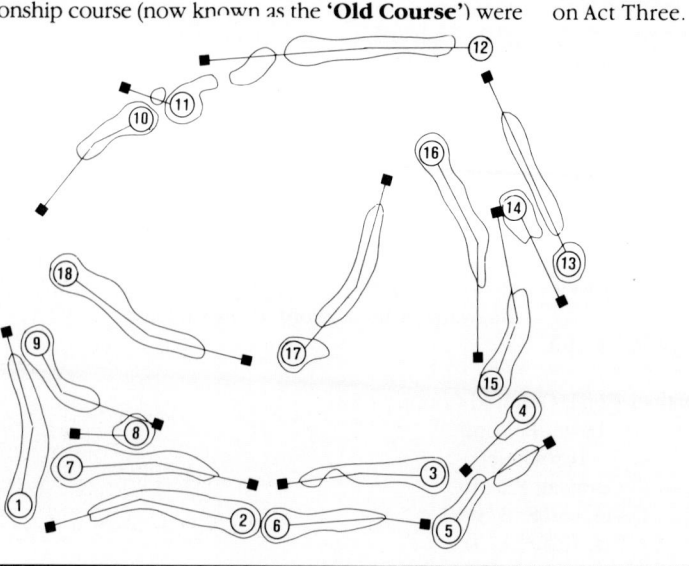

Nicklaus Course

Hole	Yards	Par	Hole	Yards	Par
1	400	4	10	410	4
2	518	5	11	181	3
3	356	4	12	525	5
4	175	3	13	361	4
5	315	4	14	158	3
6	420	4	15	411	4
7	480	5	16	520	5
8	135	3	17	426	4
9	375	4	18	460	4
Out	**3.174**	**36**	**In**	**3.452**	**36**
			Out	**3.174**	**36**
			TOTALS	**6.626**	**72**

ST MELLION LODGES & HOTEL

St Mellion is a modern golf and country club situated in the Caradon District of South East Cornwall, offering a stunning variety of sporting facilities to both its members and guests. The golf at St Mellion is truly second to none with the Old Course and the Jack Nicklaus Championship Course available for all guests to enjoy. The Old Course here offers a challenging and enjoyable round to the club golfer and is in pleasant contrast to the more demanding Nicklaus course, home of the Benson and Hedges International Open.

Guests can enjoy a full range of indoor and outdoor facilities: all weather tennis courts, squash courts, indoor heated leisure pool, jacuzzi and sauna, snooker, even an archery club. Guests can also take advantage of the multi-gym and solarium. However if you just like to walk, the five hundred acre estate offers some relaxing strolls along streams and lakes. There is much to explore in the surrounding Cornish countryside, with picturesque villages and sandy beaches but a short distance away.

The St Mellion Hotel has everything to make the guest's stay enjoyable and comfortable. The bedrooms are attractively furnished with bathroom en-suite, colour television and tea/coffee making facilities. The superb restaurant in the Club house serves a first class menu of International cuisine and a wide choice of fine wines. However some may prefer the comfort and luxury of the St Mellion Lodges, beautifully equipped and furnished with all the requirements for up to eight people. Luxury fitted kitchens, en-suite bathrooms, television and video are standard and most lodges have an inbuilt sauna room.

Whether you are a keen golfer, or just looking for a relaxing break, St Mellion will reward you with the holiday of a life time. Situated only ten miles from Plymouth, St Mellion is easily accessible by road, rail or air.

St Mellion Golf and Coutry Club
Saltash
Cornwall PL12 6SD

Tel: Liskeard (0579) 50101
Fax: Liskeard (0579) 50116

ST ENODOC
CHAMPIONSHIP GOLF

'It lay content
Two paces from the pin;
A steady putt and then it went
Oh, most securely in.
The very turf rejoiced to see
That quite unprecedented three.'

I suppose only Cornwall, and probably only St. Enodoc come to that, could have inspired someone to write a poem about a birdie. Actually, it wasn't just 'someone' it was the Poet Laureate **Sir John Betjeman** who loved, and in later years lived, beside the glorious west country links.

Everyone who visits St. Enodoc, it seems, falls under a spell of some sorts. So why is it such a favourite and what are these charms?

Imagine a really classic links course: huge sandhills; meandering, tumbling fairways; plenty of humps and hillocks; the odd awkward stance and blind shot perhaps but firm, fast greens and plenty of invigorating sea air. This is St. Enodoc to a tee. Exhilarating, dramatic scenery? St. Enodoc most definitely, being situated on the northern coast of Cornwall and not too far from Padstow and Trevose the views could hardly be mundane. The chance of a good score? Again yes – providing you stay on the fairways! St. Enodoc, unlike all too many of today's courses won't put your length of drive on trial. It will, however, more than likely test every golf club in your bag. The holes are all very individual and bristle with old fashioned character. And then the accompanying atmosphere? Well according to Sir John Betjeman even the turf finds time to rejoice in this splendidly relaxed environment. In short, St. Enodoc is a sheer delight.

Doing his best to ensure that St. Enodoc stays lost in this wonderful golfing time warp is the Club's secretary, **Mr L Guy.** He can be contacted by writing to the **St Enodoc Golf Club, Rock, Wadebridge, Cornwall, PL27 6LB** or by telephoning **(020 886) 3216**. Individual visitors are welcome throughout the week, although not surprisingly it is likely to be difficult to arrange a tee time for the weekend. Bookings (up to 4 days in advance) should be made through the Club's professional, **Nick Williams**, tel **(020 886) 2402**. Golfing Societies, or parties of 12 or more will need to make arrangements with the secretary.

Since 1982 there have been two 18 hole courses at St. Enodoc. The main course is now named the **Church Course** and the newer (and considerably less testing) one is called the **Holywell Course**. To play on the Church Course visitors must possess handicaps of 24 or less. Green fees in 1992 for the Church Course were set at £22 a round midweek and £35 a day with £12 a round and £18 a day payable on the Holywell Course. Junior golfers pay half the standard fees. There are also various reductions available for those wishing to purchase weekly or fortnightly 'temporary memberships'.

St. Enodoc is much less remote and more easily reached than many people imagine. Coming by road the two towns to look for on the map are Bodmin and Wadebridge. The former is linked to Exeter by the A30 and to Plymouth by the A38. Wadebridge is 7 miles north of Bodmin. At Wadebridge the B3314 should be taken to St Minver and then a left turn should be taken at this village to Rock.

The Church Course takes its name from the tiny, half-sunken church which is situated near the far end of the links. Many years ago the church was barely visible after a violent storm practically covered it in sand. It is well worth inspecting and Sir John Betjeman is buried in the graveyard. The church almost comes into play on the celebrated **10th** hole, the toughest par four on the 6207 yards par 69 layout (the Holywell Course measures 4165 yards, par 62). As well as being the most difficult two shot hole on the course it is also one of the most memorable. The drive is downhill, but it must carry almost 200 yards to find a narrow, heavily contoured fairway; off to the left is a marshy area and a stream and to the right, steep sand dunes and uncompromising rough. The second shot to the green is almost as daunting as the tee shot!

Betjeman's birdie came at the **13th** but the other hole that everyone talks about is the **6th**; here the golfer must confront the **'Himalayas'**, 'the highest sand hill, to the best of my belief, I have ever seen on a golf course' remarked the famous golf writer **Bernard Darwin** (another who was thoroughly enchanted by St. Enodoc) This prodigious 'bunker' must be flown from the tee and failure isn't worth contemplating. With holes like the 6th it isn't difficult to see why St. Enodoc is so often likened to Prestwick.

The area around Padstow is most fortunate in having both St. Enodoc and Trevose so close at hand. Together they make a marvellous pair and offer two very different challenges. It is difficult to imagine anyone playing St. Enodoc and not relishing a return visit; and who knows what an unexpected birdie might inspire!

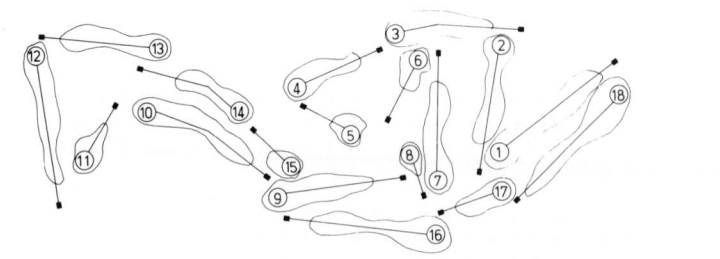

Hole	Yards	Par	Hole	Yards	Par
1	518	5	10	457	4
2	438	4	11	178	3
3	436	4	12	386	4
4	292	4	13	360	4
5	160	3	14	355	4
6	378	4	15	168	3
7	394	4	16	482	5
8	155	3	17	206	3
9	393	4	18	446	4
Out	**3,164**	**35**	**In**	**3,043**	**34**
			Out	**3,164**	**35**
			TOTALS	**6,207**	**69**

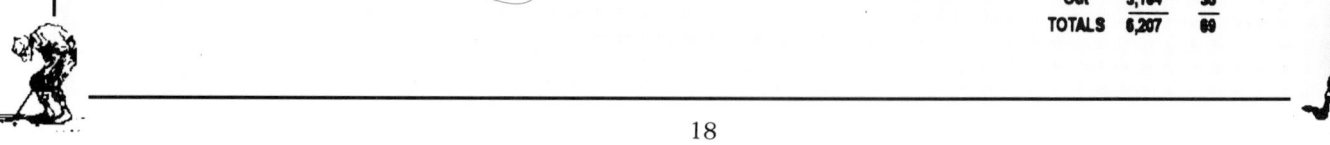

TREVOSE
CHAMPIONSHIP GOLF

To some, mention of the north coast of Cornwall will invoke thoughts of golden sandy beaches and cool, inviting seas. For others, it may conjure up images of romantic coves, wild, spectacular cliffs and incessant crashing waves. Either way, the place has a certain magic; after all it was here that King Arthur is said to have met Merlin. Such is the setting of the Trevose Golf and Country Club.

Located near the quaint little fishing port of Padstow, Trevose is an ideal spot for a golfing holiday – or any kind of holiday come to that, but those who haven't made space in the boot for the golf clubs are missing out on something rather special. The Club boasts a splendid 18 hole Championship course plus an adjacent 9 hole short course. In addition a further 9 hole course of par 35 is under construction.

A gentleman by the name of Dr Williams founded the Trevose Golf Club back in the 1920's. Today, all administrative matters are in the capable hands of **Messrs Peter Gammon** and **Lionel Grindley**. Both can be contacted by telephone on **(0841) 520208** and by fax on (0841) 521057. The Club's professional **Gary Alliss**, can be reached on **(0841) 520261**. Not surprisingly the course (or courses) are at their busiest during the summer months, but whatever the time of year visitors looking for a game would be wise to make a quick telephone call before setting off, they should find the Club very accommodating. Societies are also welcomed at Trevose. Those organising, should address written applications to the Secretary at **Trevose Golf and Country Club, Constantine Bay, Padstow, Cornwall PL28 8JB**. Proof of handicap is required to play on the Championship course.

The 1992 green fee varies according to the time of year with major reductions available to those wishing to obtain temporary membership of the Club. From November to mid-March a day's golf on the 18 hole course can be purchased for £18. From mid-March to the end of May, plus the month of October, the green fee is £25 per day, whilst between June and September (inclusive) the same is priced at £27. The green fee for a day's golf on the 9 hole course is set at £8 during the winter months with £10 payable at all other times. Junior golfers can obtain 50% reductions on all the above rates. Finally, as an example of temporary membership, a fortnight's golf on the Championship course during the peak summer period can be obtained for £140 per person.

Whereas the image of north Cornwall may be a romantic one, the same could hardly be said of the journey to get there! Travelling to this part of the West Country however, is not the painful slog it once was. The roads have been improved and there are regular flights from Heathrow to nearby Newquay Airport (six miles from the Golf Club). Motorists will normally head for Bodmin (via the A30 from Exeter or the A38 from Plymouth). From Bodmin the A389 should be taken towards Padstow. The Club is about four miles west of Padstow off the B3276. Finally, those approaching from the St Austell area may find the B3274 helpful.

From the Championship tees the 18 hole course measures 6608 yards (par 71, s.s.s. 72). The forward tees reduce the length by about 150 yards, while the ladies play over 5713 yards, par 73. The course can properly be described as a golf links though the visitor need not distress himself with fears of having to carry Himalayan-like sandhills, and as a rule the rough is kept fairly short. The latter should ensure that the golfer spends more time admiring the scenery than searching for his golf ball – and a word about the views: they are indeed tremendous, particularly those across Booby's Bay which provide such a dramatic backdrop to the **4th** green.

The wind at Trevose can often play a decisive role and prevent low scoring (no one, at least at the time of writing, has bettered 66). There are a great number of well-positioned bunkers and a stream meanders through much of the course. Trevose certainly provides a good test for any standard of golfer.

The Clubhouse with its prime situation overlooking the course offers a whole range of first class facilities. There is a large comfortable Bar and a Dining Room which can cater for over a hundred people. Breakfast, lunches and dinners are served daily in the Dining Room and in addition light snacks can be obtained at all times. For children, a separate games room is provided. Swimming, snooker and tennis are also all very much a part of the Country Club scene – what's more, there's even a trendy boutique!

There is an unmistakably relaxed, holiday flavour about Trevose. The atmosphere is perhaps best epitomised by the story of four lady Members involved in a foursomes game: apparently, when playing the short **16th** they arrived at the green only to discover that they had been so busy chattering not one of them had remembered to tee off.... so much for women drivers!

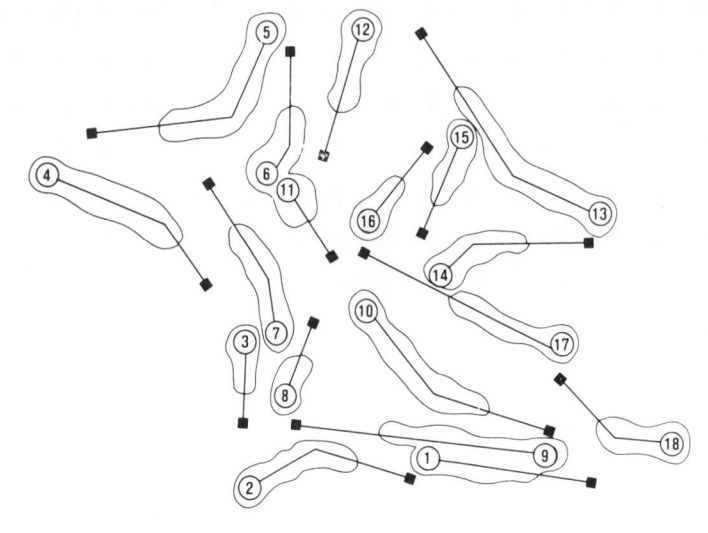

Hole	Yards	Par	Hole	Yards	Par
1	443	4	10	467	4
2	386	4	11	199	3
3	166	3	12	448	4
4	500	5	13	507	5
5	461	4	14	317	4
6	323	4	15	327	4
7	428	4	16	225	3
8	156	3	17	388	4
9	451	4	18	416	4
Out	3,314	35	In	3,294	35
			Out	3,314	35
			TOTALS	6,608	70

CORNWALL
COMPLETE GOLF

Bodmin G. & C.C.
(0208) 73600
Bodmin
(18) 6137 yards/***/D

Bude and North Cornwall G.C.
(0288) 352006
Burn View, Bude
Just outside town on A39.
(18)6202 yards/***/D

Budock Vean Hotel G.C.
(0326) 250288
Mawnan Smith, Falmouth
Between Falmouth and Helston
on A394.
(9)5007 yards/***/D

Cape Cornwall G. & C.C
(0736) 788611
St Just, Penzance
(18) 5788 yards/***/D

Carlyon Bay Hotel G.C.
(072681) 4228
Carlyon Bay, St.Austell.
(18)6463 yards/***/D/M

China Fleet G.C
(0752) 848668
Saltash
(18)6551 yards/***/F/H

Falmouth G.C.
(0326) 311262
Swanpool Rd. Falmouth
Just outside town centre.
(18)5581 yards/***/D/M

Launceston G.C.
(0566) 3442
St. Stephens, Launceston
Turn left opposite church on
B3254.
(18)6357 yards/***/D/H

Looe G.C.
(05034) 571
Widegates, Looe
Between Liskeard and Looe on
B3253.
(18)6104 yards/***/D

Lostwithiel G. & C.C.
(0208) 873550
Lostwithiel
(18)6500 yards/***/C

Mullion G.C.
(0326) 240276
Curry, Helston
5 miles from Helston on B3296.
(18) 5616 yards/***/D/H

Newquay G.C.
(0637) 872091
Tower Rd. Newquay
Just outside town centre.
(18)6140 yards/***/F

Perranporth G.C.
(0872) 573701
Budnick Hill, Perranporth
Just outside town on B3285.
(18)6208 yards/***/D/H

Praa Sands G.C.
(0736) 763445
Germoe Crossroads, Penzance
Between Helston and Penzance
on A394.
(9)4036 yards/***/E/H

St.Austell G.C.
(0726) 74756
Tregongeeves Lane, St.Austell
1 mile from St.Austell off A390
(18)5725 yards/***/D/M/H

St.Enodoc G.C.
(020886) 3216
Rock, Wadebridge
(18)6207 yards/***/F/H(24)

St. Mellion G.& C.C.
(0579) 50101
St. Mellion, Saltash
3 miles from Callington on A388
(18)6626 yards/***/A/H
(18)5927 yards/***/D

Tehidy Park G.C.
(0209) 842208
Cambourne
2 miles north of Cambourne on B3300
(18)6222 yards/***/D/H

Tregana Castle Hotel
(0736) 795254
St Ives
(18) 3549 yards/***/E

Trevose G.& C.C.
(0841) 520208
Constantine Bay, Padstow
(18)6608 yards/***/F/H
(9)1357 yards/***/F

Truro G.C.
(0872) 72640
Treliske, Truro
(18)5357 yards/***/D/H

West Cornwall G.C.
(0736) 753401
Lelant, St Ives
(18)5854 yards/***/D/H

Whitsand Bay Hotel G.C.
(0503) 30470
Portwrinkle, Torpoint
Outside Crafthole on B3247
(18)5367 yards/***/D/L

"Stymied!"

Captain Lionel Edwards   STYMIED!   Burlington Gallery

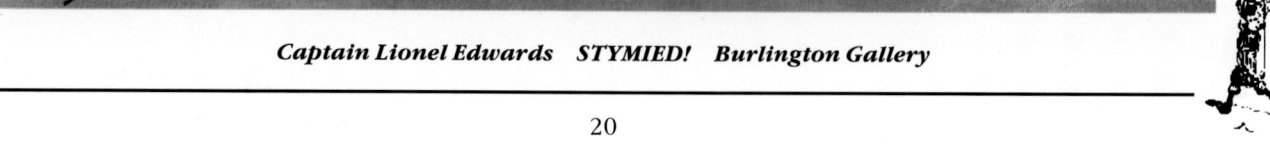

DEVON

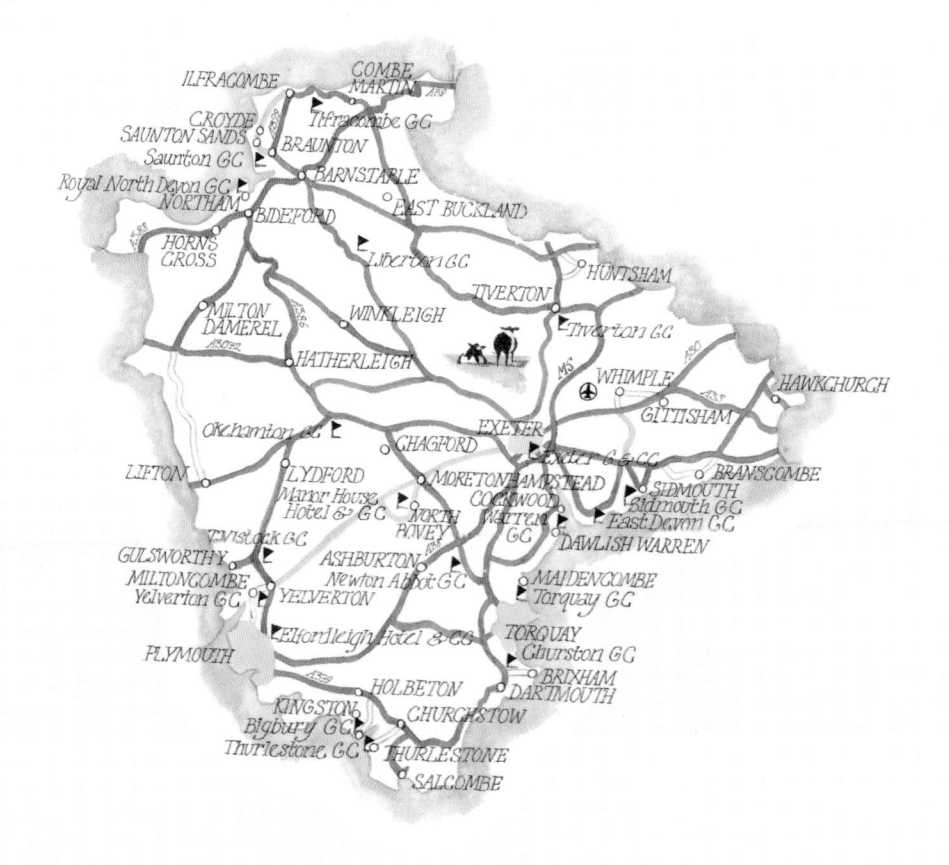

Robert Guy **WESTWARD HO!** *Burlington Gallery*

HIGHBULLEN

Highbullen is a splendid Victorian Gothic mansion complete with parkland, carriageways, home farm and outbuildings. The house was designed and built by William Moore of Exeter in 1879 near the site of old 17th century farmhouses known as Whitehall and Mountjoy. He and his family lived there until 1923. In more recent times cannon balls were discovered nearby, suggesting the site was the scene of a skirmish in Commonwealth days.

The hotel stands on high ground between the Mole and Taw Valleys in wooded seclusion, yet with fine views over surrounding country. A spectacular 9 hole golf course is set in the 60 acres of parkland.

An indoor swimming pool now occupies the old coach-house and the home farm and outbuildings have been discreetly converted into guest rooms.

Rowcliffes, 300 yards down from the home farm, has five more bedrooms with its own heated open-air pool and lovely views. There is also a self-contained 2 bedroom cottage.

The adjoining property, Whitehall, set in a country style garden is 200 yards away and has five elegant bedrooms and its own sitting room.

All thirty seven bedrooms, 12 of which are in the House, are centrally heated, and have their own private bathrooms.

The extensive cellars are now the social and gastronomic heart of the hotel, with the bar opening onto a pretty courtyard. The restaurant has appeared in all the reputable guides for over 25 years. Light lunches are available in the bar or courtyard every day.

The breakfast room opens out from the restaurant and has a magnificent view of the valley. Both the breakfast room and the restaurant are non-smoking areas.

Life at Highbullen is informal and relaxed. We tend to clear breakfast soon after 10 am and not take orders for dinner after 9 pm but, that apart, there are no rules.

Whatever the season, it's a perfect place for doing nothing, with many quiet hideaways - the drawing room, conservatory and library inside and many secluded corners in the grounds. But if you incline to a more active leisure style you can sample the heated outdoor pool, the squash court, the 9 hole par 31 golf course, the hard tennis court or the indoor court, which is floodlit and has an Escotennis carpeted surface.

More gentle pursuits are croquet and billiards, sauna, spa bath, sunbed, steamroom, table tennis and indoor putting green. Massage and hairdressing are available by arrangement. There is a comprehensively stocked golf and sports shop.

Highbullen Hotel
Chittlehamholt
Umberleigh
North Devon EX37 9HD
Tel: (0769) 540561
Fax: (0769) 540492

WHITECHAPEL MANOR

In a hurried and increasingly impersonal world Whitechapel Manor is a quiet tribute to calm, solitude, and peace. From the moment that you arrive you will be absorbed by its pure enchantment.

Whitechapel, as you will discover, is set in terraced walled gardens of lawn and clipped yew hedges surrounded by meadow and woodland.

Listed Grade 1, it is quintessentially English. The entrance hall displays a perfect Jacobean carved oak screen and throughout the rest of the house the William and Mary plasterwork and panelling, complete with painted overmantels, is remarkable for its beauty and lusty country character.

The Great Hall is where you are welcome to relax with a magazine and afternoon tea, which might include home-made Devon honey cake or freshly baked scones with raspberry jam and local clotted cream. It is also here, by a fragrant fire, that you can enjoy canapes and pre-dinner drinks while choosing from the evenings menu. The cuisine at Whitechapel Manor has won international recognition and many British Awards. It is Devon's only Michelin starred hotel restaurant. You may begin your dinner with sauteed Cornish scallops with a basil and tomato sauce or roasted quail with broad beans and a rhubarb sauce. Options on the main course include fillet of Devon beef with wild morels and a Madeira sauce or sauteed breast of Gressingham duck with a confit of turnip and coriander. Desserts are a speciality - strawberry millefeuille with a strawberry coulis or warm apple tart with caramel ice cream. The cuisine is complemented by a carefully selected list of wines, liqueurs and digestifs.

You may wish to stay in one of our large bedrooms overlooking the gardens or a smaller cosy room looking out over trees and bank, all are beautifully appointed with a great deal of thought for your comfort and respite. A superb country breakfast awaits. Crisp lightly smoked bacon, herb sausages and home-made chutneys. Eggs? scrambled, poached, boiled, pan fried or omelletes. Or oak smoked kippers if you prefer. You also have home-made breads, croissants and brioche with our own blackcurrant jam or orange marmalade.

After breakfast our guests go their different ways, some to enjoy the surrounding area, some to unwind in our gardens followed by a relaxing lunch and other to return refreshed to the real world. Our visitors book is a silent testimony to the many delights of Whitechapel Manor, many guest promise to return - you will notice that several names do appear more than once - a promise many guests keep.

Whitechapel Manor is the ideal base to explore the National Park of Exmoor, the numerous gardens, picturesque villages and National Trust properties. If golfing is one of your favoured pastimes then there is a choice of 8 courses within 40 minutes to choose from including the championship courses at Saunton Sands and England's oldest links course at Westward Ho! If you are interested in a golfing holiday a golfing package is available on request.

Special breaks are available throughout the year.

Whitechapel Manor
South Molton
North Devon EX36 3EG
Tel: (0769) 573377
Fax: (0769) 573797

Glorious Devon they call it – beaches to the north, beaches to the south and Dartmoor in the middle. Well, amidst all the glory are some thirty golf courses, the majority of which lie either directly on the coast or within a mile or so of it. The two most widely known are both located to the north of the county: **Royal North Devon** (or Westward Ho! as it is commonly known) and **Saunton**. The greater number of courses, however, are on the southern coast, or to put it another way, while North Devon may have the cream, most of the tees are to be found in the south.

Firstly though, what about golf in the middle? The beautiful setting of the **Manor House** Hotel Golf Course at Moretonhampstead (see feature page) is known to many. However, it is not the sole course within Dartmoor; **Okehampton** is another moorland type course and whilst not overly long, has a number of interesting holes making it well worth a visit. Away from Dartmoor, but still fairly centrally located is the parkland course at **Tiverton**, easily reached from the M5 (junction 27), and a little closer to Exeter and adjacent to Woodbury Common is an exciting new development at **Woodbury Park**, including an 18 hole championship course designed by Hamilton Stutt, and opened in 1992.

With its many Tudor buildings, historic Guildhall and impressive Cathedral, Exeter makes an attractive county town. Golfwise, the city has an 18 hole course at Countess Wear, south of the town off the A377. A fairly short parkland course, **Exeter** Golf and Country Club has a very grand clubhouse and the course is renowned for its beautifully maintained greens, undoubtedly among the best in Devon. There are many outstanding places in which to spend a night or two when visiting this part of the world. Exeter is a likely base and here the Royal Clarence Hotel (0392) 58464 is extremely comfortable and enjoys a splendid position overlooking Cathedral Square. Also in the city, The White Hart (0392) 79897 on South Street is a delightful old inn with good accommodation. One of the oldest and best known pubs in Exeter is The Ship on St Martins Lane – ideal unless you're over six feet tall!

On Dartmoor, the striking Manor House Hotel (0647) 40355 at Moretonhampstead is where many golfers will choose to hang up their spikes, but a number of splendid alternatives are at hand. Chagford offers the exceptional Gidleigh Park (0647) 432367 and the Mill End Hotel (0647) 432282. In nearby Frenchbeer, Teignworthy House is marvellously relaxing.

Towards Okehampton in Lydford, Lydford House Hotel (0822) 82347 is pleasant as is The Castle (0822) 82242. Whilst we are in the area, a visit to Huntsham is also in order: Huntsham Court (039 86) 210 is a rambling Gothic Hotel, with many quaint old fashioned touches. After a game at Manor House, two pubs to note are The White Hart in Moretonhampstead and The Ring of Bells in North Bovey.

SOUTH DEVON

Suitably refreshed, more golf awaits along Devon's southern coast. On the east side of the River Exe and only half an hour's drive from Exeter are the courses at **Sidmouth** and Budleigh Salterton (**East Devon**). Both are on fairly high ground providing panoramic views out to sea. Sidmouth is perhaps more of a typical cliff top course with well wooded fairways and 'springy' turf, while East Devon is a cross between downland and heathland with much heather and gorse. East Devon's delights are detailed ahead.

To the west of the Exe estuary, the friendly **Warren** Golf Club at Dawlish offers the only true links golf in South Devon. Laid out on a narrow peninsula and covered in gorse and numerous natural bunkers this is Devon's answer to St Andrews – and if this sounds a little far-fetched just inspect the aerial photographs at the 19th! It is a much improved course with an interesting finishing hole that will have the wayward hitter threatening both the Members in the Clubhouse and/or quite possibly the passengers on a passing London to Penzance 125. A fairly near neighbour of The Warren is **Teignmouth** Golf Club. It may be near, but Teignmouth offers a totally different challenge, being situated some 900 feet above sea level on Haldon Moor. Teignmouth can become shrouded in fog during the winter, but when all is clear, it's a very pleasant course and most attractive too.

Those seeking a memorable 19th hole on their way to the south coast may have sped past Gittisham – a mistake, for Combe House (0404) 42756 provides great elegance and style. In Sidmouth, The Riviera (0395) 515201 is grand, The Torbay Hotel (0395) 513456 good value, while for a family holiday, The Westcliff (0395) 513252 may be the best choice. Just east of Sidmouth, The Masons Arms at Branscombe (029780) 300 is perfect for a relaxing dinner and a stopover if required. The Royal Beacon Hotel in Exmouth (0395) 264886 also offers the highest standards of comfort. In Dawlish Warren, most convenient for the golf links is The Langstone Cliff Hotel (0626) 865155 (just roll down the hill and you're almost there). Not too far from the many courses of east Devon at Hawkchurch, near Axminster, the comfortable Fairwater Head Hotel (02977) 349 is recommended. Just to the north west of Newton Abbot in Haytor lies the Bel Alp House Country Hotel (03646) 661217, an elegant country house offering genuine tranquillity to our doubtless exhausted golfers. Another local favourite, worthy of its popularity, is The Moorland Hotel (0364) 661407.

The three handiest courses for those holidaying in the Torbay area are probably **Churston, Torquay** and **Newton Abbot**. The first two mentioned offer typical (and good quality) downland – clifftop type golf and a very different game from Newton Abbot's course at Stover where abundant heather, woods and a meandering brook are likely to pose the most challenges. Mention must also be made of the excellent new **Dartmouth Golf and Country Club**, which seems set to rival the area's very best courses.

One of the most pleasant and convenient places to stay in this area is The Orestone Manor House (0803) 328098 in Maidencombe. In Torquay itself, there are numerous fine hotels – the most famous is the Imperial (0803) 294301, which offers all manner of splendid facilities but charges for it! The Palace Hotel (0803) 200200 is less costly, but courtesy still prevails. Perhaps the best value to be found is at Homers Hotel (0803) 213456 with its first class restaurant. And in Teignmouth, we would recommend the Coombe Bank Hotel (0626) 772369.

The Quayside Hotel (08045) 55751 in the popular resort of Brixham is charming and the town retains a much quieter atmosphere than its neighbour across the bay. In Dartmouth, two restaurants merit special comment: The Cherub

Dining Rooms (0803) 832571 which has delicious seafood as a speciality, and The Carved Angel (0803) 832465. Just outside Dartmouth, in Dittisham, Fingals at Old Coombe Manor (080422) 398 is well worth the short trip and finally, we can recommend The Holne Chase Hotel (03643) 471 in Ashburton – a glorious setting with a restaurant to match.

Heading further down the coast, the picturesque village of **Thurlestone** has one of the most popular courses in Devon. It is yet another superb cliff top course with several far-reaching views along the coast. **Bigbury** lies a short distance from Thurlestone and although perhaps a little less testing it is nevertheless equally attractive and looks across to Burgh Island, a favourite (or hopefully an ex-favourite) haunt of smugglers. Both Thurlestone and Bigbury can be reached from Plymouth via the A379, or from the Torbay region via the A381.

The Thurlestone Hotel (0548) 560382 is a perfect base not only for playing the two nearby courses, but also for exploring what is a delightful part of Devon. It also has its own very pleasant short 9 hole course. The Buckland Hotel (0548) 853055 at Kingsbridge is also worthy of inclusion on any itinerary. For lovers of the country mansion, Holbeton offers The Alston Hall Hotel (075 530) 259, but if a good pub is sought The Pilchard on Burgh Island is one of the best – but beware the tide!

Golfers in Plymouth have probably been noting with interest the recent developments at nearby **St. Mellion**, just over the border in Cornwall. Also not far from the great seafaring city, the **Elfordleigh Hotel**'s 9 hole golf course at Plympton is very pleasant – and certainly not as demanding! and towards Dartmoor, **Yelverton** is one not to be missed. Designed by Herbert Fowler, the architect of Walton Heath, Yelverton lies midway between Plymouth and Tavistock on the A386. It is a classic moorland type course and very attractive too, with much gorse and heather. No shortage of ponies either! All in all, a tremendous test of golf.

Tavistock is also not far from Plymouth. **Tavistock** Golf Club is perhaps not as challenging as Yelverton, but well worth a visit all the same. A second golf course in Tavistock, **Hurdwick** Golf Club has recently been opened. For a good place to stay, The Moorland Links Hotel (0822) 852245 at Yelverton needs little explanation and for a place to celebrate one's birdie at the eighteenth, The Who'd of Thought It at Milton Combe sounds highly appropriate – it really is an excellent pub and serves outstandingly good value lunches.

NORTH DEVON

From Plymouth, the north coast of Devon is about an hour and a quarter's drive; from Exeter, a little less. Unless there is some urgency a leisurely drive is recommended for the scenery is truly spectacular. A few suggestions for breaking the journey include Milton Damerel, where The Woodford Bridge (040926) 481 is a first rate hotel, Hatherleigh for the handsome George Hotel (0837) 810454 and Winkleigh, where the Kings Arms is a praiseworthy pub in an attractive village. Just beyond Winkleigh, towards Barnstaple, there is a fine new 18 hole course at **Libbaton** near Umberleigh – again definitely worth breaking the journey for.

North Devon can boast one of the oldest Golf Clubs in England, the **Royal North Devon** Club at Westward Ho!, foun-

ded in 1864, it can also claim to have seen the lowest known score for eighteen holes of golf. In 1936 the Woolacombe Bay professional recorded a 55 on his home course – 29 out and 26 back, including a hole in one at the last! As this took place on the 1st January, one cannot help wondering quite what he did the night before! Unfortunately, there is no longer a course at Woolacombe, but there is one at nearby **Ilfracombe** (and has been for over a hundred years). Situated several hundred feet above sea level, it offers many outstanding views of the North Devon coastline. The best hole is the par four 13th and there is an interesting selection of par three holes, one of which is played across a plunging ravine but measures a mere 81 yards. Whilst in the area, two hotels for golfing breaks in Ilfracombe are St Brannochs House Hotel (0271) 863873 and the Seven Hills (0271) 862207 while another very recent addition to the county's golfing scene is the **Clovelly** Country Club near the famous 'sleepy village.'

Both **Saunton** and Westward Ho! deserve more than a fleeting visit and are featured ahead; Westward Ho! is a place for pilgrimage, but Saunton provides the more modern championship challenge. There are two fine courses at Saunton, The East (which is the championship course) and the greatly improved West. Large sandhills dominate both courses, and when the wind blows.....

Sleeping in the dunes is strictly out of bounds so here are a few ideas for the 19th. Visitors to North Devon should consider Yelden House (0237) 474400 in Bideford, whilst in Saunton Sands, the hotel of the same name is first class and enormously popular with golfers (0271) 890212. A noted nearby eating place is Otters Restaurant (0271) 813633 in Braunton. The Preston House Hotel (0271) 890472 is also close to Saunton's links and is very comfortable. At Fairy Cross, near Bideford, the Portledge Hotel (0237) 451262 is for the lover of peace and quiet, while in Northam the Durrant House Hotel (0237) 472361 is great for recuperating after an excursion to Westward Ho! More thoughts? Recommendations are many and various: in Westward Ho! Culloden House (0237) 479421 is small but friendly and there is also the Highfield House Hotel (02374) 73970. The small town of Umberleigh provides yet another worthy establishment in the shape of Northcote Manor (0769) 60501. Woolacombe offers the superb Woolacombe Bay Hotel (0271) 870388 and at Combe Martin is the relaxing Coulsworthy Country House (0271) 882463. Then there is The Penhaven Country House (02375) 711, a lovely old rectory transformed into a hotel at Parkham near Bideford and the elegant Halmstone Manor (0271) 830321 at Bishops Taunton near Barnstaple. Finally a mention too for the Knoll House Hotel (027188) 2548 in Kentishbury, famed for its tremendous fayre.

Among a number of good eating places in the area is Gray's Country Restaurant (0271) 812809 in Knowle. For those who prefer to cater for themselves in one of the many pretty cottages that abound in Devon, Country Holidays (0282) 445566, and Devon and Dorset Cottages (0626) 333678 are both worth contacting.

A final thought as we leave North Devon – should it actually happen and for some peculiar and presumably non-golfing reason you do get stranded in the dunes at Saunton, the chances are you will wake up to a glorious sunrise. If this is the case let's just hope the morning's golf is equally spectacular.

MOORLAND HOTEL

The Moorland Hotel, Haytor, stands in one of the most beautiful and majestic parts of the British Isles. Set amid a delightful aspect of moors, and nestling within a copse of firs at the southern foot of Haytor rocks, the hotel commands spectacular views across the rolling Devon countryside towards Teignmouth, Torbay and South Hams.

Set within the Dartmoor National Park, the moor offers a wide range of outdoor activities, including walking, riding, fishing and golf. The Moorland Hotel is the ideal place to relax and unwind after such exertions, a haven of comfort and hospitality.

The bedrooms in the hotel are designed to ensure a high degree of comfort for guests. All rooms have en suite facilities, colour television, direct dial telephone and hot drinks for the discerning visitor. For a real treat, two of the rooms have a traditional four poster bed, whilst all rooms command stunning views of gardens and moors, most with panoramic sea views in the distance.

Guests can enjoy the cosy, hunting lodge atmosphere of the Moorland Pine Bar or the elegance and style of the Agatha Christie lounge, named after the famous author who completed her first detective novel 'The Mysterious Affair at Styles' whilst staying at the Moorland Hotel, and found the hotel an ideal retreat as she recalls in her autobiography.

The restaurant offers varied table d'hote and a la carte menus, with an emphasis on fresh seasonal produce. The patio restaurant is ideal for bar meals, coffee or perhaps a cream tea.

Another delight of the Moorland Hotel is the self contained appartments, which provide a comfortable location for an 'away from it all' holiday. Each includes a comfortably furnished lounge with colour television and direct dial telephone, fully equipped kitchen and bathroom, with linen, heating and electricity provided.

There is much for guests to see and visit in the vicinity. The town of Bovey Tracey is close by, Widecombe in the Moor is another popular attraction, and Exeter, Newton Abbot and Plymouth are within easy reach. Alternatively, if guests prefer to keep the pace of their holiday at a more leisurely tempo, Haytor itself, a craggy outcrop of granite rocks, is virtually on the doorstep, and the village of Haytor is worth exploring, with its pretty hamlet of cottages, village post office and inn.

Whether you wish to use the hotel as a base for exploring or prefer just to relax in the hotel and its delightful gardens, you are assured of a warm welcome and precious memories of Devon hospitality.

The Moorland Hotel
Haytor
Dartmoor
South Devon
TQ13 9XT

Tel: (0364) 661407

HOLNE CHASE HOTEL

Your hosts at Holne Chase, now in their 22nd year at the Hotel, have an excellent knowledge of local facilities - particularly:-

GOLF: Kenneth Bromage has compiled a list of no fewer than 15 courses within a hour of the Hotel, plus three others of International Standing within about 90 minutes. Other courses, recently built but said to be good, he has not listed because he has not yet played over them.

Small golfing parties staying at the Hotel will find flexibility in meal times to help them plan their golfing tour.

HORSE RACING: Newton Abbot is England's most Westerly race course, National Hunt meeting run from early August through to late May. Frequently, meetings at Newton Abbot are followed/preceded by meetings at Devon and Exeter Race-course. Holne Chase is handy for both.

FISHING: The Dart is, arguably, one of Britain's loveliest rivers. Certainly, it is a challenge to the ardent fly fisherman. Holne Chase has a single bank beat of about a mile, which is available to residents at no extra charge.

Holne Chase became an hotel in 1934. The surrounding woodlands were partly laid out as Arboretum in 1878 and so afford many interesting walks taking in an old mine shaft (c.1790), an iron age fortified camp and early 20th c. charcoal burners hearths.

The woodlands abound with wildlife including roe and red deer, badger, fox, rabbit and otter. Buzzard, heron, kingfisher and even a flight of shellduck which have colonised a stretch of the river.

The Bromage family took the hotel in 1972 and have been working on it ever since. All 14 bedrooms have bath and/or shower en suite. The Hotel is classified 4 Crown 'Highly Commended' by the English Tourist Board and has won many awards over the years, both in the kitchen and in the cellar. The Head Chef is an expert Mycologist which helps add extra variety to the late summer menus.

Holne Chase is an exceptional place in which to relax. Deep, comfy sofas and armchairs, a well stocked library, blazing fires on winter evenings make relaxation easy. Dartmoor itself is wonderful walking country and guided walks can be arranged at all times of the year. We can also arrange riding from some of the best stables on Dartmoor all within 20-30 minutes from the hotel. Expert tuition is available.

Holne Chase is 3 miles north of the Ashburton. To find the hotel, take the Two Bridges/Princetown turning off the A38 and follow the road for approximately 3 miles. The hotel turning is on the right, just after the road crosses the River Dart.

Holne Chase Hotel & Restaurant
Nr Ashburton
Devon
TQ13 7NS
Tel: (03643) 471
Fax: (03643) 453

ROYAL NORTH DEVON (WESTWARD HO!)
CHAMPIONSHIP GOLF

This is a Club truly steeped in the history of the game. Westward Ho!, as it is commonly known, was the first English links course and being founded in **1864** the Royal North Devon Golf Club lays claim to being the oldest English Club still playing over its original land. Furthermore it boasts the oldest Ladies Golf Club in the world, the Westward Ho! Ladies Golf Club which was established in **1868**.

Originally designed by **Tom Morris**, and reconstructed by **Herbert Fowler**, the 18 holes are situated on Northam Burrows. The Burrows is a vast, exposed and relatively flat area of common land which stretches along the coast a couple of miles north of Bideford between Westward Ho! and Appledore.

Several of Britain's historic courses, particularly those in Scotland, have fascinating ties with common land and associated local rights which have existed since time immemorial, but whilst the inhabitants of St Andrews no longer use their hallowed turf for practising archery upon, nor put their washing out to dry on the banks of the Swilcan Burn, the locals of Northam village still graze their sheep and horses on the Burrows. There can surely be no other Championship course in the world where you can have teed up on the first, taken a few steps backward to survey the drive ahead only to see a sheep wander up and peer inquisitively at your ball! One shouldn't get too alarmed though, the animals are well-versed in the etiquette of the game – they generally keep a respectful distance from the fairways and greens, they take care not to bleat when you putt and what's more they certainly won't contemplate stealing your golf ball as I'm told the crows do at Royal Aberdeen.

Seriously, golf at Westward Ho! is a rich experience and given the warm welcome visitors receive, definitely to be recommended. Presently responsible for continuing the tradition of friendliness is the Secretary, **John Linaker**. Mr. Linaker can be contacted via **The Royal North Devon Golf Club, Golf Links Road, Westward Ho! Bideford, Devon EX39 1HD. Tel (0237) 473817**.

If you are considering a trip to the Club you may find it advisable to telephone first in order to check if any tee reservations have been made. Fine weather can make the course particularly popular during the holiday season. Societies are also welcomed and bookings can be arranged with the Secretary. In 1992, a green fee of £19 entitled the visitor to a single round with £23 payable for a full day's golf. The weekend rate was set at £23, while for juniors, the green fee was a mere £5 – excellent value. The Club's professional is **Graham Johnston** and he can be reached by telephone on **(0237) 477598**.

The course can be approached from both East and West via the A39, although travellers from the West may be able to avoid the busy town of Bideford by joining the B3236 near Abbotsham. Visitors travelling from the Dartmoor region should take the A386 road which runs from Okehampton to Bideford, whilst those coming from Exeter should follow the A377 to Barnstaple, thereafter joining the A39 as above.

From the medal tees the course measures 6449 yards (the Championship course is some 200 yards longer) and is divided into two fairly equal halves. Westward Ho! has a traditional out and back layout and there are some panoramic views across Bideford Bay, especially from the **6th** tee where, on a clear day, the Isle of Lundy can be seen. In theory, the links receives a degree of protection from the elements from a large bank of shingle which separates the Burrows from the beach. I say in theory for this is surely one of Britain's most windswept courses. However, the wind is not the only factor that can make scoring extremely difficult. There are numerous ditches and hidden pot bunkers and then of course, there are the **Great Sea Rushes**. To the uninitiated a word of caution – these giant marshland reeds, unique to Westward Ho!, can literally impale golf balls, so do as the sheep do – stay clear!

Westward Ho! is not only known for its golf course, it has literary fame as well. The village was founded a year before the Golf Club and was named after **Charles Kingsley's** adventure novel about Elizabethan seafarers. A decade or so later **Rudyard Kipling** attended the local college and remembered his days there in Stalky and Co. Alas, there is no record to suggest that Mr. Kipling was an exceedingly good golfer but while he was studying, a young boy from Northam was out on the course caddying for sixpence a round. The boy was destined to become Open Champion on five occasions. **John H. Taylor** learnt his game at Westward Ho! and his great affection for the Club remained throughout his long life. In 1957 the Club elected him their President.

In addition to a friendly and unpretentious atmosphere, the Clubhouse offers some excellent catering. It also houses the Club's own **museum.** It is most interesting and contains a great variety of golfing memorabilia, ranging from one of Tom Watson's gloves to some near priceless art.

For the golfer who has confined himself to playing on gentle heathland fairways, sheltered from any wind by tall trees, a visit to Westward Ho! would probably create quite a shock to the system. But clearly, for those with even a moderate interest in the history of the game and, of course, who are not afraid of a stiff challenge, Westward Ho! is a golfing must.

Hole	Yards	Par	Hole	Yards	Par
1	478	5	10	376	4
2	410	4	11	368	4
3	425	4	12	425	4
4	354	4	13	440	4
5	137	3	14	201	3
6	410	4	15	434	4
7	395	4	16	145	3
8	197	3	17	554	5
9	479	5	18	416	4
Out	**3,285**	**36**	**In**	**3,359**	**35**
			Out	**3,285**	**36**
			TOTALS	**6,644**	**71**

THE WESTCLIFF HOTEL

Westcliff Hotel

Surrounded by superb golfing country, and with the additional attractions of Devon's lanes and moors nearby, The Westcliff Hotel offers its guests an ideal base for exploring this beautiful part of Britain. Discounted Green Fees have been negotiated at the Sidmouth and Woodbury Park Golf Clubs, and at the time of writing, negotiations are proceeding with Honiton Golf Club.

Just as Sidmouth is the jewel of East Devon, so is Westcliff the jewel of Sidmouth. Situated in beautiful, spacious grounds, facing South and enjoying spectacular coastal views over Lyme Bay, Westcliff is the closest hotel to the much admired Connaught Gardens, Golf Club and Western Beach, yet is still within an easy stroll along the Esplanade to the town centre.

Outdoor facilities include a putting green, mini tennis, croquet, a heated pool and ample free parking. Indoors, elegantly refurbished lounges, restaurant and cocktail bar, all with magnificent sea views, await you. All 40 bedrooms have private facilities, are fitted to a high standard and most have sea views. Indoor facilities include a games room, pool or snooker, jacuzzi, solarium, exercise room and lift to all floors. A new, full-colour brochure is available on request. The Westcliff is privately owned and family run.

The Westcliff is an Ashley Courtenay Recommended Hotel.

Westcliff Hotel
Manor Road
Sidmouth
Devon
EX10 8RU
Tel: (0395) 513252

SAUNTON
CHAMPIONSHIP GOLF

At a time when the likes of **John H Taylor** and **Horace Hutchinson** were striding the windswept fairways on **Northam Burrows**, across the Taw Estuary on the **Braunton Burrows** other men were busy trapping rabbits. It took more than thirty years for matters to be put right.

Saunton Golf Club was founded in 1897 some three decades after Westward Ho! In common with many great Clubs, Saunton's beginnings were rather modest. At first there were only nine holes and the original Clubhouse was a single room next to the local Post Office. Although the course was extended to 18 holes before the First World War (and a new Clubhouse acquired) it wasn't until after the War that Saunton's reputation really gained momentum. Chiefly responsible for this was golf architect **Herbert Fowler**, who having reshaped Westward Ho! performed a similar task at Saunton.

In 1932 the course was selected to stage the British Ladies Championship and this was followed by the English Amateur Championship of 1937. Unfortunately the links didn't fare too well during the Second World War as it was considered the perfect place for a Battle School and concrete and barbed wire covered the fairways. Reconstruction didn't begin until 1951, **C.K. Cotton** this time directing matters. Once restored the course quickly re-established itself as one of Britain's leading Championship links. In the early seventies a second 18 holes were added and today the two are known as the **East** (the former 'Old Course') and the **West** Course.

The Secretary at Saunton can be reached by telephone on **(0271) 812436**, and the Professional, **Jimmy McGhee**, can be contacted on **(0271) 812013**. Other than being able to provide proof of handicap there are no general restrictions on visitors – however prior telephoning is strongly recommended. Golfing Societies are equally welcome at Saunton; those wishing to make written applications to the Club should address correspondence to the Secretary at **The Saunton Golf Club, Saunton, Braunton, Devon EX33 1LG.**

The green fees for 1992 were set at £25 per day to play either the Championship East Course or the West Course, or both, with a slight increase to £30 on Saturdays, Sundays and on Bank Holidays. Juniors are offered a fifty per cent reduction.

Although on the map Saunton and Westward Ho! appear to be very neighbourly, travelling from one to the other is in fact about a 20 mile trip via Barnstaple. The Club's precise location is off the B3231 south of Saunton village. The B3231 can be picked up at Braunton, with Braunton in turn being joined to Ilfracombe in the north and Barnstaple to the south by the A361. Those travelling from further afield should aim for Barnstaple. The town can be reached from Exeter by the A377 and from Tiverton on the new M5 link road while for those approaching from the north of Cornwall the A39 is likely to prove of most assistance.

At 6703 yards, par 71 (s.s.s. 73) from the Championship tees, the East Course is nearly 350 yards longer than the West (6356 yards par 71). Both, however, provide a fairly stiff challenge with large sand hills being the dominant feature on each.

The East Course could hardly be described as one of those that breaks you in gently: the first four holes all measure over 400 yards. There are several notable par fours early in the round, but perhaps the best are the **14th**, with its ever-narrowing fairway, and the **16th** which demands a tee shot over a vast sand hill with the second needing to be carried over a deep bunker in front of the green. The course record on the East Course stands at 66.

Since its reopening in 1951 Saunton has hosted several important Championships, both professional and amateur. On three occasions the English Open Amateur Stroke Play Championship has been played on the East Course and in 1966 the PGA Championship was held at Saunton. The St Andrews Trophy was also played here in 1984, as was the 1992 British Ladies Matchplay event.

On more than one occasion I have read that if Saunton had a different geography it would be an **Open Championship** venue. Maybe I'm missing the point, but I've never fully appreciated the 'geography argument'. If it's a question of remoteness, surely North Devon is no more remote than certain parts of the east and west coasts of Scotland – especially now that a motorway runs as far as Exeter (one hour's drive away). Attendance figures? Such is the popularity of golf in modern times it seems most unlikely that the crowds wouldn't flock to the area, and as for accommodation North Devon abounds with places to stay. Come to think of it, what better place for a week's holiday in July?

East Course

Hole	Yards	Par	Hole	Yards	Par
1	470	4	10	337	4
2	476	5	11	362	4
3	402	4	12	418	4
4	444	4	13	136	3
5	112	3	14	461	4
6	370	4	15	485	5
7	428	4	16	430	4
8	380	4	17	202	3
9	382	4	18	408	4
Out	**3,464**	**36**	**In**	**3,239**	**35**
			Out	3,464	36
			TOTALS	6,703	71

WOOLACOMBE BAY HOTEL

Woolacombe Bay itself, surely one of the most beautiful and magical settings for any hotel. Family run, the Woolacombe Bay Hotel with six acres of spacious lawns running down to the beach, set in a secluded valley between rolling green hills, the spectacular rugged coastline giving way to a breathtaking three mile expanse of wide golden sands with grassy dunes, rock pools and boisterous rolling surf provides the complete, the perfect, holiday setting. The views in all directions are magnificent, Lundy Island on the horizon, craggy headlands in the distance and the beautiful National Trust countryside supplying a magnificent backdrop to this outstanding elegant hotel with the mellow Devonian landscape.

This distinctive Edwardian building which is the Woolacombe Bay Hotel was built in the days of gracious living and exudes a feeling of luxury and traditional style, combining comfort and service with a range of truly modern amenities. Accommodation is available to suit all requirements single, doubles, family suites etc., every bedroom en suite, central heating, direct dial telephone (with baby listening facilities), colour television (with satelite TV), radio, tea and coffee making facilities, towelling robes, hairdryers etc. Some rooms have spa bath, exceptional sea views and balcony overlooking the bay. The hotel's public rooms are restful, generously proportioned, comfortable and welcoming.

The elegant chandeliered restaurant provides a relaxed ambience for the serious pleasure of eating. The table decor and the unobtrusive attention of the silver service waiting staff, sets the standard for the unhurried enjoyment of full English breakfast (available early for the serious golfer) and seven course dinner for which the hotel is justly famous. Many dishes comprise fresh, local fish, meats and vegetables all carefully selected and expertly prepared by our Chef, this supplemented with a fine wine chosen from the wine cellar makes each meal an outstanding and memorable part of a visit to this stylish friendly hotel.

For the evenings there is no shortage of entertainment either in the bar or the hotel's magnificent ballroom ensuring enjoyment to end another eventful day.

Relaxation is easy, but for those with boundless energy there is a tremendous opportunity with unlimited use of our extensive sporting facilities which include tennis, squash, snooker, indoor and outdoor heated pools, spa bath, sauna, solarium, bowls, croquet, gym and pitch and putt. We have our own power boat for charter. Massage, hairdressing, horse riding, and clay pigeon shooting are also available. Special reduced green fees have been arranged at Saunton Sands the nearby championship course, only six miles away. Short breaks are our speciality.

Woolacombe Bay Hotel
Woolacombe
Devon
EX34 7BN
Tel: (0271) 870388
Fax: (0271) 870388

EAST DEVON
CHAMPIONSHIP GOLF

Most cliff top courses are essentially downland or parkland in nature, very often they are beautifully situated but the quality of the golf offered isn't quite out of the top drawer. East Devon at Budleigh Salterton is quite a rarity, for this is where heathland golf meets the sea. Some of the holes here look as if they have been plucked from Surrey or Berkshire; the 6th and 7th for instance where a touch of Walton Heath (heather, gorse and silver birches) is followed by a touch of The Berkshire (tall pines and total seclusion.) But of course, what these famous courses cannot offer are spectacular seascapes. Laid out on cliffs some 250 to 400 feet above sea level there are breathtaking views out to sea and along the South Devon coast in both directions. The views inland, mind you, are just as expansive, with the rolling Devon countryside presenting itself in all its glory. East Devon is now beginning to sound a little like Bamburgh Castle in Northumberland, often rated as Britain's most beautiful golf course. This comparison is especially valid in that both Budleigh and Bamburgh are famed for an abundance of wild flowers including some rather rare orchids, a feature that adds even more charm and colour to the setting.

But what is really special about East Devon is that the golf course takes full advantage of the location and the natural splendour of the terrain. East Devon is not as testing as somewhere like Walton Heath; it is not as long for a start, although at 6,214 yards (par 70) it is not exactly short either, and the heather and gorse do not encroach to the point where they intimidate the golfer as on several of the south east's Championship courses; however, variety and challenge present themselves at every hole. The layout is such that the course continually rises and falls, twists and turns; there are a couple of uphill drives and many dramatic downhill tee shots and there are some fine left and right dog-leg holes. Precise shot making is well rewarded at East Devon! Finally, there is the all year round quality of the putting surfaces – the best in Devon many players reckon – and for this the Club must thank its excellent green keeper, who in turn must thank Mother Nature.

The Secretary at East Devon is the very able **John Tebbet** who may be contacted at **The East Devon Golf Club, North View Road, Budleigh Salterton, Devon EX9 6DR** and by telephone on **(0395) 443370.** The Club's professional, **Trevor Underwood** can be reached on **(0395) 445195.** Subject to being able to provide proof of handicap visitors are welcome most days after 10.00am. However to avoid any possible disappointment prior contact with the Secretary's office is recommended. The green fees for 1992 were £22 per round, £26 per day during the week with a slight increase to £26 per round and £30 per day at weekends and Bank Holidays.

Many of the country's prettiest golf courses are by definition somewhat hidden away from their nearest towns and can be rather difficult to find. This is not the case with East Devon. The entrance to the Club is clearly signposted from the main road which runs through Budleigh Salterton, the golf course being located on the Exmouth side of the town. Budleigh is linked to Exmouth by the A376 although motorists travelling from the Exeter area can avoid journeying through the heart of Exmouth (not a good idea in summer!) by picking up the B3179 at Clyst St George. If Budleigh is being approached from the north and east then the A3025 which joins Lyme Regis to Exeter is likely to be helpful (exiting just north of Sidmouth.)

As the driver pulls into the Golf Club car park, the Clubhouse and 1st tee are immediately ahead. A quick look to the right and there is the rolling countryside, to the left the view is down over the ocean which, if the sun is out, is sure to be shimmering. In between countryside and sea are great swathes of gorse and undulating fairways carved out of heather and bracken. The normal reaction to all this is a quickening pulse. Perhaps it is fortunate then that the two opening holes are the tamest on the course.

Probably the most outstanding sequence of holes at East Devon comes between the 6th and the 9th. What makes the par five **6th** so spectacular is the choice facing the golfer after a good drive. The fairway narrows all the way to the green; out of bounds lurks to the right, thick woodland menaces to the left and if that isn't sufficiently fear-inducing, twenty yards short of the green is a natural gulley full of humps and hillocks. The sensible shot is to lay up but the devil-may-care golfer will not be able to resist the challenge.

After a short walk through the woods, the magnificent back tee for the **7th** is reached. The tree-lined fairway dog-legs sharply to the left 50 feet below and you can't see the green as you drive. The approach is slightly uphill and the amphitheatre-like green is protected by a mischievously placed deep bunker. The next hole is a tough par three measuring over 200 yards – miss the green to the right here and a par will be a major achievement. The **9th** tumbles 450 yards downhill all the way and is perhaps the best of many exhilarating downhill holes at Budleigh. In 1934, a player actually drove to the edge of the green.

Maybe 'exhilarating' is indeed the best word to sum up East Devon: if there is a more splendidly situated and more attractive golf course in England I would like to see it, and if there is a course that offers greater variety and sheer pleasure, I would like to play it.

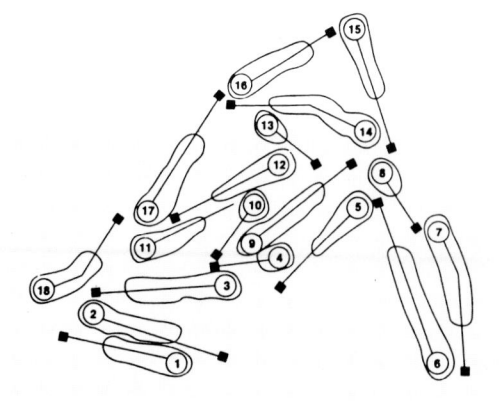

Hole	Yards	Par	Hole	Yards	Par
1	343	4	10	155	3
2	341	4	11	337	4
3	414	4	12	483	5
4	151	3	13	143	3
5	361	4	14	404	4
6	524	5	15	301	4
7	392	4	16	402	4
8	206	3	17	453	4
9	464	4	18	340	4
Out	**3,196**	**35**	**In**	**3,018**	**35**
			Out	**3,196**	**35**
			Totals	**6,214**	**70**

WOODBURY PARK GOLF CLUB

A short drive away from Exeter there is a rambler's paradise. It is difficult to imagine a more beautiful place for a gentle Sunday afternoon stroll than Woodbury Common in South East Devon. This is English moorland at its most intimate. Golden gorse flickers in a soft breeze as the purple heather-studded terrain tumbles towards the not so distant coastline. Sparkling seascapes and stunning landscapes jostle for prominence: 'Glorious Devon' at its finest.

Now let us talk golf. A short drive away from Woodbury Common - little more than a medium iron perhaps for the big hitters - there is the makings of a golfer's paradise. Welcome to Woodbury Park.

J. Hamilton-Stutt, widely acknowledged as one of Europe's foremost golf course architects, has recently created a 27 hole masterpiece immediately adjacent to Woodbury Common. Both courses, the Championship 18 hole Oaks Course (6707 yards, par 72) and the shorter 9 hole Acorns Course (2297 yards, par 33) opened for play in late Spring, 1992. Here is where dazzling white bunker-strewn terrain tumbles towards the not so avoidable water hazards. Wonderfully mature oaks and beach trees frame the fairways while golfers and wildlife jostle for prominence.

Woodbury Park is reached by way of a winding country lane

(clearly signposted off the A3052 Exeter to Sidmouth road) and there is a great feeling of peace and privacy about the place. The Golf Club however is anything but 'private' in the traditional golfing sense, and all players (addicts and newcomers, individuals and societies) are welcome to make bookings (tel: (0395) 33382) for anytime of day, seven days a week. In additional to 27 highly challenging holes, Woodbury Park also boasts a 24 bay driving range with tuition available from leading local professionals. Golf equipment, including sets of clubs, can be hired from the Golf Shop.

The Championship Course offers an intriguing blend of 'typically British' moorland, parkland and heathland type golf with a 'taste of America' - excellent conditioning and four or five daring water carries thrown in for good measure: it makes for a marvellously enjoyable mix. We feel very confident that the golfer who has driven across the plunging valley fairway at the 17th, through an avenue of bluebells and ancient oak trees, before pitching to the green beyond a veritable sea of sand traps; and then tacked the tricky par three 18th with its dramatic tee shot over a picturesque lake to a semi-island green will want to return as soon as possible - if only to admire the views and to get even with the course! And we'll guarantee him or her a warm and friendly welcome.

Woodbury Park Golf Club
Woodbury Castle
Woodbury
Exeter EX5 1JJ
Tel: (0395) 33382
Fax: (0395) 33384

NORTHCOTE MANOR

The Brown family offer a warm welcome to their Country Manor Hotel, set in the seclusion and tranquillity of 12 acres of gardens and woodland. The oldest part of the house was built in 1716 and the most recent development in 1870 so within the house the Georgian and Victorian eras are still prominent and one can imagine how the local squire lived!

We offer 11 luxurious bedrooms (one with a four poster bed) all with en suite facilities, R.C. colour television, telephone, radio, hairdryer and hospitality tray. Our restaurant serves a varied menu of excellent cuisine using fresh local produce of which much is organically homegrown and a fine selection of wines from many countries.

The atmosphere is relaxed and friendly where we hope guests will feel more like house guests than paying customers.

There are many golf courses in our surrounding area including the championship courses at Saunton and a new course, Libbaton, just 2 miles away. Others include the Royal North Devon, Tiverton, Holsworthy, Torrington, Bude, Crediton and Ilfracombe. Visitors are welcome at all clubs by prior arrangement with the club secretaries.

But there's not only good golf nearby, there are many beautiful and historical places of interest to visit from glassblowing at Dartington Crystal to tasting local scrumpy at the Cider Press. Or perhaps you would prefer to investigate the Castle ruins at Tintagel or explore the most recently built castle in this country at Drogo.

We feel sure the service and ambience at the Manor and the freshness of the Devon countryside will leave no doubts in anyones mind that a truly memorable and relaxing holiday should be repeated.

Northcote Manor
Burrington
Nr Umberleigh
North Devon
EX37 9LZ
Tel: (0769) 60501
Fax: (0769) 60770

FINGALS AT OLD COOMBE MANOR FARM

The River Dart, one of the prettiest in England flows past the little unspoilt village of Dittisham in South Devon. Upstream it is about a mile wide, narrowing as it reaches the village allowing the ferryman to carry his passengers to the Torbay side. Nothing could be better than a summer's day spent visiting riverside pubs, picnicing, fishing, or simply enjoying its wildlife and tranquillity.

Resting in a valley set back from the river is Fingals, holding court over its beautifully landscaped garden, a perfect sun-trap where guests can be as energetic or relaxed as they wish. Old Coombe Manor, the site of this establishment, boasts a Queen Anne facade, although parts of the original house date back to the 16th and 17th centuries; the site itself is listed in the Domesday Book. Over the last ten years the building has been restored, renovated and extended using traditional methods by the owner Richard Johnston personally. The predominantly wood decor complements old country furniture and classical paintings to give an inviting, cosy feeling to the house.

Each of the nine bedrooms at Fingals is decorated with individual style and character; all have en-suite bathrooms and telephones; television sets are available on request. Children are always welcome and there is one family suite available, consisting of two interconnecting rooms. The hotel's sitting-room has a well-stocked library and an adjoining television-video room.

The latest addition is a magnificently structured, self-catering oak barn built in old wood building technique. Situated by the pool it is ideal for families who can enjoy the hotel restaurant and bar without abandoning their children. The facilities at Fingals ensure that you have plenty to occupy you when not exploring locally. The beautiful tiled pool with adjoining sauna and jacuzzi is half glazed for Summer fresh air but can be covered for the Autumn and Spring.

Snack lunches are available but the gastronomic highlight of the day is the superb four-course dinner, prepared with only the freshest ingredients and the best local produce. Dinner in the guests' dining room is served at one long table while a separate dining room is available should families wish to eat together in the evening or for guests planning a more intimate meal.

If you are looking for a hotel with reception desk, lobby and cocktail lounge with uniformed barman, then keep looking. Fingals is a unique and unconventional place. Staff dress informally, surnames are dispensed with and you are free to add your drinks to your bar tab any time of the day or night. if this sounds sloppy it is far from it. The staff are totally attentive, friendly and dedicated to the concept of this special feel-at-home atmosphere.

Fingals at Old Coombe Manor Farm
Dittisham
Dartmouth
TQ6 0JA
Tel: (080422) 398
Fax: (080422) 401

MANOR HOUSE (MORETONHAMPSTEAD)
CHAMPIONSHIP GOLF

Bleak and mysterious, **Dartmoor** may seem an unlikely setting for one of Britain's finest golfing gems but the Manor House Hotel course, near Moretonhampstead, is nothing less than that. Within howling distance of the Baskerville legends, it lies beneath a backdrop of granite tors and rolling hills.

Manor House itself is a vast and impressive Jacobean-style mansion, built between the Wars as a home for the W.H. Smith family. The golf course dominates the grounds of what is now a superbly refurbished hotel and country club; part of the Principal Group. Indeed, immediately on entering the gates, the driveway will take you alongside the 13th and 14th fairways. However, it is only on reaching the mansion (clubhouse somehow doesn't seem appropriate) that the full beauty of the surroundings can be appreciated. From here, the view out across the course is quite simply stunning, and the bracing moorland air should inject a sense of joie de vivre into even the most wretched of souls!

One gentleman who would appear to have no cause to be a wretched soul is **Mr. Richard Lewis.** As **Golf Manager** he effectively runs the administrative side of things and all correspondence relating to golfing matters should be addressed to him at **The Manor House Hotel Golf and Country Club, Moretonhampstead, Devon.** Mr. Lewis is also the resident PGA professional, and can be reached by telephone on **(0647) 40355.** Golfers wishing to visit the course are always made very welcome and are permitted to play on any day of the week. During the summer months it is essential to book a starting time and although the course is often pleasantly uncrowded, a quick telephone call to check for any tee reservations is always advisable, particularly at weekends. Manor House is not surprisingly a popular meeting place for golfing societies.

In 1992 the green fee payable was £22.50 per round or £28.50 for a full day, with half-rates for juniors. Unless it is impossible for some reason, a day ticket is strongly recommended and if the prospect of 36 holes is a little daunting one could always consider the merits of hiring one of the electric-powered buggies that line up outside the pro-shop. Whilst Moretonhampstead may look somewhat remote on the map (the Hotel is 2 miles west of the town) the splendid scenery of these parts should make the journey a particularly pleasant one. The B3212 is the most direct as well as the most scenic route from Exeter – a distance of approximately 14 miles. The Club's entrance is immediately off this road and is clearly signposted. Persons approaching from the Plymouth region may also find the B3212 helpful, while those

travelling from further west and from the Torbay area will probably need to use the A30/A38.

At 6016 yards the course in not particularly long by modern standards – refreshingly so, some might say – nevertheless the par of 69 is a fairly strict one and there is only one five on the card. (From the ladies tees the course measures 5010 yards, par 70). To be frank though, length is really one of the last things the golfer should be concerned about when he comes to tackle this course – the sight from the elevated first tee should make this abundantly clear. The trout-filled River Bovey meanders its way through the centre of the course and is the dominant feature on the first seven holes. It takes a 'Seve type' to try and carry it from the tee on the **1st**; it runs immediately in front of the green on the dog-leg **2nd** and all the way along the right hand side of the narrow **3rd**. This tricky par three, with its overhanging trees to the left is surely one of the finest short holes in the country. At the back of the green, and circling round to the left, lie a profusion of rhododendrons and azaleas which in early summer burst into a kaleidoscope of colour: pinks and purples, yellows, reds, vivid blue and peach colours – as someone aptly remarked on seeing it, 'Augusta comes to Devon'!

The **4th** hole is the lone par five, and a genuine one at that with the river having to be carried from the tee, trouble all the way down the left and a raised green. The river crosses again in front of the **5th** green and reappears on the **7th**, where it twice cuts across the fairway. If you can reach the **8th** tee without having once gotten wet you're a better man than most! The 8th itself is fairly unspectacular but the **9th**, after a steep climb to the tee, gives you a chance to open the shoulders as you drive across a deep valley. Two fairly difficult par threes sandwich the **11th**, the longest par four on the course. The **13th** and **14th** are what television commentators might describe as potential birdie holes, but the closing stretch is quite tough, particularly the challenging **18th** with its acutely angled fairway and blind second. As you walk off the final green and sound the iron bell to signal all clear you should be left in no doubt that you've played a very special golf course.

The Hotel acts as a rather grand 19th. An excellent and very full range of catering is offered with additional light snacks being available throughout the day in the new golfer's bar. But the balcony terrace, with its extensive views over the course and surrounding Hotel gardens is a must on a warm day .... imagine sitting out there on a bright and clear day in June, with just a hint of breeze and a cool drink in your hand .... joie de vivre? I should say so!

Hole	Yards	Par	Hole	Yards	Par
1	293	4	10	172	3
2	375	4	11	450	4
3	151	3	12	207	3
4	517	5	13	320	4
5	403	4	14	279	4
6	156	3	15	385	4
7	384	4	16	337	4
8	399	4	17	379	4
9	400	4	18	409	4
Out	**3,078**	**35**	**In**	**2,938**	**34**
			Out	**3,078**	**35**
			TOTALS	**6,016**	**69**

DUNSFORD MILLS

Resting on the original Ford of Dunsford this 17th century converted flour mill is set in countryside of breathtaking natural beauty. A short walk takes the visitor into the protected splendour of the National Trust, Devon Wildlife Trust, The Nature Conservancy Council, Devon Wildlife Trust and the magnificent Dartmoor National Park.

The hotel itself is set in a rolling valley with its own river banks populated by a fascinating variety of wildlife; from salmon and sea trout to ducks, dippers and herons. Animals frequent the tranquillity of the surrounding countryside; wild deer, kingfishers, and sometimes, for the lucky observer, mink. Domestic animals fill the fields, sheep, lambs and cattle all graze the lush vegetation while in the spring the lanes are ablaze with wild daffodils, primroses, foxgloves, wild violets, bluebells and host of glorious colour.

The hotel's main room, has a king-size, four-poster bed and en suite luxury bathroom. The writing table commands a panoramic view over the River Teign with the Bridford Woods rising up over the valley. Add to this the gurgling of the river and Mill stream and it creates the perfect setting for the true romantic. The ten spacious, luxury bedrooms all offer en suite facilities and furniture hand-built by local craftsmen. Half of them boast views overlooking the river whilst others gaze out over surrounding farmland and the charming village of Dunsford. All have remote control television. A drink before dinner in the comfortable lounge bar can be enjoyed surrounded by antiques and paintings by local artists; overlooking the river it has the natural charm of a large stone open fireplace and oak beams. The restaurant itself is located within the original working area of the flour mill. Here the water flows under the building through the original 15 foot working waterwheel, now enclosed in a glass and oakbeam case, setting the scene and atmosphere for the whole hotel. The young, imaginative Head Chef prepares the delicious cuisine, complemented by a choice from the ever expanding wine list.

The surrounding area is a walkers' paradise, offering a chance to explore Dartmoor, one of England's last great wildernesses. For the golfer two courses are available nearby along with a driving range. There is a host of activities for the sportsman, from clay and game shooting to deer stalking, fly fishing, archery and even a four-wheel drive course. Not far away are the Devon and Exeter and Newton Abbot Racecourses. Sites of historic interest abound, including the 14th century Exeter Cathedral, 12th century Guildhall, Buckfast Abbey and majestic castles.

Dartmoor takes on a completely different look during Winter, Autumn and Spring. Come and enjoy good brisk walks, returning to your hotel with large open fires, plenty of hot water, fully central heated and a cosy atmosphere.

Dunsford Mills Country House Hotel
Dunsford
Dartmoor
Devon EX6 7EF
Tel: (0647) 52011
Fax: (0647) 52988

BUCKLAND-TOUT-SAINTS HOTEL

1990 was the tri-centenary of the restoration of Buckland-Tout-Saints; William, Prince of Orange and Mary were then on the throne of England. Even in 1690 this grand Estate had been in existence 600 years before being extensively restored by Sir John Southcote. Now, located within 7 acres of beautiful parkland in the heart of the South Devon countryside, Buckland-Tout-Saints offers you a tradition that has grown out of the lavish Country House entertaining of bygone days, when the owner of a Country Estate would invite his guests down to be wined and dined and waited upon. Today, that feeling of being a privileged guest in a private house, in an atmosphere that is elegant yet informal, is something Buckland-Tout-Saints tries hard to preserve for you.

Only 20 miles from the City of Plymouth, and 30 minutes drive from the A38 dual-carriageway which links directly onto the M5 motorway at Exeter the Hotel is conveniently located. It offers many country house pursuits including croquet and its own Putting Green. Bird-watching, canoeing, clay-pigeon shooting, fishing, golf, horse riding, hot air-ballooning, sailing, squash, surfing, swimming, tennis and wind-surfing can all be arranged by the hotel with prior notice. The Dartmouth Golf and Country Club is close by, it is a beautiful course with a fine club house and many modern facilities, the hotel will be pleased to arrange your days golfing.

Plymouth attracts many major theatrical productions and tickets can be arranged - with prior notice - at the Theatre Royal.

Buckland-Tout-Saints Hotel
Goveton
Kingsbridge
Devon TQ7 2DS
Tel: (0548) 853055
Fax: (0548) 856261

DARTMOUTH GOLF AND COUNTRY CLUB

Beautifully carved from 225 acres of rolling South Devonshire countryside, the Dartmouth Golf and Country Club is one of the finest new golf facilities in the country, providing for its members the perfect golfing environment.

Built without compromise in an area of outstanding natural beauty this 27 hole golf and leisure complex is designed and built to Championship standard. Despite the demands of such a course, the strategic positioning of its tees guarantees that the course will provide an exciting, exacting and enjoyable challenge to golfers of all abilities. Spectacular views of Torbay and the surrounding South Hams countryside spread out below the dramatic contours of a course carefully designed to offer truly memorable golf.

Above all, the course was designed with the existing natural surroundings closely in mind; characteristics such as water features have been greatly enhanced during the construction phase and this, together with the planting of several thousand semi-mature tress and the introduction of many new species of flora, has created a variety of habitats and encouraged wildlife to take up home on the site.

The concept of the Clubhouse was to represent the hallmark of the Dartmouth Golf and Country Club and, sure enough, an atmosphere of relaxed elegance extends over its 2000 square metres of luxurious accommodation. Commanding an elevated position on the site of an old stone quarry, the Clubhouse holds sway over panoramic scenes of the 10th and 18th holes of the Championship course, along with sweeping views along the valley towards Torbay.

The interior design of the clubhouse, with its fine furnishings and elegant fixtures, reflects the standards of style and comfort that it has set for itself. A fully equipped leisure facility, with the emphasis firmly on relaxation, has been incorporated into the ground floor providing an extensive range of facilities from swimming pool, jacuzzi, saunas and solarium, to beauty treatments and fitness studio. Particularly thoughtful is the creche facility allowing parents to make full use of the range of amenities. The first floor of the Clubhouse accommodates the general day to day golfing needs, including the reception area, changing facilities, club rooms (incorporating lounge bar and stud bar) and fully stocked professional's shop. This floor also houses the function suite, easily capable of seating 300 people making it by far the largest of its kind in the South Hams; with its own bar and kitchens it is able to cater for private parties, wedding receptions, conferences, and corporate golf days without disturbance. The interior layout allows it to be altered in order to hold several private parties at one time, while the latest in audio-visual equipment guarantees all the necessary business support.

Along with a billiards room, the extensive dining facilities on the second floor have been carefully designed to enable private functions to be hosted without causing inconvenience to members. The superb a la carte restaurant is now also open evenings to non-members.

In short, the Dartmouth Golf and Country Club is proud to offer some of the finest facilities in the country and, whether on the course or in the clubhouse, the ultimate golfing experience.

Dartmouth Golf and Country Club
Blackawton
Totnes
Devon TQ9 7DG
Tel: (080421) 686
Fax: (080421) 628

ROYAL BEACON HOTEL

Situated in Exmouth, the oldest seaside resort in Devon, the Royal Beacon has long been established as a premier hotel. An elegant building, it was originally a Georgian posting house. The early traditions of hospitality, good fare and comfort have continued throughout the years, adapting, evolving and modernising to meet the expectations of today's sophisticated guests.

The quiet location is magnificent, facing south and looking down across our own gardens immediately to the beach, the sea and the Devon coastline.

Beautiful surroundings and comfortable furnishings are not everything - our staff create the real atmosphere. Courtesy, friendliness and professionalism are a matter of pride for them all.

The lounge and bar are spacious and there is a superb snooker room for the enthusiast ... and outside there's Devon! The perfect place for windsurfing, bird-watching, fishing, walking, visiting the theatre or playing a round of golf. Exmouth is an ideal centre from which to explore an area rich in natural and man-made beauty from the estuary's flocks of sea birds and the beautiful flower and tree displays at Bicton Gardens to the colour and excitement of Exeter Maritime Museum or the splendour of Exeter Cathedral.

End the day at the hotel's exceptional Fennels Restaurant which reflects the Victorian period in its charm and elegance. Traditional Devon cream teas are served in the afternoon and in the evening you are invited to choose from our thoughtfully planned table d'hotel or extensive a la carte menu complemented by fine wines.

Retire for the night to one of the Royal Beacon's superbly appointed, spacious rooms, many of which enjoy sea views. All have en suite facilities and colour television, radio, direct line telephone, tea and coffee making facilities, hair drier and trouser press. Each room has its own distinctive style and individuality.

Royal Beacon Hotel
The Beacon
Exmouth
Devon
EX8 2AF
Tel: (0395) 264886/265269
Fax: (0395) 268890

DEVON
COMPLETE GOLF

KEY

*** Visitors welcome at most times
** Visitors usually allowed on weekdays only
* Visitors not normally permitted (Mon, Wed) No visitors on specified days

APPROXIMATE GREEN FEES

A – £30 plus
B – £20 – £30
C – £15 – £25
D – £10 – £20
E – Under £10
F – Green fees on application

RESTRICTIONS

G – Guests only
H – Handicap certificate required
H(24) – Handicap of 24 or less required
L – Letter of introduction required
M – Visitor must be a member of another recognised club.

Axe Cliff G.C.
(0297) 24371
Axmouth, Seaton
1 mile east of Seaton.
(18)5000 yards/**/D

Bigbury G.C.
(0548) 810207
Bigbury-on-sea, Kingsbridge
(18)6076 yards/***/D/H

Chumleigh G.C.
(0769) 80519
Leigh Rd. Chumleigh
Between Exeter and Barnstaple on A377.
(18)1450 yards/***/E

Churston G.C.
(0803) 842218
Churston, Nr. Brixham
3 miles from Paignton on A379
(18)6219 yards/***/F/H/M

Downes Crediton G.C.
(0363) 773991
Hookway, Crediton
(18)5868 yards/***/D/M

East Devon G.C.
(03954) 2018
North View Rd. Budleigh
5 miles from Exmouth on A376.
(18)6214 yards/***/B/H/L

Elfordleigh Hotel G. and C.C.
(0752) 336428
Cobrook, Plympton, Plymouth
Off A38, 5 miles N.of Plymouth.
(9)56095 yards/**/D

Exeter G. & C.C.
(0392) 874139
Countess Wear, Exeter
On A379 to Exmouth.
(18)6061 yards/**/C/H

Great Torrington G.C.
(02372) 22229
Weare Trees, Torrington
1 mile north of Gt. Torrington.
(9)4418 yards/***/E

Holsworthy G.C.
(0409) 253177
Kilatree, Holsworthy
Take A3072 to Bude.
(18)5935 yards/***/E

Honiton G.C.
(0404) 44422
Middlehills, Honiton
2 miles south of town.
(18)5931 yards/***/D/H/M

Ilfracombe G.C.
(0271) 863328
Hele Bay, Ilfracombe
On A399 past Hele.
(18)5857 yards/***/D/H

Manor House G. and C.C.
(0647) 40355
Moretonhampstead,
(18)6016 yards/***/D

Newton Abbot (Stover) G.C.
(0626) 52460
Bovey Rd. Newton Abbot
Take A382 to Bovey Tracey.
(18)5834 yards/***/C/M

Okehampton G.C.
(0837) 52113
Okehampton
(18)5163 yards/***/F

Royal North Devon G.C.
(0237) 473824
Westward Ho! Bideford
On Bone Hill Rd. near Northam.
(18)6662 yards/***/C/H

Saunton G.C.
(0271) 812436
Saunton, Nr. Braunton
Take B3231 to Croyde Bay.
(18)6703 yards/***/C/H
(18)6356 yards/***/C/H

Sidmouth G.C.
(0395) 513023
Peak Hill, Cotmaston Rd.
(18)5166 yards/***/D/H

Staddon Heights G.C.
(0752) 402475
Staddon Heights, Plymstock
5 miles from Plymouth on A379.
(18)5861 yards/***/D/H

Tavistock G.C.
(0822) 612049
Down Rd. Tavistock
(18)6250 yards/***/D/H

Teignmouth G.C.
(0626) 774194
Exeter Rd. Teignmouth
2 miles from Teignmouth on B3192.
(18)6142 yards/***/C/H/M

Thurlestone G.C.
(0548) 560405
Thurlestone, Nr. Kingsbridge
Take A379 to Thurlesrtone.
(18) 6303 yards/***/C/H/M

Tiverton G.C.
(0884) 252187
Post Hill, Tiverton
(18) 6263 yards/***/C/H

Torquay G.C.
(0803) 37371
Petitor Rd. St. Marychurch
North of Torquay on A379
(18)6192 yards/***/C/H

Warren G.C.
(0626) 862255
Dawlish Warren, Dawlish
East of Dawlish on A379.
(18)968 yards/**/D/H

Woodbury Park G.C.
(0395) 33382
Woodbury Castle, Woodbury, nr. Exeter
M5 Jct. 30, then follow A3052
(18)6707 yards/***/C

Wrangaton G.C.
(03647) 3229
Wrangaton, South Brent
Off A38 between S. Brent and Bittaford.
(9)5790/**/F

Yelverton G.C.
(0822) 852824
Golf Links
5 miles S of Tavistock on A386
(18)6288 yards/***/C/M

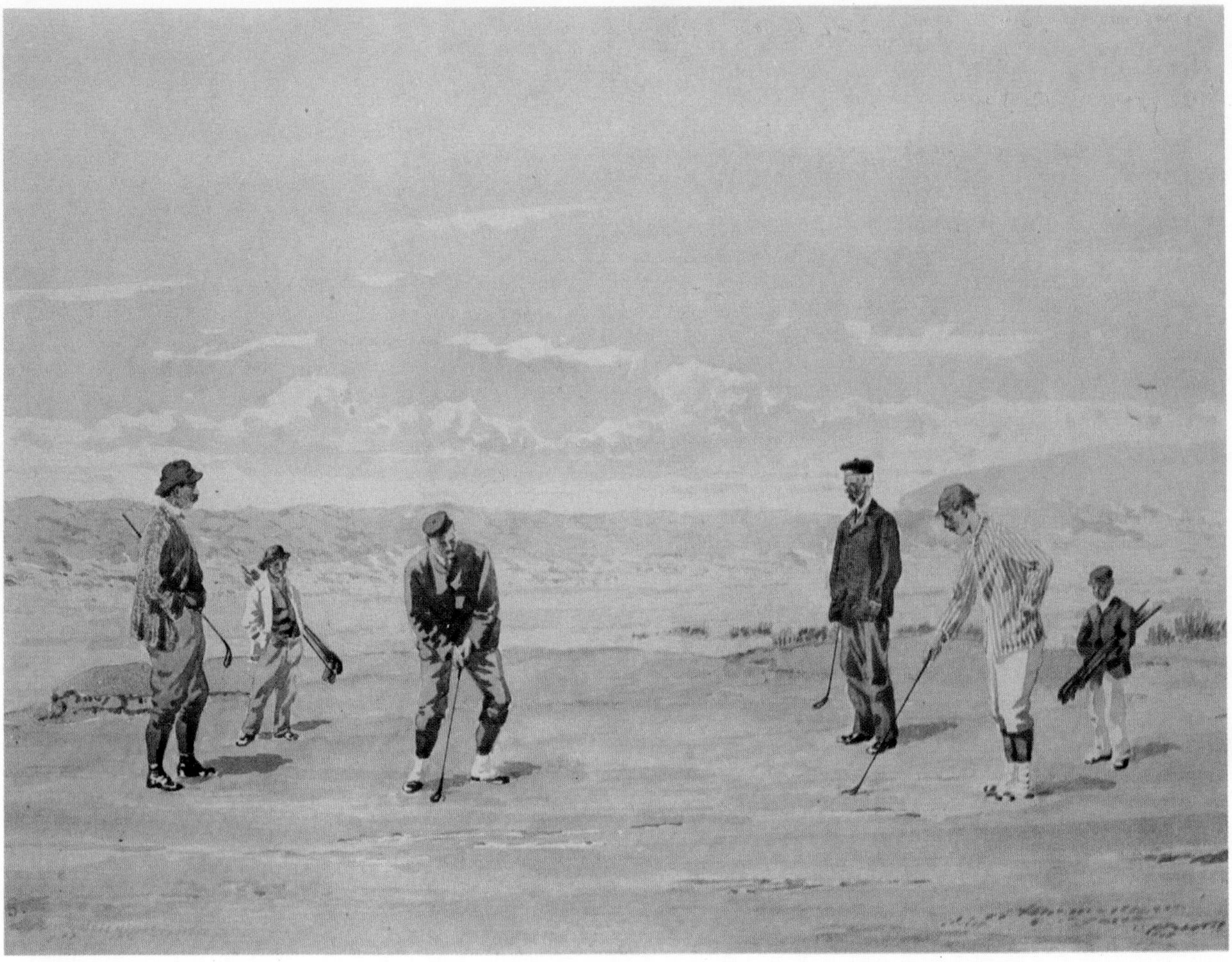

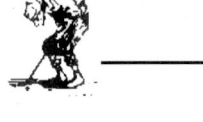

Major Hopkins A FOURSOME AT WESTWARD HO! Burlington Gallery

SOMERSET, AVON, DORSET & WILTSHIRE

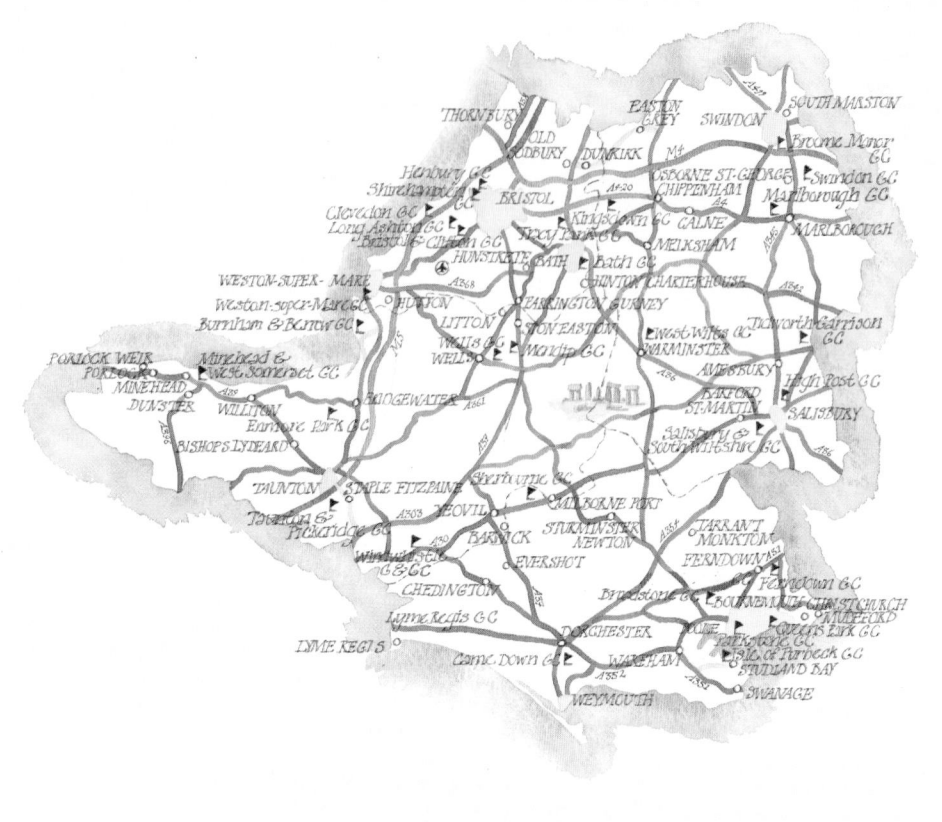

Robert Wade   **THE CADDIE**   *Rosenstiel's*

SOMERSET, AVON, DORSET & WILTSHIRE
CHOICE GOLF

From the wild beauty of Exmoor to the mystery of Stonehenge. The Quantocks and the Mendips; Lyme Regis and Bath; Avebury, Chesil Beach and Lulworth Cove. The West Country offers so much, no wonder those of us who do not live there are more than a little envious.

The golf too can be equally spectacular. There may not be a Wentworth or a St. Georges here but the region offers a considerable variety and there is certainly no shortage of challenge. There is a true Championship links at Burnham and Berrow and a magnificent cliff top course at the Isle of Purbeck. Excellent downland golf can be enjoyed at Long Ashton and Bath while Bournemouth offers some majestic heathland and parkland type courses. We shall tee off in Somerset.

SOMERSET

Burnham and Berrow (featured ahead) is without doubt the finest course in the county and the place where John H. Taylor wielded his famous mashie to great effect. The two holiday towns of **Minehead** and **Weston-Super-Mare** house the region's other two links courses. The Minehead and West Somerset Golf Club has more than a hundred years of history – it therefore remembers the quieter days in the years 'Before Butlins'. A fairly flat and windy course, it is situated on the eastern side of the town. Visitors are welcome, though during the peak season a quick telephone call to the Club is advisable. The same can be said of Weston – a slightly longer, well-maintained course, located just off the main A370 Bristol road.

After an arduous day's golf at Burnham, visitors can find more than adequate accommodation in the Club's Dormy House. Some quite incredible steaks are served in the clubhouse, 'worth killing for!' according to one of my mashie wielding friends. Further up the scale, Weston has a number of hotels, with the Grand Atlantic situated on the seafront (0934) 626543, and bordering the resort is Hutton Court (0934) 814343, a magnificent 15th century manor house. Minehead offers the York Hotel (0643) 705151 and the Periton Park Hotel (0643) 706885, both within easy reach of the local course. The Gascony (0643) 705939 and the Alcombe House Hotel (0643) 705130 are also suitable resting places, whilst slightly farther afield, the Luttrell Arms (0643) 821555 in Dunster is a superb hostelry.

Taunton's golf course is at Corfe, the **Taunton and Pickeridge** Golf Club. It is located close to the town's race track and is fairly undulating. In Taunton The Castle (0823) 272671 is a super place to stay and a nearby pub of note is the Greyhound at Staple Fitzpaine. For the more energetically minded, The Cedar Falls Health Farm (0823) 433233 at Bishops Lydeard makes it all the easier to indulge elsewhere. In Yeovil the delightful Manor Hotel (0935) 23116 is very handy for Sherborne Golf Club over the border in Dorset.

More golf is found near Bridgwater. **Enmore Park**, located to the south of the town is a very pleasant medium length affair. The course enjoys a delightful setting and nestles around the foothills of the Quantocks. The White House Hotel (0984) 32306 at Williton is convenient for the Golf Club. Moving from the Quantocks to the Mendips, the **Mendip** Golf Club at Gurney Slade offers possibly the most spectacular vistas of any course in the South West. From its 4th fairway, almost 1,000 feet above sea-level, on a clear day it is possible to sight the Cotswolds and the Quantocks,

the Welsh Mountains and the Purbeck Hills, Glastonbury Tor and Westbury's White Horse... need I go on? Mendip is an enjoyable course and very visitor friendly. An agreeable pub to note in Gurney Slade is The George Inn.

The city of **Wells** is always worth inspecting. The Cathedral is splendid and after a round on the Wells golf course a pleasant lunch can be enjoyed at the Ancient Gate House (0749) 72029. One final course to mention in Somerset is the magnificently titled **Windwhistle** Golf and Squash Club at Chard. The golf course is another laid out on high ground and offering extensive views. It's also close to the famous Cricket St. Thomas Wildlife Park, where birdies and eagles abound.

AVON

The golf course at **Clevedon** stares spectacularly out across the mouth of the Severn. Clevedon is a cliff top course rather than a links and is well worth visiting. By travelling inland from Clevedon towards Bristol along the B3128, two of the city's best courses are reached before the famous Suspension Bridge. **Long Ashton** is actually immediately off the B3128, while to find **Bristol and Clifton** a left turn should be taken along the B3129. There is probably little to choose between the two, both being particularly attractive examples of downland golf. **Henbury** Golf Club is closer to the centre of Bristol, about 3 miles to the north to be precise, in the quiet suburb of Westbury-on-Trym. Henbury is a very mature parkland course with an abundance of trees making for some very attractive and challenging holes. One final club to recommend in Bristol is **Shirehampton** – always beautifully maintained.

Perhaps the most stylish hotel in Bristol is the aptly named Grand Hotel (0272) 291645 on Broad Street. Two recommended restaurants are Harveys (0272) 277665 and Restaurant Lettonie (0272) 686456 in Stoke Bishop. An excellent base to the north of the city at Thornbury is the tudor styled Thornbury Castle (0454) 418511.

Anyone travelling from Bristol to Bath (or vice versa) is likely to pass within a few miles of the **Tracy Park** Golf and Country Club at Wick. If possible a detour is strongly recommended. Tracy Park is a newish course, built in the mid- seventies around a 400 year old mansion which acts as a rather impressive clubhouse. It offers a very good test of golf.

Everybody, they say, falls in love with Bath – the Romans did, the Georgians did and the Americans think it's cute. For visiting golfers, if the other half should come under the spell, the City has two attractive propositions: **Bath** Golf Club and **Lansdown** Golf Club. The former, commonly known as Sham Castle because of its situation adjacent to Bath's greatest fraud (there is a beautiful castle frontage but nothing else!) is laid out high above the city and provides tremendous views over the surrounding countryside. Lansdown occupies flatter ground adjacent to Bath Races.

Staying in Bath is a sheer delight. With the Roman Baths, the Abbey, The Pump Rooms, a wealth of museums and galleries, the Royal Crescent and the Theatre Royal – there are so many attractions. The hotels in the city are among some of the finest in the country. The Royal Crescent (0225) 319090 takes pride of place but The Apsley House (0225) 336966, the Paradise House Hotel (0225) 317723 and The Priory (0225) 331922 can

SOMERSET, AVON, DORSET & WILTSHIRE

also be recommended with confidence. The Hotels themselves house excellent restaurants but other popular eating places in Bath include Popjoys (0225) 460494, The Clos du Roy (0225) 744447 and Garlands (0225) 442283. Only a short distance to the south of Bath, and set in the heart of some glorious countryside, are a number of other outstanding establishments. Ston Easton Park (076 121) 631 boasts a considerable reputation as does Hunstrete House (07618) 578. Another gem is The Homewood Park Hotel (0225) 723731 in Hinton Charterhouse. North of Bath the marvellously named Old Sodbury offers The Cross Hands Hotel (0454) 313000 and Dunkirk, The Petty France Hotel (045423) 361. Just outside Bath at Colerne is Lucknam Park (0225) 742777 a delightful early 18th century mansion converted into an hotel.

WILTSHIRE

Five years ago there were only a dozen golf courses in Wiltshire; by the end of 1993 there should be at least 20. Perhaps the two developments that have attracted most attention are the beautiful Dave Thomas designed course at **Bowood Park**, just off the A4 between Calne and Chippenham, and the more private but equally impressive **Castle Combe** project north west of Chippenham, the handiwork of Peter Alliss and Clive Clark.

In **Wooton Bassett**, just west of Swindon, Alliss and Clark have constructed another new course, thus giving Swindon's golfers 3 courses close to the town; the 2 others are **Broome Manor** and the **Swindon** Golf Club, both are situated south of the town. The latter at Ogbourne St George, despite its name, is in fact closer to Marlborough than Swindon. It is an undulating, downland type course – very typical of the county's more established courses. Broome Manor is a public course and thus probably more accommodating to the visiting golfer.

Swindon is one of the fastest growing towns in the British Isles. A comfortable place to stay here is The Wiltshire (0793) 528282 and in Blunsdon is the charming Blunsdon House (0793) 721701. The Robin Hood Inn at Ogbourne St George is very handy after a game at Swindon.

Marlborough Golf Club is a near neighbour of Swindon Golf Club, being situated to the north west of the town on the Marlborough Downs. It offers similarly wide ranging views (and is similarly breezy!) The Sun (0672) 512081 in Marlborough is an ideal 19th – it offers good food in addition to reasonably priced accommodation. Also worth a visit is The Ivy House (0672) 515333 – extremely comfortable. A pleasant drive westwards will take you to Lacock near Chippenham where the Sign of The Angel is a tremendous 15th Century Inn and still further west there is a good golf course at **Kingsdown**. An excellent hotel in Chippenham is The Manor House (0249) 782206.

Dropping down the county, near Warminster, the **West Wilts** Golf Club is quite popular; the new 'pay and play' **Erlestoke Sands** course, south west of Devizes should prove to be, and t'other side of Stonehenge, **Tidworth Garrison** is certainly one of Wiltshire's top courses. It lies on Salisbury Plain and is owned by the Army. (Note the excellent Antrobus Arms (0980) 623163 in Amesbury).

Salisbury offers two fine challenges, to the north, **High Post** and to the south west **Salisbury and South Wilts**. High Post is generally considered to be the leading course in the county. It's another classic downland type. Salisbury and South Wilts offers some splendid views of Salisbury's Cathedral. One's best base in Salisbury is probably either The Rose and Crown Hotel (0722) 27908 or The Old Bell Hotel (0722) 327958. Finally, yet another new 18 hole course scheduled to open in 1992 is at **Hamptworth Park** in the south east of the county, near Landford.

DORSET

The better golf courses in Dorset lie within a ten mile radius of the centre of Bournemouth. Having said all that, **Sherborne** in the far north of the county is undoubtedly one of the prettiest inland courses to be found anywhere in Britain. In nearby Gillingham, you can stay at the Stock Hill House Hotel (0747) 823626 which comes with our highest recommendation and boasts an excellent restaurant to boot. Also, in Evershot, The Summer Lodge is a fine restaurant and in Sturminster Newton stands Plumber Manor (0258) 72507 a gorgeous country house.

In the south west of the county, **Lyme Regis**, famed for its fossils and more recently its French Lieutenant's Woman, has a fairly hilly 18 hole course which lies to the east of the town. The road between Lyme Regis and Weymouth provides dramatic views over Chesil Beach and passes through some of the most beautiful villages in England. The area north of Weymouth is Thomas Hardy country. Dorchester stands in the middle of it all and **Came Down** Golf Club is well worth noting when in these parts as is the **Mid Dorset** Golf Club at Blandford Forum. Yalbury Cottage (0305) 262382 in Dorchester offers good accommodation and the surrounding countryside has remained gloriously unspoilt. If one chooses to stay in Lyme Regis, The Fairwater Head Country House Hotel (02977) 349 is an excellent bet and The Pilot Boat is a good pub. The excellent Chedington Court (0935) 891265 in Beaminster should also be considered.

Like Burnham and Berrow, the **Isle of Purbeck** and **Ferndown** are featured ahead but **Parkstone** and **Broadstone** also fall in the 'must be visited' category. They are beautiful heathland courses with much heather, gorse and pine trees and each is kept in immaculate condition. In addition to a game on one or more of these great courses, there are a handful of other easier-to-play courses around Bournemouth and Poole, including the new **Bulbury Woods** Golf Club at Lytchett Matravers west of Poole; Bournemouth's public courses shouldn't be overlooked either: **Meyrick Park** is very good while **Queens Park** is often described as the finest public course in England.

The Bournemouth – Poole – Swanage area abounds with hotels and restaurants. Here are just a few suggestions: In Bournemouth, The Swallow Highcliff (0202) 557702, Royal Bath (0202) 555555 and The Hotel Collingwood (0202) 557575 are all good whilst Crusts (0202) 551430 is an excellent restaurant; in Poole, The Mansion House (0202) 685666 and Barrie's Seafood restaurant (0202) 708810 are recommended. Swanage offers The Pines (0929) 425211 and Christchurch, Splinters restaurant (0202) 483454. Ferndown golfers can look to the comfortable Dormy Hotel (0202) 872121 and Parkstone players can enjoy superb food at both Isabels (0202) 747885 and The Warehouse on the quay (0202) 677238. People wishing to get away from the sea and sand, or the water hazards and bunkers should visit Tarrant Monkton. Here in the popular Langton Arms (025889) 225, a converted stables makes for a really splendid little restaurant.

LUCKNAM PARK

Lucknam Park is a magnificent country house, situated six miles from the Georgian City of Bath, set in extensive parkland of two hundred and eighty acres. A focus of fine society and gracious living for over 250 years, Lucknam Park now recreates, as a luxurious hotel, the elegance and style of an era long ago.

Guests approach the hotel along a mile-long beech-lined avenue, leading to the house and its honey-toned stonework. Wide lawns, abundant fresh flowers and an aura of quiet and calm promise a very individual welcome. Whether you are a traveller, a gourmet or simply a romantic, guests will find at Lucknam Park an elegance and tranquillity born out of a sense of everything being right and well ordered.

The eleven suites and thirty-one bedrooms are furnished with a delicate sense of historical context, but also with the luxury and facilities demanded of a first class country-house hotel. Individually designed, with generous space and splendid views, each one enjoys the comfort and charming service which help to make Lucknam Park an extra special hotel.

The award-winning restaurant (recently receiving its first Michelin Star) is set with exquisite porcelain, silver and glass, reflecting the sumptuous but discreet atmosphere and service. Our highly acclaimed Head Chef, Michael Womersley, provides a frequently changing menu of Modern English cuisine using only the freshest ingredients. Wine can be chosen from an impressive list of over 350 wines and our Sommelier is delighted to assist and advise on the perfect choice.

For relaxing and unwinding the Leisure Spa facilities at Lucknam Park are second to none, providing a superb balance between gentle exercise and total pampering. In the style of a Roman Villa and set within the walls of the old garden the Leisure Spa opens up another world: indoor swimming pool and jacuzzi, saunas and steam room, a fully equipped gymnasium, snooker room, beauty salon and tennis courts are all of the highest standards.

The Beauty Salon offers all Clarins Beauty products and treatments. These treatments range from '6 minute' makeovers, using the new Le Maquillage range to full Paris Method massages, known as the 'Rolls Royce' of treatments.

Guided tours with personal guide can be arranged to explore the splendours of the glorious City of Bath and surrounding countryside. The delightful villages of Castle Combe, Lacock and the stately homes of Bowood House and Corsham Court are all close by. Many other activities are available too. Take your pick from Hot Air Ballooning, Golf, Motor Racing, Horse Riding, Clay Pigeon Shooting, Fishing, Archery and Boating. The magnificent Theatre Royal in Bath even holds private seats for guests at Lucknam Park.

Lucknam Park epitomises a country house hotel at its best. The hotel is less than two hours drive from London and guests can be sure that their memories of Lucknam Park will stay with them for a long time to come.

Lucknam Park
Colerne
Wiltshire SN14 8AZ
Tel: (0225) 724777
Fax: (0225) 743536

BURNHAM & BERROW
CHAMPIONSHIP GOLF

I wonder how many people have travelled along the M5 between Bristol and Exeter and wondered what lay beyond the great Iron Age fort that rises out of level ground, like something from out of 'Close Encounters', midway between Weston-Super-Mare and Bridgwater. Well, many golfers will know that a short distance behind the great hill lies one of England's finest links courses.

Burnham and Berrow appeared on the golfing map in 1891 and the first professional the Club engaged was a no lesser a man than **John H. Taylor**. The great man was then in fact a lad of 19 although within three years he was to win the Open Championship at Sandwich – the first of his five victories. John Henry thought very highly of what, until quite recently, had been a 'wild rabbit infested waste of sandhills' for he said it was here, at Burnham, that he was 'given the splendid opportunity of developing my mashie play' (as the course) 'necessitated very accurate approach play.'

The present day visitor to the North Somerset club is most unlikely to confront a gathering of wild rabbits (at least of the animal variety) nor, one assumes, will he possess a mashie amongst his armoury. However, despite a number of alterations made over the years, the towering sandhills remain by far the course's most dominant feature.

Not surprisingly Burnham and Berrow is a popular course and whatever the time of year visitors would be wise to telephone the Club before setting off. **Mrs. E.L.Sloman** is the Secretary and she can be contacted on **(0278) 785760**. The Club's professional, **Mark Crowther-Smith**, can be reached on **(0278) 784545**. Persons interested in organising a Society meeting are advised to write to the Secretary, the Club's full address being, **Burnham and Berrow Golf Club, St Christopher's Way, Burnham- on-Sea, Somerset TA8 2PE**.

Green fees for 1992 were set at £28 for weekdays and £40 at weekends, fees being payable in the clubhouse. For juniors the fees were half the above rates. Persons holidaying in the vicinity (Weston-Super-Mare is less than 10 miles away) might well consider the merits of a weekly ticket (£165 in 1992) or a fortnightly ticket (£320 in 1992). Furthermore, in addition to the 18 hole Championship Course there is also an adjacent 9 hole course situated alongside the sea. Whilst probably not quite up to the standard of the full Championship Course, at 3275 yards, par 36, it certainly represents a fine challenge and the green fee of £8 would appear to be excellent value.

Approaching by car from both North and South the M5 is the most direct route, leaving at exit 22. Thereafter one should follow the B3140. The course is situated about a mile north of Burnham-on-Sea and is well signposted.

Right from the **1st** hole the premium on accuracy becomes apparent. Anything short of a straight tee shot will leave a blind, not to mention very awkward second. At one time the layout of the course demanded the playing of several blind shots. However, today, accurate driving will largely eliminate such difficulties although on a number of holes the base of the flagstick will not be visible when playing the approach shot. As he or she stands on the 1st green, two features, in addition to the omnipresent sandhills will strike the first time visitor. The one is the condition of the greens – quite superb: the other is the surrounding tangling rough – buckthorn it's called – avoid it like the plague (if you can!) Burnham's **2nd** is a good straight hole played from an elevated tee, whereas the **3rd**, at least from the back, is one of those 'bite-off-as-much-as-you-dare' holes with the fairway dog-legging sharply to the left towards a sunken punch–bowl green. From the **4th** tee there is the first of several panoramic views of the Bristol Channel and distant Wales as the course moves nearer the sea. There are two par threes on the front nine, the **5th** and the **9th**, the latter is surely one of the finest short holes to be found anywhere.

On reaching the turn anyone claiming to have mastered the large sandhills may well have to eat his words after playing the **10th**: a minor mountain must be carried from the tee and there is a severe drop away to the right – be warned! If the front nine is perhaps the more interesting of the halves, the second nine is probably the more testing. The **11th** is a long par four and the **12th** and **13th** require very precise second shots; both the short holes are exceptionally tricky and the **18th** needs a couple of mighty big hits if it is to be reached in two. A good score at Burnham certainly has to be earned, but is immensely satisfying if achieved.

Visitors should find the clubhouse atmosphere pleasantly informal. The catering is of a high standard and is offered daily between the hours of 11 am and 6 pm. With prior notice both breakfast and dinner can be arranged. Visitors might also wish to note the Club's Dormy House which can sleep eight persons. Burnham and Berrow is a friendly Club and well worth a visit. Clearly the message to all golfers who pass down the M5 oblivious to what goes on beyond the great hump is quite simply, come on over!

Hole	Yards	Par	Hole	Yards	Par
1	381	4	10	370	4
2	396	4	11	422	4
3	384	4	12	388	4
4	480	5	13	475	5
5	160	3	14	181	3
6	397	4	15	438	4
7	450	4	16	329	4
8	483	5	17	201	3
9	163	3	18	449	4
Out	3,294	36	In	3,253	35
			Out	3,294	36
			TOTALS	6,547	71

CHEDINGTON COURT

Chedington Court is a traditional country house hotel built in the local mellow hamstone, nestling below the leafy ridge of a Dorset hillside on the edge of Thomas Hardy country. The view from the house is one of the most spectacular in the south of England. The ten-acre garden with its terraces, balustrades, pools, some rare trees and shrubs which attract a huge variety of birdlife and butterflies, combines a subtle blend of the well-tended and the wild. A reputed thousand year old yew tree is set among the tombstones in the old churchyard which forms part of the gardens, which also feature a massive sculptured yew hedge.

The welcoming interior of the house creates an atmosphere of comfortable yet distinctive informality with its old Persian rugs, stone fireplaces, fine brass fittings and antique furniture. Ten spacious bedrooms and their bathrooms, all different, feature most attractive fabrics and furniture.

The renowned restaurant offers a limited choice of French and English style cooking with carefully prepared well chosen raw materials with the accent on taste and popularity. Vegetarians and special diets are catered for. The acclaimed wine list shows over 500 wines from around the world, many half bottles, many at modest prices.

The golf course is 9 holes, par 74, built on 90 acres of parkland bisected by an ancient droveway. It measures 3425 yards and it is one of the longest 9-hole courses in the country. All the holes have very different characteristics and present their own individual challenge. Described as one of the best of the newer golf courses, it makes use of the natural features of the beautiful rolling countryside. The course is particularly attractive in the spring with the wild flowers in the rough and blossom in the hedgerows. Preservation of wildlife and the natural fauna and flora are of prime concern in the working management of the course. The surrounding wooded hills provide a sensational backdrop of changing colours through-out the year.

Anyone wishing to learn the game can start on the associated 780 yard pitch and putt course and there are two practice areas, one for chipping and one for driving.

Fly fishing, horse-riding, shooting and ballooning are some of the activities that can be arranged. The many fascinating places to visit, both the well documented and the remote, offer the visitor a wonderfully worthwhile interesting memorable holiday.

Chedington Court
Chedington
Beaminster
Dorset DT8 3HY
Tel: (0935) 891265
Fax: (0935) 891442

THE MANOR HOUSE

Time stands still in the Bybrook valley at the southern tip of the Cotswolds. Renowned as one of the prettiest villages in England, picturesque Castle Combe nestles in this delightful wooded valley where nothing has changed for the past 200 years. Rough-hewn limestone cottages, ancient market cross and a packbridge over the Bybrook, described in 1458 as 'the great town bridge', are the epitome of a peaceful English village.

Certainly there can be no lovelier approach to any village than the narrow lane winding its way down to Castle Combe through a green tunnel of interlocking branches.

To the enchantment of this hidden village, the Manor House lends an extra fairy tale dimension. Steeped in history, with parts of the house dating back to the 14th century and added to by the Jacobeans in 1664, it is the quintessential English manor. A symphony of chimneys, mullioned windows and creeper covered walls and inside welcoming log fires and inviting sofas.

There is rich wood panelling, and gleaming glass and silver in the candlelit 'Bybrook' restaurant. There are bedrooms tucked away in romantic attics, or boasting an Elizabethan fireplace and triple aspect views. They are all luxurious, some with four poster beds, others with Victorian style bathrooms. All the rooms in the main house have been restored and refurbished during the past two years to an exceptional degree, revealing hidden beams, stonework and a grain drying kiln.

Croquet, tennis and a heated outside swimming pool are all available for guests, with trout fishing on the one mile stretch of the Bybrook flowing through the 26 acres of gardens and parkland.

The Manor House is surrounded by countryside designated as an area of outstanding natural beauty. There are suggested walks through neighbouring woodland, or for the more energetic there are cycles to hire for visits to the many delightful nearby Cotswold villages.

Set in 200 acres of wooded valley and downland, an exceptional new golf course has been created. Castle Combe Golf Club, dominated by ancient oak and beech woods is only two minutes driving distance from the Manor House.

Guests staying at the Manor House are welcomed at the Golf Club and the 6,200 yard, par 71 course, designed by Peter Allis, will provide interesting and challenging golf for the average golfer and good player alike.

Although lost in the heart of the Cotswold countryside, access is not difficult. The M4 motorway is only 15 minutes away and the journey from London by road takes but 1 hour, 40 minutes. The intersection with the M5 is only 20 minutes away, linking the Midlands, the North and South West for ease of access.

The Manor House
Castle Combe
Chippenham
Wiltshire
SN14 7HR
Tel: (0249) 782206
Fax: (0249) 782159

ISLE OF PURBECK
CHAMPIONSHIP GOLF

Most people are a little surprised when they learn that the Isle of Purbeck Golf Club was founded as long ago as 1892 – a decade before Sunningdale and Walton Heath. They are probably even more surprised when they hear that Enid Blyton and her husband were once owners of the Club. Originally only a 9 hole course, there are now 27 holes comprising the 18 hole **Purbeck** Course and an adjacent, shorter 9 hole course, The **Dene**. In 1966 a superb new Clubhouse was built using the local Purbeck stone and it was around this time that more and more people began to consider seriously the quality of the golf here as well as the sheer beauty of the Club's setting.

Today the Club is owned and managed by the Robinson family. **Mrs. Joan Robinson** is Managing Director and she can be contacted on **(0929) 44361**. All written communications should be addressed to her at **The Isle of Purbeck Golf Club, Swanage, Dorset, BH19 3AB**. The Club's Professional, **Kevin Spurgeon** can be contacted on **(0929) 44354**.

Visitors to the Isle of Purbeck are welcome to play on both courses although those wishing to play on the Purbeck course must possess a handicap. Green fees for 1992 were set at £22.50 per round and £30 per day to play on the Purbeck course during the week, with £27.50 (£35) payable at weekends and Bank Holidays. Junior golfers pay £13 for a weekday round on the Purbeck course. The Dene course can be played for £10 during the week or £12 at the weekend, with a reduction for those teeing off after 4.30pm. Buggies are for hire at an extra £25 per round.

Swanage has become a very popular holiday centre and keen golfers might consider the merits of a temporary membership of the Club. In 1992, a week's golf on the Purbeck course was set at £165, two weeks at £240, and three at £275. There are reductions for joint membership and for those wishing to limit their golf to the Dene course. Visitors may also wish to note that the Club stages a limited number of open competitions during the summer. Information concerning these can be obtained from Mrs. Robinson. Golfing Societies are encouraged to come to the Isle of Purbeck and those organising should find the Club very accommodating.

Getting to the Isle of Purbeck may present the biggest headache. This is hardly the most accessible of Britain's golf clubs – not that the Club can be blamed for that! Anyway, the best routes are probably as follows: from the West the A35 runs from Honiton through Dorchester and joins the A351 at Lytchett Minster near Poole. The A351 should be followed as far as Corfe Castle from which the B3351 Studland road should be taken. The Club is situated just off this road. Travelling from the North the A350 also joins the A351 near Poole and from the Bournemouth/Poole area a car ferry operates between Sandbanks and Shell Bay and avoids the drive around Poole Harbour.

Any of the aforementioned headaches will surely be dispelled on arrival at the Clubhouse. The south coast possesses a number of scenic courses, but one would be very pushed to find an equal to the magnificent views provided by the Isle of Purbeck. The view from the **5th** on the Purbeck Course, 'Agglestone' is particularly outstanding as you tee off from the top of an ancient Saxon burial mound. The par three **11th**, Island, with its backdrop of pines and two tier green is also an exceptional hole.

For those who find the modern day monster courses somewhat tedious with the great emphasis they place on brute force (and ignorance?) the Purbeck Course should prove rather refreshing. From the back tees it measures 6248 yards (par 71) whilst from the forward tees the course is reduced to 5823 yards (par 69). From the Ladies tees the course measures 5648 yards (par 73).

On returning to the Clubhouse, the golfer will find that a full range of catering is offered and that the food and service is of a high standard. The Clubhouse has recently undergone total refurbishment, with a new bar, restaurant and showers. Breakfast and dinner can be arranged and lunch and high teas are offered daily. A jacket and tie must be worn for dinner and Sunday lunch. Again, some splendid views are to be enjoyed from the Clubhouse.

When in South Dorset many visitors like to take in a spot of fossil hunting. Lyme Regis and Charmouth are within easy reach, however, golfers need not look beyond the four walls of the Clubhouse – it is full of old fossils. Lest I be accused of insulting the Members, I should quickly explain: when the Clubhouse was built several fossilised dinosaur footprints and some massive ammonites were incorporated into the interior walls. It therefore follows – and golf historians please note – that to a limited extent the Isle of Purbeck could be said to possess the oldest Clubhouse in the world!

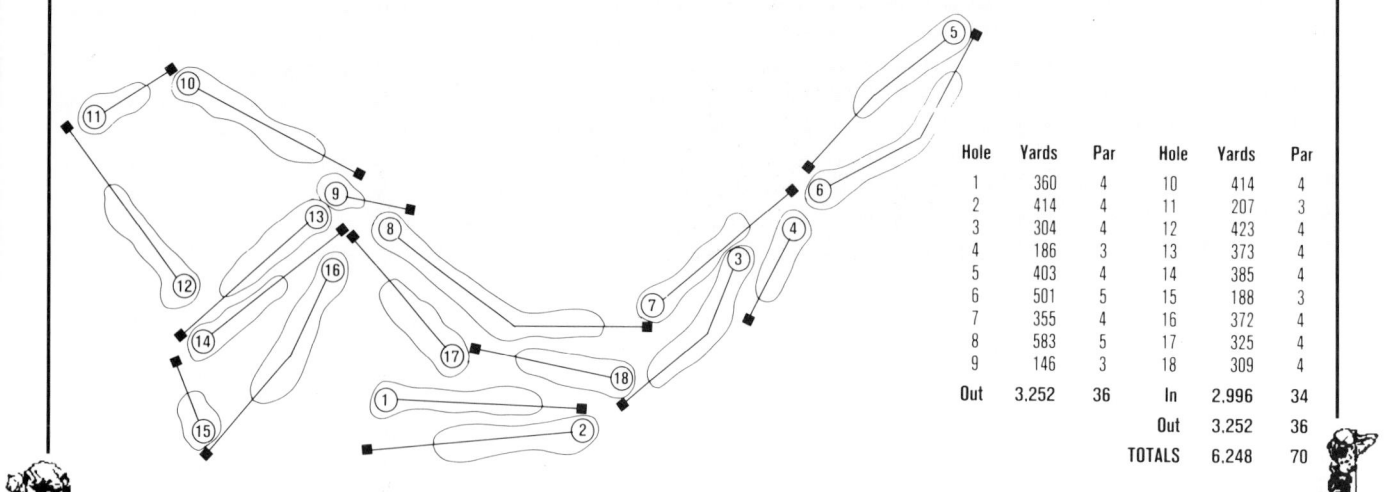

Hole	Yards	Par	Hole	Yards	Par
1	360	4	10	414	4
2	414	4	11	207	3
3	304	4	12	423	4
4	186	3	13	373	4
5	403	4	14	385	4
6	501	5	15	188	3
7	355	4	16	372	4
8	583	5	17	325	4
9	146	3	18	309	4
Out	3.252	36	In	2.996	34
			Out	3.252	36
			TOTALS	6.248	70

FERNDOWN
CHAMPIONSHIP GOLF

Ask a group of golfers to give an example of a beautifully conditioned golf course and the chances are they'll cite the likes of Augusta National and Muirfield Village. There is little doubt that when it comes to perfectly manicured fairways and quick, ultra-true greens the American courses tend to be superior to their British counterparts. Ferndown, however, is a definite exception. Indeed the fairways and greens are often among the best kept in the whole of Britain. Someone clearly deserves a mighty large pat on the back!

There are in fact two courses at Ferndown, the **Old** and the **New**. The Old Course was originally designed in 1912 by **Harold Hilton**, who was twice Open Champion before the turn of the century. The shorter New Course, which has nine holes but eighteen tees, has a much more recent history being designed in 1969 by **J. Hamilton-Stutt** and opened two years later.

The Secretary at Ferndown is **Mr. Eddie Robertson**, Tel **(0202) 874602**. Visitors to the Club are welcome on any week day provided prior permission is first obtained. Societies are limited to Tuesdays and Fridays and written applications should be addressed to the Secretary at **Ferndown Golf Club, 119 Links Road, Ferndown, Wimborne, Dorset, BH22 8BU**. All visitors and Society members must be prepared to produce a handicap certificate or alternatively a letter of introduction from their home Club.

To play the Old Course the green fee set in 1992 was £35 during the week with £40 payable at the weekend – this sum applies for a single round or a full day's golf. The green fee for the New Course is £15 during the week or £20 at weekends.

Doug Sewell, the professional at Ferndown, can be reached on **(0202) 873825)**. A former Walker Cup player and very fine professional, I once read that in an Alliance Meeting at Ferndown he played the course in 60 strokes – enough said! Ferndown has indeed been very fortunate with its professionals; Percy Alliss served the Club for over 25 years and it was here that his son Peter learnt to play.

Located approximately six miles north of Bournemouth, Ferndown is quite easily reached from all directions. Motoring from the West of England the A35 from Dorchester, which suddenly becomes the A31 near Bere Regis passes through Ferndown very close to the Golf Club. Approaching from the East, from London the M3 runs to Southampton which in turn is linked to Ferndown (or Trickett's Cross to be

precise) by the A31. The left fork should be taken at Trickett's Cross and this leads on to Golf Links Road, the course being immediately on the left. From the North the route is via Salisbury where the A338 should be followed as far as Ringwood and thereafter the A31 as above. Finally anyone who happens to possess their own jet may wish to note that Bournemouth has a small airport at Hurn, again very close to the Golf Club.

The Old Course at Ferndown measures 6442 yards from the back tees, par and standard scratch both being 71. From the forward tees the length is reduced by a little over 200 yards. The layout is essentially one of two loops, an inner loop comprising holes one to eight and the outer containing the ninth to the eighteenth.

Ferndown's fairways are of the sandy, heathland type and are gently undulating throughout. The rough consists mainly of heather and together with the many pines and fir trees gives the course a most attractive appearance. There are a considerable number of dog-leg holes necessitating much thought from the tee. The toughest holes on the course are possibly the uphill **6th**, which is normally played into the wind, the dog-leg **9th** and the **11th** – all fairly lengthy par fours from the back tees. One should also mention the **5th**, an excellent par three where the rhododendrons provide a splash of colour in season and the **16th** named 'Hilton's Hole' after its illustrious architect. At 5604 yards (par 70) the New Course is less demanding in terms of length but it too has its challenges and is set in equally beautiful surroundings.

Ferndown's Clubhouse has a prime location grandly surveying the course from its elevated position. On a clear day there are views across the course to the Isle of Wight. The facilities are excellent with lunches being offered daily. Both breakfast and dinner can be arranged with prior notice and a jacket and tie should be worn in public rooms at all times.

In recent years, the Club has played host to many competitions and tournaments, such as the Women's English Amateur Championship in 1985 and the Hennessy Cognac Cup, a four man team competition, played over the Old Course in 1982 and 1984. The Ladies European Open visited the course in 1987, while in 1989 large crowds flocked to Ferndown to watch a most exciting Ladies British Open, won by leading American player **Jane Geddes** with an impressive four round total of 274.

Old Course

Hole	Yards	Par	Hole	Yards	Par
1	396	4	10	485	5
2	175	3	11	438	4
3	398	4	12	186	3
4	395	4	13	488	5
5	206	3	14	152	3
6	409	4	15	398	4
7	480	5	16	305	4
8	304	4	17	397	4
9	427	4	18	403	4
Out	3,190	35	In	3,252	36
			Out	3,190	35
			TOTALS	6,442	71

HUTTON COURT

For most golfers, a great golfing break involves not just the game, but also the 'base camp': a place to relax and enjoy good company, food and drink before the triumphs and frustrations of tomorrow's game.

Gleneagles springs to mind; but what of the West Country, and what about non-golfing companions or days off the course? The championship links of Burnham & Berrow in Somerset is less than twenty minutes from the manor of Hutton, itself just five miles off the M5, two and a half hours by car or train from London.

With a history going back before the Norman Conquest, Hutton Court is now a hotel and restaurant in the classic country house style. You sleep in bedrooms dating from the 17th century, with modern comforts added, and dine in the great hall of the 1450s. Local meat, fish, game and venison of the region are specialities. Cuisine befits the best British tradition, substantial yet refined, and matched by over a hundred wines from a dozen countries, ranging from house wines to classics like Cheval Blanc and Petrus.

The key to the place is its relaxed atmosphere, and service that makes you a personal house guest rather than a paying customer with a room number. Serious golfers can not only play Burnham and Berrow, but three other courses within twenty minutes drive. The area offers much more than golf, however. The cathedral cities of Wells, Bath with its splendid shopping and Bristol are all in easy reach. You can walk or ride on the Mendips, explore Cheddar, Wookey, Glastonbury and the Somerset levels, or potter around antique shops and old country pubs.

You can fish the trout lakes of Blagdon and Chew, and there is sea angling on the Bristol Channel. Naturalists watch buzzards, sparrow hawks or even the odd peregrine or goshawk in and around the hotel! grounds, which foxes and badgers visit.

At Hutton Court, we'll do everything to ensure you get the most from your stay, whether you're a glutton for action or just want a lazy few days. Special rates are available for individual or party breaks, and we'll tailor food and drink to your requirements, from packed lunches to full-scale banquets. Ring us for information: we promise you a warm West Country welcome.

Hutton Court,
Church Lane,
Hutton,
Avon BS24 9SN

Telephone: Bleadon (0934) 814343

SOMERSET, AVON, DORSET & WILTS
COMPLETE GOLF

KEY

*** Visitors welcome at most times
** Visitors usually allowed on weekdays only
* Visitors not normally permitted (Mon, Wed) No visitors on specified days

APPROXIMATE GREEN FEES

A – £30 plus
B – £20 – £30
C – £15 – £25
D – £10 – £20
E – Under £10
F – Green fees on application

RESTRICTIONS

G – Guests only
H – Handicap certificate required
H(24) – Handicap of 24 or less required
L – Letter of introduction required
M – Visitor must be a member of another recognised club.

SOMERSET

Brean G.C.
(0278) 751595
Coast Rd. Brean, Burnham-on-Sea
Brean Leisure Centre.
(18)5436 yards/***/E/H

Burnham and Berrow G.C.
(0278) 785760
St.Christophers, Burnham-on-Sea
1 mile north of town.
(18)6327 yards/***/B/M/H

Enmore Park G.C.
(027867) 481
Enmore, Bridgewater
3 miles from Bridgewater.
(18)6443 yards/D/M/H

Mendip G.C.
(0749) 840570
Gurney Slade, Bath
3 miles N. of Shepton Mallet on A37
(18)5982 yards/**/D

Minehead and West Somerset G.C.
(0643) 702057
The Warren, Minehead
Just outside Minehead town centre.
(18)6130 yards/***/D

Taunton and Pickeridge G.C.
(082342) 240
Corfe, Taunton
Just past Corfe on B3170A.
(18)5927 yards/**/D

Vivary Park G.C.
(0823) 289274
Taunton
Situated in town centre.
(18)4620 yards/***/E

Wells G.C.
(0749) 72868East Horrington Rd. Wells
1 mile east of the city.
(18)5354 yards/***/D/H

Windwhistle G.C.
(046030) 231
Cricket St. Thomas, Chard
3 miles from Chard on A30.
(18)6055 yards/***/D

Yeovil G.C.
(0935) 22965
Sherborne Rd. Yeovil
1 mile from town on A30.
(18)6139 yards/***/D/H

Weston-Super-Mare G.C.
(0934) 621360
Uphill Road North, Weston-Super-Mare
(18)6225 yards/***/B

Worlebury G.C.
(0934) 623214
Worlebury, Weston-Super-Mare
2 miles from Weston-Super-Mare.
(18)5945 yards/**/C/H

AVON

Bath G.C.
(0225) 425182
Sham Castle, North Rd.
South of city off A36
(18)6369 yards/***/C/H

Bristol and Clifton G.C.
(0275) 393117
Beggar Bush Lane, Failand
Off A3969 to Bristol.
(18)6270 yards/***/C/H

Chipping Sodbury G.C.
(0454) 319042
Chipping Sodbury, Bristol,
Turn off Wickwar Rd. to Horton.
(18)6912 yards/***/D/H

Clevedon G.C.
(0275) 874057
Castle Rd. Clevedon
Just outside town off Hodley Lane.
(18)5887 yards/***(Mon,Wed)/D/H/M

Entry Hill G.C.
(0225) 834248
Entry Hill, Bath
South of the town on A367
(9)4206 yards/***/E

Filton G.C.
(0272) 694169
Golf Course Lane, Filton, Bristol
(18)6277 yards/***/D

Fosseway G.C.(0761) 412214
Charlton Lane, Midsomer Norton
Take A367 to Charlton.
(9)4246 yards/***/D

Henbury G.C.
(0272) 500044
Henbury Hill, Westbury-on-Trym
3 miles north of Bristol.
(18)6039 yards/**/D/H

Knowle G.C.
(0272) 770660
Fairway, Brislington
3 miles south of Bristol.
(18)6016 yards/**/D/H

Landsdown G.C.
(0225) 422138
Landsdown, Bath
Next to Bath racecourse.
(18)6267 yards/***/D/H

Long Ashton G.C.
(0275) 392316
Long Ashton, Bristol
Take B3128 to Long Ashton.
(18)6051 yards/***/C/H

Mangotsfield G.C.
(0272) 565501
Carsons Rd. Mangotsfield
(18)5337 yards/***/E

Saltford G.C.
(0225) 873220
Golf Club Lane, Saltford
Off A4 between Bath and Bristol.
(18)6081 yards/***/D/H

Shirehampton G.C.
(0272) 822083
Park Hill, Shirehampton
2 miles from village.
(18)5493 yards/**/D/H

Tall Pines G.C.
(0275) 472076
Downside, Backwell
(18) 4250 yards/***/D

Tracy Park G. and C.C.
(027582) 2251
Bath Rd. Wick, BristolTake A420 to Wick.
(18)6800 yards/***/D
(9)5200 yards/***/D

DORSET

Ashley Woods G.C.
(0258) 452253
Wimbourne Rd. Blandford Forum
Take B3082 to Wimbourne Minster
(18)5246 yards/***/C/H

Bridport and West Dorset G.C.
(0308) 22597
East Cliff, West Bay, Bridport
Take A35 from Bridport onto B3157.
(18)5246 yards/***/C/H

Broadstone G.C.
(0202) 692595
Wentworth Drive, Broadstone
Between Wimbourne & Poole on A349
(18)6151 yards/***/A/H

Bulbury Woods G.C
(092945) 574
nr Poole
(18) 6020 yards

Came Down G.C
(030581) 3494
Came Down, Dorchester
On A354 from Dorchester to Wimbourne
(18)6224 yards/***/C/H

Chedington Court G.C
(0935) 891413
Nr Beaminster, Dorset
A356 4 miles
(9) 3500 yards/***/E

East Dorset G.C
(0929) 472244Hyde, Wareham
(18)6640 yards/**/D/I
(9)2440 yards/**/D/I

Ferndown G.C.
(0202) 874602
119 Golf Links Road, Ferndown
Onto A348 from A31 to Tricketts Cross
(18)6442 yards/***/A/H

Highcliffe Castle G.C.
(04252) 72210
107 Lymington Rd, Highcliffe-On-Sea
Off A35 from Bournemouth
(18)4732 yards/***/D/M

Isle Of Purbeck G.C
(092944) 361
Studland
On B3351 between Studland and Swanage
(18)6248 yards/***/C/H
(9)2022 yards/***/E

Knighton Heath G.C
(0202) 572633
Hyde, Wareham
(18)6108 yards/***/D

Lyme Regis G.C
(02974) 2963
Timber Hill, Lyme Regis
(18)6262 yards/***/C

Meyrick Park G.C
(0202) 290871
Parks Dept. Bournemouth
(18)5885 yards/***/E

Mid Dorset G.C
(0258) 861386
Blandford Forum
(18) 6500 yards/***/C

Parkstone G.C
(0202) 707138
Links Road, Parkstone, Poole
Turn S off A35 to Poole
(18)6250 yards/**/B/H

Queens Park G.C
(0202) 396198
Queens Park, South Drive, Bournemouth
(18)6505 yards/***/E

Sherborne G.C
(0935) 812475
Higher Clatcombe, Sherborne
Take B3145 N of town
(18)5758 yards/***/D

Wareham G.C
(09295) 54147
Sandford Rd, Wareham
(18)5603 yards/**/C

Weymouth G.C
(0305) 773981
Links Rd, Westham, Weymouth
(18) 5979 yards/***/E

WILTSHIRE

Brinkworth G.C.
(066641) 277
Longman's Farm, Brinkworth, Chippenham
(9)6086 yards/***/E

Bremhill Park G.C
(0793) 782946
Shrivenham, Swindon
East of village
(18)5880 yards/***/E

Broome Manor G.C
(0793) 532403
Pipers Way, Swindon
1 mile from Swindon old town
(18) 6359 yards/**/D

Chippenham G.C
(0249) 652040
Malmebury Road, Chippenham
(18)5540 yards/***/C/M/H

High Post G.C
(072273) 356
Great Durnford, Salisbury
Between Salisbury and Amesbury on A345
(18)6267 yards/***/C/H

Kingsdown G.C
(0225) 742530
Kingsdown, Corsham
(18)6254 yards/***/D/H

Marlborough G.C(0672) 512147
The Common, Malborough
1 mile from town on A345
(18)6440 yards/B/H

North Wiltshire G.C.
(0380) 860257
Bishops Cannings, Devizes
(18)6450 yards/***/F/H

Salisbury and Wiltshire G.C
(0722) 742645
Netherhampton, Salisbury
1 mile from Wilton on A3094
(18)6146 yards/***/B/H

Shrivenham Park G.C
(0793) 783853
Penny Hooks
(18) 5889 yards/***/D

Swindon G.C
(67284) 217
Ogbourne St George
Take A345 towards Marlborough
(18)6226 yards/**/C

West Wiltshire G.C
(0985) 212702
Elm Hill, Warminster
Half a mile from Warminster on A350
(18)5701 yards/***/B/H

HAMPSHIRE & THE CHANNEL ISLANDS

C.E. Brock   THE PUTT   Sotheby's

HAMPSHIRE & THE CHANNEL ISLANDS
CHOICE GOLF

HAMPSHIRE

Even if the Isle of Wight and the Channel Islands were taken away from this region it would still score top marks, both for the quality of the golf and the quality of the accompanying scenery. With the New Forest to the south, the Downs to the north and Winchester Cathedral standing proudly in the middle, Hampshire is arguably the fairest of all English counties. And amongst all this finery stand the likes of Liphook, Old Thorns, North Hants, Blackmoor and Brokenhurst Manor – five of the country's leading inland courses.

Hampshire's traditional 'big three' of **Liphook**, **North Hants** and **Blackmoor**, lie towards the east of the county close to the boundary with Surrey. Not surprisingly they are staunch members of the heathland club – silver birch and pine, fir, heather and a dash of gorse. Liphook is possibly the pick of the three, though it's a close thing, and both North Hants (at Fleet) and Blackmoor annually stage major amateur events – North Hants the Hampshire Hog and Blackmoor the Selborne Salver. Each measures between 6,200 and 6,300 yards and is maintained in superb condition. The **Army** Golf Club, just north of Aldershot is another fine and quite lengthy heathland type course with a reputation for separating the men from the boys although it is perhaps not quite in the same league as the illustrious trio above. The final mention in this area goes to one of the county's newest recruits, the **Old Thorns** Golf and Country Club, situated south of Liphook. Old Thorns is featured on a later page.

There's no shortage of comfortable hotels in the north of Hampshire and often quite hidden in the countryside are some delightful pubs and restaurants. Inns to ease your slumber include two first rate establishments; The Crown and Cushion in Minley and The Chequers in Well. Fleet dissects these two villages and The Lismoyne Hotel (0252) 628555 is ideally located. In Passfield, The Passfield Oak does good food and some popular real ales, while in Grayshott, Woods (0428) 605555 is an excellent little restaurant and it sounds perfect for golfers. In Liphook, as well as the superb Old Thorns (0428) 724555, the Links Hotel (0428) 723773 is very handy for the 9th and 10th tees on the Liphook course. An Indian Restaurant nearby, The Bombay (0428) 722095 is recommended (and its celebrated curries are reputed to add 20 yards to your drive!)

Basingstoke isn't Hampshire's most attractive town – too much London overspill these days. A very good new course nearby however is the **Sandford Springs** Golf Club at Wolverton, built on the site of a former Roman shrine, and officially opened in 1989 by Nick Faldo.

Winchester golfers, like those at Liphook, are doubly fortunate having two first class courses at hand: **Royal Winchester** and **Hockley**, located two miles south of the city on the A333. Both are well kept downland type courses. A recent, and most attractive addition to the Winchester / South Hampshire area is the **Botley Park** Hotel and Country Club (0489) 780888. Some excellent golfing weekend packages are offered.

In Ampfield, south of Winchester, and Romsey, also south of the Cathedral town, two establishments catch the eye. In the former Potters Heron (0703) 266611 is comfortable and convenient for the A31 and The Old White Horse (0794) 512431 is a welcoming inn located in Romsey's market place. In Winchester there are numerous restaurants, perhaps the best

is The Old Chesil. Also in Winchester The Forte Crest (0962) 61611 is not cheap but particularly comfortable. North west of the city is Sparsholt, where one finds one of those exquisite English Country House Hotels, Lainston House (0962) 63588. More modest accommodation can be found at the Aeire Guesthouse (0962) 862519. In Stockbridge, The Game Larder (0264) 810414 is excellent and The Sherrif House (0264) 810677 also offers outstanding food. People coming from or returning to the west should note Middle Wallop – more specifically – Fifehead Manor (0264) 781565, a delightful manor house with a good restaurant. Finally, I must point pub lovers in mid-Hampshire in the direction of Ovington where The Bush is tremendous fun.

Returning to the fairways, and switching nearer to the south coast, the **Rowlands Castle** parkland course occupies a peaceful setting. The course can play fairly long, especially from the back markers. While we're on the subject of length, a hundred years ago the excellent links at **Hayling Island** is said to have measured 7,480 yards – so much for the modern-day monster courses! Today the course is less frightening but still quite a challenge and visitors are warmly received.

Another drink is needed and two fine pubs are at hand – The Old House at Home (superb name) in Havant and The Royal Oak in Langstone, both ideally situated for Rowlands Castle. Another establishment to sample in this area of Hampshire is the notable Old House Hotel (0329) 833049 in Wickham. Trekking northwards one comes to Botley, here Cobbett's (0489) 782068 is a fine French restaurant.

Stoneham is without doubt the pick of the courses in the Southampton area, it is located just 2 miles north of the town. The venue of the first Dunlop Masters tournament back in 1946, it is quite undulating with an ample sprinkling of gorse and heather which, though appealing to look at is often the curse of the wayward hitter. Just outside of Portsmouth a fine 18 hole course to note is **Waterlooville**, although there are in fact a number of courses (including some very reasonable public courses, such as **Fleming Park** at Eastleigh) in and around Southampton and Portsmouth.

Midway between Portsmouth and Southampton (M27 junction 7) is the **Meon Valley** Golf and Country Club. A fairly new parkland course, designed by J. Hamilton Stutt, it too has an attractive setting, not a million miles from the New Forest. For a night's rest the Meon Valley Hotel (0329) 833455 is the obvious selection – both comfortable and highly convenient.

I'm afraid I know very little about William the Conqueror but I understand there are at least two things we should thank him for – one is the Domesday Book and the other is the New Forest, without doubt one of the most beautiful areas in Britain. There are two real golfing treats in the New Forest, one is **Bramshaw** Golf Club which is owned and run by the owners of the charming Bell Inn (0703) 812214 – two fine 18 hole courses here, The Manor and The Forest courses, and the second is **Brokenhurst Manor,** a superb heathland course. Both venues are decidedly worth inspecting. A short distance from the New Forest, **Barton-on-Sea's** exposed cliff top course is also well worth a visit if in the area. Not overly long, but with enough challenges and some spectacular views across to the Isle of Wight and Christchurch Bay.

A few ideas for the 19th hole, and we make a start at Lyndhurst

HAMPSHIRE & THE CHANNEL ISLANDS
CHOICE GOLF

and The Parkhill House Hotel (0703) 289244 – a pleasant spot with a good restaurant as well. Two B's now, but before you get offended, I refer to Beaulieu and Brockenhurst. In the former, the Montagu Arms (0590) 612324 and its fine restaurant is ideal to hang up one's clubs and in the latter a number of places should be considered; two to include are Carey's Manor (0590) 23551, a great all rounder and The Forest Park (0590) 22844. In nearby Sway, The Tower (0590) 683034 is another that can be unfailingly recommended. Further south on the A337 we arrive at Lymington. In another good hotel setting stands The Passford House (0590) 682398. Among other things, The South Lawn Hotel (0590) 643911 is convenient for ferries leaving for the Isle of Wight, while Limpets also in Lymington is a tasty restaurant. In New Milton, we find the county's (quite probably the country's) finest country house hotel, Chewton Glen (0425) 275341. Finally, New Forest Cottages (0590) 675595 should be contacted if you want first class self-catering accommodation in this area.

ISLE OF WIGHT

There are no fewer than seven golf courses on the Isle of Wight. There are two 18 hole courses, **Shanklin and Sandown** is the better of the two (beautifully wooded with heather and gorse) and the other is **Freshwater Bay** (more a downland / cliff top course.) Of the 9 holers, **Osborne** is the most scenic but a visit to any is appealing. All courses welcome visitors and green fees tend to compare favourably with those on the mainland.

In Shanklin, The Cliff Tops (0983) 863262 and Luccombe Hall (0983) 863082 stand out, though there are many good hotels on the island. Two pubs to visit in Shanklin include The Fisherman's Cottage – good food and a fine setting and The Crab – more seafood and a high street position. Elsewhere on the island, Cowes of course is busy and fun, especially during Cowes week itself, but for our purposes Bonchurch beckons, where The Peacock Vane (0983) 852019 is a delightful restaurant with some rooms. There is also a tremendous selection of moderately priced establishments on the island; suggestions include, Gambits Private Hotel (0983) 402649, Blenheim House (0983) 752858 at Freshwater, The Culver Lodge Hotel (0983) 403819 and the excellent St Catherine's

Hotel (0983) 402392, both at Sandown.

THE CHANNEL ISLANDS

If the Isle of Wight is good for golf, the Channel Islands are even better. Not that there is a proliferation of courses – indeed they could do with a couple more – but three of them, **La Moye, Royal Jersey** and **Royal Guernsey** are particularly outstanding. Unfortunately the German troops didn't share this opinion during the island's four year occupation: they demolished La Moye's Clubhouse and dug up the fairways at Royal Guernsey. Both have long since recovered and all three provide tremendous holiday golf. La Moye's links, the regular venue for the Jersey Open, is featured ahead.

When it comes to hotels one is quite simply spoilt for choice. In Guernsey St Peter's Port offers a whole handful of excellent establishments, generally good value as well. The St Pierre Park (0481) 728282 is the most luxurious hotel, and for real character La Fregate Hotel (0481) 724624 is an 18th century manor house overlooking the harbour. The Old Government House (0481) 724921 is again beautifully stylish while The Flying Dutchman (0481) 725308 has a good restaurant to match a friendly welcome. For a good seafood restaurant try the unfortunately named Absolute End (0481) 723822.

In Jersey, St Brelade's Bay offers the superb Atlantic Hotel (0534) 44101 (ideal for La Moye links). Other recommended hotels here are the Hotel L'Horizon (0534) 43101 and the Little Grove Hotel (0534) 25321. St Helier boasts the outstanding Grand Hotel (0534) 22301 – note especially the restaurant – and St Peter, The Mermaid (0534) 41255. Perhaps the best restaurant on the island is to be found at St. Saviours – Longueville Manor (0534) 25501. In St. Martin, one and a half miles from Royal Jersey, is the comfortable Les Arches Hotel (0534) 53839. The intrepid guesthouse brigade will find more than sufficient to please them at Millbrook House (0534) 33036 in St Helier and Bryn-y-Mor (0534) 20295 in St. Aubin. Finally in Grouville Bay where the Royal Jersey Golf Club is situated is La Hougue Grange (0534) 51899, a charming country house and one of those great treats where the words 'fore' and 'fare' can be combined so happily!

John Goodall "THE FIRST" *Rosenstiel's*

OLD THORNS
CHAMPIONSHIP GOLF

There are two reasons why we have selected Old Thorns as one of our 100 featured courses in this edition of Following the Fairways. Firstly, it is because a visit to Old Thorns can fairly be described as a unique experience and the purpose of this book, after all, is to illustrate the wealth and variety of golfing challenges that these islands have to offer. The second, just as important, is that Old Thorns is both exceptionally attractive and visitor-friendly. Nature, with a little help from course designers Peter Alliss and Dave Thomas, is chiefly responsible for the beauty of the situation. The visitor-friendly aspect is a direct result of the fact that Old Thorns isn't a Golf Club as such. Like The Belfry, there are no members for whom tee times must be reserved.

What about the unique experience?

Old Thorns is where East meets West, not just on the Golf course but at the 19th hole. Old Thorns is owned by a large Japanese publishing company, **Kosaido** who acquired the course and accompanying hotel only two years after its official opening in 1982. The Japanese inherited a very English set up. The centre piece of the clubhouse and hotel is a converted 150 year old tithe barn, a delightful building. The new owners have maintained, even enhanced, its traditional 'log fires in winter' ambience, but they have also added a Japanese Centre which includes a charming Japanese garden. The buildings have been extended generally to an extent that Old Thorns now boasts a splendid range of luxury facilities. The hotel has 27 well appointed rooms and guests can enjoy a genuine Japanese Shiatsu massage!

Golfers wishing to visit Old Thorns should contact the Club in advance. The address to write to is **Old Thorns, Longmoor Road, Liphook, Hampshire GU30 7PE.** The General Manager is **Mr. G. Jones** but telephone enquiries of a golfing nature can usually be handled by the professional **Philip Loxley** and his staff on **(0428) 724555**.

Subject to booking a tee time visitors can play on any day of the week. In 1992, the green fees were £24 per round, £39 per day midweek and £35 per round at the weekend. Incidentally, something like two thirds of all visitors on a Sunday are either Japanese or Korean and there is a thoroughly international atmosphere. Hotel residents pay reduced green fees while golf buggies and sets of clubs can be hired from the professional.

Located approximately one hour's drive from London (less from Heathrow and Gatwick airports) and very close to the A3, Old Thorns is very easy to find. The A3 runs through neighbouring Liphook's golf course! The B2131 Longmoor Road should be joined close to the centre of Liphook village, near the Royal Anchor Hotel. Old Thorns is found about one mile down this road.

Just an hour's drive perhaps, but London can seem a world away when you arrive at the course. The surrounding countryside is some of Britain's finest; a great spread of oaks, beech trees, chestnuts and pines adorn the landscape and the golf course winds its way through the woods, gently rising and falling. Natural springs abound and much use has been made of them! Water hazards are numerous at Old Thorns; there are many streams and several times the golfer is asked to play over or across the edge of a small lake. The course is maintained in tremendous condition all year round and the greens have a reputation for being quick.

From the back markers the course measures 6533 yards, par 72; from the forward tees it is a less daunting 6129 yards, par 72 and from the ladies tees the course measures 5342 yards, par 74. It is difficult to single out individual holes at Old Thorns but first timers often remember the holes around the turn, especially the **9th, 10th,** and **11th,** where on each hole a miss-hit shot can cause the sight every golfer dreads – ripples on water! Avoid the water at Old Thorns though and a good score is always a possibility; the rough is rarely punishing and the bunkers not too difficult to play out of.

Old Thorns has an excellent finish with the par three **16th** and the dramatic two-shot **17th** being perhaps the best holes of all.

After holing out successfully on the tricky **18th** green a stiff drink at the 19th may be in order – a shot of saki perhaps? A good meal may also be sought and some people reckon that this is where Old Thorns really comes into its own. There is a superb selection of European and Japanese cuisine in its very characterful restaurants. If you have never tried Japanese food before then the renowned Nippon Kan Restaurant and the Teppan Yaki Bar are the perfect places for an introduction. Old Thorns is guaranteed to charm you from the moment you arrive to the time you leave.

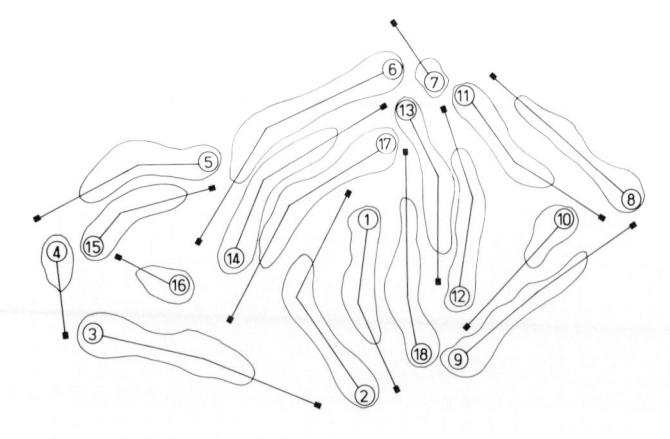

Hole	Yards	Par	Hole	Yards	Par
1	339	4	10	221	3
2	497	5	11	359	4
3	444	4	12	435	4
4	157	3	13	364	4
5	320	4	14	510	5
6	543	5	15	268	4
7	162	3	16	162	3
8	370	4	17	483	5
9	390	4	18	423	4
Out	3,222	36	In	3,225	36
			Out	3,222	36
			TOTALS	6,447	72

CHEWTON GLEN

In verdant parkland on the southern edge of the New Forest stands a magnificent country house hotel. Chewton Glen and its combination of splendour, elegance and comfort affords the discerning visitor every amenity they could wish for. The public areas are beautiful decorated, such as the light, airy main sitting room looking out onto the garden and the cosy inner lounge with its marble fireplace.

Our suites and double bedrooms have bathrooms ensuite, colour television, direct dial telephone and radio. They are furnished with antiques, attractive painted furniture and luxurious fabrics.

Guests can stroll around the thirty acre grounds or play tennis, croquet, golf or alternatively bathe in the heated outdoor swimming pool or off the shingle beach nearby. The hotel has an indoor tennis centre, health club with indoor pool, and its own nine-hole golf course.

Once the appetite has been whetted, the Marryat Room, the Hotel's Michelin-rosetted restaurant offers sumptuous fare. Our distinguished modern only by the quality of the service.

To find us leave the A35 on the Walkford Road and once through Walkford turn left down Chewton Farm Road.

Your stay will be a pleasant one; we hope it will be a long one. Whether you have enjoyed a day at the races or a round of golf at one of the many nearby golf courses we know that Chewton Glen will make your day that extra special.

Chewton Glen
New Milton
Hampshire

Tel: (0425) 275341
Fax: (0425) 272310

LA MOYE
CHAMPIONSHIP GOLF

England is part of the Channel Islands. Yes, England is part of the Channel Islands – at least this is what an islander will tell you. Apparently, the islands belonged to **William**, **Duke of Normandy** some time before he came over and added England to his territories.

So what of the golf in the 'mother country', the land where the great **Harry Vardon** was born? In short, there are three very fine courses: Royal Guernsey, Royal Jersey and La Moye. The first two certainly offer a marvellous day's golf but the general consensus is that La Moye sneaks it as the pick of an excellent trio. Its setting alone makes the course stand out, laid out two hundred and fifty feet above St. Ouen's Bay, Jersey's finest beach, on the south west tip of the island. From such a vantage point there are some tremendous views to be enjoyed from the course, particularly perhaps from the 13th where the four sister islands of Guernsey, Sark, Herm and Jetou can all be seen. Add to this a warm climate and of course, the quality of the championship links itself and you can see why people want to play golf here!

La Moye Golf Club was founded in 1902 by the then headmaster of the local school, one **George Boomer**. A course was laid out but it didn't really take shape until **James Braid** added his skilful craftsmanship. Thereafter the course was left more or less untouched, so to speak, until 1977 when major alterations were made resulting in an improved and, when played from the back tees, much longer course.

The current Secretary/Manager at La Moye is **Mr. Pat Clash**; he can be contacted by telephone on **(0534) 43401** or by writing to: **La Moye Golf Club, La Moye, Jersey, Channel Islands.** The Club professional, **David Melville** can be reached on **(0534) 43130**.

In addition to being a superb Championship course, La Moye doubles as a very popular holiday course in the best sense of the word. Visitors are always made most welcome. The only specific requirement is that they must be members of a recognised Golf Club. It isn't essential to book a tee time but during the summer months the course can become extremely busy. Making an early start is always a good idea (whether this fits in with the holiday schedule is another matter!)

The green fees for 1992 were set at £30 during the week and £35 during the weekend when afternoon play only is permissable. For junior golfers a reduced fee of £15 is payable, or £17.50 at the weekend. A weekly ticket may well be preferred and can be purchased for £145.

As for finding the course, there really should be no problem. La Moye is only a mile or so from St. Brelade and just five minutes by road from Jersey's Airport. The island is such a size that it shouldn't take much more than half an hour to travel between La Moye and Royal Jersey in Grouville, though of course it depends on the traffic and on how much of Jersey you want to take in along the way.

From the Championship tees, the course can be stretched to beyond 6700 yards, as it is for the **Jersey Open**. The medal tees however, are less exacting and the total yardage is 6464 yards, par 72: no pushover certainly, and there is often a very stiff wind. From the ladies tees the course measures 5903 yards, par 74. La Moye is a typical links type course – large sand hills, pot bunkers, the odd blind shot, gorse bushes and punishing rough (though it's not as punishing as at some). It really is full of variety with a number of dog-legs and plateau greens. Apart from the **13th** and its enchanting views, many will probably remember the **17th** hole best of all: it is a lengthy par four with the green dramatically set on the edge of the cliffs, rather like the famous 5th hole at Portrush.

The Jersey Open is a very popular event on the European Tour and the pros, inspired by the surroundings, have produced some very good scores although La Moye has never been torn apart. Some well known names have won the Jersey Open here including; **Sandy Lyle, Tony Jacklin, Bernard Gallacher, Howard Clark, Ian Woosnam** and **Sam Torrance**. So some of the best golfers in the world have played at La Moye and they may soon be joined by the best golfer to have played on the moon! Alan Sheppard, now Admiral Sheppard, has recently become an honourary member at La Moye. One suspects he is a rather good bunker player!

All golfers, terrestrial and non-terrestrial are sure to enjoy the Club's excellent 19th. A spacious new Clubhouse, it is one of a series for the Club. The original burned down while the second was destroyed by German soldiers during the island's war-time occupation. Let's just wish the new one the best of British luck!

Hole	Yards	Par	Hole	Yards	Par
1	148	3	10	356	4
2	495	5	11	489	5
3	179	3	12	128	3
4	418	4	13	386	4
5	434	4	14	179	3
6	476	5	15	330	4
7	363	4	16	476	5
8	403	4	17	420	4
9	402	4	18	382	4
Out	**3,318**	**36**	**In**	**3,146**	**36**
			Out	**3,318**	**36**
			Totals	**6,464**	**72**

LA PLACE HOTEL

Based on a farmhouse first mentioned in the King's Rentes of 1640, La Place preserves its ancient charm with pink granite lintels, corner stones, large open fireplaces and wood beams. Set amidst the peace and beauty of Jersey the hotel combines such surroundings with all the amenities the modern guest has come to expect, including private facilities, colour television, radio and telephone.

For the golfer the hotel is ideal, being only minutes away from La Moye Golf Course, highly rated by the Sunday Express Good Golf Guide. The Gourmet Golf section of the same guide recommended La Place hotel, its restaurant justly renowned even on this island, famed as it is for its high culinary standards. For the guests unwilling to interrupt their sunbathing, poolside snacks are served, or alternatively, alfresco meals are available in the south-facing old Courtyard.

La Place Hotel
Route du Coin
St. Brelade
Jersey
Channel Islands
Tel: (0534) 44261

THE WATER'S EDGE HOTEL

A mere stone's throw from the sea, The Water's Edge is one of Jersey's most celebrated hotels. Occupying an unsurpassed site on this already idyllic island it has been the unique location for films and much has already been written and said about it.

Such a marine location offers breathtaking views across the bay, whilst the unexpectedly spacious gardens allow peaceful relaxation and alfresco dining.

The forty square miles of Jersey are the home to an exceptional variety of land and seascapes, from lazy beaches to craggy cliffs, from valleys and woods to flower filled meadows. For the golfer the size of the island makes it ideal, since nowhere is very far from the justly renowned facilities.

Water's Edge Hotel
Bouley Bay
Trinity
Jersey
JE3 5AS
Tel: (0534) 862777
Fax: (0534) 863645

THE TOWER

Set in Hampshire farmland between the New Forest and the Solent, The Tower offers some of the most select and unusual accommodation in the south of England. Stretching 200 feet above the barrow on which it was built over a hundred years ago, the listed building has magnificent views of the surrounding countryside.

Set on five floors, the accommodation is outstanding. The ensuite bedrooms each take up a separate floor, and are reached by an enclosed spiral staircase. Retaining the elegance of a bygone era, each bedroom has its own individual character, complete with modern comforts such as satellite TV and direct dial telephone with ansaphone. Exquisite Table d' Hote menus are served by candle light.

An all weather tennis court is available in the grounds and the 20 metre indoor pool tempts guests after a hot day exploring the surrounding countryside and sights. Nearby, Bucklers Hart and Lymington provide much to sample and see. Winchester Cathedral, Salisbury and Stonehenge are within an hour's drive. Ancient Beaulieu with its famous motor museum is also close to hand. For keen golfers, the area may need no introduction, and for the uninitiated offers many treats, such as the courses at Lymington and Brockenhurst.

Other activities in the area include yacht charter, sailing courses, even aircraft hire. The New Forest offers miles of secluded trails over varied terrains, full of wildlife and surrounded by superb views - rambling maps can be provided and cycle and car hire are nearby.

All in all, your visit to The Tower at Sway is sure to be a pleasant, memorable and unique experience.

The Tower
Sway
Hants. SO4 16DE
Tel: (0590) 682117
Fax: (0590) 683785

HAMPSHIRE & THE CHANNEL ISLANDS
COMPLETE GOLF

HAMPSHIRE

Alresford G.C.
(0962) 733746
Cheriton Rd. Alresford
1 mile south of the town.
(11)6038 yards/**/D

Alton G.C.
(0420)82042
Old Odiham Rd. Alton
(9)5744 yards/***/D

Ampfield Par Three G.C.
(0794) 68480
Winchester Rd. Ampfield, Romsey
3 miles from Hursley on A31.
(18)2478 yards/***/E/H

Army G.C.
(0252) 541104
Laffans Rd. Aldershot
(18)6579 yards/*/G/F

Barton-on-Sea G.C.
(0425) 615308
Marine Drive, Barton-on-Sea, New Milton
1 mile from New Milton.
(18)5565 yards/***/C/H

Basingstoke G.C.
(0256) 465990
Kempshott Park, Basingstoke
3 miles west of town on A30.
(18)6284 yards/**/C/H

Basingstoke Hospitals G.C.
(0256) 20347
Aldermaster Rd. Basingstoke
2 miles north of town centre.
(9)5455 yards/***/E

Bishopswood G.C.
(0734) 81513
Bishopswood Lane, Tadley
Off A340 west of Tadley.
(9)6474 yards/**(Mon,Wed)/E

Blackmoor G.C.
(04203) 2775
Golf Lane, Whitehill, Bordon
(18)6232 yards/**/C/H

Botley Park Hotel & G.C.
(0489) 780888
6 miles east of Southampton on B3354
(18)6026 yards/***/C/H

Bramshaw G.C.
(0703) 813433
Brook, Lyndhurst
1 mile from Cadnam on B3078.
(18)6233 yards/***/D
(18)5774 yards/***/D

Brokenhurst Manor G.C.
(0703) 23332
Sway Rd. Brockenhurst
1 mile outside village.
(18)6212 yards/**/D/H(24)

Burley G.C.
(04253) 2431
Burley, Ringwood
(9)6149 yards/**/D

Corhampton G.C.
(0489) 877279
Sheeps Pond Lane, Droxford
1 mile from Corhampton on B3135
(18)6088 yards/**/D/H

Dibden G.C.
(0703) 845596
Dibden, Southampton
(18)6206 yards/***/E

Dunwood Manor G.C.
(0794) 40549
Shootash Hill, Romsey
(18)6004 yards/**/D

Fleming Park G.C.
(0703) 61297
Magpie Lane, Eastleigh
1 mile north of Eastleigh airport.
(18)4402 yards/***/F

Gosport and Stokes Bay G.C.
(0705) 527941
Military Rd. Halsar, Gosport
(9)5806 yards/**/E

Great Salterns G.C.
(0705) 664549
Portsmouth Golf Centre, Eastern Rd.
(18)5970 yards/***/E

Hartley Whitney G.C.
(025126) 4211
London Rd. Hartley Whitney
(9)6096 yards/**/D

Hayling G.C.
(0705) 464446
Ferry Rd. Hayling Island
(18)6489 yards/C/H/M/L

Hockley G.C.
(0962) 713165
Twyford, Winchester
(18)6279 yards/G/F

Leckford and Longstock G.C.
(0264) 810710
Leckford, Stockbridge
(9)3251 yards/*/F

Lee-on-the-Solent G.C.
(0705) 551170
Brune Lane, Lee-on-the-Solent
(18)6022/**/C

Liphook G.C.
(0428) 723271
Wheatsheaf Enclosure, Liphook
(18)6250 yards/**/B/H/M

Meon Valley G. and C.C.
(0329) 833455
Sandy Lane, Shedfield, Southampton
(18)5748 yards/***/C

New Forest G.C.
(042128) 2450
Lyndhurst
(18)5748 yards/***/D

North Hants G.C.
(0252) 616443
Minley Rd Fleet
(18)6251 yards/***/H/M

Old Thorns G.C.
(0428) 724555
London Kasaido G. & C.C.
Longmoor Rd. Liphook
(18)6629 yards/***/B

Petersfield G.C.
(0730) 62386
Heath Rd. Petersfield
(18)5720 yards/***/D

Portsmouth G.C.
(0705) 372210
Crookhorn Rd. Widley, Portsmouth
(18)6259 yards/***/E

Romsey G.C.
(0703) 734637
Nursling , Southampton
(18)5759 yards/**/F/H

Rowlands Castle G.C.
(0705) 412784
Links Lane, Rowlands Castle
(18)6627 yards/**/C

Royal Winchester G.C.
(0962) 52462
Sarum Rd. Winchester
(18)6218 yards/**/C/H

Sandford Springs G.C.
(0639) 297881
Wolverton, Basingstoke
Between Basingstoke and Newbury on A339
(18)6064 yards/**/C/G

Southampton G.C.
(0703) 568407
Golf Course Rd. Bassett, Southampton
(18)6218 yards/***/F
(9)2391 yards/***/F

Southwick Park G.C.
(0705) 380131
Pinsley Drive, Soutwick, Fareham
(18)5855 yards/**/E

Southwood G.C.
(0252) 548700
Ively Rd. Cove, Farnborough
(18)5553 yards/***/F

Stoneham G.C.
(0703) 768151
Bassett Rd, Bassett, Southampton
(18)6310 yards/**/C/H

Tidworth Garrison G.C.
(0980) 4231
Tidworth
Tidworth 1 mile on Bulford Road
(18) 5990 yards/**/C

Tylney Park G.C
(0256) 762079
Rotherwick, Basingstoke
(18)6138 yards/***/C/H

Waterlooville G.C
(0705) 263388
Cherry Tree Avenue, Cowplain, Portsmouth
(18)6647 yards/**/C/H

ISLE OF WIGHT

Cowes G.C
(0983) 292303
Crossfield Avenue, Cowes
(9)2940 yards/***/D

Freshwater Bay G.C
(0983) 752955
Afton Down, Freshwater Bay
2 miles from Yarmouth on A3056
(18)5662 yards/***/D

Newport G.C
(0983) 525076
St Georges Down, Newport
(9)5704 yards/***/D/H

Osborne G.C
(0983)295421
Osborne, E Cowes
(9)6304 yards/**/D/H

Ryde G.C
(0983) 614809
Binstead Rd, Ryde
(9)5200 yards/***/F/H

Shanklin & Shandown G.C
(0983) 403217
The Fairway, Sandown
Near Sandown bus station
(18)5980 yards/C/H

Ventor G.C
(0983) 853326
Steephill Down, Ventor
North of Ventor on A3055
(9)5752 yards/***/E

CHANNEL ISLANDS

Alderney G.C
(048182) 2835
Routes des Carriers, Alderney
1 mile E of St Annes
(9)2528 yards/***/D

La Moye G.C
(0534) 43401
La Moye, St Brelade
(18)6464 yards/***/A

Royal Guernsey G.C
(0481) 47022
LAncresse, Guernsey
3 miles from St Peter Port
(18)6206 yards/***(Thurs,Sat pm,Sun(H))/F

Royal Jersey G.C
(0534) 54416
Grouville, Jersey
On coast, 4 miles from S Helier
(18)6106 yards/***(W/Epm)/F

St Clements G.C
(0524) 21938
St Clements
Nr St Helier off A5
(3)3972 yards/***(Sunpm)/D

Major Hopkins   LADIES GOLF   Burlington Gallery

SUSSEX

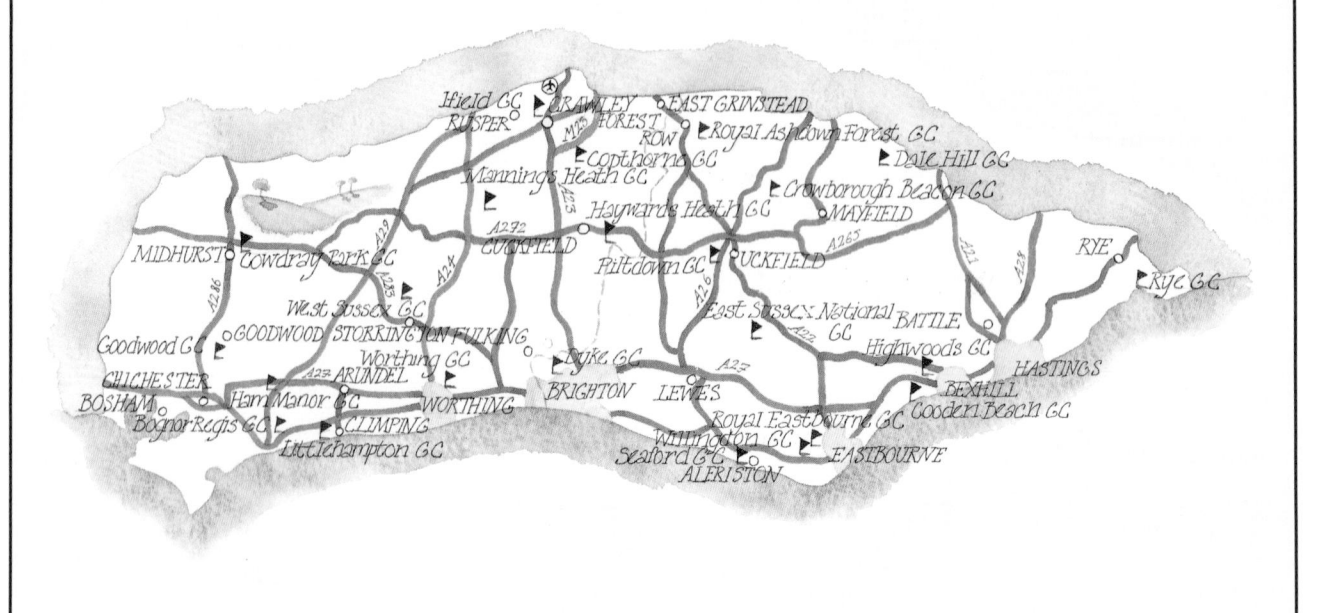

Henry Sandham *THE CLUB'S THE THING* **Rosenstiel's**

Sussex, where the South Downs tumble gently towards spectacular chalk cliffs or as Tennyson wrote, 'Green Sussex fading into blue'. Here is the county of downland and weald, of dramatic rollercoasting cliffs, the Seven Sisters and Beachy Head.

The situation in Sussex is superb. The golf is glorious as is the countryside all around, while at no time can you claim to be isolated – except perhaps when you visit the gorse at Ashdown Forest. West Sussex is as charming an area as one could find – the golf course of the same name is delightful and reflects the quality of some splendid nearby country house hotels. While in Rye, the golfer must visit with a packed wallet in order to seduce a member in a local drinking haunt and thus secure that elusive thing – a round of golf at Rye – a more spectacular day could not be wished for.

Tempting as it is to think of Sussex as one region, there are of course two counties, East and West, and between them they possess over forty courses, many of which are outstandingly good. Golfers in these parts can count themselves pretty fortunate!

CLOSE TO THE COAST

On a selective tour of some of the better courses on or near the Sussex coast, there seems no more logical a place to commence than in the region's south west corner, and **Goodwood** – glorious Goodwood to racegoers, though the golf course is in a similarly idyllic spot, nestling in the southern foothills of the South Downs. Some four miles north of Chichester on the A286 it is in fact located just below the race course and has a magnificent 18th century clubhouse.

In Goodwood itself, Goodwood Park Hotel (0243) 775537 is an excellent place to stay and very convenient for the course, but the delights of Chichester are also close at hand. Here there are a variety of attractions including numerous antique shops and the excellent Festival Theatre (0243) 781312. The Dolphin and Anchor (0243) 785121 opposite the cathedral near the Market Cross is most welcoming (great bar snacks) and a fine place for an overnight stop is Clinch's (0243)789915. A theatre of the open air variety can be found at Bosham as can the pleasant Millstream Hotel (0243) 573234.

Staying in the south west of the region **Bognor Regis** is worth a visit – a flattish but attractive parkland course with several testing par fours. Note the Royal Norfolk (0243) 826222 in town as well as the many near Chichester. The course at **Littlehampton** lies about seven miles east of Bognor Regis off the A259. It is the nearest one gets to a true links course in West Sussex and is always kept in first class condition. Further along the A259 at Angmering is the friendly club of **Ham Manor**, like Bognor it is a parkland course with an interesting layout of two distinct loops.

This corner of West Sussex is renowned for its tremendous hotels and after a day's golf there can be no better place to visit than Arundel where The Norfolk Arms (0903) 882101, a Georgian Coaching Inn has welcomed travellers for over two hundred years and the tradition continues today. Also found in Arundel are many pleasant guesthouses and inns, among them The Arden Hotel (0903) 882544, Bridge House (0903) 882142 and the Swan Hotel (0903) 882314. South of Arundel, lies Climping, here Bailiffscourt (0903) 723511, a 13th century replica offers superb comforts and an excellent restaurant.

As a town Worthing is somewhat overshadowed by neighbouring Brighton (though apparently it inspired Oscar Wilde) – overshadowed or not, it has one of the leading clubs in Sussex. **Worthing** has two eighteen hole courses, the Lower and the Upper. Both are exceptionally fine tests of golf. There is a reasonable public course too at Worthing, **Hill Barn**, while for a convenient 19th hole our recommendation in town is The Chatsworth Hotel (0903) 36103.

Moving into East Sussex and the town of Brighton; probably the best course in the area, and there are a number to choose from, is **The Dyke** Golf Club, located five miles north of the town centre. One of the more difficult courses in Sussex, it is on fairly high ground and provides some splendid views.

As arguably the most famous resort in Britain, it isn't surprising to find literally hundreds of hotels. Among the best are the Sheridan Hotel (0273) 23221 with its excellent sea food restaurant and The Grand Hotel (0273) 21188. Brighton naturally has accommodation to suit everyone's taste and pockets and slightly less expensive are the Allendale Hotel (0273) 672994, The Croft Hotel (0273) 732860 and The Trouville Hotel (0273) 697384. Another restaurant well worth a visit is Langans Bistro (0273) 606933.

A short distance along the ubiquitous A259 is Seaford. One of the older clubs in Sussex, the **Seaford** Golf Club at East Bletchington celebrated its centenary in 1987. A fair sprinkling of gorse and hawthorn is the feature of this outstanding downland course. The views too are quite spectacular being perched high above the town and overlooking the Channel. Also worth noting is the dormy house adjacent to the course.

As we continue to trek in an easterly direction, passing near to Beachy Head we arrive at Eastbourne where there are two fine courses – **Royal Eastbourne** and **Willingdon**. The former is situated very close to the town centre with the enviable address of Paradise Drive. Willingdon, north of the town off the A22, is quite a hilly course and very tough. Its interesting design has been likened to an oyster shell with the Clubhouse as the pearl. In the area around Bexhill, both **Cooden Beach** and **Highwoods** are well established courses. Hotels in the area are less plentiful than in Brighton but Eastbourne does offer the exceptionally fine Lansdowne (0323) 25174, while in Battle, Netherfield Place (04246) 4455 is extremely elegant. Convenient guesthouses include the Bay Lodge Hotel (0323) 32515 and Mowbray Hotel (0323) 20012.

Before heading inland a quick word on **Rye**. It is unquestionably one of the greatest and most natural links courses in Britain – in many people's opinion the equal of Deal and Sandwich. However, visitors are normally only permitted to play if accompanied by a Member – hence the rather flippant remark in the second paragraph! Where might such a seduction take place then? In Rye itself, The Mermaid Inn (0797) 223065 is an historic establishment standing in a steep cobbled street, while for a cosy guest house, try The Old Vicarage (0797) 222119. Another charming inn nearby is The Hayes Arms (0797) 253142 in Northiam.

FURTHER INLAND

If the majority of the leading courses in Sussex are located either

on the coast or within a few miles of it, perhaps the most attractive courses are to be found a few more miles inland. **Piltdown**, two miles to the west of Uckfield, is a good example. Piltdown is a natural heathland course with a beautiful setting and somewhat unusually, though it shares the curiosity with Royal Ashdown, it has no bunkers – though there are certainly enough natural hazards to set the golfer thinking.

Leaving the Piltdown Men and crossing the boundary from East to West, moving from Uckfield to Cuckfield, **Haywards Heath** stands right in the middle of Sussex. A very good heathland course this, but the pride of West Sussex is undoubtedly Pulborough – The **West Sussex** Golf Club. Along with Royal Ashdown and East Sussex National it is featured on a later page – suffice to say here that its reputation extends far beyond the bounds of East and West Sussex. Not too far from Pulborough, Brian Barnes has been the driving force behind the fine new development at **West Chiltington** and where the possibility of a weekend game is a definite bonus! Still in the West two more to note are in the north of the county, and very convenient for Gatwick, the **Ifield** Golf and Country Club and **Copthorne**. Another popular course is found at **Cowdray Park** – very pleasant and ideal of course, should you happen to play polo as well! There is also a good course at **Mannings Heath** (parkland golf despite the name.) The newest addition to the heart of Sussex is the magnificent **East Sussex National** (see ahead).

Places to stay? For Cowdray, The Spread Eagle (073081) 6911 at Midhurst – the hotel and restaurant are both excellent, as is the Park House Hotel (0730) 812880; for Pulborough, Little Thakeham (0903) 744416 at Storrington and Abbingworth Hall (0798) 813836 at Thakeham – sounds confusing? Fear not, both are outstanding; as is the well known Horsted Place (0825) 75581 which is adjacent to the 9th green on the West Course at East Sussex National. The South Lodge Hotel (0403) 891711 at Lower Beeding is centrally situated for most of the above courses.

Towards the north of East Sussex, **Dale Hill** is a much improved course with a new hotel (0580) 200112 attached. Considerable investment at this prestigious development have resulted in both a course of challenging quality and a hotel of the highest calibre. Next comes a classic pair: **Royal Ashdown Forest** and **Crowborough Beacon** – two wonderfully scenic courses where the heather and gorse simply run riot. Crowborough's course is situated some 800 feet above sea level and on clear days the sea can be glimpsed from the Clubhouse. Sir Arthur Conan Doyle would have taken in this view on many occasions for he lived adjacent to the course and was Captain of the Golf Club in 1910. It really is the most beautiful of courses and has in the par three 6th one of the best short holes in Britain.

The 16th century Middle House Hotel (0435) 872146 at Mayfield is recommended for a stay near Crowborough. As for Royal Ashdown two ideas here: for convenience (and considerable comfort) The Ashdown Forest Hotel (034282) 4866 which has its own fine course in addition to being adjacent to the Royal club, while nearer East Grinstead is glorious Gravetye Manor (0342) 810567. East Grinstead also boasts an excellent guesthouse in the shape of the Cranfield Lodge Hotel (0342) 321251.

In the course of our brief trip no doubt several splendid 19th hole hotels have been omitted, but such is life. In order to fit in more restaurants, please forgive this somewhat hasty apprai-

sal of some of the best in both counties: Le Francais at Brighton is busy while Byrons (0323) 20171 at Eastbourne is fishy. In Rusper, Ghyll Manor (0293) 871571 provides a comfortable resting place. Returning to Alfriston, we see Moonrakers (0323) 870472 – try a Hot Sussex Smokie! In Herstmonceux, The Sundial (0323) 832217 is French, whilst Jevington's Hungry Monk (03212) 482178 is outstanding. In Midhurst try Mida (073086) 3284, in Pulborough plump for Stane Street Hollow (0798) 87219 (this should be a 6 figure number, not 5) while in Poynings Au Petit Normand (079156) 346 should answer your prayers. But for a finale to end this array, try Manley's (0903) 742331 in Storrington – (if you can get a table!).

No trip to the heart of Sussex would be complete either without a visit to one of the many country houses, castles, pubs or inns. Here are a few more random thoughts for life beyond the 18th green: The White Horse Inn (024359) 215 in Chilgrove has an excellent restaurant, while The Shepherd and Dog in Fulking and the Lickfold Inn at Lickfold are also good. Aside from the antiques of Chichester – Arundel, (an excellent castle to see here) and Petworth which offers the superb Petworth House, there is a summer of unsurpassed opera at Glyndebourne. In contrast, a totally flamboyant place to spend time is Brighton. The streets in the old town offer several bargains while The Grand Pavilion is as striking as ever. Returning to the subject of castles, Bodiam in East Sussex is not too widely known, but nonetheless quite majestic. Any thoughts for the player who had trouble in the groping gorse at Ashdown? Well, Blackboys, the pub in the village of the same name is welcoming and resuscitating as is the Wild Boar in Crowborough and The Roebuck in Wych Cross. But perhaps the best plan is to return to Alfriston where the Smugglers and The Star are both great value. Sussex, in short, is a true delight, both on and off the fairways.

H.Rountree   BULLDOG BREED   Burlington Gallery

SOUTH LODGE HOTEL

One of the best kept secrets in West Sussex, South Lodge Hotel captures the essence of Victorian style and elegance, with an atmosphere of warmth and hospitality, hidden amongst 90 acres of beautiful gardens and parkland, with views over the rolling South Downs.

Built in 1883, this grey stoned mansion, strewn with wisteria, was once the home of the Godman family; Fredrick Ducane Godman, a keen botanist and explorer, collected hundreds of rare shrubs and trees and an outstanding variety of rhododendron and camellia, which today make the gardens at the hotel such a delight.

Dining at South Lodge is always a special occasion. In the elegant wood panelled dining room guests enjoy innovative menus created by top chef Anthony Tobin, featuring local meat, game and fish, with herbs and soft fruits grown in the hotels own walled garden.

Each of the 39 bedrooms and suites is perfectly appointed. All are individually decorated in the true country house style, sympathetically incorporating all the modern amenities one expects to find at a first class hotel.

South Lodge, situated in Lower Beeding, near Horsham, West Sussex, is only a short drive from the challenging 18 hole, par 73 Mannings Heath Golf Club, where hotel guests enjoy special privileges. The hotel will reserve tees at the course for guests during their stay.

Other activities at the hotel include tennis, coarse fishing, putting, croquet or petanque, and horse riding can be arranged at the local stables.

South Lodge is also an ideal base to explore the countryside and wealth of English heritage that Sussex has to offer, with many fine National Trust houses and exquisite gardens to discover. The Georgian coastal town of Brighton, with its famous lanes, is only 30 minutes away, and both Petworth and Arundel are within easy distance.

South Lodge Hotel
Lower Beeding
Near Horsham
West Sussex
Tel: (0403) 891711
Fax: (0403) 891766

WEST SUSSEX (PULBOROUGH)
CHAMPIONSHIP GOLF

'Concentrate your mind on the match until you are dormy. Then look at the surrounding scenery and expatiate on its beauties.'

(A.J. Robertson)

In the opinion of many, **West Sussex**, or **Pulborough** as it is commonly known, is quite simply the most beautiful course in England. The setting is the South Downs and seclusion is total. **Commander George Hillyard** founded the Club in 1930 having conceived the idea, so the story goes, as he looked out of his bathroom window one day while taking his morning shave! (His house, it should be explained, over-looked the present layout). The course was designed by **Sir Guy Campbell** and **Major C.K. Hutchinson** and opened for play in October 1930.

In a similar vein to Woodhall Spa in Lincolnshire, Pulborough has often been described as something of an oasis, the surrounding countryside being predominantly meadow and marshland with the course lying on sandy soil and heather running throughout. Heather naturally adds charm to any golf course but it is perhaps the magnificent spread of pines, oaks and silver birch trees that are most striking at Pulborough.

Mr. G.R. Martindale is the present Club Secretary; he may be contacted via the **West Sussex Golf Club, Pulborough, West Sussex RH20 2EN,** telephone **(0798) 872563**. Visitors are welcome, but strictly by appointment only; the same applies to golfing Societies. It should also be noted that three ball and four ball matches are not generally permitted – singles and foursomes being preferred. The only specific restrictions on times visitors can play are before 9.30am (throughout the week), on Tuesdays and at weekends. The green fees for 1992 were set at £27.50 for a single round or £38 for a day ticket. One final introduction: **Tim Packham** is the Club's professional, and he may be reached by telephone on **(0798) 872563**.

While Pulborough may enjoy a gloriously peaceful setting situated right in the heart of the Sussex countryside, it could hardly be described as remote and is easily accessible from all directions. The Club's precise location is about 2 miles east of Pulborough just off the A283 road to Storrington. The A283 links Pulborough to the outskirts of Brighton on the south coast and to Milford (near Guildford) to the north. For those approaching from westerly directions the A272 from

Winchester is likely to prove of most assistance before joining the A283 at Petworth approximately five miles from Pulborough. Motoring from the London area the quickest route is probably to take the M23 towards Gatwick joining the A264 at Crawley and travelling through Horsham. The A264 merges into the A29 near Billingshurst which in turn joins with Pulborough.

One of the features of Pulborough is its conspicuous absence of a par five beyond the first hole – a hole which in any event becomes a four when played from the tees of the day. At 6221 yards, s.s.s. 70, the par of 68 is a difficult one to match. With none of the par fours being overly short there aren't any really obvious birdie opportunities. Perhaps the best known hole on the course is the par three **6th**; measuring 224 yards it requires an exceptionally accurate tee shot across water to a green that has an out-of-bounds to the right and tall trees directly behind it. **Henry Longhurst**, a great admirer of Pulborough, very aptly said of the 6th, 'If ever there was an all or nothing hole, this is it.' Immediately after the potential disaster of the 6th, the **7th** requires a long uphill drive to carry over some thick heather and scrub not to mention an enormous sand bunker. With holes of such a nature and quality as the 6th and 7th it isn't unrealistic to draw a comparison between this corner of Pulborough and Pine Valley in New Jersey. It is a brave comparison (and an enormous compliment) because the North American course is generally considered to be the finest and perhaps most naturally beautiful course in the world.

The **13th** and **15th** are two more outstanding holes and the round finishes with a pair of testing par fours.

As for its 19th, West Sussex has a very comfortable Clubhouse offering full catering facilities including two bars. A jacket and tie should be worn in all public rooms.

Henry Longhurst is only one of a number of celebrated admirers of Pulborough and the late **Bobby Locke**, four times the Open Champion considered it his favourite English course. While no major professional tournament has been played over the course (again there is a parallel to be drawn with Pine Valley) the Club has hosted both the English Ladies Amateur Championship and the British Ladies Championship. It also staged the English Seniors Championship in 1989.

Hole	Yards	Par	Hole	Yards	Par
1	481	5	10	405	4
2	411	4	11	448	4
3	371	4	12	210	3
4	351	4	13	363	4
5	146	3	14	434	4
6	220	3	15	132	3
7	442	4	16	365	4
8	183	3	17	441	4
9	350	4	18	403	4
Out	2,955	34	In	3,201	34
			Out	2,955	34
			TOTALS	6,156	68

PARK HOUSE HOTEL

Park house has been run by the O'Briens for nearly 45 years and still retains the distinctive atmosphere of a private country house, where all guests receive unparalleled hospitality and maximum comfort. All the amenities of an English country house are available, yet the hotel is just fifty-two miles from London.

Set in nine acres of garden, Park House is a blend of 16th century manor and late Victorian mansion. The large and elegant public rooms include a drawing room lined with books and ornaments and a long dining room with polished tables. Great pride is taken in the nutritious and satisfying food served for the guests' delight.

All the bedrooms are individually furnished, overlooking the gardens and grass tennis courts, and include private bath-rooms, colour television and radio telephones. In addition there is a fully-serviced cottage annexe with a sitting-room, double bedroom, dressing-room and bathroom adjoining Park House.

For racegoers who can tear themselves away from the delights of the hotel, Goodwood Racecourse is only six miles away, and golfers are amply served by the range of first-class golf courses in the locality. Indeed guests can even practise at their leisure on the hotel's own 9-hole pitch and putt course. Cowdray Park in Midhurst is the centre of English polo and the famous Chichester Festival Theatre is within easy reach.

This gem of a hotel cannot be recommended too highly for a week-end away, but guests may find that this is simply not long enough!

Park House Hotel
Bepton
Midhurst
Sussex GU29 OJB
Tel: (0730) 812880
Fax: (0730) 815643

EAST SUSSEX NATIONAL
CHAMPIONSHIP GOLF

Move over Sunningdale, Wentworth and Walton Heath! These three great championship venues, all situated in the magnificent heathland belt of Surrey and Berkshire, are now having to make room for a newcomer from the heart of rural Sussex.

So what are we getting so excited about? East Sussex National has two great golf courses, the **East** and **West** which were officially opened for play as recently as April 1990. Both were designed by the American, **Robert E Cupp,** formerly Jack Nicklaus' Senior designer. For the first time in Great Britain, bent grasses have been used throughout from tee to green and the result is golf course conditioning of a type never witnessed before in this country. The fairways are genuinely carpet-like and the teeing areas are better than most golf course greens! Both courses measure in excess of 7,000 yards from their Championship tees and are similarly challenging but quite different in appearance. The East Course is the 'stadium' course and was specifically designed with a view to its staging big events, hence the gentle 'gallery mounding' very evident around the 18th green. The West Course is more intimate than the East. The landscape rises and falls quite sharply in parts; the surrounding woodland is more dense but because of the climbs there are many spectacular views over the South Downs.

East Sussex National was first conceived in the mid 1980s when a Canadian entrepreneur purchased Horsted Place, an elegant Victorian manor house which he immediately converted into one of Britain's leading country house hotels. Various parcels of adjoining land were also acquired which, when pieced together, totalled a massive 1,100 acres of prime Sussex countryside. Construction began in May 1988 on the two 18-hole Championship courses and, only 23 months later, opened for play. The summer prior to this, in July 1989, the Great Britain and Ireland Walker Cup team came to East Sussex National to prepare on what could only be described as the nearest equivalent to a top American-style golf course. When they returned victorious from Georgia they were quick to acknowledge the value of their having had the opportunity of practising at East Sussex.

Aside from the golf courses, and of course Horsted Place, East Sussex National boasts superb golf practice facilities including three academy holes – a par three, par four and par five with 15 sets of practice tees; one of the best golf shops in the country and, (under construction at the time of writing), a new 27,000 sq ft clubhouse.

One of the courses at East Sussex National, and it may be either as they alternate, is always reserved for Club Members and their guests, but visitors are welcomed on the other course (the 'Village' Course at is it known). Bookings can be made seven days in advance by telephoning the Starter at the Golf Shop on **(0825) 841217**. The visitors' green fee in 1992 was £60 for 18 holes and £80 per day. All membership and corporate enquiries can be dealt with through the Golf Shop on the above number (7 days a week) or by calling the Administration Office on **(0825) 750577** (Monday to Friday). The address for written correspondence is **East Sussex National Golf Club, Little Horsted, Uckfield, East SussexTN22 5TS.**

There are many outstanding holes on the East Course but perhaps the par fives are especially memorable; three of the four, the **7th**, **10th** and **14th** are as good a trio as one is likely to find on any course, anywhere. Of these, only the 10th is realistically reachable in two shots and then only after a brave downhill second is successfully hit over water – a hole not too dissimilar to the 15th at Augusta. Although the challenge isn't necessarily any greater on the West Course, in most people's minds it has by far the greater number of 'pretty' holes, in fact, 'provocatively spectacular' might be the description of some. Anyone wishing to put together a 'dream nine holes' could do worse than select the **1st, 2nd, 3rd, 9th, 10th, 12th, 13th, 14th** and **18th** on the East Sussex National West Course. This collection would provide two outstanding short holes, on both of which the tee shot must flirt with water; a pair of genuine par fives and five two-shot holes ranging from a drive and a short iron (the dog-leg 1st) to a truly intimidating stroke one hole (the monstrous 14th). And what a glorious finishing hole the 18th provides! In his course notes, architect Robert Cupp gives an interesting commentary on the closing holes of the West Course. Having metaphorically walked on to the back tee at the 18th he holds his breath and surveys the view ahead:

'The player has been restricted at fourteen, tempted at fifteen, devilled at sixteen and exhausted at seventeen. Now, he stands on the elevated tee, looking across a deep chasm to a fairway lined right and left by giant oaks, and a green guarded by huge bunkers and the Clubhouse beyond. The word here is 'test'. The reaction in tournament conditions is clammy hands'.

Many are likely to experience the full range of sensations in September 1993 when East Sussex stages the prestigious **G.A. European Open**. It is clearly a testimony to the quality of the Club's facilities, especially its two courses, that it has acquired a major event so soon. September 1993 – The Ryder Cup at The Belfry and the European Open at East Sussex National – my hands are becoming clammy at the prospect!

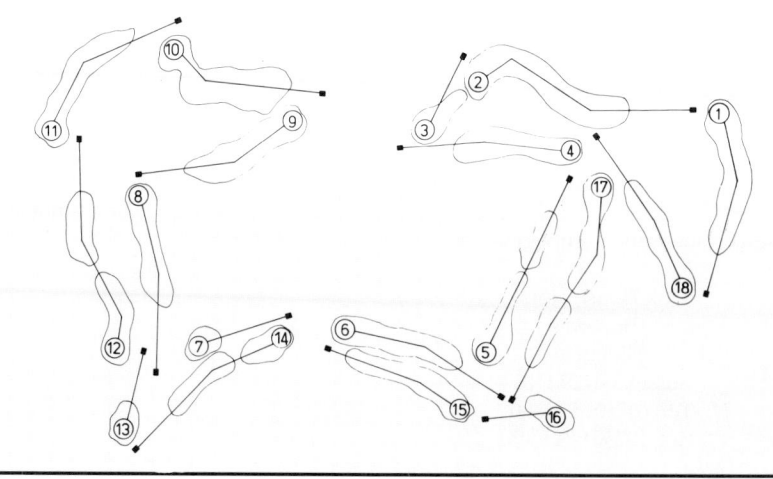

West Course

Hole	Metres	Par	Hole	Metres	Par
1	363	4	10	404	4
2	517	5	11	423	4
3	136	3	12	520	5
4	354	4	13	184	3
5	504	5	14	450	4
6	396	4	15	365	4
7	192	3	16	117	3
8	408	4	17	566	5
9	392	4	18	365	4
Out	**3,262**	**36**	**In**	**3,394**	**36**
			Out	**3,262**	**36**
			TOTALS	**6,656**	**72**

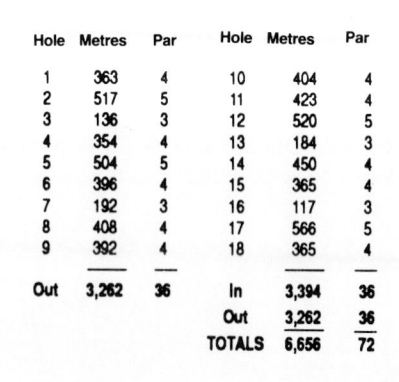

EAST SUSSEX NATIONAL GOLF CLUB AND HORSTED PLACE

Occupying a majestic setting in twenty three acres of land-scaped Sussex countryside, Horsted Place offers an enviable combination of modern facilities in a delightful and elegant form. Individually decorated suites, a magnificently appointed main dining room, two private dining rooms, executive meeting and conference libraries, a heated indoor swimming pool, a tennis court and helicopter landing area are all designed to more than cater for the needs of the modern traveller. Rated as one of the best hotels in the British Isles by the Guide Michelin and also renowned for its culinary prow-ess, Horsted Place provides unequalled standards of service and facilities for visitors, golfers and the business community. Over one thousand acres of rolling countryside surrounding Horsted Place have now been transformed into two golf courses which have quickly become established as two of Britain's finest inland challenges. If quality is the cornerstone of excellence, East Sussex National sets a standard that will not easily be equalled. American course designer Robert E. Cupp, has coaxed out of the beautiful Sussex countryside two layouts that offer a stern competitive challenge, as well as some memorably beautiful holes. The East course features gallery mounding for the benefit of spectators, the area of the eighteenth green alone being able to accommodate up to 30,000 spectators. The West course, meanwhile, is like the East over 7,000 yards from the gold tees and features nine holes where water comes perilously into play. The special qualities of the courses have been recognised by top players on the PGA European Tour resulting in the East course being chosen to host the 1993 GA European Open. The momentous challenge posed by both courses is made slightly less awesome by the provision of a three hole Teaching Academy and fabulous practice facilities.

Visitors to East Sussex National and Horsted Place are imme-diately struck by both a glorious setting and an attention to detail that result in an ambience of all-round excellence. Every visit is guaranteed to become a memorable encounter-contact the numbers below for your own taste of a unique leisure experience.

East Sussex National Golf Club and Horsted Place
Little Horsted
Uckfield
East Sussex, TN22 5TS
Tel: (hotel) (0825) 750581
Tel: (golf) (0825) 841217
Fax: (hotel) (0825) 750459
Fax: (golf) (0825) 841282

ROYAL ASHDOWN FOREST
CHAMPIONSHIP GOLF

Although it is now less than an hour's drive from the frantic chaos of Greater London, Ashdown Forest is a place of great beauty, charm and tranquillity. And so it should be, for it was here, somewhere deep in this secluded forest of pine and silver birch, that the most famous of all 'Golden Bears' Winnie The Pooh pursued his never ending quest for honey. Such is the setting for one of Britain's most fortunate golf clubs.

In 1988 Royal Ashdown Forest celebrated its centenary. It was on Christmas Eve just over a hundred years ago that the **Reverend A.T. Scott** teed up his ball and struck the very first shot. The course has changed little over the years, a fact which clearly speaks volumes for the original layout. The Club acquired the title Royal during Queen Victoria's reign and long before the turn of the century had established itself as one of the finest tests of golf in southern England.

Many great players have been associated with Royal Ashdown Forest over the years. The Cantelupe Club, the associate club connected to Royal Ashdown, included **Abe Mitchell** and **Alf Padgham** among its ranks and several noted amateurs have improved their technique on this most challenging course.

Casual visitors are welcomed at Royal Ashdown – rather more so, it must be said, than at some of the south east's leading courses. A recognised club handicap is, however, a requirement and it is normally advisable to telephone the Club before finalising any plans. Not surprisingly the course is very popular in the summer months.

The Club Secretary, **David Scrivens**, can be contacted via the **Royal Ashdown Forest Golf Club, Forest Row, East Sussex RH18 5LR** Tel: **(034282) 2018**. Those wishing to organise a Society meeting should write to Mr. Scrivens at the above address. Societies can normally be accommodated during the week, Tuesday being an exception. The green fees for 1992 were set at £33 for weekdays with £38 payable at weekends and on Bank Holidays. Visitors should note that singles and foursomes are preferred. The club professional is **Martyn Landsborough** who took over in 1990 from Alf Padgham's nephew Hector, who had been the professional for over 40 years. Martyn can be reached on **(034282) 2247**.

The Club is located within Ashdown Forest, approximately 4 miles south of East Grinstead. Motoring from London and the North the A22 is by far the most direct route. This can be joined from the M25 at Junction 6. The A22 should be followed for some 4 miles beyond East Grinstead as far as Forest Row. There one should take the B2110 Hartfield road turning left after a quarter of a mile on to Chapel Lane where the Club can be found. Approaching from the South the A22 can be joined from a number of roads north of Eastbourne.

The generally held view is that Royal Ashdown Forest is a particularly difficult course. On several holes a lengthy tee shot will be required in order to find the safety of the fairway. The ever present stream and the considerable scattering of gorse and heather create a multitude of problems for the wayward golfer – and as if they were not enough, on several of the holes the fairway is exceptionally narrow and that beautiful forest will gratefully accept the result of a slice or a hook. So the message is, hit it hard and hit it straight!

Despite the variety of hazards, of all the country's leading courses Royal Ashdown Forest must surely be unique in not possessing a single bunker. **Bernard Darwin** is doubtless not the only golfer who failed to discover this fact until the conclusion of his game; as he put it, 'It is only at the end of a round that we realise with a pleasurable shock that there is not a single hideous rampart or so much as a pot bunker.' The Club was prevented long ago by the Forestry Commission, or the then equivalent, from creating bunkers and their absence now forms part of the character and charm of the course; furthermore, the undulating nature of the landscape produces some truly magnificent views over the Forest and beyond.

The attractive Clubhouse offers a very high standard of catering. A light lunch, such as a ploughman's, can be obtained whilst a full four course meal can also be arranged. During the months of November and December a full English breakfast is available – a welcome facility which many clubs would do well to copy: golfers, like the Forest's most famous inhabitant are hungry animals and some are more than quick to claim that the missed three footer is a result of a missed breakfast!

Old Course

Hole	Yards	Par	Hole	Yards	Par
1	332	4	10	485	5
2	384	4	11	249	3
3	327	4	12	558	5
4	356	4	13	367	4
5	509	5	14	200	3
6	126	3	15	310	4
7	365	4	16	407	4
8	498	5	17	472	4
9	142	3	18	352	4
Out	3,039	36	In	3,400	36
			Out	3,039	36
			TOTALS	6,439	72

DALE HILL HOTEL & GOLF CLUB

Unique comfort, style and location, together with superb facilities, can be found at the Dale Hill Hotel and Golf Club. This modern hotel is set in 300 spectacular acres, on an established, highly acclaimed parkland golf course. From the covered portico entrance, through to the open plan, two storey classic reception area, the warmth and charm of this hotel is already established. The Quedley Restaurant, from its unusual elevated situation, commands wonderful views and serves outstanding, award winning cuisine, together with a fine selection of wines. The highest standards of decor are apparent throughout the hotel, creating a stylish, sophisticated atmosphere. Each of the attractive 25 bedrooms are appointed with every facility required by the discerning guest, and most of the rooms enjoy breathtaking views. The Golf Course itself has been up-graded over the past few years, and you can enjoy unlimited golf during your stay at Dale Hill. Professionally coached golfing sessions can be arranged. The many amenities offered in the luxurious health complex are all appointed to very high standards, and for the ultimate in relaxation, massage and selected beauty treatments are available. Full conference facilities and technical equipment are ready for use, and support and advice provided, ensures the success of any meeting. This truly first class hotel is within easy reach of Tunbridge Wells and the stunning Sussex countryside where you will find historic medieval forts and castles. A stay at Dale Hill is highly recommended, whether on business or pleasure. Room and breakfast from £38.50.

Dale Hill Hotel & Golf Club
Ticehurst
Wadhurst
East Sussex TN5 7DQ
Tel: (0580) 200112
Fax: (0580) 201249

EAST & WEST SUSSEX
COMPLETE GOLF

WEST SUSSEX

Bognor Regis G.C.
(0243) 821929
Downview Rd. Felpham, Bognor Regis
(18)6238 yards/**/B/H

Copthorne G.C.
(0342) 712508
Bovers Arms Rd. Copthorne, Crawley
(18)6550 yards/**/C

Cottesmore G.C.
(0923) 528256
Buchan Hill, Pease Pottage, Crawley
1 mile from M23 on Horsham Rd.
(18)6100 yards/***/C
(18)5400 yards/***/D

Cowdray Park G.C.
(073081) 3599
Midhurst
1 mile east of Midhurst on A272.
(18)5972 yards/***/C

Effingham Park G.C.
(0342) 716528
West Park Rd. Copthorne
(9)1749 yards/***/E

Goodwood G.C.
(0243) 774968
Goodwood, Chichester
Take A286 to Goodwood racecourse.
(18)6318 yards/***/B/H

Goodwood Park G. & C.C.
(0243) 775987
4 miles north of Chichester
(18)6530 yards/***/D

Ham Manor G.C.
(0903) 783288
Angmering
Between Worthing and Littlehampton
on A259.
(18)6243 yards/***/B/H

Haywards Heath G.C.
(0444) 414457
High Beech Lane, Haywards Heath
2 miles north of Haywards Heath.
(18)6206 yards/***/C/H

Hill Barn G.C.
(0903) 237301
Hill Barn Lane, Worthing
N.of Worthing off the Upper Brighton Rd.
(18)6224 yards/***/D

Ifield G. and C.C.
(0293) 520222
Rusper Rd. Ifield, Crawley
(18)6289 yards/**/C

Littlehampton G.C.
(0903) 717170
170 Rope Walk, Riverside, Littlehampton
(18)6244 yards/***/C

Mannings Heath G.C.
(0403) 210228
Goldings Lane, Mannings Heath
3 miles south of Horsham off A281.
(18)6404 yards/**/C/H

Paxhill Park G.C.
(0444) 484467
1 mile north of Lindfield
(18) 6196 yards/***/D

Pycombe G.C.
(0273) 845372
Pycombe, Brighton
6 miles N of Brighton on A272
(18) 6234 yards/***/C

Selsey G.C.
(0243) 602203
Golf Links Lane, Selsey, Chichester
7 miles south of Chichester on B2145.
(9)5402 yards/***/D

Tilgate Forest G.C.
(0293) 530103
Titmus Drive, Tilgate, Crawley
(18)6359 yards/***/D

West Chiltington G.C.
(0798) 813574
Broadford Bridge Road, W. Chiltington
2 miles E of Pulborough
(18) 5969 yards/***/D

West Sussex G.C.
(0798) 872563
Pulborough
2 miles east of Pulborough on A283
(18)6156 yards/**/F/H/L

Worthing G.C.
(0903) 260801
Links Rd. Worthing
At junction between A27 and A24.
(18)6477 yards/***/B/H
(18)5243 yards/***/B/H

EAST SUSSEX

Aldershaw G.C.
(0424) 870898
Sedlescombe
(18) 6218 yards/***/D

Ashdown Forest Hotel G.C.
(0342) 824869
Chapel Lane, Forest Row
(18)5510 yards/***/C

Brighton and Hove G.C.
(0273) 556482
Dyke Rd, Brighton
2 miles north of Brighton.
(9)5722 yards/***/D

Cooden Beach G.C.
(04243) 2040
Cooden Sea Rd. Cooden
(18)6450 yards/***/C

Crowborough Beacon G.C.
(08926) 61511
Beacon Rd. Crowborough
8 miles south of Tunbridge Wells on A26.
(18)6279 yards/**/B/H/L

Dale Hill G.C.
(0580) 200112
Ticehurst, Wadhurst
(18)6055 yards/***/C

Dyke G.C.
(0273) 857296
Dyke Rd. Brighton
4 miles north of Brighton.
(18)6212 yards/***(Sun)/C

Eastbourne Downs G.C.
(0323) 20827
East Dean Rd. Eastbourne
On A259 west of Eastbourne.
(18)6635 yards/***/D

East Brighton G.C.
(0273) 604838
Roedean Rd. Brighton
Opposite Brighton Marina off A259.
(18)6304 yards/***/C

East Sussex National G.C.
(0825) 75577
Little Horsted, Uckfield
(18)7081 yards/***/F
(18)7154 yards/*/F

Hastings G.C.
(0424) 852981
Battle Rd. St.Leonards-on-Sea
3 miles N.W. of Hastings on A2100.
(18)6248 yards/***/E

Highwoods G.C.
(0424) 212625
Ellerslie Lane, Bexhill-on-Sea
2 miles west of Bexhill on A259
(18)6218 yards/***/C

Hollingbury G.C.
(0273) 552010
Ditchling Rd. Brighton
(18)6502 yards/***/D

Horam Park G.C.
(04353) 3477
Chiddingly Rd. Horam, Heathfield
(9)2844/***/D

Lewes G.C.
(0273) 473245
Chapel Hill, Lewes
Between Lewes and Eastbourne on A27.
(18)5951 yards/**/D

Peacehaven G.C.
(0273) 514049
Brighton Rd. Newhaven
1 mile west of Newhaven on A259.
(9)5007 yards/***/F/H

Piltdown G.C.
(082572) 2033
Piltdown, Uckfield
3 miles west of Uckfield.
(18)6059 yards/**/B/H/L

Royal Ashdown Forest G.C.
(034282) 2018
Chapel Lane, Forest Row, E.Grinstead
(18)6439 yards/**/B/H

Royal Eastbourne G.C.
(0323) 30412
Paradise Drive, Eastbourne
Half-mile from town centre.
(18)6109 yards/***/C
(9)2147 yards/***/D

Rye G.C.
(0797) 225241
Camber, Rye
(18)6301 yards/*/F

Seaford G.C.
(0323) 892103
East Blatchington, Seaford
N of Seaford off A259
(18)6233 yards/**/F

Seaford Head G.C.
(0323) 890139
Southdown Rd, Seaford
12 miles from Brighton
(18)5348 yards/***/E

Waterhall G.C.
(0273) 508658
Mill Rd, Brighton
(18)5692 yards/***/D

West Hove G.C.
(0273) 413411
Old ShorehamRd, Hove
(18)6038 yards/**/C

Willingdon G.C.
(0323) 410983
Southdown Rd, Eastbourne
(18)6049 yards/**/C

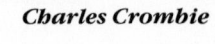

Charles Crombie ***WHAT SHALL I TAKE FOR THIS?***
Rosenstiel's

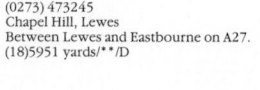

KENT

Julian Barrow   **ROYAL ST GEORGE'S**   *Burlington Gallery*

KENT
CHOICE GOLF

From the mysterious and desolate lands of Romney Marsh to the famous White Cliffs of Dover. From the rich orchards of the Garden of England to the outskirts of Greater London, a county of great contrast. From the windswept links of Sandwich and Deal to the secluded Parks of Belmont and Knole, a county of great contrast.

Kent's reputation as one of the country's greatest golfing counties has been built around a three mile stretch of links land lying midway between St Margaret's Bay and Pegwell Bay. Within this short distance lie three Open Championship courses: **Princes** (1932), **Royal Cinque Ports** (1909 and 1920) and **Royal St Georges** (too numerous to list!) Kent has a few other fine links courses but the golfer who sticks hard to the coast will be missing out on some of the most enjoyable inland golf Southern England has to offer.

GOLFING INLAND

In common with each of the counties that border Greater London many of Kent's courses are gradually finding themselves more in London than in Kent. When the Blackheath golfers left their famous Common and set up base at Eltham they were doubtless surrounded by the green fields of Kent. Even Charles Darwin's village of Orpington is now feeling the pinch but happily the **West Kent** Golf Club and nearby **Lullingstone Park** provide pleasant retreats.

Enough grousing! The ancient town of Sevenoaks is categorically in Kent and a very fortunate place too with **Wildernesse** Golf Club to the north and **Knole Park** to the south. The former is arguably the finest inland course in the county; with narrow fairways and quite thickly wooded, it is also one of the toughest. Knole Park is one of several Kentish courses that enjoy stately surroundings, being laid out in the handsome deer park of Lord Sackville. Both Wildernesse and Knole suffered during the great hurricane of October '87 but then so did many courses in southern England.

In the south west of the county, Tunbridge Wells is a very pretty, if congested, old town; **Nevil** Golf Club is nearby and there are 36 holes at the **Edenbridge** Golf and Country Club.

For a stop-over in Sevenoaks The Royal Oak Hotel (0732) 451109 is comfortable, as is The Bull Hotel (0732) 885522 in nearby Wrotham Heath. A number of fine restaurants are also close at hand; they include La Cremaillere (0732) 851489 in Hadlow (french cooking), The Gate Inn in Hildenborough (good sea food) and the outstanding Thackeray's House (0892) 511921 in Tunbridge Wells. If you are short of a place to stay in Tunbridge Wells, The Royal Wells (0892) 511188 is particularly good value, and for a second place to eat try Eglantine's (0892) 24957. Finally in the south western corner of the county there is an outstanding pub – great for lunches – at Speldhurst, namely the 13th century George and Dragon.

To the north of the county, both **Mid Kent's** downland course at Gravesend and **Rochester and Cobham Park** are handy for those travelling along the A2. Further along this road is the attractive town of Faversham and south of the town off the A251 is Belmont Park, the estate of Lord Harris and the home of **Faversham** Golf Club. Here golf is played in the most tranquil of settings and it is particularly delightful in autumn when the fairways abound with countless strolling pheasants.

Beyond the 18th green a few ideas emerge for a 19th hole. In Shorne, the Inn On The Lake (047482) 3333 is a most pleasant place to stay. An alternative for pub lovers is the Dickensian Leather Bottle (0474) 814327 in Cobham which also has some comfortable bedrooms. More expensive accommodation is located near Ash Green in the alarmingly named village of Fawkham where The Brandshatch Place (0474) 872239 offers tremendous comfort and a very good restaurant. Two more pubs to note in the area are the Golden Eagle in Burham and the particularly pleasant and aptly named Little Gem in Aylesford. Over towards Faversham two fine places to rest the spikes are Trowley House (0795) 539168 at Sheldwich and The Tanyard Hotel (0622) 744705 at Boughton Monchelsea. If it's just quality fayre that is required, then Faversham itself houses the extremely popular Reads (0795) 535344.

Leaving Faversham, famous pheasants and all, we must make a pilgrimage. The **Canterbury** Golf Club, situated to the east of the beautiful cathedral city along the A27 is well worth a visit. Very undulating, it is a first class parkland course – one of the best in the county. South of Canterbury (via A2 and A260) at Barham is the **Broome Park** Golf and Country Club, set in the grounds of yet another famous country house – this time a beautiful 300 year old mansion, the former home of Lord Kitchener. It too is a very pleasant parkland course and quite lengthy. Whether it's the proliferation of nearby golf courses (Sandwich and Deal are just 15 miles away) or the Cathedral, or even the glorious Kent countryside that attracts most, Canterbury deserves more than a short visit. Perhaps the leading hotel which also houses a commendable restaurant is The County (0227) 766266. The House of Agnes Hotel (0227) 472185 can also be recommended in Canterbury and just outside the city, Howfield Manor (0227) 738294 at Chartham Hatch is a charming small country house hotel. Ersham Lodge (0227) 463174 and Magnolia House (0227) 765121 also receive many favourable reports. The aforementioned glorious countryside is riddled with village pubs: two of note are The Duck Inn at Petts Bottom and The White Horse at Chilham Castle.

Maidstone may not have the appeal of Canterbury but to the south east of this busy commuter town is one of England's most attractive golf courses, **Leeds Castle**. The castle itself was described by Lord Conway as the most beautiful in the world and the setting really is quite idyllic. There are nine very individual holes and as it's a public course (like Lullingstone Park, mentioned above, and **Cobtree Manor Park** on the Chatham Road) there are no general restrictions on times of play. Another recent golfing addition to the area is **Tudor Park** near Bearsted. Like Broome Park it is part of a Country Club; the golf course was designed by Donald Steel and is especially popular with golfing societies.

The golf course at **Ashford** is pretty much in the middle of the county, and is another strongly worth inspecting. Ashford is a heathland type course, which in itself is fairly unique to Kent and where visitors are always made to feel welcome. We're now in the heart of the Kent Downs and a variety of fine establishments beckon. Eastwell Manor (0233) 635751 takes pride of place. Elegant and relaxing with a splendid restaurant – in fact outstanding in every way. In Wye, The Wife of Bath (0233) 812540 is a tremendous restaurant. An ideal tavern is The Compasses at Side Street and for a pub with good value accommodation The Bell near Smarden is recommended.

Back to the fairways and a word for **Cranbrook**, a very pleasant and greatly improved parkland course. This was the scene of Bing Crosby's last round in England. Apparently he was close to purchasing the course before his untimely death in Spain. Also in Cranbrook is one of Kent's most popular hotels, The Kennel Holt Hotel (0580) 712032 – excellent for dinner and equally convenient for **Lamberhurst** Golf Club.

AROUND THE COAST

Switching from the rich countryside of Kent we now visit the coast. **Littlestone** is the first port of call, and it's quite a contrast. Situated on the edge of the flatlands of Romney Marsh, it enjoys a somewhat remote setting. Littlestone is a splendid links and an Open Championship qualifying course, which doesn't deserve to be overshadowed by Kent's more illustrious trio further along the coast. Littlestone's best holes are saved for near the end of the round – the par 4 16th and par 3 17th typify all that's best (and frightening!) about links golf.

Not too far from Littlestone is the town of Hythe where the large Hythe Imperial (0303) 267441 is a fine base, especially as there are 9 holes in the 'back garden'!

North of Sandwich is the **North Foreland** Club at Broadstairs, also an Open qualifying course, although its 27 holes are more strictly clifftop than links in nature. The Royal Albion Hotel (0843) 68071 in Broadstairs is another fine place to stay, as is the intimate Rothsay Hotel (0843) 62646. To the south of Deal is **Walmer and Kingsdown**, a downland course providing splendid views.

Perhaps not surprisingly, where there is one great golf links there is often another nearby: Troon, Turnberry and Prestwick in Ayrshire; Birkdale, Hillside and Formby in Lancashire. Kent's famous three, **Royal St Georges**, **Royal Cinque Ports** and **Prince's** are all featured ahead.

Despite the great quality of golf on offer there aren't too many places along the famous three mile stretch where one can put the feet up (or the golf clubs for that matter). Anyway, in Sandwich The Bell Hotel is very comfortable and convenient (0304) 613388; its quayside setting is handy for The Fisherman's Wharf Restaurant (0304) 613636. St. Crispin's Inn (0304) 612081 is a charming alternative. Two pubs to note in Sandwich are the King's Arms (0304) 617330 and the Fleur-de-Lis (0304) 611131. In Deal, The Black Horse Hotel (0304) 374074 is a popular golfing haunt. St Margaret's Bay, located on National Trust land is worth a look and the Cliffe Tavern (0304) 852749 nearby is a good place to wet one's whistle and stay if you wish. The Guildford House Hotel (0304) 375015 located on Beach Street in Deal is another ideal 19th hole if you're playing the famous courses nearby. As a final tip it might be a good idea to take the car on a short drive to Westcliffe, where Wallett's Court (0304) 852424 is supremely welcoming (despite its name!) As we conclude our trip another thought emerges.... Hardelot, Le Touquet... Why, we could nip down to Lydd where an airplane can whisk us off to Le Touquet quicker than we can drive back to London. Vive le golf!

F.P. Hopkins   CROOKHAM   Burlington Gallery

ROYAL ST. GEORGES (SANDWICH)
CHAMPIONSHIP GOLF

Two monumental events are scheduled to take place on the Kent Coast in 1993. The most important is that the **Open Championship** returns to Sandwich. Secondly, the Channel Tunnel is due to be opened. Hordes of French will be streaming over by the Citroen load. The French of course have recently gone potty over golf and commentators are predicting that a French golfer will soon win the Open. It has happened before mind you – although that was way back in 1907. Could St Georges in 1993 be the next occasion? St Georges that bastion of English golf. Perish the thought!

The Club was founded in **1887**, rather ironically by two Scottish gentlemen, **Dr. Laidlaw Purves** and **Henry Lamb** after what can only be described as a rather eccentric venture. Like all good Scotsmen they had been bitten by the bug; however, both were presently living in Victorian London which meant that their golf was more or less confined to the various commons where the game was played alongside every conceivable activity imaginable. To them golf was meant to be played on a links by the sea. Hence the pair found themselves at Bournemouth setting off in an easterly direction looking for a suitable site. Having reached the eastern shore of Kent they had drawn the proverbial blank (one presumes that they experienced one of those infamous Victorian pea-soupers, the day they passed through Rye); with patience no doubt wearing thin, suddenly 'land ahoy!' Doctor Purves sights a vast stretch of duneland at Sandwich. The story is that he 'spied the land with a golfer's eye' from the tower of St Clement's Church. Quite what he was doing at the top of the tower is irrelevant – St. Georges had been located. Within seven short years the Open Championship had 'come south' and St. Georges was the first English venue.

More than one hundred years on **Gerald Watts** is the Secretary at St Georges and he can be contacted by telephone on **(0304) 613090**. All written communication should be directed to him at **The Royal St. Georges Golf Club, Sandwich, Kent CT13 9PB**. As a general guide visitors are welcome between Mondays and Fridays; gentlemen must possess a handicap of no more than 18 and ladies no more than 15 and introductions are required. There are no ladies tees and other points to note are that the 1st tee is reserved daily for Members until 9.45am and between 1.15pm and 2.15pm; however, the 10th tee is usually free in the early mornings. St. Georges is essentially a singles and foursomes Club and three ball and four ball matches are only permissible with the

agreement of the Secretary.

The green fees for 1992 were set at £45 per round, £65 per day. During the months of December, January and February the £45 fee is applicable for a full day's golf. Should there be a wish to hire golf clubs, a limited supply are for hire through the professional, **Niall Cameron**, telephone **(0304) 615236**. Finally, the services of a caddie can be booked via the Caddiemaster on **(0304) 617380**.

Please excuse the awful pun but finding Sandwich should be a 'piece of cake.' The town is linked to Canterbury to the west by the A257, a distance of approximately 15 miles and to Deal, 6 miles south east of Sandwich by the A258. Motoring from London, the most direct route is to head for Canterbury using a combination of the A2 and M2 and thereafter following the A257 as above. For those coming from the south coast Ashford is the place to head for: Ashford is joined to Canterbury by the A28. Sandwich can also be reached by train.

Since its first Open of 1894, won by **John H. Taylor**, the Championship has been held at Sandwich on ten further occasions, most recently of course in 1985 when **Sandy Lyle** became the first British winner for 16 years. The visitor will not have to tackle the course from the Open Championship tees but he'll still have to confront the many dunes, the great undulations and the awkward stances that St. Georges is so famous for.

Having done battle with the elements the golfer will find the Clubhouse welcoming. Excellent lunches are served daily and both breakfasts and dinners can be obtained with prior arrangement. A jacket and tie must be worn in all public rooms.

St. Georges has seen many great happenings: **Walter Hagen** winning the Championship in 1922 and then promptly handing his winnings straight to his caddie; **Henry Cotton's** opening 67-65 in the 1934 Championship and then the **Harry Bradshaw** broken bottle episode of 1949. After a gap of 32 years the Open returned to St. Georges in 1981 when the 'forgotten' American **Bill Rogers** won.

So who will win in 1993? A Frenchman? Hardly. An American? No, patriotism rules the heart and so I predict that once again Faldo will follow Lyle – and St. Nick will win at St. Georges.

Hole	Yards	Par		Hole	Yards	Par
1	448	4		10	401	4
2	377	4		11	218	3
3	215	3		12	367	4
4	471	4		13	445	4
5	422	4		14	509	5
6	157	3		15	468	4
7	532	5		16	165	3
8	420	4		17	427	4
9	391	4		18	470	4
Out	**3,433**	**35**		**In**	**3,470**	**35**
				Out	3,433	35
				TOTALS	**6,903**	**70**

ROYAL CINQUE PORTS (DEAL)
CHAMPIONSHIP GOLF

In the year 55 B.C. **Julius Caesar** landed on the coast near Deal. In 1920, an American invader by the name of **Walter Hagen** came to Deal to play in his first Open Championship. Both came, both saw, but neither conquered. In fact both returned from whence they came, tails firmly between legs – small wonder Deal is often considered the toughest of all England's Championship links!

The Royal Cinque Ports Golf Club was founded in February 1892 by **Major General J.M.Graham** whilst at lunch in Deal's Black Horse Hotel. The 18 hole course was opened in 1895 and has required very few alterations during its distinguished history. Today the gentleman responsible for the efficient organisation of the Club is the Secretary; **Mr. C Greaves**. Mr. Greaves may be contacted at the **Royal Cinque Ports Golf Club, Golf Road, Deal, Kent CT14 6RF.** Tel **(0304) 374007**. **Andrew Reynolds** is the professional and he can be reached on **(0304) 374170**.

Visitors with official handicaps (maximum 20) are welcome to play the famous links, although prior booking with the Secretary is essential. As with a number of the more traditional Clubs, three and four ball matches have no standing on the course; indeed they are rarely permitted and only by arrangement with the Secretary.

In 1992 a green fee of £40 entitles the visitor to a full day's golf, and persons arriving after 1 pm can obtain a £10 reduction. The Club also offers a twilight green fee where there is a 50% reduction for those teeing off after 5pm. An early start in winter with a later start in summer would appear to be the best bets. Sadly, weekend bookings are seldom possible.

The golf course is situated approximately one mile north of the town. Probably the best route from London is to take the A2/M2 as far as Dover. There, one should pick up the A258 which takes you to Deal. Also worth noting is Deal Railway Station which is on the northern side of the town near the pier.

Very often it is Mother Nature who provides the greatest challenge at Deal. Strong winds billowing in from the sea, capable of changing direction several times during a round, can turn what appear to be modest holes into monsters. The course measures 6407 yards from the medal tees (par 70) with the Championship tees extending the course to some 6741 yards (par 72). From the ladies tees the course measures 5675 yards, (par 74). The outward nine is generally considered the

easier half – **Michael Bonallack** turned in 31 during his record amateur score of 65 (a record which has stood for more than a quarter of a century). Certainly the back nine is longer and Deal is renowned for its tough finish, the classic par five **16th** perhaps being the most difficult (and best) hole on the course. The fairways are humpy and hillocky and well bunkered. The rough is often thick and many of the greens stand on natural plateaux. On a clear day there are some magnificent views across the course towards the English Channel and to the distant white cliffs beyond Pegwell Bay.

Two **Open Championships** have been held at Deal, in 1909 and in 1920. The 1909 Championship was won by the Englishman **John H. Taylor**, his fourth victory in the event. The 1920 Open has already been referred to – the luckless Hagen in fact finished fifty third in a field of fifty four. Also entitled to feel somewhat peeved that year was **Abe Mitchell** who allowed **George Duncan** to come from thirteen strokes behind him to snatch victory. Plans to stage a third Championship at Deal in 1949 had to be abandoned when extensive flooding led to a temporary closure of the course.

The Royal Cinque Ports Club has also twice been selected to host the **Amateur Championship**, firstly in 1923 and again in 1982. In 1992 both the English Amateur and the St Andrews Trophy were staged at Deal. One of the annual highlights on the Club's calendar is the Halford Hewitt Challenge Cup. An Old Boys competition, usually played in April, the Halford Hewitt is thought to be the largest Amateur tournament in the world – over 600 players participate.

The Members of Royal Cinque Ports are doubly fortunate. Blessed with such a fine course, they also possess an excellent Clubhouse. The facilities are first class and both the early starter and our twilight golfer will be glad to find that hot and cold snacks are normally available at all times. With prior notice both breakfast and dinner can be arranged. For those just wanting a quick drink in between rounds (a stiff one may be in order!) a bar is provided.

It would not of course be fair, either to the Romans or Mr Hagen, to leave Deal without recording that both did eventually achieve their ambitions. The Romans returned a century later and conquered the Brits, and as for Walter, he didn't have to wait quite so long, for in 1922 he won the first of four Open Championships, none of which though, alas, was at Deal.

Hole	Yards	Par	Hole	Yards	Par
1	361	4	10	362	4
2	399	4	11	398	4
3	492	5	12	437	4
4	153	3	13	420	4
5	502	5	14	222	3
6	315	4	15	455	4
7	385	4	16	506	5
8	154	3	17	372	4
9	404	4	18	407	4
Out	3,165	36	In	3,579	36
			Out	3,165	36
			TOTALS	6,744	72

PRINCE'S
CHAMPIONSHIP GOLF

For many years **Gene Sarazen,** now aged 90, has performed the traditional honour of hitting the first tee shot at the US Masters tournament. It is a moving occasion and one sadly, rarely shown on British television. Sarazen is one of golf's greatest characters and certainly one of the finest players ever to have graced the sport. This popular American is one of only four golfers in history (Nicklaus, Hogan and Player are the others) to have won all four of golf's grand slam events, yet he will probably be remembered best for two single strokes. The first took place on the par five 15th at Augusta in the final round of the 1935 Masters. Three shots behind the leader at that stage, Sarazen holed a four wood for an albatross, or double eagle two. Needless to say, he went on to win the tournament. The second took place at Troon thirty eight years later and this time the television cameras were there to witness the 71 year old holing in one at the Postage Stamp, 8th hole. And Sarazen's link with Prince's? It was the scene of his one **British Open** victory in **1932** which, no thanks to Adolf Hitler, was Prince's one and only Open Championship.

Sarazen's total score of 283 was then a record for the Open Championship but today's golfer cannot properly walk in Sarazen's footsteps for the 18 hole links was dismembered during the last War (as indeed was its predecessor during the First World War) – perhaps not surprisingly given its geography and the continuous fear of invasion. For a while it looked possible that golf would never return to Prince's as there were plans to turn the links into a permanent military training site.

Fortunately for you and me, golf won the day and in 1950, **Sir Guy Campbell** and **John Morrison** were invited to restore the links. Remarkably, given the heavily scarred landscape, 17 of the pre-war greens could still be used. Campbell and Morrison decided however, that they could best utilise the available land by creating three loops of nine holes and this lay out is what greets the present day visitor to Prince's.

I'm not sure that 'greets' is actually the right terminology. Prince's may have lost its Open Championship status, but it has not lost its teeth. The three nines: the **Dunes, Himalayas** and **Shore** are each tremendously testing and, being a fairly flat and relatively exposed links the golfer is often at the mercy of the elements.

The Golf Club however, most definitely 'greets' the visitor. This must be one of southern England's most welcoming clubs and subject to availability, visitors with handicaps can generally play at all times. It is worth noting that they can stay overnight at the nearby Bell Hotel (0304) 613388 which has recently been acquired by the owners of Prince's Golf Club. Both individuals and golfing societies (the club can cater for over 100 persons in its spacious clubhouse) should contact **Mr Geoff Ramm**. The address to write to is **Prince's Golf Club, Sandwich Bay, Sandwich, Kent CT13 9QB**. The telephone number is **(0304) 611118**. Also most helpful is the club's professional, **Philip Sparks**. He can be reached on **(0304) 613797**.

For 1992, the cost of a single round (ie. 18 holes) at Prince's is £26.50 midweek and £31 at weekends. However, for an extra £2.50 midweek (rising to £3 on Saturdays and £8 on Sundays) you can enjoy a full day's golf. Apart from being exceptionally good value, a full day here is strongly recommended for this way all 27 holes can be tackled.

Golfers playing 36 holes will play two eighteens from the following three combinations: Dunes/ Himalayas 6506 yards, par 71; Himalayas/ Shore 6510 yards, par 72 and Dunes/ Shore 6690 yards, par 72. (For these composite courses the distances given are from the medal tees.) Each course is of a similarly high standard with a plethora of plateaued greens, ridges, humps and hollows but not too many bunkers. The paucity of sandtraps is a feature of golf at Prince's and unlike neighbouring St George's where there are many blind shots, the fairways tend to run parallel with the dunes as opposed to clambering over the top of them. If there is a preferred nine, most people tend to select the Himalayas Course. As the name implies, it is the more naturally rugged of the three. Here, the par three **7th** is often singled out for special praise (or chastisement!) It is a very difficult hole, usually played directly into the wind.

Situated four and a half miles from Sandwich railway station, visitors should approach the course via St George's Road which, in turn, leads into Sandown Road, King's Avenue and finally, Prince's Drive. Sandwich is linked to Canterbury by the A257 and to Deal by the A258. Motoring from London, Canterbury can be reached by way of the A2 and M2.

Prince's most celebrated son is undoubtedly **P.B.Laddie Lucas**. A Walker Cup player and Captain he was also a noted war-time Fighter Pilot. Wing Commander Lucas is a son of Prince's in more ways than one for he was actually born in the old clubhouse. Today, Prince's annually stages the Laddie Lucas Spoon, an open event for children aged between 8 and 13. Entries are received from all over Britain and France – and who knows, perhaps amongst this year's entrants there is a budding Gene Sarazen.

Himalayas			Shore			Dunes		
Hole	Yards	Par	Hole	Yards	Par	Hole	Yards	Par
1	386	4	1	430	4	1	457	4
2	415	4	2	511	5	2	167	3
3	184	3	3	176	3	3	491	5
4	355	4	4	410	4	4	414	4
5	400	4	5	386	4	5	418	4
6	580	5	6	408	4	6	498	5
7	195	3	7	562	5	7	373	4
8	415	4	8	184	3	8	208	3
9	391	4	9	425	4	9	429	4
Out	3,321	35	In	3,492	36	Out	3,455	36

THE HYTHE IMPERIAL

This four star, 100 bedroom, privately owned hotel set in its own 50 acre estate with extensive sport and leisure facilities, has been welcoming guests since 1880. Whether coming to Hythe for business or pleasure, the Hythe Imperial will provide the facilities and warm welcome that one would expect from a hotel of this calibre.

A gracious country house atmosphere pervades the hotel. Part of its charm lies in the individually designed bedrooms and suites, so that all guests are made to feel special and at home. Guests can be accommodated in a wide variety of rooms from a suite with jacuzzi and bath to a standard single or a suite suitable for a family. All bedrooms enjoy a sea, golf course or garden view, and are equipped with colour TV, radio, direct dial telephone and tea/coffee making facilities. However, as one would expect room service is available if required.

Excellent cuisine and a fine wine cellar are hallmarks of the Hythe Imperial. The superb restaurant is the ideal choice for more formal occasions, whilst the hotel bars and leisure centre offer delicious lighter meals. The leisure facilities are truly excellent, with a nine hole golf course, grass tennis courts, two all weather floodlight tennis courts, a 45 foot indoor pool, squash, sauna and steam room - the list is endless.

Guest can enjoy the croquet lawn and putting green or be pampered by a massage or beauty treatment available by appointment.

The surprisingly challenging level links course offers interesting golf for all standards with well placed bunkers and water hazards on both northern and southern boundaries. When playing the eighteen holes alternative tees are available on each hole and in three cases, alternative greens. The ladies' 5172 yards red tees, par 71, the gentleman's 5421 yards yellow tees, par 68 and the white 5533 yards tees stretch the scratch golfer as much as the novice.

A handicap and knowledge of the rules and etiquette of golf is necessary and a green card must be obtained in advance from the hotel reception. It is advisable to book starting times in advance, particularly at weekends - as indeed are golf lessons with our resident Professional. Luxurious clubhouse, lounge bar and professional's shop.

The Hythe Imperial
Princes Parade
Hythe
Kent
CT21 6AG
Tel: (0303) 267441
Fax: (0303) 264610

KENT
COMPLETE GOLF

Ashford G.C.
(0233) 622655
Sandyhurst Lane, Ashford
Off A20, 1/2 mile N. of Ashford
(18)6246 yards/***/C/H

Austin Lodge G.C.
(0322) 863000
Off A225, nr Eynsford Station
(18)6600 yards/***/D

Barnehurst G.C
(0322) 523 746
Mayplace Road, East Barnehurst
(9)5320 yards/***/F

Bearsted G.C
(0622) 38198
Mill Lane, Enderby, Leicester
Take junction 21 roundabout off M1/M69
(18)6253 yards/**/C/H/L

Broome Park Golf & Country Club
(0227) 831701
Barham, Canterbury
Leave M2 for A2, turn onto A260
(18)6610 yards/***/C/H

Canterbury G.C
(0227) 453532
Scotland Hills, Canterbury
1 mile from town centre on A257
(18)6249 yards/**/C/H

Cherry Lodge G.C
(0959) 72250
Jail Lane, Biggin Hill
Leave Bromley on A233 to Westerham
(18)6652 yards/**/B

Chestfield G.C
(022 779) 4411
103 Chestfield Road, Whitstable
Take A229 to roundabout nr. station, turn S.
(18)6080 yards/**/D

Cobtree Manor G.C
(0622) 53276
Maidstone
Leave M2 or M20 at A229
(18)5701 yards/***/E

Cranbrook G.C.
(0580) 712833
Cranbrook
(18) 6351 yards/**/C

Cray Valley G.C
(0689) 831927
Sandy Lane, St. Pauls Cray, Orpington
Leave A20 at Ruxley roundabout
(18)5624 yards/***/D

Darenth Valley G.C
(09592) 2944
Station Road, Shoreham
Take A225, club is 4 miles N. of Sevenoaks
(18)6356 yards/***/E

Dartford G.C
(0322) 23616
Dartford Heath
On Dartford Heath, 2 miles from city centre
(18)5914 yards/**/H/M

Deangate Ridge G.C
(0634) 251180
Hoo, Rochester
Take A228 from Rochester to Isle of Grain
(18)6300 yards/***/E

Edenbridge Golf & Country Club
(0732) 865097
Crouch House Road, Edenbridge
From A25 at Westerham take B2026
(18)6643 yards/***/D

Faversham G.C
(079589) 251
Belmont Park, Faversham
Leave M2 at junction 6 and take A251
(18)5979 yards/**/E

Gillingham G.C
(0634) 850999
Woodlands Road, Gillingham
M2 to junction 4, north to A2
(18)5911 yards/**/E

Hawkhurst G.C
(0580) 752396
High Street, Hawkhurst, CranbrookOn A268 2 miles from A21 at Flimwell
(9)5769 yards/**/D

Herne Bay G.C
(0227) 374097
Eddington, Herne Bay
Take A291 Thanet Way Road to Herne Bay
(18)5466 yards/***/D/H

High Elms G.C
(0689) 58175
High Elms Road, Downe
Take A21 from Bromley, right on Shire Lane
(18)5626 yards/***/E

Holtye G.C
(0342) 850635
Holtye Common, Cowden, Edenbridge
On A264 near East Grinstead
(9)5289 yards/***/D

Hythe Imperial G.C
(0303) 267441
Princes Parade, Hythe
Turn off M20 for Hythe
(9)5511 yards/***/D/H

Knole Park G.C
(0732) 452150
Seal Hollow Road, Sevenoaks
On N.E of Seven Oaks, down Seal Hollow Road
(18)6249 yards/**/B/H

Lamberhurst G.C
(0892) 890241
Church Road, Lamberhurst
Take A21 S. from Tonbridge towards Hastings
(18)6277 yards/**/B

Leeds Castle G.C
(0622) 765400
Maidstone
M20 from Maidstone and onto A20
(9)2910 yards/***/E

Littlestone G.C
(0679) 62310
St. Andrews Road, Littlestone, New Romney
A20 to Ashford, B2070 to New Romney
(18)6424 yards/**/F/H

Lullingstone Park G.C
(0959) 34542
Park Gate, Chelsfield, Orpington
Take A20 to Swanley, B258 to Park Gate
(18)6674 yards/***/E
(9)2445 yards/***/E

Mid Kent G.C
(0474) 568035
Singlewell Road, Gravesend
Off A2 S. of Gravesend
(18)6206 yards/**/F/H

Nevill G.C
(0892) 25818
Benhall Mill Road, Tunbridge Wells
1 mile S.E of Tunbridge Wells
(18)6336 yards/**/B/H

North Foreland G.C
(0843) 62140
Convent Road, Broadstairs
1 mile from Broadstairs station
(18)6382 yards/**/C/H

Poult Wood G.C
(0732) 364039
Higham Lane, Tonbridge
2 miles N. of town centre off A227
(18)5569 yards/***/E

Princes G.C
(0304) 611118
Sandwich Bay, Sandwich
4 miles from Sandwich through town centre
(27)(3x9)***/B

Rochester & Cobham Park G.C
(047 482) 3411
Park Lane, by Rochester
South onto B2009 from A2
(18)6467 yards/**/B/H

Royal Cinque Ports G.C
(0304) 374007
Deal, Sandwich
Take A258 from Sandwich to Upper Deal
(18)6744 yards/**/A/H

Royal St Georges G.C.
(0304) 613090
Sandwich Bay Rd, Sandwich
(18)6857 yards/**/A/H

Ruxley G.C.
(0689) 871490
Sandy Lane, St Pauls Cray, Orpington
(18)4885 yards/***/E

St Augustines G.C.
(0843) 590333
Cottingham Road, Cliffsend, Ramsgate
2 miles S W of Ramsgate
(18)5138 yards/***/C/H

Sene Valley G.C.
(0303) 68513
Sene, Folkestone
A20 from Folkestone
(18)6320 yards/***/C

Sheerness G.C
(0795) 662585
Power Station Rd, Sheerness
A249 then A250 towards Seerness
(18)6500 yards/**/D/H

Sittingbourne & Milton Regis G.C.
(0795) 842261
Wormdale, Newington, Sittingbourne
Leave M2, exit 5 for A249
(18)6121 yards/**/D/H/L

Tenterden G.C.
(05806) 3987
Woodchurch Rd, Tenterden
1 mile E of Tenterden on B2067
(18)6030 yards/**/D

Tudor Park G.& C.C.
(0622) 34334
Ashford Rd, Bearsted
Leave M20 at junction 8 for A20
(18)6000 yards/**/B/H

Tunbridge Wells G.C.
(0892) 523034
Langton Rd, Tunbridge Wells
Adjacent to Spa Hotel
(9)4684 yards/**/B/H

Upchurch River Valley
(0634) 360626
Upchurch, Sittingbourne
(18)6160 yards/***/E

Walmer & Kingsdown G.C.
(0304) 373256The Leas, Kingsdown, Deal
Off A258, S of Deal
(18)6465 yards/***/C

Westgate & Birchington G.C.
(0843) 31115
Domneva Rd, Westgate On Sea
A28 near Birchington
(18)4926 yards/***/D/L

West Kent G.C.
(0689) 853737
West Hill, Downe, Orpington
A21 to Orpington and Downe vill.
(18)6392 yards/**/C/H/L

West Malling G.C.
(0732) 844785
London Rd, Addington, Maidstone
Take A20 from London to Maidstone
(18)6142 yards/**/C
(18)6011 yards/**/C

Whitstable & Seasalter G.C
(0227) 272020
Collingwood Road, Whitstable
Leave A299 for Thanet Way at Borstal Hill
(9)5276 yards/**/B

Wildernesse G.C
(0732) 61526
Seal, Sevenoaks
Take A25 from Sevenoaks towards Maidstone
6478 yards/**/B/H/L

Woodlands Manor G.C
(09592) 3805
Tinkerpot Lane, Sevenoaks
Leave M25 at junction 3 and take A20
(18)5858 yards/***/D/H

Wrotham Heath G.C
(0732) 884800
Seven Mile Lane, Comp, Sevenoaks
On B2016, S. of junction with A20
(9) 5959 yards/**/C/H

F.P. Hopkins   A PAINSTAKING PUTTER   Burlington Gallery

GREATER LONDON & SURREY

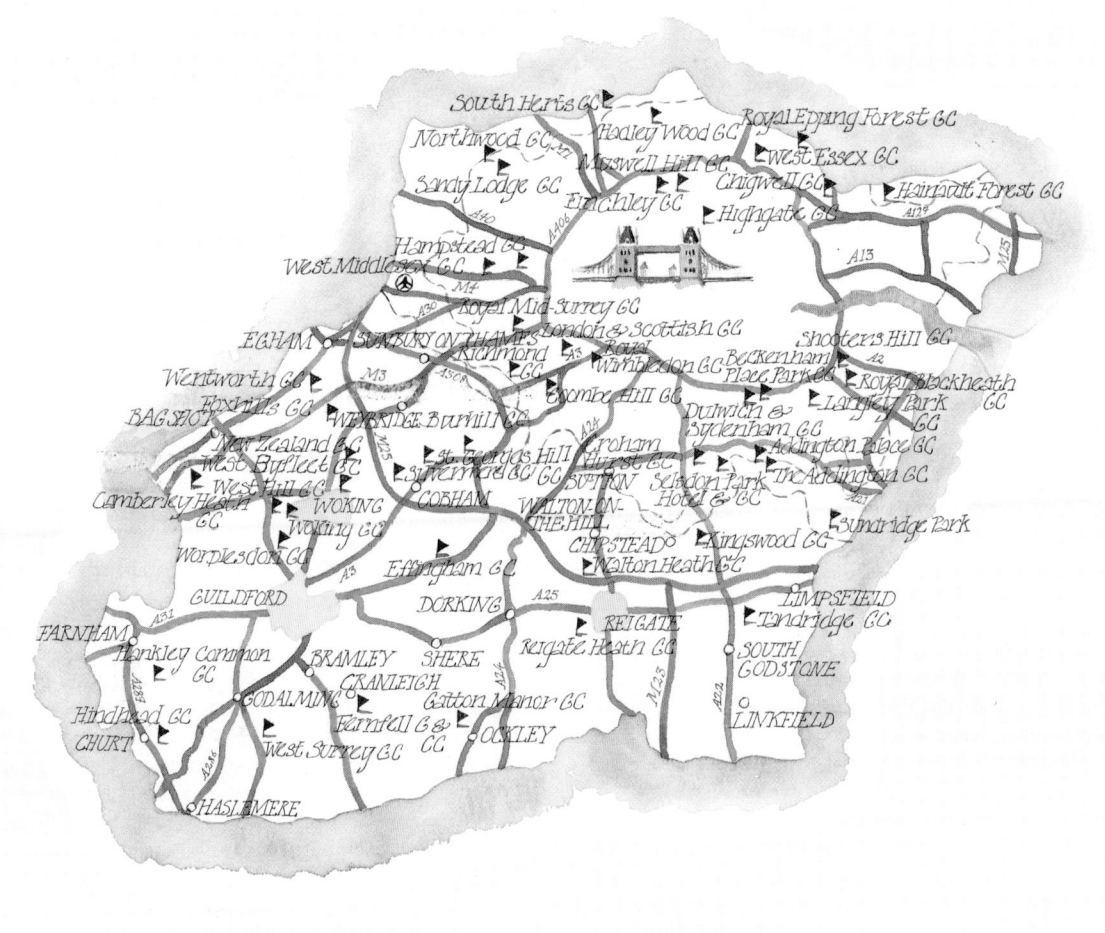

Julian Barrow **WALTON HEATH** *Burlington Gallery*

GREATER LONDON & SURREY
CHOICE GOLF

GREATER LONDON

Records suggest that golf was first played in England in **1608**; the venue was **Blackheath** in London but the participants were Scottish not English. James I (James VI of Scotland) and his courtiers are generally credited with bringing the game south of the border. The exact date that the English caught the bug is unclear, certainly in the 18th Century it was still pretty much an alien pastime – in his first English dictionary compiled in 1755 Dr Samuel Johnson described golf as, 'a game played with a ball and a club or bat'.

During its formative years golf in London was largely confined to the public commons such as those at Blackheath, Clapham, Chingford and Tooting Bec, the golfers having to share their rather crudely laid-out courses with 'nurse-maids, dogs, horses and stubborn old ladies and gentlemen'.

Not surprisingly when the first Golf Clubs started to form the tendency was to retreat from the public stage. The **Royal Blackheath** Golf Club, fittingly enough the first English Club to be founded (it dates from 1787) eventually moved from the Heath and now plays on a private course at Eltham. Golf is no longer played (or at least shouldn't be!) on the commons at Clapham and Tooting Bec. However, golf does survive on those at **Wimbledon** and Chingford, the latter being the home of **Royal Epping Forest** and where golfers are still required to wear red clothing in order that they can be distinguished from other users of the common.

The majority of London Clubs are for obvious reasons set in deepest suburbia and with many it is often far from clear as to whether they fall within Greater London or not. In anyone's book **Muswell Hill** is in London, which for present purposes is just as well because it's an excellent course. Measuring close to 6,500 yards, and quite undulating, it represents a fairly stiff test from the back tees. Other good 18-hole courses to the north of London include **Finchley** (with its elegant Victorian clubhouse), **Mill Hill** (which has something of a heathland feel to it) and **Highgate** (which is particularly pretty), while **Hampstead** has an enjoyable 9 holes.

A cluster of fine courses lie a little further to the north west of the capital. Near neighbours of one another are **Northwood** and **Sandy Lodge**. The latter could be said to be Sandy by name, sandy by nature – a heathland course but it can play more like a golf links at times. Anyway, it's certainly an exceptionally fine course and hosts many top class events. Northwood is in parts parkland, in parts heathland with an exceptionally good back nine. A mention also for **West Middlesex**, one of West London's better parkland courses.

The other side of the M1 one finds **South Herts** and **Hadley Wood**. South Herts is somewhat tucked away in Totteridge but well worth finding. The Club can boast having both Harry Vardon and Dai Rees among its past professionals. Hadley Wood, near Barnet is a very beautiful course designed by Alister Mackenzie, with lovely tree-lined fairways. The Clubhouse is very elegant too. Over towards Essex, Royal Epping Forest has been mentioned; also within Epping Forest itself, **West Essex** is a fine parkland course and there are two first rate public courses at **Hainault Forest**.

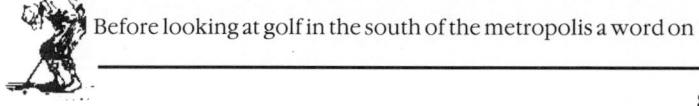

Before looking at golf in the south of the metropolis a word on some of London's better hotels. Finding real value in the capital isn't easy – local knowledge helps and it may be a case of rub of the green. The following appraisal is dedicated to the American and Japanese visitor – and to any of us who have a generous expense account!

In Park Lane, The Inn on the Park 071-499 0888 is quite excellent and its restaurant, The Four Seasons is outstanding. Luxury of the highest order is also offered in The Dorchester 071-629 8888 as it proudly overlooks Hyde Park (alas no golf). The Grill Room and The Terrace are both restaurants of distinction. The international class of the Ritz 071-493 8181 is obvious – one can quite simply sniff the style. Nearby, Browns 071-493 6020 is contrastingly English and justifiably proud of it. A few more? Well how about The Savoy 071-836 4343, note the delightful settings of its restaurants The Grill Room and The River Restaurant. Another member of the Savoy group is Claridges 071-629 8860, traditional to a tee but still extremely popular.

For people not wishing to stay in Central London these hotels may be of some help: in Hadley Wood The West Lodge Park 081-440 8311 is a superb 19th Century mansion – very convenient for the many courses of South Hertfordshire. A galleried hall is one of the features of The Mansion House at Grim's Dyke 081-954 4227. The former home of W.S.Gilbert, this hotel is located in Harrow Weald – ideal for playing (or spectating) at Moor Park. Golfers will also find Selsdon Park Hotel very comfortable and convenient 081-657 8811. If the above are slightly out of the price range of the majority of ordinary mortals then it goes without saying that London provides a veritable feast of accommodation at vastly varying rates. Two highly recommended establishments combining comfort and value are Aston Court 071-602 9954 and The Peacehaven Hotel 081-202 9758.

Among the city's leading restaurants are the Roux Brothers Le Gavroche 071-408 0881 and Rue St Jacques 071-637 0222 (very French), and the Hungarian Gay Hussar 071-437 0973. For lovers of seafood try Le Suquet 071-581 1785 or La Croisette 071-373 3694. A little less expensive than London's top restaurants but still very good are Gavvers 071-730 5983 (French), Simpsons 071-836 9112 (exceedingly English) and Leiths 071-229 4481 which sounds perfect for golf historians.

Those looking for a game in south west London might consider looking in the Wimbledon area where there are several courses. **Royal Wimbledon** is just about the best in London but golfers may find it easier to arrange a game (during the week at any rate) on the nearby course at Wimbledon Common, home of the **London Scottish Club**, located two miles from Wimbledon railway station. **Coombe Hill** is another of the capital's most prestigious clubs – its well manicured fairways are just about visible from Royal Wimbledon. A little further out at Richmond, games can be enjoyed at **Royal Mid Surrey** (two courses here, an Outer and an Inner) and at **Richmond** Golf Club with its superb Georgian Clubhouse; there is also a public course at Richmond. A quick mention must be made here of Cannizaro House 081-879 1464, a truly delightful hotel on Wimbledon Common; it is perfect for the London and Surrey golfer. Due West of London, **Ealing** offers a reasonable test and there are again a number of public courses in the vicinity.

South of London the Croydon area is another that is thick with Clubs. **Addington** is generally considered the best, a lovely heathland course covered in heather, pines and silver birch and has in the par 3,13th one of golf's toughest and most beautiful short holes. **Addington Palace** is also well thought of, as indeed is **Croham Hurst**. To make up a four, especially if one requires a base, **Selsdon Park** must be the selection; a pleasant parkland course set around the Selsdon escarpment. Seldson Park is very popular with societies. Not far from Croydon, the course at **Coulsdon Court** has a welcoming reputation and an extraordinary selection of trees. Two of the better courses towards the south east of London are **Langley Park** (at Beckenham) – heavily wooded with a particularly good series of holes towards the end of the round including an attractive par 3 finishing hole featuring a fountain and small lake, and **Sundridge Park** where indeed there are two good courses, an East and West.

Elsewhere in the south east there is a popular public course at **Beckenham Place Park** (very cheap green fees) and there are interesting layouts at **Shooters Hill** and **Dulwich and Sydenham**, but the final mention goes to **Royal Blackheath**. The Club has a great sense of history and the course is full of character. Early in the round one may confront the famous 'Hamlet Cigar bunker' while its 18th isn't so much difficult as unusual, requiring a pitch over a hedge to the green. In some ways it's unfortunate that the Club ever had to leave its famous common – Blackheath village is quite charming – but then the author of this tome may just be a little biased!

SURREY

When Providence distributed land best suited for building golf courses it wasn't done in the most democratic of spirits. Take for instance the quite ridiculous amount of majestic links land to be found along the coast of Lancashire – its enough to make every good Yorkshireman weep. And then there's Surrey, blessed with acre upon acre of perfect inland golfing terrain – what a contrast to poor Essex!

Though very different in appearance, it is probably safe to suggest that **Walton Heath** and **Wentworth** are the county's two leading courses. (Sunningdale – at least according to the postman – being just over the border in Berkshire). But Walton and Wentworth (both featured on later pages) are only two of Surrey's famous 'W Club' – there's also **Worplesdon** and **Woking, West Hill, West Surrey**, **West Byfleet** and to this list we can now add **Wisley** and **Wildwood** – two of the country's newest and most exclusive developments.

Located off the A32 to the west of Woking, Worplesdon, West Hill and Woking Golf Clubs lie practically next door to one another. Indeed it might be possible to devise a few dramatic cross – course holes – though in view of the value of some of the adjacent properties that would have to be driven over it's perhaps not such a good idea! West Hill is generally considered the most difficult of the three, the fairways at times being frighteningly narrow; Worplesdon with its superb greens is probably the most widely known (largely due to its famous annual foursomes event), while Woking, founded a century ago, perhaps possesses the greatest charm. Whatever their particular merits, all three are magnificent examples of the natural heathland and heather type course.

Marginally closer to the capital and still very much in the heart of stockbroker-belt country is a second outstanding trio of courses centred around Weybridge: **St George's Hill, New**

Zealand and **West Byfleet**. Once again, these are heathland type courses where golf is played amidst heavily wooded surroundings, the combination of pines, silver birch, purple heather and, at New Zealand especially, a magnificent spread of rhododendrons, making for particularly attractive settings. St George's Hill is in fact one of the more undulating courses in Surrey and calls for several spectacular shots – indeed, many people rate it on a par with Wentworth and Walton Heath. No course in England however, I would suggest, has a better sequence of finishing holes than those at New Zealand, the 14th, 15th and 16th being especially memorable.

Golf in Surrey isn't of course all heathland and heather. **Tandridge** is one of the best downland courses in Southern England while just a short drive from Weybridge is the delightful parkland course at **Burhill**, situated some two miles south of Walton-on-Thames. Burhill's Clubhouse is a particularly grand affair – at one time it was the home of the Dowager Duchess of Wellington. Much less grand but to some of equal interest, is the Dick Turpin cottage sited on the course and reputed to have been used by the infamous highwayman. Also worth noting is a nearby public course, **Silvermere**, located midway between Byfleet and Cobham where it may be easier to arrange a game – at least in theory, as it does get very busy – and where green fees are naturally lower.

Some thoughts for the 19th hole are required. Surrey is a rich county – in more ways than one. Quality golf comes in abundance, so too do first class country houses, pubs, hotels and restaurants. Here are a few suggestions. In Walton-on-the-Hill, very convenient for Walton Heath is Ebenezer Cottage (073 781) 3166 – a super restaurant. More fine fare is found at Sutton; Partners 22 (081) 644 7743 is the place, and at Chipstead where Dene Farm (0737) 552661 has a delightful country setting. Also in Egham one can stay at the enchanting Runnymede Hotel (0784) 436171. It is situated on the river near Bell Weir Loch and is ideal for trips to Wentworth and Sunningdale.

After a day's golf on any of the courses in the Woking area The Wheatsheaf Hotel (0483) 773047 is a good spot to collect one's thoughts. Another relaxing hotel is The Oatlands Park Hotel (0932) 847242 – centrally located and extremely pleasant. An attractive guesthouse in Woking is Glencourt (0483) 764154 whilst in nearby Reading, The Aeron Private Hotel (0734) 424119 will not empty your purse either. The Cricketers (0932) 862105 on Downside Common, Cobham is a sporting little pub. Two outstanding restaurants are La Bonne Franquette (0784) 39494 in Egham and Casa Romana (0932) 843470) in Weybridge, and in Reigate La Barbe (0737) 241966 also comes highly recommended. Finally, two of the county's (and the country's) finest country house hotels are in this area, again convenient for Wentworth – Pennyhill Park (0276) 71774 near Bagshot and Great Fosters (0784) 433822 near Egham.

Generally speaking golf in the Home Counties and golf in America have precious little in common. However, the **Foxhills** Club at Ottershaw (off the A320) can make a genuine claim to have married the two successfully. A Jacobean-styled manor house run on American country club lines including an outstanding range of leisure facilities, it has two Championship length heathland type courses. Not surprisingly, Foxhills is a very popular haunt for golfing societies. Another fairly newish set up in this area is the highly recommended **Fernfell Golf and Country Club** at Cranleigh just south of Guildford.

GREATER LONDON & SURREY
CHOICE GOLF

The country club scene may not of course appeal to all types and excellent golf, in an extremely sedate atmosphere, can be enjoyed at **Gatton Manor** situated in Ockley near Dorking. The course has a very scenic layout running through woods and alongside lakes. One doesn't have to look too far for a good night's rest – the Manor House is now a very relaxing hotel with golf obviously very much on the menu. Note also the Punch Bowl in nearby Oakwood Hill – an excellent country pub.

Heading towards Walton Heath, if a game cannot be arranged over one of its famous courses then there is golf of a similarly challenging nature at **Reigate Heath** and not too far away, at **Kingswood,** there is a fine parkland course.

The rich heathland seam runs the breadth of the county and over to the west, practically straddling the three counties of Surrey, Berkshire and Hampshire, lies the superb **Camberley Heath** course, (there is also a first rate public course in Camberley, **Pine Ridge**, which opened in 1992) while down in the south-west corner there is yet another outstanding trio of clubs: **Hindhead, West Surrey** and **Hankley Common**.

Hankley Common was for many years a favourite of the late South African Bobby Locke, four times Open Champion, who once owned a house adjacent to the course. Hankley Common is widely known for its spectacular 18th hole – one of the greatest closing holes in golf. A vast gulley which seems to possess magnetic powers looms in front of the green – nine out of ten first timers fail to reach the putting surface.

The south-west corner of Surrey is particularly scenic. The hustle and bustle of London seems a world away – and of course in a way it is. In Bramley, The Bramley Grange Hotel (0483) 893434 is an ideal base from which to explore the countryside. Close to the Sussex borders lies Haslemere and another fine hotel, a timbered farmhouse on this occasion, The Lythe Hill Hotel (0428) 651251 where bedrooms in the original house have great character. People who have still not found a restaurant to visit must surely do so here for Morels (0428) 51462 offers some simply splendid dishes and a most delightful atmosphere.

Cecil Aldin   CHIPPING TO THE FLAG   Burlington Gallery

WENTWORTH
CHAMPIONSHIP GOLF

It is autumn. A reddish gold leaf scurries across the 18th green. The huge gallery is silent. Fully fifty yards away, to the right of the fairway, close to the trees and in the rough is young **Severiano Ballesteros.** He is one shot down to the legendary Arnold Palmer and he needs a miracle. The blade flashes, and the ball flies towards the green. It pitches, it rolls and it drops … the eagle has landed.

A stunningly beautiful place, Wentworth is set in the heart of the famous Surrey heathland belt. The name first appeared on the golfing map in the mid 1920s when the great **Harry Colt** was commissioned to design two eighteen hole courses. The **East Course** was the first to open in 1924, with the **West Course** following two years later. Now in the 1990s a third 18 hole Championship course has just been added. Officially opened by **HRH The Duke of Edinburgh** in July 1990, the new **Edinburgh Course** (also known as the South Course) winds its way attractively through Wentworth Estate's Great Wood and several outstanding holes have been created. It was designed by **John Jacobs, Gary Player** and current European Ryder Cup Captain, **Bernard Gallacher.**

Before the War, it was the East Course that captured the limelight by staging the Club's first important events: in 1926 an unofficial match between British and American teams and in 1932 the first ever playing of the Curtis Cup. In the period since 1945, the longer West Course has grabbed most of the glory. In the 1950s came the Ryder Cup and the World Cup and in the 1960s, the World Matchplay Championship.

The owners of the club, **Wentworth Group Holdings** are making substantial investment into both the facilities and the courses. Under Chairman Elliott Bernerd and Chief Executive Willy Bauer, standards are being raised to match the best clubs in the world. Following the completion of the Edinburgh Course, a computerised irrigation system has been installed on the West Course. Future plans include major expansion and refurbishment of the famous castellated Clubhouse and the incorporation of Bernard Gallacher's professional shop into the main building. The great range of associated leisure and business facilities are continually being expanded.

General Manager **Keith Williams** and his staff ensure that all Members and visitors feel welcome. However, it is advisable for visitors to Wentworth to pre-book a starting time. Unless they are accompanied by a Member, visitors are restricted to weekdays and must have a handicap of 20 or less for men and 30 for ladies. Enquiries to the Club should be addressed to **Wentworth Golf Club, Virginia Water, Surrey.** Tel: **(0344) 842201.**

In 1992 green fees were set at £80 for the West Course, £65 for the new Edinburgh Course and £55 for the East Course. Special packages are available for parties of 20 or more. Optional extras from a caddy and club hire to a photographer and a golf clinic are available from the professional's shop. Wentworth also has a 16-bay driving range.

Travelling to Wentworth ought not to present too many difficulties, the area being well served by major roads. The entrance to the Wentworth Estate is on the main A30 road, some two miles west of Staines. The M3, M4 and M25 all pass close to the course making access easy from any direction. Finally Heathrow Airport is no more than twenty minutes drive away.

The West Course or 'Burma Road' as it has become known, is arguably England's best known golf course thanks to the enormous television exposure it has received. The cameras have captured many magical moments, especially during the annual Volvo PGA Championship and the Toyota sponsored World Matchplay Championship. For many, the World Matchplay is the most exciting tournament in the golfing calendar; in recent years it has certainly produced some thrilling finals, none more so than in 1989 when **Nick Faldo** came from 3 behind with 7 to play to defeat **Ian Woosnam** with a 3 at the last. The PGA has also seen plenty of drama in recent years and 1991's event will go down as a vintage..........

It is spring. The PGA Championship is reaching a nailbiting climax as the two players walk down the 1st fairway in the sudden death play off. A decade has passed and the legendary Ballesteros hasn't won for some time. He desperately needs a victory. The blade flashes and a 5 iron is struck 200 yards towards the green. It lands, skips, rolls and finishes 2 feet from the pin.... El Gran Senor is back!

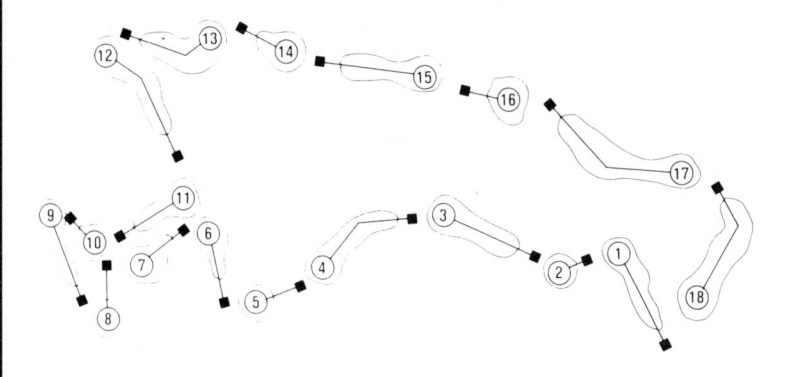

West Course

Hole	Yards	Par	Hole	Yards	Par
1	471	4	10	186	3
2	155	3	11	376	4
3	452	4	12	483	5
4	501	5	13	441	4
5	191	3	14	179	3
6	344	4	15	466	4
7	399	4	16	380	4
8	398	4	17	571	5
9	450	4	18	502	5
Out	3,361	35	In	3,584	37
			Out	3,361	35
			TOTALS	6,945	72

RUNNYMEDE HOTEL

Set in 12 acres of landscaped gardens on the very banks of the Thames, the Runnymede combines modern facilities with old fashioned service and courtesy. Built on the site of the 17th Century Anglers Rest Inn, it has a special atmosphere that makes it an attractive and pleasant place to stay.

For weekend breaks, private meetings or simply to relax, the Runnymede offers 172 air-conditioned bedrooms, many of which have fine river views and feature refinements such as satellite television, in-house movies, hairdryer and trouser press, towelling bathrobe, together with a mini bar and tea and coffee making facilities.

Guests can enjoy a drink on the terrace overlooking the bustling Bell Weir lock or a view of the lush banks of the river whilst dining in the River Room Restaurant - with an enviable reputation for excellent food and immaculate service. A La Carte and Table d'Hote menus are available for lunch and dinner, and for a leisurely outing, special riverboat cruises with on-board lunch or dinner parties prepared by the Chef are available by arrangement.

In August 1992 the Runnymede Hotel opened a luxurious health and fitness spa with a 18m x 9m pool, jacuzzi, gymnasium, hair and beauty salon, dance studio, steam, sauna and solarium and a full sized snooker room. There is also a croquet and putting lawn.

For those with a sporting inclination, the famous golf courses of Wentworth, Sunningdale and Foxhills are a few minutes drive away, while racegoers will find the Runnymede an ideal base: Ascot, Kempton Park, Sandown Park, Windsor and Epsom are all in close proximity.

Runnymede Hotel
Windsor Road
Egham
Surrey TW20 0AG
Tel: (0784) 436171
Fax: (0784) 436340

WALTON HEATH
CHAMPIONSHIP GOLF

Gavrilo Princip may have pulled the trigger that ignited the Great War but our history books tell us that tension in Europe had sometime earlier reached boiling point. In their Palaces in St. Petersburg and Berlin the Czar and the Kaiser pondered the strength of their armies. Meanwhile the great statesmen of Britain were engaged in battles of a different nature......

All square as they reach the 18th green on the Old Course at Walton Heath, **Churchill** turns to **Lloyd-George** and says, 'Now then, I will putt you for the Premiership'.

Herbert Fowler once said, God builds golf links and the less man meddles the better for all concerned. Herbert Fowler designed Walton Heath. However, before the opening of the Old Course in May 1904, at least a little meddling was called for. The glorious heathland through which the emerald fairways were cut was once covered, or nearly covered in thick heather, in parts as much as two feet thick (the Members will tell you it still is!) While many of Britain's leading Clubs took several years to establish their reputations, that of Walton Heath was assured months before the first stroke was even played; in January 1904 **James Braid** agreed to become Walton's first professional. Braid initially signed a seven year contract, his performances in the next seven Open Championships were: 2nd, 1st, 1st, 5th, 1st, 2nd and 1st, after which he became the first ever golfer to win five Opens. Hardly surprisingly his contract was extended and so indeed began an association with the Club that was to last for nearly fifty years.

In the years immediately before the First War, Walton Heath Members included no fewer than 24 M.Ps (including Winston Churchill and Lloyd-George) and 21 Members of the Lords. Another famous Walton golfer was **W.G. Grace** (who it is said compiled as many hundreds on the Heath as he did at the Oval). After the War a more Royal Flavour dominated with the **Prince of Wales** becoming an Honorary Member in 1921 and Captain in 1935.

Time to leap forward to the present and introduce the Club's Secretary: **Group Captain Robbie James**. He may be contacted at **The Walton Heath Golf Club, Tadworth, Surrey KT20 7TP**. Tel: **(073781) 2380**. Subject to prior arrangement with the Secretary, golfers are welcome to visit Walton Heath between Mondays and Fridays. Proof of both Club Membership and an official handicap is required. The green fees for 1992 were set at £55 for a full day's golf, with a reduced rate of £45 available if teeing off after 11.30am. The hire of golf clubs can be arranged through the Club's popular professional, **Ken MacPherson**, tel: **(073781) 2152**.

Located south of London, motoring to the Club is assisted greatly by the M25. Those approaching on this motorway should leave at junction 8 turning north on to the A217. The A217 should be followed for approximately 2 miles after which a left turn should be taken on to the B2032. The Golf Club is situated a mile or so along this road. Travelling from further afield, the M25 is linked to the M23 to the South, the M20 to the East and to the North and West by the M3, M4 and M1.

There are two great courses at Walton Heath, the **Old** and the **New** (the latter first appearing as nine holes in 1907 but later extended to the full 18). Lying adjacent to one another, each possesses the same classical heathland characteristics: heather, bracken, gorse, pines and silver birch. The Old Course is slightly longer than the New, their respective distances being 6801 yards (par 73) and 6609 yards (par 72). The finishing three holes on the Old are thought by many to be the finest on any course. The **16th** is a very mild dog-leg to a raised green which slopes from left to right, with the right side of the green heavily guarded by bunkers. The par three **17th** has sand traps practically encircling the green, creating a near island effect and the **18th** requires a testing second to carry an enormous cross bunker.

Over the years Walton Heath has played host to many important tournaments. The major amateur championships have included the English Amateur and both the Ladies English Amateur and the Ladies British Open Amateur Championships. Among the professional events, twenty-two of the PGA Match Play Championships were staged at Walton Heath and in recent years **The Ryder Cup** of 1981 as well as five **European Open Championships**.

Walton Heath has a fine Clubhouse with an excellent restaurant and lounge. A jacket and tie should be worn in all public rooms after 11am. Lunches are served between 12.00 pm and 2.30pm.

Understandably wherever you turn in the Clubhouse you are likely to see a reminder of the long association with James Braid. One small note sent to him from the Prince of Wales conveys a message all golfers can appreciate. It relates how the Prince came to the 18th requiring a four for a 79. After explaining how his second finished just through the green he tells how, 'with the chance of breaking 80, I couldn't stand the nerve-strain and fluffed the chip and took two putts...' How the mighty fall!

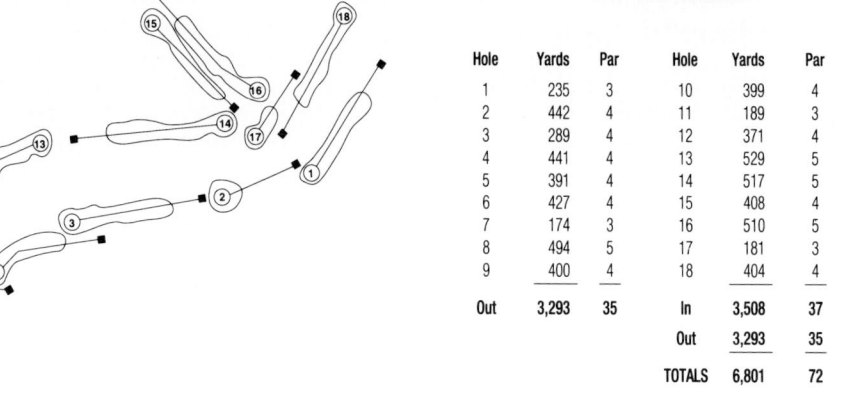

The Old Course

Hole	Yards	Par	Hole	Yards	Par
1	235	3	10	399	4
2	442	4	11	189	3
3	289	4	12	371	4
4	441	4	13	529	5
5	391	4	14	517	5
6	427	4	15	408	4
7	174	3	16	510	5
8	494	5	17	181	3
9	400	4	18	404	4
Out	3,293	35	In	3,508	37
			Out	3,293	35
			TOTALS	6,801	72

PENNYHILL PARK

Just 50 minutes from central London in the full splendour of the English countryside lies the little village of Bagshot and Pennyhill Park.

At the end of the winding driveway the stone-fronted, creeper-clad house stands surrounded by 112 acres of parkland and lake. This is Pennyhill Park, built in 1849 by the pioneering Canadian bridge-builder, James Hodge. The building has been altered several times to suit the individual tastes and requirements of its various owners.

The total commitment to service at Pennyhill complement the traditions of its historic past. On entering the main hallway and with the stately sweep of the period staircase a warm welcome awaits you from attentive staff. Trained to Edwardian standards of courtesy they provide impeccable and discreet service.

Peace and tranquillity surround this house which, though old, provides every modern amenity.

You can watch polo at Smiths' Lawn Windsor; Sunningdale and Wentworth are just two of the nearby prestigious golf courses. Pennyhill Park also has its own nine-hole golf course and other sporting facilities including tennis courts, a Roman-styled swimming pool, clay pigeon shooting and horse riding stables with professional coaching. The sauna and solarium are housed in the Pennyhill Park orangery, and the three-àcre lake is annually stocked with brown and rainbow trout for those in search of more tranquil pursuits.

The award winning Latymer restaurant provides all the elegance amd quiet dignity expected of its surroundings. The food, of mainly British produce, is served in the traditional way; and the service, known to many, is complemented by an outstanding selection of fine wines.

There are 76 bedrooms and suites in this fine example of the English country house, all individually designed and beautifully furnished. Each room is named after a shrub or flower, save for the most luxurious Hayward suite, the namesake of the last permanent occupant of this English country manor house. Every room at Pennyhill Park is furnished and decorated using soft, elegant fabrics and comforting themes such as walnut and oak.

Pennyhill Park Hotel and Country Club,
London Road,
Bagshot,
Surrey. GU19 5ET
Tel: (0276) 71774

GREATER LONDON & SURREY
COMPLETE GOLF

GREATER LONDON
(including Middlesex)

Arkley G.C.
(081) 4490394
Rowley Green Rd. Barnet
2 miles from Barnet.
(9)6045 yards/**/C/H

Ashford Manor G.C.
(0784) 252049
Fordbridge Rd. Ashford
2 miles east of Staines.
(18)6343 yards/***/B/H/M

Beckenham Place Park G.C.
(081) 6502292
Beckenham Hill Rd. Beckenham
1 mile from Catford.
(18)5722 yards/***/E

Bexley Heath G.C.
(081) 3036951
Mount Row, Mount Rd. Bexley Heath
(9)5239 yards/**/D

Brent Valley G.C.
(081) 5671287
Church Rd. Cuckoo Lane, Hanwell
(18)5426 yards/***/E

Bushey G. and C.C.
(081) 9502283
High Street, Bushey
On the A411.
(9)3000 yards/***(Wed)/D

Bush Hill Park G.C.
(081) 3605738
Bush Hill, Winchmore Hill
(18)5809 yards/**/C

Chigwell GC.
(081) 5002059
High Rd. Chigwell
(18)6279 yards/**/A/H

Chingford G.C.
(081) 5292107
158 Station Rd. Chingford
(18)6336 yards/***/E

Chislehurst G.C.
(081) 4672782
Camden Park Rd. Chislehurst
(18)5128 yards/**/C/H

Crews Hill G.C.
(081) 3636674
Cattlegate Rd. Crews Hill, Enfield
(18)6230 yards/**/F/H/M

Dulwich and Sydenham Hill G.C.
(081) 6933961
Grange Lane, College Rd.
(18)6051 yards/**/D/H(22)

Dyrham Park G.C.
(081) 4403361
Galley Lane, Barnet
2 miles from Barnet off A1.
(18)6369 yards/*/C/G

Ealing G.C.
(081) 9970937
Perivale Lane, Greenford
(18)6216 yards/**/B/H

Elstree G.C.
(081) 9536115
Watling Street, Elstree
1 mile north of Elstree on A5183.
(18)6100 yards/***/B

Eltham Warren G.C.
(081) 8501166
Bexley Rd. Eltham
(9)5840 yards/**/B/H/M

Enfield G.C.
(081) 3633970
Old Park Road South, Enfield
1 mile north east of Enfield.
(18)6137 yards/**/B/H/M

Finchley G.C.
(081) 3462436
Nether Court, Frith Lane, Mill Hill
(18)6411 yards/***/A

Fulwell G.C.
(081) 9772733
Wellington Rd. Hampton Hill
2 miles south of Twickenham on A311.
(18)6490 yards/**/A/H

Grims Dyke G.C.
(081) 4284539
Oxhey Lane, Hatch End, Pinner
2 miles west of Harrow on A4008.
(18)5598 yards/**/B/H

Hadley Wood G.C.
(081) 4494486
Beech Hill, Barnet
(18)6473 yards/**/A/H/M

Hainault Forest G.C.
(081) 5002097
Chigwell Row, Hainault
(18)5754 yards/***/E
(18)6600 yards/***/E

Hampstead G.C.
(081) 4557089
Winnington Rd. Hampstead
(9)5821 yards/**/C/H

Harefield Place G.C.
(0895) 231169
The Drive, Harefield Place, Uxbridge
2 miles north of Uxbridge off A40.
(18)5753 yards/***/D/L

Hartsbourne G. and C.C.
(081) 9501133
Hartsbourne Ave. Bushey Heath
(18)6305 yards/*/F/G
(9)5432 yards/*/F/G

Haste Hill G.C.
(09274) 22877
The Drive, Northwood
On A404.
(18)5753 yards/***/E

Hendon G.C.
(081) 3466023
Devonshire Rd, Mill Hill, NW7
(18)6241 yards/***/B/M

Highgate G.C.
(081) 3403745
Denewood Rd. Highgate
(18)5982 yards/**(Wed)/B/H

Hillingdon G.C.
(0895) 33956
18 Dorset Way, Hillingdon
(9)5459 yards/**(Thu)/C/H/M

Home Park G.C.
(081) 9772423
Hampton Wick, Richmond-upon-Thames
(18)6519 yards/***/C

Horsenden Hill G.C.
(081) 9024555
Woodland Rise, Greenford
(9)3236 yards/***/E

Hounslow Heath G.C.
(081) 5705271
Staines Rd. Hounslow
Adjacent to Hounslow Heath.
(18)5820 yards/***/E

Ilford G.C.
(081) 5542930
291 Wanstead Park Rd. Ilford
(18)5414 yards/***/D

Langley Park G.C
(081) 650 2090
Beckenham
(18) 6488 yards/**/A

London Scottish G.C.
(081)7897517
Windmill Enclosure, Wimbledon Common
2 miles from Wimbledon next to the windmill.
(18)5436 yards/**/D/H

Mill Hill G.C.
(081) 9592339
100 Barnet Way, Mill Hill
1 mile south of Stirling Corner.
(18)6286 yards/***/A

Muswell Hill G.C.
(081) 8881764
Rhodes Ave. Wood Green
(18)6474 yards/**/B/H(24)

North Middlesex G.C.
(081) 4451604
Friern Barnet Lane, Whetstone
5 miles north of Finchley on A1000
(18)5611 yards/***/B

Northwood G.C.
(0923) 825329
Rickmansworth Rd. Northwood
Between Rickmansworth and North Hills on
A404
(18)6493 yards/**/C/H

Old Fold Manor G.C.
(081) 4409185
Hadley Green, Barnet
Just outside Barnet on Potters Bar Rd.
(18)6449 yards/**/B

Perivale Park G.C.
(081) 5758655
Ruislip Road East. Greenford
Between Greenford and Perivale on Ruislip Rd.
East
(9)2667 yards/***/E

Pinner Hill G.C.
(081) 8660963
South View Rd. Pinner Hill
1 mile west of Pinner Green.
(18)6293 yards/**(Wed, Thurs)/F

Roehampton G.C.
(081) 8765505
Roehampton Lane SW15
(18)6011 yards/**/C/G

Royal Blackheath G.C.
(081) 8501795
Court Rd. Eltham SE9
(18)6214 yards/**/B/H

Royal Epping Forest G.C.
(081) 5292195
Forest Approach Chingford E4
Just south of Chingford station.
(18)6620 yards/***/D/H

Royal Wimbledon G.C.
(081) 9462125
29 Camp Rd. Wimbledon SW19
1 mile west of Wimbledon village.
(18)6300 yards/**/A/H(18)/L

Ruislip G.C.
(0895) 632004
Ickenham Rd. Ruislip
(18)5500 yards/***/D

Shooters Hill G.C.
(081) 8546368
Eaglesfield Rd, SE18
1 mile from Welling.
(18)5718 yards/**/B/H/M

Shortlands G.C.
(081) 4602471
Meadow Rd. Shortlands, Bromley
(9)5261 yards/*/D/G

Sidcup G.C.
(081) 3002150
7 Hurst Rd. Sidcup
Half a mile past Sidcup station.
(9)5692 yards/***/D/H

South Herts G.C.
(081) 4452035
Links Drive, Totteridge N20
(18)6432 yards/**/F/H

Stanmore G.C.
(081) 9542599
Gordon Ave. Stanmore
(18)5881 yards/**/D/H

Strawberry Hill G.C.
(081) 8940165
Wellesley Rd. Twickenham
Next to Strawberry Hill station.
(9)2381 yards/**/D

Sudbury G.C.
(081) 9023713
Bridgewater Rd. Wembley
(18)6282 yards/**/B/H/M

Sundridge Park G.C.
(081) 460278
Garden Rd. Bromley
1 mile from Bromley on A2212.
(18)6410 yards/**/A/H
(18)6028 yards/**/A/H

Trent Park G.C.
(081) 3667432
Bramley Rd. Southgate N14
Opposite Oakwood tube.
(18)6008 yards/***/E

Twickenham G.C.
(081) 7831698
Staines Rd. Twickenham
Situated on A305.
(9)6014 yards/***/E

Wanstead G.C.
(081) 9893938
Overton Drive, Wanstead
(18)6211 yards/**(Wed,Thu)/B/H

West Middlesex G.C.
(081) 5743450
Greenford Rd. Southall
2 miles from Greenford.
(18)6242 yards/**/D

Whitewebbs G.C.
(081) 3634454
Beggars Hollow, Clay Hill, Enfield
1 mile north of Enfield.
(18)5881 yards/***/F

Wimbledon Common G.C.
(081) 9467571
Camp Rd. Wimbledon Common SW19
1 mile north west of Wimbledon village.
(18)5486 yards/***/F

Wimbledon Park G.C.
(081) 9461250
Home Park Rd, Wimbledon SW19
(18)5465 yards/***/B/H/L/M

Wyke Green G.C.
(081) 5608777
Syon Lane Isleworth
Just north of Gillette corner.
(18)6242 yards/***/A/H

SURREY

Addington G.C.
(081) 7771055
Shirley Church Rd, Croydon
(18)6242 yards/**/F

Addington Court G.C.
(081) 657 0281
Featherbed Lane, Addington
2 miles east of Croydon.
(18)5577 yards/***/D
(18)5513 yards/***/F

Addington Palace G.C.
(081) 6543061
Gravel Hill, Addington Park,Croydon
2 miles from East Croydon on A12.
(18)6282 yards/***/B

Barrow Hills G.C.
(0932) 848117
Longcross, Chertsey
4 miles west of Chertsey.
(18)3090 yards/*/F

Betchworth Park G.C.
(0306) 882052
Reigate Rd. Dorking
(18)6266 yards/**(Tue,Wed)/A

Bramley G.C.
(0483) 893042
Bramley, Guildford
4 miles south of Guildford on A281.
(18)5910 yards/**/B/H

Burhill G.C.
(0932) 227345
Walton-on-Thames
(18)6224 yards/**/A/H/L

Camberley Heath G.C.
(0276) 23258
Golf Drive, Camberley
1 mile south of Camberley.
(18)6402 yards/**/C/H

Chipstead G.C.
(0737) 551053
How Lane, Coulsdon
Situated next to Chipstead station.
(18)5454 yards/**/B

Coombe Hill G.C.
(081) 9422284
Kingston Hill.
(18)6286 yards/***/A

Combe Wood G.C.
(081) 9423828
George Rd. Kingston Hill
1 mile north of Kingston-on-Thames.
(18)5210 yards/**/F/H
(9)1655 yards/***/E

Coulsdon Court G.C.
(081) 6600468
Coulsdon Rd. Coulsdon
2 miles south of Croydon.
(18)6030 yards/***/D

Crondall G.C.
(0252) 850880
Oak Park, Hoalte Lane, Crondall, West Farnham
(18)6278 yards/***/C

Croham Hurst G.C.
(081) 6575581
Croham Rd. South Croydon
(18)6274 yards/**/C

Cuddington G.C.
(081) 3930952
Banstead Rd. Banstead
Next to Banstead station.
(18)6282 yards/**/A/H/L

FERNFELL

Fernfell Golf and Country Club is located just out of Cranleigh. Guildford is 8 miles away and travelling from London is a straightforward journey on the A3 to Guildford and the A281 to Cranleigh. Turning into the drive, one's eye is immediately drawn to the view across the parkland 18 hole course to the surrounding woodland. The drive winds up to the Club House, a 400 year old Sussex barn which we are told must be one of the most impressive club houses in the country.

During the summer the interior is light and airy. When the nights draw in, the beams, huge log fire and leaded windows combine to create a warm and welcoming atmosphere. The snooker table is an added point to remember. Members, golf societies, green fee players and those attending company golf days all comment on the catering and the efficient, friendly staff.

The 18 hole, 5599 yards, par 68 course is interspersed with fine specimen trees, white sanded bunkers and a picturesque stream runs through the course to challenge the golfer. The holes that linger in the memory are the 1st, 13th and 16th. The 1st is a par 3 from an elevated tee across the stream which runs in front of an elevated green. Elevation and elation are the key words here. There is woodland both on the course and surrounding it, which abounds with wildlife. A past golf captain, who has written papers on various aspects of ornithology, has counted 72 species of birds, amongst which the mandarin dune, woodpigeon, tawny owl and green wood-

pecker are worth mentioning. During the spring, vast splashes of blue appear when the bluebells open. The Club House, the course and the Surrey countryside, make an exceptional golfing day. Company golf day organisers and golf societies should make particular note of Fernfell and its easy access from London. The golf professional can organise golf clinics and make video recording of parts of a golf day. Three, en-tout-cas, hard tennis courts and an open air swimming pool are all part of the facilities.

Fernfell is one of three group golf courses, the other being Westerwood Golf and Country Club at Cumbernauld near Glasgow and Murrayshall Country House Hotel and Golf Course at Scone, near Perth. Westerwood boasts a Seve Ballesteros designed Championship Golf Course, 6721 yards par 73; Laura Davies gave advice on the ladies tees. Murrayshall Golf Course is 6434 yards, par 73 set in undulating parkland, has a rich variety of trees, water hazards and breathtaking views. The Westerwood and Murrayshall Hotels offer exceptional facilities for those on Golfing Breaks, vacation or business. Please refer to the feature pages within this guide book for details.

Corporate golf is now recognised as the most effective method of corporate entertaining and staff incentives. All three courses offer corporate membership. Golf Societies and Green Fee Payers are welcome.

Fernfell Golf and Country Club
Barhatch Lane
Cranleigh
Surrey
Tel: (0483) 268855
Fax: (0483) 267251

GREATER LONDON & SURREY
COMPLETE GOLF

Dorking G.C.
(0306) 889786
Chart Park, Dorking
1 mile south of Dorking on A24.
(9)5210 yards/**/D

Drift G.C.
(04865) 4641
The Drift, East Horsley
(18)6404 yards/**/C

Effingham G.C.
(0372) 452203
Guildford Rd. Effingham
4 miles from Leatherhead.
(18)6488 yards/**/B/H

Epsom G.C.
(03727) 21666
Longdown Lane, Epsom
Just north of Epsom Downs station.
(18)5668 yards/**/D

Farnham G.C.
(02518) 2109
The Sands, Farnham
1 mile east of Farnham off A31.
(18)6313 yards/**/B

Farnham Park G.C.
(0252) 715216
Folly Hill, Farnham
1 mile north of Farnham.
(9)1161 yards/***/E

Fernfell G.C.
(0483) 268855
Barhatch Lane, Cranleigh
1 mile from Cranleigh off A281.
(18)5561 yards/***/D

Foxhills G.C.
(093287) 2050
Stonehill Rd. Ottershaw
Behind St. Peters Hospital
(18)6880 yards/**/A
(18)6747 yards/**/A

Gatton Manor G.C.
(030679) 555
Ockley, Dorking
2 miles south west of Ockley off A29.
(18)6902 yards/***/D

Goal Farm G.C.
(04867) 3183
Pirbright.
Between Woking and Guildford on A322.
(9)1283 yards/***/E

Guildford G.C.
(0483) 575243
High Path Rd. Merrow, Guildford
(18)6080 yards/**/C

Hankley Common G.C.
(025125) 2493
Tilford Rd. Tilford, Farnham
(18)6403 yards/**/B/H

Hindhead G.C.
(0428) 604614
Churt Rd. Hindhead
2 miles north of Hindhead on A287.
(18)6349 yards/***/A

Hoebridge G.C.
(0483) 722611
Old Woking Rd. Old Woking
Between Old Woking and West Byfleet on B382.
(18)6536 yards/***/D
(18)2230 yards/***/E
(9)2900 yards/***/E

Kingswood G.C.
(0737) 832188
Sandy Lane, Kingswood
4 miles south of Sutton.
(18)6821 yards/***/B/H

Laleham G.C.
(0932) 564211
Laleham Reach, Chertsey
(18)6203 yards/**/C

Leatherhead G.C.
(037284) 3966
Kingston Rd. Leatherhead
(18)6088 yards/***/A

Leatherhead Golf Centre
(0372) 843453
Oaklawn Road, Leatherhead
(9)1752 yards/***/E

Limpsfield Chart G.C.
(0883) 723405
Limpsfield, Oxted
Between Oxted and Westerham on A25.
(9)5718 yards/**(Thu)/F

Lingfield Park G.C.
(0342) 834602
M25 junction 6, beside racecourse
(18) 6500 yards/B

Malden G.C.
(081) 9420654
Traps Lane, New Malden
1 mile from New Malden centre.
(18)6201 yards/**/B

Mitcham G.C.
(081) 6481508
Carshalton Rd. Mitcham Junction
Next to Mitcham Junction station.
(18)5935 yards/**/D/H(18)

Moore Place G.C.
(0372) 463533
Portsmouth Rd. Esher
1 mile from Esher on A3.
(9)3512 yards/***/E

New Zealand G.C.
(09323) 45049
Woodham Lane, Woodham, Weybridge
(18)6012 yards/**/A

North Downs G.C.
(0883) 653298
Northdown Rd. Woldingham, Caterham
(18)5787 yards/**/F/H

Oak Park G.C.
(0252) 850880
Crondall, nr Farnham
(18)6437 yards/***/D

Oak Sports Centre
(081) 643 8363
Woodmansterne Rd. Carshalton
1 mile south of Carshalton Beeches station on B2032.
(18)5975 yards/***/D
(9)1590 yards/***/E

Purley Downs G.C.
(081) 6578347
106 Purley Downs Rd. Purley
(18)6243 yards/**/B/H/M/L

Puttenham G.C.
(0483) 810498
Heath Rd. Puttenham, Guildford
4 miles west of Guildford on A31.
(18)5367/**/B/H

R.A.C. Country Club
(03722) 763111
Woodcote Park, Epsom
1 mile from Epsom station.
(18)6702 yards/*/F/G
(18)5474 yards/*/F/G

Redhill and Reigate G.C.
(0737) 244626
Clarence Lodge, Pendleton Rd. Redhill
(18)5238 yards/***/D

Reigate Heath G.C.
(0737) 242610
Reigate Heath, Reigate
(9)5554 yards/**/F

Richmond G.C.
(081) 9404351
Sudbrook Park, Richmond
(18)5965 yards/**/A

Richmond Park G.C.
(081) 876 3205
Roehampton Gate, Richmond Park
(18)5940 yards/***/E
(18)5969 yards/***/E

Royal Mid Surrey G.C.
(081) 9401894
Old Deer Park, Richmond
(18)5544 yards/***/A/G/L
(18)6052 yards/***/A/G/L

St. Georges Hill G.C.
(0932) 842406
St. Georges Hill, Weybridge
(18)6492 yards/**/A/H

Sandown Park G.C.
(0372) 63340
Moor Lane, Esher
Situated in Sandown Park racecourse.
(9)5656 yards/***/E
(9)1193 yards/***/E

Selsdon Park Hotel G.C.
(081) 6578811
Sanderstead, South Croydon
3 miles south of Croydon on A2022.
(18)6402 yards/***/B

Shillingee Park G.C.
(0428) 653237
Chiddingford, Godalming
(9)2500 yards/***/D

Shirley Park G.C.
(081) 6541143
194 Addiscombe Rd. Croydon
2 miles from East Croydon.
(18)6210 yards/**/B/H

Silvermere G.C.
(0932) 867275
Redhill Rd. Cobham
(18)6333 yards/***/D

Surbiton G.C.
(081) 3983101
Woodstock Lane, Chessington
2 miles east of Esher off A3.
(18)6211 yards/***/A/H

Tandridge G.C.
(0883) 712273
Oxted
(18)6250 yards/**(Tue,Fri)/B

Thames Ditton and Esher G.C.
(081) 3981551
Portsmouth Rd. Esher
Off A3 close to Sandown racecourse.
(9)5606 yards/***/D

Tyrrells Wood G.C.
(0372) 376025
Tyrrells Wood, Leatherhead
(18)6219 yards/***/A/H

Walton Heath G.C.
(0737) 812060
Tadworth
(18)6813 yards/**/A/H/L
(18)6659 yards/**/A/H/L

Wentworth G.C.
(09904) 2201
Virginia Water
Just off the A30 near the A329 junction.
(18)6945 yards/**/A/H
(18)6176 yards/**/A/H
(18)7000 yards/**/A/H

West Byfleet G.C.
(09323) 45230
Sheerwater Rd. West Byfleet
1 mile west of West Byfleet on A245
(18)6211 yards/**/B

West Hill G.C.
(04867) 4365
Bagshot Rd. Brookwood
On A322 between Guildford and Bagshot.
(18)6368 yards/**/B/H

West Surrey G.C.
(0483) 421275
Enton Green, Godalming
(18)6247 yards/**/B/H

Windlemere G.C.
(0276) 858727
Windlesham Rd. West End, Woking
Opposite Gordon Boys School entrance.
(9)5346 yards/***/D

Wisley G.C.
(0483) 211022
1 mile from M25 junction 10
27 (3x9)/*/

Woking G.C.
(0483) 760053
Pond Rd, Hook Heath, Woking
(18)6322 yards/**/B/H/M

Woodcote Park G.C.
(081) 6682788
Meadow Hill, Bridle Way, Coulsdon
(18)6624 yards/**/B/H

Worplesdon G.C.
(0483) 489876
Heath House Rd. Woking
4 miles from Guildford.
(18)6422 yards/**/A/H/L

Charles Crombie   RULE XXXIII   Rosenstiel's

HERTS, BEDS & ESSEX

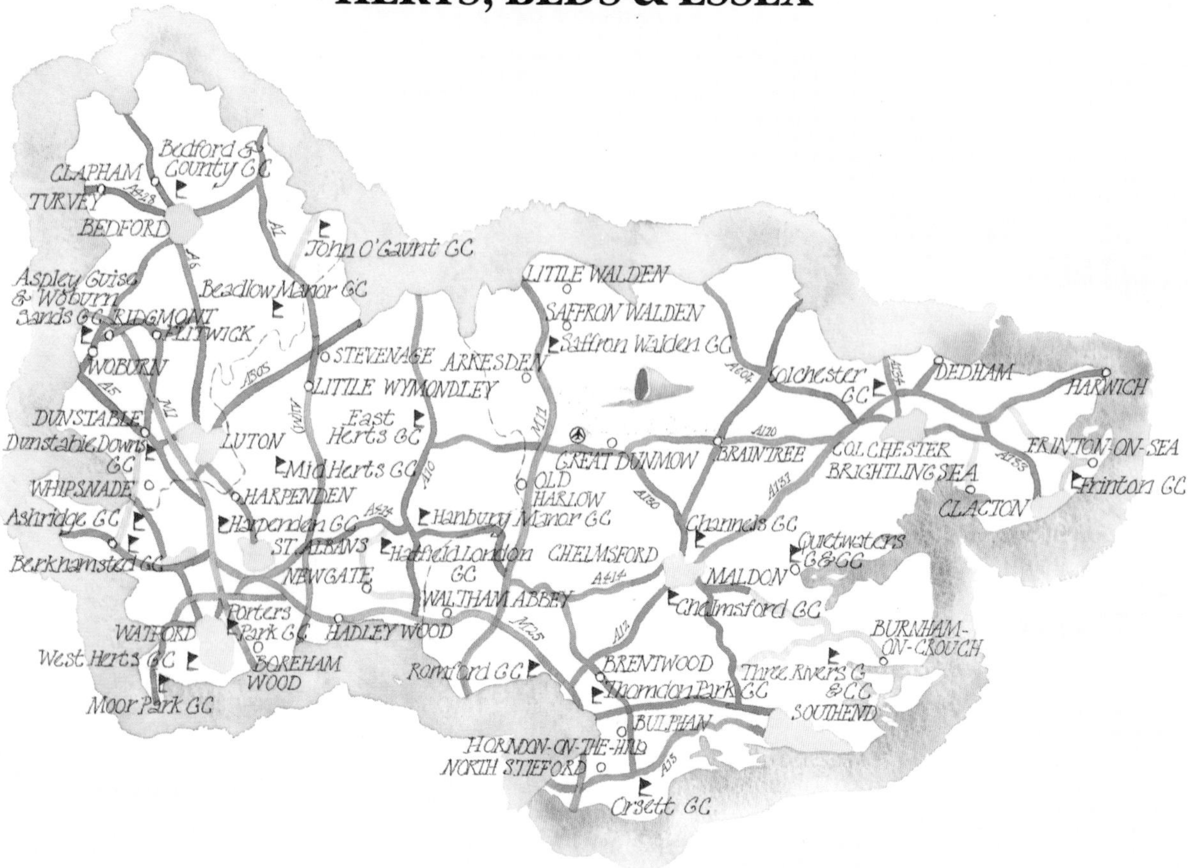

Robert Guy OPEN FAIRWAYS Burlington Gallery

HERTS, BEDS & ESSEX
CHOICE GOLF

Unfortunately, for all too many the first and often lasting impression of a place can be determined by the great blue ribbons that now stretch the length and breadth of the country – Britain's ever expanding motorway network. The M1 (not to mention the M25) cuts through the heart of Hertfordshire and slices off the left ear of Bedfordshire. Between London and Luton it is a fearsome animal at the best of times and passing beyond these two counties one often draws a sigh of relief. The greater expanse of Essex fares a little better, escaping with a few nasty scratches, but in all three counties, the deeper realms are not as often explored as they might be, except needless to say by those who live there.

The golfing breed is a little more fortunate than most. In every county in Britain he, and she, can visit golf courses that are tucked away in the most secluded and tranquil of settings and even in the, 'there's an open space – lets build on it, 90s' Hertfordshire, Bedfordshire and Essex are not exceptions to the rule.

HERTFORDSHIRE

A glance at the map tells you that **Ashridge** in Hertfordshire isn't all that great a distance from London and the M1 but it occupies a particularly peaceful spot and the approach road which runs near **Berkhamsted** Golf Club passes through some glorious countryside – the kind that once covered much of this part of the world. Both are delightful heathland/parkland courses. Berkhamsted is best known for its conspicuous absence of bunkers, though like Royal Ashdown Forest in Sussex has more than enough natural hazards to test the courage of any golfer, while Ashridge is perhaps most famed for its long association with Henry Cotton, for many years the Club's professional. There are many fine par fours at Ashridge, the 9th and 14th being two of the best; the approach to the latter bears an uncanny resemblance to the 17th at St. Andrews – the mischievously positioned bunker front left and the road behind the green – though it's not quite as frightening! Both courses are decidedly worth a visit.

There is certainly no shortage of golf courses in Hertfordshire. In the upper realms of the county, Harpenden, convenient for those motoring along the M1, has two fine courses, **Harpenden** and **Harpenden Common**, the former at Hammonds End being perhaps the pick of the two. A short distance away at Wheathampstead is the **Mid Herts** Golf Club, while on the other side of the country's most famous blue ribbon lies **East Herts** near Buntingford, also worth noting if travelling along the A10. In the far north of the county a 45 hole development is taking shape at **Malton** near Royston and right in the heart of Hertfordshire stands the exclusive new **Brocket Hall** Golf Club near Welwyn. The greater concentration of courses, however, perhaps not surprisingly, is in the area just north of London. **Moor Park**, featured a few pages on, is the most widely known though nearby **Porters Park** (in the quiet of Radlett) and **West Herts** (on the edge of Watford, yet similarly peaceful) also strongly merit attention.

West Herts was once more commonly known as Cassiobury Park after its location. Bernard Darwin in his famous 'Golf Courses of the British Isles' sang its praises highly; 'Of all the race of park courses, it would scarcely be possible in point of sheer beauty, to beat Cassiobury Park near Watford.' One other course to note in Hertfordshire is the first class public course at Essendon, confusingly called **The Hatfield London Country Club.**

It is possible to view the county's best courses from a London base. This isn't to say, however, that a number of excellent establishments can't be found beyond the city limits. In Thundridge, near Ware, **Hanbury Manor** (0920) 487722 is a very fine Country House Hotel which can boast among many things, a golf course first laid by Harry Vardon in the 1920's and recently completely redesigned by Jack Nicklaus Jnr. This new course is explored on a separate page in this chapter. In **Hadley Wood**, where there is a well established 18 hole course, The West Lodge Park is an elegant mansion house 081-440 8311, while Boreham Wood carries a restaurant to note – Signor Battis.

The best bet if you are playing Moor Park is the Mansion House at Grims Dyke 081-954 4227 in Harrow Weald. St Albans and Harpenden, where the traffic races through, are both littered with good pubs off the busy high streets. St Albans offers its superb Cathedral and the delightful St Michael's Manor (0727) 864444 which lies in its shadow. Harpenden's Moat House (05827) 64111 is a little pricey but extremely well thought of. An idea for East Herts – The Redcoats Farmhouse (0438) 729500 at Little Wymondley – very cosy.

For golfers seeking genuine excellence – a true pinnacle perhaps – The Briggens House Hotel (027979) 2416 and its elegant restaurant at Ware should serve admirably. Briggens House has its own 9 hole golf course and is only 6 miles away from Hanbury Manor.

BEDFORDSHIRE

Arguably the two leading Clubs in Bedfordshire are **John O'Gaunt** at Sandy and **Beadlow Manor** near Shefford: both have more than one course. The former is more established, its two courses, the Championship John O'Gaunt course and the shorter Carthegena are curiously very different in character, the John O'Gaunt being a very pretty parkland type, the Carthegena, a heathland course. Visitors to both John O'Gaunt and Beadlow Manor can expect first class facilities and a friendly welcome and for the latter the Beadlow Manor Hotel (0525) 60800 is naturally very convenient.

Another of the better courses in Bedfordshire is **Dunstable Downs**, laid out on high ground, offering remarkably extensive views – both Surrey to the south and Warwickshire to the north west can be sighted. It is a classic downland type course.

In Berkhamsted, The Swan Inn is a great little place to stay. (It's actually in Herts, but as well as being convenient for Berkhamsted and Ashridge is also handy for the leading courses of South Bedfordshire.) In Whipsnade, the Zoo is excellent while the downs nearby are a good place to get rid of some energy. In Dunstable's town centre The Old Palace Lodge (0582) 662201 is well worth an overnight visit.

Elsewhere in the county, **Aspley Guise and Woburn Sands** (the more famous Woburn Golf and Country Club lies over the border in Buckinghamshire), is another that provides far reaching views and a word also for the **Bedford and County** Golf Club, just north of the county town off the A6 and near St Neots in Cambridgeshire, but just within Bedfordshire **Wyboston Lakes** is a pleasant pay and play course.

In Woburn some excellent hotels can be found as well as the delightful House and game reserve. The Paris House (0525)

290692 is an outstanding restaurant while the Bedford Arms (0525) 290441 is a welcoming Georgian coaching inn. The Black Horse and The Bell are notable pubs to visit. Outside the town, Moore Place (0908) 282000 in Aspley Guise is extremely relaxing and in Flitwick, the 17th Century Flitwick Manor (0525)712242 and its restaurant are tremendous. En route to the county town the Rose & Crown (052528) 245 in Ridgmount serves a good pint and bar snacks. In Bedford itself we call upon the services of the Moat House group – The Bedford Moat House (0234) 355131. For grander accommodation The Woodlands Manor (0234) 363281 in Clapham offers a delightful hotel with a quality restaurant. Finally, in the corner of Bedfordshire, Turvey offers two fine restaurants, The Three Fyshes (02306) 264 and Laws (023064) 655; some accommodation is available in the latter.

ESSEX

Not much of Essex could be described as 'natural golfing country' yet of all England's counties this is the one witnessing perhaps the biggest explosion in golf course site applications. Strange, isn't it? Two of the top courses in the county are **Thorndon Park** (2 miles South of Brentford) and **Orsett** (2 miles East of Grays and in the wonderfully named area of Mucking and Fobbing). Neither is a great distance from the M25 and both can be reached via the A128. Thorndon Park, as its name suggests, is a parkland type course situated in a former deer park belonging to Thorndon Hall – a quite stunning mansion, whereas Orsett is much more of the heathland variety with sandy subsoil.

In a similar vein to neighbouring Hertfordshire, a number of the county's better courses are being gradually swallowed up by Greater London – the fine parkland course at **Abridge** with its splendidly luxurious Clubhouse being one of them, now lying the wrong side of the M25 (as does the famous course at **Epping Forest.**) **Romford** is one that holds its Essex identity. A well bunkered and fairly flat course, Romford was the home of James Braid before he moved to Walton Heath.

Further afield, both **Colchester** (the oldest town in England) and **Saffron Walden** have courses set in very pretty surroundings and for lovers of seaside golf there is a pleasant (though windy!) course at **Frinton-on-Sea**. One of the county's newest attractions is the beautifully named **Quietwaters** Club at Tolleshunt D'Arcy, not far from Maldon where there are 36 holes. Peaceful perhaps, but much has happened here of late including the construction of a European Tour Championship Course. Finally, for those visiting Chelmsford, both the **Chelmsford** Golf Club, to the south of the town and the **Channels** Golf Club to the north with its superb Elizabethan Clubhouse can be recommended along with The **Three Rivers** Golf and Country Club nearby in Purleigh (two courses here).

Essex is blessed with many outstanding hotels and restaurants. Dedham presents an ideal starting point. Here we find the superb La Talbooth (0206) 323150. This is a monument to good food, an ideal place to celebrate a special round of golf. Close by, The Maison Talbooth (0206) 322367 offers stylish accommodation. This delightful village with its views of the Stour also offers the Dedham Vale Hotel (0206) 322273 and its first class restaurant. All are also convenient for the many Suffolk courses. Resisting the temptation to venture further up the Stour and discover the delights of Constable's country

we arrive at the coast and Harwich – heading directly for The Pier (0255) 241212, here as you may suspect the seafood is the speciality of the house. Golfers taking in the course at Frinton may wish to sample a local hotel, The Rock Hotel (0255) 677194. The area remains quiet and its sandy beaches appeal. Further up the coast in Brightlingsea, a restaurant and a pub should be pointed out; Jacobs (020630) 2113 is the restaurant, the Cherry Tree is the pub.

More thoughts and in Arkesden a thatched pub, The Axe & Compasses provides good food and a cheerful hostelry. Saffron Walden offers the Saffron Hotel (0799) 22676 – nothing grand, but extremely comfortable. Another Walden, this time a Little one, north of Saffron; in the quiet village lies The Crown – good bar food. Another Essex hotel handy for a motorway, the M11, is The Green Man (0279) 442521 in Old Harlow – situated opposite the village green, the hotel totally belies the proximity of the nearby autoroute. Not particularly close to the county's best golf courses, but well worth a trip is The Whitehall Hotel (0279) 850603 in Broxted where the restaurant is excellent.

Finally we visit Great Dunmow, not far from Stansted Airport and where the legendary Flitch trials take place. The Saracens Head Hotel (0371) 873901 in town is smallish but very pleasant. If you are rushing home and cannot spend a night in the area then dinner at The Starr (0371) 874321 may still be a possibility. Incidentally for those unfamiliar with the Flitch trials, the basic idea is to test (by some rather interesting methods) the suitability of man and woman. Not apparently a necessity for selecting one's golf partner......but it's a thought!

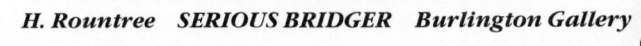
H. Rountree **SERIOUS BRIDGER** *Burlington Gallery*

MOOR PARK
CHAMPIONSHIP GOLF

I don't suppose many would dispute that the R&A Clubhouse at St Andrews is the best known 'nineteenth' in the world. However, for the title of 'most magnificent' or 'most grand' it is doubtful whether Moor Park can have many serious rivals. The **Moor Park Mansion** dates from the **13th century**. In its illustrious history it has been the home of Earls, Dukes, Cardinals, Archbishops and even a Queen – Catherine of Aragon living there in the 16th century. During the last war the Mansion was requisitioned, becoming first the headquarters of the Territorial Army, then of the A.T.S. and later of the American 2nd Airborne Corps and it was from within Moor Park that preparations were made for the ill-fated invasion of Arnhem in 1944.

Golf first came to Moor Park in 1923, **Lord Ebury** founding the Golf Club just four years after the estate had been purchased by Lord Leverhulme. **Harry Colt** was called in to design three golf courses, two of which remain with the Club, **The High** and **The West** courses, the third now being a public course (Rickmansworth) although it is in fact maintained by the Moor Park Club.

The Club's current Secretary is **Mr. John Davies**; he may be contacted by telephone on **(0923) 773146**. The professional, **Ross Whitehead** can also be contacted at this number. Visitors are welcome at Moor Park between Mondays and Fridays although it is essential to telephone the Club in advance in order to book a starting time and visitors should note that proof of handicap is required. The only general restrictions during the week are on Tuesday and Thursday mornings, when both courses are reserved for members between 8.30am and 10am. Moor Park is extremely popular with Golfing Societies and up to 110 players can normally be catered for. Those organising must make prior arrangements with the Club, written applications to be addressed to **The Secretary, Moor Park Golf Club, Rickmansworth, Herts WD3 1QN**. In 1992 the green fee for a full day's golf was priced at £50, entitling the visitor to a round over both courses. For junior golfers the fees were half the normal rate.

Situated on the north western outskirts of Greater London, Moor Park is very accessible from all parts of the country. Its precise location is off the A404 Northwood to Rickmansworth road. Those travelling from afar should find the M25 of great assistance with junctions 17 or 18 probably being the best points of exit. As for rail stations, Moor Park is the nearest at a distance of approximately three-quarters of a mile from the Golf Club (a good uphill walk mind you!) Rickmansworth is also less than two miles away.

The major Championships staged at Moor Park are all played over the High Course. Measuring 6713 yards (par 72, sss 72) it is some 900 yards longer than the West Course, though this at 5815 yards (par 69, sss 68) is certainly no 'pushover'. The High Course begins with a fairly straightforward, slightly uphill **1st** but the **2nd** which dog-legs to the right, is one of the toughest 'fours' of the round. Towards the middle of the front nine a sliced tee shot will send a ball into some particularly pleasant properties whose gardens border the fairways (attempting to retrieve your ball is not recommended!) The back nine contains three excellent short holes including the **12th** where the attractive two-tiered green is surrounded by willows and is surely one of the best par threes in the country.

Within two years of the Club being founded, Moor Park played host to the 1925 PGA Matchplay Championship, won by Archie Compston. Since then, several memorable professional tournaments and pro-ams have been played here. However, perhaps the best known game of golf at Moor Park took place back in 1928. A 72 hole challenge match was played between the American **Walter Hagen**, the leading professional of the day, and the aforementioned **Archie Compston**, one of Britain's finest players. With only one hole completed of the final round the match was all over, Hagen having been defeated 18 up with 17 to play – the greatest margin of victory ever recorded in a match play event. Ironically, a few weeks later Hagen won his third Open Championship at Sandwich, finishing three strokes ahead of Compston – poor Archie, he never did win the Open.

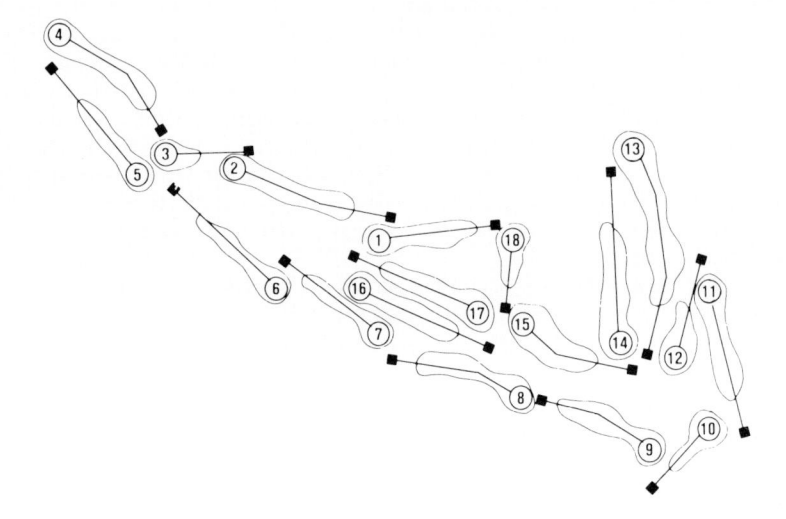

High Course

Hole	Yards	Par	Hole	Yards	Par
1	371	4	10	145	3
2	418	4	11	393	4
3	165	3	12	210	3
4	426	4	13	507	5
5	334	4	14	435	4
6	493	5	15	430	4
7	362	4	16	517	5
8	467	4	17	408	4
9	480	5	18	152	3
Out	3.516	37	In	3.197	35
			Out	3.516	37
			TOTALS	6.713	72

HANBURY MANOR

Hanbury Manor, recently awarded a much sought after 5 star rating by the AA, is a country house experience to be savoured. A lovingly restored mansion with 96 bedrooms and 10 conference suites, turn-of-the-century charm blends with every modern comfort and service that is always friendly and courteous.

The beautiful 200 acre estate provides a vast array of amenities, including a championship golf course, tennis, squash, snooker and a fully equipped Health Club.

The perfect place to relax or to combine business with pleasure, Hanbury Manor is easily accessible, only 25 miles north of London. The elegantly appointed bedrooms spoil the most discerning traveller, whilst fine dining is available in three enticingly different restaurants including the gourmet Zodiac Restaurant and the casual Vardon Grill.

One of many highlights of a stay at Hanbury Manor will undoubtedly be the magnificent 18 hole golf course, created out of rolling Hertfordshire countryside by Jack Nicklaus II, of Golden Bear Associates. The course measures a testing 7011 yards from the championship tees, with a number of strategically placed bunkers and several picturesque water hazards providing a series of challenges for all levels of players.

The contrasting nature of the Downfield nine - beautifully sculpted out of existing meadowland and an old quarry site - and the inward half - set in breathtaking parkland with mature trees - provides a remarkable variety of panoramic scenery that make for a whole series of spectacular memories. The careful design and conditioning of the course makes Hanbury Manor one of the most beautifully manicured layouts anywhere in Britain.

Whether toning-up or winding down, Hanbury provides the perfect environment for relaxing after a game on the championship standard golf course. Indoors or out, the variety of freely accessible leisure activities are numerous, making Hanbury Manor a genuine resort property. The centrepiece of the magnificently equipped leisure facilities is undoubtedly the 17m x 7m swimming pool where a warm welcome is tendered to all aquaphiles, under a stunning Romanesque canopy. Steam rooms, Swedish sauna, and a jacuzzi are offered as wonderful wet alternatives and vie with the Hanbury Beauty Studio and sumptuous gymnasium for guests' attention.

Hanbury Manor has set out to offer guests a level of facilities and service that re-define traditional standards. Whether as a hotel guest, or as a member of our Golf and Leisure Sections, Hanbury Manor is quite simply an experience not to be missed.

Hanbury Manor
Thundridge
Nr Ware
Hertfordshire SG12 0SD
Tel: (0920) 487722
Fax: (0920) 487692y

HANBURY MANOR
CHAMPIONSHIP GOLF

There can be few golfing venues in Europe where 'Old' meets and marries 'New' as successfully and interestingly as it appears to have done at Hanbury Manor in Hertfordshire.

The 'Old' is the manor itself, which since the late 19th century has been dominated by a striking Jacobean styled mansion, and its wonderful grounds which since 1918 have included a nine hole parkland golf course. The 'New' is the very recent conversion of the estate into the Hanbury Manor Golf and Country Club including restoration and transformation of the mansion into an extremely elegant five star country house hotel and the complete redesign of the golf course into an 18 hole championship length 'American style' golf course.

The original Hanbury Manor course was designed by Englishman **Harry Vardon**. Vardon was the greatest of the 'Great Triumvirate' of Vardon, Braid and Taylor who dominated golf between 1894 and 1914. The architect of the new Hanbury course is American **Jack Nicklaus II**, eldest son (or chief cub) of the 'Golden Bear', the greatest of the big three of Nicklaus, Palmer and Player who dominated golf from the late 1950s until the mid 1970s.

So how new, how good and how American is the new course at Hanbury Manor? The official opening took place in the summer of 1991; Jack Jnr. was present of course, and so were **Tony Jacklin** and **Dave Stockton** who played a friendly match billed as 'The Ryder Cup Captains' Challenge' and which, like the real thing, was won by Stockton. Both Stockton and Jacklin were very complimentary of both the condition of the course and its design. Stockton was also quoted as saying that it was, 'by far the best course I've played outside of the United States'. A shade rash you might think, especially given that it was uttered by someone who played in several Open Championships – a comment in fact that must rank alongside Paul Azinger's description of Woburn which began, 'I came here expecting a links...'(!). But Hanbury Manor undoubtedly has great potential and while the superior conditioning of the course and the extravagant use of water hazards give the course a very American feel the surrounding countryside is unmistakably rural England.

Hanbury Manor is located approximately 25 miles north of London, directly off the A10, just north of the Ware turn off. It is important to note that golf is restricted to hotel residents, Club members and their guests. The residential green fees in 1992 were £35 midweek and £40 at the weekend. The hotel offers a number of 'packaged residential golf breaks' and those interested should telephone the hotel on **(0920) 487722** for details. The Club Manager, **Meriel Riches** and the professional, **Peter Blaze** can also be contacted via the above number. Written correspondence should be addressed to **Hanbury Manor Golf and Country Club, Ware, Hertfordshire SG12 0SD**.

Only the very brave (or rash?) should attempt to tackle Hanbury Manor from the championship tees: at 7011 yards it is monstrously long and many of the par fours are beyond the reach of most mortals. From the medal tees, 6633 yards (par 72) is much more realistic while the forward tees and ladies tees reduce the course to 6080 yards and 5363 yards (par 72) respectively. As well as the mix of an American type course in a very English setting, Hanbury Manor offers two very different challenges within an 18 hole round. The two nines are laid out on opposite sides of the mansion; the first nine has a much newer feel as here the Nicklaus team had to shape virgin golfing terrain (essentially farmland prior to its development) whereas on the back nine they built over the existing mature parkland of the Vardon layout. The degree of challenge, however, is comparable and both nines contain a number of dramatic and beautifully sculptured holes.

The threat of water looms as early as the twisting, downhill **2nd**, one of two outstanding par fives on the front nine. The green at this hole has been raised and built at such an angle with fronting traps that even the biggest hitters are unlikely to attempt the water carry with their second shot. A small lake also features on the par three **6th** and the very difficult par four **8th**, but for my money the **7th** and **9th** are better holes.

On the back nine both the **10th** and **15th** fairways are bordered by a splendid variety of trees and the **13th** and **17th** call for do-or-die shots over water. Respite comes at the **18th** for though there is yet more water to be carried from the tee, it is not a big carry – besides, the opulent comforts of Hanbury's 19th hole are now within sight.

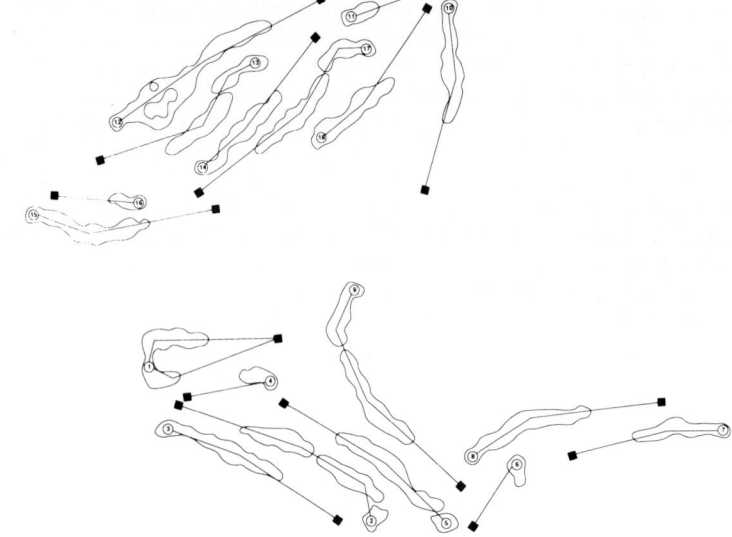

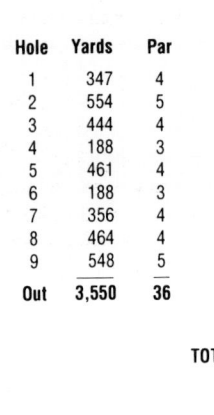

Hole	Yards	Par	Hole	Yards	Par
1	347	4	10	409	4
2	554	5	11	212	3
3	444	4	12	543	5
4	188	3	13	416	4
5	461	4	14	397	4
6	188	3	15	406	4
7	356	4	16	186	3
8	464	4	17	498	5
9	548	5	18	394	4
Out	**3,550**	**36**	**In**	**3.461**	**36**
			Out	**3,550**	**36**
			TOTALS	**7,011**	**72**

STOCKS HOTEL AND CLUB

Stocks, an historically elegant country house hotel located in the heart of the Chiltern Hills, dates back to 1176 and was the former home of entrepreneur Victor Lownes, who turned the house into a training school for his 'Bunny Girls'. The house is situated amidst twenty acres of parkland, surrounded by 10,000 acres of National Trust Estate. Stocks however, is not only a peaceful house for unwinding and enjoying the delightful relaxing atmosphere and excellent cuisine, but also offers sporting and leisure facilities that are second to none.

Construction of an 18 hole championship golf course started in May 1992. The course will be 7185 yards long and has been skilfully designed to blend with the layout of the already established parkland, using the natural features and many of the existing fine old trees. The work has been timed to take advantage of the summer growing season and it is anticipated that the course will be available for some limited play by advance members in the Autumn of 1993. The official opening will be in Spring 1994.

For companies who require corporate entertainment or hospitality days, hot air ballooning, clay pigeon or laser shooting and off-the-road driving events, are all available. One can take advantage of the riding and livery stables, four tennis courts (one floodlit), gymnasium or squash court, croquet, table tennis, volley ball, cricket, five a side football and heated outdoor swimming pool (May to October). However, if you prefer more gentle pursuits, there is also the country's largest jacuzzi or a snooker table to while away an hour or so.

The bedrooms are most luxurious and are beautifully furnished and equipped with all amenities including such niceties as towelling robes.

The Tapestry Restaurant is inviting with its crisp linen, features a seasonal a La Carte menu and a table d'hote menu (changes daily), making good use of fresh ingredients and offers an exceptional cheese-board to finish. Here you can sample some of the finest cuisine in the Home Counties. The Tapestry Restaurant is open daily for lunch and dinner. breakfast is served in the Conservatory with wonderful views of the Chilterns.

There is also a terrace, situated beside the swimming pool, where lunch or afternoon tea can be served on warm summer days. A visit to Stocks is thoroughly recommended whether on business or pleasure; you will find the staff are pleasant and helpful. Your 'Home from Home' in the country.

Stocks Country House Hotel
Stocks Road
Aldbury
Nr Tring
Hertfordshire HP23 5RX
Tel: (044285) 341
Fax: (044285) 253

HERTS, BEDS & ESSEX
COMPLETE GOLF

HERTFORDSHIRE

Aldenham G. and C.C.
(0923) 853929
Radlett Rd. Aldenham, Watford
(18)6344 yards/***/B

Ashridge G.C.
(044284) 2244
Little Gaddesden, Berkhamstead
North of Northchurch on B4506.
(18)6508 yards/***/A

Batchwood Hall G.C.
(0727) 52101
Batchwood Drive, St. Albans
North West St. Albans.
(18)6463 yards/***/E

Berkhamstead G.C.
(0442) 863730
The Common, Berkhamstead
(18)6568 yards/***/A/H/M

Bishops Stortford G.C.
(0279) 654027
Dunmow Rd. Bishops Stortford
Just to the east of Bishops Stortford.
(18)6449 yards/**/C/H

Boxmoor G.C.
(0442) 242434
18 Box Lane, Hemel Hempstead
2 miles from Hemel Hempstead.
(9)4854 yards/***(Su)/D

Brickendon Grange G.C.
(099286) 228
Brickendon, Hertford
3 miles south of Hertford.
(18)6315 yards/**/C/H

Brookmans Park G.C.
(0707) 52487
Golf Club Rd. Hatfield
(18)6454 yards/**/C

Bushey Hall G.C.
(0923) 225802
Bushey Hall Drive, Bushey
1 mile south east of Watford.
(18)6071 yards/**/C/H

Chadwell Springs G.C.
(0920) 463647
Hertford Rd. Ware
Between Hertford and Ware on A119.
(9)3209 yards/**/C

Cheshunt G.C.
(0992) 24009
Park Lane, Cheshunt
(18)6608 yards/***/E

Chorleywood G.C.
(0923) 282009
Common Rd. Chorleywood
3 miles west of Rickmansworth.
(9)2838 yards/**/(Tue,Thu)/D

East Herts G.C.
(0920) 821923
Hamels Park, Buntingford
1 mile north of Puckeridge on A10.
(18)6449 yards/**(Wed)/B/H/M

Family Golf Centre
(0462) 482929
Jack's Hill, Graveley, Stevenage
(18)6630 yards/***/D

Hanbury Manor Hotel & G.C.
(0920) 487722
Thundridge, Ware
8 miles north of M25 junction 25
(18)6900 yards/***/A

Harpenden G.C.
(0582) 712580
Hammonds End, Redbourne Lane, Harpenden
4 miles north of St. Albans.
(18)6363 yards/**/C/H

Harpenden Common G.C.
(0582) 712856
East Common, Harpenden
(18)5659 yards/**/C

Knebworth G.C.
(0438) 814681
Deards End Lane, Knebworth
1 mile south of Stevenage on B197.
(18)6428 yards/**/F/H

Letchworth G.C.
(0462) 683203
Letchworth Lane, Letchworth
Near Willian Village.
(18)6181 yards/**/B/H/M

Little Hay G.C.
(0442) 833798
Box Lane, Hemel Hempstead
(18)6610 yards/***/E

London Hatfield Country Club
(0707) 32624
Essendon
(18)6500 yards/***/C

Mid Herts G.C.
(058283) 2242
Gustard Wood, Wheathampstead, St. Albans
6 miles north of St. Albans.
(18)6060 yards/**/F

Moor Park G.C.
(0923) 773146
Moor Park Mansion, Moor Park,
Rickmansworth
Between Rickmansworth and
Northwood on A404.
(18)6713 yards/**/F
(18)5815 yards/**/F

Panshanger G.C.
(0707) 338507
Herns Lane, Welwyn Garden City
1 mile north east of Welwyn.
(18)6538 yards/***/E

Porters Park G.C.
(0923) 854127
Shenley Hill, Radlett
(18)6313 yards/**/A/H

Potters Bar G.C.
(0707) 52020
Darkers Lane, Potters Bar
North of Barnet off A1000
(18)6273 yards/**/F/H

Redbourn G.C.
(0582) 793493
Moor Lane, Rickmansworth
(18)6407 yards/**/D
(9)1361 yards/**/E

Rickmansworth G.C.
(0923) 775278
Moor Lane, Rickmansworth
(18)4412 yards/***/E

Royston G.C.
(0763) 242696
Baldock Rd. Royston
Between Baldock and Royston on A505.
(18)6032 yards/**/C

Sandy Lodge G.C.
(0923) 825429
Sandy Lodge Lane, Northwood
Next to Moor Park Station
(18)6340 yards/**/B/M/H

Stevenage G.C.
(043888) 424
Aston Lane, Aston, Stevenage
(18)6451 yards/***/E

Verulam G.C.
(0727) 53327
London Rd. St. Albans
(18)6432 yards/**/C

Welwyn Garden City G.C.
(0707) 325243
Mannicotts, High Oaks Rd. Welwyn
(18)6200 yards/**/B

West Herts G.C.
(0923) 224264
Cassiobury Park, Watford
2 miles south of Watford on A412.
(18)6488 yards/**/C/H

Whipsnade Park G.C.
(044284) 2330
Studham Lane, Dagnall
Between Dagnall and Studham.
(18)6735 yards/**/C

BEDFORDSHIRE

Aspley Guise and Woburn Sands G.C.
(0908) 583596
West Hill, Aspley Guise, Milton Keynes
Between Aspley Guise and Woburn Sands
on A5130.
(18)6248 yards/**/C/H

Aylesbury Vale G.C.
(0525) 240196
Wing, Leighton Buzzard
(18)6711 yards/***/C/H

Beadlow Manor Hotel G. & C.C.
(0525) 60800
Beadlow, Shefford
(18)6238 yards/***/F
(9)6042 yards/***/F

Bedford and County G.C.
(0234) 352617
Green Lane, Clapham
Off A6 north of Bedford.
(18)6347 yards/**/B/H

Bedfordshire G.C.
(0234) 53241
Bromham Rd. Biddenham
2 miles from Bedford on A428.
(18)6172 yards/**/B

Dunstable Downs G.C.
(0582) 604472
Whipsnade Rd. Dunstable
(18)6184 yards/**/F

John O'Gaunt G.C.
(0767) 260360
Sutton Park, Sandy
On B1040 to Potton.
(18)6513 yards/***/A/H
(18)5882 yards/***/A/H

Leighton Buzzard G.C.
(0525) 373811
Plantation Rd. Leighton Buzzard
(18)5454 yards/**(Tue)/C/H

Charles Crombie   RULE XV   Rosenstiel's

99

EPPING FOREST GOLF AND COUNTRY CLUB

Only minutes from Junction 5 of the M11, Epping Forest Golf and Country Club boasts one of the finest all round leisure centres in Southern England, with a host of indoor and outdoor activities to complement the 170 majestic acres that surround it. This impressive site is currently being developed into a superb 18-hole championship golf course which will include two luxurious club houses, changing facilities, dining area and a pro-shop.

The main Elizabethan house, Woolston Hall, overlooks the outdoor heated swimming pool, open all year round and set amidst a landscaped enclosure beneath exotic palm trees. Only a few seconds walk from the pool are five outdoor floodlit hard tennis courts, with professional coaching available. At Gina's, the health and sports complex visitors can choose from a range of vigorous or relaxing activities including squash, the fully equipped gymnasium, aerobics, badminton, table tennis and a sauna and steam room.

Evening entertainment comes in the exciting shape of a stylishly refurbished nightclub, which caters for all tastes and ages. The first floor restaurant provides a mouth-watering selection of meals throughout the evening.

The centre piece of Epping Forest Golf and Country Club is the

magnificent 18-hole golf course, designed by Neil Coles M.B.E. ready for play in early 1994. The course boasts superb natural hazards in the form of an existing river, mature trees in copses and woodland, and three beautiful lakes have been added. At 6435 yards, Par 72, it is ideal for club members and will offer an enjoyable yet challenging experience for all standards of golfer. The 18th hole will perhaps provide the most abiding memory - a par four of modest length, the green sits close by a lake with bunkers beyond, thus ensuring a finale not only for player, but also for spectators looking out from the terrace and the clubhouse.

To complete the picture the course is complemented by a floodlit golf range, chipping green and practice bunker. A flexible range of memberships are available and are sure to prove tremendously popular at this first class Golf and Sporting Complex.

For further information please contact:

Caroline Carter - Golf Membership 081-500 2549

Paul Gilbert - Golf Pro. (0836) 34516 (Mobile)

Epping Forest Golf and Country Club
Woolston Hall
Abridge Road
Chigwell
Essex
Tel: 081-501 0011
Fax: 081-559 8409

Millbrook G.C.
(0525) 404683
Millbrook, Ampthill
In Millbrook village.
(18)6473 yards/**(Thu)/D

Mowsbury G.C.
(0234) 216374
Cleat Hill, Kimbolton Rd
2 miles north of Bedford.
(18)6514 yards/***/E

South Beds G.C.
(0582) 591500
Warden Hill Rd. Luton
3 miles from Luton.
(18)6342 yards/**/C/H
(9)2590 yards/**/E/H

Stockwood Park G.C.
(0582) 413704
Stockwood Park, London Rd. Luton
(18)5964 yards/***/E

Tilsworth G.C.
(0525) 219722
Dunstable Rd. Tilsworth, Leighton Buzzard
(9)5443 yards/***/E

Wyboston Lakes G.C.
(0480) 212501
Wyboston Lakes, Wyboston
South of St. Neots off A1.
(18)5721 yards/***/C

ESSEX

Abridge G. and C.C.
(04028) 396
Epping Lane, Stapleford Tawney, Abridge
(18)6703 yards/**/A/H

Ballards Gore G.C.
(07022) 58917
Gore Rd.Canedon, Rochford
2 miles east of Rochford.
(18)7062 yards/**/C

Basildon G.C.
(0268) 533297
Clay Hill Lane, Basildon
(18)6122 yards/***/E

Belfairs Park G.C.
(0702) 526911
Eastwood Road North, Leigh-on-Sea
(18)5871 yards/***/E

Belhus Park G.C.
(0708) 854260
Belhus Park, South Ockendon
(18)5900 yards/***/E

Bentley G.C.
(0277) 373179
Ongar Rd. Brentwood
4 miles north of Brentwood.
(18)6709 yards/**/C/H/L

Birch Grove G.C.
(0206) 34276
Layer Rd. Colchester
2 miles south of Colchester.
(9)4076 yards/***/E

Boyce Hill G.C.
(0268) 793625
Vicarage Hill, South Benfleet
7 miles west of Southend-on-Sea.
(18)5882 yards/**/B

Braintree G.C.
(0376) 46079
Kings Lane, Sisted, Braintree
2 miles north of Braintree on A120.
(18)6026 yards/**/C

Bunsay Downs G.C.
(0245) 412648
Little Baddow Rd. Woodham Walter, Maldon
2 miles west of Woodham Walter.
(9)2913 yards/***/D

Burnham-on-Crouch G.C.
(0621) 782282
Ferry Rd. Creeksea, Burnham-on-Crouch
(9)5350 yards/**/C/M

Canons Brook G.C.
(0279) 421482
Elizabeth Way, Harlow
(18)6462 yards/**/B

Castle Point G.C.
(0268) 510830
Somnes Avenue, Canvey Island
(18)5627 yards/***/E

Channels G.C.
(0245) 440005
Belsteads Farm Lane, Little Waltham, Chelmsford
(18)6100 yards/**/B/H

Chelmsford G.C.
(0245) 256483
Widford Rd. Chelmsford
(18)5912 yards/**/B/M

Clacton-on-Sea G.C.
(0255) 421919
West Rd. Clacton-on-Sea
1 mile west of Clacton pier.
(18)6244 yards/***/B/H

Colchester G.C.
(0206) 853396
Braiswick, Colchester
1 mile north of town on B1508.
(18)6319 yards/***/C

Earls Cone G.C.
(0787) 224466
Earls Cone, Colchester
(18)6842 yards/***/C

Fairlop Waters G.C.
081-500 9911
Barkingside, Ilford
(18)6288 yards/***/E

Forrester Park G.C.
(0621) 891406
Beckingham Rd. Great Totham, Maldon
3 miles north of Maldon.
(9)2675 yards/***/D

Frinton G.C.
(0255) 674618
Esplanade, Frinton-on-Sea
(18)6259 yards/**/B/H

Gosfield Lakes G.C.
(0787) 474747
7 miles north of Braintree
(18)6512 yards/**/C/H
(9)1354 yards/***/E

Hanover G. & C.C.
(0702) 230033
Hullbridge Road, Rayleigh
(18)6800 yards/**/B

Hartswood G.C.
(0277) 218714
King George's Playing Fields, Brentwood
(18)6238 yards/***/E

Harwich and Dovercourt G.C.
(0255) 3616
Station Rd. Parkeston, Harwich
(9)5692 yards/***/F/H

Havering G.C.
(0708) 741429
Risebridge Chase, Lower Bedfords Rd. Romford
2 miles from Gallows Corner off A12.
(18)5237 yards/***/D

Langdon Hills G.C.
(0268) 548061
Bulphan
SW of Basildon, M25 junction 29
(18)6485 yards/***/B/H

Maldon G.C.
(0621) 853212
Beeleig, Langford, Maldon
2 miles north of Maldon on B1019.
(9)6197 yards/**/C/H

Maylands G. and C.C.
(04023) 73080
Colchester Rd. Harold Park, Romford
Between Romford and Brentwood on A12.
(18)6182 yards/**/C/M

Orsett G.C.
(0375) 891352
Brentwood Rd. Orsett
(18)6614 yards/**/B/H

Pipps Hill G.C.
(0268) 23456
Cranes Farm Rd. Basildon
(9)2829 yards/***/F

Quietwaters Hotel & C.C.
(0621) 860410
Tolleshunt Knights, nr Maldon
(18)6194 yards/***/C
(18)6765 yards/***/A

Rochford Hundred G.C.
(0702) 544302
Rochford Hall, Hall Rd. Rochford
4 miles north of Southend.
(18)6255 yards/**/B/H

Romford G.C.
(0708) 740007
Heath Drive, Gidea Park, Romford
2 miles from Romford off A12.
(18)6365 yards/**/B/H/M

Saffron Walden G.C.
(0799) 522786
Windmill Hill, Saffron Walden
(18)6608 yards/**/B/H

Skips G.C.
(04023) 48234
Horsemanside, Tysea Hill, Stapleford
(18)6146 yards/*/F

Stapleford Abbots G.C.
(04023) 81108
3 miles north of Romford
(18)6487 yards/**/C
(18)5965 yards/**/C
(9)1140 yards/**/C

Stoke-by-Nayland G.C.
(006) 262836
Keepers Lane, Leavenheath, Colchester
(18)6471 yards/***/B/H/M
(18)6498 yards/***/B/H/M

Theydon Bois G.C.
(0992) 813054
Theydon Rd. Epping
1 mile south of Epping off B172.
(18)5472 yards/***/A/H/M

Thorndon Park G.C.
(0277) 810345
Ingrave, Brentwood
2 miles south of Brentwood on A128.
(18)6455 yards/**/A

Thorpe Hall G.C.
(0702) 582205
Thorpe Hall Ave. Thorpe Bay
(18)6286 yards/**/B/H

Three Rivers G. and C.C.
(0621) 828631
Stow Rd. Purleigh, Nr. Chelmsford
(18)6609 yards/**/C/H
(9)2142 yards/**/C/H

Toot Hill G.C.
(0277) 365523
Toot Hill, Ongar
(18)6013 yards/*/G

Towerlands G.C.
(0376) 552487
Panfield Rd. Braintree
Just out of town on B1053.
(9)2698 yards/***/E
(18)5406 yards/***/D

Upminster G.C.
(04022) 20249
114 Hall Lane, Upminster
(18)5926 yards/**/C/M

Warley Park G.C.
(0277) 224891
Magpie Lane, Little Warley
M25 junction 29
(27)(3 x 9)/**/B

Warren G.C.
(024541) 3258
Woodham Walter, Maldon
6 miles east of Chelmsford on A414.
(18)6211 yards/**/B

West Essex G.C.
081-5290928
Sewardstonebury, Chingford
(18) 6289 yards/**/B/H

Woodford G.C.
081-5040553
2 Sunset Ave. Woodford Green
10 miles from London.
(9)5806 yards/**/C

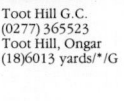

A.B Frost   TEMPER   Rosenstiel's

BERKS, BUCKS & OXON

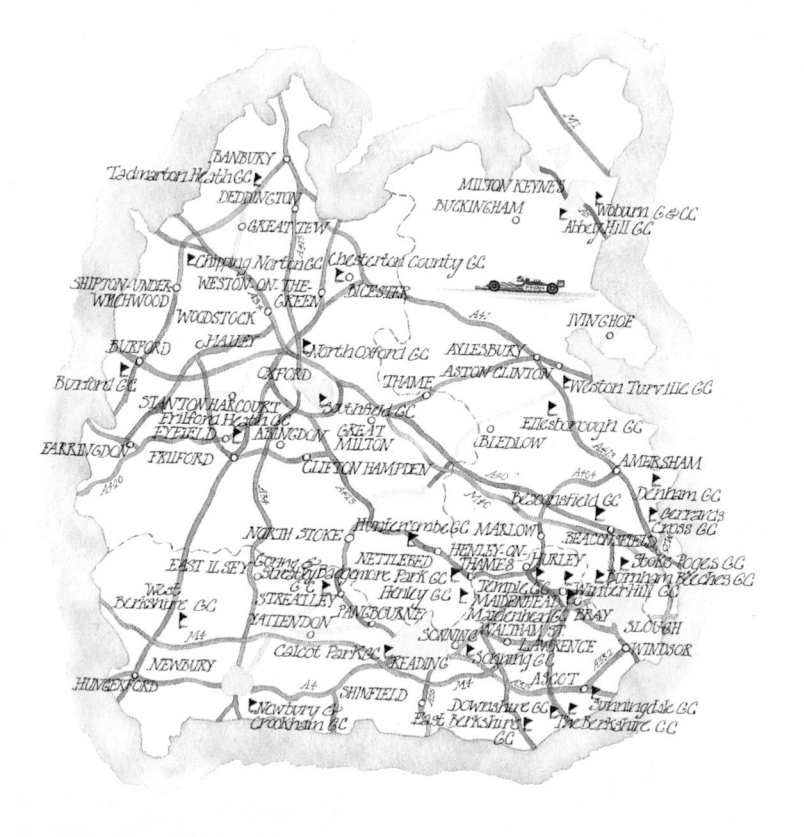

H. Rountree STOKE POGES Sarah Baddiel's Book Gallery

BERKS, BUCKS & OXON
CHOICE GOLF

Berkshire, Buckinghamshire and Oxfordshire – three very English counties, don't you think? From Burnham Beeches to Banbury Cross, the region extends from the edge of the Chilterns to the edge of the Cotswolds and occupies a very prosperous part of southern Britain.

OXFORDSHIRE

We start at **Huntercombe**, a charming Golf Club which has enjoyed an interesting history. In the early years of the century three rather old Daimler motor cars were used to ferry Members to and from the local station and later a thirty seater bus was acquired for the same purpose. The course itself has passed through various owners – at first a property company, then an insurance company (the Norwich Union) and later Viscount Nuffield before finally becoming a Members Club in 1963. Situated on the edge of the Chilterns at some 700 feet above sea level there are some marvellous views across the Oxford Plain. The course itself is fairly flat and is always kept in first class condition. Nearby in Henley there are two courses worth inspecting, the more established **Henley** Golf Club and **Badgemore Park**, a fairly new course but one that has settled down quickly.

A suitable 19th hole? In Henley The Red Lion (0491) 572161 is a commendable hotel. In Nettlebed, the White Hart (0491) 641245 is a pleasing inn with some good value bedrooms (very handy for Huntercombe) and North Stoke offers the excellent Spring Hotel (0491) 36687 with its first class restaurant, the Fourways (not Fairways).

As The Berkshire has a Red and Blue, so **Frilford Heath** has a Red and a Green. Both of Frilford's 18 hole challenges – and challenge is certainly the word – are exceptionally fine heathland courses and the Club can proudly and justly boast the best golf in the county. Frilford Heath is featured later in this chapter. Good food and drink can be found in nearby Fyfield at The White Hart and in Frilford itself at Noah's Ark (0865) 391470. A short trip to Abingdon can also be recommended, here the Upper Reaches Hotel (0235) 522311 is most welcoming.

Oxford is actually not all that far away. There are two courses either side of the town – **North Oxford** and **Southfield** both are certainly worth a game. The latter is the home of Oxford University. The Randolph (0865) 247481 is the pick of the Oxford hotels, and for first class restaurants, the Cherwell Boathouse (0865) 52746 is certainly among the best. Oxford, naturally, is more than a little used to visitors of all tastes and for reasonably priced accommodation, try Cotswold House (0865) 310558. Outside in Cumnor, The Bear and Ragged Staff serves good food while a little further afield in Stanton Harcourt, The Harcourt Arms (0865) 310630 has a tremendous atmosphere, a good restaurant and excellent accommodation. Another fine restaurant which is near Oxford and within striking distance of Frilford is The Plough at Clanfield (036781) 222. A final recommendation in this area is for the golfing/culinary connoisseur and it is to visit Great Milton and Le Manoir Aux Quat' Saisons (0844) 278881 – possibly the country's finest restaurant.

Back on the fairways (suitably fed one hopes!) and beyond Oxford, there is a flattish parkland course near Bicester, The **Chesterton** Golf Club and a much improved course at **Burford**. Inching up towards the Cotswolds there is a

pleasant course at **Chipping Norton** but the best in the north of the county is clearly **Tadmarton Heath**. At less than 6000 yards in length, it is fairly short by modern standards, but the narrow fairways and a great spread of gorse can make it a very difficult test. It also has a wonderfully remote setting. Not far away, the village of Deddington provides an admirable place to rest the heather-clad spikes, more specifically, the Holcombe Hotel (and restaurant) (0869) 38274 while Burford offers the Lamb (099382) 3155, a truly charming Cotswold inn.

BUCKINGHAMSHIRE

Moving into Buckinghamshire, **Woburn** stands rather alone in the far north of the county. The Golf and Country Club is featured ahead, but a brief thought on where to stay: in Woburn Park itself The Paris House (0525) 290692 is highly recommended as is Moore Place (0908) 282000 in nearby Aspley Guise and in Woburn village try the friendly Bedford Arms (0525) 290441. In Milton Keynes, overlooking the **Abbey Hill** public golf course, is the suitably named Friendly Lodge Hotel (0908) 561666. The Red Lion Country Hotel (0908) 583117 is also guaranteed to please.

Heading 'down the county' **Ellesborough**'s golf course is another with rather stately surroundings being located on part of the property of Chequers. Quite a hilly course and rather testing, it is well worth inspecting and not only because there are some commanding views across the Buckinghamshire countryside. Elsewhere in the centre of the county, there is a fairly lengthy parkland course at **Weston Turville**, south of Aylesbury.

Ideas for a 19th hole in these parts include in Ivinghoe, The Kings Head (0296) 668388, a splendid restaurant in a 17th century inn and two 'Bells', The Bell (0296) 89835) in Aylesbury's market place and The Bell (0296) 630252 in Aston Clinton (note the superb wine list here). A couple of good pubs to savour are The Rising Sun at Little Hampden and The Fox at Dunsmore.

It is in Southern Buckinghamshire where most of the county's better courses are to be found. **Stoke Poges** has staged many leading amateur events, not at all surprisingly, this being one of the finest parkland courses in the south of England. We have explored Stoke Poges on a later page, but note also **Farnham Park**, a nearby public course.

Denham is a close neighbour of Stoke Poges lying some 3 miles north of Uxbridge, and as an old Club handbook will tell you 'half an hour's drive from Marble Arch'. (Add an extra sixty minutes nowadays if you're attempting the journey during 'Rush Hour'). It is worth making the escape though for Denham enjoys a beautiful setting, deeply secluded amidst some glorious countryside. The Clubhouse is a most unusual building having been built around a 16th century tithe barn.

In equally beautiful surroundings is the **Burnham Beeches** Golf Club, situated approximately 4 miles west of Slough. Always immaculately kept, it has some prodigiously difficult rough. Others to note in southern Buckinghamshire include **Beaconsfield**, **Harewood Downs** (at Chalfont St. Giles) and **Gerrards Cross**, each is again within fairly easy access of the capital.

There are a number of very comfortable hotels in the area.

BERKS, BUCKS & OXON
CHOICE GOLF

These include The Bell-house Hotel (0753) 887211 just outside Beaconsfield, The Burnham Beeches Hotel (0628) 603333, a former hunting lodge – ideal for the golf course, and The Compleat Angler Hotel (0628) 484444 at Marlow Bridge – a superb riverside setting. In Farnham Common, Oscar's (0753) 646211 is an informal restaurant while two good pubs are The Kings Arms in Amersham and The Lions at Bledlow.

BERKSHIRE

Berkshire – or should one say 'Royal Berkshire' – is often described as being cigar-shaped. Now whilst this may not say much for the present day talents of cigar-makers it does serve as a fairly rough description in as much as the county is indeed peculiarly long and thin. When it comes to surveying the county's twenty or so golf courses it is tempting to adopt another cigar analogy in that one end could be said to glow rather more brightly than the other.

To the east of the county there is a famous heathland belt and it is here that the twin pearls of **Sunningdale** and **The Berkshire** are to be found. Both Clubs possess two 18 hole courses which for sheer enjoyment can stand comparison with anything that golf has to offer.

Sunningdale is better known than The Berkshire but it is difficult to imagine a more delightful setting than the tranquil, tree-lined fairways of The Red and The Blue Courses at The Berkshire – and so close to London too. Both Clubs are featured ahead. **Swinley Forest** is the other outstanding heathland course in the area, a veritable paradis terrestre indeed. However this is a very private club and visitors are only permitted to play as guests of Members. Still in heather and pine country is the very attractive **East Berkshire** course at Crowthorne. Also in close proximity is the popular **Downshire** public course where the green fees are naturally less expensive than the above mentioned courses. Windsor is where many visiting the area will choose to spend a night or two. Pride of place must go to Oakley Court (0628) 74141; its comfortable rooms are complemented by splendid grounds and a delightful dining room, The Oak Leaf. Melrose House (0753) 865328 meanwhile, will delight those for whom money is far from no object!

In the Ascot area there are a number of good establishments. The Thatched Tavern (0344) 20874 is a pleasant place to have lunch or dinner while The Berystede Hotel (0344) 23311 is an outstanding place to stay. In Sunninghill, near Ascot, the Royal Berkshire (0344) 23322 is perhaps the creme de la creme and admirably reflects the quality of the nearby courses. However, a night spent in Ascot does not have to be extravagantly expensive; for affordable comfort try The Highclere Hotel (0344) 25220. A good local pub is the Slug and Lettuce in Winkfield Row – a fine atmosphere and a charming restaurant. This area of Berkshire of course borders Surrey and we shouldn't forget its many delights. One tip is Pennyhill Park (0276) 71774 in Bagshot – a superb hotel and very convenient (not to mention appropriate) for the likes of Sunningdale.

Time for some more golf and **Temple's** fine course can be glimpsed from the main A23 Maidenhead to Henley Road. It has an interesting layout with many fine trees and lush fairways. Designed by Willie Park early this century, it was for a number of years the home of Henry Cotton. The course is always maintained in first class condition.

The golf course at **Winter Hill** is on fairly high ground – apparently its name derives from the particularly chilling winds that sweep across in winter (I have no explanation for nearby Crazies Hill!) From the course there are some spectacular views over the Thames – definitely worth a visit. So for that matter is classy **Sonning**, situated further towards Reading. Beyond the boating villages of Goring and Streatly, lies the fairly tough **Goring and Streatly** course also well worth inspecting if in the vicinity.

In Maidenhead, Frederick's Hotel (0628) 35934 has a considerable reputation for comfort, its dining room is also highly acclaimed while in nearby Bray, The Waterside Inn (0628) 20691 is a quite outstanding restaurant. The Boulters Lock Hotel (0628) 21291 on Boulters island, is a delightful place to stay. In Maidenhead, Shoppenhangers Manor (0628) 23444 is a splendid French restaurant located in a charming English Manor and west of Maidenhead, Littlewick Green and the Warrener Restaurant (0628) 822803 are also very highly thought of. North of here in Hurley one finds yet another gem, Ye Olde Bell (062882) 5881, a very popular Norman inn. Meandering further down the Thames, recommended hotels include The White Hart at Sonning (0734) 692277 with its charming Elizabethan courtyard and also in Sonning, The French Horn (0734) 692204 is a super restaurant. Reading offers the reasonably priced Thames House Hotel (0734) 507951. In Streatly, The Swan Diplomat (0491) 873737 has a splendid riverside setting. The restaurant here is extremely good. In need of a pub? A visit to The Bell at Aldworth should do the trick. Another nearby local is the Crown and Horns at East Ilsley.

Finally, two locations with good hotel and restaurant combinations are Pangbourne, The Copper Inn (0734) 842244 and Yattendon, The Royal Oak (0635) 201325.

On the western edge of Reading **Calcot Park** golf course poses many interesting challenges; it can boast Guinness Book of Records fame too in that one sterling fellow sprinted round the course in a motorised cart in just over 24 minutes – a more leisurely round is recommended!

Newbury is of course better known for its racing than its golf, but the **Newbury and Crookham** Golf Club close to Greenham Common is one of the oldest Clubs in Southern England and is again strongly recommended. The course is hilly and well-wooded, though not overly long.

Before leaving Berkshire it is worth noting one of the county's more recent additions, **West Berkshire**, situated just south of the village of Chaddleworth. It is a splendid downland course, but not exactly one for the weak-kneed – it stretches to around the 7000 yard mark with one par five measuring well over 600 yards – a hearty breakfast before playing here is a must!

SUNNINGDALE
CHAMPIONSHIP GOLF

On seeing the spectacularly beautiful 18th hole at **Killarney** during one of his visits to Ireland, the late **Henry Longhurst** declared, 'What a lovely place to die'. Now whilst one rarely wishes to dwell on the subject of meeting our maker, golfers have been known to indulge in a considerable amount of speculation as to the type of course they might find on the arrival of such an occasion. There is a story of one heated discussion which involved, quite by chance, an Englishman, a Scotsman and an American. The latter argued with great conviction that a large number of the holes would, as sure as hell, resemble **Augusta**, whilst the Scotsman vehemently insisted that even the most minute deviation from the **Old Course** at **St Andrews** would constitute an act of heresy; as for the Englishman, he naturally had no doubts whatsoever that he could stroll through the Pearly Gates and meet a second **Sunningdale**.

Well, perhaps the heavenly blend is a mixture of all three, but in any event, the gentleman in charge of the terrestrial Sunningdale is the Secretary, **Stewart Zuill**. Mr. Zuill may be contacted on **(0344) 21681**. **Keith Maxwell** is the Club's resident professional and he can be reached on **(0344) 20128**. As with neighbouring Wentworth and The Berkshire there are two eighteen hole courses, the **Old**, designed in 1900 by **Willie Park** and the **New** which was constructed by **Harry Colt** in 1922. Both are splendid, and many would say the leading examples of the famous Berkshire/Surrey heathland type course. The holes wind their way through glorious forests of conifer and pine with heather, bracken and gorse bordering each fairway. All around there are splashes of silver sand.

With its great reputation and close proximity to the capital, Sunningdale is not surprisingly very popular. Unless accompanied by a Member visitors are restricted to weekdays and must make prior arrangement with the Secretary. A letter of introduction is also required. All written communications should be addressed to Mr. Zuill at **The Sunningdale Golf Club, Ridgemount Road, Sunningdale, Berkshire SL5 9RW**. In 1992 the green fee was set at £84. This entitled the visitor to a full day's golf, enabling a round over both courses. Sets of clubs can be hired from the professional shop should the need arise. Persons keen to organise a Society meeting are also advised to approach Mr. Zuill via the above address.

Sunningdale is situated just off the A30, about 28 miles West of

London. Motoring from the South and West the M3, (leaving at junction 3) and the M4 (junction 10) may be of assistance, while from the North both the A332 and the A330 pass through nearby Ascot. The Club's precise location is some 300 yards from Sunningdale Railway Station.

When golfers talk of Sunningdale, invariably it is the Old Course they have in mind, this despite the fact that a large number of people consider the New to be its equal. The former has acquired such pre-eminence largely as a result of the many major professional and amateur tournaments that have been staged there. However the Old Course is perhaps best known for a single round of golf played by the legendary **Bobby Jones**. In qualifying for the 1926 Open Championship, which he in fact went on to win, the great man put together what has often been described as the finest 18 holes of golf ever seen. Jones' record 66, a remarkable achievement in the 1920s, comprised twelve fours and six threes – 33 for the front nine and 33 for the back nine. More amazingly Jones played only 33 shots from tee to green and took 33 putts – as Bernard Darwin put it, 'incredible and indecent'.

In more recent years Sunningdale has been repeatedly selected to host the prestigious European Open. During the 1970s the finest lady golfers assembled for the Colgate sponsored European WPGA Championship and in 1987 the Walker Cup was played at Sunningdale.

At 6341 yards (par 70) the Old Course is more than three hundred yards shorter than the New (6676 yards, par 70). The respective distances from the Ladies tees are 5825 yards and 5840 yards (both being par 74). It seems somehow wrong to single out individual holes, each course possessing its own wealth of variety and charm. The views from the **5th** and **10th** tees on the Old Course are, however, particularly outstanding and the **18th** also provides a spectacular closing hole as it gently dog-legs towards the green and the giant spreading oak tree, very much the symbol of Sunningdale.

Sunningdale's glorious setting has been described as both 'heavenly' and 'hauntingly beautiful'. Certainly the golfer privileged to stroll up the final fairway on a summer's evening as the sun begins its leisurely dip, can be forgiven if he amends the words of Henry Longhurst and declares 'What a lovely place to be alive!'

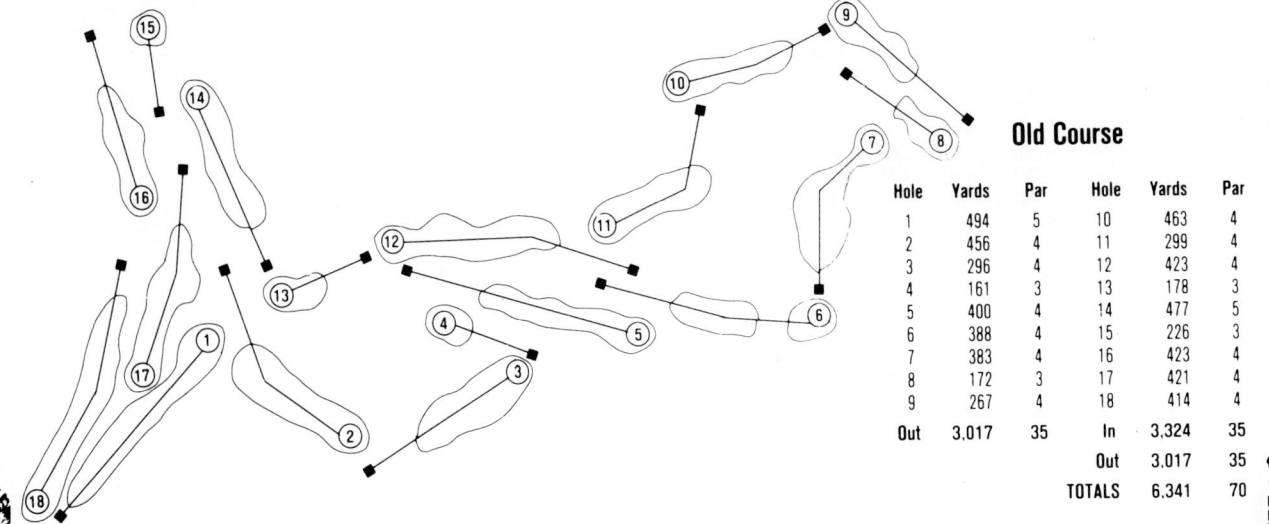

Old Course

Hole	Yards	Par	Hole	Yards	Par
1	494	5	10	463	4
2	456	4	11	299	4
3	296	4	12	423	4
4	161	3	13	178	3
5	400	4	14	477	5
6	388	4	15	226	3
7	383	4	16	423	4
8	172	3	17	421	4
9	267	4	18	414	4
Out	3,017	35	In	3,324	35
			Out	3,017	35
			TOTALS	6,341	70

THE BERKSHIRE
CHAMPIONSHIP GOLF

The horse racing, golf playing residents of Ascot must number among the luckiest folk in England for right on their door steps lie the cream of each sport. They have of course, three golfing pearls close at hand, Sunningdale, Wentworth and The Berkshire, the youngest of the illustrious trio.

The two eighteen hole courses of The Berkshire, the **'Red'** and the **'Blue'**, were designed in 1928 by **Herbert Fowler** – a master among golf architects whose other great works include Walton Heath and Saunton. They occupy some 400 acres of Crown Land over which Queen Anne's carriage used to pass en route to the hunting in Swinley Forest.

Today, both courses give the appearance of having been hewn out of a dense forest, rather in the way that the Duke and Duchess courses were created at Woburn. This, in fact, was not the case, as much clearing of the ancient forest occurred during the First World War when the land was used for military purposes and most of the present thick woodland is of comparatively recent origin.

The Berkshire has been described as being primarily a 'Members' Club', this largely through the conspicuous absence of any big-time professional golf tournament. Perhaps the Club does not wish to have its tranquillity stirred or its rough trampled over by hordes of excited spectators, but this does not imply that the club closes its doors to the outside world, or makes visitors unwelcome. Indeed, The Berkshire is a busy and popular Club with a great number of Societies the large majority of which choose to return year after year. For individual visitors, no less than Societies, booking with the Secretary is essential and **Major P.D. Clarke** is the gentleman in question. He can be contacted at **The Berkshire Golf Club, Swinley Road, Ascot, Berkshire, SL5 8AY.** Tel: **(0344) 21496**. It should be emphasised that unless otherwise invited, visitors are only permitted to play the course during weekdays. Green fees for 1992 were set at £40 for a single round with £55 payable for a day ticket, this securing a game on both courses – something to be strongly recommended. If clubs need to be hired the professional, **Keith MacDonald** can assist – some forewarning is advisable. He can be contacted on **(0344) 22351**.

The Berkshire can be reached easily from London. It lies just off the A332 road between Ascot and Bagshot. The A332 can be joined from Windsor to the north and Guildford to the south, while motoring from Reading and the West, the M4 should be left at junction 10 and the A329 followed to Ascot.

The two courses are of fairly similar length – the Red slightly longer, measuring 6369 yards to the Blue's 6260 yards, although the latter's par is one fewer at 71. The Red course is perhaps the better known of the two, to some extent due to its comprising an unusual six par threes, six par fours and six par fives. In any event, most people agree that there is little to choose between the two, both in terms of beauty and degree of difficulty, moreover there are many who claim that the golf at The Berkshire is as good, if not better than that offered by its more celebrated neighbours.

The Berkshire is especially famed for its glorious tree-lined fairways. There is a splendid mix of mature pines, chestnuts and silver birch and both courses are kept in the most superb condition. Much of the rough consists of heather ensuring that the wayward hitter is heavily punished.

The Club may have avoided professional tournaments, but it does play host to a number of important amateur events. The Berkshire Trophy is one of the annual highlights on the amateur calendar and before turning professional Messrs. **Faldo** and **Lyle** were both winners. It is an open event for players with a handicap limit of one. A major ladies amateur open, the Astor Salver, is also played at The Berkshire, with a handicap limit of six.

As for its 19th hole, the Club possesses one of the country's largest and grandest Clubhouses; furthermore, it has a reputation for providing the most stupendous roast lunches. A fine fellow by the name of Sam is responsible for these veritable feasts. So then, how about 18 holes on the Blue, one of 'Sam's specials' and then 18 on the Red – can you think of a better way to spend a day?

Red Course

Hole	Yards	Par	Hole	Yards	Par
1	517	5	10	188	3
2	147	3	11	350	4
3	480	5	12	328	4
4	395	4	13	486	5
5	178	3	14	434	4
6	360	4	15	477	5
7	195	3	16	221	3
8	428	4	17	532	5
9	478	5	18	175	3
Out	3,178	36	In	3,191	36
			Out	3,178	36
			TOTALS	6,369	72

Blue Course

Hole	Yards	Par	Hole	Yards	Par
1	217	3	10	199	3
2	344	4	11	477	5
3	475	5	12	355	4
4	153	3	13	154	3
5	330	4	14	363	4
6	476	5	15	406	4
7	364	4	16	452	4
8	404	4	17	378	4
9	310	4	18	403	4
Out	3,073	36	In	3,187	35
			Out	3,073	36
			TOTALS	6,260	71

WOBURN
CHAMPIONSHIP GOLF

A magnificent stately home housing one of the finest art collections in the world, the largest wildlife safari park in Europe and two of the finest inland golf courses in Britain – quite a place Woburn!

The Stately Home is of course **Woburn Abbey** which since the reign of Henry VIII has been the home of the Dukes of Bedford, while the Wildlife Park and the golf courses lie within the grounds of the great estate.

In a game that prides itself on its antiquity **The Woburn Golf and Country Club** might be described as a remarkably precocious youngster. It was founded as recently as 1976 and its two courses, aptly named the **Duke's** and **Duchess**, were not opened until 1977 and 1979 respectively. In such a short period of time Woburn has acquired an enviable reputation.

In charge of all golfing matters at Woburn is **Alex Hay** whose Celtic tones are well-known to millions of television viewers. Mr. Hay acts as both Managing Director and resident professional. In the former capacity he may be contacted on **(0908) 370756** and when donning his golf professional hat can be reached by telephone on **(0908) 647987**, and by fax on (0908) 378436

Visitors, Societies and Company Days are all welcome from Monday to Friday at Woburn, although prior booking is essential. In addition, visitors must be Members of recognised golf clubs and be able to provide proof of handicap. All written enquiries should be addressed to the **Managing Director, Woburn Golf and Country Club, Bow Brickhill, Milton Keynes, MK17 9LJ**. The green fees for 1992 were set at £89.35 per person per day for parties of nine and above, and £65 for parties of less than nine. This fee is inclusive of golf and lunch while dinner can also be arranged if there are 24 people or more.

Having booked a game, travelling to Woburn ought not to present too many problems. The Club is located approximately 45 miles from London and 73 miles from Birmingham and is well-served by major roads. Both the M1 (junction 13) and the A5 pass close by. For those using British Rail, Bletchley Station, some 4 miles away has good connections from both London and Birmingham. Luton and Heathrow Airports are also within fairly easy reach. The town of Woburn and the Abbey are both actually within the county of Bedfordshire while the Golf and Country Club lies a short distance over the boundary in Buckinghamshire; presumably the lions amble from county to county.

Twenty years ago if someone had suggested that a Championship Course (never mind two) could have been built on the Woburn Estate, the famous lions would probably not have been the only ones to roar. The present site was then a dense forest, with giant trees and bracken restricting vision beyond a few yards. Golf architect **Charles Lawrie** of Cotton Pennink was called in and plans were drawn up. The bulldozers soon arrived and from amidst the pines and the chestnuts great avenues were carved. The fairways flourished on the sandy subsoil and within two years of opening, The Duke's Course was considered fit to stage a major professional tournament. It proved a popular decision and a succession of sponsors decided to follow suit. Following its opening the Duchess matured with equal rapidity and Woburn soon possessed two precious gems.

The tournaments held at Woburn have included numerous British Masters Championships, The Ford Ladies Classic and the Weetabix Women's British Open. Under the sponsorship of Dunhill, Woburn has in fact become something of a home for the British Masters event, and winners have included such great names as **Trevino, McNulty, Ballesteros, Lyle** and **Faldo**. During the 1992 event, won in such thrilling style by **Christy O'Connor Jnr**, Bernhard Langer was quoted as saying of the Duke's Course, 'It is as good a golf course as we play all year'.

From the back markers (or tiger tees?) the Duke's Course stretches to 6940 yards (par 72), while the Duchess measures 6616 yards (par 71). The corresponding distances for the ladies are 6065 yards (par 75) and 5831 yards (par 74). The best hole at Woburn? Not easy when there are 36 to choose from, but many single out the picturesque short **3rd** on the Duke's Course; for my money however, the **13th** is one of the best par fours in the country.

As one might expect from a modern Golf and Country Club the facilities at Woburn are excellent. The newly rebuilt and refurbished Clubhouse offers a full complement of catering, though dinners must be pre-arranged. For the sporty types there is tennis and an open-air heated swimming pool. The majority of golfers, however, will probably head for one of the two Bars.....and toast the Duke and the Duchess.

Duke's Course

Hole	Yards	Par	Hole	Yards	Par
1	514	5	10	404	4
2	385	4	11	502	5
3	134	3	12	193	3
4	395	4	13	419	4
5	510	5	14	565	5
6	207	3	15	432	4
7	464	4	16	449	4
8	409	4	17	425	4
9	177	3	18	356	4
Out	**3,195**	**35**	**In**	**3,745**	**37**
			Out	3,195	35
			Totals	**6,940**	**72**

MOORE PLACE

When Francis Moore built his elegant Georgian mansion in the tranquil Bedfordshire village of Aspley Guise in 1786 he could never have imagined it would be such a focal point for hospitality 200 years later. Thoughtfully renovated and extended, the original house now has a Victorian style conservatory restaurant, and a collection of new bedrooms which create a courtyard effect, featuring a rock garden and water cascade. The hotel's attractive day rooms – including an airy, glass roofed reception and relaxing bar-lounge – are decorated and furnished in handsome period style.

The 54 prettily decorated bedrooms all have ensuite bathrooms, direct dial telephone, colour television, tea and coffee making facilities and hairdryer.

There are 3 private function rooms in this charming Georgian house, where banquets and conferences are well provided for. The rooms are traditionally decorated, yet equipped with full audio-visual facilities.

The highly acclaimed restaurant is an outstanding success. Accomplished cooking in the modern mode can be enjoyed in the beautiful, picture windowed restaurant. Excellent cuisine is complemented by a good selection of fine wines. Moore Place is surrounded by interesting places to visit, such as the Duke of Bedford's Woburn Abbey, Dunstable Downs and Whipsnade Zoo. Woburn golf course is also nearby.

Moore Place,
Aspley Guise,
Nr Woburn, Beds MK17 8DW
Tel: (0908) 282000
Fax: (0908) 281888

STOKE POGES
CHAMPIONSHIP GOLF

'The first thing we do, let's kill all the lawyers.' Never utter this Shakespearean line at Stoke Poges. Not only will it insult some of the members but it will likely stir the former Lord of the Manor. **Sir Edward Coke**, the first Lord Chief Justice of England (and the judge who put paid to Guy Fawkes) once owned the estate on which Stoke Poges Golf Club now stands and his presence is still greatly felt for his towering monument can be seen from many parts of the course.

While no one seriously disputes that the best golf in the Home Counties is to be found south west of London, especially in the celebrated heathland belt of Surrey and Berkshire, to continually visit the heather and gorse can get a little frustrating at times. For this reason alone there is good cause for investigating Stoke Poges, near Slough in southern Buckinghamshire. But there are many better reasons for doing so.

Stoke Poges is arguably the finest parkland course in the south of England; it is certainly one of the loveliest and its palatial mansion Clubhouse is one of the most historic and attractive that any keen follower of the fairways is likely to come across.

Writing in 1910, just a year after golf first came to Stoke Poges, **Bernard Darwin** gave his opinion on the merits of the site. 'It is a beautiful spot, and there is very good golf to be played here; the club is an interesting one, moreover, as being one of the first and most ambitious attempts in England at what is called in America, a Country Club, there are plenty of things to do at Stoke besides playing golf. We may get very hot at lawn tennis or keep comparatively cool at bowls or croquet, or, coolest of all, we may sit on the terrace or in the garden and give ourselves wholly and solely to loafing.'

Well, the good news is it's still a marvellously relaxing place!

Visitors who wish to play golf, as opposed to loaf, should first approach the Club's Secretary, **Mr. R.C. Pickering**. He and his very helpful staff may be contacted by telephone on **(0753) 526385** or by writing to **The Stoke Poges Golf Club, North Drive, Park Road, Stoke Poges, Slough SL2 4PG**. Visitors (including Societies) are welcome between Mondays and Fridays with the exception of Tuesday mornings. All players must possess a handicap. Stoke Poges professional **Kim Thomas** can be reached on **(0753) 523609.**

The green fees for 1992 are £27 per round, £37 per day. A reduced rate of £20 is payable after 5pm. Junior golfers under the age of 14 and accompanied by an adult pay £10 per round.

The precise location of the golf course is 2 miles from the centre of Slough via the B416. Travellers from London should head towards Stoke Poges using either the M4 (junction 6) or the A40 (leaving at Gerrards Cross). Approaching from the south and west the M3 (junction 3) and the M4 (junction 6) are likely to prove helpful while from the north and midlands the route is by way of the M1 (junction 8) then through Chesham, Amersham and Beaconsfield.

Stoke Poges is a fairly medium-length course: it will not wear you out but it will definitely challenge you to play some precise shots. **Harry Colt** planned the course, and Colt probably put more thought into the courses he designed than any other architect before or since. At Stoke Poges he made magnificent use of a very wooded landscape and some of the short holes he created here are among the most seductive in England. The **7th** is the most talked about; it is not an especially long par three but the tee shot must be measured to perfection for the narrow green has been built at an angle and is fronted by a brook, surrounded by trees and has a devilishly positioned bunker at the back of the 'safest' side of the green. There are at least half a dozen very good two-shot holes, and here one might single out the **3rd**, **6th**, **8th**, **12th**, **17th** and **18th**.

The 19th hole at Stoke Poges is the spectacular mansion referred to in the third paragraph (a famous illustration of it by **Harry Rountree** is reproduced at the beginning of this chapter). 'A dazzling vision of white stone' was Darwin's description. It was built in 1775 by one of the Penn family of Pennsylvania fame and was assaulted by Odd Job after his evil master, Goldfinger, had been caught cheating by James Bond. (A pity Lord Coke didn't catch him.) Some fine refreshment is available within (phone the catering manager on (0753) 526385 before 11am to reserve an a la carte lunch) and again as we have already commented, it has a marvellously relaxed ambience. 'Begging your pardon m'Lord, what I meant to say was, The first thing we do, let's kill all the loafers!'

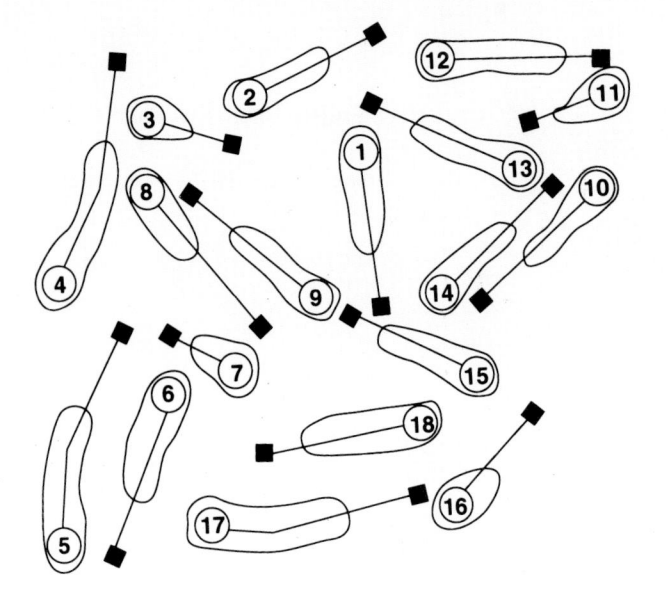

Hole	Yards	Par	Hole	Yards	Par
1	502	5	10	390	4
2	411	4	11	156	3
3	198	3	12	435	4
4	425	4	13	502	5
5	496	5	14	429	4
6	412	4	15	326	4
7	150	3	16	187	3
8	354	4	17	421	4
9	454	4	18	406	4
Out	**3,402**	**36**	**In**	**3,252**	**35**
			Out	**3,402**	**36**
			Totals	**6,654**	**71**

FRILFORD HEATH
CHAMPIONSHIP GOLF

In 1910, just two years after the Golf Club was founded, **Bernard Darwin** described Frilford Heath as, 'A wonderful oasis in a desert of mud. The sand is so near the turf,' he enthused, 'that out of pure exuberance it breaks out here and there in little eruptions'.

The sand must be the only thing that has ever erupted at Frilford Heath. Peaceable and peaceful, this is one of England's most pleasant and understated golfing retreats. I would also suggest that it is one of England's most underrated venues. In Darwin's day there was only one 18 hole course, today the club has 36 holes – two quite marvellous tests of golf – and though in 1987 it was honoured with hosting the **English Amateur Championship** its reputation is still not as widespread or as great as it merits; moreover the condition and quality of both courses has improved significantly since the late 1980s and for this Frilford's fortunate golfers owe a considerable debt to their course manager, **David Heads**. It is always pleasing to see the construction of new tees and the careful planting of indigenous trees but at Frilford additional gorse and heather have also been introduced, and of course, there is an important difference between placing new hazards and positioning new hazards. A lot of thought has gone into all the many subtle alterations and when added to the fact that the greens at Frilford have never been better and the rough really is rough (so rare these days) there is certainly much to admire.

Visitors wishing to inspect one or both courses, the **Red** and the **Green** as they are known, should make arrangements with the Club's secretary, **Mr J.W.Kleynhans**, preferably by telephoning in advance on **(0865) 390864**. Handicap certificates are required and play is not normally permitted before 10am. The professional at Frilford is **Derek Craik**, tel **(0865) 390887** and the Club's full address is **Frilford Heath Golf Club, Abingdon, Oxford OX13 5NW**. The green fees in 1992 were set at £37 for Monday to Friday with £47 payable at weekends and on Bank Holidays. A reduced fee is payable after 5pm (£25 in 1992).

The Golf Club is located three miles west of Abingdon off the A338 Oxford to Wantage road (an old Roman Road). It is only a few minutes from the A420, the A415 and the A34, the latter linking Oxford to the M4.

It is sometimes said that the Red and Green Course are very different in character: I would not use the word 'very'. It is certainly fair to say that the Red is the more exacting (for it is 700 yards longer) and that the Green has the greater number of 'pretty' holes but there is a fair distribution of challenge and charm on both courses.

The **Red Course** (6768 yards, par 73 from the back markers and 6495 yards from the forward tees) opens rather modestly with three medium length par fours and a well bunkered short hole. Arguably the best sequence of holes comes between the 5th and the 9th. The **5th** is a tough par five with a fiendish cross bunker that regularly comes into play on the second shot as the prevailing wind is against. If the wind is blowing then the **6th**, also a par five is reachable in two, although its green, like most at Frilford is heavily contoured. The **7th** is a difficult par four – the key here being a long and accurate drive, and the stroke one **8th** has a hog's back shaped fairway, making it a veritable 'beast' of a hole. Beauty follows beast though in the form of the par three **9th** where the tee shot is struck over a picturesque pond. On the back nine the golfer confronts a two-tiered green on the short **11th** and a saucer-shaped green on the **13th**. Two other notable holes are the **12th**, with its backdrop of magnificent trees – a kaleidoscope of colours in Autumn, and the **16th** where a new back tee has turned the hole into a very good dog-leg.

The **Green Course** (6006 yards, par 69) begins more impressively than the Red with a heavily wooded, sweeping par five followed by a most attractive par three. The **2nd** is in fact one of two outstanding short holes on the front nine, the other being the **6th**. The dog-leg **11th** is perhaps the most memorable of the two-shot holes on this course, the drive here is over a natural lake, and there is a trio of lengthy par fours starting at the **14th**, but in the right conditions the **18th** is just about driveable – the perfect opportunity to show-off in front of the clubhouse!

Well, if you cannot enjoy your golf at Frilford Heath you must be a rather desperate individual and I suggest you skip the club's welcoming 19th hole and visit the 'local' down the road – it's called The Dog House.

Frilford Heath Red Course

Hole	Yards	Par	Hole	Yards	Par
1	361	4	10	552	5
2	377	4	11	157	3
3	405	4	12	486	5
4	190	3	13	378	4
5	518	5	14	338	4
6	487	5	15	424	4
7	412	4	16	313	4
8	472	4	17	388	4
9	189	3	18	321	4
Out	3,411	36	In	3,357	37
			Out	3,411	36
			TOTALS	6,768	73

LE MANOIR AUX QUAT'SAISONS

Le Manoir aux Quat'Saisons is situated in 27 acres of gardens and parkland in the Oxfordshire village of Great Milton. Easily accessible from London or Birmingham via the M40 motorway, this internationally acclaimed country house hotel and restaurant is one of only nine establishments in the World to be awarded the Relais & Chateaux Gold and Red shields. This is their highest classification and confirms the overall standard of excellence and hospitality at this magnificent 15th century Cotswold manor house.

There are nineteen elegant bedrooms at Le Manoir aux Quat'Saisons. Each one has been individually designed and captures the atmosphere of warmth and friendliness by the use of beautiful fabrics and antique furnishings. Many of the luxurious bathrooms feature whirlpool baths or steam showers. In the converted stable block, most of the bedrooms have a private terrace overlooking the gardens and orchard. Even the medieval dovecote has been transformed into a romantic suite.

Chef/Patron Raymond Blanc is one of the World's finest chefs

and Le Manoir is widely acknowledged as Britain's finest restaurant. The extensive vegetable and herb gardens in the grounds provide the kitchen with a great variety of produce. An extensive wine list, the work of Restaurant Director, Alain Desenclos, complements Raymond Blanc's cuisine.

Before or after your meal, a stroll through the gardens at Le Manoir is a delight. Colourful herbaceous borders line the paths, the water gardens and lake attract wildlife and, in the private swimming pool garden, residents can relax, sip a cool drink and soak up the sun. More energetic guests can enjoy a game of tennis.

Private lunch or dinner parties can be held in the Cromwell Room where up to 46 guests can enjoy the specially priced party menus created by Raymond Blanc.

Le Manoir aux Quat'Saisons - a unique combination of exceptional cuisine and comfort.

Le Manoir aux Quat'Saisons
Great Milton
Oxford
OX9 7PD
Tel: (0844) 278881
Fax: (0844) 278847

BERKS, BUCKS & OXON
COMPLETE GOLF

KEY

*** Visitors welcome at most times
** Visitors usually allowed on
weekdays only
* Visitors not normally permitted
(Mon, Wed) No visitors on
specified days

APPROXIMATE GREEN FEES

A – £30 plus
B – £20 – £30
C – £15 – £25
D – £10 – £20
E – Under £10
F – Green fees on application

RESTRICTIONS

G – Guests only
H – Handicap certificate required
H(24) – Handicap of 24 or less
required
L – Letter of introduction required
M – Visitor must be a member of
another recognised club.

BERKSHIRE

Bearwood G.C
(0734) 760060
Mole Road, Sindlesham
Leave M4 at junction 10 for B3030
(9) 2814 yards/**/D/H

The Berkshire G.C
(0344) 21495
Swinley Road, Ascot
Leave M3 at junction 3 or M4 at junction 10
(18) 6356 yards/**/A/L
(18) 6258 yards/**/A/L

Calcot Park G.C
(0734) 427124
Bath Road, Calcot, Reading
Leave M4 at junction 12 for A4 to Reading
(18) 6283 yards/**/F

Donnington Valley G.C
(0635) 32488
Old Oxford Road, Donnington
North of Newbury
(18) 4002 yards/***/F

Downshire G.C
(0344) 424066
Easthampstead Park, Wokingham
Take M3 or M4 to Bracknell & to
Easthampstead Park
(18) 6382 yards/***/E

East Berkshire G.C
(0344) 772041
Ravenswood Avenue, Crowthorne
Take M3 or M4 to Bracknell, onto A3095
then B3348
(18) 6315 yards/**/B/H

Goring & Streatley G.C
(0491) 873229
Rectory Road, Streatley-on-Thames
10 miles N.W of Reading
(18) 6255 yards/**/B

Hawthorn Hill G.C
(0628) 771030
Drift Road, Nr Maidenead
Leave M4 at exit 8/9, take A330 to Bracknell
(18) 6212 yards/***/E

Hurst G.C
(0734) 345143
Sandford Lane, Hurst, Wokingham
3 miles from Wokingham on B3030
(9) 3013 yards (men)/ 2906 (ladies)/***/E

Lavender Park G.C
(0344) 884074
Swinley Road, Ascot
4 miles S.W of Ascot on A332
(9) 1104 yards/***/E

Maidenhead G.C
(0628) 24693
Shoppenhangers Road, Maidenhead
Take A4 or M4 to Maidenhead, onto A308
(18) 6360 yards/**/B/H

Mill Ride G.C
(0344) 886777
Mill Ride, North Ascot
(18) 6639 yards/***/A/H

Newbury & Crookham G.C
(0635) 40035
Burys Bank Road, Greenham, Newbury
2 miles S.E of Newbury off A34
(18) 5880 yards/**/B/M

Reading G.C
(0734) 472909
17 Kidmore End Road, Emmer Green, Reading
2 miles N. of Reading off B481
(18) 6212 yards/**(not Friday)/B

Royal Ascot G.C
(0344) 25175
Winkfield Road, Ascot
Leave M3 at junction 3, take A332 N.
(18) 5653 yards/***/F

Sonning G.C
(0734) 693332
Duffield Road, Sonning-on-Thames
Take A4 from Reading to Maidenhead
(18) 6345 yards/**/F/H

Sunningdale G.C
(0990) 21681
Ridgemount Road, Sunningdale, Ascot
28 miles W. of London off A30
6586 yards/**/A/H
6676 yards/**/A/H

Sunningdale Ladies G.C
(0990) 20507
Cross Road, Sunningdale
Off A30 from M3 or M4
(18) 3622 yards/***/D (men extra)

Swinley Forest G.C
(0344) 20197
Coronation Road, S. Ascot
Take M3 or M4 to Ascot
(18) 6011 yards/*/F/G/H

Temple G.C
(0628) 824248
Henley Road, Hurley, Maidenhead
1 mile E. of Hurley on A423
(18) 6206 yards/**/A/H

West Berkshire G.C
(048 82) 574
Chaddleworth, Newbury
Leave M4 at junction 14, take A338 N.
(18) 7053 yards/**/C

Winter Hill G.C
Grange Lane, Cookham, Maidenhead
4 Miles from Maidenhead via M4 (junction 9)
(18) 6408 yards/**/C

BUCKINGHAMSHIRE

Abbey Hill G.C
(0908) 563845
Monks Way, Two Mile Ash, Stony Stratford
2 miles south of Stony Stratford.
(18) 6193 yards/***/E

Beaconsfield G.C
(0494) 676545
Seer Green, Beaconsfield
(18) 6469 yards/**/A/H

Buckingham G.C
(0280) 815566
Tingewick Rd. Buckingham
2 miles from town on A421.
(18) 6082 yards/**/B/M

Burnham Beeches G.C.
(0628) 661448
Green Lane, Burnham
(18) 6415 yards/**/A/H

Chesham and Ley Hill G.C.
(0494) 784541
Ley Hill, Chesham
(9) 5240 yards/**/D

Chiltern Forest G.C.
(0296) 630899
Aston Hill, Halton, Aylesbury
5 miles south of Aylesbury off A41.
(18) 6038 yards/**/D

Datchet G.C.
(0753) 43887
Buccleuch Rd. Datchett, Slough
2 miles from Slough.
(9) 5978 yards/**/C/H

Denham G.C.
(0895) 832022
Tilehouse Lane, Denham
(18) 6451 yards/**(Fri)/A

Ellesborough G.C.
(0296) 622114
Butlers Cross, Aylesbury
1 mile west of Wendover on A413.
(18) 6271 yards/**/F/H

Farnham Park G.C.
(0753) 647065
Park Rd. Stoke Poges
(18) 5787 yards/***/E

Flackwell Heath G.C.
(06285) 520929
Treadaway Rd. Flackwell Heath, High
Wycombe
(18) 6150 yards/**/B/H

Gerrards Cross G.C.
(0753) 885300
Chalfont Park, Gerrards Cross
(18) 6021 yards/**/A/H

Harewood Downs G.C.
(0494) 762308
Cokes Lane, Chalfont St. Giles
3 miles south of Amersham off A413.
(18) 5448 yards/**/B/H

Hazelmere G. and C.C.
(0494) 718298
Penn Rd. Hazelmere, High Wycombe
3 miles from High Wycombe on B474.
(18) 6039 yards/***/B

Iver G.C.
(0753) 655615
Hollow Hill Lane, Langley Park Rd. Iver
(9) 6214 yards/***/E

Little Chalfont G.C.
(0494) 764877
Lodge Lane, Little Chalfont
(9) 2926 yards/***/E

Stoke Poges G.C.
(0753) 526385
Stoke Park, Park Rd. Stoke Poges
3 miles from Slough on B416.
(18) 6654 yards/**/B/H

Stowe G.C.
(0280) 813650
Stowe, Buckingham
4 miles from Buckingham on A413.
(9) 4573 yards/**/E/G

Wavendon Golf Centre
(0908) 281811
Wavendon, Milton Keynes
1 mile from M1 junction 13
(18) 5800 yards/***/E

Weston Turville G.C.
(0296) 24084
New Rd. Weston Turville, Aylesbury
(18) 6782 yards/***/D

Wrexham Park G.C.
(0753) 663271
Wrexham Street, Wrexham, Slough
(18) 5836 yards/***/D
(9) 2383 yards/***/E

Whiteleaf G.C.
(08444) 3097
The Clubhouse, Whiteleaf, Aylesbury
(9) 5391 yards/**/C/H

Windmill Hill G.C
(0908) 378623
Tannenhoe Lane, Bletchley
(18) 6773 yards/***/E

Woburn G. and C.C.
(0908) 370756
Bow Brickhill, Milton Keynes
2 miles from Woburn.
(18) 6913 yards/**/F/H
(18) 6641 yards/**/F/H

Wycombe Heights G.C
(0494) 816686
Rayners Avenue, Loudwater, High Wycombe
(18) 6300 yards/***/E

OXFORDSHIRE

Badgemore Park G.C.
(0491) 572206
Badgemore Park, Henley-on-Thames
1 mile from Henley.
(18) 6112 yards/***/B/H

Burford G.C.
(099382) 2583
Burford
(18) 6405 yards/**/B/H

Cherwell Edge G.C
(0295) 711591
Chacombe, Banbury
East of Banbury on B4525
(18) 5925 yards/***/E

Chesterton G.C.
(0869) 241204
Chesterton, Bicester
(18) 6224 yards/***/C/H

Chipping Norton G.C.
(0608) 2383
Southcombe, Chipping Norton
1 mile south of Chipping town centre.
(18) 6283 yards/***/C

Frilford Heath G.C.
(0865) 390864
Frilford Heath, Abingdon
3 miles west of Abingdon off A338.
(18) 6768 yards/***/A/H
(18) 6006 yards/***/A/H

Hadden Hill G.C
(0235) 510410
Wallingford Road, Didcot
(18) 6563 yards/***/D

Henley G.C.
(0491) 575742
Harpsden, Henley-on-Thames
1 mile from Henley.
(18) 6330 yards/**/A/H

Huntercombe G.C.
(0491) 641207
Nuffield, Henley-on-Thames
6 miles from Henley off A423.
(18) 6108 yards/**/A/H

North Oxford G.C.
(0865) 54415
Banbury Rd. Oxford
3 miles north of City centre.
(18) 5805 yards/***/B/H

Southfield G.C.
(0865) 242158
Hill Top Rd. Oxford
(18) 6230 yards/**/B/H

Tadmarton Heath G.C.
(0608) 737278
Wiggington, Banbury
5 miles west of Banbury on B4035
(18) 5917 yards/**/B/H

RULE XIII

Worm casts may
be removed ·
· · · · without
penalty · · ·

Charles Crombie **RULE XIII** *Rosenstiel's*

GLOS, HEREFORD & WORCESTER

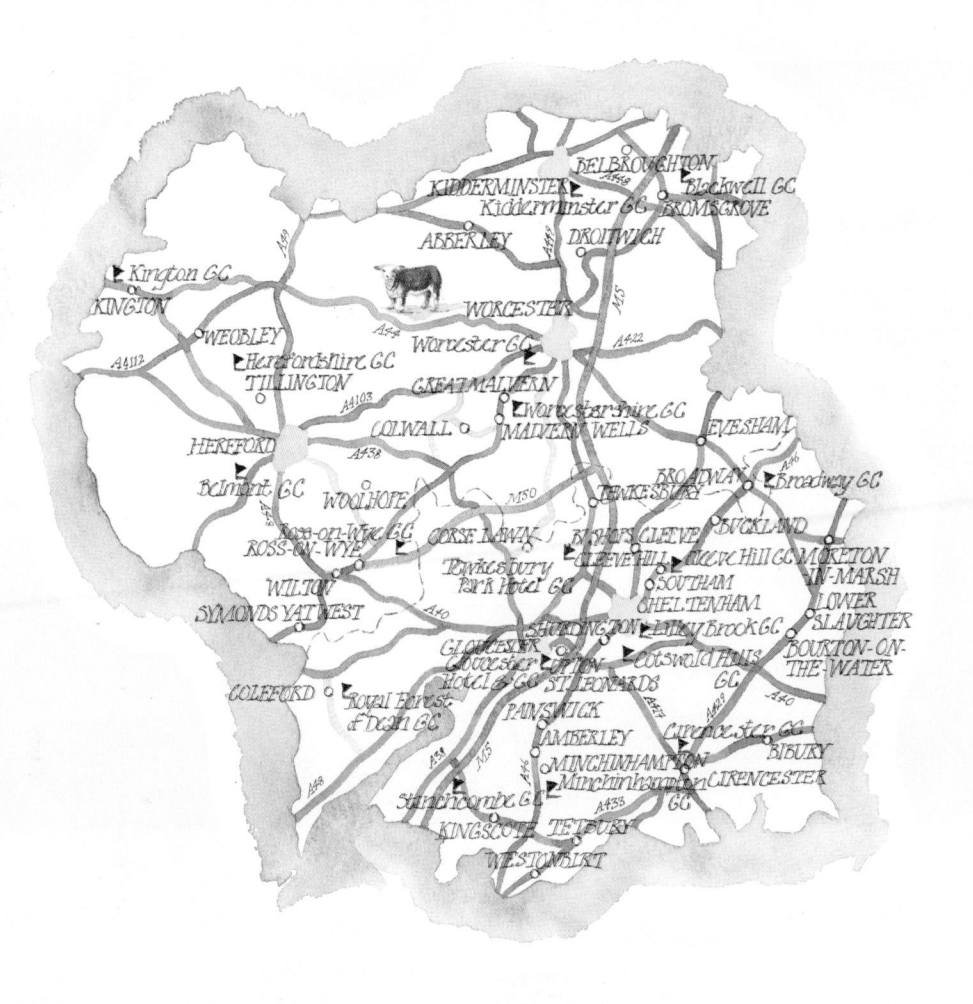

C.E. Brock   THE DRIVE   Sotheby's

CALCOT MANOR

If, in the course of your everyday life, you long for the peace of rolling hills, fields of flower-filled hedgerows, open log fires, delicious meals taken in friendly company and comforts to console even the most jaded, then the spirit of Calcot Manor has already invaded your life.

Originally part of Kingswood Abbey, founded by the Cistercians in 1158, this farmhouse and its beautiful stone barns and stables stands in one of the most unusual parts of England. Part of its estate includes a 14th century tithe-barn that is among the oldest in the country and yet further proof that time here really does stand still.

At Calcot you're in the very heart of the Cotswolds, nestling among one of the richest areas for the simple delights of touring and exploring; taking along, of course, a delicious hamper from the Manor. Staying at the hotel still leaves the choice of heated outdoor swimming pool fringed by evergreens and brilliant shrubbery, croquet on the lawn, or simply a sunny or shady retreat for reading, dreaming, or even working, before lunch in the light airy restaurant or on the terrace overlooking the lush green countryside.

Dinner is a civilised affair with a consistently surprising and delightful menu that makes full use of the fresh, local produce, prepared and presented by the highly covetable chef; the formal, but relaxed, atmosphere extends out for coffee and drinks on the terrace or elegant sitting rooms.

At the end of a long day the bedrooms at Calcot wait ready to welcome you; each one has private bathroom and its own unique character and decor echoing a particular aspect of the region. The Master Bedroom is particularly enticing, with its canopied and draped four-poster bed and whirlpool bath.

The area around Calcot has much to offer the sportsman. For the golfer two breathtakingly beautiful courses are mere minutes away and, of course, special arrangements can be made for guests, these include a two or three day golf package with green fees and tuition with a local professional. There is racing at nearby Bath, Cheltenham and Newbury, along with horse trials at Badminton and Gatcombe. Clay pigeon shooting is available in the hotel grounds, including tuition, while the fisherman has the choice of coarse in the local lakes or trout fishing in the chalk streams of the Wyle and Avon. The hotel can also arrange cycling, walking, watersports, ballooning and gliding, as well as offering help with the numerous Arts Festivals and theatres in the region, including the famous Theatre Royal at nearby Bath.

Calcot Manor also offers a variety of special-interest breaks, ranging from antiques and country gardens to a day with the resident chef; details are available on request.

Calcot Manor
Nr Tetbury
Gloucestershire GL8 8YJ
Tel: (0666) 890391
Fax: (0666) 890394

PENRHOS COURT

Penrhos Court stands on the hill between Lyonshall and the ancient border town of Kington. The earliest part is a cruck hall built around 1280, when Edward the First took Kington away from the Welsh. Sometime about the year 1400 a post & truss, timber-frame house was butted onto the East-side and again in 1590 there was another major addition to complete the house as it stands today. Barns and stables have since been added to form a courtyard, adapting Penrhos over the ages to meet the demands of the times.

In recent years Penrhos has once again evolved to survive. During 1974 a restaurant was started in the cowbyre. This quickly gained a local reputation, won national awards and received acclaim in the food guides. Since opening, this business has provided a stable background to the project of re-building the whole complex of derelict buildings.

Daphne Lambert is the leader of this justly renowned kitchen. Using only the finest of raw ingredients, home-grown herbs and vegetables she turns her craft into an art.

Although her main aim is to run a high-standard, 20th-century restaurant, Daphne has quite naturally turned her attention to the food and cooking of the medieval ages. She has made a deep study of the subject and runs six or seven special medieval banquets each year on the dates of their original holidays; Mid-summer, Michaelmas, Martinmas etc. Using medieval recipes and traditional entertainment, each banquet is full of interesting flavours and variety, enormous fun and spectacular to behold, producing an event no doubt very close to some of the special feasts that were perhaps held at Penrhos some 600 or 700 years ago. Her knowledge and enthusiasm mixed with the practical creativity that a chef has with food and cooking, has helped to dispel the ridicule that some historians have put on medieval food.

Now as the repair of Penrhos Court reaches its completion there emerges one of the most delightful hotels you could hope to find anywhere, catering for all sorts of special events and countryside holidays.

Penrhos Court Hotel and Restaurant
Kington
Herefordshire
HR5 3LH
Tel: (0544) 230720
Fax: (0544) 230754

THE CHELTENHAM PARK HOTEL

The Cheltenham Park Hotel is a beautiful Regency Manor House set in nine acres of landscaped gardens with a natural trout lake and waterfalls. The hotel has superb views over the Leckhampton Hills and the Lilleybrook Golf Course.

This luxury hotel was recently totally refurbished and extended to 154 luxuriously appointed bedrooms. These include the Presidential Suite and Executive Rooms which command superb views over the attractively landscaped gardens, with their meandering walkways, gentle waterfalls, romantic arbours and classically inspired gazebo.

The Lakeside Restaurant offers the best of modern English cuisine with a choice from either our Table d'Hote or our a la Carte menus, using only the freshest of produce. Your meal will be complemented with a selection of fine wines from our cellars.

There are two bars to choose from; the Tulip Bar with its marble fireplaces, original oak panelling and large patio overlooking the golf course, or the congenial Lakeside Bar with its terraces down to the lake.

The Cheltenham Park hotel is only two miles from the town centre and is therefore only a short drive from the Racecourse. Access to and from all parts of the country is quick and easy as Cheltenham Spa lies at the hub of the country's motorway/ dual carriageway network with excellent rail and coach services as well as its own airport at Staverton.

The hotels location lends itself to ease of access to a wide range of attractions including the famous Pittville Pump Rooms in Cheltenham where the spa waters may be taken and the Gloucester Dockland areas which have recently undertaken major works to restore them to their former grandeur.

This beautiful hotel is right next door to the well known Lilleybrook Golf Course and only minutes away from Cotswold Hills Golf Course - a perfect golfing location. Alternatively a day at the races, a luxury break away from it all, or a peaceful environment for a business meeting, the Cheltenham Park Hotel is the ideal choice.

Cheltenham Park Hotel
Cirencester Road
Charlton Kings
Cheltenham GL53 8EA
Tel: (0242) 222021
Fax: (0242) 226935

PUCKRUP HALL

Standing in just over one hundred acres of lawns and rolling parkland between the Cotswold and Malvern Hills, Puckrup Hall is a grand Regency house offering the ideal location for a touring base, quiet break or management retreat. To the north are Worcester and Great Malvern, while to the east the Vale of Evesham lads to Shakespeare country. Just to the west of the hotel the great river Severn meanders for three miles to Tewkesbury and its magnificent Abbey.

The emphasis at Puckrup Hall is on a relaxing and luxurious stay. There is a remarkable air of light and spaciousness throughout the hotel, perhaps influenced by the design and decor of the delightful Orangery and Conservatory. Leading off from the elegant hallway is the Worcester Room, a beautifully proportioned meeting or dining room for up to 16 guests and an integral part of the original house. The magnificent Ballroom is second to none and can cater for up to 200 people for private dining or company entertaining.

Each of Puckrup Hall's delightful, well appointed en suite bedrooms is individual, both in shape and interior design. This is reflected in that each of the twelve double or twin bedrooms is given a name, after the month of the year, while the four suites, including two with four poster beds, are named after the four seasons, with interior designs to catch the colours of the year.

The gourmet will certainly not be disappointed with the cuisine at the hotel. Dining in an atmosphere of soft intimate colours, be prepared for imaginative menus which are changed daily and a much acclaimed a la carte menu which changes with each season, emphasising the freshness and quality of the best from the Vale of Evesham and the finest produce available at the time.

For a memorable stay in an idyllic country setting, Tewkesbury Hall is hard to beat. The hotel is just two miles north of Tewkesbury Centre on the A38 and only a few minutes from junction 8 of the M5, via junction 1 of the M50, making it easily accessible from Birmingham, Bristol and South Wales.

Puckrup Hall
Puckrup
Tewkesbury
Gloucestershire GL20 6EL

Tel: Tewkesbury (0684) 296200 Fax: (0684) 850788

GLOS, HEREFORD & WORCESTER
CHOICE GOLF

A hush descends as you ponder your first swing in old Worcestershire. Apple and cherry trees are in blossom and in the distance a herd of white faced Herefords appraise your stance. You're fortunate, for several hundred years ago the air in these parts was thick with the clatter of sword against sword but now there is peace. Crack! Straight down the fairway – the echo resounds and then dies – you're on your way.

Herefordshire, Worcestershire and Gloucestershire – what a lovely trio! Bordering the Principality the region is arguably the most tranquil in England. It is an area of rich pastures and cider orchards, of small market towns and sleepy villages rather than crowded cities and encompasses the Cotswolds and the Malverns, the beautiful Wye Valley and the splendid Vale of Evesham. Truly a green and pleasant land!

HEREFORD & WORCESTER

Herefordshire and Worcestershire are no more – at least according to the modern county boundaries – Hereford and Worcester it is now, no doubt a compromise to the two county towns.

Golf courses aren't exactly plentiful, but those there are tend to be very scenic, often hidden away deep in the glorious countryside. To the north west of Hereford, **Kington** and **Herefordshire** are two typical examples and both clubs welcome visitors. Kington is further towards Wales and is reputed to be the highest course in either country. It is a place where poor golf can always be blamed on the rarefied atmosphere. To the south of Hereford is another attractive course, **Belmont**, one of the newer courses in the region, but one that has already gained a good reputation.

Hereford is a natural base when golfing in the area and there are a number of good hotels. The Graftonbury Hotel (0432) 356411 is a charming garden hotel with easy access to Belmont Golf Club. The Green Dragon Hotel (0432) 272506 is particularly comfortable – note the many four-poster beds – and in nearby Much Birch, The Pilgrim Hotel (0981) 540742 is a splendid former rectory. The Hopbine Hotel (0432) 268722 and the White Lodge Hotel also offer reasonably priced accommodation near to Hereford city centre. A short drive to Weobley reveals the Red Lion (0544) 318419, a 14th century Inn in the centre of a delightful village – very handy for Herefordshire Golf Club. Near the same golf course is a good pub, The Bell at Tillington, while for Belmont, The Butchers Arms is recommended (some accommodation here too). Kington has a first class restaurant, Penrhos Court (0544) 230720, and also boasts The Oxford Arms Hotel (0544) 230322, a 16th Century Coaching Inn near to the golf course. Visitors to this pleasant area should also consider the excellent Allt-yr-yns Hotel (0873) 890307 in Walterstone.

Ross-on-Wye is a renowned beauty spot and the town's golf course reflects the reputation. Set in the heart of the Wye Valley and surrounded by a blaze of colour, it's hard to believe that the M50 is under a mile away (junction 4). If staying a few days in the area, The Pengethley Manor Hotel (098987) 211 is most charming, alternatively try the New Inn (0989) 87274 in St Owens Cross, where you are sure to receive a warm welcome.

Worcester is an attractive city with a very beautiful Cathedral which overlooks the famous county cricket ground. Only a mile from the town centre off the A4103 is the **Worcester** Golf and Country Club. The oldest course in the county, and probably the finest is the appropriately name **Worcestershire** Golf Club, situated two miles south of Great Malvern. There are extensive views from the course towards the Malverns, the Severn Valley and the Cotswolds. Elsewhere in the county, **The Vale** Golf Club near Evesham has recently opened and boasts 27 testing holes and there is a reasonable course at **Kidderminster**. The final recommendation in Worcestershire is the popular **Blackwell** Golf Club near Bromsgrove.

Near Worcester, The Elms Hotel (0299) 896666 at Abberley is an outstanding country house while Malvern Wells offers two excellent restaurants, The Croque-en-Bouche (06845) 65612 and The Cottage in the Wood (06845) 73487. Worcester itself contains the stylish Fownes Hotel (0905) 613151 and the moderately priced THF Giffard Hotel (0905) 726262. Browns Restaurant (0905) 26263 is also well worth a visit. Great Malvern provides a charming 19th century coaching inn, The Foley Arms (0684) 573397, whilst a particularly highly recommended hotel in Redditch is Abbey Park (0527) 63918. A final suggestion for the area is to visit Colwall Village, here the Colwall Park Hotel (0684) 40206 is exceptionally good value.

GLOUCESTERSHIRE

Heading into Gloucestershire, I trust that when Doctor Foster went to Gloucester he wasn't a well travelled golfer. Again the county has very few courses and Gloucester itself didn't possess one at all until as recently as 1976. Neighbouring Cheltenham has been a little more fortunate but granted one or two exceptions, the quality of the golf in the county doesn't exactly match up to the undeniable quality of its scenery.

The county's two best known courses are probably **Cotswold Hills** and **Lilley Brook**, located to the north and south of Cheltenham respectively. Both offer commanding views of the Gloucestershire countryside, especially perhaps Lilley Brook, one of southern England's most undulating courses. Each is well worth a visit.

Cleeve Hill is Cheltenham's third 18 hole course. Situated on high ground to the north of the town it can get rather cold in winter. One anonymous person said that when visiting Cheltenham he enjoyed a game at Lilley Brook in the summer as half of him was mountain goat, and at Cleeve Hill in the winter because the other half of him was eskimo!

The Cheltenham area has many fine hotels, but perhaps the best known is the Queens Hotel (0242) 514724. Lypiatt House (0242) 224994 is a popular alternative. A good hotel in the surrounding hills is the simply splendid Greenway (0242) 862352 in Shurdington. This hotel offers a warm welcome, a first class menu and beautiful grounds. In Cleeve Hill, the Malvern View Hotel (024267) 2017 is well thought of, its name self – explanatory, and a little further north in Bishops Cleeve, Cleeveway House (024267) 2585 has a small number of rooms and an outstanding restaurant.

Outside of Cheltenham, **Minchinhampton** has the biggest reputation. A Club of great character, it celebrated its centenary in 1989. There are two courses here, an Old and a New, the latter was constructed in the 1970's. A quick word for another course in the south of the county, **Stinchcombe Hill** which is

also very well thought of. A first class place to stay is Burleigh Court (0453) 883804, while to the north The Amberley Inn (0453) 872565 in Amberley with its fine views over Woodchester Valley has considerable charm. For a good pub visit Painswick, The Royal Oak – a short golf course here too.

The 18 hole course at **Cirencester** is probably the nearest one gets to golf in the Cotswolds. Cirencester is certainly a pleasant enough place but to most of us the real Cotswolds are the many wonderfully named villages: Bourton-on-the-Water, Stow-on-the-Wold, Upper Slaughter and Lower Slaughter.

Gloucester's newish course lies within the grounds of **The Gloucester Hotel** (0452) 25653 at Robinswood Hill. A luxurious Country Club, there are in fact 27 holes here plus all manner of accompanying leisure facilities. The 18 hole course enjoys a pleasant setting and has matured very rapidly. The same can be said of **Tewkesbury Park** Hotel's golf course (0684) 295405 which is laid out on the site of the famous Roses Battle of 1471. Both hotels are comfortable and their courses are open to residents and non-residents alike, although booking in advance is preferred. However, for a special occasion, we can recommend a stay at Puckrup Hall (0684) 296200

(previously known as Tewkesbury Hall), an elegant Regency house set in 40 acres of parkland, and at Upton St Leonards, near Gloucester, Hatton Court (0452) 617412 is most relaxing.

The Forest of Dean is our next port of call – another beauty spot and some good golf too at the **Royal Forest of Dean** Golf Club in Coleford. In Coleford itself there is a lovely 16th century Manor house by the name of Portway House (0594) 833937 which is well worth an overnight treat. A notable inn nearby is The Speech House (0594) 822607. Staying a few days in the area is recommended: the countryside is splendid and just 8 miles away lies Chepstow and the delights of **St Pierre**.

Last but not least, **Broadway** Golf Club – the course being a mile and a half or so from 'the loveliest village in England'. It really is a beautiful part of the world and those wishing to do some exploring will find several superb hotels, any of which will make an ideal base. The Lygon Arms (0386) 852255 in Broadway with its outstanding frontage probably takes pride of place but for excellent value the Collin House Hotel (0386) 858354 takes some beating. Both have very fine restaurants. True to form there are again some marvellous views from the golf course – this time looking out across that splendid Vale of Evesham.

THE NEW INN

Resting in the heart of unspoiled Herefordshire countryside, The New Inn has been welcoming travellers since around 1540. Built as the main coaching inn on the Chepstow to Hereford route it still retains its original character with hosts of beams and timbers.

The lounge bar and restaurant crackle to the sound of warming log fires in winter; all there to complement the fine food and ales from which the inn has gained its worthy reputation. Homemade food using fresh local produce is the speciality, with a bar offering an extensive selection of wines and spirits.

The beautifully maintained beer garden overlooks the rolling Herefordshire countryside, with views stretching away to the Black Mountains in the distance.

The New Inn boasts two, romantic, four-poster suites, each charmingly retaining the warmth and character of a wealth of oak beams, and offering the modern amenities of colour television, tea/coffee making facilities and ensuite bathrooms. The oak suite also offers a private lounge and dining area to further enhance the tranquil privacy of this most delightful of country inns.

The New Inn
St Owens Cross
Herefordshire HR2 8LQ
Tel: 0989 87 274

ABBEY PARK

Set within 230 acres of parkland, Abbey Park is a well-established Golf and Country Club and an ideal location for a holiday, weekend, special occasion or business meeting. Guests and visitors alike can enjoy an unrivalled range of sports, health and leisure facilities, as well as bars, sumptuous restaurants, bedrooms and conference suites. With an emphasis on style and service, Abbey Park is hard to beat.

Abbey Park boasts 30 standard bedrooms, stylishly furnished and featuring ensuite facilities, remote control T.V., free video channel and tea and coffee making facilities. There are also two 'executive' rooms which feature, among other comforts, a king-sized bed and a sunken whirlpool bath.

Hotel guests are more than welcome to use the fully equipped leisure suite, including the attractive, indoor, heated pool - not only is this illuminated, but the pool area also has a whirlpool spa bath, splash pool, power shower, sauna, steam room and solarium. If you can tear yourself away, an aerobics suite and a conditioning suite beckon, featuring some of the most technically advanced computer-controlled health, toning and conditioning equipment in the UK. After a full health check our team of consultants will personally check and monitor a fitness programme which has been specifically designed for you.

The golf course at Abbey Park is a sportsman's dream. The 18-hole, 6411 yard, Par 71 course is further enhanced by a beautifully sculptured landscape and natural water hazards; a well-stocked golf shop is on site and a resident golf pro is nearby to help give that edge to your game.

An ideal location for business conferences, meetings, seminars or product launches, Abbey Park offers a choice of five different meeting rooms and a full range of the latest audio-visual equipment.

Conveniently located close to the M5, M40 and M42, Abbey Park is within easy reach of many of England's most popular tourist centres, including Stratford-upon-Avon, Malvern, Warwick and the Cotswolds. The nearest British Rail station is Redditch and both Birmingham International and East Midlands International airports are easily accessible.

Abbey Park Golf & Country Club Hotel
Dagnell End Road
Bordesley
Redditch
Worcestershire B98 7BD
Tel: (0527) 63918/584140
Fax: (0527) 65872

ALLT-YR-YNYS

Allt-yr-Ynys, situated on wooded river banks in Herefordshire, and standing in an acre of well-established gardens, is an elegant country hotel with a fascinating history. Robert Cecil came to this beautiful spot in 1091, after the conquest of Glamorgan, and it is said that Elizabeth I was once a house guest here. The historical appeal of the hotel remains intact - Allt-yr-Ynys as it is today was built in 1550, and retains much fine craftsmanship of the period. Moulded ceilings, oak panelling and door pillars feature throughout the house, yet at the same time the hotel offers the very finest of modern comforts.

All the bedrooms are individually furnished - the Master Suite, for example, has a Jacobean fourposter, and each has an ensuite bathroom, telephone, colour television and radio. Ancient outbuildings have been converted to provide additional luxury accommodation.

Much attention is paid to personal service at the hotel - guest are warmly and genuinely welcomed and the staff do their utmost to meet the particular needs of every guest. The Chef is only too happy to prepare special dishes, and the hotel caters for weddings and functions of all kinds. Great care is taken with the quality and presentation of food, using only the finest cuts of meat and the freshest of vegetables and other ingredients.

Guest can enjoy the indoor heated swimming pool and jacuzzi at Allt-yr-Ynys, or perhaps the Clay Shooting Centre, ideal for corporate entertaining. Realising that nobody wants to be ankle-deep in mud in wet weather clothes and wellingtons, the stands and observation area are conveniently situated under one roof.

The setting is every bit as magnificent as the hotel. On the border between England and Wales, on the English side, the rolling wooded farmland of Herefordshire gives way to the Malvern Hills beyond. On the Welsh side the Fwddog Ridge dominates the landscape. Part of the Black Mountains, it runs north to Hay-on-Wye, all within the Brecon Beacons National Park. Houses and castles of historic interest abound in the area - just as a taster, the ancient castle at Chepstow, which looks down the River Wye, and Llanthony Abbey in the Black Mountains. If you are a keen golfer Allt-yr-Ynys is conveniently situated for Abergavenny, Monmouth, Chepstow and Hereford Golf Courses.

Allt-yr-Ynys is many things to many people: Conference Centre, country retreat, holiday hotel or activity holiday location. The common thread is the personal involvement of owners and staff - you as a guest will find that your interests are always paramount.

Allt-yr-Ynys
Walterstone
Herefordshire
Tel: (0873) 890307
Fax: (0873) 890539

GLOUCESTERSHIRE, HEREFORD & WORCESTER
COMPLETE GOLF

KEY

*** Visitors welcome at most times
** Visitors usually allowed on weekdays only
* Visitors not normally permitted (Mon, Wed) No visitors on specified days

APPROXIMATE GREEN FEES
A – £30 plus
B – £20 – £30
C – £15 – £25
D – £10 – £20
E – Under £10
F – Green fees on application

RESTRICTIONS
G – Guests only
H – Handicap certificate required
H(24) – Handicap of 24 or less required
L – Letter of introduction required
M – Visitor must be a member of another recognised club.

GLOUCESTERSHIRE

Cirencester G.C.
(0285) 2465
Cheltenham Rd. Bagendon, Cirencester
2 miles from Cirencester on A435.
(18)6100 yards/***/C/H

Cleeve Hill G.C.
(024267) 2592
Cleeve Hill, Nr. Prestbury, Cheltenham
3 miles north of Cheltenham on A46.
(18)6217 yards/***/D

Cotswold Hills G.C.
(0242) 515264
Ullenwood, Cheltenham
3 miles south of Cheltenham.
(18)6716 yards/***/F/H/M

Gloucester Hotel G. and C.C.
(0452) 411331
Matson Lane, Robinswood Hill
2 miles south of Gloucester on B4073.
(18)6135 yards/***/B/H

Lilley Brook G.C.
(0204) 526785
Cirencester Rd. Charlton Kings
3 miles from Cheltenham on A435.
(18)6226 yards/***/B/H/M

Lydney G.C.
(0594) 842614
Lakeside Ave. Lydney
(9)5382 yads/**/D

Minchinhampton G.C.
(045383) 3866
Minchinhampton, Stroud
5 miles south of Stroud.
(18)6675 yards/***/C/H
(18)6295 yards/***/C/H

Painswick G.C.
(0452) 812180
Painswick, Stroud
1 mile north of Painswick on A46.
(18)4780 yards/**/D

Royal Forest of Dean G.C.
(0594) 32583
Lords Hill, Coleford
(18)5519 yards/***/D

Stinchcombe Hill G.C.
(0453) 2015
Stinchcombe Hill, Dursley
1 mile from Tetbury.
(18)5710 yards/**/C

Tewkesbury Park Hotel G.C.
(0684) 295404
Lincoln Green Lane, Tewkesbury
1 mile south of town on A38.
(18)6533 yards/***/B/H

Westonbirt G.C.
(0666) 88242
Westonbirt, Tetbury
(9)4504 yards/***/E

HEREFORD & WORCESTER

Abbey Park G.C.
(0527) 63918
Abbey Park, Dagnell End Rd. Redditch
North of Redditch on B4101.
(18)5857 yards/***/D

Belmont G.C.
(0432) 35266
Belmont House, Belmont
2 miles south of Hereford on A465.
(18)6448 yards/***/F

Blackwell G.C.
(021445) 1994
Blackwell, Bromsgrove
3 miles east of Bromsgrove.
(18)6202 yards/**/A/H

Broadway G.C.
(0386) 853683
Willersey Hill, Broadway
3 miles east of Broadway off A44.
(18)6122 yards/***(Sat)/B/H

Churchill and Blakedown G.C.
(0562) 700200
Churchill Lane, Blakedown, Kidderminster
3 miles north of Kidderminster.
(9)5399 yards/**/D

Droitwich G. and C.C.
(0905) 774344
Westford House, Ford Lane, Droitwich
1 mile north of Droitwich.
(18)6040 yards/**/C/H

Evesham G.C.
(0386) 860395
Cray Combe Links, Fladbury, Pershore
4 miles west of Fladbury.
(9)6415 yards/**/C/H

Habberley G.C.
(0562) 745756
Habberley, Kidderminster
3 miles north of Kidderminster.
(9)5104 yards/**/D/M

Herefordshire G.C.
(0432) 71219
Ravens Causeway, Wormsley
(18)6200 yards/***/C

Kidderminster G.C.
(0562) 822303
Russel Rd. Kidderminster
1 mile south of town off A449.
(18)5659 yards/**/C/M

Kington G.C
(0544) 230340
Bradnor Hll, Kington,
1 mile north of Kington on B4355.
(18)5726 yards/***/D

Leominster G.C.
(0568) 2863
Ford Bridge, Leominster
(9)5250 yards/***/F

Little Lakes G.C.
(0299) 266385
Lye Head, Rock, Bewdley
3 miles west of Bewdley.
(9)6247 yards/**/D

Pitcheroak G.C.
(0527) 41054
Plymouth Rd. Redditch
(9)4724 yards/***/E

Redditch G.C.
(0527) 43309
Lower Grintsy, Green Lane, Callow Hill
3 miles west of Redditch.
(18)6671 yards/**/F/M

Ross-on-Wye G.C.
(098982) 267
Two Park, Gorsley, Ross-on-Wye
(18)6500 yards/***/B/H/M

Tolladine G.C.
(0905) 21074
Tolladine Rd. Worcester
1 mile east of Worcester.
(9)5134 yards/**/D

Worcester G.and C.C.
(0905) 422555
Boughton Park, Worcester
Just east of Hereford city centre.
(18)5946 yards/**/B/H

Worcestershire G.C.
(0684) 575992
Wood farm, Malvern Wells
(18)6449 yards/***/C/H/M

Charles Crombie   RULE IV   Rosenstiel's

RULE·IV·
If a player play when his partner should have done so ....
• • • • • • • • • • • •

EAST & WEST MIDLANDS

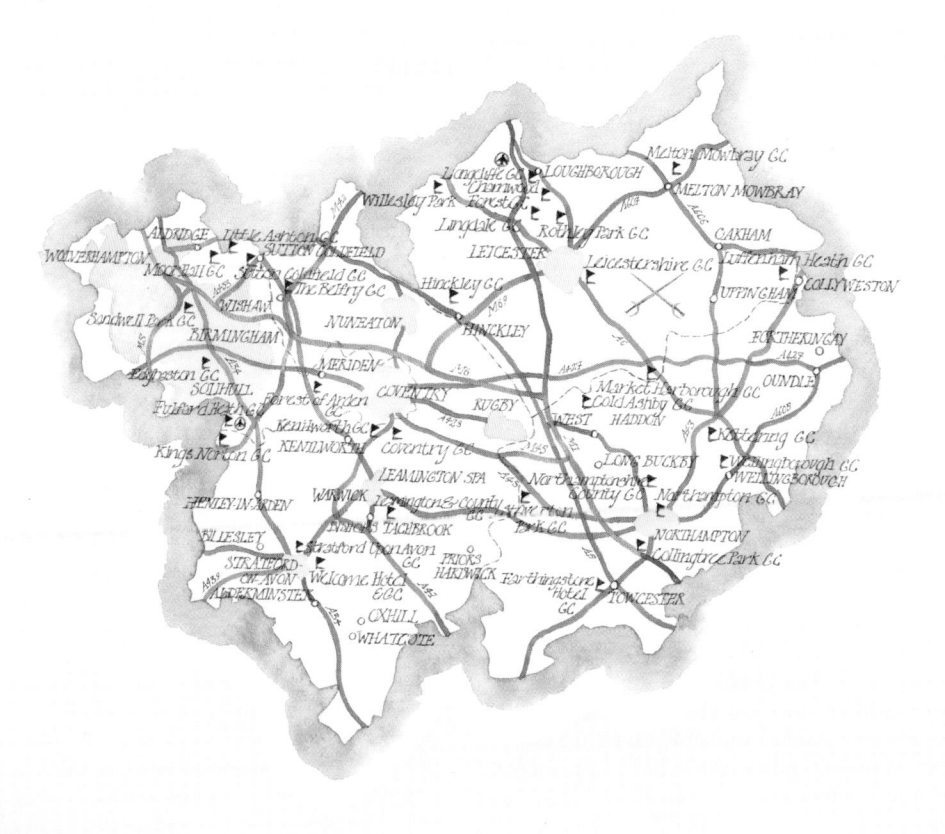

Bill Waugh   **THE BALLESTEROS HOLE**   *Burlington Gallery*

WEST & EAST MIDLANDS
CHOICE GOLF

'GREATER BIRMINGHAM'

Golfers in the City of London have often been known to get frustrated at having to travel many a mile for a decent game of golf. In 1919 one obviously disgusted individual teed up at Piccadilly Circus and proceeded to play along The Strand, through Fleet Street and Ludgate Hill firing his last shot at the Royal Exchange. Such behaviour is, as far as I'm aware, unknown in Birmingham – the Bull Ring and the NEC in their admittedly shorter existence, have never been peppered with golf balls, this I suspect may be because the needs of its golfing citizens have been properly attended to.

Within a sensible distance (ie. easy access) of the town centre lie the likes of **The Belfry** and **Little Aston** to the North, **Fulford Heath**, **Copt Heath** and **Kings Norton** to the South, and **Sandwell Park** and **Edgbaston** lying somewhere in the middle. Golfers north of Birmingham are indeed particularly fortunate for in addition to The Belfry and Little Aston there is also **Sutton Coldfield** and **Moor Hall**. All provide extremely pleasant retreats from the noise and confusion of England's second largest city. One need hardly add that there are also a number of public courses dotted around the outskirts of Birmingham.

Despite its relative youth, **The Belfry** (featured on a following page) has become the area's best know golfing attraction thanks largely of course to the thrilling **Ryder Cup** encounters staged there. However, **Little Aston** has long been regarded as one of Britain's finest inland courses and has hosted numerous major events – both amateur and professional. Little Aston's back nine is particularly outstanding. As at The Belfry there is an abundance of trees and the golfer must confront water, but it offers a much more subtle challenge than the Belfry. It is also a very 'traditional' Club – no nightclubs and boutiques here! Looking in and around Birmingham for places to stay a few obvious thoughts emerge. The Belfry Hotel (0675) 470301 is most luxurious and ideal for its own two courses (as well as the plethora of golf courses in the Sutton Coldfield area). It offers practically every activity under the sun. (When does the sun ever shine in Birmingham, you ask!). Moor Hall (021) 3083751 also provides a most comfortable and convenient 19th hole – an attractive mansion this. Still in Sutton Coldfield Penns Hall (021) 3513111 enjoys a peaceful lakeside setting while a short distance away in Aldridge is another alternative, The Fairlawns Hotel (0922) 55122.

Solihull to the south of Birmingham is surrounded by good golf. The George Hotel (021) 7112121 here is a modernised coaching inn and a very comfortable place in which to stay. Liaison (021743) 3993 is a pleasant spot to have dinner. Another suburb of Birmingham, on this occasion Edgbaston, provides the restaurant Sloans (021) 4556697. Two pleasant and popular pubs to track down when visiting the West Midlands include The Bear at Berkswell and another beast, The White Lion in Hampton-in-Arden.

Staying more centrally in Birmingham, The Albany (021) 6438171 is a first rate hotel while close to the National Exhibition Centre The Birmingham Metropole (021) 780 4242 is also good. On the other side of the cost coin, The Bridge House Hotel (021) 706 5900 makes for an excellent base. Perhaps the best word for Birmingham's restaurants is cosmopolitan, a huge range can be sampled.

Like Birmingham, the city of Coventry has been removed from Warwickshire and now bears the West Midlands label. **Coventry** Golf Club enjoys a decidedly peaceful setting at Finham Park, two miles south of the city along the A444. The course is good enough to have recently staged the British Seniors Championship. To the north west of Coventry at Meriden, the **Forest of Arden** Golf and Country Club offers a marvellous day's golf – 36 holes to savour here with the beautiful Aylesford and Arden courses – while the leisure facilities at the Country Club Hotel (0676) 23721 are outstanding.

The major tourist attraction in Coventry is undoubtedly the spectacular Cathedral. A fine piece of modern architecture sadly not reflected in the city's hotels – but then Coventry is no different from most. De Vere Hotel (0203) 633733, near the Cathedral is perhaps the best in the city, although The Post House (0203) 402151 is also well thought of. The Hearsall Lodge Hotel (0203) 674543 offers more modest accommodation, but is perfectly pleasant and comfortable and very convenient for **Coventry Hearsall** Golf Club, just south of the city off the A46. Another recommendation is Nailcote Hall (0203) 466174, situated west of Coventry in Berkwell.

WARWICKSHIRE

Birmingham and Coventry removed, Warwickshire has been left with only a handful of courses. The county's two most popular towns (tourist wise) are unquestionably Stratford and Warwick. Whilst **Warwick** has only a nine hole course located inside its race track, Shakespeare-spotters who've sneaked the clubs into the boot will be well rewarded. There are two fine 18 hole courses in Stratford, **Stratford** Golf Club and the **Welcombe Hotel** Golf Course, and a little beyond the town there are plans to build a 27 hole course at Bidford on Avon.

The Welcombe Hotel (0789) 295252 is a beautiful mansion with comfortable rooms and a good restaurant. But there are many outstanding alternatives for those spending a night or two in the Stratford area. Pride of place must go to Billesley Manor (0789) 400888 to the west of the town: quite simply majestic – and with a superb restaurant to boot. Of the countless guest houses and B&B's in the vicinity, two that are frequently acclaimed are Moonraker House (0789) 299346 and Oxtalls Farmhouse (0789) 205277. For pubs, a short drive towards Oxhill is recommended where The Peacock and The Royal Oak (in Whatcote village) will provide excellent sustenance.

Warwick has a famous castle and a good restaurant to note nearby is Randolphs. **Kenilworth** also has a castle (and a pretty reasonable golf course too). Here The Clarendon House (0926) 57668 is the place to stay and a restaurant to savour is The Restaurant Bosquet (0926) 52463. Wooton Court, at Leek Wooton, near Kenilworth has recently been acquired by a consortium which has ambitious plans to build a 36 golf and leisure centre. Lastly we visit Leamington Spa. It may not have the attractions of a Stratford or a Warwick but it does have a very fine golf course. **Leamington and County** is a hilly parkland course, situated to the south of Leamington. After an enjoyable round at Leamington, The Lansdowne (0926) 450505 is a smallish well-priced hotel in town and Crandon House (029577) 652 a comfortable farmhouse but if one is looking to spoil oneself then we recommend a trip to Bishops Tachbrook and Mallory Court (0926) 330214 – superb rooms and a terrific restaurant await.

124

WEST & EAST MIDLANDS
CHOICE GOLF

LEICESTERSHIRE

As we move from the West to the East Midlands let us start with the best course in Leicestershire.

Luffenham Heath lies over to the far east of the county within what was formerly Rutland and very close to the border with Lincolnshire. It is without question one of the most attractive heathland courses in England and being in a conservation area something of a haven for numerous species of wildlife. It isn't the longest of courses but then, thankfully, golf isn't always a question of how far you can belt the ball! A visit here is strongly recommended and there is no shortage of spectacular 19th holes nearby. The splendid Rutland countryside reveals many outstanding establishments. In Oakham, Hambleton Hall (0572) 756991 is quite tremendous. If you cannot spend the night here the restaurant is equally superb. By contrast, but also very enjoyable, is The Whipper Inn Hotel (0572) 75697 in Oakham's Market Square. A fine inn with good beers, snacks and some comfortable accommodation too. Note that this is Ruddles country and some excellent country pubs lie in wait. The King's Arms in Wing is a good example and there's a nearby maze in which to lose the children before a round of golf or a pint of County.

Rothley Park Golf Club, adjacent to the 13th century Rothley Court (0533) 374141 is one of Leicestershire's most picturesque parkland courses and is within easy access of Leicester, lying some 7 miles to the north west of the city, off the A6. Leicester is well served by golf courses and there are no fewer than three 18 hole municipal courses within four miles of the centre of Leicester, **Western Park** perhaps being the best of these. **Leicestershire** Golf Club is situated just 2 miles from the city centre along the A6. It is one of the top courses in the county; try to avoid the ubiquitous stream that runs through it. Leicester may not be the country's most attractive city but it does have its good points. The Haymarket Theatre offers a variety of productions while the Art Gallery includes works by English sporting artists and if you have business in town the Grand Hotel (0533) 555599 will prove the best selection. The Scotia Hotel (0533) 549200 is also popular with tourist and business people alike.

Looking further afield, in the north of the county the ancient town of **Melton Mowbray** has a fine nine hole course sited on high ground to the north east of the town and Loughborough possesses an 18 hole heathland type course, **Longcliffe**, which is heavily wooded with a particularly testing front nine.

In the south of the county, **Market Harborough**'s nine hole course offers extensive views across the surrounding countryside. North-west of Leicester, Charnwood Forest is one of the Midland's most pleasant retreats, an area where heath and woodland confront rocky craggs and granite outcrops. The village of Woodhouse Eaves lies on the eastern edge of the Forest and has two extremely pleasant courses at hand, **Lingdale** and **Charnwood Forest**. Though they are less than two miles apart they offer quite different challenges. Lingdale (which has recently been extended from 9 holes to 18) has a parkland setting with a trout stream flowing through it, while Charnwood Forest is a heathland type course – nine

holes, no bunkers but several outcrops of granite around which one must navigate.

Hinckley is linked to the centre of Leicester by the A47. Hinckley's golf course is a fairly new creation, built over the original nine hole Burbage Common layout. Several lakes and much gorse have to be confronted making this potentially the toughest in the county. The final mention for a round in Leicestershire goes to **Willesley Park** at Ashby-de-la-Zouch. A parkland-heathland mix this and well worth a visit.

Some ideas for life beyond the 18th fairway. If a pork pie and a piece of Stilton is what you're after then Melton Mowbray is an answer to your prayers – try The George (0664) 62112 – a charming inn with comfortable rooms. In the Loughborough area The Kings Head (0509) 23222 is popular and for two good restaurants, try The Old Schoolhouse (050981) 3941 in Sileby and The Cottage in the Woods (0509) 890318, Woodhouse Eaves. Finally, The Crown in Old Dalby is another good pub.

NORTHAMPTONSHIRE

The much admired **Northamptonshire County** course is situated some five miles north of Northampton at Church Brampton, and indeed is often referred to locally as Church Brampton. Famed for its many testing par fours, it is a splendid heather and gorse type with a fair few undulations in its 6,500 yards. Rather like Liphook in Hampshire a railway line bisects the course. In the past it has staged the British Youths Championship. Things are certainly happening around Northampton. At **Collingtree Park** Johnny Miller's spectacularly designed course has recently been opened to the public (see feature page) while **Northampton's** golfers are planning to leave their course and move to another venue. One final mention for visitors to the county town is the **Delapre** Golf Complex where a game should be easily arranged.

If looking to stay overnight in Northampton, The Moat House Hotel (0604) 22441 is modern but comfortable and handy for the centre, while the Westone Moat House (0604) 406262 is a mansion with modern additions. For value and friendly service, Garenden Park Hotel (0509) 236557 is highly recommended.

Elsewhere in the county there is a reasonable course at **Kettering** and not far away there is a better course at **Wellingborough,** two miles east of the town and set around the former Harrowden Hall. Quite hilly, it has several lakes and a mass of mature trees. It is certainly one of the best courses in the county. Others include **Staverton Park** at Daventry, **Cold Ashby** (near the site of the famous Battle of Naesby of 1645) with its superb views across the Northamptonshire Uplands, and the popular **Farthingstone Hotel** Golf and Leisure Centre near Towcester.

Pleasant countryside surrounds the towns of Wellingborough and Kettering. Perhaps the best bet for accommodation near the former is The Hind (0933) 222827. In the south of the county, The Crossroads (0327) 40354 at Weedon and The Saracens Head (0327) 50533 at Towcester are both welcoming although Farthingstone Hotel (0327) 36291 must be the best bet here.

COLLINGTREE PARK
CHAMPIONSHIP GOLF

In recent years we have grown accustomed to watching Australian Greg Norman tear golf courses apart: 62s at Doral and Glen Abbey; 63s at St Andrews and Turnberry and 64s at Augusta and Troon. A tournament isn't over they say, whilst Greg Norman is within seven shots of the leader. In the 1970s the man with a similar reputation for shooting extraordinary, par shattering rounds was American **Johnny Miller**. Twice in as many weeks in 1975 he returned a score of 61. That year he won the first 3 tournaments he entered in America, all by very large margins and he finished one shot away from catching Jack Nicklaus in The Masters after closing rounds of 65 and 66. In 1973, he stormed through the field with a final round of 63 to win the US Open; the score still stands as the lowest ever to win a major. In 1974 he won eight tournaments on the US tour and in 1976 charged around a dry and dusty Royal Birkdale in a course record equalling 66 on the final day of the Open, to win by six strokes. He was a dashing champion whose hobby (like Norman's) was driving super fast cars. Johnny Miller is also the man who has designed Collingtree Park.

Opened in May 1990, it is Miller's first course in Europe; hitherto he has been responsible for impressive layouts in the United States and Japan. Without question, Miller has produced a dramatic golf course which, in time, will surely be considered one of the finest in England. It is certainly one of the most challenging with 11 acres of lakes to be negotiated and more than 72,000 imported trees and shrubbery in a layout that can be stretched to close on 7,000 yards.

Collingtree Park is much more than an exciting new golf course; it claims to be 'Britain's first golf, housing and leisure village'. In addition to Miller's creation, there is a Golf Academy which includes three full length practice holes, a 16 bay floodlit driving range and an indoor video teaching room and computerised custom fitting centre. Luxury homes are being constructed around the golf course and, if all goes to schedule, a stunning five star 150 bedroomed country house hotel will soon form the centre of the village.

Persons wishing to learn more about the grand scheme at Collingtree Park might wish to contact the Operations Dir-ector, Geoffrey Hillman on (0604) 700000. All golf enquiries should be made to the Golf Director, **John Cook** and his professional staff; they may be contacted on **(0604) 701202**. The address for written correspondence is **Collingtree Park Golf Course, Windingbrook Lane, Northampton NN4 0XN**.

Summer green fees for 1992 were set at £35 per round during the week and £50 at the weekend. It is of course wise to telephone the Club in advance to find out how busy the course is likely to be. Handicap certificates are required. Details of Corporate Day packages and tuition courses can be obtained by telephoning (0604) 700000.

Travelling to Collingtree Park should be fairly straight forward. Very centrally located in the heart of England, it is just on the outskirts of Northampton, one of Britain's fastest growing towns and very close to the M1. Junction 15 is the exit to use, immediately picking up the A5108 road to North-ampton. This road should be followed for about half a mile and Collingtree Park's entrance is the second turning on the left. The golf course is 65 miles from London, 35 miles from Birmingham and about 20 miles from Milton Keynes.

When Johnny Miller first viewed the site in 1986 it is doubtful that he could have thought it the most natural setting for a golf course he had ever seen. Part meadowland, part wasteland it required a massive amount of work. With the support of Jack Nicklaus' technical services team it certainly received it. Work commenced in 1987 with the movement of over 350,000 cubic metres of earth. A positive drainage system with 16 miles of underground piping was installed and then the course was landscaped.

'I designed the course along American lines, but not without respect for the English countryside. I wanted Collingtree to combine the best of both English and American course ideas' said Miller. At 6821, yards from the championship tees (6692 yards from the medal and 5416 yards from the ladies) it is a formidable challenge, but with the lakes, the verdant fairways and the variety of trees it is an attractive one and there are of course the special holes. There isn't a bad hole at Collingtree Park but on the front nine the par three **5th** across the edge of a lake and the **9th** – one of those par fives that can be reached with two good shots but where disaster awaits the failed attempt – are especially memorable and on the much more difficult back nine there is the glorious finishing hole, probably the most dramatic in Great Britain. The **18th** measures close to 600 yards from the back tees and the third shot (you won't be going for this one in two) must be played to an island green – Florida comes to Northamptonshire! It is Miller's master stroke and you can guarantee that almost all conversation at the 19th hole will centre around 'how did you fair at the last?' And I dare say there will be one or two tall stories.

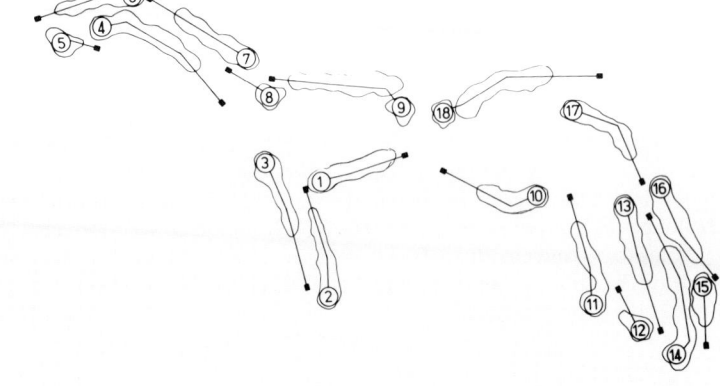

Hole	Yards	Par	Hole	Yards	Par
1	348	4	10	348	4
2	386	4	11	387	4
3	431	4	12	192	3
4	533	5	13	423	4
5	179	3	14	542	5
6	367	4	15	170	3
7	388	4	16	392	4
8	166	3	17	401	4
9	498	5	18	541	5
Out	3,296	36	In	3,296	36
			Out	3,296	36
			TOTALS	6,692	72

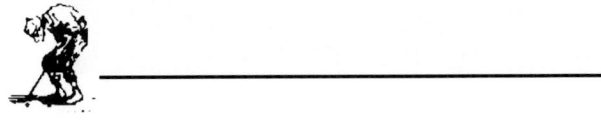

THE BELFRY
CHAMPIONSHIP GOLF

To adopt lawyers' jargon, it is 'beyond any reasonable doubt' that the game of golf was invented in Scotland. A handful of golfing pioneers brought the game south and today with the exception of a few notable areas in the north, where to live is to play golf, the sport is almost as popular south of the border.

One cannot help wondering quite what those early pioneers would have made of the 'Belfry project'.....'American-style target gowff?'....'and what d'ya mean artificial burns with man-made mounds and lakes!'.....'more than 7,000 yards did ya say?'....'Too many whiskies m'friend, you must be out o'your wee mind!'

The 'Belfry project' involved not only a plan to build a Championship course on American lines where in due course the **Ryder Cup** could be staged, but also the siting of a new headquarters for the P.G.A. **Peter Alliss** and **Dave Thomas** were given the task of designing the show piece and a very great task it was, for the land they were given was flat, uninteresting and comprised one small lake, a stream and numerous acres of potato fields.

Well, the boys didn't hang about: earth mountains were moved, the potatoes disappeared and hundreds of trees were planted – the end result in fact produced two 18 hole courses, opened in June 1977. The feature course was named the **Brabazon**, after Lord Brabazon a former President of the P.G.A. and the shorter, easier course, the **Derby**.

June 1977 – the month when Hubert Green survived a death threat to win the US Open and a month before Nicklaus and Watson fought out the 'Duel in the Sun' at Turnberry. So much has happened since then and to cite the history of The Belfry since its creation is almost to chart the rise of European golf; they are of course indelibly linked. Of all Europe's successes around the world the **1985 Ryder Cup** triumph at The Belfry will perhaps be remembered best of all. It was, after all, the first time the Americans had been defeated in nearly 30 years, and no other single event has been more responsible for generating the golf boom that has swept right across the Continent. So successfully staged was the tied match in **1989** that The Belfry has been awarded the match in **1993** for the third time in succession.

A key feature of The Belfry is that it is a Club without any Members. Both courses open their doors to the general public at all times all the year round. Not surprisingly the Brabazon is particularly busy and before setting off it is important to telephone and book a starting time. The Golf Manager, **Robert Maxfield**, and the two resident golf Professionals, **Peter McGovern** and **Simon Wordsworth** run the show efficiently. They can be contacted on **(0675) 470301**. Persons wishing to make a written enquiry should address a letter to the Golf Manager at **The Belfry, Lichfield Road, Wishaw, North Warwickshire, B76 9PR**.

In 1992 the green fees payable for a round on the Brabazon course were £46 for weekdays and £51 for weekends. This contrasted with £20.50 for a weekday round on the Derby course with £26 payable at weekends. For the fitter among us intent on tackling the pair in a day a weekday ticket cost £56, with £66 payable at weekends. In addition to being a luxury hotel with a full complement of facilities, the Belfry Hotel has public bars and restaurants open to the general public. If after a meal and a few drinks you're still not satisfied with your golf there's a final opportunity to put things right on the impressive floodlit covered driving range.

Situated close to the country's industrial heart there is surely no golfing complex in Britain better served by communication networks. The Belfry is one mile from the M42 (junction 39), five miles from the M6 (junction 4), nine miles from Birmingham city centre and less than ten minutes from Birmingham International Airport and the N.E.C. Railway Station. The exact positioning of the Golf Club is at the apex of the A446 and A4091.

Apart from the sheer length of the Brabazon Course the many water hazards are likely to present the greatest challenge. Two of its holes are guaranteed to excite; the short par four **10th** where almost everyone tries to be famous for five seconds before spending five minutes trying to fish his or her ball out of the lake, and the thrilling **18th** where **Christy O'Connor Jnr** hit that magnificent 2 iron in the 1989 Ryder Cup, and where American dreams of victory in the same match met a watery grave.

Mention has been made of how this American-styled extravaganza was created out of a field of potatoes; well interestingly, the American legend **Sam Snead** on first viewing St. Andrews declared that it looked like 'the kind of real estate you couldn't give away'.... obviously the message is clear – let's plough the old place up, fill the Road Hole Bunker with water, plant a few trees, create a lake out of the Valley of Sin......

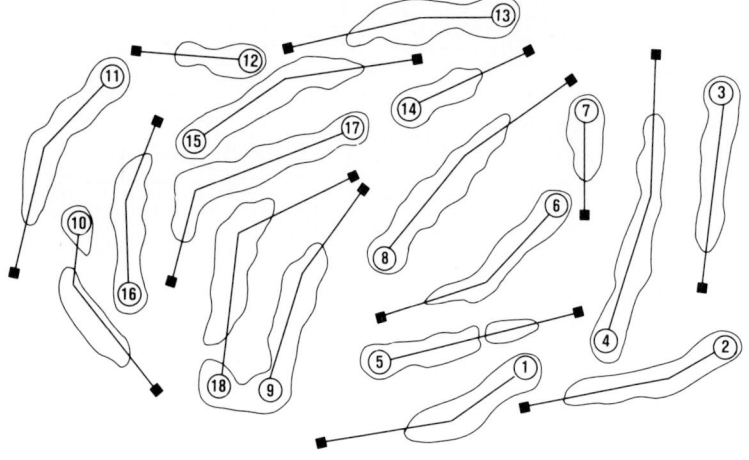

Brabazon Course

Hole	Yards	Par	Hole	Yards	Par
1	408	4	10	301	4
2	340	4	11	365	4
3	455	4	12	225	3
4	569	5	13	364	4
5	389	4	14	184	3
6	386	4	15	540	5
7	173	3	16	400	4
8	476	5	17	555	5
9	390	4	18	455	4
Out	**3,586**	**37**	**In**	**3,389**	**36**
			Out	**3,586**	**37**
			TOTALS	**6,975**	**73**

WEST AND EAST MIDLANDS
COMPLETE GOLF

NORTHAMPTONSHIRE

Cherwell Edge G.C.
(0295) 711591
Chacombe, Banbury
3 miles east of Banbury on A442.
(18)5322 yards/***/D

Cold Ashby G.C.
(0604) 7400548
Cold Ashby, Northampton
(18)5898 yards/***/C

Collingtree Park G.C
(0604) 700000
Windingbrook Lane, Northampton
(18)6692 yards/***/A

Daventry and District G.C.
(0327) 702829
Norton Rd. Daventry
1 mile north of Daventry.
(9)5582 yards/***/D

Delapre G.C.
(0604) 764036
Eagle Drive, Nene ValleyWay, Northampton
Just south of town.
(18)6293 yards/***/D

Farthingstone Hotel G. C
(0327) 36291
Farthingstone, Towcester
(18)6500 yards/***/C

Hellidon Lakes Hotel & CC
(0327) 62550
Hellidon
(18)6691 yards/***/B

Kettering G.C.
(0536) 512074
Headlands, Kettering
(18)6036 yards/**/C/H

Kingsthorpe G.C.
(0604) 710610
Kingsley Rd. Northampton
2 miles from town off A508.
(18)6006 yards/**/B/H

Northampton G.C.
(0604) 845155
Kettering Rd. Northampton
Just north of town on A43.
(18)6002 yards/**/C/H

Northamptonshire County G.C.
(0604) 843025
Sandy Lane, Church Brampton, Northampton
5 miles from Northampton off A50.
(18)6503 yards/***/A/H

Oundle G.C.
(0832) 273267
Benefield Rd. Oundle, Peterboro
2 miles west of Peterborough.
(18)5507 yards/**/F

Priors Hall G.C.
(0536) 60756
Stamford Rd, Weldon
2 miles east of Weldon off A43.
(18)6677 yards/***/E

Rushden and District G.C.
(0933) 312581
Kimbolton Rd. Chelveston, Wellingborough
2 miles east of Higam Ferrers on old A45.
(9)6381 yards/**/C

Staverton Park G.C.
(0327) 705911
Staverton, Daventry
1 mile south of Daventry on A425.
(18)6204 yards/***/C

Wellingborough G.C.
(0933) 677234
Horrowden Hall, Great Horrowden
North of Wellingborough on A509.
(18)6604 yards/**/C/H

Woodlands Vale G.C.
(032736) 291
Woodlands Vale, Farthingstone, Towcester
3 miles west of Weedon.
(18)6330 yards/***/C

LEICESTERSHIRE

Birstall G.C.
(0533) 674322
Station Rd. Birstall, Leicester
3 miles north of Leicester off A6.
(18)5988 yards/***/B/H

Charnwood Forest G.C.
(0509) 890259
Breakback Lane, Woodhouse Eaves,
Loughborough
(9)6202 yards/***/C/H

Cosby G.C.
(0533) 864759
Chapel Lane, Cosby
(18)6277 yards/**/F/H

Enderby G.C.
(0533) 849388
Mill Lane, Enderby
(9)4356 yards/***/E

Glen Gorse G.C.
(0533) 714159
Glen Rd. Oadby
Just outside Oadby on A6.
(18)6641 yards/**/F/H

Greetham Valley G.C.
(078086) 666
Off B668 in Greetham
(18) 6656 yards/***/C

Hinckley G.C.
(0455) 615124
Leicester Rd. Hinckley
1 mile north of Hinckley on A47.
(18)6592 yards/**(Tue)/F/H

Humberstone Heights G.C.
(0533) 764674
Gipsy Lane, Leicester
3 miles east of Leicester on A47.
(18)6444 yards/***/D

Kibworth G.C.
(0533) 792301
Weir Rd. Kibworth Beauchamp
8 miles south of Leicester on A6.
(18)6282 yards/**/C

Kirby Muxloe G.C.
(0533) 393457
Station Rd. Kirby Muxloe
4 miles west of Leicester on A47.
(18)6303 yards/**/F/H

Leicestershire G.C.
(0533) 738825
Evington Lane, Leicester
2 miles south of Leicester.
(18)6312 yards/***/B

Leicestershire Forest G.C
(0455) 824800
Markfield Rd, Botcheston
(18)6111 yards/***/D

Lingdale G.C.
(0509) 890703
Joe Moores Lane, Woodhouse Eaves
(9)6114 yards/***/C

Longcliffe G.C.
(0509) 239129
Shells Nook Lane, Nanpantan, Loughborough
(18)6551 yards/**/B/H]

Luffenham Heath G.C.
(0780) 720205
Ketton, Stamford
6 miles south of Stamford.
(18)6254 yards/***/A/H

Lutterworth G.C.
(0455) 552532
Rugby Rd. Lutterworth
(18)5570 yards/**/C

Market Harborough G.C.
(0858) 463684
Oxendon Rd. Market Harborough
1 mile south of Market Harboro on A508.
(9)6080 yards/**/D

Melton Mowbray G.C.
(0664) 62118
Waltham Rd. Thorpe Arnold, Melton Mowbray
2 miles north of Melton Mowbray on A607.
(9)6200 yards/***/C/M

Oadby G.C.
(0533) 700326
Leicester Rd. Oadby
1 mile south of Oadby on A6.
(18)6228 yards/***/E

Rothley Park G.C.
(0533) 302809 Westfield Lane, Rothley
6 miles north of Leicester off A6.
(18)6487 yards/***/B/H/M

R.A.F. North Luffenham G.C.
(0780) 720041
North Luffenham, Oakham
(9)5998 yards/*/E/G

Scraptoft G.C.
(0533) 418863
Beeby Rd. Scraptoft, Leicester
(18)6146 yards/***/B/H

Ullesthorpe G.C.
(0455) 209023
Frolesworth Rd. Ullesthorpe
(18)6206 yards/**/C/H

Western Park G.C.
(0533) 872339
Scudmore Rd. Braunstone Frith
2 miles west of Leicester on A47.
(18)6532 yards/***/E

Whetstone G.C.
(0533) 861424
Cambridge Rd. Cosby
Just south of Leicester.
(18)5795 yards/***/D

Willesley Park G.C.
(0530) 414596
Tamworth Rd. Asby-de-la-Zouch
2 miles south from Asby-de-la-Zouch on A453.
(18)6304 yards/**/B/H/M

WEST MIDLANDS

Belfry G.C
(0675) 70301
Lichfield Road, North Wishaw, Sutton Coldfield
On junction of A4091 and A446
(18) 6975 yards/***/A
(18) 6077 yards/***/D

Bloxwich G.C.
(0922) 405724
Stafford Road, Bloxwich, Walsall
4 miles from Walsall centre off A34
(18) 6286 yards/**/D/H

Boldmere G.C. 021-354 3379
Monmouth Drive, Sutton Coldfield
6 miles N.E of Birmingham on A452
(18) 4463 yards/***/E

Brand Hall G.C
021-552 2195
Heran Road, Oldbury, Warley
Leave M5 at junction 2 for A4123
(18) 5813 yards/***/E

Calderfields G.C.
(0922) 640540
Aldridge Road, Walsall
Leave M6 at junction 7 for the A454
(18) 6700 yards/***/E

City of Coventry G.C
(Brandon Wood)
(0203) 543133
Brandon Lane, Brandon, Coventry
6 miles S. of Coventry on A45
(18) 6530 yards/***/F

Cocks Moor Woods G.C
021-444 3584
Alcester Road South, Kings Heath, Birminham
On A435 near city boundary
(18) 5742 yards/***/E

Copt Heath G.C
(0564) 772650
Warwick Road, Knowle, Solihull
Leave M42 at junction 5 for A41
(18) 6504 yards/**/B/H/M

Coventry G.C
(0203) 414152
Finham Park, Coventry
2 miles S. of Coventry on A444
(18) 6613 yards/**/C/H

Dartmouth G.C
021-588 2131
West Bromwich
Off the West Bromwich-Walsall Road
(9) 6060 yards/**/D

Druids Heath G.C
(0922) 55595
Stonnal Road, Aldridge
Between Sutton Coldfield and Walsall off A452
(18) 6914 yards/**/C/H

Dudley G.C
(0384) 233877
Turners Hill, Rowley Regis, Warley
One mile from town centre
(18) 5715 yards/*/E

Edgbaston G.C.
021-454 1736
1 mile south of city centre
(18) 6118 yards/***/B

Enville G.C
(0384) 872074
Highgate Common, Enville, Stourbridge
Take A458 Bridgnorth Road
(18) 6541 yards/**/C/H
(18) 6207 yards/**/C/H

Forest of Arden Golf & Country Club
(0676) 22335
Maxstoke Road, meriden, Coventry
10 miles W. of Coventry off A45
(18) 6962 yards/***/B/H
(18) 6500 yards/***/B

Fulford Heath
(0564) 822806
Tanners Green Lane, Wythall, Birmingham
1 mile from main Alcester road
(18) 6216 yards/**/D/H

Gay Hill G.C
021-430 6523
Alcester Road, Hollywood, Birmingham
7 miles from city centre on A435
(18) 6522 yards/**/C/H

Grange G.C
(0203) 451465
Copsewood, Coventry
3 miles from city centre on A428
(9) 3001 yards/**/E

Great Barr G.C
021-358 4376
Chapel Lane, Great Barr, Birmingham
Adjacent to exit 7 of M6
(18) 6546 yards/**/D/H

Hagley G.C
(0562) 883701
Wassel Grove, hagley, Stourbridge
Off A456 Kidderminster-Birmingham Road
(18) 6353 yards/**/D

Halesowen G.C
021-501 3606
The Leasowes, Halesowen
(18) 5754 yards/**/D

Handsworth G.C
021-554 0599
11 Sunningdale Close, Handsworth,
Birmingham
3 miles N.W of city centre off A41
(18) 6312 yards/**/C/H

Harborne G.C
021-427 3058
40 Tennal Road, Birmingham
3 miles W. of city centre off A4040
(18) 6240 yards/**/C/H

Harborne Church Farm G.C
021-427 1204
Vicarage Road, Harborne, Birmingham
Follow harborne Road to Vicarage Lane
(9) 4514 yards/***/F

Hatchford Brook G.C
021-743 9821
Coventry Road, Sheldon, Birmingham
On A45 road to Coventry
(18) 6164 yards/***/F

Hearsall G.C
(0203) 713470
Beechwood Avenue, Coventry
Off A45, 2 miles S. of city centre
(18) 5963 yards/**/C/H

Hilltop G.C
021-554 4463
Park Lane, Handsworth, Birmingham
Take Birmingham road from M5
(18) 6114 yards/***/E

Himley Hall G.C
(0902) 895207
Log Cabin, Himley Hall Park, Dudley
Turn onto B4176 from A449
(9) 3090 yards/***/E

Kings Norton G.C
(0564) 826789
Brockhill Lane, Weatheroak, Alvechurch,
Birmingham
2 miles from junction 3 of M42
(27) **/D/H

Ladbrook Park G.C
(05644) 2264
Poolhead lane, Yanworth-in-Arden, Solihull
4 miles from Hockley Heath on A4023
6407 yards/***(prior arrangement)/D/H

Lickey Hills G.C
(021) 453 3159
Rose Hill, Old Birmingham Road, Rednal,
Birmingham Road
10 miles S.E of city centre
(18) 6010 yards/***/E

Little Aston G.C
(021) 353 2066
Streetly, Sutton Coldfield
3 miles N. of Sutton Coldfield
(18) 6724 yards/**/F

Maxstone Park G.C
(0675) 64915
Castle lane, Coleshill, Birmingham
From A446 take B4147 to Nuneaton
(18) 6437 yards/**/D

Moor Hall G.C
021-308 6130
Moor Hall Drive, Four Oaks, Sutton Coldfield
2 miles from Sutton Coldfield on A453
(18) 6219 yards/**/B

Moseley G.C
021-444 2115
Springfield Road, Kings Heath, Birmingham
E. of Alcester Road on Birmingham ring-road
(18) 6227 yards/B/H/L

North Warwickshire G.C
(0676) 22259
Hampton Lane, Meriden
1 mile from Stourbridge on B4102
(9) 3186 yards/**(not Thurs)/C

North Worcestershire G.C
021-475 1047
Frankley Beeches Road, Northfield,
Birmingham
(18) 5919 yards/**/D

Olton G.C
021-705 1083
Mirfield Road, Solihull
7 miles S. of Birmingham on A41
(18) 6229 yards/**(not Weds)/D/H

Oxley Park G.C (0902) 20506
Bushbury, Wolverhampton
2 miles from town centre off A449
(18) 6168 yards/***/D

Patshull Park
(0902) 700100
Burnhill Green, Pattingham, Wolverhampton
Take exit 3 from M54 to Albrighton and Patshull
(18) 6460 yards/***/F

Penn G.C
(0902) 341142
Penn Common, Penn, Wolverhampton
2 miles S.W of town off A449
(18) 6465 yards/**/D

Pype Hayes G.C
021-351 1014
Eaglehurst Road, Walmley, Sutton Coldfield
Take junction 6 from M6, take Tyburn road to
Eaglehurst
(18) 5811 yards/***/E

Robin Hood G.C
021-706 0061
St. Bernards Road, Solihull
6 miles S. of Birmingham on A41
(18) 6609 yards/**/F/H

Rose Hill G.C
021-453 3159
Lickey Hills, Rednal, Birmingham
Leave M5 by junction 4 to Lickey Hills
(18) 6006 yards/***/E

Sandwell Park G.C
021-553 4637
Birmingham Road, West Bromwich
(18) 6470 yards/**/F

Shirley G.C
021-744 6001
Stratford Road, Solihull
7 miles S. of Birmingham on A34
(18) 6445 yards/**/C

South Staffordshire G.C
(0902) 751065
Tettenhall
(18) 6653 yards/**/B

Stourbridge G.C
(0384) 395566
Pedmore
(18) 6178 yards/**/C

Sutton Coldfield G.C
021-3539633
Streetly
(18)6541 yards/***/B

Swindon G.C
(0902) 897031
Bridgnorth Rd, Swindon
(18) 6042 yards/**/C

Walmley G.C
021-373 0029
Wylde Green
(18)6537 yards/**/B

Walsall G.C
(0922) 613512
The Broadway, 0ff A34
(18) 6243 yards/**/A

Windmill Village Hotel & G.C
(0203) 407241
Birmingham Rd, Coventry
(18) 5200 yards/***/D

WARWICKSHIRE

Atherstone G.C
(0827) 713110
The Outwoods, Atherstone
Half mile out of Atherstone on Colehill Road
(18) 6239 yards/**/C/H

Kenilworth G.C
(0926) 50517
Crew Lane, kenilworth
Off A429 from Kenilworth to Coventry
(18) 6408 yards/***/F/H

Leamington & County G.C
(0926) 425961
Golf Lane, Whitnash, Leamington Spa
2 miles from town centre on A452
(18) 6425 yards/***/F

Newbold Comyn G.C
(0926) 421157
Newbold Terrace East, Leamington Spa
Off B4099 Willes Road
(18) 6259 yards/***/D

Nuneaton G.C (0203) 347810
Golf Drive, Whitestone, Nuneaton
2 miles from town centre off B4114
(18) 6412 yards/**/C/H

Purley Chase G.C
(0203) 393118
Ridge lane, Atherstone, Nuneaton
Take A5 to Mancetters Island and onto Pipers
Lane
(18) 6604 yards/***/F/H

Rugby G.C
(0788) 542306
Clifton Road, Rugby
Off the Rugby-Market Harborough Road
(18) 5457 yards/***/E

Stratford-Upon-Avon G.C
(0789) 205749
Tiddlington Road, Stratford-upon-Avon
Half-mile from River bridge on B4089
(18) 6309 yards/**/F/H

Warwick G.C
(0926) 494396
The Racecourse, Warwick
Half-mile pat junction of A41 and A46
(9) 2682 yards/***(not Sundays)/E

Welcombe Hotel G.C
(0789) 295292
Warwick Road, Stratford-Upon-Avon
2 miles from Stratford on A46 to Warwick
(18) 6600 yards/**/C/H

Charles Wagstaff **GOLFERS** *Rosenstiel's*

EAST ANGLIA

Julian Barrow   **BRANCASTER**   *Burlington Gallery*

EAST ANGLIA
CHOICE GOLF

The counties of East Anglia, which for our purposes comprise Norfolk, Suffolk and Cambridgeshire, stretch from Constable Country in the south, through the Fens and the Broads to the tip of the Wash. For golfers this means it stretches from Felixstowe Ferry, through Thetford to Hunstanton. There are numerous other combinations capable of whetting the golfing appetite, for East Anglia is one of the game's richest regions; certainly for quality and variety it has few equals. It is also a corner of Britain where golf has long been a popular pastime.

NORFOLK

It is doubtful whether any county in England can surpass Norfolk's great range of outstanding courses. In short it offers the golfer a bit of everything. There are the magnificent links courses at **Hunstanton** and **Brancaster**, some terrifically scenic golf along the cliffs at **Sheringham** and **Cromer** and a number of superb inland courses of which **Thetford**, **Barnham Broom** and **Kings Lynn** are prime examples.

However, the title of 'Oldest Club' in Norfolk goes to **Great Yarmouth and Caister**, founded in 1882. A fine seaside links, it is located to the north of Great Yarmouth close to the old Roman town of Caister-on-Sea and near to the start of the A149 coastal road. Punters may wish to note that the golf course is actually situated inside part of Great Yarmouth race course. Anyone who does think of combining the two might look to Gorleston-on-Sea for a night's rest at the Cliff Hotel (0493) 662179 or in Yarmouth itself we recommend the Imperial Hotel (0493) 851113 which is a family run hotel and the Bradgate Hotel (0493) 842578.

Cromer, some 25 miles north along the A149 is apparently famed for its crabs – the town, not the golf course I hasten to add – and also for its 150 year old lighthouse. The latter is a feature of **Royal Cromer's** attractive cliff top course. The 14th, the 'Lighthouse Hole', was played by Tony Jacklin during his '18 holes at 18 different courses helicopter round'. Several elevated tees and a generous spread of gorse makes for a very interesting game.

Sheringham is only five miles further along the coast and is Norfolk's other great cliff top course. Founded some three years after Cromer in 1891 it is perhaps less exacting than its neighbour but certainly no less scenic. The view from the 5th hole is particularly stunning looking out across the rugged north Norfolk coastline – we have featured Sheringham on a later page.

A glorious day's golf (followed perhaps by some early evening bird watching? – don't forget the binoculars) and time to relax. Well, in Sheringham, The Burlington (0263) 822224, The Beacon (0263) 822019 and the Beaumaris (0263) 822370 are handy whilst in nearby Weybourne The Swiss Restaurant (0263) 70220 is a splendid eating place and Maltings Hotel (026370) 731 is a perfect base. However, if you were intending to stay over in Cromer we would suggest the Anglia Court Hotel (0263) 52443. On the road towards Brancaster (still the A149) the Blakeney area offers a glorious coastline and two beautifully situated hotels, The Manor (0263) 740376 and The Blakeney (0263) 740797.

And so on to Brancaster and Hunstanton, an outstanding pair to put it mildly. We have featured both courses, or both links to be precise, later in this section. Once again, there's no shortage of places in which to relax and reflect on the day's golf. In Old Hunstanton, adjacent to the links, is the very relaxing Lodge Hotel (04853) 2896 and on Golfhouse Road Le Strange Arms (0485) 53441 is also highly thought of. The village of Thornham lies between Hunstanton and Brancaster and here one might consider The Chequers Inn (048526) 229 or The Kings Head (048526) 213. To the south east of Brancaster The Old Rectory (0328) 820597 at Great Snoring sounds like the perfect place for a particularly long rest and a little nearer at Brancaster Staithe, the Jolly Sailors (0485) 210314 is a good pub with an accompanying restaurant. Further accommodation can be found at Titchwell, the Titchwell Manor (0485) 210221 and for two outstanding seafood restaurants we recommend the Moorings in Wells and Fishes in Burnham Market. Finally, a really homely country house, The Holly Lodge (0485) 70790 at Heacham takes some beating.

Kings Lynn is our next port of call, and another very good golf course. Although the **Kings Lynn** Golf Club was founded back in 1923, it has played at Castle Rising to the north of the town since 1975. An Alliss-Thomas creation, it's very heavily wooded and quite a demanding test of golf. Returning to the town itself suggestions for an overnight stay might include The Dukes Head Hotel (0553) 774996 and Russett House (0553) 773098. A short journey to Grimston and one finds a real gem in Congham Hall (0485) 600250, an elegant and very well run Georgian Manor House Hotel.

The golfing visitor to Norwich, one of England's more attractive county towns, should have little difficulty in finding a game. **Sprowston Park** is a welcoming club on the edge of the city while for a fine combination of the old and the new try **Royal Norwich** and **Barnham Broom**. Both clubs have excellent parkland courses. Barnham Broom is part of an Hotel and Country Club complex and has two courses with numerous accompanying leisure facilities; it is featured ahead. If Norwich is to be the base though, then The Maids Head Hotel (0603) 761111 is most comfortable. Slightly less imposing, but no less comfortable, are the Grange Hotel (0603) 34734 and the Marlborough House Hotel (0603) 628005. Among many good restaurants are Marcos (0603) 624044, The Anchor Quay Bar (0603) 618410 and Greens Seafood (0603) 623733.

Last but not least we must visit **Thetford**, right in the very heart of East Anglia and close to the Norfolk-Suffolk boundary. Thetford is surely one of England's most beautiful inland courses. Set amid glorious oaks, pines and silver birch trees it is also a great haven for wildlife (rather like Luffenham Heath in Leicestershire). Golden pheasant abound and one can also sight red deer and even, so I'm told, Chinese Water Deer (whatever they may be!) The green fee here is always money well spent. The second place to invest the cash is at The Bell Hotel (0842) 754455 in Thetford – a jolly good place to rest the spikes.

SUFFOLK

Of the twenty or so Golf Clubs in Suffolk, about half were founded in the 19th Century and the **Felixstowe Ferry** Golf Club which dates from 1880 is the fifth oldest club in England. Given its antiquity, and the fact that it was here that the 'father of golf writers' Bernard Darwin began to play his golf, Felixstowe Ferry is as good a place as any to begin our brief golfing tour of Suffolk.

The course lies about a mile to the north east of Felixstowe and is a classic test of traditional links golf. This part of Suffolk is fairly remote and at times it could easily be imagined that one was playing one of the better Scottish links courses. The greens are first class and the wind is often a major factor. Those looking to spend some time in this area (the courses at Ipswich and Woodbridge are only a short drive away) should note the Marlborough Hotel (0394) 670724 in Felixstowe.

The A45 links Felixstowe with Suffolk's largest town. The **Ipswich** Golf Club at Purdis Heath, three miles east of Ipswich, was designed by James Braid and is a fine parkland course. Always well-maintained, the fairways wind their way between two large ponds and are bordered by an attractive assortment of hardwood trees and silver birches. **Woodbridge** provides an excellent contrast to Purdis Heath (and to Felixstowe for that matter). Like the Ipswich course it's beautifully mature but is much more undulating and is of the heather and gorse variety as opposed to parkland. The Golf Club is located two miles east of Woodbridge along the B1084 Orford road.

The Ipswich-Woodbridge area is blessed with some outstanding places to stay and the seafood served in these parts is some of the best in Britain. In Woodbridge, Seckford Hall (0394) 385678 is superb while Melton Grange (0394) 384147 also appeals. For those who enjoy their lobster Orford should be visited, more particularly the Butley-Orford Oysterage (0394) 450277. In Ipswich another Marlborough Hotel (0473) 257677 is both comfortable and good value and to the west of the town at Hintlesham is 16th century **Hintlesham Hall** (047387) 334, where a glorious country house with an excellent restaurant and a fairly new golf course await – gourmet golf personified! Other hotel suggestions in the Ipswich area would definitely include the good value Bentley Tower Hotel (0473) 212142.

A little further up the Suffolk coast lie two delightful holiday courses: **Thorpeness** and **Aldeburgh**. Although close to the sea both are again heather and gorse types. The town of Aldeburgh is of course famed for its annual music festival and Benjamin Britten once lived next to the Club's 14th fairway. Thorpeness, yet another James Braid creation, is about two miles north of Aldeburgh and is especially scenic. One hole that everyone remembers is the par three 17th, played across an attractive pond. On the 18th an unusual water tower (the 'House in the Clouds') and a restored windmill provide a unique background. Thorpeness Golf Club has its own Golf Hotel (0728) 452176 which is naturally very convenient, but in Aldeburgh there are a number of alternatives, many of which specialise in golfing breaks. Ideas here include the Wentworth (0728) 452312, the White Lion (0728) 452720 and the Uplands Hotel (0728) 452420. Also worth a visit is the White Horse Hotel (0728) 830694 in nearby Leiston. A final thought before moving inland is The Crown (0502) 722275 at Southwold to the north of Thorpeness – some pleasant rooms and some very good beer!

Over to the west of Suffolk the two courses that stand out are **Bury St. Edmunds** and **Royal Worlington**. The former is a fairly tough parkland course. Royal Worlington and Newmarket, to give the latter its full title, is located two miles from Mildenhall, midway between Cambridge and Bury St. Edmunds. A marvellous course, essentially heathland but with an almost links feel it was once generously described as the finest nine holes in the world. Bury St. Edmunds offers a first rate hotel in The Angel

(0284) 753926 while to the south of the town two cosy establishments are The Bull at Long Melford with its 15th Century frontage and the popular Swan (0787) 247477 at Lavenham.

CAMBRIDGESHIRE

Having ventured west it is time to inspect the land of the fens and the courses of Cambridgeshire. Not exactly a county renowned for its golf, the courses tending, as one might expect, to be rather flat. One great exception though is the **Gog Magog** Golf Club situated to the south east of Cambridge which offers a tremendously enjoyable test of golf. The Club takes its name from the ridge of low hills on which it lies. Apparently taking a line due east from here the next range of hills one comes across is the Ural Mountains! Among many fine holes, the par four 16th stands out and is surely one of the best (and toughest!) two-shot holes in the country. A second good course, close to the famous University City belongs to the **Cambridgeshire Moat House Hotel** (0954) 780555. It is a particularly tough course when played from the back tees with a lake and several ditches providing the challenges.

Cambridge with its magnificent colleges is a marvellous place to spend a day or two and the Moat House is just one of many fine hotels. Of the others The Garden House Hotel (0223) 63421 perhaps takes pride of place and is particularly welcoming. It also possesses a first class restaurant. Another good eating place in town is The Marguerite (0223) 315232. Among the less expensive hotels, both Bon Accord House (0223) 411188 and the Lensfield Hotel (0223) 355017 are recommended. Some notable hostelries in the county include The Plough and Fleece at Horningsea, The Three Horse Shoes at Madingley and The Green Man at Grantchester. Other courses in Cambridgeshire which can be recommended include **Ramsey, St Ives, St Neots** and a duo just outside of bustling Peterborough, **Peterborough Milton** and the public course, **Thorpe Wood**. Finally, in Ely there is the attractive **Ely City** course which provides some excellent views of the stunning 12th Century cathedral and where the course record is held by one Lee Trevino.

Lance Thackeray THEIR LAST BALL Burlington Gallery

THORPENESS GOLF CLUB HOTEL

Two miles north of Aldeburgh in the heart of Suffolk's Heritage Coast lies the unspoilt Thorpeness, one of Britain's most unusual villages. Many years ago its remote seclusion made it the haunt of smugglers who carried their contraband ashore to bury it for collection in safer times.

Glencairn Stuart Ogilvie, with visionary genius, decided to create a model village. His project began in 1910 with the construction of the Meare, a beautiful 60 acre lake which now flanks the course. During the First World War the golf club was commandeered for defence purposes, and work was not resumed until 1918.

The course, as it exists now, was laid out by James Braid in 1925. Set in 175 acres of lovely gorse and heather country, studded with spinneys of silver birch and clumps of tree lupin, the 6,241 yard, par 69 round is attractive enough to provide a treat for amateurs and challenging enough to test the best.

There are a few holes to watch out for; the short 145 yard seventh, hit across a small lake, the 500 yard 14th which dog-legs sharply to the left, and the 18th, which features the Windmill and House in the Clouds - a former water tower now converted to a holiday home.

Ten years ago a purpose built accommodation block was added to the club. Its twenty-two rooms, all with private facilities, welcome families. In addition to these the club offers a large private lounge which is ideal for conferences of up to forty delegates.

A new conservatory has recently been added to the oak-panelled bar and has been proving very popular with both visitors and guests. The Dining Room, also panelled, serves traditional English food with the delicious speciality of local, freshly caught fish.

For the non-golfer, or simply for a relaxing change, the unspoilt beauty of the surrounding area offers endless opportunities for inland or coastal walks, with peaceful beaches for swimming and fishing. For the avid music-lover, the Snape Maltings annual music festival, initiated by Sir Benjamin Britten, is a nearby treat.

Thorpeness Golf Hotel
Thorpeness
Suffolk IP16 4NH
Tel: (0728) 452176
Fax: (0728) 452868

ROYAL WEST NORFOLK (BRANCASTER)
CHAMPIONSHIP GOLF

Excluding those which have staged an Open Championship, there are perhaps two courses in Britain that exude a sense of tradition, history and character above all others. One is **Westward Ho!** and the other is **Brancaster** or, to give them their correct titles, **Royal North Devon** and **Royal West Norfolk**.

Apart from their rather geographical names, they have much in common; both enjoy a wondrously remote setting yet are still fairly close to a superb Championship links (Saunton and Hunstanton); both have a unique hazard (Devon's sea rushes and Norfolk's tidal marshes) and both are particularly friendly Clubs, emphasising that tradition need not accompany aloofness.

Brancaster is something of a golfers' Camelot. Having reached the attractive little village there is every possibility that a high tide will have flooded the road that leads to the course. Indeed, many choose to leave their car in the village and walk the remainder of the journey. (Dont worry, it's not that far!) The golf course lies in a range of sand hills between marshland and sea. There is a story that the course was laid out on the suggestion of the **Prince of Wales** (later King Edward V11), having conceived the idea while out shooting on the land. Certainly it was he who bestowed patronage upon the Club immediately on its foundation in 1891. The Royal flavour has continued and there have been no fewer than four Royal Captains, most recently the **Duke of Kent** in 1981.

The Secretary at Brancaster is **Major Nigel Carrington Smith** and he can be contacted on **(0485) 210223**. The Club's full address is **The Royal West Norfolk Golf Club, Brancaster, Nr. Kings Lynn, Norfolk, PE31 8AX**. Individual visitors and societies are both welcome at Brancaster although all visiting parties must make prior arrangements with The Secretary – an introduction is preferred. Due to increased demand, no visitors are received at any time, unless playing with a member, during the last week in July and until the end of the first week in September.

In 1992, the green fee was set at £30 during the week and £40 at weekends and on Bank Holidays. The preferred days for golfing societies are Mondays, Wednesdays and Fridays. The Professional at Brancaster, **Mr. R.E. Kimber**, can be contacted on **(0485) 210616**.

The problem of being wondrously remote is that travelling to the course can be a lengthy journey. Brancaster is approximately eight miles from Hunstanton and twenty-five miles from Kings Lynn, to the south and south west respectively, and about thirty miles from Cromer to the east. Linking each to the other is the A149.

Like our friend Westward Ho!, Brancaster has the traditional out and back links layout. A quick glance at the scorecard tells us that one nine is considerably shorter than the other, the outward half measuring 3369 yards to the inward's 3059 yards. However, as at every good seaside course, wind direction is all important and on many occasions the back nine can play, or at least seem much longer. In total, the 6428 yards, par 71 represents a considerable test of golf. From the ladies tees the course measures 5927 yards, par 75.

As well as the tidal marshes which come into play around the **8th** and **9th**, Brancaster is famed for its great wooden sleepered bunkers. Many are cross bunkers, which as Sir Peter Allen observed: '... can be alarming to play over and frightening to play out of.' The course has received very few alterations over the years although two greens were lost to the sea in 1939 and 1940. There is no gentle beginning; the first three holes all measure over 400 yards and the great cross bunkers are introduced on the **3rd** hole, one of the most difficult on the course. The bunker is fifty yards short of the green, which itself sits on a plateau. The **4th** is a short par three but is deceptively tricky, especially into the wind. The 8th and 9th have been mentioned and the marshes must be carried twice on the 8th and from the tee on the dog-legged 9th which has a cross bunker in front of the green. The **11th** and **12th** are played deep amid the dunes but the **14th** is perhaps the most difficult hole, with the **18th** close behind – a hole with sleepered bunkers both to the front and back of the green.

The Clubhouse, which is only a year younger than the course, is decidedly comfortable and is separated from the sea only by a sea wall. This famous last line of defence had to be repaired in 1991, after high seas reaped havoc in 1990. The Clubhouse also has a lovely verandah from which there are some glorious views. The setting really is something special and nobody described it better than the late **Tom Scott**.

'It has a quiet and restful beauty, and when you leave the Clubhouse and drive across the marsh to the main road in the dusk of a summer evening, look back for a minute and perhaps you will be rewarded, as I have frequently been, with a view of the red sun setting over the sea with a golden glow. You will see too, the long shadows cast by the great sand hills, and you will hear the call of the many birds across the marshes, a sound to my mind typical of Norfolk.'

Hole	Yards	Par	Hole	Yards	Par
1	410	4	10	151	3
2	449	4	11	478	5
3	407	4	12	386	4
4	128	3	13	317	4
5	421	4	14	432	4
6	186	3	15	188	3
7	486	5	16	346	4
8	478	5	17	377	4
9	404	4	18	384	4
Out	**3,369**	**36**	**In**	**3,059**	**35**
			Out	**3,369**	**36**
			TOTALS	**6,428**	**71**

HUNSTANTON
CHAMPIONSHIP GOLF

Imagine you are standing on the tee of a particularly difficult par three hole. It is a difficult hole on a still day – 188 yards long and with six deep bunkers encircling the green – but it is particularly tough on this day because the wind is dead against. You select a one iron and hit the perfect shot; so perfect that it lands a few feet from the flag and rolls into the hole. Marvellous, but what a pity this is only a practice round! A day later, in the tournament itself, you reach the 16th but this time the wind is with you. You choose a six iron and incredibly you repeat the trick – in it goes for a second hole in one. Much celebration follows at the 19th. The next day (the second of the tournament) the wind is once more at your back as you walk onto the tee of what is now your favourite hole. If a six iron was good enough yesterday, it must be good enough today you reckon. Your calculations are entirely accurate and your well struck shot never really looks like missing. Three aces in three days at the same hole! Are you a liar, a dreamer..... or Robert Taylor?

Taylor performed this remarkable feat in the summer of 1974 on the **16th** at **Hunstanton**. Nobody has ever matched his extraordinary achievement and probably never will.

Founded over a hundred years ago, Hunstanton Golf Club celebrated its centenary in 1991. Although it is situated on the east coast of England the course actually faces north west and looks over The Wash towards Lincolnshire. Hunstanton has the kind of geography that causes its Members to loose sleep over talk of global warming. It is a very good golf course – in the opinion of many, the east coast's finest 18 hole challenge between Sandwich and Muirfield, a distance of about 400 miles. It is a boast regularly expressed by Hunstanton's Members when a player from Brancaster happens to be within earshot. But theirs is a valid claim, for Hunstanton is a truly classic links course. Like Brancaster, the course runs out and back although not rigidly so, rather it meanders away from the Clubhouse, reaches the 8th green and meanders its way home. The outward holes have the River Hun for company, normally it is off to the right and the inward ones are closer to the shore. At first glance, the links looks very flat, and indeed there aren't any major climbs, up or down, but the course has more than its fair share of subtle undulations and there are a number of elevated tees and plateau greens, some of which offer extensive views of both sea and country.

It isn't the views though that are likely to be best remembered after a round at Hunstanton, it is the greens and bunkers. The putting surfaces are as quick (and usually as well prepared) as any in Britain – including the Open Championship courses. As for the bunkers, they are numerous, strategically (and sometimes sadistically) placed and often quite deep. Avoid the bunkers and putt well and you'll probably score well here!

The Club is very happy to receive visitors on weekdays and occasionally at weekends. All must be members of Golf Clubs and have current handicaps. It is worth noting that the 1st tee is reserved on weekdays before 9.30am, but in any event it is a good idea to contact the club a few days prior to any visit. The Secretary at Hunstanton, **Mr R.H. Cotton** can be approached by writing to; **The Hunstanton Golf Club, Old Hunstanton, Norfolk PE36 6JQ.** Mr Cotton can also be contacted by telephone on **(0485) 532811. Mr J Carter** is the Club's professional and he can be reached on **(0485) 532751.**

The green fees in 1992 were £28 per day during the week and, when available, £34 per day at weekends. Junior golfers paid half the above rates.

From the Championship tees, Hunstanton measures 6,670 yards, par 72 (s.s.s 72); while from the medal tees it is reduced by some 350 yards to 6,318 yards, although it then becomes a par 70, and for Ladies the course measures 5,986 yards, par 75. We have already referred to the ingenious and severe bunkering and the four par three holes emphasise this: the **4th** is only 165 yards in length but has eight bunkers; the **7th** is a similar length and only has one trap, but what a trap! The tee shot is an attractive one over a gully to a plateau green, anything short is almost certain to plummet into a deep, yawning bunker that almost runs the entire width of the entrance – a low runner is not the desired shot here. The **14th** requires a blind tee shot of 200 yards plus and again eight bunkers are waiting to greet the player who fails to find the putting surface.

The par four holes at Hunstanton offer a range of challenges. The **3rd**, for instance, demands a very long approach shot if the prevailing wind is up to its tricks; by contrast, the **6th** is a modest length hole but a deft touch is required to pitch onto the plateau green. The finishing holes are all quite interesting but the best hole on the course is generally considered to be the **11th** which runs parallel to the shore. A high tee gives a spectacular view of both the hole and the surrounding countryside. At 439 yards it needs two perfectly hit shots along an ever narrowing valley-fairway to reach the green.

Numerous major amateur events have been staged at Hunstanton over the years, including the 1990 British Boys Amateur Championship won by the highly promising Michael Welch.

Hole	Yards	Par	Hole	Yards	Par
1	343	4	10	372	4
2	532	5	11	439	4
3	443	4	12	356	4
4	165	3	13	387	4
5	424	4	14	216	3
6	332	4	15	476	5
7	162	3	16	188	3
8	483	5	17	446	4
9	508	5	18	398	4
Out	**3,392**	**37**	**In**	**3,278**	**35**
			Out	**3,392**	**37**
			Totals	**6,670**	**72**

SHERINGHAM
CHAMPIONSHIP GOLF

I suspect that most golfers have, at one time or another, worked out their eclectic score for the 18 holes on their home course. Recently, a friend of mine from Withington Golf Club in Cheshire, boasted after his first ever hole in one that his first four holes now ran 2-2-2-1. Not bad, I told him, but what about **Ernie Riseboro**. Never heard of him came the rather terse reply. Ernie Riseboro was one of the first professionals at Sheringham; the Club was founded a century ago in 1891 and he served the club from 1907 until his retirement in 1958. Apart from longevity of service, Ernie's great claim to fame was that his best ball score for Sheringham comprised nothing higher than a 2 .... and have you seen the par fours at Sheringham! .....

Sheringham's splendid cliff top course is situated in one of the more remote parts of Britain, tucked away on Norfolk's northern coast, staring out across the bleak North Sea. The course has long been regarded as one of the finest on the east coast of England and as long ago as 1920 was selected to host the English Ladies Championship – more of which a little later – an event which returned in 1991 during the Club's Centenary year, when 18 year old **Nicola Buxton** triumphed over 17 year old **Karen Stupples**. Famous early members of the Club included two of Britain's greatest heroes: **Robert Falcon Scott** and **Douglas Bader** – snowshoes and spitfires at Sheringham.

Today, visitors are very welcome at Sheringham, although they are required to be in possession of a Club handicap. It is always advisable to make an advance telephone call to the Secretary, **Mr. M.J. Garrett**, to check whether any tee reservations are planned. Mr Garrett may be contacted on **(0263) 823488**.

Green fees for 1992 were set at £25 on weekdays with £30 payable at weekends and on Bank Holidays. Reduced rates are available for junior golfers. Golfing societies are also encouraged and may make weekday bookings through the Secretary, written applications to be addressed to Mr Garrett at the **Sheringham Golf Club, Weybourne Road, Sheringham, Norfolk NR26 8HG**.

Anyone approaching Sheringham should be travelling along the A149 as the course is located immediately off this road, half a mile west of the town. Coming directly from Norwich motorists should take the A140 before joining the A149 at Cromer, Sheringham being signposted off to the left on the B157 about 4 miles before Cromer is reached. A level crossing heralds the entrance to the Golf Club.

The current professional at Sheringham is **Richard Emery**, tel **(0263) 822980**. Before stepping out onto the 1st tee it might be a good idea to step into his well-stocked pro shop and top up on the supply of golf balls – not forgetting that this is very much a cliff top course!

So having got to the 1st tee what are we confronted by? In short, from the medal tees, 6464 yards of challenging, varied and at times most spectacular golf. The par for the men is 70 (s.s.s.71) while for the ladies the course measures 5807 yards, par 73. The course has been laid out on a strip of land sandwiched between the cliffs on the one side and the North Norfolk Steam Railway line on the other. The turf is of that springy, seaside nature and there is an abundant smattering of heather and gorse. Whereas the sea can beckon on some of the front nine holes so the railway line becomes very much a feature on the home stretch.

The opening two holes, a short four followed by a par five, may well provide a solid start and dare I suggest, the chance of beginning 3-4? The next five holes run close to the cliff edges and are possibly the most enjoyable of the round; certainly the views here are tremendous. Particularly memorable is the panoramic view from the **5th** fairway, looking out across the north Norfolk coastline – not a hole to be hurried. On the next seven holes the gorse becomes the most likely devil to wreck a promising card, perhaps the most testing holes being the **10th** and **12th**. Sheringham has an exacting finish and with the railway line acting as a continuous boundary to the right now is not the time to suddenly develop a slice.

Special mention must be made of the **17th**, a hole made famous by the great **Joyce Wethered**, now Lady Heathcote-Amery, when playing in her first English Ladies Championship in 1920. Aged only 19, she reached the final to play the overwhelming favourite, **Cecil Leitch**. On the 17th green (which was then much closer to the railway line) Miss Wethered faced a short putt to win the match. Just as she prepared to strike the ball the 4.20 train from Sheringham thundered past, but no matter she duly sunk the putt. Questioned as to why the train hadn't put her off at all she apparently replied, 'What train?'!

After her win at Sheringham Miss Wethered's career blossomed, indeed she won the next four English Ladies titles as well and was never beaten in that event. How great a player was she? According to Bobby Jones she was the best golfer in the world of either sex, but then Jones always was modest, and besides, I bet she never took on Ernie Riseboro at Sheringham.

Hole	Yards	Par	Hole	Yards	Par
1	335	4	10	444	4
2	543	5	11	163	3
3	424	4	12	425	4
4	327	4	13	351	4
5	418	4	14	354	4
6	217	3	15	195	3
7	490	5	16	349	4
8	157	3	17	405	4
9	410	4	18	423	4
Out	3,321	36	In	3,109	34
			Out	3,321	36
			TOTALS	6,430	70

UFFORD PARK

Whatever your reason for visiting Ufford Park, you will delight in the tranquility of some of Suffolk's most beautiful countryside.

Set in 120 acres of parkland the hotel provides a perfect setting for the holiday and business visitor.

For those with time on their hands, there are facilities like the 18 hole golf course and extensive leisure club, while the conference organiser will find Ufford Park to be one of the area's foremost venues for all sizes of business meeting.

Ufford Park's location makes it an ideal place to work, play and stay. Sited near the historic market town of Woodbridge, the complex is only minutes away from the main A12 London road. By the same token, you are a short drive from the region's Heritage Coastline, with beauty spots like Dunwich, Snape and Southwold all within easy reach.

The 18 hole golf course has been designed to professional standards and offers a rewarding challenge for all standards of player. Greens and other areas are maintained by experienced ground staff, while many natural features are retained from the original ancient parkland. The course is 6,335 yards par 71.

No less challenging - for those who require it - is our leisure club. Open to hotel guests and local members, it features a luxurious deck level swimming pool - complete with jet stream - a steam room, a fitness studio with assessment room, dance studio, solarium, spa, bath, sauna, beautician and hair salon. All our leisure club facilities are professionally staffed on a full - time basis.

All 25 hotel bedrooms have their own bathroom/shower, colour television, radio, direct dial telephone, trouser press, hair dryer and full tea and coffee making facilities. Additional accommodation is available in the Golf Lodge which caters for business, private and golfing parties up to 20.

Visitors using the Ufford Cedar Restaurant can enjoy a full English breakfast, lunch and the chef's choice of a la carte or carvery meal for dinner. A variety of family snacks can be ordered from the hotel bar, while special arrangements can be made for weddings, conferences and other functions.

Facilities cover anything from a boardroom meeting or training workshop to conferences for up to 120 delegates and corporate golf days, tailored to suit the individual needs of the client.

Two day 'get away' breaks start from £90 per person for dinner, bed and breakfast. For further information please contact:

Ufford Park Hotel, Golf and Leisure
Yarmouth Road
Ufford
Woodbridge
Suffolk IP12 1QW
Tel: (0394) 383555
Fax: (0394) 383583

HINTLESHAM HALL GOLF CLUB

Hintlesham Hall's 18 hole championship standard golf course provides excellent golf in an uniquely privileged environment. Designed by well known golf course architect Martin Hawtree, the course measures 6630 yards from the medal tees with a Par of 72. Blending perfectly with the surrounding mature parkland of this prestigious location, the course was allowed the unusually long period of two full years to mature before opening for full scale use in September 1991. As a result, golfers are pleasantly surprised to find a beautifully manicured course with well defined fairways and consistently paced greens.

The Hintlesham course has been constructed to challenge the professional, while remaining enjoyable and rewarding to high handicap golfers. Practice facilities include a putting green, a short game pitching area and practice drive ground. Year round play is ensured by the quality of construction and the natural advantages of the site.

The brand new clubhouse, a bright and airy building designed with a frontage in the style of an Edwardian pavilion, includes services and facilities well above the standards of those ordinarily provided at a golf club. Large lounge, dining area and separate stud bar are bordered by a full width verandah providing extensive views over this beautiful, undulating parkland course.

Both the men's and women's changing areas are light and spacious with separate saunas, a shared steam room and large spa bath which look onto an internal courtyard.

With equal status for ladies and gentlemen, both on the course and in the clubhouse, Hintlesham Hall Golf Club provides a traditional high level of service to its members and their guests commensurate with the standards at the adjacent hotel.

Hintlesham Hall Golf Club has a growing national reputation for the total organisation of every facet of a golfing day, whether small or large scale. Alastair Spink, the Club Head Professional can offer a programme of indoor and outdoor tuition and golf clinics whilst Club Secretary, Peter Smith, as well as looking after the membership, is on hand to arrange tournaments and golf days. Green Fee players are welcome subject to reserving tee-off times.

For further information about Membership, Green Fee Play, Organised Golfing Days or Golfing Breaks, pleas contact the Club Secretary on (047 387) 761.

Hintlesham Hall and its Golf Club are located 4 miles west of Ipswich on the A1071. Hintlesham is 10 minutes drive from the A45 and A12 trunk roads.

Hintlesham Hall Golf Club
Hintlesham
Ipswich
Suffolk IP8 3NS
Tel: (047 387) 761
Tel: Hotel: (047 387) 334
Fax: (047 387) 463

HINTLESHAM HALL

Hintlesham Hall, originally built in the 1570's, with a stunning Georgian facade offers the best in country house elegance and charm. Gracious living, good food and wine, attentive service and tranquil relaxation greet every guest to the hotel.

The Hall is set in over 170 acres of rolling Suffolk countryside some of which is devoted to a beautiful 18-hole championship full-length golf course, and has 33 luxurious bedrooms and suites, of different shapes and sizes, some with four poster beds. Thoughtful attention to detail pervades the hotel, and this includes the restaurant. Head Chef, Alan Ford, believes good food starts with good produce. French truffles, Scottish salmon, Cornish Scallops and Suffolk lobsters are just some of the enticements on the menu which changes seasonally. There is an award-winning 300 bin wine list which ranges the world from France to Australia.

All moods are reflected in Hintlesham's fine reception rooms - the intimate book-lined Library, the tranquil spacious Garden room and the cool entrance Arcade. The Hall is just 45 minutes drive from Newmarket and is an ideal base from which to explore East Anglia, be it the medieval wool villages of Lavenham and Kersey, Long Melford and Woodbridge with their wealth of antique shops or Dedham and Flatford Mill famous for their Constable associations. The cathedral city of Norwich and the University colleges of Cambridge are also close by. However, perhaps most importantly, Hintlesham Hall is the perfect retreat for those who wish to go nowhere at all.

Hintlesham Hall
Hintlesham
Suffolk IP8 3NS
Tel: Hintlesham (047 387) 334
Fax: Hintlesham (047 387) 463

BARNHAM BROOM
CHAMPIONSHIP GOLF

'Yes, nice place to go for a holiday, Norfolk – quaint villages, splendid country houses, Norwich Cathedral, The Norfolk Broads, a spectacular coastline... oh, and plenty of invigorating sea air.' What about a golfing holiday? 'Well yes, there are some tremendous seaside courses aren't there – Hunstanton, where the greens are faster than a marble staircase and Brancaster, a glorious reminder of how golf used to be: plus fours, sleepered bunkers, pitch and run and all that; and some fabulous cliff-top golf further along the coast at Sheringham and Cromer. Apart from Thetford though, which is almost in Suffolk anyway, there's nothing much inland is there? – too flat and too exposed I imagine.'

Barnham Broom Hotel, Golf & Country Club has shattered the illusion: thirty six marvellous holes of golf set in 250 acres of rolling parkland and a fine hotel in which to rest the weary bones overnight. As for being 'too flat and too exposed', well the two courses are called **The Hill** and **The Valley** and on both the golfer is protected from nature's worst habits by a good and varied collection of trees.

Barnham Broom actually arrived on the scene in the late 1970s at a time when the phrase 'Hotel, Golf & Country Club' was greeted somewhat suspiciously by this country's golfing fraternity. 'An American joint is it? – lots of water and 18 enormously long holes. Just like the Belfry I suppose!'

There were only 18 holes at the time – the present day Valley Course – but 1989 saw the opening of The Hill Course and they complement each other perfectly. There is a fair amount of water at Barnham Broom but it is not overdone, nor is it entirely artificial, the ubiquitous River Yare being chiefly responsible for the many watery duels. The only overtly American look to the place is the conditioning of the courses: they are beautifully maintained – unlike all too many courses these days in Britain. Certainly they deserve inspection.

Very able to assist you with your enquiries is the senior professional and Golf Director, **Peter Ballingall**. He can be approached either by writing to Barnham Broom, the full address being **Barnham Broom Golf & Country Club, Honingham Road, Barnham Broom, Norwich NR9 4DD** or by telephone on **(060545) 393**. Also extremely helpful is golf professional **Steve Beckenham** who can also be contacted via the above telephone number.

In 1992, the green fees to play at Barnham Broom were set at £25 per round, £30 for a full day. These rates apply seven days per week. It is important to telephone the club in advance to book a starting time – Barnham Broom has become very popular with golf societies and hotel guests may have reserved tee times. Reduced green fees are available to hotel residents and weekend breaks are good value, especially now there are 36 holes to play.

Barnham Broom is situated 7 miles from Norwich, almost due west of the county town mid way between the A11 and the A47. The latter is likely to be the best road to take out of Norwich; an alternative is the B1108. Travelling from further afield, Norwich has been brought much closer to London by the M11 (which should be left at junction 9 for the A11). The A467 links the city with the Midlands to the west and Great Yarmouth to the east. A combination of the A45/A140/A43 should be taken from Ipswich.

The two courses are of similar length, the Valley Course measuring 6470 yards, par 71 from the back markers against the Hill Course's 6628 yards, par 72. From the tees of the day the difference in total is just 28 yards (6241 yards and 6269 yards). For ladies, each course measures a shade under 6000 yards and is a par 74. Both courses open with par fives. The **2nd** on the Valley Course is a tremendous dog-leg where a miss hit shot can end up in a small lake; but the challenge is even greater on the **3rd** which is the stroke index one. Another fine hole on the Valley Course is the **6th** although it has lost some of its sting since the January 1990 storms removed an obstructing tree.

On the Hill Course, which is maturing rapidly, the outstanding hole is probably the par five **6th** which is played along a valley. Just in front of the green the river meanders severely and gives the impression of practically surrounding the golfer as he putts (hopefully) for a memorable birdie.

Memorable birdies at the 6th or not, it is likely that when the golfer walks from the 18th green he will have enjoyed a memorable round. Barnham Broom really is a delightful place to visit. The atmosphere is extremely relaxed, not at all stuffy, and the golf is par excellence. We have mentioned the hotel only briefly but it really does make a superb base and offers the sporting types a whole host of leisure facilities.

Yes, nice place for a golfing holiday, Norfolk – beside the sea and in the heart of the country.

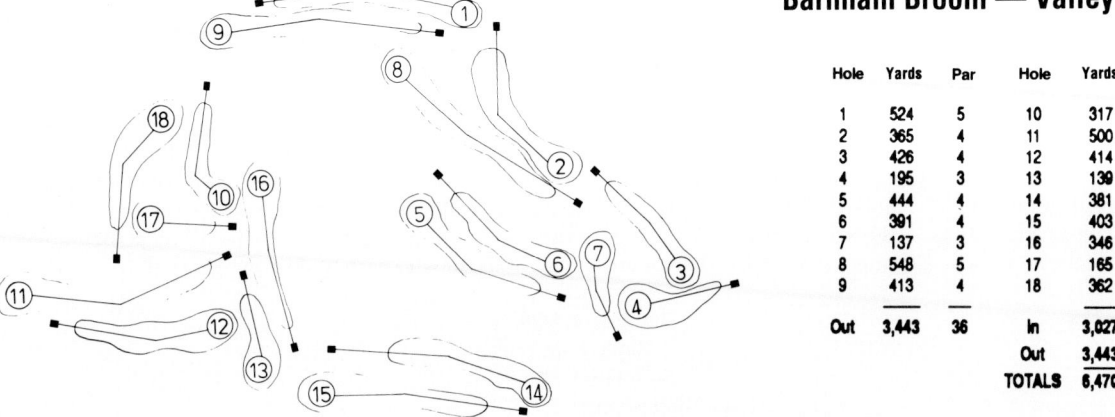

Barnham Broom — Valley Course

Hole	Yards	Par	Hole	Yards	Par
1	524	5	10	317	4
2	365	4	11	500	5
3	426	4	12	414	4
4	195	3	13	139	3
5	444	4	14	381	4
6	391	4	15	403	4
7	137	3	16	346	4
8	548	5	17	165	3
9	413	4	18	362	4
Out	3,443	36	In	3,027	35
			Out	3,443	36
			TOTALS	6,470	71

EAST ANGLIA
COMPLETE GOLF

CAMBRIDGESHIRE

Abbotsley G.C.
(0480) 215153
Eynesbury Hardwicke, St. Neots
(18)6150 yards/***/C

Cambridgeshire Moat House Hotel G.C.
(0954) 780555
Bar Hill
4 miles north of Cambridge off A604.
(18)6734 yards/***/B/L/M

Ely City G.C.
(0353) 662751
Cambridge Rd. Ely
Just south of Ely on A10.
(18)6686 yards/**/B

Girton G.C.
(0223) 276169
Dodford Lane, Girton
3 miles north of Cambridge off A604.
(18)6085 yards/**/C

Gog Magog G.C.
(0223) 247626
Shelford Bottom
2 miles south of Cambridge on A13107.
(18)5354 yards/**/F/H
(9)5833 yards/**/F/H

Hintlesham Hall G.C.
(047387) 334
Hintlesham
(18)6630 yards/**/A

March G.C.
(0354) 52364
Frogs Abbey, Grange Rd, March
(9)6200 yards/**/D

Orton Meadows G.C.
(0733) 237478
Ham Lane, Peterborough
2 miles west of Peterborough.
(18)5800 yards/***/D

Peterborough Milton G.C.
(0733) 380489
Milton Ferry, Peterborough
2 miles west of Peterboro on A47.
(18)6431 yards/**/F/H

Ramsey G.C.
(0487) 812600
4 Abbey Terrace, Ramsey, Huntingdon
(18)6136 yards/**/C/H

St. Ives G.C.
(0480) 68392
Westwood Rd. St. Ives
5 miles east of Huntingdon off A604.
(9)6052 yards/**/C/H

Lakeside Lodge G.C.
(0487) 740540
Fen Road, Pidley
(18)6600 yards/E/***

St. Neots G.C.
(0480) 72363
Crosshall Rd. St. Neots
2 miles west of St. Neots off A1.
(18)6027 yards/**/F

Thorpe Wood G.C.
(0733) 267701
Thorpe Wood, Peterborough
(18)6595 yards/***/D

SUFFOLK

Aldeburgh G.C.
(0728) 452890
Saxmundham Rd. Aldeburgh
1 mile from town centre on A1094.
(18)6330 yards/***/F/H
(9)4228 yards/***/F/H

Beccles G.C.
(0502) 712244
The Common, Beccles
(9)2696 yards/**/C

Bungay and Waveney Valley G.C.
(0986) 892337
Outney Common, Bungay
Just outside Bungay on A143.
(18)6615 yards/**/C/H

Bury St. Edmunds G.C.
(0284) 755979
Tuthill, Bury St. Edmunds
2 miles from Bury on A45.
(18)6615 yards/***/B/H

Cretingham G.C.
(0728) 685275
Cretingham, Woodridge
(9)1955 yards/***/D

Felixstowe Ferry G.C.
(0394) 286834
Ferry Rd. Felixstowe
(18)6042 yards/***/C/H

Flempton G.C.
(0284) 728291
Flempton, Bury St. Edmonds
4 miles from Bury.
(9)6074 yards/**/C

Fornham Park G.C.
(0284) 706777
Fornham St. Genevive, Bury St. Edmunds
2 miles from Bury.
(18)6212 yards/***/F

Haverhill G.C.
(0440) 61951
Coupals Rd. Haverhill
(9)5680 yards/***/C

Ipswich G.C.
(0473) 728941
Purdis Heath, Bucklesham Rd.
3 miles east of Ipswich off A45.
(18)6405 yards/**/B/H(18)
(9)3860 yards/***/D

Links G.C.
(0638) 663000
Cambridge Rd. Newmarket
1 mile south of Newmarket opposite
racecourse.
(18)6162 yards/***/F/H

Newton Green G.C.
(0787) 77217
Newton Green, Sudbury
3 miles east of Sudbury on A134.
(9)5488 yards/**/D/H

Rookery Park G.C.
(0502) 560380
Beccles Rd. Carlton Coleville, Lowestoft
2 miles west of Lowestoft on A146.
(18)6649 yards/***/C/H

Royal Worlington and Newmarket G.C.
(0368) 71226
Worlington, Bury St. Edmonds
(9)3105 yards/**/B

Rushmere G.C.
(0473) 725648
Rushmere Heath, Ipswich
East of Ipswich off A1214.
(18)6287 yards/***/C/H

Southwold G.C.
(0502) 723234
The Common, Southwold
(9)6001 yards/***/C/H

Stowmarket G.C.
(0449) 736473
Lower Rd. Onehouse, Stowmarket
(18)6101 yards/***/C/H

Thorpeness G.C.
(072845) 2176
Thorpeness
(18)6241 yards/**/B/H

Waldringfield Heath G.C.
(0473) 36768
Newbourne Rd. Waldringfield
5 miles north of Ipswich off A12.
(18)5837 yards/***/C

Woodbridge G.C.
(03943) 2038
Bromeswell Heath, Woodbridge
2 miles east of Woodbridge off A12.
(18)6314 yards/**/B/H
(9)4486 yards/**/B/H

Wood Valley G.C.
(0502) 712244
The Common, Beccles
(9)2781 yards/**/D/H

NORFOLK

Barnham Broom G. and C.C.
(060) 545393
Norwich, Norfolk
8 miles south of Norwich.
(18)6603 yards/***/B
(18)6470 yards/***/B

Bawburgh G.C.
(0603) 746390
Long Lane, Bawburgh, Norwich
Behind Royal Norfolk Showground.
(9)5278 yards/***/D

Costessey Park G.C.
(0603) 746333
Costessey Park, Costessey, Norwich
3 miles west of Norwich.
(18)5853 yards/***/C

Dereham G.C.
(0362) 695900
Quebec Rd. Dereham
1 mile from Derehamon B1110.
(9)6225 yards/**/C/H

Diss G.C.
(0379) 642847
Stuston Rd. Stuston Common, Diss
1 mile town centre.
(9)5900 yards/***/D

Eaton G.C.
(0603) 51686
Newmarket Rd. Norwich
(18)6125 yards/**/B/H

Fakenham G.C.
(0328) 2867
Sports Centre, The Racecourse, Fakenham
1 mile south of Fakenham off A1065.
(9)5879 yards/***/C

Gorleston G.C.
(0493) 661911
Warren Rd. Gorlestone, Gt.Yarmouth
3 miles south of Gt. Yarmouth off A12.
(18)6400 yards/***/C/H

Great Yarmouth and Caister G.C.
(0493) 728699
Beech House, Caister-on-Sea, Gt.Yarmouth
2 miles north of Gt.Yarmouth on A149.
(18)6235 yards/***/F

Hunstanton G.C.
(0485) 532811
Golf Course Rd. Old Hunstanton
(18)6670 yards/***/A/H

Kings Lynn G.C.
(0553) 631654
Castle Rising, Kings Lynn
(18)6646 yards/**/A/H

Links Country Park Hotel G.C.
(026375) 691
West Runton
Betweeen Cromer and Sheringham
on A149.
(9)2407 yards/***/C

Mundesley G.C.
(0263) 720279
Links Rd. Mundesley
1 mile from Mundesley.
(9)5410 yards/***/C

R.A.F. Marham G.C.
(0760) 337261
RAF Marham, Kings Lynn
(9)5244 yards/*/D/G

Richmond Park G.C.
(0953) 881803
Saham Rd, Watton
(18)6300 yards/***/D/H

Royal Cromer G.C.
(0263) 512884
145 Overstrand Rd. Cromer
1 mile east of Cromer on B1159.
(18)6508 yards/***/B/H

Royal Norwich G.C.
(0603) 429928
Drayton High Rd. Hellesdon
(18)6603 yards/**/F/H

Royal West Norfolk G.C.
(0485) 210087
Brancaster, Kings Lynn
(18)6428 yards/**/A/H

Ryston Park G.C.
(0366) 383834
Denver, Downham Maret
1 mile south of Downham on A10.
(9)6292 yards/**/D

Sheringham G.C.
(0263) 823488
Weybourne Rd. Sheringham
1 mile from town on A149.
(18)6464 yards/***/F/H

Sprowston Park G.C.
(0603) 410657
Wroxham Rd. Sprowston
(18)5985 yards/**/B/H

Swaffham G.C.
(0760) 721611
Cley Rd. Swaffham
1 mile from Swaffham.
(9)6252 yards/**/C

Thetford G.C.
(0842) 752169
Brandon Rd. Thetford
(18)6879 yards/**/B/H

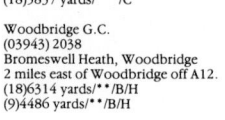

Charles Crombie   RULE XXIII   Rosenstiel's

DERBY, NOTTS & LINCS

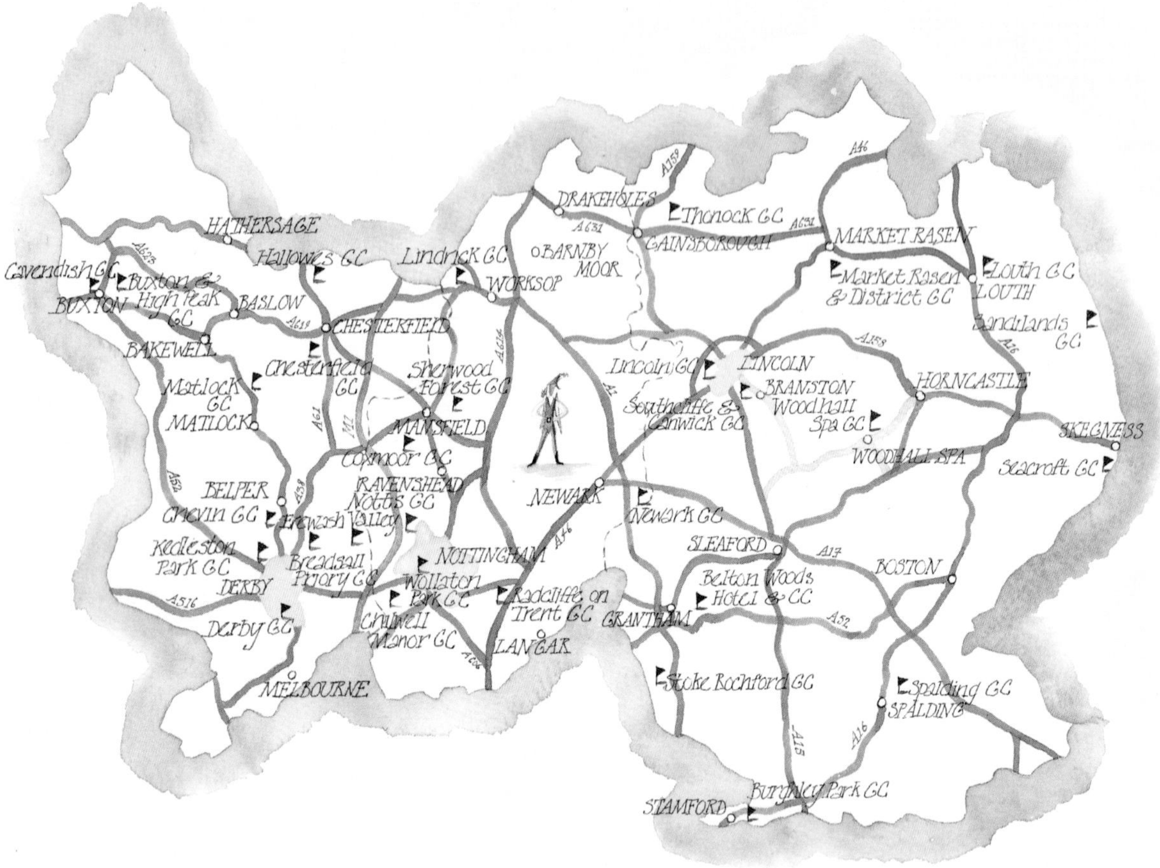

Map of the region showing golf courses including: Cavendish GC, Buxton & High Peak GC, BUXTON, BAKEWELL, Matlock GC, MATLOCK, BELPER, Chevin GC, Kedleston Park GC, DERBY, Derby GC, MELBOURNE, HATHERSAGE, Hallowes GC, BASLOW, CHESTERFIELD, Chesterfield GC, Sherwood Forest GC, Coxmoor GC, MANSFIELD, Ravenshead Notts GC, Erewash Valley GC, Breadsall Priory GC, Wollaton Park GC, Chilwell Manor GC, NOTTINGHAM, Radcliffe on Trent GC, LANGAR, Lindrick GC, WORKSOP, DRAKEHOLES, BARNBY MOOR, Thonock GC, GAINSBOROUGH, MARKET RASEN, Market Rasen & District GC, Louth GC, LOUTH, Sandilands GC, Lincoln GC, LINCOLN, Branston, Woodhall Spa GC, HORNCASTLE, Southcliffe & Canwick GC, WOODHALL SPA, SKEGNESS, Seacroft GC, NEWARK, Newark GC, SLEAFORD, Belton Woods Hotel & CC, BOSTON, GRANTHAM, Stoke Rochford GC, Spalding GC, SPALDING, STAMFORD, Burghley Park GC

Michael Brown   PREPARING TO PLAY   Burlington Gallery

142

DERBYSHIRE, NOTTINGHAMSHIRE & LINCS
CHOICE GOLF

DERBYSHIRE

Not wishing to be unkind but Derby the town isn't one of Earth's more inspiring places – nor for that matter are most of the Midland's industrial sprawls – but Derbyshire the county is a different matter altogether. The Peak District is without question one of the most scenic regions in Britain and commencing only a short distance north of Derby, it covers the greater part of the county – the Pennine Way of course starts in Derbyshire.

As well as being the beginning of all things beautiful the area just north of Derby is where three of the county's leading golf courses are to be found: Kedlestone Park, Breadsall Priory and Chevin. Located approximately 4 miles from Derby off the A111 (and well signposted) **Kedleston Park** golf course occupies a beautiful situation and is generally rated as the finest course in Derbyshire. Quite lengthy from the back tees, it has a variety of challenging holes. Eyeing the course from across a lake is the impressive Kedleston Hall, historic home of Lord Scarsdale.

I'm not sure what the 13th century monks would have made of the **Breadsall Priory** Golf and Country Club, 3 miles north east of Derby at Morley, but for heathens of the 20th century it provides an ideal setting for one of the most enjoyable games in the Midlands. Golfwise Breadsall Priory has only been on the map since 1976 but the undulating parkland course with its imported Cumberland turf greens has matured rapidly; indeed a second 18 holes have recently been completed and they admirably complement a new plush leisure centre.

Chevin lies slightly further north off the A6 at Duffield; it has an interesting layout, the first ten holes are a steady climb towards a spectacular vantage point after which holes eleven to eighteen gently bring you down to earth (or at least to Duffield!) Another course to recommend in the south of the county and over towards Nottingham is the wooded layout at **Erewash Valley**, noted for its two quarry holes.

If Derby has to be one's base then The Crest Hotel (0332) 514933 in Littleover is comfortable enough. The Georgian House Hotel (0332) 49806 is an elegant, comfortable and reasonably priced alternative. In Belper, Remys (0773) 822246 is a very good French restaurant – a perfect place to celebrate one's closing birdie at Chevin. **Breadsall Priory** (0332) 832235 itself of course offers a most satisfying 19th hole.

Moving 'up country', the picturesque town of **Matlock** has a fairly short but pleasant course situated north of the town off the Chesterfield road, and if heading in that direction **Chesterfield's** course at Walton is also well worth a visit and there are two public courses also close to the town centre. Two recommendations for a memorable night are: Riber Hall (0629) 582795 near Matlock and The New Bath Hotel (0629) 583275 in Matlock Bath.

The town of Buxton lies in the heart of the Peak District and is for many people their idea of the perfect town. This may have something to do with the fact that some of the finest pubs in England are located round about, but it is also helped by the fact that there are two excellent golf courses either side of the town – **Buxton and High Peak** and **Cavendish**. Of similar length it is difficult to say which is the better, in any event both warmly welcome visitors at green fees that should leave a few pennies for celebrating nearby. After a day on the fairways

(not to mention an evening in a Buxton pub) a suitable hotel is required. Again there are two thoughts: The Palace Hotel (0298) 22001 and The Lee Wood Hotel (0298) 70421 which overlooks the cricket ground.

Having done my bit for the Buxton tourist board another suggestion for this delightful area is in Hassop, Hassop Hall (062 987) 488. Other good locals include The Old Bulls Head, Little Hucklow; in Hathersage, The George, and in Beeley, The Devonshire Arms which is near to Chatsworth and no trip to the area would be complete without visiting this incredible stately home, perhaps England's finest.

NOTTINGHAMSHIRE

Moving into Nottinghamshire, the famous **Notts** Golf Club at Hollinwell is featured separately on a later page; however, in addition to this rather splendid 'Nottingham gorse affair' those visiting the county town should strongly consider the merits of **Wollaton Park**, an attractive course set amidst the deer park of a stately home, surprisingly close to the centre of Nottingham, and the city's two 18 hole municipal courses are also fairly good. Slightly further afield but well worth noting are the parkland courses at **Chilwell Manor** (A6005) and **Radcliffe on Trent** (A52 East of the town).

Nottingham has no shortage of comfortable modern hotels and The Albany (0602) 470131 and The Royal (0602) 414444 are both first rate and centrally located. To the north of the city at Arnold, The Bestwood Lodge (0602) 203011 is less stylish but good value while to the south lovers of the country house scene should delight in Langar Hall (0949) 60559 at Langar (seems to have a golfing ring to it, don't you think?) The best known pub in town is probably the Olde Trip to Jerusalem – said to be the oldest in England.

Two of the county's finest courses lie fairly close to one another near the centre of Nottinghamshire, **Coxmoor** and **Sherwood Forest**. The former is a moorland type course situated just south of Mansfield at Sutton-in-Ashfield. The Sherwood Forest course is more of a heathland type – well wooded, (as one might expect given its name) with much tangling heather. Measuring over 6,700 yards it is quite a test too.

Over towards the border with Lincolnshire is the attractive town of Newark with its twelfth century castle and cobbled market square. **Newark** Golf Club lies four miles east of the town off the A17. Reasonably flat and quite secluded the golf is a little less testing than at some of the county's bigger clubs. An attractive place to stay is the Old Rectory, north of Newark in Kirkton. Also in town The Old Kings Arms is a fine pub (0636) 703416.

Before inspecting Lincolnshire, a brief word on **Lindrick**. Although its postal address is in Nottinghamshire the majority of the course lies in South Yorkshire. In any event, it is featured ahead. If a night's rest is required 'this side' of the border, then Ye Old Bell Hotel at Barnby Moor (0777) 705121 is a pleasant coaching inn and The Angel in Blyth is a friendly pub with some accommodation also.

LINCOLNSHIRE

Lincolnshire is a large county. It used to be even larger before Grimsby, Scunthorpe and Cleethorpes were all snatched away

DERBYSHIRE, NOTTINGHAMSHIRE & LINCS
CHOICE GOLF

by that upstart Humberside. Still, by my reckoning there are at least twenty golf courses left. Woodhall Spa is of course head and shoulders above the rest but although the county as a whole is unlikely to be the venue for many golfing holidays there are certainly a handful of courses well worth a visit.

Woodhall Spa is featured ahead. For those fortunate enough to be able to spend a few days playing the course, here are some suggestions. The appropriately named Golf Hotel (0526) 53535 (a sister to the Manor House Hotel, Moreton-hampstead) is probably the most popular and convenient place in which to stay, but The Abbey Lodge (0526) 52538 and The Petwood (0526) 52411 are also recommended and The Dower House (0526) 52588 is very pleasant. Lincoln of course may be a base and for those not minding a bit of a drive The George (0780) 55171 at Stamford is quite excellent – a charming atmosphere with a very fine restaurant. Stamford in fact is a delightful town: Burghley is found here, an outstandingly attractive Elizabethan House. **Burghley Park** Golf Club is noted for its greens and its links with Mark James, while just over the county boundary in Leicestershire lies **Luffenham Heath**, a truly splendid golf course.

Lincoln was briefly mentioned, it really is an attractive city – a beautiful cathedral, a castle and a wealth of history. The White Hart (0522) 526222 is a noted hotel and there are some fine restaurants – one of the best is Whites. Simpler food and a great pub can be found in the Wig and Mitre (0522) 535190. The award winning D'Isney Place Hotel (0552) 538881 will lure many and disappoint none. Outside the city in Branston, The Moor Lodge Hotel (0522) 791366 is good value. The best golf to be found in **Lincoln** is at Torksey just to the north west of the city. It's a fairly

sandy, heathland type course with a lovely selection of trees. It is probably the second best course in the county after Woodhall Spa. **Southcliffe and Canwick**, on the opposite side of Lincoln is a shorter parkland course, but challenging in its own way.

Three courses of note towards the north of the county are at **Gainsborough** (Thonock), **Market Rasen** and **Louth**. All are very welcoming, Thonock is a classic parkland layout, Market Rasen is a very good woodland type course while Louth has an attractive setting in a local beauty spot, the Hubbards Hills. The Limes Hotel (0673) 842357 is ideal for Market Rasen, and in Louth, The Priory (0507) 602930 offers a comfortable stop-over. (There are some fine pubs in Louth too, note especially The Wheatsheaf).

Skegness is a famous resort, perhaps not everyone's cup of tea, but a game here is certainly recommended for those who like their links golf. **Seacroft** is the place; flattish, windy and plenty of sand dunes. Further up the coast, a less severe challenge is offered at **Sandilands** where the Grange and Links Hotel (0507) 441334 is adjacent to the course. The south of the county comprises much rich agricultural land but not too much in the way of golf. **Stoke Rochford** is a popular parkland course and **Spalding** is worth inspecting particularly at the time of year when the famous bulbs have flourished. An 18 hole course here, and in the south west, the new **Belton Woods** Hotel & Country Club (0476) 593200 has a delightfully peaceful setting outside Grantham. It has two eighteen hole courses, (as well as a multitude of other facilities) the Lancaster and Wellington, and there is a lot of water to be negotiated – a few Barnes Wallis type shots may be called for!

Drummond Fish   THE SECOND   Burlington Gallery

NOTTS (HOLLINWELL)
CHAMPIONSHIP GOLF

For many people Nottinghamshire is simply mining country, part of the 'black country'. To more romantic souls, it's the land of Robin Hood, Little John and Friar Tuck, not of course forgetting Maid Marion. But for those of us who thrash a little white ball around the counties of the realm, talk of Nottingham will invariably invoke thoughts of Hollinwell, home of the Notts Golf Club and one of the finest inland courses in the Kingdom.

1987 was an important landmark for the Notts Golf Club, it being centenary year, although the Club's first home was in fact nearer to Nottingham itself at Bulwell Forest. Apparently the proposed move from Bulwell to Hollinwell which occurred around the turn of the century initially met with considerable opposition. However, undeterred, the radicals invited **Willie Park Jnr** to design the new course and by the time **John H. Taylor** had added some finishing touches, not a squeak of discontent was to be heard. Messrs. Park and Taylor had presented the members with a masterpiece.

The gentleman presently looking after the interests of the Notts golfers is the Secretary, **Mr. J.R. Walker**. Visitors seeking a game are advised to contact him some time in advance of intended play. Mr. Walker can be contacted by telephone on **(0623) 753225** while the address for written correspondence is **The Notts Golf Club, Hollinwell, Derby Road, Kirkby-in- Ashfield, Nottinghamshire, NG17 7QR**.

As a general guide, visitors can play between Mondays and Fridays although it should be noted that Friday is Ladies Day. The first tee is reserved for members between 12.00pm and 1.00pm on Mondays and Tuesdays, and on Wednesdays and Thursdays between 12.00pm and 2.00pm or 11.30am and 1.30pm during the winter months. Societies are welcome with Mondays and Tuesdays being the favoured days. In 1992, the green fees were set at £30 per round or £38 per day. Another thing visitors might wish to note is the Club's popular driving range.

Since the Club's move to Hollinwell in 1900 it has had, somewhat remarkably, only four professionals. The present incumbent is **Brian Waites** probably our best known club pro and one who made history in 1983 by becoming the oldest British player to make his debut in the Ryder Cup. Now a member of the Seniors Tour, Waites recently played for the Rest Of The World Seniors against the American Seniors in the United States. He and his staff may be contacted on **(0623) 753087**. The course is located to the north west of Nottingham on the A611. Approaching from either the North or South of England, the M1 is very convenient. The motorway should be left at junction 27 at which the A608 should be followed until it joins the A611. The Club is then two miles away and is signposted off to the right.

From the Championship tees, the course is something of a minor monster stretching to a shade over 7000 yards (7020 yards, par 72). Even from the forward tees, it represents a formidable test at 6609 yards. The ladies course measures 5882 yards, par 75. If Hollinwell is a monster, then it's a pretty one (if there can be such a creature!) with a wealth of heather and gorse lining the fairways, together with some superb oaks and silver birch trees; certainly a splendid setting in which to enjoy a day's golf.

Similar to Woodhall Spa the **1st** at Hollinwell is relatively straightforward and has been described as 'ideal for the early morning top!' – something to be avoided on the lengthy **2nd**, a hole famed for the huge rock which guards the back of the green known as Robin Hood's Chair. Another notable hole on the front nine is the **8th**, perhaps not so intimidating from the forward tee, but from the medal tee it requires a very straight and solid drive to carry an attractive lake. Half hidden by trees to the right of the tee is the 'holy well' from which the name Hollinwell derives. Whether its waters will give you divine inspiration to tackle the back nine is debatable but it's worth a look. Actually, a prayer or two, or at least a little luck may be required when the downhill **13th** is confronted. One of only three short holes, although short is hardly apt, it was once called 'an absolute terror', having 'trouble everywhere'. The **15th** is another challenging hole and the round ends with a stiff par four which if achieved, will certainly earn you a drink at the club's comfortable nineteenth.

Championship golf regularly visits Hollinwell. Both **Sandy Lyle** and **Nick Faldo** have triumphed here, Lyle winning the 1975 English Open Stroke Play Championship (an event which returned to Hollinwell in 1992) as a precocious seventeen year old, and Faldo the European Tournament Players Championship of 1982. Arguably the most celebrated event was the 1970 John Player Classic when **Christy O'Connor** pocketed a cheque for £25,000, at the time a world record first prize – no doubt a few Irish eyes were smiling.

Hole	Yards	Par	Hole	Yards	Par
1	376	4	10	362	4
2	430	4	11	365	4
3	511	5	12	433	4
4	455	4	13	236	3
5	193	3	14	403	4
6	533	5	15	440	4
7	403	4	16	355	4
8	410	4	17	480	5
9	178	3	18	457	4
Out	3,489	36	In	3,531	36
			Out	3,489	36
			TOTALS	7,020	72

LINDRICK
CHAMPIONSHIP GOLF

There are two golf courses in England whose names will be forever linked with the Ryder Cup: one is **The Belfry**, the other is **Lindrick** – and they couldn't be more different. The Belfry (perhaps one should be precise and say the Brabazon Course) is a big strapping youngster still in its teens, immature in some ways though agreeable in others. Lindrick is the seasoned campaigner; it's seen a lot in its lifetime (and in fact is old enough to have received a telegram in 1991.) It is no giant but it is charming, subtle and full of challenge.

Before the Ryder Cup came to Lindrick in 1957, many golfing enthusiasts knew very little of this great course, indeed some knew nothing at all; by the end of that heady, wind-swept week in October, none present would ever forget it. It was the last time an exclusively British and Irish team would ever beat the mighty men from across the sea.

Lindrick lies close to the boundaries of Yorkshire, Nottinghamshire and Derbyshire. In fact, in places it actually forms the boundary. The majority of the course lies in Yorkshire, but some holes are in Nottinghamshire, and to the considerable annoyance of every Yorkshireman, the postal address is Lindrick, Notts!

The golf course occupies the best part of 200 acres of typical 'dog-walking' common land – Lindrick Common, and is essentially heathland in nature, lying on top of limestone rock. There is a mass of gorse which when in bloom adds great colour (though it can be a devil if you land in it!) and a wealth of pine, oak and silver birch – a delightful setting to be sure.

Visitors are very welcome to test their skills in this splendid environment, although prior arrangement with the Club is required. The Secretary is **Mr. G. Bywater**, who may be contacted by telephone on **(0909) 475282**. Written correspondence should be addressed to **Lindrick Golf Club, Lindrick Common, Worksop, Notts, S81 8BH.** All bookings should be made through the Secretary's office, but as a general guide, visitors are not permitted to play on Tuesday mornings and the first tee is normally reserved for Members

for an hour around lunch time, but again it's best to check.

The green fees at Lindrick vary according to the season and the following are the figures for summer 1992: £35 per day during the week, or £45 for a round at the weekend. Reductions of 50% are available to junior golfers if accompanied by an adult. The Club's Professional is **Peter Cowen.**

Although Lindrick Common may look a little isolated on the map, strangers shouldn't have too much difficulty in locating the course. Those coming from the south should find the M1 and the A1 of great assistance. The Club is actually situated just off the A57 Worksop to Sheffield road, to the west of the former and is well signposted.

From the Championship tees, the course measures 6615 yards, with the par a fairly tight 71. Quite refreshingly, it is not a long hitter's course, the fairway shots to the green being what Lindrick is all about, and there are some excellent par fours. The **2nd**, with its slightly uphill approach, the **5th** and the **10th**, where there is a potentially punishing cross bunker, are three noted holes, others include the troublesome **12th** and **13th**, but perhaps the best known hole at Lindrick is the par five **4th**. This requires a blind approach to a low lying green backed by trees and behind which the River Ryton flows. The green has a magnificent stage-like setting and it was here that the boundaries of Yorkshire, Derbyshire and Nottinghamshire once merged. In days of old, the stage was used for bare fist-fighting and cockfighting, contestants and spectators being able to step into a convenient county whenever unfriendly law authorities showed up. The round concludes with some very testing holes. During the 1982 Martini International tournament **Greg Norman** ran up a 14 at the **17th**! While the par three **18th** regularly ensures a climactic finish.

The Clubhouse at Lindrick provides golfers with a fine view of the 18th green and many a drama will have been witnessed; but I don't suppose there will ever be anything to equal the scenes of 1957 and the time when **Dai Rees** and his boys made the old campaigner smile.

Hole	Yards	Par	Hole	Yards	Par
1	401	4	10	368	4
2	359	4	11	173	3
3	163	3	12	464	4
4	480	5	13	438	4
5	433	4	14	557	5
6	141	3	15	362	4
7	434	4	16	486	5
8	318	4	17	397	4
9	435	4	18	206	3
Out	**3,164**	**35**	**In**	**3,451**	**36**
			Out	**3,164**	**35**
			Totals	**6,615**	**71**

WOODHALL SPA
CHAMPIONSHIP GOLF

Between them, **Sunningdale** and **Walton Heath** have seventy two holes, each with an Old and a New. Many may disagree but if a composite eighteen were created, taking the best eighteen holes from the four courses I still don't think we would see a better (or more challenging) course than the round offered at **Woodhall Spa** - and I certainly don't view Sunningdale and Walton Heath as anything less than outstanding.

Woodhall Spa Golf Club was founded in 1905. The course itself was originally laid out by **Harry Vardon** although substantial alterations were made firstly by **Harry Colt** and later by **Colonel Hotchkin**.

As one of the country's greatest (and most beautiful) heathland courses, Woodhall Spa is understandably extremely popular and visitors looking for a game must make prior arrangements with the Club's Secretary. (This applies to individual visitors and Golfing Societies alike). **Mr. B.H.Fawcett** is the very helpful gentleman in question and he may be contacted via **The Woodhall Spa Golf Club, Woodhall Spa, Lincolnshire**, telephone **(0526) 52511**. The Club's professional, **Peter Fixter** can be reached on **(0526) 53229**.

The green fees at Woodhall Spa for 1992 were set at £22 per round during the week with £32 payable for a full day's golf and £25 per round at weekends, or £35 for a full day. Reduced rates are available to junior golfers, but only if accompanied by a member.

Glancing at the map, Woodhall Spa looks fairly close to Lincoln. By road the distance is in fact, at least twenty miles. Those approaching from the cathedral city should take the B1188 towards Sleaford, taking a left fork onto the B1189 towards the village of Martin. At Martin the B1191 road should be picked up and followed to Woodhall Spa, the Club being directly off this road. Those travelling from further north will probably need to use a combination of motorways before joining the A15 – this road links Lincoln to the M180 (junction 4). Persons motoring from the south may have to do even more map-reading but the following is hopefully of assistance: the A1 is likely to be a good starting point; it should be left just north of Colsterworth and the B6403 then taken towards Ancaster and R.A.F. Cranwell. Just beyond R A F Cranwell the A15 can be joined. A right fork should be taken towards the wonderfully named hamlet of Ashby de la Launde on to the B1191. The B1191 takes us to Martin – remember Martin? The B1191 runs from Martin to Woodhall Spa.

The journey across Lincolnshire will have taken the traveller alongside many miles of flat agricultural land – hardly golfing country. Suddenly, everything changes as Woodhall Spa looms on the horizon like a glorious golfing mirage. Often described as the ultimate golfing oasis, Woodhall Spa has all the classic heathland characteristics; sandy subsoil, heather running riot and glorious tree lined fairways.

The course measures a lengthy 6907 yards, par 73 or, from the ladies tees, 5771 yards par 73. It is arguably most renowned for its vast cavernous bunkers and while it is almost impossible to select individual holes, perhaps those that particularly stand out are to be found towards the middle of the round, between the **9th** and the **13th**. Indeed, the **11th** is quite possibly the finest par four in the country and certainly one of the prettiest. A plaque beside the **12th** tee records how in March 1982 two Members halved the hole in one.

Another feature of Woodhall Spa is the remarkable variety of wildlife which the golfer is likely to come across (especially the more wayward hitter!) One hawkish, but obviously dedicated individual, claimed after hitting a rather poor drive to the **18th** that he was 'distracted by the merry gathering of partridges and pheasants to the right of the tee and by the squirrel who was chasing a magpie across the fairway.'

Although none of the major professional tournaments has visited the course (primarily a result of its isolation) numerous major amateur events have. These have included the Youths Amateur Championship, the English Amateur Championship, and the English Ladies Amateur Championship.

The Members are fortunate in having a wonderfully intimate Clubhouse. The atmosphere is both friendly and informal and there's an almost Colonial feel about the place – a Raffles in Lincolnshire perhaps? A full complement of catering is offered throughout the week with a variety of very reasonably priced meals.

I referred earlier to the often alarmingly deep bunkers; apparently a competitor in the 1974 English Amateur Championship, in his endeavours to find the exit to the Club drove his car straight into a huge bunker beside the 4th green.....one wonders whether this might have had a little to do with the aforementioned friendly atmosphere to be found at the 19th!

Hole	Yards	Par	Hole	Yards	Par
1	363	4	10	333	4
2	408	4	11	442	4
3	417	4	12	157	3
4	415	4	13	437	4
5	155	3	14	489	5
6	506	5	15	325	4
7	435	4	16	398	4
8	193	3	17	322	4
9	560	5	18	544	5
Out	**3,452**	**36**	**In**	**3,447**	**37**
			Out	3,452	36
			Totals	6,899	73

KEY

*** Visitors welcome at most times
** Visitors usually allowed on
weekdays only
* Visitors not normally permitted
(Mon, Wed) No visitors on
specified days

APPROXIMATE GREEN FEES
A – £30 plus
B – £20 – £30
C – £15 – £25
D – £10 – £20
E – Under £10
F – Green fees on application

RESTRICTIONS
G – Guests only
H – Handicap certificate required
H(24) – Handicap of 24 or less
required
L – Letter of introduction required
M – Visitor must be a member of
another recognised club.

DERBYSHIRE

Alfreton G.C
(0773) 832070
Wingfield Rd, Oakesthorpe
1 mile N of Alfreton
(9) 5012 yards/**/D

Allestree Park G.C
(0332) 550616
Allestree Hall, Derbyshire
3 miles N of Derby off A6
(18) 5749 yards/***(Sun am)/E

Ashbourne G.C
(0335) 42078
Clifton, Ashbourne
1 mile S of Ashborne
(9) 5359 yards/***/D

Bakewell Golf Club
(062981) 2307
Station Rd, Bakewell
E of Bakewell off A619
(9) 4808 yards/***/E

Breadsall Priory G.& CC
(0332) 832235
Moor Rd, Morley, Derby
3 miles N of Derby off A61
(18) 6402 yards/***/C

Burton On Trent G.C
(0283) 44551
Ashby Road East, Burton On Trent
(18) 6555 yards/***(H)/F

Buxton & High Peak G.C
(0298) 23453
Fairfield, Buxton
N of Buxton off A6
(18) 5954 yards/***/F

Cavendish G.C
(0298) 23494
Gadley Lane, Buxton
1 mile W of Buxton
(18) 5815 yards/***/C

Chapel-en-le-Frith G.C.
(0298) 812118
Manchester Road
(18)6089 yards/***/D

Chesterfield G.C
(0246) 279256
Walton, Chesterfield
(18) 6326 yards/**/C

Chesterfield Municipal G.C
(0246) 73887
Crow Lane, Chesterfield
(18) 6044 yards/***/E

Chevin G.C
(0332) 841864
Golf Lane, Duffield
5 miles N of Derby, off A6
(18) 6043 yards/**/C

Craythorne G.C
(0293) 64329
Stretton, Burton On Trent
Off A38
(18) 5164 yards/***/D

Derby G.C
(0332) 766323
Sinfin, Derby
(18) 6183 yards/***/E

Erewash Valley G.C
(0602) 323258
Stanton By Dale, Ilkeston
Junction 25 off M1
(18) 6444 yards/**/C

Glossop & District G.C
(04574) 3117
Sheffield Rd, Glossop
1 mile from Glossop off A57
(18) 5726 yards/***/E

Horsley Lodge G.C.
(0332) 780838
Smalley Mill Road
(18)6434 yards/***/C

Ilkeston Borough G.C
(0602) 320304
West End Drive, Ilkeston
(18) 6636 yards/***/E

Kedleston Park G.C
(0332) 840035
Kedleston, Quarndon, Derby
4 miles N of Derby off A11
(18) 6636 yards/**(H)/B

Matlock G.C
(0629) 582191
Chesterfield Road, Matlock
Off A632
(18) 5871 yards/**/C

Mickleover G.C
(0332) 518662
Uttoxeter Rd, Mickleover
3 miles W of Derby off A516
(18) 5621 yards/***(Sun)/D

Ormonde Fields G & CC
(0773) 742987
Nottingham Rd, Codnor, Ripley
Off A610
(18) 6007 yards/***/B

Pastures G.C
(0332) 513921
Pastures Hospital, Mickleover
3 miles W of Derby
(9) 5005 yards/*/F

Renishaw Park G.C
(0246) 432044
Station Rd, Renishaw
(18) 6253 yards/***/C

Shirland G. & C C
(0773) 834935
Lower Delves, Shirland
(18) 6021 yards/***/D

Sickleholme G.C
(0443) 51306
Barnford
(18) 6064 yards/***/C

Stanedge G.C
(0246) 566156
Walton, Chesterfield
5 miles S of Chesterfield
(9) 4867 yards/**(pm)/D

Tapton Park G.C.
(0246) 239500
Murray House, Tapton
(18)6010 yards/***/E

NOTTINGHAMSHIRE

Beeston Fields G.C
(0602) 257062
Beeston Fields, Nottingham
4 miles W of Nottingham
(18) 6404 yards/***/F

Bulwell Forest G.C
(0602) 278008
Huchnall Rd, Bulwell
4 miles N of Notts off A611
(18) 572 yards/***/C

Chilwell Manor G.C
(0602) 258958
Chilwell, Nottingham
(18) 6379 yards/**/C

Coxmoor G.C
(0623) 557359
Coxmoor Rd, Sutton In Ashfield
3 miles SW of Mansfield
(18) 6501 yards/**(H)/B

Edwalton Municipal G.C
(0602) 234775
Edwalton, Nottingham
(9) 6672 yards/***/E

Kilton Forest G.C
(0909) 472488
Blyth Rd, Worksop
2 miles N of Worksop
(18) 6772 yards/***(Sun)/E

Lindrick G.C
(0909) 475282
Lindrick Common, Worksop
4 miles W of Worksop off A57
(18) 6615 yards/***/Winter B/A

Mapperley G.C
(0602) 265611
Mapperley Plains, Nottingham
5 miles NE of Notts
(18) 6224 yards/***/D

Newark G.C
(0636) 626282
Coddington, Newark
(18) 6486 yards/**/C

Nottingham City G.C
(0602) 278021
Bulwell, Nottingham
NW of city
(18) 6120 yards/***/E

Notts G.C
(0623) 753225
Hollinwell, Kirkby In Ashfield
3 miles N of Notts off A611
(18) 7020 yards/**(H)/A/B

Oakmere Park G.C
(0602) 653545
Oaks Lane
(18) 7100 yards/***/C
(9) 3400 yards/***/E

Oxton G.C
(0602) 653545
Oxton, Southwell
(18) 6630 yards/***/D

Radcliffe On Trent G.C
(0602) 333000
Cropwell Road, Radcliffe On Trent
7 miles W of Notts
(18) 6423 yards/**(Tues)/C

Retford G.C
(0777) 703733
Ordsall, Retford
Off A620
(9) 6230 yards/**/F

Ruddington Grange G.C
(0602) 846141
Wilford Road
5 miles south of Nottingham
(18) 6500 yards/**/C

Sherwood Forest G.C
(0623) 26689
Eaking Road, Mansfield
3 miles S of Mansfield
(18) 6709 yards/***(Mon, Thurs, Fri)/B

Ruchcliffe G.C.
(0509) 852959
Stocking Lane
(18)6020 yards/**/B

Stanton On The Wolds G.C
(06077) 2006
Stanton On The Wolds, Keyworth
7 miles S of Notts off A606
(18) 6379 yards/**(Tues)/C

Wollaton Park G.C
(0602) 787574
Wollaton Park, Nottingham
(18) 6494 yards/**/D

Worksop G.C
(0909) 472696
Windmill Lane, Worksop
S of Worksop, off A57
(18) 6651 yards/***/C

LINCOLNSHIRE

Belton Park G.C
(0476) 67399
Belton Lane, Grantham
2 miles from Grantham.
(18) 6420 yards/***/C

Belton Woods G.C
(0476) 593200
(18) 7021 yards/***/D
(18) 6875 yards/***/D
(9) 1184 yards/***/E

Blankney G.C
(0526) 20263
Blankney, Lincoln
1 mile S of Metheringham on B1188.
(18) 6402 yards/**/C

Boston G.C
(0205) 350589
Cowbridge, Horncastle Rd. Boston
2 miles N of Boston on B1183.
(18) 5825 yards/***/B

Burghley Park G.C
(0780) 53789
St. Martins Without, Stamford
(18) 6200 yards/***/B

Canwick Park G.C
(0522) 522166
Canwick Park, Washingborough Rd.
2 miles S of Lincoln on A158.
(18) 6257 yards/**/D

Carholme G.C
(0522) 23725
Carholme Rd. Lincoln
1 mile from Lincoln on A57.
(18) 6114 yards/***(Sun)/F

Gainsborough G.C
(0427) 613088
Thonock, Gainsborough
1 mile NE of Gainsboro.
(18) 6504 yards/***/B

Horncastle G.C.
(0507) 526800
West Ashby
(18) 5782 yards/***/D

Lincoln G.C
(042771) 210
Torksey, Lincoln
(18) 6400 yards/***/B/H/L

Louth G.C
(0507) 603681
Crowtree Lane, Louth
(18) 6502 yards/***/C/M

Market Rasen and District G.C
(0673) 842416
Legsby Rd. Market Rasen
(18) 6043 yards/**/F

Millfield G.C
(042771) 255
Laughterton, Lincoln
(18) 5583 yards/***/E

North Shore G.C
(0754) 763298
North Shore Rd. Skegness
1 mile N of Skegness.
(18) 6134 yards/***/C/M

R.A.F. Waddington G.C
(0552) 720271
Waddington, Lincoln
(18) 5223 yards/***/E/L

Sandilands G.C
(0521) 41432
Sea Lane, Sandilands, Sutton-on-Sea.
4 miles S of Mablethorpe on A52.
(18) 5995 yards/***/C/H

Seacroft G.C
(0754) 3020
Drummond Rd. Skegness
1 mile S of Skegness
(18) 6478 yards/***/C/H/M

Sleaford G.C
(05298) 273
South Rauceby, Sleaford
W of Sleaford off A153.
(18) 6443 yards/***/C/H

Spalding G.C
(077585) 474
Surfleet, Spalding
4 miles N of Spalding off A16.
(18) 5847 yards/***/C/M

Stoke Rochford G.C
(047683) 275
Stoke Rochford, Grantham
5 miles S of Grantham off A1.
(18) 6204 yards/***/B/H

Sutton Bridge G.C
(0406) 350323
New Rd. Sutton Bridge, Spalding
(9) 5804 yards/**/C/H

Woodhall Spa G.C
(0526) 52511
The Broadway, Woodhall Spa
6 miles S of Horncastle on B1191.
(18) 6866 yards/***/B/H

STAFFS, SHROPSHIRE & CHESHIRE

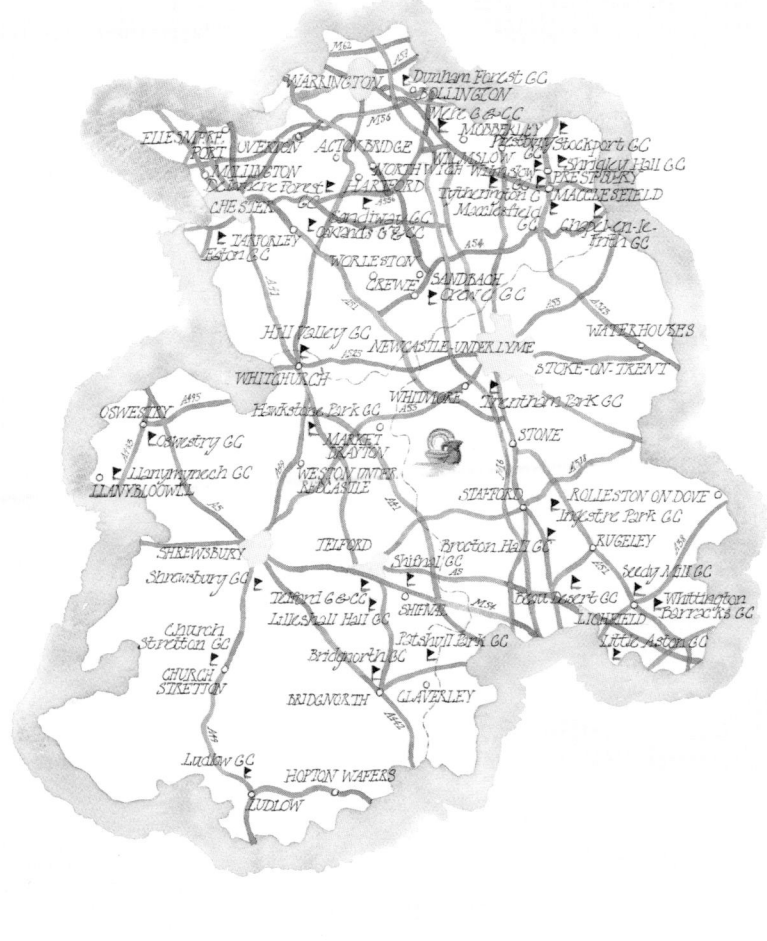

H. Rountree   PERFECTLY PLACED   Burlington Gallery

STAFFS, SHROPSHIRE & CHESHIRE
CHOICE GOLF

Staffordshire, Shropshire and Cheshire: three essentially rural counties. Staffordshire shares a boundary with the West Midlands and Cheshire has two rather ill-defined borders with Greater Manchester and Merseyside. As for Shropshire it enjoys a splendid peace, broken only perhaps by the mooing of cows and the cries of fore! from the county's many lush fairways.

Each of the three has a great deal to offer the visiting golfer: in Staffordshire, Beau Desert and Whittington Barracks are two of the best (and prettiest) courses in the Midlands; Cheshire offers Tytherington, Mere and some heathland gems (we have described Hoylake and the Wirral courses in the 'Lancashire' section) while Shropshire, in addition to possessing the likes of Hawkstone Park and Patshull Park can boast at having produced two US Masters champions – both Sandy Lyle and Ian Woosnam were bred if not born in the county.

STAFFORDSHIRE

Making a start in Staffordshire, **Whittington Barracks** and **Beau Desert** have already been mentioned. The former, located near Lichfield off the A51 is a heathland type course with fine views towards the three spires of Lichfield Cathedral; it is quite possibly the county's toughest challenge. Beau Desert Golf Club near Hazel Slade occupies an unlikely setting in the middle of Cannock Chase. Surrounded by fir trees and spruces it is, as its name implies, quite a haven. Perhaps a mixture of heathland and woodland, and less testing than Whittington Barracks, it is nonetheless equally enjoyable.

After a relaxing day on the golf course, some thoughts for a suitable 19th hole are in order. In Lichfield The Angel Croft (0543) 258737 is a comfortable hotel for a night's stay and Thrales (0543) 255091 is a particularly good restaurant. The George Hotel (0543)414822, an old coaching inn, is also recommended. (Note also the new 18 hole pay-and-play course in Lichfield, the charmingly named **Seedy Mill.**) After a round at Beau Desert, Rugeley may be the place to head for, here the Cedar Tree Hotel (0889) 584241 is welcoming but if a restaurant is sought then nearby Armitage offers the Oakleigh House Hotel (0543) 255573. On the other side of Lichfield, in Tamworth, the Castle Hotel (0827) 57181 is a more than fair bet.

From the heart of Cannock Chase to the heart of the Potteries, there are a number of courses in and around Stoke-on-Trent. **Trentham** and **Trentham Park**, near neighbours to the south of the city, are both well worth a visit, particularly perhaps the latter where the course is well-wooded and there are many delightful views. Probably the best hotel in Stoke is The North Stafford (0782) 744477, however as the recommended courses are south of the town Stone may be the most convenient place to spend a night. Two suggestions here, The Crown Hotel (0785) 813535 and The Stone House (0785) 815531, both are comfortable. The Star is a good local pub. East of Stoke, The Old Beams (0538) 308254 in Waterhouses is an excellent restaurant while in nearby Cauldon The Yew Tree is a superb hostelry.

Stafford, the county town, is pretty much in the middle of things. Once again a pair of 18 hole courses to note here; to the south of Stafford is **Brocton Hall** and to the north east, set in the grounds of the former home of the Earl of Shrewsbury is **Ingestre Park**. Both offer a very relaxing game. There is also an enjoyable 9 holer at Stafford Castle. If a bed is needed then Tillington Hall (0785) 53531 in Stafford is pleasant and, although a bit of a drive away, Rolleston on Dove offers the engaging Brookhouse Inn (0283) 814188, a splendidly converted farmhouse.

SHROPSHIRE

Moving into Shropshire, many will wish to head straight for **Hawkstone Park** (featured ahead) and given its two highly acclaimed courses and fine Hotel (093 924) 611 this is understandable. (Incidentally, note also the Reach Tree (0743) 246600, a great restaurant to visit after playing golf). However, Shropshire has a lot more than Hawkstone Park on the menu. **Patshull Park** makes a marvellous starter, especially considering its closeness to the Midlands – an ideal retreat in fact. As at Hawkstone golf is played amid very peaceful and picturesque surroundings and overnight accommodation is immediately at hand, tel. (0902) 700100. The delightful setting of Patshull Park owes much to the fact that the land was originally landscaped by 'Capability' Brown.

Shrewsbury is a pleasant county town with many charming half-timbered buildings. **Shrewsbury** Golf Club is situated about five miles from the town centre off the A49. It is an interesting course with a railway track running through the middle. The Prince Rupert Hotel (0743) 236000 in Shrewsbury itself is good value for an overnight stay and the oak beams and sloping floors add character. Fieldhouse Hotel (0743) 353143 has no pretensions of grandeur but is extremely comfortable.

Travelling a little further down the A49 into southern Shropshire, **Church Stretton**, set amidst the Long Mynd Hills, is well worth a visit. Not the longest course in Britain but one that offers quite outstanding views. The Stretton Hall Hotel (0694) 723224 is an obvious but comfortable base and those needing to quench their thirst might note the Royal Oak in Cardington (some accommodation also).

The largest town in Shropshire is Telford. It's a strange mixture of the old and the new: a modern centre yet surrounded by a considerable amount of history – Brunel's famous Ironbridge is here. **Telford Hotel** Golf and Country Club (0952) 585642 is situated near to the Ironbridge Gorge, high above it in fact, and is easily accessible from the M54 (junction 4 or 5). Full leisure facilities are offered at the Hotel.

Further south of Telford, towards Bridgnorth, **Lilleshall Hall's** golf course can also be recommended.

To the east of Telford, **Shifnal's** course is set in a glorious park and an old manor house serves as an impressive Clubhouse. The Park House Hotel (0952) 460128 in Shifnal is an excellent place for a stop-over and the hotel's restaurant, The Idsall Rooms is particularly good.

In the middle of Shropshire, **Bridgnorth** is one of the oldest and longest courses in the county (note the distinguished Haywain (0746) 780404 restaurant in town), and in the far south is historic **Ludlow**. It's now a fairly quiet market town but in former times was the capital of the West Marches. The golf course takes you around the town's race course – or is it vice versa? – Anyway it's an interesting challenge and if a

round of golf is being combined with a weekend's racing then The Feathers (0584) 875261 in Ludlow provides an ideal place in which to relax – note the outstanding Jacobean facade. In Brimfield, near Ludlow, you might stop at the Roebuch (058472) 230 – a nice summer pub with a fine restaurant. Not too great a distance from Ludlow is Hopton Wafers where The Crown offers some first rate cooking and a fine drop of ale.

To the north west of Shropshire three courses are strongly recommended. **Oswestry** is one clearly to note – if only because this is where Ian Woosnam relaxes when he's not winning The Masters. Close to the Welsh border, **Llanymynech** lies on high ground and is very up-and-down. On the 4th hole you stand on the tee in Wales and drive into England (always good for the ego). After a game here, a visit to The Bradford Arms (0691) 830582 in Llanymynech is essential as it boasts a particularly fine restaurant. Still high in the hills another 'Llany', not Wadkins but Blodwel: Llanyblodwel is where excellent refreshment can be found – The Horseshoe, with its spectacular setting. **Hill Valley** near Whitchurch, brings us down to earth. We may get wet as well with water affecting many holes on this fairly new American-style course. As well as the water there are many other challenges and it's well worth inspecting. Terrick Hall Hotel (0948) 3031 is practically adjacent to the course. In Whitchurch itself there is the Hollies Hotel (0948) 2184, ideally situated perhaps for keen golfers wanting to play both Hill Valley and Hawkstone Park.

CHESHIRE

Cheshire could be described as the Surrey of the North. In many parts it's decidedly affluent, with a great band of commuter towns lining its northern fringes. There's also a sand belt where heathland golf is found – no Sunningdale here perhaps but **Delamere Forest** and **Sandiway** would certainly be at home in either Surrey of Berkshire. Delamere is particularly good. A creation of Herbert Fowler, who also designed Walton Heath and The Berkshire, it's a marvellous heather and gorse type course – some superb trees also. The words 'temporary green' do not exist at Delamere Forest (something winter-golfers might wish to bear in mind) nor apparently does the word 'par' – the old fashioned term 'bogey' being preferred as a more realistic yardstick of a hole's difficulty – at least for the non-pro.

There are a number of first class places in which to stay in the area but pride of place must go to Rookery Hall (0270) 626866 in Worleston near Nantwich. Part Georgian, part Victorian, it's a wonderful hotel with a restaurant to match. Nantwich also offers the reasonably priced Burland Farmhouse (0270) 74210. Nearer to Sandiway in Hartford, Hartford Hall (0606) 75711 is very pleasant whilst in Sandiway itself, Minsmere Hall (0606) 889100 is very convenient and comfortable. In Acton Bridge, The Rheingold Riverside Inn (0606) 852310 offers some really stylish food. Finally, a handy pub for Delamere is The Ring of Bells at Overton.

Mere is certainly one of the best courses in Cheshire. Al-

though fairly close to Sandiway and Delamere, Mere is a classic parkland course, and a beautiful one too with a testing closing stretch including the spectacular par five 18th, where a new green has been built on the edge of a small lake. After eagling the 18th at Mere the perfect place for celebration is in Lower Peeover at The Bells of Peeover (0565) 722269 (pronounced 'Peever' I'm assured).

The area around Wilmslow is fairly thick with Clubs. **Wilmslow** itself and **Prestbury** have two of the better courses. For many years the former was the venue of The Greater Manchester Open. Both are extremely well kept. Again there are many fine hotels nearby to choose from, one strong recommendation though is **Mottram Hall** (0625) 828135 at Mottram St Andrews – quite magnificent. The hotel now also boasts a challenging 18 hole course, designed in fine style by Dave Thomas.

Stockport provides a dramatic contrast to rural Cheshire – not the prettiest of places perhaps but full of character (with a wonderful market my mother tells me). Offerton is where **Stockport** Golf Club is found. It's a good test and well worth visiting; so for that matter are the two courses at Bramhall, **Bramhall** and **Bramhall Park**, which just failed to make it onto our crowded map! **Macclesfield's** course offers some extensive views and between Macclesfield and Prestbury is the fairly new, but highly acclaimed **Tytherington** Club which is featured ahead. **Shrigley Hall** (0625) 575757 in Pott Shrigley, again near to both Prestbury and Macclesfield, has another newish golf course in a wonderful setting with magnificent views over the Cheshire Plain.

Over to the far east of Cheshire, close to the Derbyshire border and the splendid Peak District is **Chapel-en-le-Frith**. A really friendly Club this and some enjoyable golf too. From the far east to the far west, Chester demands inspection – a fascinating Roman city with all manner of attractions. The best place to swing a club is at **Eaton**, a parkland course to the south of the city. The best hotel by far is The Chester Grosvenor (0244) 324024 (note the superb restaurant). An interesting alternative though is The Blossoms Hotel (0244) 323186 where Ghost Hunting and Murder Weekends are organised! In Wilmslow, meanwhile, Stanneylands Hotel (0625) 525225 is both popular and extremely comfortable. South East of Chester near Tarporley is the **Oaklands** Golf and Country Club, one of the latest additions to Cheshire's many golfing attractions.

In the middle of the county, **Crewe** offers a pleasant 18 holes and a few miles outside of the town Weston Hall is being converted into a £50 million golf complex which promises to include a 'European Tour' purpose built stadium course. Back towards the north of the region, **Ringway** Golf Club is a good parkland challenge and our final visit takes us to the end of a very leafy lane in Altrincham – the impressive **Dunham Forest** Golf and Country Club. Only two miles from the M56 (junction 7) and not all that far from the whirl of Manchester it nonetheless delights in an incredibly tranquil setting. The beautifully mature tree-lined fairways are a sheer delight to play on and if you cannot enjoy your golf here, well, let's just say you've got problems!

HAWKSTONE PARK HOTEL

Even a fairly detailed map is unlikely to show Weston-under-Redcastle, but ask a golfer for the location and it is possible he will direct you there blindfolded! The Hawkstone Park Hotel, where Sandy Lyle learned his game, sits in an exquisite 300-acre estate and is more than just a golfers' paradise. It features one fine eighteen-hole golf course and one 9 hole golf course. The Hawkstone Course is over fifty years old, set in wooded, undulating parkland which includes several antiquities, such as the thirteenth-century Red Castle, and is bordered on one side by the beautiful Hawk lake.

The hotel, situated just a chip shot from the course, is steeped in history. It was built as an elegant and spacious hostelry in 1790 and was then known as the Hawkstone Inn. It has been developed into a really superb hotel complex which provides a catalogue of sporting and leisure facilities, including a tennis court, a croquet lawn, an open-air swimming pool, a sauna, a solarium and a trimnasium.

Where better to reflect on a round or two of golf than in the tastefully designed restaurant, which offers traditional English cuisine? Hawkstone's renown has spread far and wide and many visitors arrive expecting that the wealth of facilities at Hawkstone Park will impress them most.

However, it is the pleasantness and efficiency of the staff which really linger longest in the mind. Kevin Brazier, Company Operations Executive, proudly declares that the hotel's motto is 'client loving care' and this approach is apparent throughout the hotel. You will find Hawkstone Park fourteen miles north of Shrewsbury, off the A49 road.

Hawkstone Park Hotel
Weston under Redcastle
Shrewsbury
Shropshire SY4 5UY
Tel: (0939) 200611
Fax: (0939) 200311

HAWKSTONE PARK
CHAMPIONSHIP GOLF

What is a man to do when his two daughters, his pride and joy, tell him that they wish to leave home? Well, such was the dilemma facing a certain **Sir William Gray** in 1921. His solution you might think was an admirable one .... he promised to build them a golf course. For two young ladies much bitten by the bug it proved irresistible – clearly bribery of the highest calibre. In 1921 the ingenious Sir William owned Hawkstone Park, and the golf course, the subject of this tale, grew from an original nine holes to the present day Hawkstone course.

Today probably every golfer from Land's End to John O'Groats has heard of Hawkstone Park – nothing to do with the 'golfing Grays', but one **Sandy Lyle**, Open Champion of 1985 and U.S. Masters Champion of 1988. Sandy's association with Hawkstone Park has been life-long. Whilst there is probably no truth in the rumour that he was born adjacent to the first tee he certainly grew up nearby. For many years his father Alex served as professional and in every sense it was here that Sandy learnt his game.

Hawkstone Park is, of course, much more than the birthplace of Sandy Lyle. There are in fact two 18 hole courses, the **Hawkstone** and the **Weston** and both are set in the beautiful grounds of the Hawkstone Park Hotel. The hotel itself is certainly a grand affair. In a guide book of 1824 it was described as 'more like the seat of a nobleman than an hotel' and the grounds are not only exceptionally beautiful – exotic plants and flowers abound – but they are also steeped in history and legend.

The hotel runs the golf courses and other than an early morning tee reservation for residents there are no general restrictions on visitors, but starting times must be pre-booked. This can be done either by telephoning the Hotel on **(0939) 200611** or by contacting the professional shop on **(0939) 200209**. Parties of twelve or more are deemed to be golfing societies, subject again to making prior arrangements. They are equally welcome and written applications may be made in writing to the **Banqueting Manager, Hawkstone Park Hotel, Weston-under-Redcastle, Nr Shrewsbury SY4 5UY**.

In keeping with their policy of continual improvement, major alterations are being carried out to the Weston course by Brian Hugget Design, with the result that for the next year at least, only nine holes of this course will be open for play. Revised green fees for the Weston course start at £7.50, with a round on the Hawkstone available from £20. Golf buggies and electric trolleys can be hired through the professional shop. Those not playing in Societies should pay their green fee to the professional **Keith Williams**, who is the Director of Golf at Hawkstone Park and also an English Golf Union coach.

It has been said that one of the reasons for Hawkstone Park enjoying such a delightfully peaceful setting is that it is 'miles from anywhere' – not strictly true: it is only seven miles south of Whitchurch, or if you prefer, 12 miles north of Shrewsbury, and is easily accessible. The A49 is the best route when approaching from either of these towns. Shrewsbury itself is linked to the West Midlands by way of the M54 and the A5, while those motoring from the north will find the M6 of assistance.

At 6465 yards (par 72) from the medal tees, the Hawkstone course is 1,000 yards longer than the Weston (5368 yards, par 66); both courses, however, are maintained in superb condition and if possible a round over both should be attempted. It need hardly be added that Sandy Lyle holds the Hawkstone amateur course record with an impressive 65.

The hotel and golf course complex combine well to provide a good level of facilities for golf meetings at a corporate or local level. A wide range of golfing breaks are offered throughout the year and many golfers regularly travel great distances to sample the delights of this Shropshire paradise. It's all come a long way since the days of Sir William Gray and his golf-mad daughters, but one suspects that they would approve.

Hawkstone Course

Hole	Yards	Par	Hole	Yards	Par
1	364	4	10	525	5
2	398	4	11	441	4
3	217	3	12	147	3
4	322	4	13	373	4
5	367	4	14	476	5
6	362	4	15	317	4
7	436	4	16	255	4
8	481	5	17	386	4
9	188	3	18	410	4
Out	3,135	35	In	3,330	37
			Out	3,135	35
			TOTALS	6,465	72

THE STANNEYLANDS HOTEL

A handsome Country House, Stanneylands is set in several acres of impressive gardens, which feature a unique collection of trees and shrubs.

Classically furnished Public Rooms give an atmosphere of quiet luxury. The tasteful bedrooms, with all the expected modern amenities offer delightful views over the extensive grounds or the rolling Cheshire Countryside.

The restaurant, renowned as one of the best in the Manchester area, where attentive staff serve the finest of English contemporary cuisine and live 'occasional' music enhances the enjoyment. In addition, Stanneylands offers two distinctive meeting rooms, making the Hotel an excellent location for seminars, conferences, formal and informal dinner parties. The private Oak panelled dining room can accommodate up to 50 people, the Stanley Suite up to 100 guests. A full range of audio and visual equipment is also available.

Stanneylands is ideally located with many fine golf courses in the area - several only a few minutes away; the 1991 British Open Championship Courts at Birkdale is less than 40 minutes drive. Arrangements can be made through the hotel for those wanting to play at the well known Mere Golf and Country Club near Knutsford or the Tytherington club at Macclesfield. For non golfing partners there is a wide range of attractions to make your time at Stanneylands a truly enjoyable experience, including visits to Historic Houses, Museums, Art Galleries, Wildlife and Heritage Centres as well as walking, fishing and many more sports.

Situated only 3 miles from Manchester's International Airport, access to and from Stanneylands is quick and convenient via the M6, M56 and M62 motorways, whilst the nearby Wilmslow Station provides an inter-city service to London in just over 2 hours. Manchester city centre is a mere 10 miles away.

The Stanneylands Hotel
Wilmslow
Cheshire
SK9 4EY
Tel: (0625) 525225
Fax: (0625) 537282

TYTHERINGTON
CHAMPIONSHIP GOLF

When the first edition of Following The Fairways was put to bed one frantic summer's day in 1986, the Tytherington Club had barely raised its flag to appear on the nation's golfing map. Since then the course has quickly established itself as one of the finest parkland challenges in the north west of England. It stands proudly in an area inundated with a wealth of fine courses including the likes of Mere, Wilmslow, Prestbury and Delamere Forest.

An important development that has taken place since 1986, and one that has put the spotlight firmly on Tytherington, is the growth of the **Women Professional Golfers' European Tour** (WPGET.) It has greatly affected Tytherington because this is where the Tour's headquarters are based; Executive Director **Andrea Doyle** and her team directing its destinies from within the red bricked walls of the large clubhouse.

An important reason behind the WPGET's decision to base itself at the Cheshire Club is its ideal location close to Manchester Airport and the guarantee of easy access to the city's extensive motorway network. Notwithstanding the foregoing, Tytherington is a fairly peaceful place and is certainly surrounded by attractive countryside – famous Alderley Edge is just down the road and the Peak District is also close by. The 18 hole course makes the most of a gently rolling, well wooded landscape. Golfers who enjoy American style target golf will find Tytherington a rare treat; there is a fair amount of water on the course and the greens are traditionally fast and holding.

Visitors wishing to play at Tytherington are made very welcome and there are no specific restrictions on the times they may play. Handicap certificates are required however. The Club requests visitors to book tee times in advance. For individuals this means telephoning the **Starter** on **(0625) 434562.** The green fees for 1992 were set at £22 per round, £32 per day midweek and £26 per round and £36 per day at the weekend. Golfing Societies should make arrangements with the Club's Managing Director, **Patrick Dawson,** who may be contacted by writing to **The Tytherington Golf Club, Macclesfield, Cheshire SK10 2JP** and both he and the Professional **Sandy Wilson** can be reached via the above telephone number.

We have already referred to Tytherington's convenient situation; its precise location is directly off the A523 Stockport Road, two miles north of Macclesfield's town centre. Travellers approaching from the south of England should use the M6 leaving at the Holmes Chapel exit, which is junction 18, and thereafter follow the A535 and A537 which connect Holmes Chapel to Macclesfield.

From its Championship tees, Tytherington can be stretched to a lengthy 6737 yards, par 72. Off the medal tees it is much less daunting at 6362 yards, par 72 while the LGU tees measure the course at 5621 yards, par 74. The ladies tees were certainly brought back when Tytherington staged the WPGET English Open in September 1991. Victory went to **Katrina Douglas**, who won at the third extra hole from Switzerland's **Evelyn Orly**, after shooting an impressive final round of 70.

If you are going to put a good score together at Tytherington it is nigh on imperative that you get off to a flying start. The two nines each comprise a balanced two par threes, two par fives and five par fours but from the back tees the inward nine is more than 300 yards longer. It is also where the most difficult and daring shots are called for. Notable holes include the dog-legged **10th,** where the tee shot must carry a small lake and the par five **12th** which has a stream running along the left hand side of the fairway and which crosses it about 50 yards in front of the green. A good drive here sets up an exciting second shot to the green. Exciting or nerve-wracking? The **18th** is a fine finishing hole and celebration or recuperation can take place at the Club's excellent 19th. Tytherington's Pavillion Restaurant has a tremendous reputation and many will want to take advantage of the attractive conservatory.

Hole	Yards	Par	Hole	Yards	Par
1	465	4	10	420	4
2	507	5	11	217	3
3	164	3	12	520	5
4	401	4	13	156	3
5	196	3	14	439	4
6	382	4	15	402	4
7	301	4	16	540	5
8	320	4	17	412	4
9	480	5	18	415	4
Out	3,216	36	In	3,521	36
			Out	3,216	36
			TOTALS	6,737	72

STAFFS, SHROPSHIRE & CHESHIRE
COMPLETE GOLF

STAFFORDSHIRE

Alsager G. and C.C.
(0270) 875700
Andley Rd. Alsager, Stoke-on-Trent
(18)6206 yards/**/C/M

Barlaston G.C.
(078139) 2795
Meaford Rd. Barlaston, Stone
1 mile north of Stone off A34.
(18)5800 yards/***/C

Beau Desert G.C.
(0543) 422626
Hazelslade, Hednesford, Cannock
(18)6300 yards/**/B/H

Branston G.C.
(0283) 43207
Burton Rd. Branston, Burton-upon-Trent
(18)6458 yards/**/C/H

Brocton Hall G.C.
(0785) 661901
Brocton
4 miles south of Stafford off A34.
(18)6095 yards/***/B/H

Burslem G.C.
(0782) 837006
Wood Farm, High Lane, Tunstall
(9)5527 yards/**/D

Burton-upon-Trent G.C.
(0283) 4451
43 Ashby Road East, Burton-uponTrent
3 miles from Burton on A50.
(18)6555 yards/***/B/H/L/M

Craythorne G.C.
(0283) 64329
Craythorne Rd. Stretton
2 miles north of Burton off A38.
(18)5230 yards/***/D/H

Drayton Park G.C.
(0827) 251139
Drayton Park, Tamworth
(18)6414 yards/**/B/H

Golden Hill G.C.
(0782) 784715
Mobberley Rd. Golden Hill, Stoke-on-Trent
Between Tunstall and Kidgrove on A50.
(18)5957 yards/***/D

Greenway Hall G.C.
(0782) 503158
Stockton Brook, Stoke-on-Trent
5 miles from Stoke off A53.
(18)5676 yards/*/F/G

Ingestre Park G.C.
(0889) 270304
Ingestre, Stafford
6 miles east of Stafford off A51.
(18)6376 yards/**/B/H

Lakeside G.C.
(0889) 583181
Rugeley Power Station, Rugeley
2 miles south off Rugeley on A513.
(9)4768 yards/*/E/G

Leek G.C.
(0538) 384779
Cheddleton Rd. Leek
1 mile from Leek on A520.
(18)6229 yards/**/B/H

Newcastle Municipal G.C.
(0782) 627596
Keele Rd. Newcastle
(18)6256 yards/***/E

Newcastle-under-Lyme G.C.
(0782) 618526
Whitmore Rd. Newcastle-under-Lyme
2 miles south of Newcastle-under-Lyme on A53.
(18)6427 yards/**/B/H

Patshull Park Hotel & G.C
(0902)700100
Beside A464
(18)6400 yards/***/B

Perton Park G.C.
(0902) 380103 Wrottesley Park Road
West of Wolverhampton
(18)7036 yards/***/E

Seedy Mill G.C
(0543) 417333
Elmshurst, north of Litchfield
(18)6247 yards/***/F

Stafford Castle G.C.
(0785) 223821
Newport Rd. Stafford
(9)6347 yards/**/D

Stone G.C.
(0785) 813103
Filley Brooks, Stone
1 mile north of Stone on A34.
(9)6140 yards/**/C

Tamworth G.C.
(0827) 53850
Eagle Drive, Tamworth
(18)6083 yards/***/F

Trentham G.C.
(0782) 658109
14 Barlaston Rd. Trentham
(18)6644 yards/***/B/H

Trentham Park G.C.
(0782) 658800
Trentham Park. Trentham
4 miles south of Newcastle-under-Lyme off A34.
(18)6644 yards/**/B/H

Uttoxeter G.C.
(0889) 564884
Wood Lane, Uttoxeter
Next to Uttoxeter Racecourse.
(18)5695 yards/***/C

Westwood G.C.
(0538) 383060
Newcastle Rd. Walbridge, Leek
Just west of Leek on A53.
(18)6100 yards/**/D

Whittington Barracks G.C.
(0543) 432317
Tamworth Rd. Lichfield
3 miles from Lichfield on A51.
(18)6457 yards/**/B/H/L

Wolstanton G.C.
(0782) 622413
Dimsdale Old Hall, Hassam Parade
(18)5807 yards/**/F/H

SHROPSHIRE

Bridgnorth G.C.
(0746) 763315
Stanley Lane, Bridgnorth
1 mile from Bridgnorth
(18)6668 yards/***/B

Church Stretton G.C.
(0694) 722281
Hunters Moon, Trevor Hill, Church Stretton
(18)5008 yards/***/C

Hawkstone Park Hotel G.C.
(093924) 611
Weston under Redcastle, Shrewsbury
(18)6203 yards/***/C/H
(18)5063 yards(restricted play)/***/E/H

Hill Valley G. and C.C.
(0948) 3584
Terrick Rd. Whitchurch, Salop
1 mile north of Whitchurch.
(18)6050 yards/***/B/H
(9)2553 yards/***/D

Lilleshall Hall G.C.
(0952) 603840
Lilleshall, Newport, Salop
(18)5906 yards/**/C/H

Llanymynech G.C.
(0691) 830983
Pant, Oswestry
6 miles south of Oswestry.
(18)6114 yards/***/C/H

Ludlow G.C.
(058477) 285
Bromfield, Ludlow
(18)6239 yards/***/F/H

Market Drayton G.C.
(0630) 652266
Sutton, Market Drayton
(18)6214 yards/**/C

Meole Brace G.C.
(0743) 64050
Meole Brace, Shrewsbury
(12)5830 yards/***/E

Oswestry G.C.
(069188) 535
Aston Park, Oswestry
2 miles south of Oswestry.
(18)6046 yards/***/C/H/M

STAFFS, SHROPSHIRE & CHESHIRE
COMPLETE GOLF

Shifnal G.C.
(0952) 460330
Decker Hill, Shifnal
(18)6422 yards/**/C/H

Shrewsbury G.C.
(074372) 2976
Condover
9 miles south of Shrewsbury.
(18)6212 yards/***/C/H

Telford Hotel G. and C.C.
(0952) 585642
Great Hay, Telford
4 miles south of Telford.
(18)6274 yards/***/B/H

Wrekin G.C.
(0952) 244032
Ercall Woods, Wellington, Telford
(18)5657 yards/**/C

CHESHIRE

Alderley Edge G.C.
(0625) 585583
Brook Lane, Alderley Edge
(9)5839 yards/***/C/H

Alsager G. & C.C.
(0270) 875700
Audley Road, Alsager
(18)6200 yards/**/F

Astbury G.C.
(0260) 272772
Peel Lane, Astbury, Congleton
(18)6277 yards/**/C/H/M

Avro G.C.
(061) 4392709
British Aerospace, Woodford
(9)5735 yards/E/G/H

Birchwood G.C.
(0925) 818819
Kelvin Close, Risley, Warrington
(18)6808 yards/**/C/H

Chapel-en-le-Frith G.C.
(0298) 813943
The Cockyard, Manchester Rd.
Chapel-en-le Frith
(18)6065 yards/***/C/H

Chester G.C.
(0244) 677760
Curzon Park North, Chester
1 mile from Chester.
(18)6487 yards/***/C/H

Congleton G.C.
(0260) 273540
Biddulph Rd. Congleton
(18)5704 yards/***/F

Crewe G.C.
(0270) 584099
Fields Rd. Haslington, Crewe
1 mile south of Haslington on B5077.
(18)6181 yards/**/C/H

Davenport G.C.
(0625) 876951
Worth Hall, Middlewood Rd. Higher
Poynton
(18)6066 yards/***/B/H

Delamere Forest G.C.
(0606) 882807
Station Rd. Delamere, Northwich
(18)6287 yards/***/F

Disley G.C
(0663) 62071
Jackson's Edge, off A6
(18)6051 yards/**/F

Dukinfield G.C.
(061) 3382340
Yew Tree Lane, Dukinfield
(16)5544 yards/**/F/H

Eaton G.C.
(0244) 680474
Eaton Park, Ecclesford
2 miles south of Chester on A483.
(18)6446 yards/***/B/H

Ellesmere Port G.C.
(051) 3397689
Chester Rd. Hooton, S.Wirral
9 miles north of Chester on A41.
(18)6432 yards/***/E

Hazel Grove G.C.
(061)4833978
Buxton Rd. Hazel Grove, Stockport
(18)6300 yards/**/F

Helsby G.C.
(0928) 722021
Towers Lane, Helsby, Warrington
(18)6262 yards/***/C

Knights Grange G.C.
(06065) 52780
Grange Lane, Winsford
(9)6210 yards/***/E

Knutsford G.C.
(0565) 3355
Mereheath Lane, Knutsford
(9)6288 yards/**/F

Leigh G.C.
(092576) 2943
Kenyon Hall, Broseley Lane, Culcheth
(18)6861 yards/***/C/H

Lymn G.C.
(092575) 5020
Whitbarrow Rd., Lymn
5 miles south of Warrington.
(18)6319 yards/***/C/H

Macclesfield G.C.
(0625) 23227
The Hollins, Macclesfield
(9)5974 yards/**/C/H

Malkins Bank G.C.
(0270) 765931
Betchton Rd. Sandbach
(18)6071 yards/***/E

Mere G. and C.C.
(0565) 830155
Chester Rd. Mere, Knutsford
(18)6849 yards/**(Wed,Fri)/A/H/L

Mottram Hall Hotel & G.C
(0625) 828135
Mottram St. Andrews
(18)6900 yards/***/B

New Mils G.C.
(0663) 43485
Shaw Marsh, New Mills, Stockport
(9)5707 yards/***(Sun)/F

Oaklands G. & C.C.
(0829) 733884
Tarporley
(18)6169 yards/**/B

Onneley G.C.
(0782)750577
Onneley, Crewe
1 mile from Woore.
(9)5584 yards/**(Tue)/C

Portal G.C.
(0829) 733933
Tarporley
(18)7145 yards/***/B

Poulton Park G.C.
(0925) 812034
Dig Lane, Cinnamon Brow, Warrington
3 miles from Warrington
(9)5512 yards/***/D

Prestbury G.C.
(0625) 829388
Macclesfield Rd. Prestbury
(18)6359 yards/**/B/H

Queens Park G.C.
(0270) 666724
Queens Park Gardens, Crewe
2 miles from Crewe
(9)5370 yards/***/E

Runcorn G.C.
(09285) 72093
Clifton Rd. Runcorn
(18)6035 yards/**/C/H

St. Michael Jubilee G.C.
(051) 4246230
Dundark Rd. Widnes
(18)5612 yards/***/E

Sandbach G.C.
(0270) 21177
117 Middlewich Rd. Sandbach
(9)5614 yards/**/C/H

Sandiway G.C.
(0606) 883247
Chester Rd. Sandiway, Northwich
4 miles from Northwich.
(18)6435 yards/***/F/H/L

Shrigley Hall G.C.
(0625)575757
Shrigley Park, Pott Shrigley
(18)6305 yards/***/B

Tytherington G.C.
(0625) 434562
Near Macclesfield.
(18)6737 yards/***/B/H

Upton-by-Chester G.C.
(0244) 381183
Upton Lane, Upton-by-Chester
2 miles north of Chester.
(18)5875 yards/***/C/H

Vicars Cross G.C.
(0244) 335174
Tarvin Rd. Littleton
2 miles east of Chetster off A51.
(18)5876 yards/***/C

Walton Hall G.C.
(0925) 63061
Warrington Rd. Higher Walton
(18)6801 yards/***/F

Warrington G.C.
(0925) 65431
London Rd. Appleton, Warrington
(18)6217 yards/***/B/H
(18)5890 yards/***/B/H

Widnes G.C.
(051) 4242440
Highfield Rd. Widnes
(18)5688 yards/**/F/H

Wilmslow G.C.
(056587) 2148
Great Warford, Mobberley, Knutsford
2 miles from Wilmslow.
(18)6611 yards/**/F

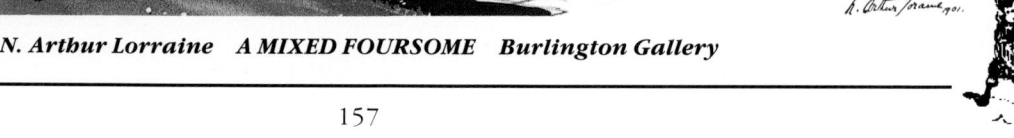

N. Arthur Lorraine   **A MIXED FOURSOME**   *Burlington Gallery*

LANCASHIRE & THE ISLE OF MAN

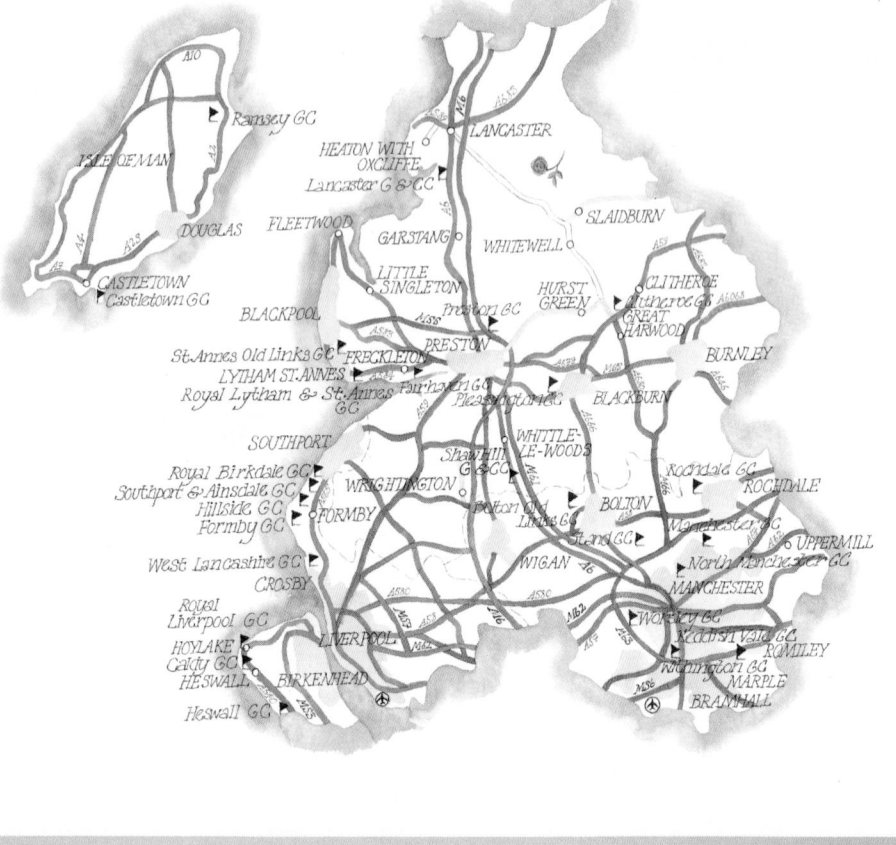

Bill Waugh   **ROYAL LYTHAM & ST ANNES**   *Burlington Gallery*

LANCASHIRE & THE ISLE OF MAN
CHOICE GOLF

'Caddies are not allowed on the greens when wearing clogs' – recorded in the Minutes of a Lancashire Golf Club, 1894.

THE 'LANCASHIRE' COAST

I don't suppose they appreciate it in the slightest but the many horses that race across the sands near Southport early each morning (and the donkeys that do their best to race across the same sands) are performing within a few yards of one of the greatest stretches of golfing country in the world. On the Lancashire coast between Liverpool and Blackpool lie a magnificent collection of natural golfing links. Being more specific, between **Hoylake** on the Wirral Peninsula and Lytham St Annes (a distance of less than 40 miles) are to be found the likes of **Wallasey, West Lancashire, Formby, Southport and Ainsdale, Royal Birkdale, Hillside, Royal Lytham, Fairhaven** and **St Annes Old Links**. A truly formidable list. Hoylake, Birkdale and Lytham have, of course, each staged the Open Championship on a number of occasions, while the Amateur Championship has been played at both Hillside and Formby, and Southport and Ainsdale has twice hosted the Ryder Cup. When the wind hammers across from the Irish Sea any of the links mentioned can become treacherously difficult and the famous Lancashire sandhills rarely provide shelter from the elements. **Hoylake, Birkdale, Hillside, Formby** and **Lytham** are each featured on later pages but a visit to any of the above will certainly not meet with disappointment (though it may result in a little damaged pride!)

Having done battle with the elements, and perhaps after visiting the treacherous Gumbley's bunker at S and A or the heather and pines at Formby a drink will be in order. A good meal and a comfy bed for the night may also be required. Here are some suggestions. In Southport, The Scarisbrick Hotel (0704) 543000 and The Prince of Wales (0704) 536688 are probably the pick of the hotels but there are numerous others. The Metropole Hotel (0704) 36836 and the Bold Hotel (0704) 325578 are also worth a visit and amongst the lesser lights, Upton Fields House (0636) 812203 and The Sunningdale Hotel (0704) 538673 will not disappoint. In Formby, The Tree Tops Motel (0704) 879651 is an ideal base.

Lytham St. Annes is another golfer's paradise. It's a pleasant town and hotels to note are The Chadwick (0253) 720061 on the seafront, The Clifton Arms Hotel (0253) 739898 and the Dormy House (0253) 724206. Endsleigh Private Hotel (0253) 51937 and Strathmore (0253) 725478 also have good reputations. Fleetwood, to the north, also has to be mentioned and one of the best fish restaurants here is The Trafalgar (0253) 872266; another good restaurant (but less fishy) is The Cromwellian (0772) 685680.

Blackpool, famed for its 'golden mile', its great tower and impressive funfair is more of a paradise for children than golfers, but then if golf is being sneaked in on the family holiday it may be the best choice for a stay. On the North Promenade are two of the town's best hotels, The Pembroke (0253) 23434 and The Imperial (0253) 23971. Comfort here is guaranteed but there are numerous, slightly cheaper alternatives and pot luck may be the order of the day. The Sunray Private Hotel (0253) 51937 and The Surrey House Hotel (0253) 51743 fall into the less glamorous category but offer first-class food and accommodation and on Shaftesbury Avenue, you can find the Brebyns Hotel (0253) 54263, noted for its good food.

It may be that some business in Liverpool has to be dealt with before one can put on one's plus fours and stride out onto the fairways. If you are staying in the Liver city then the Britannia Adelphi 051-709 7200 and the Atlantic Tower 051-227 4444 are both good, while first class leisure facilities can be found in The Liverpool Moat House 051-709 0181. The city has a reputation for splendid Indian and Chinese food but two European establishments are our recommendations. On the one hand The Armadillo 051-236 4123 and on the other La Grande Bouffe 051-236 3375. The nearest of the great links courses is West Lancashire, although Formby too is within easy reach. The A565 is the road to take out of Liverpool.

For the purposes of this piece Liverpool and Manchester have been included in Lancashire, a county to which they both once belonged (and still do in spirit). As the whole of Merseyside has been included – it's here that Royal Birkdale and Royal Liverpool are now situated – parts of former Cheshire are also included. Confused? Lets visit the Wirral. For such a relatively small area the peninsula is fairly thick with Golf Clubs. In addition to the famous links at Hoylake, **Wallasey** offers another tremendous seaside test amid some impressive sand dunes while **Heswall** offers a quite outstanding parkland challenge. Situated alongside the River Dee off the A540, it's a medium length course, beautifully maintained with views towards the distant Welsh hills. A strong word also for **Caldy** which is a parkland-cum-clifftop course, similarly well-kept and similarly scenic. If an hotel and restaurant are sought on the Wirral here are some recommendations – for an hotel, the splendidly named Bowler Hat Hotel 051-652 4931 at Birkenhead is most comfortable, while Les Bougies 051-342 6673 at Heswall is a fine French restaurant. Beadles in Birkenhead is another good restaurant – ideal for a spot of lunch before playing Royal Liverpool perhaps.

INLAND GOLF IN LANCASHIRE

Looking to play more centrally in Lancashire, The **Shaw Hill** Golf and Country Club is most definitely one to note if travelling along the M6. Located just north of Chorley, despite its proximity to the motorway, it enjoys a very peaceful setting and is a particular favourite of golfing societies. Visitors are welcome throughout the week, and there is some high-quality accommodation immediately beyond the 18th green (02572) 69221.

On the other side of the M6, **Pleasington** Golf Club enjoys similarly secluded and picturesque surroundings. The course is situated three miles west of Blackburn along the A59 and is undoubtedly one of the best parkland courses in the North of England. Still moving 'up' the country, **Preston** has a pleasantly undulating course, just north of the town, it too can easily be reached from the M6 (junction 32).

Another of the better inland courses in the county is **Clitheroe** Golf Club which is situated on the edge of the Forest of Bowland. The course lies approximately two miles south of the town with views across to Pendle Hill.

Lancashire wouldn't be complete without mentioning its county town. There are a number of Clubs at hand, perhaps the best being the **Lancaster** Golf and Country Club located three miles south of the city on the A588 at Stodday. An attractive parkland course, it is laid out close to the River Lune estuary (and can be breezy!)

LANCASHIRE & THE ISLE OF MAN
CHOICE GOLF

A few ideas for the 19th now follow: The city of Lancaster lies west of some majestic moorland scenery. The M6 carves its way through, and near to junction 34 The Post House Hotel (0524) 65999 is ideal for travellers. Recommended alternatives include Edenbreck House (0524) 32464 and Lancaster Town House (0524) 65527. A little further north in Heaton with Oxcliffe a pub with a splendid riverside setting is The Golden Ball – well worth a visit when in these parts. In Morecombe The Midland Hotel (0524) 417180 is welcoming. At Whitewell, amid the delightful Forest of Bowland lies the Inn at Whitewell (0200) 8222 which offers excellent bar snacks, a first rate restaurant and some charming bedrooms. If you are looking for a self catering holiday in the region, we recommend you contact either Red Rose Cottage Holidays (0200) 27310, or Country Holidays (0282) 445533.

More thoughts for celebrating after a day at Preston or Clitheroe. In Hurst Green The Shireburn Arms Hotel (0254) 826518 is well worth a visit. Not only can you enjoy the splendid Ribblesdale countryside but also some tremendous cuisine. An alternative eating establishment, a restaurant on this occasion is Tiffany at Great Harwood, where the fish is particularly good. In Clitheroe itself, The Swan and Royal Hotel (0200) 23130 is convenient and nearby in Slaidburn is The Parrock Head Farm Hotel (02006) 614. In Preston, both the Gibbon Bridge (0995) 61456 and Tulketh Hotel (0772) 726250 offer excellent facilities.

GREATER MANCHESTER

And so to Manchester. The city itself is famed the world over for the liberal amount of rain that falls. Mancunians will tell you that this is pure poppy-cock (or something like that). Of course, the only time that rain can be guaranteed these days is during the five days of an Old Trafford Test Match. If you do happen to get caught in the rain, be it on the streets or the fairways, here are a few superior shelters. You ought to be able to find a room in The Britannia Hotel 061-228 2288 for there are 365 (one for every day of the year?) Alternatives include the Hotel Piccadilly 061-236 8414, West Lynne Hotel 061-721 4866 and The Horizon Hotel 061-445 4705.

Outside the conurbation, there are many options. To the north in Egerton, The Egerton House (0204) 57171 is good value especially at weekends and a country setting can be enjoyed. The well respected restaurant adds appeal. Another thought is The Bramhall Moat House 061-439 8116; it is ideal for the many courses in northern Cheshire. Altrincham has a trio to consider: The Cresta Court 061-928 8017 is modern but well equipped, The Bowdon 061-928 7121 is Victorian and comfortable, while a former coaching inn, the George and Dragon 061-928 9933 has most charm.

Some of the very best restaurants in the Manchester area include The Bonne Auberge 061-437 5701 in Heald Green, the French 061-941 3355 in Altrincham, and Peppers 061-832 9393 in Bridge Street (handy for the Opera).

It is probably a fair assessment to say that for golf courses, Manchester, rather like London, gets top marks for quantity but is a little shaky on the quality score. Certainly it compares unfavourably with Liverpool and Leeds; it is a shame because historically Manchester was the scene of some of the earliest golf outside Scotland: The **Old Manchester** Club was founded back in 1818. Its current status is 'temporarily without a course' – one can only hope that its Members have found somewhere else to play ... **North Manchester** perhaps? Only four miles from the city centre this is one of the best in the county.

A close neighbour of North Manchester is the excellent **Manchester** Golf Club. Elsewhere in Manchester, **Stand** (Whitefield) and **Worsley** (Eccles) are fine courses while to the north, **Rochdale** is well worth travelling to. There is a cluster of courses close to the River Mersey in the Didsbury – Sale area; the best is perhaps **Withington**, and there are about 10 public courses in and around the city centre. Over towards Stockport, there is a very enjoyable course at **Reddish Vale** and the area around Bolton again boasts a number of courses of which **Bolton Old Links** is probably the finest. It is a tough and interesting moorland course at which visitors are always made welcome. As for the title 'Links' it may sound a bit quaint – but there again, what are we to make of Wigan Pier?

THE ISLE OF MAN

A very brief word here for that tax haven the Isle of Man. There are five 18 hole courses on the island, with the links courses at **Castletown** and **Ramsey** particularly standing out. With fairly modest green fees and numerous relaxing places to stay the island would appear to be an ideal place for a golf holiday – ask Nigel Mansell who brought Greg Norman here! In Castletown, there are two excellent restaurants, Silverburn Lodge (0624) 822343 and La Rosette (0624) 822940, whilst the Castletown Golf Links Hotel (0624) 822201 is very comfortable and its name more than hints at what takes pride of place on the menu! Castletown golf course is featured ahead. At the other end of the island, Ramsey offers the large Grand Island Hotel (0624) 812455 and The Harbour Bistro (0624) 814182, an informal and friendly restaurant.

Lawson Wood   A BAD LIE   Rosenstiel's

ROYAL BIRKDALE
CHAMPIONSHIP GOLF

Back in 1889 your average J.P. was possibly not the most popular man in town. However, in a certain **Mr. J.C. Barrett**, Birkdale possessed a man of rare insight and one clearly cognisant of the finer things in life. Mr. Barrett was a golfer. On the 30th July, 1889, he invited eight fellow addicts to his home and together they resolved to form a Golf Club. One can imagine their enthusiasm as they formulated their plans, perhaps over a brandy and cigars, I know not but very quickly a clubhouse was secured – a single room in a private residence at a four shilling per week rental! Land (at £5 per year rental) was acquired and soon a 9 hole course was laid out. It all sounds rather unsophisticated, but compared with today's problems of first finding a suitable site and then obtaining planning permission, I suppose it was relatively straightforward.

Although no one could question its present day status as one of the country's leading Championship courses, historically Birkdale set off rather like the proverbial tortoise. Forced eviction in 1897 led to the Club's rerooting in its present position where a full eighteen holes were immediately available. During the 1930's a modern style Clubhouse was built and **John H. Taylor** and **Fred Hawtree** were commissioned to redesign the course. As one would expect they made a splendid job of it and it was now only a question of time (and the small matter of a world war) that prevented Birkdale from staging an Open Championship.

Since the War our golfing tortoise has left many of the hares behind. No fewer than seven **Open Championships** have now been held at Birkdale (1991 being the most recent) in addition to numerous other major events.

Golfers wishing to play at Birkdale must belong to a recognised Golf Club and produce a current handicap certificate. Visitors must make prior arrangements with the Secretary, **Norman Crewe**. This applies to individual visitors as well as those hoping to organise a Society game. Mr. Crewe can be contacted at **The Royal Birkdale Golf Club, Waterloo Road, Birkdale, Southport, Merseyside PR8 2LX**. Tel. **(0704) 67920**. Golf clubs may be hired from the professional, **Richard Bradbeer, (0704) 68857** and it may also be possible to obtain the services of a caddy. Individual visitors may play from Monday to Friday, green fees in 1992 being £50 per round, or £70 per day. Societies are welcome on Wednesdays and Thursdays.

The Club is situated approximately 2 miles from the centre of Southport close to the main A565 road. From the North this road can be reached via the A59, leaving the M6 at Preston and from the South via the M62 and M57 or alternatively, as when travelling from Manchester and the East, by taking the A580 and then following the A570 into Southport.

Whilst the course possesses many of the towering sand hills so familiar with good links golf, the holes tend to wind their way between and beneath the dunes along fairly flat and narrow valleys. From the fairways the awkward stance and blind shot are the product of poor golf, not poor fortune. Fair it may be, but easy it certainly is not! From the medal tees the course measures 6703 yards and is a stiff par 72; from the Championship tees, Birkdale stretches to 6940 yards. From the red tees the Ladies course is 5777 yards and has a par of 75.

With its par fives the back nine is probably the easier half – at least to the longer hitter – although with the menacingly thick rough and narrow strategically bunkered fairways the wild long hitter will be severely penalised. A journey into the rough on the 16th, however, is recommended although only to visit **Arnold Palmer's plaque** – placed in memory of the great man's miraculous 6 iron shot when he somehow contrived to find the green after driving deep into the undergrowth.

Birkdale may have a relatively short history as an Open course, but her list of Champions is as impressive a list as can be found anywhere: **Peter Thomson** (twice), **Arnold Palmer, Lee Trevino, Johnny Miller, Tom Watson**, who claimed his fifth title in nine years when winning in 1983 and **Ian Baker-Finch** who set alight the 1991 championship with a brilliant front nine of 29 on the final day. The course has indeed thrown up more than its fair share of drama. Perhaps most notably in 1969 when **Jack Nicklaus**, ever the sportsman, conceded **Tony Jacklin's** very missable putt on the 18th green, so tying the **Ryder Cup**. In 1961, Palmer's Open, an almighty gale threatened to blow the tented village and all inside far out into the sea. In stark contrast was the 1976 Open when fire engines were close at hand as Birkdale (and all of Britain come to that) suffered in the drought. That 1976 Championship saw the mercurial **Miller** at his brilliant best as he shook off first the challenge of Nicklaus and then of an inexperienced and unknown 19 year old who had a name no one at the time could pronounce ...... **Severiano Ballesteros**.

Hole	Yards	Par	Hole	Yards	Par
1	448	4	10	395	4
2	417	4	11	409	4
3	409	4	12	184	3
4	203	3	13	475	4
5	346	4	14	199	3
6	473	4	15	543	5
7	156	3	16	414	4
8	458	4	17	525	5
9	414	4	18	472	4
Out	**3,324**	**34**	**In**	**3,616**	**36**
			Out	3,324	34
			TOTALS	**6,940**	**70**

ROYAL LYTHAM & ST ANNES
CHAMPIONSHIP GOLF

'There goes a hundred thousand bucks........' the immortal words of **Al Waltrous** after having witnessed the most magnificently outrageous stroke in golfing history. Imagine yourself in his shoes, striding down the 17th fairway, sharing the lead in the Open Championship; you have played two strokes and are safely on the edge of the green, your partner (and effectively opponent) has driven wildly into the rough and has found a small bunker – he faces a terrifying shot over sandhills, scrub and goodness knows what else – a blind shot of fully 170 yards....seconds later the impossible happens and his ball is lying a few yards from the hole, well inside your second. Minutes later you walk from the green having taken five to your opponent's four.

The occasion was, of course, the **1926 Open Championship** at Royal Lytham and your opponent, the incomparable **Bobby Jones**.

In February 1986, Royal Lytham and St Annes proudly celebrated its one hundredth birthday. Few Golf Clubs in the world can have enjoyed such a rich and colourful history. There have been eight Open Championships – a ninth will be staged in 1996 – two Seniors' British Opens and many other major events.

Presently in charge of all administrative matters at Lytham is the Club's Secretary, **Major Stuart Craven** and he may be contacted by telephone on **(0253) 724206. Eddie Birchenough** is the Club's professional and he may be reached on **(0253) 720094**. Visitors wishing to tread the famous fairways are asked to provide a letter of introduction from their home club, but subject to this requirement they are welcome any day between Mondays and Fridays, restrictions applying at weekends. Whilst advance booking is not essential it is clearly advisable and those wishing to write to the club should address correspondence to the Secretary at **Royal Lytham and St Annes Golf Club, Links Gate, Lytham St Annes, Lancashire FY8 3LQ.**

The green fees at Lytham were priced at £45 for a single round in 1992, or £60 for a full day's golf. Dormy house facilities are available at the 19th hole (telephone the club for details) and

Royal Lytham's Clubhouse is a marvellous Victorian building. Golfers can enjoy the excellent catering service which is offered throughout the day.

Motoring to the course is assisted greatly by the M6 and the M61. Both northbound and southbound travellers should leave the M6 at junction 32; here the M55 can be picked up. The M55 runs out of steam at junction 4 but a left turn will take you to Lytham St Annes. The M61 links the Greater Manchester area to the outskirts of Preston. From Preston, the A583 should be followed joining the A584 which also runs to Lytham St Annes. The course is situated only a mile from the centre of the town close to St Annes railway station.

The railway line is in fact a major feature of the opening holes at Lytham, forming a continuous boundary to the right. From the back markers the course measures 6673 yards par 71 (s.s.s. 73) with the ladies playing over 5814 yards par 75 (s.s.s. 75). Rather unusually, Lytham opens with a par three, which at over 200 yards is quite a testing opener although the real threat of the railway looms on the **2nd** and **3rd**. Of the other par three holes at Lytham perhaps the **12th** stands out – normally played into a prevailing wind it calls for a searching tee shot towards a raised and heavily guarded green. The back nine is generally felt to be the more difficult of the two halves although the determining factor at Lytham, as on most links courses will nearly always be the wind. The **17th** has been mentioned and a plaque marks the spot from where the Jones miracle recovery shot was played. As for the **18th** it of course invokes so many 'Open Championship memories': **Tony Jacklin's** arrow straight drive en route to winning the 1969 Championship; **Gary Player** putting left handed from up against the Clubhouse wall in 1974 and its two most recent Championships in 1979 and 1988, when the world twice watched **Ballesteros** storm home in cavalier fashion.

That 1988 Championship will always be remembered for the fantastic duel between **Nick Price** and the Spaniard. Price led by two shots going into the final round. He produced an almost flawless 69 yet lost by two. 'A round that happens once every 25 or 50 years' was Seve's description of his scintillating 65. Perhaps Nick Price alone can understand how Al Waltrous felt.

Hole	Yards	Par	Hole	Yards	Par
1	206	3	10	334	4
2	420	4	11	485	5
3	458	4	12	189	3
4	393	4	13	339	4
5	188	3	14	445	4
6	486	5	15	468	4
7	551	5	16	356	4
8	394	4	17	413	4
9	162	3	18	386	4
Out	3.258	35	In	3.415	36
			Out	3.258	35
			TOTALS	6.673	71

FORMBY
CHAMPIONSHIP GOLF

According to the traditionalist, as opposed to the pure pleasure-seeker, there is only one genuine form of golf and that is the sort played on a links. To this person golf might be just as enjoyable (and probably a darn sight easier when the wind blows!) on an inland course but it is not quite the real thing: Sunningdale, Gleneagles, Wentworth – all wonderful places but ..... From the pure pleasure-seeker's point of view the above mentioned courses may be more attractive, not because the challenge is probably less intimidating but because many of the best links courses tend to be fairly bleak places: Carnoustie, Lytham, Hoylake and Sandwich immediately spring to mind. Here the golfer is exposed. Trees are either very rare or non-existent; often the layout of the course is a tiresome 'straight out and straight back' and any heather doesn't seem to turn quite such a delicate shade of purple on a links as it does at Gleneagles or Sunningdale.

Formby, on the Lancashire coast (and not a million miles away from either Lytham or Hoylake) is a very rare place for it is here that the traditionalist and the pure pleasure-seeker can play a round of golf together and not fall out. Formby is a links – no question about it – firm, fast seaside greens, natural sandy bunkers and some fairly prodigious sand hills. But Formby is also blessed with a plethora of pine trees which add great beauty to the scene and often considerable shelter. Many of Formby's holes weave their way a good bit below the level of the surrounding dunes, creating a feeling of privacy, or at least occasional intimacy, so rare on a links course, and Formby certainly doesn't stretch 'out and back', in fact the bird's eye view of the links reveals eleven distinct changes of direction.

Founded over a century ago, Formby has long been one of Britain's most popular courses and visitors may find it as difficult to get a game here as at either Birkdale or Lytham. Forward planning is essential. Both individual visitors and societies are welcome on Mondays, Tuesdays, Thursdays and Fridays. The Secretary, **Mr. A. Thirlwell** can be contacted by telephone on **(07048) 72164** or by writing to the **Formby Golf Club, Golf Road, Formby, Liverpool L37 1LQ.** All players must hold a current golf club handicap. In 1992 the green fee to play at Formby was set at £40. This secured either a single round or, more attractively, a full day's golf. The professional at Formby is **Clive Harrison**.

Formby is situated approximately 14 miles north of Liverpool and about 7 miles south of Southport (even less from Birkdale). Linking each to the other is the A565. Long distance travellers will likely use a combination of the M6 and either the M58 or the M62/M57. Both the M57 and M58 take the motorist to within 2 miles of the A565, just south of Formby. The M6 links with the M58 (junction 26) and with the M62 (junction 21A). There is also a train station at Formby and most who know the course well will be all too familiar with the railway line! It runs parallel to the first three fairways and is a particularly potent threat on the opening drive.

It isn't only the right hander wrestling with a slice (or the hook-happy left hander) who is likely to come to grief over the opening holes at Formby: they offer great variety and even greater challenge. Vast, gaping bunkers regularly loom in front of greens and straying from the fairways will usually be penalised heavily. If the pines don't shut you out the heather almost certainly will.

Included among most people's favourite holes at Formby are the par five **3rd** and the par three **5th**; the **7th** with its raised green and avenue of pines and the genuinely glorious **12th.** Formby's celebrated 4-3-5-4 finish calls for some very precise shot-making and at the end of the round there is every chance that the golfer will have used all 14 clubs in their bag. In total the course measures 6695 yards par 72.

The 19th at Formby is very comfortable and catering facilities are provided throughout the week with the exception of Mondays. A jacket and tie must be worn in the clubhouse.

Although the Open Championship has never visited Formby the Club regularly hosts important amateur events. Just a week after the Open was played at Royal Birkdale in 1991, the English Amateur was being staged 'down the road' at Formby. In the piece on Royal Birkdale, featured elsewhere in this chapter, we mentioned how in the Open of 1976 a raw and hitherto unknown 19 year old burst on to the scene finishing joint runner up to Johnny Miller. Arguably the high point of Ballesteros' career came in 1984 when he overcame Tom Watson to win his second Open title at St. Andrews. Later that same summer, Formby celebrating its centenary, hosted the Amateur Championship and another teenage Spaniard wrote his name into the history books: **Jose-Maria Olazabal** who produced some sensational golf to defeat a second future Ryder Cup star, **Colin Montgomerie**. Jose-Maria hasn't looked back since. Perhaps the Spanish Armada should have tried landing in Lancashire instead of Devon.

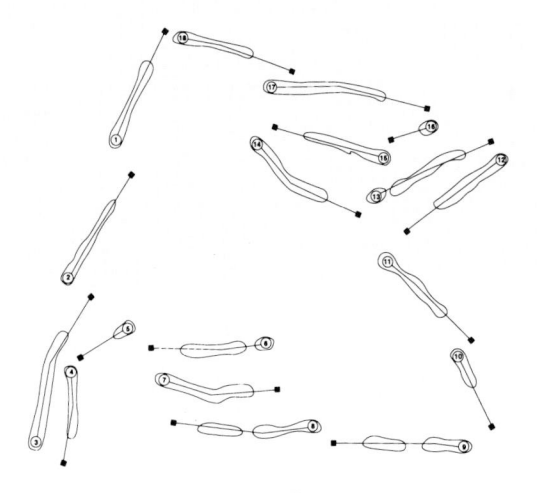

Hole	Yards	Par	Hole	Yards	Par
1	415	4	10	182	3
2	381	4	11	384	4
3	518	5	12	405	4
4	312	4	13	380	4
5	162	3	14	420	4
6	402	4	15	403	4
7	377	4	16	127	3
8	493	5	17	494	5
9	450	4	18	390	4
Out	**3,510**	**37**	**In**	**3,185**	**35**
			Out	**3,510**	**37**
			Totals	**6,695**	**72**

ROYAL LIVERPOOL (HOYLAKE)
CHAMPIONSHIP GOLF

The Royal Hotel at Hoylake (alas no longer with us) played a starring role in the early history of the Royal Liverpool Golf Club. In 1869 a meeting was held there which led to the famous Club's formation. Perhaps of greater significance that day, with no disrespect whatsoever to those founding Members, was the presence in the Hotel of a seven year old boy. **John Ball**, whose father was the Hotel proprietor, grew to become not only Hoylake's favourite son, but also the finest amateur golfer Britain has ever produced.

In the early days, golf at Hoylake must have been at times a trifle frustrating, for the Club shared the links with a racecourse and hoof prints on the fairways were a fairly common hazard. However, by 1876 the horses (doubtless equally frustrated) had found elsewhere to gallop and the golf course quickly developed into England's premier Championship test. The 1869 birthdate in fact makes Hoylake England's second oldest links course, just four years younger than Westward Ho! in Devon.

Ten **Open Championships** and sixteen **Amateur Championships** later visitors are welcome to play at Hoylake, subject to proof of handicap or letter of introduction from their home Club. The green fees as determined from April 1992 were £35 (£50) during the week and £50 (£75) at weekends. Lady visitors pay proportionally less. The tee is reserved for members until 9.30am and between 1.00pm and 2.00pm.

On weekdays, individual bookings must be made through **Robin White**, the Secretary, tel **(051) 632 3101,** who will also authorise limited weekend bookings. Organisers should address written applications to; **The Secretary, Royal Liverpool Golf Club, Meols Drive, Hoylake, Wirral, Merseyside. L47 4AL.**

John Heggarty is the Club's professional. Through him, lessons can be booked, clubs hired, and caddies obtained. Mr Heggarty can be reached on **(051) 632 5868.**

Hoylake is located at the tip of the Wirral peninsula, approximately ten miles west of Liverpool and fifteen miles north of Chester. The north west of England is particularly well served by motorway connections and finding the course shouldn't be a problem. Approaching from either the north or south the M6 is likely to be of assistance; it passes midway between Manchester and Liverpool and should be left at junction 19A. Thereafter the M56 can be followed towards Chester joining the M53 at junction 15. The M53 will then take you to the far end of the Wirral where the A553 Hoylake road should be picked up. (In a nutshell: M6 – M56 – M53 – A553).

The course occupies fairly flat ground and is very exposed to the elements. It is most unusual for the wind not to blow. (You have been warned!) It was his mastery of the wind, a skill acquired playing at Hoylake that enabled John Ball to win many of his record eight Amateur Championships. His victories were achieved between 1888 and 1912. Ball's great rival during those years, both remarkably and ironically was a fellow Hoylake man, **Harold Hilton**. Hilton himself won four Amateur Championships. In addition both Hilton and Ball won the Open Championship, Ball in 1890 and Hilton twice, in 1892 and 1897. The great Bobby Jones is the only other Amateur golfer to have won the Open title.

Even on those very rare occasions when all is calm, Hoylake is still an exceptionally difficult test. From the medal tees the course measures 6821 yards, par 72, and it can play every inch of its length. It is helpful to strike the ball, in the words of the Clubs motto, 'far and sure'. Rather like Carnoustie, Hoylake is renowned for its exacting final stretch. It contains two par fives and three par fours any of which is capable of wrecking a potentially good score. The long **16th** in particular can be cruelly punishing with its out of bounds to the right of the fairway.

The ten Opens held at Hoylake produced ten different Champions and among them some of the game's greatest names: **Harold Hilton, John H. Taylor, Walter Hagen** and **Bobby Jones**. The latter's victory in 1930 was the second leg of the historic grand slam.

The sole reason for the course being presently 'off the Open rota' (the last staging was in 1967 when **Roberto de Vicenzo** won) is that the course cannot accommodate the vast crowds that the event now attracts. Unfortunately, it is the same enthusiastic public who suffer most, for there are many who maintain that Hoylake remains the greatest of all England's Championship links.

Hole	Yards	Par	Hole	Yards	Par
1	428	4	10	409	4
2	369	4	11	200	3
3	505	5	12	395	4
4	184	3	13	157	3
5	407	4	14	516	5
6	383	4	15	460	4
7	200	3	16	509	5
8	479	5	17	391	4
9	393	4	18	395	4
Out	3,348	36	In	3,432	36
			Out	3,348	36
			TOTALS	6,780	72

HILLSIDE
CHAMPIONSHIP GOLF

If Royal Birkdale is the finest golf links in England (and every modern commentator seems to think it is) then Hillside must surely be number two. Why so? Well, firstly they occupy the very same magnificent golfing country being laid out literally side by side amid a vast stretch of sandhills near Southport and, secondly, when analysing the quality of the individual golf holes people find it very difficult to separate the two courses. Perhaps it is only Birkdale's Open Championship history which accords it precedence. And why hasn't Hillside staged the 'Big One'? Presumably it's because it is only since 1967 when Hillside's back nine holes were completely reshaped that it has deserved to be ranked alongside its more illustrious neighbour. The front nine at Hillside has long been highly regarded, but the newer second nine is really outstanding and indeed very spectacular – a bit like Ballybunion minus the Atlantic Ocean.

Since 1967 Hillside has hosted a number of important championships. In the late 1970s both the **British Ladies Championship** and the **Amateur Championship** were held here and in 1982 came the European Tour's prestigious **PGA Championship**. A great course and a great event produced a great winner when **Tony Jacklin** defeated the up-and-coming **Bernhard Langer** in a thrilling play-off after the German had 'opened the door' by four-putting the 16th in the final round. It was Jacklin's last hurrah – thereafter he turned his attention towards winning Ryder Cups!

Golfers wishing to visit Hillside should find the Club welcoming, although arrangements are best planned some time in advance. All players must be in possession of a current handicap. The weekday green fees in 1992 were £35 per round, £45 per day. No visitors are permitted on Saturdays although occasionally it is possible to make a Sunday afternoon booking (the fee was £45 in 1992). The gentleman to approach is the secretary, **John Graham**, tel **(0704) 67169**; fax (0704) 63192. The Club's full address is **Hillside Golf Club, Hastings Road, Hillside, Southport, Merseyside PR8 2LU**. The Club's professional, **Brian Seddon** can be contacted on **(0704) 68360**. (For directions on how to reach Hillside please refer to Royal Birkdale).

A quick look at the scorecard tells you that Hillside scores ten out of ten for its design balance: the two nines are of a very similar length and each comprises two par threes, two par fives and five par fours. From the back markers the links measures 6850 yards, par 72 although from the forward tees the course is a less daunting 6204 yards and from the ladies tees Hillside measures 5939 yards, par 76.

The first two holes at Hillside are fairly straightforward – provided you don't hook on to the railwayline! The **3rd** is a really first class dog-leg hole where the approach must be played over a brook to a green that is well protected by deep traps: stray to the right with your second shot and you'll land in a pond. Stray to the right at the next, the short **4th** and your ball will be greeted by one of three bunkers that are just as devilish as those on the 3rd. The **5th** is a real teaser. It is a par five that can be reached with two good blows, and you can see everything from the tee by virtue of a gap in the dunes fifty yards short of the green, the problem is that a seemingly magnetic sleepered bunker has been placed in the gap. Three of the next four holes are difficult dog-leg par fours, all measuring in excess of 400 yards. The **7th** is the breather – a lovely par three played downhill towards a generous green backed by some magnificent tall pines.

The second nine commences with another outstanding short hole, the 147 yard **10th**. Distance-wise it may not sound much but it's a much tougher green to hit than most and is ringed by a series of alarmingly cavernous bunkers – yes, Hillside is inundated with them! Of the next four holes only the 12th could be described as anything less than superb, with the par five **11th**, which is played from an elevated tee through a wonderful dune-lined valley, being possibly the best hole of the entire round. The **15th** is where Tony Jacklin defeated Langer in the 1982 PGA play-off (there was little the German could do when Jacklin almost holed his second shot); the **16th** is a big and impressive par three; the **17th**, a huge par five, which some rate as good as the 11th and the **18th** makes for a very demanding finishing hole, no thanks to the line of bunkers that traverse the fairway 250 yards from the tee. Langer drove into one of these traps in the final round of the 1982 PGA but still found the heart of the green with his second. Makes you sick doesn't it!

Hole	Yards	Par	Hole	Yards	Par
1	399	4	10	147	3
2	525	5	11	508	5
3	402	4	12	368	4
4	195	3	13	398	4
5	504	5	14	400	4
6	413	4	15	398	4
7	176	3	16	199	3
8	405	4	17	548	5
9	425	4	18	440	4
Out	3,444	36	In	3,406	36
			Out	3,444	36
			TOTALS	6,850	72

CASTLETOWN
CHAMPIONSHIP GOLF

Was the **Isle of Man** ever part of the mainland? If so, which mainland? Situated almost exactly midway between Great Britain and Ireland (and roughly equidistant, as the seagull flies, from England, Scotland, Northern Ireland and the Republic, it looks as if Providence deliberately positioned it in mid-Ocean so that no-one could really claim it as theirs and hence a strong spirit of independence flourished.

The Irish theory, however, has much appeal. One of the Emerald Isle's greatest heroes, Finn McCool, a legend in his own lifetime if ever there was one, and the Giant who started to build the famous Causeway was really responsible for its location. One day, Finn got out of bed the wrong side and started to have one of those days. Finn's personality problem was his temper – the only thing about him that was short. This particular day he completely lost his rag and Finn McCool became Finn Not-so-Cool. He grabbed the largest rock he could find and hurled it 50 miles into the sea. Today, that huge rock is known as the Isle of Man.

Enough about the geography and history of the island: what of the golf? Put Castletown aside for a second and it is pretty fair, add Castletown to the equation and it is pretty excellent. What really makes Castletown is its extraordinary location on the island. Like St. Andrews the course is laid out on a fairly thin strip of land but unlike St. Andrews it is surrounded by water on three sides, the golf links being laid out on a very unusual, triangular-shaped peninsula. This is the Langness Peninsula, more commonly known as Fort Island, situated right on the south eastern tip of the Isle of Man only a few minutes from the island's airport at Ronaldsway.

The extraordinary location produces some amazing seascapes and as the land 'between the sea' is more or less perfect links terrain the architect who designed Castletown was given a mighty head start by Mother Nature. Fortunately for you and I they didn't give the task to any old architect either; the original layout was prepared by **'Old' Tom Morris** – he of course was the chap who reckoned that Machrihanish was 'designed by The Almighty for playing golf'. What must he have thought of this site? (Interestingly there is more than hint of Machrihanish about some of the holes at Castletown). After the last war Castletown was reshaped and this time another celebrated architect was brought in to oversee the project: **Mackenzie Ross**, the man who converted Turnberry from a battle station into the majestic links it now is.

Unless one is fortunate enough to be a member of Castletown Golf Club by far the easiest way of inspecting Mackenzie's masterpiece is to stay overnight at the adjacent Castletown Golf Links Hotel. The Hotel actually owns the golf course and booking a game is much easier for Hotel guests. Residents have priority over visitors and pay reduced green fees. Non residents can only book tee times one month in advance; this is not to say that they are unwelcome at short notice, it is just that it may be a case of pot luck. Bookings may be made through the Golf Secretary, **Wendy Baxter**, tel **(0624) 822201.** Visitors who do not have a tee reservation should contact the Club's professional, **Murray Crowe**, tel **(0624) 822211**.

The green fees for 1992 are £13.50 per day for Hotel Residents,while visitors pay £19 per day between Monday and Thursday and £25 at all other times.

Because of the Hotel, its adjoining links and its course architect, Castletown has been called the 'Poor Man's Turnberry'. This is actually intended as a compliment; certainly there is nothing poor about the Hotel or its golf course, the quality of both is very high. In fact many people believe that in its way the golf at Castletown is just as enjoyable (if a little less testing) and scenically as enchanting as the famous Ailsa Course. From its championship tees the links can be stretched to 6713 yards, par 72. The respective lengths from the medal and forward tees being 6546 yards and 6137 yards.

Among the best holes on the course are two fine par threes, the **6th** and the **11th,** the sharply dog-legging **7th** and a truly spectacular pair, the **8th** and the **17th**. The former carries a famous name, 'The Road Hole.' There are no railway sheds to drive over here but terror does lurk all the way down the right side of the fairway: a sliced drive will either end up on tarmac, the beach or the sea. Take the road away and from the back tee the 8th is almost a mirror image of the 1st at Machrihanish – it is of a similar length too at 426 yards. There are no bunkers around the green but then getting there is problematical enough.

The 17th is called 'The Gully' and again a brave, long drive is needed if the direct route to the green is taken. The carry is nearly 200 yards over a deep chasm – rocks and frothy water await the miss-hit shot. You stand on the 17th tee at Castletown with the knowledge that your drive could finish up in England, Scotland, Ireland or even Wales. As the great Nigel would say, only the best drivers should stay on the Isle of Man.

Hole	Yards	Par	Hole	Yards	Par
1	252	4	10	568	5
2	390	4	11	166	3
3	557	5	12	369	4
4	388	4	13	349	4
5	497	5	14	448	4
6	135	3	15	373	4
7	383	4	16	188	3
8	426	4	17	420	4
9	386	4	18	418	4
Out	**3,414**	**37**	**In**	**3,299**	**35**
			Out	**3,414**	**37**
			Totals	**6,713**	**72**

THE CASTLETOWN GOLF LINKS

Set on Fort Island with breathtaking views across the Irish Sea, the Castletown Golf Links Hotel's very own 18 hole Championship Golf Course offers you a challenging course with the finest facilities and service to match.

The Castletown Golf Links Hotel occupies pride of place in the centre of a wild and beautiful course with the first tee directly opposite the hotel's entrance.

The Airport is only five minutes away from The Hotel. From landing on the Island, you can be collected by our courtesy car, taken to The Hotel, checked in and be on the first tee within 20 minutes.

The course offers a challenge from the beginner to the more seasoned player. Holes such as the 8th - known as 'The Road' running parallel with the main shore line driveway leading to The Hotel, the 17th - christened 'The Gully', with a 200 yard drive across the Irish Sea, are so memorable, they will surely require a post-mortem afterwards in the 19th!

The Hotel itself has been refurbished and now all bedrooms and public areas offer elegance and a luxuriously high standard of comfort that will undoubtedly appeal to the most discerning traveller. Golfer or not, the complete enjoyment experience awaits you - indoor pool, saunas, snooker room and solariums are here to pamper you, or a walk around the course and the never ending countryside has to be given time out.

As the sun goes down over the Island's mountains, enjoy the fine wines and inspirational cuisine in one of our two restaurants. Whether you choose to dine in the main restaurant or L'Orangerie, you will be sure to delve into the very best cuisine - an experience all of its own, as the Islanders will recommend.

Afterwards - the choice is your own. Relax in one of our three bars, watch satellite TV, or let us whisk you away to our sister hotel in Douglas where you can dance the night away at Toff's Night Club, or enjoy the only immediate and complimentary membership Casino in Europe.

The Isle of Man and Castletown Golf Links Hotel and golf course, have to be seen to be believed.

The Castletown Golf Links Hotel
Deryhaven
Isle of Man
Tel: (0624) 822201
Fax: (0624) 824633

LANCASHIRE & THE ISLE OF MAN
COMPLETE GOLF

KEY

*** Visitors welcome at most times
** Visitors usually allowed on weekdays only
* Visitors not normally permitted (Mon, Wed) No visitors on specified days

APPROXIMATE GREEN FEES
A – £30 plus
B – £20 – £30
C – £15 – £25
D – £10 – £20
E – Under £10
F – Green fees on application

RESTRICTIONS
G – Guests only
H – Handicap certificate required
H(24) – Handicap of 24 or less required
L – Letter of introduction required
M – Visitor must be a member of another recognised club.

GREATER MANCHESTER

Acre Gate G.C
061-748 1226
Pennybridge Lane, Flixton
from Urmston take the Flixton Road
(18) 4395 yards/***/E

Altrincham G.C
061-928 0761
Stockport Road, Timperley, Altrincham, Cheshire
1 mile E. of Altrincham on the A560
(18) 6162 yards/***/D

Ashton-In-Makerfield G.C
(09420 724229
Garswood Park, Liverpool Road, Ashton-In-Makerfield
On A58, off the M6 at junction 24
(18) 6169 yards/**(not Wed)/F/M

Ashton On Mersey G.C
061-973 3220
Church Lane, Sale, Cheshire
2 miles from Sale Station
(9) 6202 yards/**(not Tues pm)/F/H

Ashton-Under-Lyne G.C
061-330 1537
Gorsey Way, Ashton-Under-Lyne
From Ashton take the Mossley Road to Queens Road
(18) 6209 yards/**/D

Blackley G.C
061-643 2980
Victoria Ave East, Blackley
Take A64 from Middleton towards Blackley
(18) 6237 yards/**/F

Bolton G.C
(0204) 43067
Lostock Park, Chorley New Road, Bolton
Leave M6 at junction 6
(18) 6215 yards/***/D/M

Bolton Municipal G.C
(0204) 42336
Links Road, Bolton
3 miles W. of Bolton on the A673
(18) 6012 yards/***/E

Brackley G.C
061-790 6076
Bullows Road, Little Hutton, Worsley
9 miles out of Manchester on the A6
(9) 3003 yards/***/E

Bramhall G.C
061-439 4057
Ladythorn Road, Bramhall, Stockport, Cheshire
8 miles S. of Manchester on the A5102
(18) 6293 yards/***/C/M

Bramall Park G.C
061-485 3119
20 Manor Road, Bramall, Stockport
8 miles S. of Manchester leave A6 for A5102
(18) 6214 yards/***/C

Breightmet G.C
(0204) 27381
Red Bridge, Ainsworth, Bolton
3 miles out of Bolton on Bury road
(9) 6448 yards/**(not Wed)/E

Brookdale G.C
061-681 4534
Ashbridge, Woodhouse, Failsworth
5 miles N.E of Manchester
(18) 5878 yards/***/D/M

Bury G.C
061-766 4897
Unsworth Hall, Blackford Bridge, Bury
7 miles N. of Manchester on the A56
(18) 5953 yards/***/D

Castle Hawk G.C
(0706) 40841
Heywood Road, Castleton, Rochdale
Leave Rochdale via Castleton Road for Heywood Road
(18) 3158 yards/***/F

Cheadle G.C
061-428 2160
Shiers Drive, Cheadle, Cheshire
1 mile S. of Cheadle village
(9) 5006 yards/***(not Tues/Sat)D/M/H

Chorlton-Cum-Hardy G.C
061-881 3139
Barlow Hall Road, Chorlton
3 miles from the city centre, near cemetry
(18) 6003 yards/***/D

Crompton & Royton G.C
061-642 2154
Highbarn, Royton, Oldham
N. of Oldham off the A627
(18) 6212 yards/***/D

Davyhulme Park G.C
061-748 2260
Gleneagles Road, Davyhulme, Urmston
8 miles S. of Manchester near hospital
(18) 6237 yards/***/D/M

Deane G.C
(0204) 61944
off Juction Road, Deane, Bolton
2 miles from junction 5 of the M61
(18) 5511 yards/***/D//H

Denton G.C
061-336 3218
Manchester Road, Denton
5 miles from city centre on the A57
(18) 6290 yards/***/D/H

Didsbury G.C
061-998 9278
For Lane, Northenden
Signposted off the M3 at junction 9
(18) 6273 yards/***/D/H

Disley G.C
(0663) 63266
Stanley Hall Lane, Jacksons Edge, Disley, Stockport
6 miles S. of Stockport on the A6
(18) 6015 yards/***/F/H/M

Dunkinfield G.C
061-338 2340
Lyne Edge, Ashton-under-Lyne
(18) 5585 yards/**/D

Dunham Forest G.C
061-928 2605
Oldfield Lane, Altrincham, Cheshire
2 miles N. from junction 7 off M56
(18) 6800 yards/***/F/H

Dunscar G.C
(0204) 51090
Longworth Lane, Bromley Cross, Bolton
3 miles N. of Bolton off the A666
(18) 5957 yards/**/F

Ellesmere G.C
061-790 2122
Old Clough Lane, Worsley
5 miles W. of Manchester on the A580
(18) 5957 yards/(by arrangement)/E/H/M

Fairfield Golf And Sailing Club
061-370 2292
Booth Road, Audenshaw
4 miles from city centre off the A635
(18) 5654 yards/***/(not Wed pm or weekend am)/F

Flixton G.C
061-748 2116
Church Road, Flixton
6 miles S. of Manchester
(9) 6441 yards/**/D

Gathurst G.C
(02575) 2861
Miles Lane, Shevington, Wigan
1 miles S. of junction 27 of the M6
(9) 6308 yards/**(not Wed)/D/M

Gatley G.C
061-437 2091
Waterfall Farm, Styal Road, Heald Green, Gatley
3 miles from Manchester airport
(9) 5934 yards/**(not Tues)/F

Great Lever & Farnworth G.C
(0204) 62582
Lever Edge Lane, Bolton
2 miles from Bolton town centre
(18) 5958 yards/**/D

Haigh Hall G.C
(0924) 831107
Haigh Country Park, Haigh, Wigan
Take B5106 from M6 for country park
(18) 6400 yards/***/D

Hale G.C
061-980 4225
Rappax Road, Hale, Altringham, Cheshire
2 miles S.E of Altringham
(9) 5780 yards/**(not Thurs)/F

Heaton Manor G.C
061-432 2134
Heaton Mersey, Stockport, Cheshire
2 miles N.W of Stockport
(18) 5876 yards/***(not Tues/Wed)/D

Heaton Park G.C
061-798 0295
Prestwich
Leave M66 southbound by A576 roundabout
(18) 5849 yards/***/E

Hindley Hall G.C
(0942) 55131
Hall Lane, Hindley, Wigan
Leave M61 at junction 6 for for A6
(18) 5875 yards/***/F/M

Horwich G.C
(0204) 696980
Victoria Road, Horwich, Bolton
2 miles from junction 6 of the M61
(9) 5404 yards/*/F

Houldsworth G.C
061-224 5055
Wingate House, Higher Levenshulme
Leave M6 at junction 12 for A6
(18) 6078 yards/**/E

Lobden G.C
(0706) 343228
Lobden Moor, Whitworth, Rochdale
Half mile from village centre on A671
(9) 5750 yards/***(not Sat)/F

Lowes Park G.C
061-764 1231
Hill Top, Bury
Take A56 N. from Bury
(9) 6035 yards/**(not Wed)/D/M

Manchester G.C
061-643 3202
Hopwood Cottage, Rochdale Road, Middleton
7 miles N. of the city on the A665
(18) 6540 yards/**/C/H

Marple G.C
061-427 2311
Hawk Green, Marple, Stockport, Cheshire
Leave A6 at High Lane for Hawk Green
(18) 5700 yards/***/D/M

Mellor & Townscliffe G.C
061-427 2208
Tarden, Gibb Lane, Mellor, Stockport
Leave A626 7 miles S.E of Stockport
(18) 5925 yards/***(not Sat)/D

North Manchester G.C
061-643 9033
Rhodes House, Manchester Old Road, Middleton
Head for Middleton from exit 18 of the M62
(18) 6527 yards/**/F/H

Northenden G.C
061-998 4738
Palatine Road, Northenden
1 mile through Northenden
(18) 6469 yards/***(not Sat)/F/H

Oldham G.C
061-624 4986
Lees New Road, Oldham
Turn S. at Lees from the A669
(18) 5045 yards/***/E

Old Links G.C
(0204) 43089
Chorley Old Road, Bolton
N. of the A58 on the B6226
(18) 6406 yards/***/D

Pike Folds G.C
061-740 1136
Cooper Lane, Victoria Avenue, Blackley
4 miles N. of city centre off Rochdale Road
(9) 5789 yards/**/E

Prestwich G.C
061-773 4578
Hilton Lane, Prestwich
On A6044 1 mile from junction with A56
(18) 4712 yards/***/F/H

Reddish Vale G.C
061-480 2359
Southcliffe Road, Reddish, Stockport, Cheshire
1 mile N. of Stockport
(18) 6086 yards/**/F/H

Regent Park G.C
061-485 3199
Manor Rd, Bramhall
(18) 6293 yards/***/F

Ringway G.C
061-980 2630
Hale Mount, Hale Barns, Altrincham, Cheshire
Leave M6 at junction 6, follow signs for Hale
(18) 6494 yards/***/C/H

Romiley G.C.061-430 2392
Goosehouse Green, Romiley, Stockport
Signposted from village on the B6101
(18) 6335 yards/***(not Thurs)/F

Saddleworth G.C
(0457) 7872059
Mountain Ash, Ladcastle Road, Uppermill, Oldham
5 miles from Oldham, off the A670
(18) 5976 yards/***/D//H

Sale G.C
061-973 3404
Sale Lodge, Golf Road, Sale, Cheshire
1 mile from Sale station
(18) 6346 yards/***/F/M

Stamford G.C
(04575) 2126
Oakfield House, Huddersfield Road, Heyheads, Stalybridge
On the B6175, off the A6018
(18) 5619 yards/**/D

Stand G.C
061-766 2388
The Dales, Ashbourne Grove, Whitefield
1 mile N. of exit 17 of the M62
(18) 6425 yards/**/D/H

Stockport G.C
061-427 2001
Offerton Road, Offerton, Stockport
Take A627 from the A262
(18) 6319 yards/***/D/M

Swinton Park G.C
061-794 1785
East Lancashire Road, Swinton
5 miles from city centre on A580
(18) 6675 yards/***/D/M

Turton G.C
(0204) 852235
Wood End Farm, Chapeltown Road, Bromley
3 miles N. of Bolton on the A666/676
(9) 5805 yards/***(not Wed/Sat)/E

Walmersley G..C
061-764 0018
Garretts Close, Walmersley, Bury
3 miles N. of Bury on the A56
(9) 3057 yards/***(not Mon/Tues)//E

Werneth (Oldham) G.C
061-624 1190
Green Lane, Garden Suburb, Oldham
5 miles from Manchester off the A6104
(18) 5363 yards/**/D

Werneth Low G.C
061-368 2503
Werneth Low Road, Hyde, Cheshire
2 miles from Hyde town centre
(9) 5734 yards/***(not Sun)/D

Westhoughton G.C
(0942) 811085
Long Island, Westhoughton, Bolton
4 miles S.W of Bolton on the A58
(9) 5834 yards/**/F

Whitefield G.C
061-766 2904
81/83 Higher Lane, Whitefield
Leave M62 at exit 17 for Radcliffe
(18) 2580 yards/***/F/H

Whittaker G.C
(0706) 78310
Whittaker Lane, Littleborough
1 mile from the town centre
(9) 5576 yards/***(not Tues/Sun pm)/D/M

William Wroe G.C
061-748 8680
Penny Bridge Lane, Flixton
Take B5124 from exit 4 of the M63
(18) 4395 yards/***/E

Withington G.C
061-445 9544
Palatine Road, West Didsbury
3 miles from Manchester city centre
(18) 6411 yards/***/F/H

Worsley G.C
061-789 4202
Stableford Avenue, Monton, Eccles
Signposted 1 mile E. of junction 13 of M62
(18) 6217 yards/***/D/H/M

LANCASHIRE

Accrington and District G.C
(0254) 32734
New Barn Farm, Devon Avenue, West End, Oswaldthistle5 miles from Blackburn on the A679
(18) 5954 yards/***/D

THE INN AT WHITEWELL

Originally built as a manor house for the keeper of the King's deer in the 14th century, the Inn at Whitewell still belongs to the Royal family as part of the Duchy of Lancaster. As a result, it still retains its associations with field sports and grouse and pheasant shooting can be arranged in season. The Inn also has fishing rights to five miles of both banks of the River Hodder where you can fish for salmon and trout.

You will often find fresh fish on the menu, including local smoked salmon and game in season, black pudding and a foot long Cumberland sausage. The wine list is extensive and claims to be one of the best lists for a pub in the country as the proprietors are also wine-shippers.

Interestingly, the Inn has an art gallery where you can by works by artists from all over the country. You can also buy locally made shirts and shooting stockings, for which they have Royal customers, and hand lasted shoes. Despite all this, the Inn maintains a country pub atmosphere with carved stone fireplaces, oak beams, wood-panelling, oak settles and a baby grand in the corner of the lounge.

The setting is quite stunning. The Inn is set in three acres of beautiful grounds and looks straight across to the Trough of Bowland. In fine weather, you can sit outside at wooden tables, high above the river, and enjoy the peace and beauty of the country.

Shooting and horse riding can be arranged and Browsholme Hall and Clitheroe Castle are nearby. For the golfer, the splendid inland course of Clitheroe Golf Club is closeby. Situated on the edge of the Forest of Bowland amidst superb countryside the course looks across to Pendle Hill - a delightful setting. A short drive away lies Lancaster Golf and Country Club and the county of Lancashire is home to the famous Royals; Lytham and Birkdale, both within easy reach of the inn.

The Inn At Whitewell
Forest of Bowland
Clitheroe
Lancashire BB7 3AT
Tel: (02008) 222

LANCASHIRE & THE ISLE OF MAN
COMPLETE GOLF

Alt G.C
(0704) 530435
Park Road, West Southport
N. of the Marine Lake
(18) 5939 yards/***/F

Ashton and Lea G.C
(0772) 72480
Tudor Avenue, off Blackpool Road, Lea, Preston
3 miles from Preston off A583
(18) 6289 yards/**/D

Bacup G.C
(0706) 873170
Maden Road,Bacup
Half mile from Bacup centre on the A671
(9) 5652 yards/**(not Tues)/F

Baxenden and District G.C
(0254) 34555
Top o thMeadow, Baxenden
2 miles S.E of Accrington off the A680
(9) 5740 yards/***/E

Beacon Park G.C
(0695) 622700
Beacon Hill, Dalton, Up Holland, Wigan
Signposted from the centre of Up Holland
(18) 5996 yards/***/E

Bentham G.C
(0468) 61018
Robin Lane, Bentham
13 miles E. of M6 (junction 34) on B6480
(9) 5752 yards/***/E

Blackburn G.C
(0254) 51122
Beardwood Brow, Blackburn
W. side of town off Revidge Road
(18) 6100 yards/**/D/H

Blackpool North Shore G.C
(0253) 51017
Devonshire Road, Blackpool
N. of the town centre on the A587
(18) 6442 yards/***/D

Blackpool-Stanley Park G.C
(0253) 33960
North Park Drive, Blackpool2 miles E. of the town centre
(18) 6060 yards/***/E

Burnley G.C
(0282) 21045
Glen View, Burnley
Just past junction of A56 and A646
(18) 5891 yards/***(not Sat)/D

Chorley G.C
(0257) 480263
Hall othHill, Heath Charnock, Chorley
On the A673, near junction with A6
(18) 6277 yards/***/D/H

Colne G.C
(0282) 863391
Law Farm, Skipton Old Road
2 miles E. of Colne
(9) 5961 yards/***/D

Darwen G.C
(0254) 701287
Winter Hill, Darwen
2 miles from Darwen centre, off the A666
(18) 5752 yards/**/E

Dean Wood G.C
(0695) 622219
Lafford Lane, Up Holland, Skelmersdale
Leave M6 at exit 26, take A577 to Up Holland
(18) 6129 yards/**/E

Duxbury Park G.C
(02572) 65380
Wyreside, Knott End, Blackpool
Leave M55 at exit 3, take A585 then B2588
(18) 6390 yards/***/E

Fairhaven G.C
(0253)736741
2 miles from St Annes
(18) 6883 yards/**/D

Fishwick Hall G.C
(0772) 798300
1 mile east of Preston
(18) 6028 yards/**/D

Fleetwood G.C
(03917) 3114
1 mile west of Fleetwood
(18) 6723 yards/***/D

Heysham G.C
(0524) 51011
3 miles from Morecambe
(18) 6224 yards/***/D

Hindley Hall G.C
(0942) 55131
Hindley, Wigan
(18) 5840 yards/**/D/I

Ingol Golf and Squash Club
(0772) 734556
Tanterton Hall Rd, Ingol
(18) 6345 yards/***/E

Knott End G.C
(0253) 810254
Knott End on Sea
(18) 6010 yards/**/D

Lancaster G. & C. C
(0524) 751247
Ashton Hall, Ashton-with-Stodday, Lancaster
3 miles S.W of Lancaster on A588
(18) 6422 yards/**/F/H

Lansil G. C
(0524) 39269
Caton Road, Lancaster
1 mile E. of Lancaster centre on A683
(18) 5608 yards/***(not Sun am)/E/H

Leyland G.C
(0772) 421359
Wigan Road, Leyland
Off A49 from M6 exit 28
(18) 6105 yards/**/D

Longridge G.C
(077478) 3291
Fell Barn, Jeffrey Hill, Longridge, Preston
Take B6243 from Preston to Longridge
(18) 5800 yards/***/D

Lytham Green Drive G.C
(0253) 737390
Ballam Road, Lytham
1 mile from Lytham centre
(18) 6159 yards/**/C/H

Marsden Park G.C
(0282) 67525
Townhouse Road, Nelson4 miles N. of Burnley, just off A56
(18) 5806 yards/***/E

Morecambe G.C
(0524) 412841
Bare, Morecambe
Leave M6 at junctions 34 or 35 for Morecambe
(18) 5766 yards/***/F/M

Nelson G.C
(0282) 64583
Kings Causeway, Briefield, Nelson
2 miles N. of Burnley on the A682
(18) 5967 yards/**(not Thurs pm)/D

Ormskirk G.
(0695) 72112
Cranes Lane, Lathom, Ormskirk
2 miles E. of Ormskirk
(18) 6333 yards/***/C/H

Penwortham G.C
(0772) 744630
Blundell Lane, Penwortham, Preston
1 mile W. of Preston off the A59
(18) 5915 yards/**(not Tues)/D

Pleasington G.C
(0254) 22177
Pleasington, Blackburn
Leave Blackburn S.W on A674 for Pleasington
(18) 6417 yards/**/C

Poulton-Le-Fylde G.C
(0253) 892444
Myrtle Farm, Breck Roa, Poulton-Le Fylde
3 miles E. of Blackpool via Breck Road
(9) 958 yards/***/E

Preston GC
(0772) 700011
Fulwood Lane, Fulwood, Preston
N. of Preston, off Watling Street Road
(18) 6233 yards/**(by arrangement)/C/H

Rishton G.C
(0254) 884442
Eachill Links, Blackburn
3 miles E. of Blackburn off A679
(9) 6094 yards/**/F

Rochdale G.C
(0706) 43818
Edenfield Road, Bagslate, RochdaleTake A680 for 3 miles from M62 exit 20
(18) 5981 yards/***/F

Rossendale G.C
(0706) 213056
Edwood Lane, Haslingden, Rossendale
16 miles N. of Manchester off A56
(18) 6267 yards/***(not Sat)/D

Royal Lytham & St Annes G.C
(0253) 724206
Linksgate, St Annes on Sea, Lytham St Annes
1 mile from the centre of St Annes on Sea
(18) 6673 yards/**/A/H/L

St Annes Old Links G.C
(0253) 723597
Highbury Road, St Annes, Lytham St Annes
On the A584 coastal road towards St Annes
(18) 6616 yards/**(not Tues)/C/H

Shaw Hill Golf And Country Club
(02572) 69221
Whittle-le-Woods, Chorley
2 miles N. of Chorley on the A6
(18) 6467 yards/**/C/H

Silverdale G.C
(0524) 701300
Red Bridge Lane, Silverdale, Carnforth
Leave the M6 at junction 35 for Silverdale
(9) 5262 yards/***/E

Springfield G.C
(0706) 49801
Springfield Park, Bolton Road, Rochdale
(18) 5209 yards/***/E

Todmorden G.C
(0706) 812986
Rive Rocks, Cross Stone Road, Todmorden
1 mile from town centre
(18) 5818 yards/***(not Sat)/F

Towneley G.C
(0282) 38473
Todmorden Road, Burnley
1 mile from Burnley Football Ground
(18) 5862 yards/**/E

Tunshill G.C
(0706) 342095
Kiln Lane, MilnrowAlongside the M62 near junction 21
(9) 2902 yards/**(not Tues pm)/F

Whalley G.C
(025482) 2236
Portfield Road, Whalley, Blackburn
Take A59 to Whalley, turn S. of the town
(9) 5953 yards/***/F

Wigan G.C
(0257) 421360
Arley Hall, Haigh, Wigan
4 miles N. of Wigan on the B5239
(9) 6058 yards/**(not Tues)/F

Wilpshire G.C
(0254) 48260
72 Whalley Road, Wilpshire, Blackburn
4 miles E. of Blackburn on A666
(18) 5911 yards/**/D/H

MERSEYSIDE

Allerton Municipal G.C
051-428 4074
Allerton, Liverpool
Take the Allerton road from city centre
(18) 5494 yards/***/E
(9) 1845 yards/***/E

Arrowe Park G.C
051-677 1527
Arrowe Park, Woodchurch, Birkenhead
3 miles from the town centre
(18) 6377 yards/***/E

Bidston G.C
051-638 3412
Scoresby Road, Leasowe, Wirral
1 mile from Leasowe on the A551
(18) 6207 yards/***/E

Bootle G.C
051-928 6196
Dunnings Bridge Road, Bootle
5 miles N. of Liverpool on the A565
(18) 6362 yards/***/E

Bowring G.C
051-489 1901
Bowring Park, Roby Road, Huyton, Liverpool
5 miles E. of the city centre
(9) 2500 yards/***/E

Brackenwood G.C
051-608 3093
Bracken Lane, Bebington, Wirral
Signposted from junction 4 off M56
(18) 6285 yards/***/D

Bromborough G.C
051-334 2155
Raby Hall Road, Bromborough, Wirral
Half mile from Bromborough station
(18) 6650 yards/**/D

Caldy G.C
051-625 5660
Links Hey Road, Caldy, Wirral
Take A540 from Chester to Caldy
(18) 6665 yards/**/C

Childwall G.C
051-487 0654
Naylors Road, Liverpool
Take Childwall Valley Road to the Bridge Inn
(18) 6425 yards/***(not Tues)/D

Eastham Lodge G.C
051-327 3003
117 Ferry Road, Eastham, Wirral
6 miles from Birkenhead off the A41
(15) 6444 yards/**/D/H

Formby G.C
(07048) 72164
Golf Road, Formby, Liverpool
6 miles S. of Southport off the A565
918) 6781 yards/**/A/H

Formby Ladies G.C
(07048) 73493
Golf Road, Formby, Liverpool
6 miles S. of Southport of the A565
(18) 5374 yards/C/H

Grange Park G.C
(0744) 26318
Prescot Road, St Helens
1 mile from St Helens on the A58
(18) 6429 yards/**/C

Haydock Park G.C
(09252) 224389
Golbourne Park, Newton-Le-Willows
1 mile E. of junction 23 of the M6
(18) 6043 yards/**(not Tues)/D

Hesketh G.C
(0704) 36897
Cockle Dicks Lane, Southport
1 mile N. of Southport centre on the A565
(18) 6193 yards/**/C/H

Heswall G.C
051-342 1237
Cottage Lane, Gayton Heswall, The Wirral
Leave M53 at junction 4 and to Well Lane
(18) 6472 yards/***/C/H

Hillside G.C
(0704) 67169
Hastings Road, Hillside, Southport
At the end of Hastings Road off A565
(18) 6850 yards/**/F/H

Hoylake G.C
051-632 2956
Carr Lane, Hoylake
100 yards from Hoylake station
(18) 6330 yards/***/D

Huyton and Prescot G.C
051-489 3948
Hurst Park, Huyton Lane, Huyton
Off the B5199
(18) 5738 yards/**/D/M

Kirkby (Liverpool Municipal)
051-546 5435
Ingoe Lane, Kirkby
Leave M57 at junction 6
(18) 6571 yards/***/E/H

Leasowe G.C
051-677 5852
Leasowe Road, Moreton, Wirral
1 mile W. of Wallasey village
(18) 6204 yards/**/D/H

Lee Park G.C
051-487 3882
Chidwall Valley Road, Gateacre
Take A562 from Liverpool onto B5171
(18) 6411 yards/***/D

Royal Birkdale G.C
(0604) 67920
Waterloo Road, Birkdale, Southport
2 miles S. of Southport on A565
(18) 6703 yards/**/A/H/L

Royal Liverpool G.C
051-632 3101
Meols Drive, Hoylake, Wirral
10 miles W. of Liverpool off the A553
(18) 6737 yards/***/A/H/L

Sherdley Park G.C
(0744) 813149
Elton Head Road, St Helens
2 miles from town centre on the A570
(18) 5941 yards/***/F

Southport and Ainsdale G.C
(0704) 78000
Bradshaws Lane, Ainsdale, Southport
3 miles S. of Southport on the A565
(18) 6612 yards/**/B/M

Southport Municipal G.C
(0704) 35286
Park Road West, Southport
At N. end of Promenade near Marine Lake
(18) 6139 yards/***/E

Southport Old Links G.C
(0704) 28207
Moss Lane, Southport
Past the Law courts for Manchester Road
(9) 6486 yards/**(not Wed)/E

Wallasey G.C
051-691 1024
Bayswater Road, Wallasey
Take Wallasey Tunnel from Liverpool centre
(18) 6607 yards/**/C/H

Warren G.C
051-639 5730
The Grage, Grove Road, Wallasey
500 yards up Grange Road, past station
(9) 2945/**/E

West Derby G.C
051-254 1034
Yew Tree Lane, Liverpool
4 miles E. of Liverpool centre off A57
(18) 6333 yards/**/C

LANCASHIRE & THE ISLE OF MAN
COMPLETE GOLF

West Lancashire G.C
051-924 1076
Hall Road West, Blundellsands, Liverpool
Follow signs from A565 from Crosby
(18) 6756 yards/***/C/H

Wirral Ladies G.C
051-652 1255
93 Bidston Road, Oxton, Birkenhead
Leave M53 at junction 3 for the A41
(18) 6966 yards(ladies)***(by arrangement)/D/H
(18) 5170 yards/(men)***(by arrangement)D/H

Woolton G.C
051-486 2298
Doe Park, Speke Road, Woolton, Liverpool
6 miles from the city centre
(18) 5706 yards/***/D

ISLE OF MAN

Castletown G.C
(0625) 822201
Fort Island, Castletown
Towards the airport on Dreswick Point
(18) 6804 yards/***/F

Douglas G.C
(0624) 75952
Pulrose Road, Douglas
1 mile S. of Douglas on the A5
(18) 6080 yards/***/F

Howstrake G.
(0624) 20430
Groudle Road, Onchan
Take A11 from Douglas to Onchan Head
(18) 5367 yards/**/E

Ramsey G.C
(0624) 812244
Brookfield, Ramsey
5 minute from town centre
(18) 6019 yards/***/D/H

Rowany G.C
(0624) 834108
Rowany Drive, Port Erin
Course is just off the Promenade
(18) 5840 yards/***/D

Peel G.C
(0624) 834932
Rheast Lane, Peel
Inland on the A1 towards Douglas
(18) 5914 yards/**/D

Port St Mary G.C
(0624) 834932Callow Road, Port St Mary
S. from Castletown on the A7
(9) 2711 yards/***/E

Ellen Clapsadle   **THE LADY GOLFER**   *Rosenstiel's*

YORKSHIRE & HUMBERSIDE

Roy Perry **TO HALVE THE MATCH** *Rosenstiel's*

YORKSHIRE & HUMBERSIDE
CHOICE GOLF

While many consider the delights of Yorkshire to be exclusive to its northernmost area this is totally wrong. The small villages that nestle amid the southern Pennines or the Dales are delightful. The river Wharfe carves its way through south Yorkshire revealing extraordinary beauty along its trail. From the haunting howls of Haworth and the Bronte country to the jovial singing in a pub on Ilkley Moor, there is a rich tradition; Yorkshire folk are a proud breed – better reserve your best golf for the eighteenth fairway.

SOUTH YORKSHIRE

Perhaps the pick of the courses in the Sheffield area are the moorland course at **Hallamshire**, three miles west of the city off the A57, **Abbeydale**, a fine wooded parkland test to the south west and **Lees Hall**, a mix of parkland and meadowland, located south of the town centre, and occupying a lofty situation with marvellous views over the city.

Having saved your best golf for the 18th fairway a few thoughts now emerge for the 19th. The best hotel in Sheffield is probably The Grosvenor House (0742) 720041 while The Hallam Tower Post House (0742) 670067 is particularly convenient for the Hallamshire course. Sheffield also offers the comfortable Park Hall Hotel (0246) 434897. The city has many good Asian restaurants, one of the best being Nirmal's Tandoori (0742) 72054, whilst for French food enthusiasts we suggest the Restaurant Le Dauphin (0742) 620800. Finally, we ought to recommend a good pub, the area is naturally riddled with them, but try the Cross Keys in Handsworth Road.

Before noting some of the other courses in South Yorkshire, a brief word on **Lindrick** (featured separately). According to the postman it properly belongs in Nottinghamshire although the Club's administrative ties are with Yorkshire and a great number of members live in the Sheffield area. Anyway, whichever side of the fence it's on (and the larger part lies in Yorkshire) it is quite superb!

Rotherham's excellent course is located at Thrybergh Park, two miles north of the town on the A630 and is well worth inspecting. Crossing the A1 we arrive at Doncaster. The **Doncaster Town Moor** Golf Club is situated very close to the famous racetrack. Like Rotherham, it's a parkland type course though not as testing. In Doncaster, The Danum (0302) 342261 and The Grand St Ledger (0302) 364111 are the recommended establishments. In the countryside surrounding the busy railway town, Cadeby provides the cosy Cadeby Inn, while in Hatfield Woodhouse The Green Tree offers a warm welcome and some good snacks. The hotel with the most character in the area is The Crown at Bawtry (0302) 710341 – a very pleasant High Street inn. Those seeking more modern comforts should try the Moat House (0709) 364902 in Rotherham.

WEST YORKSHIRE

West Yorkshire has a greater number of golf courses. Quantity is certainly matched by quality with the area just to the north of Leeds being particularly outstanding. Within a short distance of one another are **Moortown** (featured on a later page), **Alwoodley, Sand Moor** and **Moor Allerton** all of which are of Championship standard.

Whilst Alwoodley, Moortown and Sand Moor are predominantly moorland in character, Moor Allerton, where there are 27 holes, is more strictly parkland. When travelling to any of the four Clubs, the A61 should be taken out of Leeds. Moortown and Moor Allerton are probably the most widely known courses in southern Yorkshire (if one excludes Lindrick). However, many consider Alwoodley and Sand Moor to be at least their equal. Play all four if you can! Other good courses to note around Leeds are **Roundhay, Leeds, Howley Hall** and **Temple Newsham**.

Following the Wharfe into the east of West Yorkshire one finds some superb countryside. This is the land of the Brontes. In Bramhope, a far cry from the romance of the Brontes but a particularly popular hotel for businessmen visiting Leeds, is the Leeds Post House (0532) 842911. Visiting golfers will find plenty of good but inexpensive accommodation in Leeds, The Aragan Hotel (0532) 759306 being a fine example. The gem in this area however, is a restaurant with rooms, Pool Court (0532) 842288 in Pool-in-Wharfedale.

Another concentration of good golf courses is to be found to the north of Bradford, more particularly, **Northcliffe, Keighley** and **Shipley**. Northcliffe is probably the pick with some outstanding views of the nearby moors, but each is well worth a game. Yet another trio encircles Huddersfield, with **Bradley Park** to the north, **Woodsome Hall** to the south and **Huddersfield** Golf Club to the west. It was on the latter course that Sandy Herd learnt his game. The Open Champion of 1902, Herd finished in the first five in the Championship on no fewer than twelve occasions; he would have doubtless won on several of those but for a fellow called Vardon from Ganton across the way.

Two more courses in West Yorkshire demand to be visited, the first is **Ilkley** and the second is **Otley**. They are without question two of the county's most attractive courses. Our friend, the River Wharfe, winds its way through much of the Ilkley course and is a major hazard on several of the early holes. The equally charming course at Otley nestles majestically in the Wharfe Valley.

Beyond the fairways, the river and the rough, the gourmet golfer is superbly well catered for in this area. Here are some suggestions. In Ilkley, the Edwardian Breakfast at Rombalds (0943) 603201 is legendary but the hotel itself and the restaurant are both thoroughly recommended too. Elsewhere in Ilkley, a town where delightful antique shops clutter the streets, one finds The Craiglands Hotel (0943) 607676, this has a setting adjoining that famous moor and is most comfortable. Another good value establishment is The Cow and Calf (0943) 607335 one of the county's finest restaurants – book well in advance! Also, greatly renowned for its fine cuisine is the Box Tree (0943) 608484.

Continuing in the tradition of quality and class, Kildwick Hall (0535) 632244 is a gorgeous Jacobean manor house which provides an outstanding place to stay and a first class restaurant too. Bingley, Otley – all this are is riddled with enthusiastic cricket and rugby sides as well as golfers – popular pubs for one and all include The Fox at Menston, The Malt Shovel at Harden and in Ryburn, where there would seem to be a focal point, The Old Bridge and The Over the Bridge (both provide excellent lunches – perhaps in between rounds?) Finally, for a splendid restaurant visit Golcar where The Weavers Shed (0484) 515444 has a fine setting.

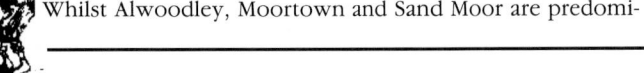

YORKSHIRE & HUMBERSIDE
CHOICE GOLF

NORTH YORKSHIRE

To the south and west the Yorkshire Dales; to the north and east the Yorkshire Moors. North Yorkshire is England's largest county and quite possibly England's most beautiful.

The Dales and the Moors may not sound like great golfing country and indeed by far the greater number of Yorkshire's golfcourses lie in the more populated and industrial regions of South and West Yorkshire. However, golfing visitors to North Yorkshire will not be disappointed; not only does the county boast the likes of Ganton and Fulford, two of England's greatest inland courses, but there are twenty five or so others, the majority of which are set in quite glorious surroundings.

York, they say, is a city everyone should visit at least once. I recommend at least twice for there are two outstanding golf courses within 3 miles of York Minster: **Fulford** to the south and York Golf Club at **Strensall** to the north. Fulford (see feature page) is perhaps the better known, but York is also a Championship course and has many admirers. It is a fine woodland type course, laid out to the edge of Strensall Common.

Staying in York really is a delight, there is a wealth of attractions – Shambles has some marvellous shops, the Minster itself is sensational, there are museums galore and some first class hotels in and around the city. The star of the show is Middlethorpe Hall (0904) 640241, a beautiful mansion house with an exquisite restaurant. The Mount Royale (0904) 6288565 is another well run hotel and is less expensive, while closer to the centre of town The Judges Lodging (0904) 38733 is particularly elegant. Hudson's Hotel and the equally relaxing Grasmead House Hotel (0904) 629996 are two more excellent value establishments. The town centre has many tea shops and small restaurants as well as some pleasant pubs. McCoys (0904) 612191 is a particularly fine restaurant. A noted pub outside the city can be found in Wighill – The White Swan – good value bar snacks. In Fulford village two pubs very handy for the famous course are The Saddle and The Plough, whilst convenient accommodation can be found in Hovingham at The Worsley Arms (0653) 628234.

Next to York, Harrogate probably offers most to both sightseer and golfer. **Pannal** and **Harrogate** are the pick of the courses in the area, the former being a fairly lengthy championship challenge. It is moorland in nature and heavily wooded. Harrogate is possibly the more attractive with its lovely setting at Starbeck near Knaresborough.

The town of Harrogate is renowned for its many fine restaurants. They include The Drum and Monkey (0423) 502650 (superb seafood) and Number Six (0423) 530585. The restaurants in the town's hotels are generally particularly good, notably The Hotel Majestic (0423) 68972, The Russell (0423) 509866 and The Studley (0423) 60425.

Before heading towards the Dales and Moors it is worth noting **Selby** in the south of the county. Laid out over fairly sandy subsoil the course could be described as part links, part parkland. An enjoyable day's golf here might be followed by a visit to Monk Fryston and its fine hotel, Monk Fryston Hall (0977) 682369.

Skipton is known as the 'Gateway to the Dales'. The ancient market town has a fine parkland course situated only a mile or so from the town centre. The views are magnificent and a mountain stream runs through the course adding to the many challenges. An appetite created, dinner is recommended at The Devonshire Arms (075671) 441 in Bolton Abbey. If a good drink is simply all that's required then The Angel at Helton may be preferable.

Ripon is another very charming place; there are only nine holes of golf here (at Ripon City) though they offer great variety nonetheless. The surrounding countryside is quite stupendous. Jervaulx Abbey, founded in 1156 is well worth inspecting (note the outstanding Jervaulx Hall Hotel (0677) 60235), as is Fountains Abbey. For accommodation, Ripon has The Ripon Spa Hotel (0765) 2172 or the more modest Crest Lodge (0765) 2331 and in nearby Boroughbridge, The Crown (0423) 322328 is a comfortable old inn. Lovers of Theakstons should make a pilgrimage to The White Bear at Masham.

Two of North Yorkshire's most beautiful courses are situated fairly close to one another in the centre of the county: **Thirsk & Northallerton** and **Bedale**. The former lies very close to Thirsk racetrack. The views here are towards the Cleveland Hills on one side and the Hambleton Hills on another. Bedale Golf Club can be found off the A684 and is known for its beautiful spread of trees.

In the north of the county, **Richmond** is yet another course that enjoys glorious surroundings. The town itself has a strange mixture of medieval, Georgian and Victorian architecture and is dominated of course by the famous Castle. Fine restaurants once again abound – in Moulton The Black Bull Inn (032577) 289 is excellent, as is The Bridge Inn (0325) 50106 at Stapleton. Firmly recommended also is The Millers House (0969) 22630 at Middleham and The Burgoyne Hotel (0428) 84292 in Reeth. Just south of Richmond, **Catterick Garrison's** Golf Club is worth noting.

Dropping back down in the county, **Malton and Norton** shouldn't be overlooked. It is also particularly convenient for those heading towards Ganton on the A64. **Ganton**, thought by many to be the finest inland course in the North of England, boasts a superb setting on the edge of the Vale of Pickering. It is explored fully on a later page.

Yorkshire's coast contrasts greatly with that of Lancashire, with spectacular cliffs rather than dunes dominating the shoreline. Not surprisingly, there are no true links courses to be found here. However, visitors to the resorts of **Filey** and **Scarborough** will be able to enjoy a game with views over sea and sand – three courses here – and near Flamborough Head there is a testing layout at **Bridlington**.

The splendid Royal Hotel (0723) 364353 in Scarborough caters for all tastes and The Hotel St. Nicholas (0723) 364101 offers fine views. Four more to note in and around Scarborough are The East Ayton Lodge, The Esplanade Hotel (0723) 360382, the Downe Arms (0723) 362471 and The Raven Hall Country House Hotel (0723) 870353 – complete with its own nine hole course – midway between Scarborough and Whitby. Slightly inland at Hackness, The Hackness Grange Country Hotel (0723) 82345 enjoys a beautiful setting and makes for a pleasant stay (there's also a pitch and putt course to sneak in some early morning practice).

YORKSHIRE & HUMBERSIDE
CHOICE GOLF

HUMBERSIDE

To Yorkshire we must tag on Humberside, much of which once belonged to Yorkshire anyway. It has been a much maligned county and it's not fair to compare Scunthorpe and Grimsby with the likes of Harrogate and York. It has its treasures like any other county: a forty mile stretch of sand; pretty villages nestling in the Wolds and the Holderness countryside; it would be difficult to imagine a more pleasant market town than Beverley and then there's the spectacular Humber Bridge and dramatic Flamborough Head.

Unfortunately, try as I may, I cannot trot off a list of wonderful golf courses. There are enough of them about but there's no Ganton or Fulford here, alas. The best in the county is arguably at **Hornsea**, famed, of course for its pottery. It is a beautiful heathland course with particularly outstanding greens. One tip – try not to kill the ducks on the 11th!

Beverley is no great distance from Hornsea and The Beverley Arms (0482) 869241 is a superb place for a nights rest. Tickton offers the excellent Tickton Grange (0964) 543666 and for a pleasant drink visit The White Horse in Brandesburton.

If one has crossed all 1,542 yards of the Humber Bridge to reach the county's largest town then the **Hull** Golf Club at Kirk Ella is probably the best choice for a game although **Hessle** is now a very good course too. The Waterfront (0482) 227222 is the most attractive hotel in town. The seafood in Hull ought to be sampled and Ceruttis (0482) 28501 is one of the best places to do so.

Across the Humber, **Elsham** is well thought of (an old haunt of Tony Jacklin's this) and slightly nearer to Scunthorpe, **Holme Hall** at Bottesford is a championship length parkland course. Finally over to the Humberside coast, both **Grimsby** and **Cleethorpes** are also worth a game. Both towns are full of character (characters as well) and if you do play at Grimsby, don't miss out on the local fish and chips – they're reckoned to be the best in Britain!

RAVEN HALL COUNTRY HOUSE HOTEL & GOLF COURSE

Standing dramatically 600 feet up on the southern most tip of Robin Hoods Bay, Raven Hall is set in 100 acres of award-winning landscaped gardens and battlements, on the site of an old Roman fortress. This 18th century country house captures the most unique, breath-taking panoramic views across towards the smugglers haunt.

Raven Hall has been referred to as 'Yorkshire's best kept golf secret' possessing its own 9 hole, cliff top golf course, free to hotel residents and open to non-residents, providing a challenge to even the keenest golfer.

For the golfer who wishes to try out other golf courses, within a radius of 20 miles there are five 18 hole courses one of which is the championship course at Ganton.

Apart from our golf course the hotel can offer numerous other sports and leisure facilities including: tennis, outdoor swimming pool, croquet, giant chess, crown bowls, putting, table tennis, full size snooker table and a Health and Beauty Salon with sauna.

Renowned for its excellent Yorkshire cuisine, provided since 1970 by Don Holmes, and the special warmth of the Gridley family's hospitality since 1961, the hotel has 53 en-suite bedrooms - all with spectacular views. Included in these are eight bedrooms situated on the third floor and named 'The Cottage'. These rooms capture the style of the traditional English country cottage complete with wooden beams and individual names.

Raven Hall is situated 12 miles north of the Victorian seaside resort of Scarborough: 15 miles south of the Historic Fishing Town of Whitby and it is only an hour away from the famous Medieval walled City of York.

Ideally sited for golfers, walkers and traditional family holidays - "Raven Hall is where coast and country meet...just waiting to be discovered."

Raven Hall Hotel
Ravenscar
Scarborough
North Yorkshire
YO13 0ET
Tel: (0723) 870353
Fax: (0723) 870072

THE MOUNT ROYALE HOTEL

The hotel is the result of the tasteful blending of two beautiful William IV detatched houses. The proprietors, Richard and Christine Oxtoby, have spent a good deal of effort on restoring the former glory of these buildings and their efforts have been well rewarded.

Any traveller having an interest in English history must surely rank the fascinating city of York at least alongside London. The capital of the north and second city of the realm, it began its long and fascinating life around AD71 as a fortress to protect the Roman 9th Legion. The marauding Vikings gave the city its name, derived from Jorvik or Yorwik. This period of history has been magnificently captured in the Jorvik Viking Centre, one of the most entertaining museums in the country. The Minster or Cathedral is the largest medieval structure in Britain. There has been a Minster on the site since the 7th century, the present one is the fourth and was started about 1220, taking 250 years to complete. The city is still protected by ancient city walls, guarded by defensive bastions, working portcullis' and barbican at the Walmgate bar.

Wander around the Micklegate bar, where traitors' severed heads were displayed or visit the National Rail Museum.

Staying in York involves mixing with some of the most fascinating sights in the world. Relaxing afterwards in the intimate cocktail bar of the Mount Royale, or enjoying a delicious meal in the restaurant overlooking the delightful garden, enhances the whole experience. Enjoying the gracious beauty of the hotel, the style and antiquity of much of the furnishings, or slipping into the secluded heated swimming pool is the perfect way to pamper the body as well as the mind.

The hotel is ideal for the small conference or private dinner party, and is only a short drive from the rolling Yorkshire Dales. The perfect base, offering peace and tranquility, practically in the heart of this wonderful city.

Mount Royale Hotel
The Mount
York YO2 2DA
Tel: (0904) 628856
Fax: (0904) 611171

MOORTOWN
CHAMPIONSHIP GOLF

Moortown enjoys an enviable situation. It lies within minutes of the town centre of Leeds, yet it also lies within minutes of the Pennines and the beauty of the Yorkshire Moors. The Club was founded in the autumn of 1909 with the course being laid out by the great **Alister Mackenzie**. Less than twenty years after its formation Moortown was selected to host the first ever **Ryder Cup** to be played on British soil. It proved a momentous occasion.

The American side in 1929 was virtually identical to the one that had crushed the British team 9-2 in the inaugural staging at Worcester, Massachusetts two years previously. It included the likes of **Walter Hagen**, then reigning British Open Champion, **Gene Sarazen**, **Johnny Farrel** the US Open Champion, **Leo Diegel** the U.S.P.G.A. Champion and **A1** (there goes a hundred thousand bucks) **Waltrous**. To cut a long story short the British side won by six matches to four. On the final day **George Duncan** defeated Walter Hagen by 10 and 8 and **Archie Compston** defeated Gene Sarazen 6 and 4. Whatever it may have done to American pride, and I note that Wall Street collapsed later that summer, it certainly secured Moortown's place in golfing lore.

Stepping forward in time, **Mr. R.H. Brown** is the Secretary at Moortown. He may be contacted by telephone on **(0532) 686521**, while the Club's professional **Bryon Hutchinson** can be called on **(0532) 683636**.

Visitors are welcome at Moortown between Mondays and Fridays. Golfing Societies are also welcome during the week although prior arrangement with the secretary is essential. All written correspondence should be addressed to Mr Brown at **The Moortown Golf Club, Harrogate Road, Alwoodley, Leeds LS17 7DB**. In 1992 the green fees were £33 for a single round or £39 for a full day's golf during the week, with weekend golf costing £39 for a round, or £44 for the day.

Moortown's aforementioned enviable situation is, in part, a product of the A61 – the Leeds to Harrogate Road which runs from the heart of the city to within yards of Moortown's front door. For those travelling from the city centre, note that if you reach Eccup Reservoir you have gone too far! Leeds itself is well served by motorway connections, the M62 linking Leeds to Greater Mancester and the M1 joining Sheffield to Leeds. Some roads which may prove helpful include the A64 (York to Leeds) and the A65 (Skipton to Leeds). Our friend the A61 approaches from the north via Ripon, Ripley and Harrogate.

With its great spread of heather and gorse Moortown can properly be described as heathland, although occasionally it is classed as a moorland type course. Either way, it is always beautifully maintained and has the fine combination of being sufficiently testing yet not too severe.

From its championship tees, the course measures a lengthy 7020 yards, par 71 (s.s.s. 74). The forward tees reduce the length to 6515 yards while for the ladies, Moortown measures 5931 yards par 75 (s.s.s. 75). The generally held view is that the front nine is much the easier of the two halves; this may have something to do with the fact that it begins with what golfers usually term a 'birdiable hole', being a short par five to a fairly open green. Perhaps Moortown's finest hole is the **10th**, a par three measuring 176 yards it calls for a shot to a plateau green built on a foundation of rock; it is called 'Gibraltar' – miss it and you're sunk. The **12th** is an excellent par five, aptly titled 'The Long' for it stretches to 554 yards; the aforementioned Archie Compston once holed out here in two strokes.

Over the years Moortown has been the venue for several major events, both amateur and professional. Three English Amateur Championships have been held at Moortown, and also the English Ladies Amateur and the Ladies British Amateur. In recent years the Car Care professional tournament has been played over the course.

Being situated directly behind the 18th green, Moortown's Clubhouse is very much a nineteenth hole. Lunches are served daily (except Mondays) and both breakfast and dinner can be arranged with prior notice.

In concluding it seems appropriate to return to the course. The difficult, dog-leg **18th** at Moortown has an alarming effect on certain people. Countless numbers, including **Severiano Ballesteros**, have been known to overclub and fire the ball over the green into the Clubhouse area. In the 1929 Ryder Cup during one of the foursomes matches, **Joe Turnesa** hooked his second behind the marquee adjoining the Clubhouse whereupon his partner promptly sailed it back over the marquee to within a yard of the hole. In the 1974 English Amateur Stroke Play tournament one player actually put his second into the Mens Bar. Opening the Clubhouse windows he played his third straight out onto the green. The Clubhouse certainly has a welcoming atmosphere but this would seem to be taking things a little too far!

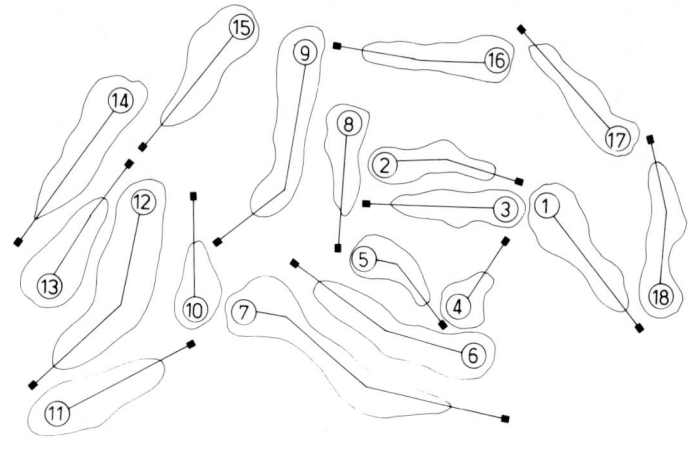

Hole	Yards	Par	Hole	Yards	Par
1	490	5	10	176	3
2	456	4	11	367	4
3	446	4	12	554	5
4	174	3	13	439	4
5	388	4	14	437	4
6	446	4	15	397	4
7	516	5	16	417	4
8	220	3	17	191	3
9	470	4	18	436	4
Out	3,606	36	In	3,414	35
			Out	3,606	36
			TOTALS	7,020	71

GANTON
CHAMPIONSHIP GOLF

They used to say at Ganton that when **Harry Vardon** played the course twice in the same day, in his afternoon round he'd often hit his tee shots into the very divots he'd created in the morning. The chances are that this was a little bit of Yorkshire bluff but then again the Members at Ganton were fortunate to witness what were probably the very finest years of Britain's greatest ever golfer.

Vardon came to Ganton in 1896, just five years after the Club's formation. Within a few weeks of his appointment he won his first **Open Championship** at Muirfield defeating the then hat-trick-seeking John H. Taylor in a play-off. In 1900 Vardon returned from America with the **U.S. Open** trophy, by which time he'd added two more Open Championships and was half way towards his record number of six victories in that event. By the time that Vardon left the Club in 1903 the name of Ganton had been firmly put on the golfing map.

Located approximately nine miles from the sea, Ganton could hardly be called a golf links in the strict sense but it is often said that it has many of the features of links golf with crisp seaside turf and sandy sub-soil. Indeed, whenever new bunkers are cut, sea-shells are often discovered lying beneath the surface – it appears that the whole of the surrounding area was once an arm of the sea.

Golfers wishing to play at Ganton must make prior arrangements with the Club's Secretary, **Air Vice Marshal Price** who may be contacted via the **Ganton Golf Club, Ganton, Scarborough, North Yorkshire YO12 4PA**, telephone **(0944) 70329**. The Club's professional, **Gary Brown**, can be reached on **(0944) 70260**. Subject to proof of handicap and prior arrangement, visitors are made most welcome and it is possible to pre-book starting times. The green fees for 1992 were set at £35 for a day's golf during the week with £40 payable at the weekend.

Travelling to the course is made straightforward by the A64. This road links the village directly with Scarborough to the north east (12 miles) and to both York (30 miles) and Leeds (60 miles) to the south west. If approaching from the Humberside region a combination of the A164 to Great Driffield and the B1249 will take you to within 2 miles of the course, while travellers from further north can avoid the city of York by heading for Thirsk and thereafter heading for Malton by way of the A170 and the B1257. Malton lies on the A64 road and like Scarborough is approximately 12 miles from Ganton.

Ganton enjoys a beautifully peaceful setting nestling on the edge of the Vale of Pickering and the Yorkshire Moors. While the golf course is indeed beautiful, particularly when the gorse is in full bloom, it is very rarely peaceful and when the winds sweep across it can become fearsomely difficult and there are few inland courses with such cavernous bunkers – 111 of them in all! In addition to the many bunkers and the great spread of gorse, there are numerous fir trees and pines which can come into play following a wayward shot, the dog-leg **18th** being a notable example and one that provides a very testing finishing hole. The finest hole on the course is thought by many to be the **4th** where the second has to be played across a plunging valley towards a plateau green that is heavily bunkered to the right.

The nineteenth at Ganton has a most welcoming atmosphere and offers an extensive range of catering. (Note the famous Ganton Cake; the origins of which are unknown and the recipe a secret!) Dress is informal in the men's bar until 4pm Monday to Friday, although a jacket and tie should be worn in all other public rooms.

Inevitably Ganton's name will always be linked with Vardon's. But another great player also developed his talents on the Yorkshire course – **Ted Ray**, the famed long hitter who won the Open in 1912 and later found fortune in America winning their Open in 1920. In winning the latter, he ironically held off the challenge of the then 50 year old Vardon. The greatest event in Ganton's distinguished history was undoubtedly the great **Ryder Cup** match of 1949 when the home team led by three matches to one at the end of the first day only to lose eventually by seven to five. **Ben Hogan**, convalescing from his near fatal accident, led the American side as non-playing captain.

Three times since the last War the **Amateur Championship** has been staged at Ganton; in 1964, 1977 and most recently in 1991, the Centenary Year for the Club. The professionals have also visited Ganton with the Dunlop Masters of 1975 won by **Bernard Gallacher** and in 1981 the P.G.A. Championship resulting in a third victory in four years for **Nick Faldo**.

Hole	Yards	Par	Hole	Yards	Par
1	375	4	10	169	3
2	416	4	11	403	4
3	334	4	12	364	4
4	406	4	13	498	5
5	157	3	14	283	4
6	447	4	15	437	4
7	430	4	16	448	4
8	392	4	17	251	4
9	494	5	18	389	4
Out	3,451	36	In	3,242	36
			Out	3,451	36
			TOTALS	6,693	72

THE FEVERSHAM ARMS HOTEL

The Feversham Arms Hotel was rebuilt in 1855 by the Earl of Feversham on the site of an older hostelry known as the Board Inn. After an interesting and varied history it was purchased in 1967 by the Aragues family who have since updated the hotel facilities whilst taking care to preserve the character and charm of the old coaching inn.

Built in Yorkshire stone, the hotel has 18 bedrooms, all with private bathroom and everything you would expect of a hotel of this calibre; some even have four poster beds. The Goya restaurant, elegant and warm, and renowned for good food, specialises in shellfish and game in season. The extensive wine list includes a good selection of French Grand Cru Classes and Spanish Gran Reservas. If your idea of a good break includes open fires and dinner by candlelight, you will not be disappointed by the Feversham Arms.

An acre of beautiful walled gardens is joined by a superb all-weather hard tennis court and a stunning outdoor heated swimming pool. If you are contemplating a round of golf, the hardest decision will be where to start. There are over twenty Golf Clubs within a radius of 35 miles, the nearest being Kirkbymoorside. Racegoers will probably find that the area needs no introduction: York, Beverley, Ripon, Thirsk, Wetherby, Pontefract and Redcar are all close to hand.

Helmsley itself is on the edge of the North York Moors National Park, which offers to the open air enthusiast over 550 square miles of panoramic views, clear waters, pine wood, steep-sided hills and rugged coastline. Villages of local stone and rich in medieaval architecture with Roman remains are situated within the Park.

The Feversham Arms Hotel is a must for the sport lover or for anyone visiting this beautiful and historic area.

The Feversham Arms Hotel
Helmsley
North Yorkshire YO6 5AG
Tel: (0439) 70766
Fax: (0439) 70346

FULFORD
CHAMPIONSHIP GOLF

These days golf is not only played in every foreign field but it is also played in the most unlikely of places. In 1971 American astronaut **Captain Alan Sheppard** struck two golf shots from the surface of the moon, becoming in the process the only man able to shank a ball 200 yards. Not to be outdone, as ever, **Arnold Palmer** in 1977 hit three golf balls off the second stage of the Eiffel Tower, while in 1981 at Fulford, York, **Bernhard Langer** decided to take golf into further alien territory by shinning up a rather large tree and playing his chip shot to the 17th green from amidst its spreading branches.

Fulford Golf Club was founded soon after the turn of the century, but it was only as recently as 1985 that the club celebrated fifty years of playing over the present course. Televised tournament golf has undoubtedly turned the North Yorkshire Club into a 'golfing household name', but in golf's more discerning circles it has for a long time possessed the reputation of having one of the country's finest inland courses.

Golfers wishing to visit Fulford – normally possible between Mondays and Fridays – must make prior arrangements with the Club's Secretary, **Judith Hayhurst**. Individuals and Society Members alike are required to belong to recognised Golf Clubs and be able to provide proof of handicap. The Secretary can be contacted by writing to the club, the full address being, **Fulford Golf Club, Heslington Lane, Fulford, York, YO1 5DY** or by telephoning **(0904) 413579**. Green fees in 1992 were £30 per day during the week and (when available) £35 at weekends. Finally the Club's professional is **Brian Hessay (0904) 412882**.

Fulford is situated about a mile to the south of York, just off the A19. For persons travelling from the south of England the A1 and M1 can assist as far as the Leeds area from where the A64 runs straight through to Fulford. Perhaps a more direct route though is to join the A19 near Doncaster. Those approaching York from the north should find their route a little more scenic, the most helpful roads again probably being the A19 (via Thirsk) and the A64 (via Malton – which incidentally passes Ganton further to the north east). Those journeying from easterly directions should either use the A1099 or the A166 before joining the A64 east of York. The famous city is well served by rail connections and the Leeds/Bradford

Airport is located approximately 30 miles to the west of York.

Fulford's homely looking Clubhouse is surprisingly spacious inside with a comfortable Lounge and Dining Room. A full catering service is provided throughout the week with the exception of Mondays. Jackets and ties should be worn in the Clubhouse after 6pm.

Measuring just a little under 6800 yards from the back tees, (par 72, s.s.s. 72) Fulford provides quite a stern test for the club golfer, but it is no more than a medium length course for the professionals. Much of the prodigiously low scoring achieved at Fulford during the Benson and Hedges and Murphys Cup events has, however, precious little to do with the length of the course. As the Members will quickly tell you, it simply reflects the superb condition in which the fairways and the putting surfaces are maintained. Fulford is renowned for its fast and very true greens. Certainly, **Ian Woosnam** found them much to his liking as he holed putt after putt during an extraordinary sequence of eight successive birdies during his final round in the 1985 B&H Tournament. Woosnam's score of 62 that day set a new course record but unfortunately it wasn't quite good enough to prevent **Sandy Lyle** from joining a distinguished list of Fulford champions. A list which includes the likes of **Tony Jacklin, Greg Norman** and **Lee Trevino**.

The B and H has since gone south to St Mellion but Fulford immediately picked up another big event, the Murphy's Cup. In keeping with the tradition of eccentricity established by Bernhard Langer in 1981, the organisers announced before the 1990 event that the first player to hole in one at the **14th** would receive 'one hours output of Murphy's Irish Stout' (estimated to be 13,750 pints)! Fulford's first two Murphy's Cup tournaments were won by the popular Zimbabwean, **Tony Johnstone.**

Most golfers probably won't be leaving Fulford with a 62 under their belt – nor one presumes will they have been shinning up the trees or downing Murphy's by the bucket load – but they are sure to be heading home contented souls having spent a day on what is unquestionably one of the country's most pleasurable golf courses.

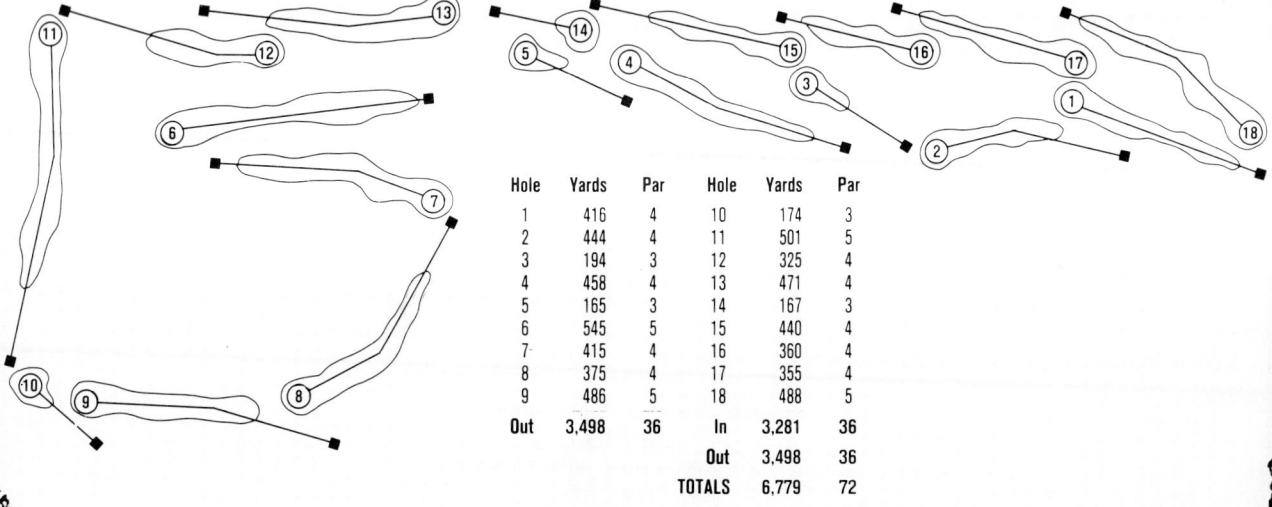

Hole	Yards	Par	Hole	Yards	Par
1	416	4	10	174	3
2	444	4	11	501	5
3	194	3	12	325	4
4	458	4	13	471	4
5	165	3	14	167	3
6	545	5	15	440	4
7	415	4	16	360	4
8	375	4	17	355	4
9	486	5	18	488	5
Out	3,498	36	In	3,281	36
			Out	3,498	36
			TOTALS	6,779	72

THE WORSLEY ARMS HOTEL

The Worsley Arms Hotel, an attractive stone-built Georgian Coaching Inn, is situated in the heart of Hovingham near York, and has a history stretching back to Roman times. The Hotel is overlooking the village green and surrounded by delightful gardens. Having been built in 1841 by Sir William Worsley, the first Baronet, it is still owned and run by the Worsley family whose home, Hovingham Hall, stands nearby in wooded parkland amidst beautiful rolling countryside.

Elegant traditional furnishings and open log fires give the Worsley Arms the welcoming and restful atmosphere of a pleasant and comfortable country house. The graceful and spacious sitting rooms are havens of peace and tranquillity and are the ideal place in which to relax over morning coffee, full afternoon tea or an aperitif. There is also a congenial bar where residents can meet both local people and other guests.

The Worsley Arms Hotel often plays host to private shooting parties, and with 500 acres of picturesque nature trails and jogging paths, created entirely by Sir Marcus Worsley, it is an ideal place for an enjoyable picnic. Executive Chef William

Dillon, is happy to provide picnic hampers and champagne for guests. William, who was trained in Geneva, offers an exquisite and imaginative menu in the Hotel's Wyvern Restaurant. With its eighteenth century paintings, delightful decor and a host of fresh flowers, the emphasis is on delicacy of preparation, with intriguing combinations of flavour and texture in the food that it serves. Specializing in local game from the Estate, when in season, the carefully selected wine list has to offer quality and fine variety.

The Chef's own herb garden is recognized in his cooking of fine fresh herbs.

Situated on the edge of the Howardian Hills, close to the Yorkshire Dales, the Wolds and the North Yorkshire Moors National Park, the Worsley Arms Hotel and Hovingham Hall are within easy driving distance from the City of York, Castle Howard and other Heritage and National Trust properties, and offers a warm and friendly personal welcome to its guests. Staff will ensure that your stay in the heart of Yorkshire is both restful and memorable.

The Worsley Arms Hotel
Hovingham
York YO6 4LA
Tel: (0653) 628234
Fax: (0653) 628130

YORKSHIRE & HUMBERSIDE
COMPLETE GOLF

NORTH YORKSHIRE

Aldwark Manor G.C
(03473) 353
Aldwark Manor, Adwark Alne, York
5 miles S.E of Boroughbridge off the A1
(9) 2569 yards/***/E

Bedale G.C
(0677) 422451
Leyburn Road, Bedale
S. of town on the A684
(18) 5599 yards/***/D

Catterick Garrison G.C
(0748) 833268
Leyburn Lane, Catterick Garrison
3 miles from Catterick Bridge off the A1
(18) 6291 yards/***/D

Crimple Valley G.C
(0423) 883485
Hookstone Wood Road, Harrogate
1 mile S. of the town centre
(9) 2500 yards/***/pm only)/E

Easingwold G.C
(0347) 21964
Stillington Road, Easingwold
12 miles from Ork off the A19
(18) 6262 yards/***/D

Filey G.C
(0723) 513293
West Avenue, Filey
1 mile S. of town centre
(18) 6030 yards/***/D/M

Forest Park G.C
(0904) 400425
Stockton on the Forest
(18)6211 yards/***/D

Fulford G.C
(0904) 413579
Heslington Lane, Heslington, York
Out of York on the A19
(18) 6779 yards/**/F/H

Ganton G.C
(0944) 70329
Ganton, Scarborough
11 miles W. of town on the A64
(18) 6693 yards/***/F/H

Ghyll G.C
(0282) 842466
Thornton-In-Craven
1 mile from Barnoldswick off the A56
(9) 5708 yards/***(not Sun)/E

Harrogate G.C
(0423) 862999
Forest Lane Head, Starbeck, Harrogate
1 mile from Knaresborough on the A59
(18) 6204 yards/***/C/M

Heworth G.C
(0904) 424618
Munaster House, Muncastergate, York
2 miles from city centre on the A1036/A64
(11) 6078 yards/**/E

Kirbymoorside G.C
(0751) 31525
Manor Vale, Kirbymoorside
On the A710 Thirsk-Scarborough road
(18) 5958 yards/***/D

Knaresborough G.C
(0423) 862690
Butterhills, Boroughbridge Road,
Knaresborough
2 miles from town centre off main
Boroughbridge road
(18) 6083 yards/***/D/H

Malton and Norton G.C
(0653) 693882
Welham Park, Malton
Off the A64 York-Scarborough road
(18) 6411 yards/***/F/H
(18) 6141 yards/***/F/H

Masham G.C
(0765) 689379
Swinton Road, Masham, Ripon
8 miles N.W of Ripon on the A6108
(9) 5244 yards/***/D

Oakdale G.C
(0423) 5671620
Oakdale, Harrogate
1 mile from town centre
(18) ***/C/M

Pannal G.C
(0423) 872628
Follifoot Road, Pannal, Harrogate
Off the A61 Leeds-Harrogate Road
(18) 6659 yards/**/M/H

Pike Hills G.C
(0904) 706566
Tadcaster road, Copmanthorpe, York
4 miles form York on the Tadcaster Road
(18) 6048 yards/**/E

Raven Hall Hotel & Golf Course
(0723) 870353
Ravenscar
Half way between Scarborough and Whitby
(9) 1938 yards/***/D

Richmond G.C
(0748) 825319
Bend Hagg, Richmond
Off the A6108 from Scotch Corner
(18) 5704 yards/***/D

Ripon City G.C
(0765) 6033640
Palace Road, Ripon
1 mile W. of town on A6108
(9) 5645 yards/***/F/M

Scarborough North Cliff G.C
(0723) 360786
North Cliff Avenue, Burniston Road,
Scarborough
2 miles N. of town centre on coast road
(18) 6425 yards/***/D/M

Scarborough South Cliff G.C
(0723) 374737
Deepdale Avenue, Scarborough
1 mile S. of Scarborough on the main Filey Road
(18) 6085 yards/***/D/H

Selby G. C
(0757) 228622
Mill Lane, Brayton Bariff, Selby
Off the A63 Leeds Road
(18) 6246 yards/**/D/M/H

Settle G.C
(07292) 3912
Buckhaw Brow, Settle
1 mile N. of Settle on A65
(9) 4600 yards/***(not Sun)/D

Skipton G.C
(0756) 793922
Skipton
1 mile from town centre on Skipton N. bypass
(18) 6191 yards/***(not Mon)/D/M

Thirsk & Northallerton G.C
(0845) 522170
Thornton-le-Street, Thirsk
2 miles N. of Thirsk
(9) 6257 yards/***/F/M/H

Whitby G.C
(0947) 602768
Low Straggpeton, Whitby
On main coastal road between Whitby and
Sandsend
(18) 5706 yards/***/D

York G.C
(0904) 491840
Lords Moor Lane, Strensall, York
6 miles N. of York
(18) 6275 yards/***/C

SOUTH YORKSHIRE

Abbeydale G.C
(0742) 360763
Twentywell Lane, Dore, Sheffield
5 miles S. of Sheffield off the A621
(18) 6419 yards/***/C

Austerfield Park G.C
(0302) 710841
Cross Lane, Austerfield, N Bawtry, Doncaster
4 miles N. of Bawtry, off the A614
(18) 6828 yards/***/D

Barnsley G.C
(0226) 382856
Waefield Lane, Staincross, N Barnsley
3 miles N. of Barnsley on the A61
(18) 6048 yards/***/D

Beauchief G.C
(0742) 367274
Abbey Lane, Sheffield
S. of Sheffield off the A621
(18) 5423 yards/***/F

Birley Wood G.C
(0742) 647262
Birley Lane, Sheffield
4 miles S. of Sheffield off A616
(9) 5200 yards/***/E

Concord Park G.C
(0742) 456806
Shiregreen Lane, Sheffield
4 miles N. of Sheffield off the A6135
(18) 4302 yards/***/E

Crookhill Park G.C
(0709) 862979
Carr Lane, Conisborough, Nr Doncaster
Leave the A1 at Doncaster for the A630 to
Sheffield
(18) 5846 yards/***/E

Doncaster G.C
(0302) 868316
278 Bawtry Road, Bessacarr, Doncaster
Between Doncaster and Bawtry on the A638
(18) 6220 yards/**/D/M

Doncaster Town Moor G.C
(0302) 535286
Neatherds House, Belle Vue, Doncaster
Near racecourse roundabout
(18) 5923 yards/***(not Sun am)/D

Dore and Totley G.C
(0742) 360492
Broadway Road, Sheffield
S. of Sheffield off the A61
(18) 6301 yards/*(prior arrangement)/D/H

Grange Park G.C
(0709) 558884
Upper Wortley Road, Rotherham
2 miles W. of the town on the A629
(18) 6461 yards/***/D

Hallamshire G.C
(0742) 302153
Sandygate, Sheffield
4 miles from city centre off A57
(18) 6396 yards/**/C/M

Hallowes G.C
(0246) 413734
Hallowes Lane, Dronfield, Sheffield
Signposted off the A61
(18)6134 yards/***/F

Hickleton G.C
(0709) 896081
Hickleton, Doncaster
7 miles from Doncaster on the A635
(18) 6361 yards/***/F/M

Hillsborough G.C
(0742) 343608
Worrall Road, Sheffield
3 miles from city centre via Middlewood Road
(18) 5518 yards/**/C/M

Lees Hall G.C
(0742) 554402
Hemsworth Road, Norton, Sheffield
3 miles S. of Shefield
(18) 5518 yards/***/D

Phoenix G.C
(0709) 363864
Pavilion Lane, Brinsworth, Rotherham
1 mile from M1 Rinsley roundabout
(18) 6145 yards/***/D/M

Renishaw Park G.C
(0246) 432044
Station Road, Renshaw, Sheffield
Leave M1 at junction 30 and follow signs
(18) 6253 yards/**/D/H/M

Rotherham G.C
(0709) 850812
Thrybergh Park, Thrybergh, Rotherham
7 miles from M1 junction 35
(18) 6323 yards/**/C/M

Roundwood G.C
(0709) 523471
off Green Lane, Rawmarsh, Rotherham
2 miles N. of Rotherham on the A633
(9) 5646 yards/***/D

Sickleholme G.C
(0433) 51306
Saltergate Lane, Bamford, Sheffield
14 miles W. of Sheffield on the A625
(18) 6064 yards/***(not Wed am)/D

Silkstone G.C
(0226) 790328
Field Head, Silkstone, Barnsley
Just beyond Dodworth village off the A628
(18) 6045 yards/**/D/H

Sitwell Park G.C(0709) 541046
Shrogswood Road, Rotherham
2 miles S.E of Rotherham off the A631
(18) 6203 yards/***/D/M

Stocksbridge and District G.C
(0742) 882003
30 Royd Lane, Townend, Deepcar, Sheffielld
9 miles from Sheffield on the A616
(15) 5055 yards/***/D/H

Tankersley Park G.C
(0742) 468247
High Green, Sheffield
1 mile off the A6135 N. of Chapeltown
(18) 3204 yards/**/D

Tinsley Park G.C
(0742) 44237
High Hazel Park, Darnall, Sheffield
Take the A57 off the M1 junction 33
(18) 6045 yards/***/E

Wath G.C
(0709) 872149
Abdy, Blackamoor, Rotherham
Take A633 to B6090, then B6089 and follow
signs
(18) 5776 yards/**/D

Wheatley G.C
(0302) 831655
Armthorpe Road, Doncaster
Leave Doncaster on the A18
(18) 6345 yards/***/D/M

Wortley G.C
(0742) 885294
Hermit Hill, Wortley, Sheffield
Leave M1 at junction 35, take A629
(18) 5983 yards/***/C/M

WEST YORKSHIRE

Alwoodley G.C
(0532) 681680
Wigton Lane, Alwoodley, Leeds
5 miles N. of Leeds via the A61
(18) 6301 yards/**/F/M

Baildon G.C
(0274) 595162
Moorgate, Baildon, Shipley
5 miles N. of Bradford
(18) 6178 yards/**/F

Ben Rhydding G.C
(0943) 608759
High Wood, Ben Rhydding, Ilkley
On S.E of town
(9) 3711 yards/***(not Sat/Sun am)/E

Bingley St Ives G.C
(0274) 562506
The Mansion, St Ives Estate, Bingley
Off the A650 towards Bingley centre
(18) 6480 yards/**/E

Bradford G.C
(0943) 875570
Hawksworth Lane, Guisele, Leeds
Take Ilkley road from Shipley for Hawksworth
(18) 6259 yards/***(not Sat/Sun am)/C

Bradford Moor G.C
(0274) 638313
Scarr Hall, Pollard Lane, Bradford
2 miles N.E of city centre off the A658
(9) 5854 yards/***/F

Bradley Park G.C
(0484) 539988
Bradley Road, Huddersfield
Leave M62 at exit 25 for Huddersfield
(18) 6202 yards/***/D

Branshaw G.C
(0535) 643235
Branshaw Moor, Keighley
2 miles S.W of Keighley on B6143
(18) 5121 yards/**/E

Calverley G.C
(0532) 569244
Woodhall lane, Pudsey
4 miles N.E of Bradford
(18) 5516 yards/***(not Sat/Sun am)/E

City of Wakefield G.C
(0924) 374316
Lupset Park, Horbury Road, Wakefield
1 mile from the city centre
(18) 6405 yards/***/E

Clayton G.C
(0274) 880047
Thornton View Road, Clayton, Bradford
2 miles S. W. of Bradford off the A647
(9) 5518 yards/***(not Sun)/E

Cleckheaton & District G.C
(0274) 851266
Bradford Road, Cleckheaton
4 miles S. of Bradford on the A638
(18) 5847 yards/***/D

Crosland Heath G.C
(0484) 653216
Felk Stile Road, Crosland Heath, Huddersfield
Take A62 from Huddersfield for 3 miles
(18) 5962 yards/***(by arrangement)/D

YORKSHIRE & HUMBERSIDE
COMPLETE GOLF

Dewsbury District G.C
(0924) 492399
The Pinnacle, Sands Lane, Mirfield
3 miles from Dewsbury
(18) 6256 yards/**/F/H

East Bierley G.C
(0274) 681 023
South View Road, Bierley, Bradford
3 miles S.E of Bradford
(9) 4692 yards/***(not Sun)/E

Elland G.C
(0422) 72505
Hammerstones, Leach Lane, Elland
Off the Blackley Road, 1 mile from junction
24 of M62
(9)5526 yards/**/F

Garforth G.C
(0532) 863308
Long Lane, Garforth, Leeds
6 miles E. of Leeds off the A642
(18)6296 yards/**/D/M

Gott's Park G.C
(0532) 638232
Armley Bridge Road, Leeds
3 miles W. of city
(18) 4449 yards/***/E

Halifax G.C
(0422) 244171
Union Lane, Ogden, Halifax
4 miles from town centre on A629
(18)6030 yards/**/D

Halifax Bradley Hall G.C
(0422) 74108
Stainland Road, Holywell Green, Halifax
Between Halifax and Huddersfield on
B61126213 yards/***/F

Halifax West End G.C
(0422) 363293
Highroad Well, Halifax
2 miles N.W of Halifax off the A646
(18) 6003 yards/***/F

Hanging Heaton G.C
(0924) 461606
White Cross Road, Bennett Lane, Dewsbury
1 mile from town centre on the A653
(9) 5874 yards/**/F/M

Headingley G.C
(0532) 679573
Back Church Lane, Adel, Leeds
5 miles from city off the A660
(18) 6238 yards/***/D

Headley G.C
(0274) 833481
Headley Lane, Thornton, Bradford
4 miles W. of Bradford on B6145
(9) 247 yards/**/E

Horsforth G.C
(0532) 586819
Layton Road, Horsforth, Leeds
After Rawdon off the A6120
(18) 6243 yards/**/C

Howley Hall G.C
(0924) 472432
Scotchman Lane, Morley, Leeds
Leave A650 for B6123 for Morley
(18) 6420 yards/***(not Sat)/D

Huddersfield G.C
(0484) 26203
Fixby Hall, Fixby, Huddersfield
Leave M62 at junction 24 for a643
(18) 6424 yards/***/D

Ilkley G.C
(0943) 600214
Myddleton, Ilkley
18 miles N.W of Leeds off the A65
(18) 6256 yards/**/B/M

Keighley GC
(0535) 604778
Howden Park, Utley, Keighley
1 mile N. of Keighley on the A650(18) 6139
yards/**/D/H

Leeds G.C
(0532) 659203
Elmete Lane, Leeds
Off the Leeds ringroad to the A58
(18) 6097 yards/**/C/M

Lightcliffe G.C
(0422) 202459
Knowle Top Road, Lightcliffe, Halifax
On the A58 Leeds-Halifax road
(9) 5388 yards/***(not Wed/Sat)/E/M

Longley Park G.C
(0484) 4522304
Maple Street, off Somerset Road, Huddersfield
Half mile from town centre
(9) 5269 yards/**(not Thurs)/E

Low Laithes G.C
(0924) 273275
Parkmill, Flushdyke, Ossett
Near to exit 40 of M1
(18) 6448 yards/***/D

Marsden G.C
(0484) 844253
Mount Road, Hemplow, Marsden, Huddersfield
8 miles from Huddersfield off the A62
(9) 5702 yards/**/E

Meltham G.C
(0484) 850227
Thick Hollins, Meltham, Huddersfield
Half mile E. of Meltham off B6107
(18) 6145 yards/***(not Wed/sat)/D

Middleton Park G.C
(0532) 700449
Middleton Park, Leeds
3 miles S. of the city centre
(18) 5233 yards/***/E

Moor Allerton G.C
(0532) 661154
Coal Road, Wike, leeds
Off the A61 Harrogate Road
(27) 6045 yards/**/B/H
6222 yards/**/B/H
6930 yards/**/B/H

Moortown G.C
(0532) 686521Alwoodley, Leeds
(18) 7020 yards/***/A

Mount Skip G.C
(0422) 892896
1 mile E. of Hebden Bridge
(9) 5114 yards/***/F

Normanton G.C
(0924) 892943
Snydale Road, Normanton, Wakefield
Half mile from Normanton on B6133
(9) 5184 yards/***(not Sun)/E

Northcliffe G.C
(0274) 596731
High Bank Lane, Shipley
Off the A650 Bradford road
(18) 6065 yards/***(not Sat/Tues)/C/H

Otley G.C
(0943) 465329
West Busk Lane, Otley
2 miles from Otley off A6038
(18) 6225 yards/***/C

Outlane G.C
(0422) 74762
Slack Lane, Outlane, Huddersfield
Out of Huddersfield off the A640
(18) 5590 yards/***/E

Painthorpe House G.C
(0924) 255083
Painthorpe Lane, Crigglestone, Wakefield
2 miles S. of city off the A636
(9) 4100 yards/***(not Sun)/E

Phoenix Park G.C
(0274) 667178
Phoenix Park, Dick Lane, Thornbury, Bradford
Off Thornbury roundabout on A647
(9) 4774 yards/**/F

Pontefract & District G.C
(0977) 792241
Park Lane, Pontefract
On the B6134 off the A1
(18) 6227 yards/**/E

Pontefract Park G.C
(0977) 702799
Park Road, PontefractBetween the town and
M62 roundabout
(9) 4068 yards/***/E

Queensbury G.C
(0274) 882155
Brighouse Road, Queensbury, Bradford
4 miles from Bradford on the A647
(9) 5102 yards/***/E/M

Rawdon G.C
(0532) 506040
Buckstone Drive, Rawdon, Leeds
6 miles from London on the A65
(9) 5964 yards/**/F

Riddlesden G.C
(0535) 602148
Howden Rough, Elam Wood Road, Riddlesden,
Keighley
Off the A650 Keighley road
(18) 4185 yards/***/E

Roundhay G.C
(0532) 662695
Park Lane, Leeds
4 miles N. of Leeds
(9) 5166 yards/***//E

Ryburn G.C
(0422) 831355
Norland, Sowerby Bridge, Halifax
Off Station road from Halifax
(9) 5002 yards/***/E/H

Sand Moor G.C
(0532) 685180
Alwoodley Lane, Leeds
About 6 miles from Leeds on A61
9180 6429 yards/**/F/M

Scarcroft G.C
(0532) 892263
Syke Lane, Leeds
N.E of Leeds on the A58
(18) 6426 yards/***/C/H

Shipley G.C
(0274) 568652
Beckfoot Lane, Cottingley Bridge, Bingley
On the A650 at Cottingley bridge
(18) 6203 yards/***(not Tues/Sat)/F

Silsden G.C
(0535) 52998
High Brunthwaite, Silsden, KeighleyOff the
A6034 to Silsden centre
(14) 4870 yards/***/E

South Bradford G.C
(0274) 679195
Pearson Road, Odsal, Bradford
Off the M606 to Odsal
(9) 6004 yards/**/D

South Leeds G.C
(0532) 700479
Gipsy Lane, Beeston Ring Road, Leeds
Off the Leeds-Dewsbury road
(18) 5890 yards/***/D/M

Temple Newsam G.C
(0532) 645624
Temple Newsam Road, Leeds
5 miles from Leeds on the A63
(18) 6448 yards/***/F
(18) 6029 yards/***/F

Wakefield G.C
(0924) 258778
Woodthorpe Lane, Sandal, Wakefield
3 miles S. of Wakefield on the A61
(18) 6626 yards/***/D

West Bowling G.C
(0274) 724449
Newall Hall, Rooley Lane, Bradford
2 miles from town centre
(18) 5770 yards/**/D

West Bradford G.C
(0274) 542767
Chellow Grange, Bradford
3 miles from Bradford on the B6144
(18) 5752 yards/**/E

West End G.C
(0422) 53608
The Racecourse, Paddock Lane, Highroad Well,
Halifax
Take A61 Burnley road from town centre
(18) 6003 yards/***/E

Wetherby G.C
(0937) 63375
Linton Lane, Wetherby
Off the A1 at Wetherby
(18) 6235 yards/***/C

Whitwood Golf & Country Club
(0977) 512835Atofts Lane, Whitwood,
Castleford
1 mile along A655 from junction 31 of M62
(9) 6282 yards/***/D

Woodhall Hills G.C
(0532) 554594
Woodhall Road, Calverly, Pudsey
6 miles from Leeds on the A647
(18) 6102 yards/***/D

Woodsome Hall G.C
(0484) 602971
Fenay Bridge, Huddersfield
5 miles S.E of Huddersfield on the A629
(18) 6068 yards/***(not Tues)/D

HUMBERSIDE

Beverley and East Riding G.C
(0482) 868757
Anti Mill, The Westwood, Beverley
1 mile from town centre on A1230
(18) 6164 yards/**/D

Boothferry G.C
(0430) 430364
Spaldington, Howden, Goole
3 miles from junction 12 of M62 on B1228
(18) 6651 yards/***/D

Bridlington G.C
(0662) 672092
Belvedere Road, Bridlington
2 miles S. of Bridlington station, off A165
(18) 6320 yards/***/D

Brough G.C
(0472) 667291
Cave Road, Brough
W. of village off A63
(18) 6035 yards/**(not Wed am)/C/H

Cleethorpes G.C
(0472) 812059
Kings Road, Cleethorpes
1 mile S. of Cleethorpes, off A1031
(18) 6015 yards/***/D

Driffield G.C
Sunderlandwick, Driffield
1 mile from town centre on A164
(9) 6227 yards/***/D

Flamborough Head G.C
(0262) 850333
Lighthouse Road, Flamborough, Bridlington
5 miles N.E of Bridlington on the B1255
(18) 5438 yards/***(not Sun am)/D/M

Ganstead Park G.C
(0482) 811280
Longdales Lane, Coniston, Hull
2 miles E. of Hull on A165
(18) 6495 yards/***(not Wed/Sun am)/D/H

Grimsby G.C
(0472) 42630
Littlecoates Road, Grimsby
Off the A46 in Grimsby
(18) 6058 yards/***/D/M

Hainsworth Park G.C
(0964) 542362
Brandesburton, Driffield
8 miles N. of Beverley on A165
(9) 5360 yards/***/E

Hessle G.C
(0482) 650171
Westfield Road, Cottingham, Hull
4 miles W. of Hull off A1105
(18) 6638 yards/***(not Tues am)/C/H

Holme Hall G.C
(0724) 862078
Holme Hall, Bottesford, Scunthorpe
Take A159 S. from Scunthorpe
(18) 6475 yards/***/D/M

Hornsea G.C
(04012) 2020
Rolston Road, Hornsea
On the road to Withernsea
(18) 6450 yards/***(not Tues)/D

Hull G.C
(0482) 658919
The Hall, 27 Packman Lane, Kirk Ella, Hull
5 miles W. of Kingston-upon-Hull off the A164
(18) 6242 yards/**/C/H

Immingham G.C
(0469) 75298
Church Lane, Immingham, Grimsby
Turn N. to Immingham, off the A180
(18) 5809 yards/**/D

Kingsway G.C(0724) 840945
Kingsway, Scunthorpe
S. of the A18
(9) 1915 yards/***/E

Normanby Hall G.C
Normanby Park, Normanby, Scunthorpe
leave B1430 5 miles N. of Scunthorpe
(18) 6548 yards/***/F

Scunthorpe G.C
(0724) 866561
Burringham Road, Scunthorpe
On the B1450, near hotel
(18) 6281 yards/**/D/M/H

Springhead Park G.C
(0482) 656309
Willerby Road, Hull
From Hull, take A1105 to Willerby
(18) 6439 yards/***/F

Sutton Park G.C
(0482) 74242
Salthouse Road, Sutton, Hull
4 miles E. of city on A165
(18) 6251 yards/***/F

Withernsea G.C
(0964) 612258
Chestnut Avenue, Withernsea
17 miles E. of Kingston-upon-Hull, S. of town
(9) 5150 yards/***/D

CUMBRIA & THE NORTH EAST

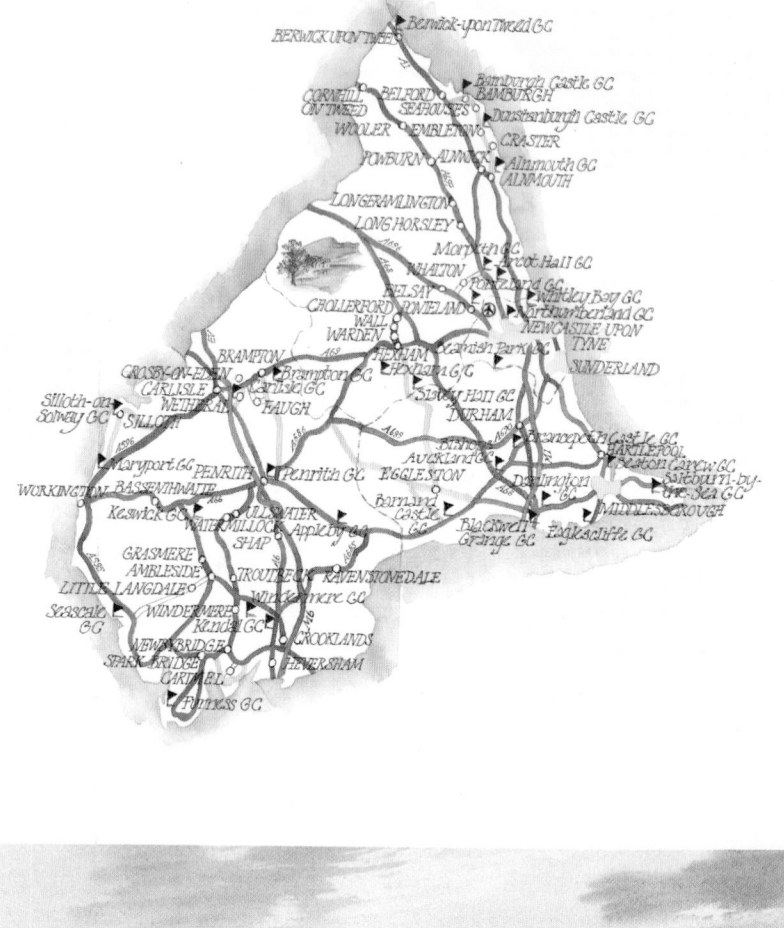

Arthur Weaver **THE GREEN** *Burlington Gallery*

CUMBRIA & THE NORTH EAST
CHOICE GOLF

Just as Devon is often viewed by holiday-makers as a mere stepping stone to Cornwall (which as a Devonian pleases me greatly!) so the far north of England is often viewed by golfers as a mere pretty pathway to the delights of Scotland – Turnberry, Gleneagles etc. Indeed some even believe that north of Lytham there's nothing much in the way of golfing challenges until the Bonnie Land is reached. To those I simply say, 'shame on you!'

Our region covers Cumbria as well as the North East. Now admittedly Cumbria is hardly perfect golfing territory. A Sunningdale in the middle of the Lake District is hard to imagine (although some spectacular holes are clearly possible!) But there are a number of golf courses in between the fells and the lakes, and furthermore Cumbria comprises more than just the Lake District. Before the counties were rearranged and renamed in the early seventies, Cumberland was the most northerly county in the West of England, and home not only to the famous sausage but to the **Silloth-on-Solway** Golf Club, which is, dare I say it, almost as good a links as you'll find anywhere in England. As for the North East, **Seaton Carew** near Hartlepool offers championship golf of a very high calibre and **Slaley Hall** is full of Northumbrian promise, while even further north along the Northumberland coast lie a string of golfing pearls – **Alnmouth, Dunstanburgh, Bamburgh** and **Goswick** – good courses with breathtaking scenery.

CUMBRIA

Let us make a start in the Lake District with the hope that in addition to the picnic hamper and the climbing boots, we've left room in the back of the car for the golf clubs.

The Lake District is the land of the poets, 'Where breezes are soft and skies are fair' (W.C. Bryant), and 'Where nature reveals herself in all her wildness, all her majesty' (S. Roger).

At Keswick the golfer can meet the poet. **Keswick** Golf Club lies 4 miles east of the lakeland town via the A66. Whilst the course now measures well over 6,000 yards, it recently held a rather dubious claim to being the shortest course in Britain – in 1976 there was a splendid Clubhouse but only five holes – no doubt some remarkable scores were returned! These days scoring is a little more difficult with several streams and some dense woodland to be avoided. As one might imagine the views are quite something and a visit will never disappoint.

Still in the Lakes, we find **Kendal**, a fine parkland course, just three-quarters of a mile from the town centre and only 2 miles from the M6 link road. Although a fair bit shorter than Keswick its first hole is often considered to be the toughest opener in Britain – 231 yards, uphill all the way, out of bounds to the left and woods to the right! Should one make it to the 2nd the holes get much easier; however there is an infamous quarry on the right of the 15th fairway which has been known to receive more than golf balls. One frustrated chap after firing ball after ball into its murky depths decided to throw in his bag for good measure. Fortunately he didn't throw himself in as well but word is he never played golf again. Who said it was only a game!

The Golf Club at **Windermere** has recently celebrated its centenary and the course has improved considerably in the last few years. An ideal place for a game of golf while on holiday in the Lakes, we have featured Windermere on a later page. Another first class course, still within the National Park

boundary is at **Penrith**; close to the A6 but a lovely setting near Ullswater and several very challenging holes.

Recommending both superior and reasonably priced establishments in the area is a difficult task to put it mildly simply because there are so many. But hopefully the following suggestions will prove of assistance. Grasmere is a personal favourite and here Michael's Nook (09665) 496 is an outstanding country hotel with an excellent restaurant. The Wordsworth (09665) 592 is another grand hotel while at White Moss House (09665) 295 – the poet's former residence – another superb restaurant can be found. Slightly nearer to Keswick, Armathwaite Hall (059681) 551 in Bassenthwaite is charming, while for a really relaxing country inn The Pheasant Inn (059681) 234 in Bassenthwaite Lake can have few equals. In Keswick itself there is The Woolpack (0539) 723852.

Penrith is a bustling town with numerous hotels. As an alternative to staying in town Ullswater naturally attracts and here the Sharrow Bay Hotel (07684) 86301 and its restaurant are particularly stylish. Cheaper accommodation is available nearby in one of the areas best pubs, The Queens Head at Askham, while The Old Church Hotel at Watermillock offers spectacular views (085 36) 204. Also worth hunting out are Brandelhow Guesthouse (0768) 64470 and The Grotto (0768) 63288.

Oh-so-popular Windermere offers a wealth of good hotels. Three certainly meriting attention are The Miller Howe (09662) 2536, the Langdale Chase and the moderately priced Applegarth Hotel (09662) 3206. Rogers (09662) 4954 in the High Street is a first class restaurant. Other ideas for a 19th hole in the Lake District must include The Old Vicarage (044852) 381 at Witherslack, The Mortal Man (05394) 33193 at Troutbeck (wake up to a glorious setting), The Wild Boar in Crook and for a really popular pub try the Masons Arms in Cartmel Fell.

To the south of Cumbria the highly rated **Furness** Golf Club lays claim to being the oldest in the county. A true links and being quite exposed, scoring well is often more difficult than the card suggests. An after-golf thought here is the excellent Abbey House Hotel (0229)838282. Also pleasant is Bridge House (022985) 239 at Spark Bridge.

Travelling along Cumbria's coast, **Seascale** is soon reached. Another links, and somewhat underrated. One shouldn't be put off by the thought of being close to the Seascale nuclear installations (and jokes about balls glowing in the dark are uncalled for): it's an excellent test of golf – some tremendous views too towards the Wasdale Screes and the Scafell Range. North of Workington (en route to Silloth) there is a fair course at **Maryport**. There is doubtless some convenient accommodation nearby but I'll recommend a trip inland to another personal favourite, Buttermere, one of the more westerly lakes, and where The Bridge Hotel (059685) 252 is very comfortable.

Silloth-on-Solway has already been referred to and is again featured separately on a later page. The course certainly deserves more than a fleeting visit and two handy hotels in the town are The Queens Hotel (06973) 31373 and The Golf Hotel (06973) 31438. Both are very comfortable and specialise in golf packages, as for that matter does the nearby Skinburness Hotel (06973) 32332.

Golfers in Carlisle are well catered for with two good courses

in the area, **Carlisle** and **Brampton** (or Talkin' Tarn as the latter is sometimes called). Brampton is located to the east of Carlisle off the B6413 and is a beautifully kept course, laid out four hundred feet above sea-level with extensive views towards the nearby hills. It is probably best described as moorland whereas Carlisle, equally well maintained, is more of a parkland type. For an overnight stop in Carlisle The Crown and Mitre (0228) 25491 is welcoming while in Brampton, Farlam Hall (06977) 46234 is an excellent hotel and The Hare and Hounds (06977) 3456 a comfortable inn. The Angus Hotel (0228) 23546 is convenient for the city centre and will not extinguish one's entire holiday budget in one go! Fantails (0228) 560239 in Wetheral is possibly the best restaurant in the area and for a pleasant water setting, Crosby-on-Eden and The Crosby Lodge (0228) 573618 is recommended.

Before leaving Cumbria, a quick mention for the somewhat isolated **Appleby** Golf Club. If you are in the vicinity it's well worth a visit. A splendid combination of moorland and heathland – very colourful. Remote, perhaps but in nearby Appleby-in-Westmoreland the Appleby Manor (07683) 51571 awaits while for a friendly inn note the Black Swan at Ravenstondale.

THE NORTH EAST

And so to the North East – and what a mixture!: Durham, Cleveland, Tyne & Wear and Northumberland. An area encompassing Tyneside, Teeside and Wearside, it also includes the Cleveland Hills, the Cheviots and the wild spectacular coast of ancient Northumbria. The four modern-day counties stretch from the far end of the Yorkshire Pennines and intrude into the Scottish Borders, the greater part of Northumberland lying north of Hadrian's Wall.

The appeal of any golf course can be affected greatly by its surroundings; nowhere in Britain does the accompanying landscape seem to dictate the enjoyment of a game as much as in this part of the world. The contrast between the industrial and rural North East is dramatic to put it mildly. The golf courses in the former tend towards the uninspiring – Seaton Carew being one great exception – whilst the likes of Bamburgh Castle and Hexham offer such magnificent scenery that the quality of the golf can often be relegated to a secondary consideration.

CLEVELAND

Beginning in the south of the region, Cleveland is one of the smallest counties in England and not surprisingly has very few courses. **Seaton Carew**, is far and away the best in the county. In fact, it is almost certainly the best links course on the East Coast of England, north of Norfolk. It is located approximately 3 miles south of Hartlepool and has a skyline dominated by far-off chimneys which at night appear like giant torches. Golf here is played amidst the dunes with gorse and devilishly thick rough lining the fairways. In recent years several important Championships have been held here, including the British Boys Championship in 1978 and 1986.

South of the Tees, despite its name, the golf course at **Saltburn** isn't right by the sea, it's about a mile west of the town and is a well-wooded meadowland course. Quite a contrast to Seaton Carew: a trifle easier, but certainly worth a visit. Around Teeside itself there are courses at Redcar (**Cleveland),** **Middlesborough** and **Billingham** but perhaps the best in

the area is found at **Eaglescliffe**, a hilly course where there are some marvellous views of the Cleveland Hills. There are a number of hotels in the county, although as everywhere some of them are modern and unfortunately rather characterless. An exception to this is The Crathorne Hall Hotel (0642) 700398 at Yarm. Most handy for Seaton Carew is probably The Grand (0429) 266345 in Hartlepool. At Saltburn an excellent pub can be recommended, namely The Ship with its splendid sea views, while a little inland at Moorsholm The Jolly Sailor offers some very good food. Those playing at Eaglescliffe can enjoy midday sustenance (or evening celebration) at The Blue Bell.

DURHAM

Crossing into Durham, people often talk of (some even whistle about) Old Durham Town, but of course it's very much a city with a cathedral that has been adjudged the most beautiful building in the world. Without doubt the course to visit here is **Brancepeth Castle**, 4 miles south west of the city and set in very beautiful surroundings. Rather like St. Pierre at Chepstow the course occupies land that was formerly a deer park and a 13th Century church and castle provide a magnificent backcloth. Perhaps the most convenient place to stay is at The Bridge Hotel (091) 3780524 in Croxdale but there are a number of good hotels in Durham itself including The Royal County (091) 3866821. Lothlorien Guesthouse (091) 3710067 meanwhile, will leave plenty of spare pennies with which to explore the region's many attractions.

Further north, **Beamish Park** near Stanley is another laid out in a former deer park (belonging to Beamish Hall) and is well worth a detour if heading along the A1. **Bishop Auckland** in the centre of the county is a pleasant parkland course. The land here belongs to the Church of England and one of the terms of the Club's lease is that the course has to close on Good Friday and Christmas Day. Play then at your peril!

To the south west of Bishop Auckland, **Barnard Castle** enjoys yet another delightful setting. More of a moorland course than anything else it has a stream that must be crossed seventeen times during a round! There are some fine establishments nearby in which to celebrate (or perhaps even dry out?) In Barnard Castle itself The Jersey Farm Hotel (0833) 38223 is excellent value for a night's stay while those just looking for a bar snack and a drink might visit the nearby villages of Cotherstone (The Fox and Hounds) and Ronaldkirk (The Rose and Crown.) A slightly longer drive to Eggleston, also possible from Bishop Auckland, and one finds The Three Tuns – famed for its pub lunches. Midway between Bishop Auckland and Darlington at Newton Aycliffe is the **Woodham** Golf and Country Club which has a growing reputation.

Darlington is the largest town in the county. It may not have the appeal of Durham but for golfers there's a twin attraction: to the north, **Haughton Grange** with its great selection of MacKenzie greens and to the south, **Blackwell Grange** with its variety of trees. Both courses are parkland and always superbly maintained. For an ideal base one doesn't really have to look further than the 17th Century Blackwell Grange Moat House (0325) 380888. However, a good French restaurant to note in the town is The Bishops House and for a drink try The Kings Head (0325) 380222.

CUMBRIA & THE NORTH EAST
CHOICE GOLF

TYNE & WEAR

Tyneside is essentially a tale of two cities, Newcastle and Sunderland – home of the Geordies and where the welcome is second to none. There are plenty of golf courses in the area but the really attractive golf lies further north along the coast. The **Northumberland** (Gosforth Park) Golf Club and **Ponteland** probably have the best two courses in Tyne & Wear. The former is situated alongside Gosforth Park Racecourse and like Seaton Carew has staged several national championships. However the visitor may find it easier to arrange a game at Ponteland (at least during the week) – a particularly well-kept course this and very convenient if you happen to be flying to or from Newcastle Airport. **Whitley Bay** is another alternative. It is quite a long, windswept course with very large greens and a wide stream that can make scoring pretty difficult.

If there's one large town in England that could really do with a good golf challenge it's Sunderland, a place of great character – golf architects please note!

Staying in and around Newcastle, the leading hotels are The Swallow Gosforth Park Hotel (091) 2364111, the Holiday Inn (091) 2365432 and the Metro Park (091) 493 2233. All offer all the mod-cons and some first class leisure facilities. Jesmond offers a multitude of less expensive hotels and guesthouses. Chirton House Hotel (091) 2730407 is but one example. Newcastle is fast becoming a mecca for good and varied eating and Jesmond is once more at the forefront. The Daraz offers quite superb Indian cuisine. Francesca's is great value while more pricey but excellent cooking is found in either The Fisherman's Lodge (091) 2813281 or The Fisherman's Wharf (091) 2321057. If you are really wishing to celebrate in style, try 21 Queens Street on the Keyside where the food is second to none on Tyneside. In Chinatown, The Ming Dynasty also has a fine reputation. Ponteland possesses two inns of note, namely The Wagon and The Rendezvous while just outside the village is a delightful country house hotel, Horton Grange with another fine restaurant.

NORTHUMBERLAND

Finally then, a look at Northumberland, a county with a splendid, almost mythical history. The first golf course on the way up, as it were, is **Arcot Hall**, 6 miles north of Newcastle and a most tranquil setting. A James Braid creation, Arcot Hall is a heathland course with a wealth of trees and a lake. The 9th here is a particularly good hole. The club has a sumptuous Clubhouse but beware of The Grey Lady who ghosts in and out from time to time! If thoroughly frightened, many peaceful villages are at hand and some very good pubs. The Highlander at Belsay is one such place (and equally convenient incidentally after a day's golf at Ponteland).

Trekking northwards again, **Morpeth** is next on the agenda. Another pleasant course designed this time by one of James Braid's old rivals – Mr. Vardon no less. One of England's finest Georgian Country Houses lies only a short distance away at Longhorsley – Linden Hall (0670) 516611. Also nearby is The Besom Barn at Longframlington – a good place for a drink with some splendid English cooking. Embleton Hall (066510) 249 at Longframlington is also recommended.

Along the rugged coast some tremendous golf lies ahead.

Alnmouth is very pleasing and in the village is the comfortable Marine House Hotel (0665) 830349. Just a little beyond are the magnificent Castle courses of **Dunstanburgh** (at Embleton) and **Bamburgh**. The golf is glorious – the scenery spectacularly superb. Dunstanburgh Castle, the ruins of which were immortalised in watercolour by Turner, occupies a wondrously remote setting. The course is a genuine links, hugging close to the shore and staring out across miles of deserted beach. Bamburgh Castle is perhaps even more special, often referred to as England's most beautiful course. Not long by any means – but the setting! Holy Island and Lindisfarne, the Cheviot Hills and a majestic castle; furthermore, the fairways are bordered by a blaze of colour, with gorse, purple heather and numerous wild orchids. Bamburgh Castle is featured ahead. Not far from here is the fairly short but underrated course at **Seahouses.**

Having placated the golfing soul a few suggestions for the body include The Dunstanburgh Castle Hotel (0665) 76203 – as its name suggests, very handy for the golf course, The Lord Crewe Arms (06684) 243 in Bamburgh – good for a drink with some accommodation also. A further good resting place is to be found in Belford, The Blue Bell Hotel (06683) 543. Among several good Northumbrian pubs are the Tankerville Arms in Wooler, The Olde Ship in Seahouses and the Jolly Fisherman in Craster.

For centuries the town of Berwick-upon-Tweed didn't know whether it was coming or going, passing between England and Scotland like the proverbial shuttlecock. However, disorientated, it has a fine links course at **Goswick**, 3 miles south of the town. Two thoughts for what may be one's last night in England – or maybe one's first? – are The Kings Arms Hotel (0289) 307454 and The Turret House Hotel.

Having sent the golfer north of Newcastle I am aware of having neglected **Hexham**, and the county's newest gem, **Slaley Hall**. Hexham Golf Club is only a short drive west of Newcastle, along either the A69 or the A695. The journey is well worth making, (Slaley Hall – see feature page – is not too far away) as the course has a glorious setting and the nearby villages with their many inns – note the Hadrian (at would you believe) Wall, the Three Wheat Heads and The Boat at Warden – cry out for inspection. Finally a restaurant of note is the Black House (0434) 604744 just south of the market town.

A golfing holiday I believe is in order – and who needs Scotland!

Gilroy **SNOW GOLF** *Burlington Gallery*

FARLAM HALL HOTEL

Farlam Hall was opened in 1975 by the Ouinion and Stevenson families who over the years have managed to achieve and maintain consistently high standards of food, service and comfort. These standards have been recognised and rewarded by all the major guides and membership of Relais and Chateaux.

This old border house, dating in parts to the 17th Century, is set in mature gardens which can be seen from the elegant lounges and dining room, creating a relaxing and pleasing environment. The fine silver and crystal in the dining room complement the quality of the English Country House food produced by Barry Ouinion and his team of chefs.

The 13 individually decorated bedrooms vary in size and shape, some have jacuzzi baths, one an antique four poster bed, and there are 2 ground floor bedrooms.

This area offers a wealth of different attractions, - miles of unspoilt country for walking, 8 golf courses within 30 minutes of the hotel, and close by are Hadrians Wall, Lanercost Priory and Carlisle with the Castle, Cathedral and Museum. The Lake District, Scottish Borders and Yorkshire Dales provide an ideal days touring.

Dogs welcome. Winter and Spring Breaks. Directions, Farlam Hall is 2.5 miles east of Brampton on the A689, not in Farlam Village.

Price Guide (including dinner) Double/Twin £170-£200, Single £95-£100.

Closed Christmas.

Farlam Hall Hotel
Brampton
Cumbria
CA8 2NG
Tel: (06977) 46234
Fax: (06977) 46683

CROSBY LODGE

Crosby Lodge was purchased by the Sedgwick family in 1970, and has been skilfully restored and converted into the romantically beautiful Country House Hotel it is today.

The front door opens into an enormous welcoming log fire, with an oak staircase leading up to the bedrooms. Each bedroom is decorated and designed individually, with en suite bathrooms. Various period pieces, such as half-tester beds, have been retained, whilst at the same time the hotel provides first class modern amenities. Crosby Lodge has an established reputation for excellence and the large spacious rooms, full of antiques and elegantly furnished, welcome guests with a comfortable and relaxed atmosphere. Overlooking tree-lined parkland, the delightful dining room, with its beamed ceiling, gleaming cutlery and long windows, is a haven for the connoisseur of good food and wine. Deliciously exciting menus feature authentic continental cuisine alongside the very best of traditional British fare. The four course Table d'hote menu has a vast choice and is complimented by a smaller A la carte menu providing such delights as steaks, scampi and Dover sole. The Crosby Lodge sweet trolley is renowned far and wide, and coffee and delicious home-made sweetmeats can be taken in the charming lounge and cocktail bar. Chef Proprietor Michael Sedgwick produces exciting dishes using fresh, mainly local ingredients, ensuring everything is to the highest standard.

To the visitor, Crosby Lodge offers untold days of pleasure, with the Lake District and Scottish Lowlands so near at hand. Historic Hadrian's Wall, stunning Cumberland and Northumberland country and the ancient border city of Carlisle await the visitor; travelling further afield, yet returning to Crosby Lodge in the evening, one can reach Edinburgh, a city steeped in history and culture. For the golfer the hotel is ideal, with arrangements easily made on the new Riverside Course, only minutes away, or indeed on a variety of courses at Carlisle, Brampton, Penrith and Silloth.

Featured in the Egon Ronay, Michelin, with three AA stars and a British Tourist four crown hotel, Crosby Lodge is fully deserving of the praise it receives. With an emphasis on comfort, relaxation, good food, traditional courtesy and old-fashioned hospitality, Michael and Patricia Sedgwick, son James and staff will ensure that you have a memorable stay and every assistance with your arrangements.

Crosby Lodge
Country House Hotel and Restaurant
Crosby-On-Eden
Carlisle
Cumbria CA6 4QZ
Tel: (0228) 573618
Fax: (0228) 573428

189

SILLOTH ON SOLWAY
CHAMPIONSHIP GOLF

One of the greatest ever lady golfers, **Miss Cecil Leitch** once said, 'If you can play Silloth you can play anywhere'. The four times British Ladies Champion and the great rival of Joyce Wethered would have been able to judge better than most for she grew up in Silloth and it was on Silloth's Championship links that she and her four golfing sisters learnt to play.

Silloth-on-Solway Golf Club celebrated its centenary in 1992. At one time there was some uncertainty as to the exact date of the Club's formation as although the first few holes were laid out in 1892, it was not until 1903 when the Club together with its 'new' Clubhouse was formally opened by the Speaker of the House of Commons, **The Rt. Hon. Edward Gully**.

Today, Silloth is perhaps one of Britain's lesser known Championship links, this doubtless a result of its somewhat remote situation 23 miles west of Carlisle. Hidden away it may be but it is a journey decidedly worth making, for not only is this one of Britain's greatest tests of golf but the Silloth Club is just about the most friendly one is likely to come across.

Helping to promote this welcoming atmosphere is the Club's Secretary, **John Proudlock**, who may be contacted by telephone on **(06973) 31304;** when making a booking visitors should ask for **Mrs Burns** who controls the diary. There are no specific restrictions on visiting golfers during the week and they can play by arrangement at almost any time. At weekends the Club restricts the number of visitors to 40 and they may play a single round subject to the tee being pre-booked for competitions etc.

The cost of a day's golf at Silloth in 1992 is priced at £18 during the week and £23 per round at weekends – for such a splendid Championship course surely excellent value. The fees for juniors are half the above rates. Weekly tickets (Monday to Friday) can be purchased for £72. Golfing Societies must book starting times either by telephoning the Club or by writing to the Secretary at **The Silloth-on-Solway Golf Club, Silloth-on-Solway, Carlisle, Cumbria CA5 4BL**. Should the need arise, sets of clubs may be hired from the professional, **John Burns**, tel: **(06973) 31304**.

With the M6 running to Carlisle, Silloth isn't actually quite as remote as many people imagine. Golfers travelling from the south should leave the M6 at junction 41 and thereafter take the B5305 to Wigton. At Wigton the B5302 should be picked up and followed to Silloth. Those who have been sensible

enough to take their golf clubs to the Lake District may find the B5300 road helpful; it runs along the coast from Maryport to Silloth. Finally those approaching from Scotland should head for Carlisle and thereafter follow a combination of the B5307 and the B5302 to Silloth.

Measuring a modest 6357 yards, par 72 (5780 yards, par 75 for Ladies), Silloth may not sound particularly frightening, and you may just be wondering what all the fuss is about. Standing on the **1st** tee with the wind hammering into your face you'll know exactly what all the fuss is about! Humbling is perhaps the best way to describe the sensation. Two shots later (hopefully!) you'll also discover why the large greens at Silloth have acquired such a marvellous reputation. The course meanders its way through and over some classic links terrain. There are occasional spectacular vantage points – the coastal views from the **4th** and **6th** tees being especially memorable – and the round calls for several demanding strokes, both going out and coming home. Of the many great holes however, perhaps the par five **13th** stands out. Appropriately named 'Hogs Back' it has an exceptionally narrow fairway that is heather lined on either side and a plateau green. Hit a good drive and you'll be tempted to go for the green in two – miss it and you're in deep trouble!

The comfortable and recently extended Clubhouse at Silloth offers full catering until 9pm after which light snacks may be obtained from the Bar. The lunchtime menu is quite outstanding and provided some pre-warning is given, a full Cumberland breakfast can be arranged.

The Club is understandably proud of the fact that twice in recent years it has been selected to host the British Ladies Amateur Championship. However, it can also be proud of the courage some of its members displayed back in 1912; for this information I am greatly indebted to the Club's former Secretary, **John Todd**. On behalf of all the Clubs in the British Isles Silloth appealed against the assessment to income tax on green fees. Unfortunately for the Golf Clubs the learned judge found in favour of the Inland Revenue; this left Silloth with the task of finding £433 12s. 9d. for legal expenses. 81 Clubs promised contributions to help towards the debt and they eventually raised £140 11s. between them, leaving Silloth with a deficiency of almost £300. One very famous Club I am told subscribed one shilling – and I bet you'd like to know which!

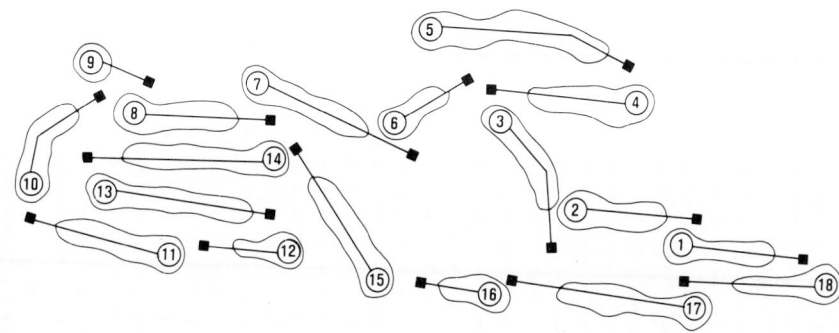

Hole	Yards	Par	Hole	Yards	Par
1	380	4	10	308	4
2	319	4	11	403	4
3	358	4	12	200	3
4	372	4	13	468	5
5	482	5	14	477	5
6	187	3	15	417	4
7	403	4	16	182	3
8	371	4	17	495	5
9	134	3	18	401	4
Out	**3,006**	**35**	**In**	**3,351**	**37**
			Out	**3,006**	**35**
			TOTALS	**6,357**	**72**

ABBEY HOUSE HOTEL

This most impressive red sandstone building is a superb and slightly unusual example of the work of the eminent English architect, Sir Edwin Lutyens. It was completed in 1914 as a business guest house and, in its conversion to a graceful hotel of the very highest calibre, virtually all of the magnificently-proportioned rooms have adapted to their new role with minimal disturbance. There is an inherent grandeur and quiet dignity about the hotel equalled only by the fourteen acres of grounds, comprising a beautifully balanced mixture of formal gardens and wooded copses. Beyond these lies a splendid vista of mature woodland and meadow interspersed with established walkways which lead to the ruins of nearby Furness Abbey. In less than half-an-hour's drive you are in the centre of the English Lake District with all the historic and picturesque places of interest in and around Grizedale Forest.

Barrow-in-Furness lies on a peninsula with a road bridge to the Isle of Walney, and some tiny isolated islands in and around sheltered bays; Sailing craft complete the coastal picture. Inland excursions bring you to the tarns, fells and pikes of the Cumbrian Mountains.

Abbey House offers impeccable accommodation for business and holiday visitors alike, and the finest a la carte English and French cuisine of the Abbey Restaurant is available to residents and non-residents.

Excellent conference and banqueting facilities can be provided.

The Hotel is also an ideal stopover for those of you who wish to have that little flutter on the horses as it is within easy reach of the Cartmel Race Course near Grange-Over-Sands or Carlisle Race Course.

Abbey House Hotel
Abbey Road
Barrow in Furness
Cumbria LA13 OPA
Tel: (0229) 838282
Fax: (0229) 820403

WINDERMERE
CHAMPIONSHIP GOLF

Whoever first coined that atrocious phrase, 'Golf is a good walk spoiled' was more than likely an idiot. One thing's for sure, he (or she) had never visited Windermere Golf Club in the Lake District. Golf not only 'takes us to such beautiful places', as **Henry Longhurst** used to say, but it also regularly guides us to some beautiful vantage points. Had our idiot stood on the **8th** tee at Windermere he would have assuredly been forced to revise the ill-informed comment. Golf, if nothing else, is a good walk with a good incentive. (Better not tell that idiot that the 8th at Windermere is called 'Desolation'!)

Windermere Golf Club celebrated its centenary in 1991. Cleabarrow Fells, the land on which the course is laid out was originally leased in 1891 from the Rector of Windermere (one who obviously gave the game his blessing) before being purchased outright by the Club in 1912. The 200 acres comprised, in addition to classically undulating lakeland terrain, a serious amount of heather, bracken and rocks. However, it was soon converted into a sporting 9 hole course and so well was this received that a further 9 holes were added before the end of 1892.

The Club's centenary booklet reveals a colourful history. In the 1920s, the course measured 4,320 yards but had a par of 72 (today it is 5,006 yards, par 67.) Holes had interesting pars in those days and our friend 'Desolation', though a similar length as now at 131 yards, was a par three and a half! In the 1930s, the fees for a caddy were 2s.2d. per round for a 'First Class Adult' ranging to 1s.1d. for a 'Second Class Schoolboy.'

Windermere has always been a popular course, perhaps never more so than at the present time, just as the Club enters its second century. Windermere has never had pretensions to becoming a Championship length course but it has always offered an enjoyable challenge, and with its outstanding views and the marvellous condition in which the course is currently maintained, it is easy to understand why more and more people are calling it a 'mini Gleneagles.' Windermere is probably worthy of such flattery.

Visiting golfers are very welcome to come and judge for themselves. Not too many foreigners associate the Lake District with the Royal and Ancient game but there can surely be few more delightful environments than this. Visitors should contact the Club in advance of intended play. **Mr K R Moffat** is the Club's Secretary and he can be approached by telephone on **(05394) 43123;** Windermere's professional **Stephen Rooke** and his staff handle all tee reservations and they can be contacted on **(05394) 43550.** The address is **Windermere Golf Club, Cleabarrow, Windermere,**

Cumbria. LA23 3NB.

As a general guide, tee times can normally be reserved between 10.00am and 12.00pm, 2.00pm and 4.30pm and before 9.00am. Players must be members of golf clubs and have official handicaps. Golf Societies (maximum 50 persons) can usually be accommodated by arrangement. The green fees in 1992 were set at £18 between Mondays and Fridays and £25 on Saturday, Sunday and Bank Holidays.

For most people travelling to the Lake District will be via the M6. The best exit point for southbound travellers is junction 37 and for northbound motorists, junction 36. The precise location of the Golf Club is a mile and a half from Bowness-on-Windermere along the Crook (Kendal) road, the B5284.

The Clubhouse is most welcoming (some excellent bar snacks are offered between Tuesdays and Saturdays) and the golf course will certainly not disappoint. With a par of 67, there are of course many par three holes and while none of the par fours is overly long the naturally rugged landscape makes up for the lack of length. As on a links type course, awkward stances and blind shots are not uncommon at Windermere, and with the greens being fairly small a well-honed short game is often the key to a good round.

We have already singled out the **8th** as Windermere's 'signature hole': from the tee the green sits roughly at eye level but in between is a deep valley of gorse. The green is in fact table-shaped and can be extremely difficult to hit. Distraction is the last thing a player really needs here but over the player's shoulder is a marvellous view of Morecombe Bay while stretching ahead are the magnificent mountains of the Lake District.

Among other notable holes at Windermere one might include the **2nd**, a very long par three; the **4th** which is the stroke one hole with its difficult drive to an acutely angled fairway and potentially even more difficult blind approach; the **6th** and **7th** where you play beside an attractive little reservoir and the three closing holes, which, according to the card run 5-4-3 – scores that most players will be happy to settle for!

Having introduced Windermere with a regrettable quote, it seems only appropriate to conclude with one of the more noble philosophies on life and reputedly first uttered by the legendary golfer **Walter Hagen**: 'You're only here for a short while; don't hurry, don't worry, but be sure to smell the flowers along the way.' At Windermere, they might even be found fluttering and dancing in the breeze.

Hole	Yards	Par	Hole	Yards	Par
1	315	4	10	199	3
2	232	3	11	259	4
3	252	4	12	291	4
4	356	4	13	306	4
5	291	4	14	146	3
6	354	4	15	187	3
7	371	4	16	480	5
8	130	3	17	356	4
9	269	4	18	203	3
Out	2,579	34	In	2,427	33
			Out	2,579	34
			Totals	5,006	67

SLALEY HALL
CHAMPIONSHIP GOLF

Why is a genial Irishman from County Galway spending an increasing amount of time in deepest, rural Northumberland? Simple, the genial Irishman is **Christy O'Connor Jnr** – he of the famous 2 iron – and the reason for his presence in Northumberland is Slaley Hall. 'Never heard of it' you say. Well the whole golfing world is going to hear of it soon. Slaley Hall is already the pride and joy of the North East. Situated 18 miles from Newcastle Airport but surrounded by some of England's most beautiful countryside, what started as an almost absurdly ambitious dream is fast becoming a reality.

Slaley Hall itself is one of those lovely old ivy-clad manors that belongs to a forgotten world. Not totally forgotten in this case it seems, for Newcastle based entrepreneurs, **Seamus O'Carroll** and **John Rourke** conceived the idea of turning the large estate into one of the world's leading golf and leisure complexes – men clearly not interested in half measures! The plan was to build an 18 hole Championship golf course around Slaley Hall and then extend the Hall by constructing an adjoining luxury hotel complete with all manner of accompanying facilities.

The Championship Golf course was designed by **Dave Thomas** and opened for play in July 1989. Let us at once say that Thomas has produced a masterpiece; he himself considers it his finest work. Immediately it opened, critics were describing it as The Woburn of the North. As for the hotel, in Autumn 1991 the 140 bedroomed, five star Slaley Hall Sheraton opened and it boasts a vast array of luxury facilities. Meanwhile, various property developments, from holiday villas to Scandinavian styled timeshare lodges have started to mushroom all over the Northumbrian landscape.

Overseeing all aspects of golf at Slaley Hall is the Director of Golf, **Stuart Brown**. He can be contacted by telephone on **(0434) 673350**. For written correspondence the Club's full address is **Slaley Hall Golf and Country Club, Slaley, Hexham, Northumberland NE47 0BY**. Assisting the Director of Golf from time to time is the Club's European Tour Professional, Christy O'Connor Jnr. who often plays a key role on corporate golf days.

Visitors are always made extremely welcome at Slaley Hall. Provided they possess a recognised handicap they may play at any time during the week and can usually book a tee time for the weekend. 1992's green fees were set at £20 per round, £25 per day midweek and £25 per round, £40 per day on Saturdays and Sundays.

Although it genuinely is situated in deepest, rural Northumberland visitors shouldn't have too much difficulty finding Slaley Hall. Its precise location is 6 miles south of Hexham and 2 miles west of the A68 road, between Corbridge and Consett. The quickest route from Newcastle (and its Airport) is to pick up the A69 towards Hexham. From Hexham, the road to take for Slaley is the B6306. Approaching from further afield the A1/M1 is likely to be of most assistance for those motoring up from the south and the midlands, while to the north Hexham is linked to Edinburgh by the A68.

From its Championship tees Slaley Hall weighs in at a fairly formidable 6995 yards, par 72. Less daunting are the medal tees from which the course is reduced to 6382 yards, par 72. From the ladies tees the course measures 5832 yards, par 76. The **1st** hole offers a chance to open the shoulders, for the fairway is fairly wide, but thereafter at least a little caution may be the order of the day. The **2nd** and **3rd** are excellent holes; the former a swinging dog-leg where, if you're too greedy from the tee, the conifers will swallow your ball. Fir trees are ever present at Slaley Hall, lining just about every fairway and giving the course something of an alpine feel. The golfer must do battle with streams and small lakes at the **4th**, **5th**, **6th** and **7th**; the **8th** is another of Slaley's swinging dog-legs and the **9th** a magnificent par four – a hint of Woodhall Spa perhaps?

On the back nine, holes **11**, **12** and **13** are highly memorable; laid out close to Slaley Hall itself cherry trees abound and they are a truly spectacular sight when in bloom. Holes **14** to **17** have a distinctly moorland feel and the **18th** is a classic, though very difficult, finishing hole.

Just a year after opening, the magazine Executive Golfer International featured Slaley Hall in its June 1990 edition, and had this to say: 'We feel confident in predicting that Slaley Hall will soon become a name synonymous with major golf events – in the same league as Wentworth, Gleneagles and Turnberry. But in addition, Slaley Hall will be the total resort for all reasons and all seasons – as they say, the ultimate dream.'

No wonder yer man was tempted.

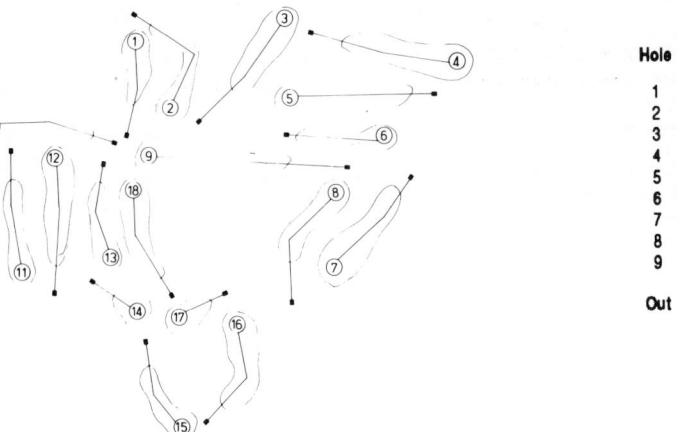

Hole	Yards	Par	Hole	Yards	Par
1	434	4	10	363	4
2	366	4	11	565	5
3	412	4	12	533	5
4	518	5	13	381	4
5	382	4	14	179	3
6	205	3	15	331	4
7	428	4	16	396	4
8	408	4	17	182	3
9	452	4	18	460	4
Out	3,605	36	In	3,390	36
			Out	3,605	36
			TOTALS	6,995	72

BAMBURGH CASTLE
CHAMPIONSHIP GOLF

In an earlier piece I quoted one of **Henry Longhurst's** most celebrated comments, namely; 'What a lovely place to die' (referring to the 18th hole at Killarney). The golf course at Bamburgh merits another from the great man; 'Golf takes you to such beautiful places.'

The setting is quite stunning. A number of Britain's golf courses fall within the gaze of nearby castles; Royal St. David's and Harlech Castle is perhaps the best known example, Cruden Bay and Dunstanburgh are others, but none is more dramatic than the situation at Bamburgh. Standing 150 feet high on a vast, rocky crag and covering over eight acres, Bamburgh is one of Britain's most spectacular castles. It towers over the village and is visible in all its majesty from the adjoining 18 hole links.

Apparently we have to thank the Normans for the splendid keep. It was they who built it, having acquired the original castle from Matilda, Countess of Northumberland, after threatening to take out the eyes of her captive husband – charming times!

Turning to less gory subjects, **Mr. T.C. Osborne** is the Secretary of Bamburgh Castle Golf Club; he may be contacted by telephone on **(06684) 321**. The Club has no golf professional but should you turn up without any balls – a fate arguably worse than that of the Count of Northumberland – fear not, a supply can be purchased in the Clubhouse.

Visitors are made extremely welcome at Bamburgh. However, they are often restricted at weekends and on Public Holidays when they must be accompanied by a Member. Handicap certificates are also required. Before setting off, golfers are advised to contact the Steward on **(06684) 378**.

The green fees at Bamburgh vary according to the season. The summer fees for 1992, applicable between the 29th March and the 20th October, are as follows: £20 per day during the week (£9 for juniors) and £25 per round, £30 per day at weekends (£12 and £10 respectively for juniors). For Autumn and Winter visitors the fees are £15 during the week and £20 at weekends. Finally, five day temporary membership can be purchased for £60 during the Summer (£35 for juniors). Golfing Societies are equally welcome at Bamburgh, though pre-booking with the Secretary is essential. All written enquiries should be addressed to Mr Osborne at **The Bamburgh Castle Golf Club, The Club House, Bamburgh, Northumberland NE69 7DE**.

Bamburgh has what might be described as an 'invigorating climate'. Situated on the north eastern coast of Northumberland, only Berwick-upon-Tweed lies further north in England and Bamburgh is a shade closer to the North Pole than either Prestwick, Turnberry or Troon. Despite its remoteness, the journey is a fairly straightforward one and is definitely worth making. Both north and southbound travellers should pick up the A1 which runs between Berwick and Alnwick, passing Bamburgh midway. It doesn't however, pass through Bamburgh. Those approaching from the north should exit left on to the B3142 at Belford, while those approaching from the south are best leaving the A1 just north of Warenford before following the B3141 to Bamburgh. Anyone motoring across the glorious Northumberland countryside may find Wooler a useful place to head for: the B6348 connects Wooler to the A1 just north of the B1341 turn off.

By any standards, Bamburgh Castle is a short course measuring 5465 yards (par 68) from the men's tees and 5064 yards from the ladies tees (par 70). Short it may be but it isn't without its tests; there are many whin bushes and several of the fairways are flanked with tangling heather. As with every seaside course, the moods of the wind must always be considered. In any event the golfer will not have come to Bamburgh to seek golf's toughest challenge, it is the splendour of the unique setting that is to be enjoyed. The Castle isn't the only sight that demands attention: there are magnificent views across to nearby Holy Island and Lindisfarne and the Cheviot Hills provide a glorious backdrop. As for the course itself, in addition to the great spread of purple heather, a number of fairways are lined with rare wild orchids. It is hardly surprising that Bamburgh is often described as Britain's most beautiful course. Especially memorable holes at Bamburgh include the short **8th** with its tee shot over a valley, the **15th** – from this tee the golfer can spy no fewer than four castles – and the **17th** which is guaranteed to bring the dreaming golfer down to earth.

What about the 19th? In short, exceptionally friendly (as one comes to expect in this part of England). There are no formal dress requirements and lunches and dinners are offered daily in addition to light snacks.

There is a saying used in many sports that 'a good big'un' is always better than 'a good little'un'; the golf course at Bamburgh demonstrates that the phrase has no meaning whatsoever in the world of golf..........besides, ask Ian Woosnam!

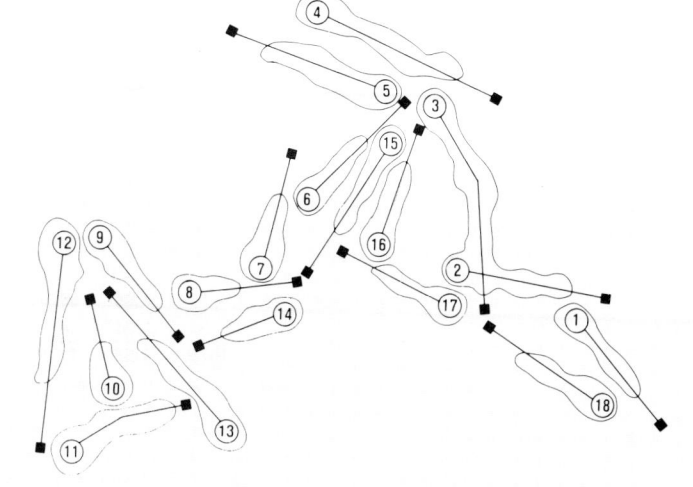

Hole	Yards	Par	Hole	Yards	Par
1	182	3	10	196	3
2	213	3	11	334	4
3	510	5	12	413	4
4	476	5	13	406	4
5	314	4	14	149	3
6	224	3	15	404	4
7	279	4	16	268	4
8	162	3	17	260	4
9	361	4	18	314	4
Out	**2,721**	**34**	**In**	**2,744**	**34**
			Out	**2,721**	**34**
			TOTALS	**5,465**	**68**

MICHAELS NOOK HOTEL

A gracious, stone-built Lakeland home, with a wealth of mahogany woodwork, Michaels Nook is quietly tucked away overlooking the Grasmere valley and surrounded by well-kept lawns and beautiful trees. It was opened as a hotel over twenty years ago by owner Reg Gifford, a respected antique dealer, and furnishings, enhanced by an abundance of flowers and plants, reflect his appreciation of English furniture, antique rugs, prints and porcelain. The Hotel retains the mellowness of the private home, and a hint of pleasing eccentricity, accentuated by the presence of a Great Dane and some exotic cats.

There are twelve, lovely, individually-designed bedrooms, all with en suite bathrooms, and two magnificent suites. Each room has colour television and direct dial telephone, and is provided with many thoughtful extra touches, such as fresh flowers, fruit, and mineral water. Full room service is available.

In the Restaurant, polished tables gleam, set with fine crystal and porcelain, and only the best fresh ingredients are used for dishes memorable for their delicate flavour and artistic presentation. Different choices are offered each day. A very extensive Wine List offers selections from all the best wine-producing areas, and makes for fascinating reading, as well as excellent drinking. The panelled Oak Room, with handsome stone fireplace and gilt furnishings, hosts Director and Senior Manager meetings and private celebrations.

Spectacular excursions, by car or on foot, start from the doorstep of this delightful house, and encompass some of Britain's most impressive scenery. Dove Cottage, Wordsworth's home during his most creative period, is close at hand, and Beatrix Potter's farm at Sawrey only a short drive away.

The Hotel itself has three acres of landscaped grounds, and a further ten acres of woodland and wild fell, plus a speciality rhododendron garden covering four acres of nearby hillside. Guests are also welcome to make use of the heated swimming pool, and other health facilities of The Wordsworth Hotel, less than a mile away, and under the same ownership. Both Hotels offer special arrangements with Keswick Golf Club, and enjoy a close proximity to some of the excellent northern links courses.

Michaels Nook
Grasmere
Ambleside
Cumbria LA22 9RP
Tel: (05394) 35496
Fax: (05394) 35765

CUMBRIA & THE NORTH EAST
COMPLETE GOLF

CUMBRIA

Alston Moor G.C
(0498) 81675
The Hermitage, Alston
2 miles S. of Alston
(9) 6450 yards/***/E

Appleby G.C
(07683) 51432
Brackenber Moor, Appleby-in-Westmorland
2 miles S. of Apppleby on the A66
(18) 5895 yards/***/E

Barrow G.C
(0229) 25444
Blakesmoor Lane, Hawcoat, Barrow-in-Furness
Take A590 to Hawcoat
(18) 6209 yards/***/F/M

Brampton G.C
(069 77) 2255
Brampton
2 miles S. off the B6413 Castle Carrock road
(18) 6420 yards/***/F/H

Carlisle G.C
(0228) 513303
Aglionby, Carlisle
3 miles E. of Carlisle
(18) 6278 yards/***/F

Cockermouth G.C
(059681) 223
Embleton, Cockermouth
4 miles out of Cockermouth
(18) 5496 yards/***/E

Dunnerholme G.C
(0229) 62675
Duddon Road, Askam-in-Furness
Leave A590 for A595 for Askam-in-Furness
(10) 6101 yards/***(not Sun)/E

Furness G.C
(0229) 41232
Central drive, walney Island, Barrow-in-Furness
Follow signs for Walney Island from town
(18) 6418 yards/***/F

Grange Fell G.C
(05395) 32536
Fell Road, Grange-Over-Sands
On the main road to Cartmel
(9) 4826 yards/***/E

Grange-Over-Sands G.C
(05395) 33180
Meathop Road, Grange-over-Sands
On left as you enter Grange itself
(18) 5660 yards/***/E

Kendal G.C
(0539) 724079
The Heights, Kendal
Leave A6 for Kendal for the B5284
(18) 5483 yards/***/D

Keswick G.C
(07687) 83324
Threlkeld Hall, Keswick
4 miles along A66 from Keswick
(18) 6175 yards/***/E

Kirkby Lonsdale G.C
(0468) 71429
Casterton Road, Kirkby Lonsdale
1 mile from town on A683
(9) 4058 yards/***(not Sun am)/E

Maryport G.C
(0900) 812605
Bank End, Maryport
On the B5300 from A596 to Workington
(18) 6272 yards/***/E

Penrith G.C
(0768) 62217
Salkeld Road, Penrith
Half mile out of Penrith on A6
(18) 6026 yards/***/D/M/H

Seascale G.C
(09467) 28202
The Banks, Seascale
N. of village, on the coast
(18) 6416 yards/***/D

Sedbergh G.C
(0587) 20993
The Riggs, Millthrop, Sedbergh
1 mile from Sedbergh on the Dent Road
(9) 4134 yards/***/E

Silecroft G.C
(0657) 4250
Silecroft, Millom
3 miles N. of Millom
(9) 5712 yards/**/E

Silloth On Solway G.C
(0965) 31304
Silloth On Solway
18 miles W. of Carlisle
(18) 6343 yards/***/F/H

St Bees School G.C
(0946) 82295
Rhoda Grove, Rheda, Frizington
4 miles S. of Whiehaven on the B5345
(9) 5082 yards/***/F

Stonyholme Municipal G.C
(0228) 34856
St Aidans Road, Carlisle
1 mile N. of Carlisle
(18) 5600 yards/***/E

Ulverston G.C
(0229) 52824
Bardsea Park, Ulverston
On the B5087 to Bardsea
(18) 6142 yards/***/D/M/H

Windermere G.C
(09662) 3123
Cleaharrow, Windermere
9 miles from Kendal off A591
(18) 5006 yards/***/F/H

Workington G.C
(0900) 603460
Branthwaite Road, Workington
2 miles S.E. of Workington off A595
(18) 6100 yards/***/E/M/H

CO DURHAM

Aycliffe G.C
(0325) 310820
School Aycliffe Lane, Newton Aycliffe
Part of Sports complex off A6072
(9) 6054 yards/***/E

Barnard Castle G.C
(0833) 38355
Harmire Road, Barnard Castle
N. of town on the B6278
5838 yards/***/F

Beamish Park G.C
091-3701133
Beamish, Stanley
Follow signs for Open Air Museum
(18) 6000 yards/***(not Sun)/F/H

Birtley G.C
091-4102207
Portobello Road, Birtley
Between Birtley and Whitelands
(9) 5154 yards/**/E

Bishop Auckland G.C
(0388) 602198
High Plains, Durham Road, Bishop Auckland
Just N. of town, on left
(18) 6420 yards/***/D

Blackwell Grange G.C
(0325) 464464
Briar Close, Blackwell, Darlington
On the A66 S. from Darlington
(18) 5587 yards/***(not Wed pm)/D

Brancepeth Castle G.C
091-3780075
Brancepeth, Durham
5 mile S.W of Durham on A690
(18) 6300 yards/**/DH

Chester-le-Street G.C
091-3883218
Lumley Park, Chester-le-Street
leave A1 for the A167 for Durham
(18) 6054 yards/**/F/L

Consett and District G.C
(0207) 502186
Elmfield Road, Consett
Off the A691 from Durham
(18) 6001 yards/weekends only/E/H

Crook G.C
(0388) 762429
Low Jobs Hill, Crook
6 miles W. of Durham city off A690
(18) 6016 yards/***/E

Darlington G.C
(0325) 463936
Haughton Grange, Darlington
N.E of the town on the A1150
(18) 6032 yards/**/D/M

Dinsdale Spa G.C
90325) 332297
Middleton St George, Darlington
2 miles from town on Neasham Road
(18) 6078 yards/**/D

Durham City G.C
091-3780069
Littleburn Farm, Langley Moor
2 miles S.W. of Durham off the A690
(18) 6211 yards/**/E

Hobson Municipal G.C
(0207) 71605
Hobson, Nr Burnopfield, Newcastle-Upon-Tyne
(18) 6582 yards/***/E

Houghton-Le-Spring G.C
091-5841198
Copt Hill, Houghton-Le-Spring
On the B1404
(18) 6450 yards/*/D/M

Mount Oswald G.C
091-3867527
South Road, Durham
S.W of Durham on the A1050
(18) 6101 yards/***/E

Roseberry Grange G.C
091-3700670
Grange Villa, Chester-Le-Street
3 miles W. of Chester-Le-Street on A693
(18) 5628 yards***/E

Seaham G.C
091-5812354
Dawdon, Seaham
6 miles S. of Sunderland off A19
(18) 5972 yards/**/E

South Moor G.C
(0207) 232848
The Middles, Craghead, Stanley
2 miles from Stanley off B6313
(18) 6445 yards/***/F/M

Stressholme G.C
(0325) 461002
Snipe Lane, Darlington
8 miles N. of Scotch Corner
(18) 6511 yards/***/E

Woodham G. & C.C
(0325) 320574
Burnhill Way, Newton Aycliffe
1 mile N. of Newton Aycliffe
(18) 6727 yards/***/D

TYNE & WEAR

Boldon G.C
(0783) 364182
Dipe Lane, East Boldon
3 miles N.W of Sunderland
(18) 6348 yards/**/F

City of Newcastle G.C
091-285 1775
Three Mile Bridge, Gosforth, Newcastle-Upon-Tyne
3 miles N. of Newcastle city centre
(18) 6508 yards/***/D

Garesfield G.C
(0207) 561278
Chopwell
Leave the A694 for the B6315
(18) 6603 yards/***/E

George Washington G.C
091-417 2626
Near Washington Moat House Hotel
Signposted from the A1
(18) 6000 yards/***/E

Gosforth G.C
091-285 3495
Broadway East, Gosforth
3 miles N. of Newcastle on A6127
(18) 6043 yards/**/D/H

Newcastle United G.C
091-286 4693
Ponteland Road, Cowgate
1 mile W. of city centre
(18) 6498 yards/**/E

Northumberland G.C
091-236 2009
High Gosforth Park
Newcastle Upon Tyne
(18)6640 yards/**/F

Ravensworth G.C
091-487 2843
Moss Heaps, Wrekenton, Gateshead
2 miles S.E. of Gateshead
(18) 5872 yards/**/E/H

Ryton G.C
091-413 3737
Stanners Drive, Clara Vale, Ryton
8 miles W. of Newcastle, off A695
(18) 6034 yards/**/E

South Shields G.C
091-456 0475
Cleadon Hills, South Shields
Take A1018 N. from Sunderland
(18) 6264 yards/***/D

Tynemouth G.C
091-257 4578
Spital Dene, Tynemouth, North Shields
W. of town off A1058 or A193
(18) 6403 yards/**/E/M

Tyneside G.C
091-413 2742
Westfield Lane, Ryton
W. of Newcastle off A695
(18) 6055 yards/***/D/H

Wallsend G.C
091-262 4231
Bigges Main, Wallsend on Tyne
Take A1058 from Newcastle
(18) 6459 yards/***/E

Wearside G.C
091-534 2518
Coxgreen, Sunderland
On S. bank of Wear
(18) 6323 yards/***/D/M/H

Westerhope G.C
091-286 9125
Whorlton Grange, Westerhope
Take A696 W. of Newcastle
(18) 6407 yards/***/E

Whickham G.C
091-4887
Hollinside Park, Whickham
5 miles W. of Newcastle
(18) 6129 yards/**/E

Whitburn G.C
091-529 2144
Lizard Lane, South Shields
Between Sunderland and South Shields off A183
(18) 6035 yards/**/E

Whitley Bay G.C
091-252 0180
Claremont Road, Whitley Bay
(18) 6617 yards/**/F

NORTHUMBERLAND

Allendale G.C
(091) 267 5875
Thornley Gate, Allendale, Hexham
Near town off B6295
(9) 4410 yards/***/E

Alnmouth G.C
(0665) 830231
Foxton Hall, Alnmouth, Alnwick
In town, off the A1068
(18) 6414 yards/***/D/H

Alnmouth Village G.C
(0665) 830370
Marine Road, Alnmouth
Leave A1 for A1068 for Alnmouth
(9) 6078 yards/***/E

Alnwick G.C
(0665) 602632
Swansfield Park, Alnwick
Leave A1 at Alnwick
(9) 5379 yards/***/F

Arcot Hall G.C
091-2362794
Dudley, Cramlington
Leave A1 for A1068 for Ashington
(18) 6389 yards/***/D

Bamburgh Castle G.C
(06684) 321
The Wynding, Bamburgh
Leave A1 for B1341 to Bamburgh
(18) 5465 yards/***/D/M

Bedlingtonshire G.C
(0670) 822457
Acorn Bank, Bedlington
Half mile W. of town
(18) 6224 yards/***/E

Bellingham G.C
(0660) 20530
Boggle Hole, Bellingham, Hexham
16 miles N. of Hexham, off B5245
(9) 5245 yards/***/E

Berwick-Upon-Tweed G.C
(0289) 87256
Goswick, Berwick-Upon-Tweed
4 miles S. of town off the A1
(18) 6399 yards/**/F

THE WORDSWORTH HOTEL

In the very heart of English Lakeland, and the centre of one of its loveliest villages, The Wordsworth combines the sophistication of a first-class Hotel with the magnificence of the surrounding countryside. Situated in two acres of landscaped grounds next to the churchyard where William Wordsworth is buried, its name honours the memory of the area's most famous son. The scenery that so inspired the Lake Poets can be enjoyed from the peaceful lounges, furnished with fine antiques , or in the Conservatory and Cocktail Bar with the aid of a favourite aperitif or specially mixed drink.

The Hotel has 35 most attractive and comfortable bedrooms, each with private bathroom, colour TV, radio, direct-dial telephone, and intercom. Some rooms have romantic four-poster beds (a honeymoon package is offered) and there are two suites. 24-hour room service is available. The facilities of the Coleridge Room are ideal for private functions of up to 100 guests, and a marquee on the lawns is not uncommon for larger parties, especially summer weddings.

The Prelude Restaurant, named after Wordsworth's famous autobiographical poem, is the place to enjoy the best of the seasonal produce skilfully prepared by the Chef and his team. The accompanying Wine List combines familiar favourites with some pleasantly surprising 'finds', and a fine selection of claret and burgundies. The Hotel's own pub - 'The Dove and Olive Branch' -is a friendly meeting place for a traditional beer or tasty snack, and has recently received accolades from The Good Pub Guide and national newspapers.

For the energetic and those wishing to pamper themselves, the Wordsworth has an indoor heated swimming pool, opening onto a sun-trap terrace, a jacuzzi, mini-gym, sauna and solarium. In the area, the sports-minded can indulge in clay shooting, fishing and all manner of water sports.

For the golfer, the Hotel can arrange free rounds from Monday to Friday at Keswick Golf Club - par 71 - in a delightful valley setting amidst spectacular mountain scenery. It is also within easy reach of several excellent links courses, such as Silloth, as well as the famous championship courses at Royal Lytham and Royal Birkdale. The Hotel Management will do whatever it can to assist with arrangements at these courses.

The Wordsworth Hotel
Grasmere
Ambleside
Cumbria LA22 9SW
Tel: (05394) 35592
Fax: (05394) 35765

CUMBRIA & THE NORTH EAST
COMPLETE GOLF

Blyth G.C
(0670) 367728
New Delaval, Blyth
14 miles N. of Newcastle off A193
(18) 6533 yards/**/E

Dustanburgh Castle G.C
(0665) 562
Embleton, Alnwick
8 miles N.E of Alnwick, off A1
(18) 6038 yards/***/F

Hexham G.C
(0434) 603072
Spital Park, Hexham
1 mile W. of Hexham, off the A69
(18) 6026 yards/***/D/H

Magdalene Fields G.C
(0289) 306384
Berwick-Upon-Tweed
5 minutes walk from town centre
(18) 6551 yards/***/E

Morpeth G.C
(0670) 519980
The Common, Morpeth
1 mile S. of Morpeth on the A197
(18) 6215 yards/***/D/H

Newbiggin-By-The-Sea G.C
(0670) 817344
Newbiggin-by-the-Sea
9 miles E. of Morpeth on the A197
(18) 6423 yards/***/E

Ponteland G.C
(0661) 22689
53 Bell Villas, Ponteland
2 miles N. of airport on A696
(18) 6512 yards/**/B

Prudhoe G.C
(0661) 32466
Eastwood Park, Prudhoe
12 miles W. of Newcastle on the A695
(18) 5812 yards/**/E

Rothbury G.C
(0669) 20718
Old Racecourse, Rothbury, Morpeth
Leave A697 for B6344 to Rothbury
(9) 5146 yards/***(not Sat)/F

Seahouses G.C
(0665) 720794
Beadnell Road, Seahouses
Take B1340 from Bamburgh for Seahouses
(18) 5336 yards/**/F

Slaley Hall G.& C.C
(0434) 673691
Slaley, Hexham
7 miles south of Corbridge off A68
(18) 6995 yards/***/F

Stocksfield G.C
(0661) 843041
New Ridley, Stocksfield
On A695 between Corbridge and Prudhoe
(18) 5594 yards/**/F/M

Warkworth G.C
(0665) 711596 Warkworth
Take A1068 from Felton to Warkworth
(9) 5856 yards/***/E

Wooler G.C
Dodd Law, Doddington, Wooler
2 miles N.E of town on the Berwick Rd
(9) 6353 yards/***/E

CLEVELAND

Billingham G.C
(0642) 554494
Sandy Lane, Billingham
Near the town centre
(18) 6034 yards/***/D

Castle Eden & Peterlee G.C
(0429) 836220
Castle Eden, Hartlepool
At junction of A19 and A181
(18) 6293 yards/***/D

Cleveland G.C
(0642) 471798
Queen Street, Redcar
Through Coatham off the A1042
(18) 6707 yards/***/D/H

Eaglescliffe G.C
(0642) 780098
Yarm Road, Eaglescliffe, Stockton on Tees
On the A135 from Stockton
(18) 6045 yards/**/D

Hartlepool G.CC
(0429) 274398
Hart Warren, Hartlepool
At N. end of Hartlepool, off King Osway Drive
(18) 6215 yards/***(not Sun)/D/H

Middlesbrough G.C
(0642) 311515/316430
Brass Castle Lane, Marton, Middlesbrough
5 miles S. of the town
(18) 6106 yards/**(not Tues)/D/M

Middlesbrough Municipal G.C
(0642) 315361
Ladgate Lane, Middlesbrough
Take A19 via A174 to Ackham
(18) 6314 yards/***/E

Saltburn-By-Sea G.C
(0287) 22812
Guisborough Road, Hobb Hill, Saltburn-by-Sea
1 mile from centre of town on the B1268
(18) 5803 yards/***/F/M

Seaton Carew G.C
(0429) 266249
Tees Road, Seaton Carew, Hartlepool
3 miles S. of the town off the A178
(18) 6802 yards/***/F/M

Teesside G.C
(0642) 616516
Acklam Road, Thornaby
1 mile from the A19 on the A1130
(18) 6472 yards/**(pm only)/E

Wilton G.C
(0642) 465265
Wilton Castle, Redcar
4 miles W. of Redcar off the A174
(18) 6019 yards/***(not Sat)/D

APPLEBY MANOR COUNTRY HOUSE HOTEL

There are two things which keep people returning time and again to the beautiful market town of Appleby-in-Westmorland.

Firstly, there's the opportunity to enjoy a memorable round of golf on the 18-hole moorland course. The panoramic views which surround you are truly splendid and the course is a pleasure to play, with superb greens and just enough variety and challenge to keep you happily satisfied for all of its 5895 yards. Secondly, there's nowhere nicer to return to after a rewarding day's golf than the relaxing and friendly three-star Appleby Manor Country House Hotel, just a few minutes drive from the course, the hotel is set in wooded grounds overlooking Appleby Castle with views which are equally impressive as those on the course.

You can relax tired muscles in a variety of ways in the hotels super little indoor leisure club equipped with a heated pool, jacuzzi, sauna, solarium and steam-room. And in the lovely restaurant you'll be pleasantly surprised by the abundance of good food served up by your talented chef.

The cocktail bar with its impressive range of over 70 single-malt whiskies will keep you occupied after dinner and you'll find everything you need in your comfortable bedroom including remote-control colour TV with film channel, tea/coffee facilities, fully-tiled private bathroom, direct-dial telephone and hair-dryer.

Great value special breaks of two days or more are available all year round at the hotel, with golf booked direct with the club. Please telephone for a full-colour brochure and all the details.

Appleby Manor Country House Hotel
Appleby-In-Westmorland
Cumbria CA16 6JD
Tel: (07683) 51571
Fax: (07683) 52888

AVON

EASTCOTE COTTAGE,
Crossways Knapp Road, Thornbury, Bristol, Tel: (0454) 413106
Three comfortable bedrooms with modern ameneties are offered by this charming, unpretentious guesthouse. The M4/M3 interchange is conveniently near, although thankfully not too near!

FOUNTAIN HOUSE,
9/11 Fountain Buildings, Lansdown Road, Bath, Tel: (0225) 338622
Fountain House is Bath's first all-suite hotel, offering a combination of the comfort of a conventional hotel with the independence and privacy of one's own home. A central situation gives quick and easy access to the city's array of historical attractions.

HIGHWAYS HOUSE,
143 Wells Road, Bath, Tel: (0225) 21238
Bath is a holiday centre that thousands of tourists make for annually, and it is a safe bet that Highways House has received a good few of them. A guest lounge and nicely decorated breakfast room are doubtless part of the attraction.

OAKLEIGH GUESTHOUSE,
19 Upper Oldfield Park, Bath, Tel: (0225) 339193
Only ten miles from the city centre, Oakleigh is a comfortable distance from the majority of Bath's architectural glories. All rooms have TV and tea/coffee making facilities and most have private bathrooms.

BEDFORDSHIRE

CHURCH,
41 High Street, Roxton, Tel: (0234) 870234
Moderate prices do not conceal moderate standard accommodation in this particular instance, and Church can be thoroughly recommended in all respects.

CLARENDON HOUSE HOTEL,
25/27 Ampthill Road, Bedford, Tel: (0234) 266054
For travellers requiring a restful bed for the night and a sensible, unpretentious meal, this hotel should fit most people's bill.

HERTFORD HOUSE HOTEL,
57 De Parys Avenue, Bedford, Tel: (0234) 50007
Mouth-watering breakfasts served on the first floor dining room are a feature of this clean, comfortable hotel. The atmosphere is invariably friendly and relaxed.

LAWS HOTEL,
Turvey, Bedford, Tel: (023 064) 213
A popular restaurant and splendid gardens are particularly notable characteristics of the Laws Hotel. It is also ideally situated for all central amenities.

BERKSHIRE

AERON PRIVATE HOTEL,
191 Kentwood Hill, Tilehurst, Tel: (0734) 424119
This well-run guesthouse is conveniently situated for the town centre and provides clean, tidy rooms all of which have colour television, direct-dial telephones and tea/coffee making facilities.

BRIDGE COTTAGE,
Station Road, Woolhampton, Reading, Tel: (0734) 713138
This picturesque riverside cottage contains exposed oak beams and an olde-worlde atmosphere gives added charm. Disabled guests are welcome.

GREEN MEADOWS,
Bucklebury, Reading, Tel: (0734) 713353
A warm welcome is guaranteed at this pleasant country manor that is set in its own substantial grounds. Bedrooms are relaxing and comfortable, and Heathrow is within easy travelling distance.

GREENWAYS,
Garden Close Lane, Newbury, Tel: (0635) 40496
Conveniently located for London bound travellers, this well-appointed country house will make every guest feel quite at home. Excellent facilities include an outdoor swimming pool and relaxing guests lounge.

LYNDRICK HOUSE,
The Avenue, Ascot, Tel: (0344) 883520
Set in a peaceful residential area, this pleasant, five bedroomed house is only ten minutes drive form Wentworth Golf Club. Meals are served in an elegant conservatory and bedrooms have colour TV and tea/coffee making facilities.

PILGRIMS REST GUEST HOUSE,
Oxford Road, Newbury, Tel: (0635) 40694
This medium-sized guesthouse provides comfortable accommodation in a convenient location, only minutes from the town centre. All rooms are tastefully furnished and ensuite accommodation is available.

ST MARYS HOUSE,
Church Steet, Kintbury, Tel: (0488) 58551
Originally a Victorian schoolhouse, this splendid establishment offers seven comfortable rooms including some that are ensuite. A TV lounge and drinks licence ensure a relaxing stay for every visitor.

SUNDIAL HOUSE,
Buccleuch Road, Datchet, Nr Windsor, Tel: (0753) 47090
Sundial House was once the coach house of the Duchess of Buccleuch. Built in the eighteenth century, it is now a tasteful and elegant guesthouse, offering four bedrooms, all with ensuite facilities. Windsor Castle is within one mile.

BUCKINGHAMSHIRE

CLIFTON LODGE HOTEL,
210 West Wycombe Road, Tel: (0494) 440095,
Recently refurbished and modernised, this small hotel offers a high standard of accommodation and food. A friendly welcome and attentive staff are other excellent features.

ELMS COUNTRY HOUSE,
The Elms, Radnage, Nr. Stokenchurch, Tel: (0494) 482175
This elegant and well appointed guesthouse offers accommodation of an uncommonly high standard. Set in an area of Outstanding Natural Beauty, the Elms reflects the atmosphere of a bygone age.

FOXHILL,
Kingsey, Tel: (0844) 291650
A farmhouse dating back to the seventeenth century, Foxhill provides elegant bedrooms and a splendid garden, complete with ornamental pond. Guests will be made most welcome.

POLETREES FARM,
Brill, Nr Aylesbury, Tel: (0844) 238276
The charm and elegance of a 500 year-old farmhouse are immediately apparent in this popular guesthouse. Accommodation is spruce and thoughtful, and the farmhouse meals are worth a visit in themselves.

CAMBRIDGESHIRE

CHISWICK HOUSE,
Chiswick End, Meldreth, Royston, Tel: (0763) 60242
This impressive black and white timbered house dates as far back as the fourteenth century. It is even believed that King James I used the house as a hunting lodge. Nowadays, the emphasis has shifted to comfortable accommodation and friendly service.

DYKELANDS GUESTHOUSE,

157 Mowbray Road, Cambridge, Tel: (0223) 244300

Both the city of Cambridge and the surrounding countryside are reached with ease from this well-appointed guesthouse. The majority of rooms are ensuite and all are equipped with radio, TV and tea/coffee making facilities.

HARTFORD COTTAGE,

Longstaff Way, Hartford, Huntingdon, Tel: (0480) 54116

Splendid gardens form an engaging backdrop to this spacious, homely guesthouse. The surrounding countryside is justifiably well documented and London is little more than an hour away.

KIRKWOOD HOUSE,

172 Chesterton Road, Cambridge, Tel: (0223) 313874

The charms of Cambridge are enough to warrant a book in itself. Suffice to say that the visitor staying at Kirkwood House is highly unlikely to suffer from boredom. The city centre is a mere ten minutes walk.

MILLSIDE COTTAGE,

9 Mill Street, Houghton, Tel: (0480) 64456

Service and cleanliness are everywhere in evidence at Millside Cottage, a tribute to the conscientious and welcoming proprietors. Houghton itself is a extremely picturesque and is surrounded by villages of equal charm.

CHESHIRE

AMBASSADOR PRIVATE HOTEL,

13 Bath Street, Southport, Tel: (0704) 543998

Selecting a hotel in Southport can be a daunting experience, but all those confused tourists can rest assured that the Ambassador will not prove an erroneous choice. All rooms are ensuite and the elegant town centre is only minutes away.

SHIRE COTTAGE,

Benches Lane, Chisworth, Hyde, Cheshire, Tel: 061-427 2377 (daytime) (04578) 66536 (after 4 pm)

This modern bungalow affords magnificent views over Etherow Country Park. An ideal location makes it convenient for Manchester Airport, city centre, the Peak District, Kinder Scout and various Stately Homes. Early breakfasts can be arranged.

SUNNINGDALE HOTEL,

85 Leyland Road, Southport, Tel: (0704) 538673

Weary golfers will find that returning from the local clubhouse to this guesthouse involves minimal effort. For lovers of less energetic pursuits, the guesthouse offers a pool table, dartboard and spacious lounge bar.

CORNWALL

AVIARY COURT,

Mary's Well, Redruth, Tel: (0209) 842256

This popular guesthouse stands on the edge of Illogen woods in its own extensive grounds. Some of the comfortable bedrooms are ensuite and guests can also enjoy a bar and real fire in an agreeable lounge.

BEACH DUNES HOTEL,

Ramoth Way, Perranporth, Tel: (0872) 57226

This family hotel is an ideal base for exploration of the fabulous Cornish coastline. Food served here is nutritious and imaginative, and vegetarians can also be catered for.

CARNSON HOUSE HOTEL,

East Terrace, Tel: (0736) 65589

Conveniently situated for the town centre and local amenites, Carnson House offers eight well-appointed bedrooms, all of which have central heating and tea/coffee makers. Many local attractions, including St Michaels Mount, are within easy reach.

EAST CORNWALL FARMHOUSE,

Fullaford Road, E.Cornwall, Tel: (0579) 50018

A former Count House set in the beautiful Silver Valley, East Cornwall Farmhouse is particularly popular for imaginative cooking prepared using local and home-grown produce. All bedrooms have colour TV and tea/coffee making facilities and two are ensuite. Cotehele House is only two miles away, whilst for golfers the tremendous St Mellion complex is only ten minutes drive away.

HIGH MASSETTS,

Cadgwith, Helston, Tel: (0326) 290571

This extremely comfortable establishment offers fabulous views over a sandy cove which offers safe bathing, fishing and skin-diving. Accommodation is equally impressive and all bedrooms have modern amenities and tea/coffee makers.

MANOR FARM,

Crackington, Nr. Bude, Tel: (08403) 304

This manor house is steeped in history. Built in the eleventh century, it belonged at one time to The Earl of Mortain, half brother to William the Conqueror. Today's accommodation is highly acclaimed and guests also have the benefit of attractive gardens.

OLD SCHOOLHOUSE,

St. Ervan, Padston, Wadebridge, Tel: (0841) 540811

Hidden away in an historic country lane, the Old Schoolhouse retains both its original character and the old school bell! Furnishings and rooms are both of a very high standard.

PERRAN HOUSE,

Fore Street, Tel: (0726) 882066

This well appointed guesthouse is extremely convenient for local amenities and places of interest for Cornwall's many tourists. Cream teas in summer are an added and tempting inducement.

RASHLEIGH ARMS,

Quay Road, Tel: (0726) 73635

Excellent value is always worth seeking out and this attractive inn will not fail to please. Rooms are modern and well-kept and real ale is always on tap (not in the bedrooms though!).

ROSEBUD COTTAGE,

Bossiney, Tel: (0840) 770861

Accommodation and food are both highly recommended at this attractive Cornish cottage guesthouse. Three comfortable bedrooms are equipped with modern facilities and tea/coffee makers.

TREVISPIAN-VEAN FARM HOUSE,

Trevispean-Vean, Erme, Truro, Tel: (0872) 79514

Twelve comfortable bedrooms, most of them ensuite, are provided for the benefit of guests at this highly recommended and picturesque farmhouse. Trevispean-Vean is perfectly situated for excursions to both coast and countryside.

CUMBRIA

BESSIESTOWN FARM,

Penton, Carlisle, Tel: (0228) 577219

A friendly Northern welcome paves the way for an enjoyable stay at this beef and sheep rearing farm that overlooks the nearby Scottish borders. All seven rooms are ensuite and are furnished with taste.

LYNWOOD GUESTHOUSE,

Broad Street, Windermere, Tel: (05394) 42550

Six nicely furnished bedrooms make this Victorian house popular with discerning Lakeland visitors. A pleasant TV lounge provides entertainment for the weary and weather-beaten.

THE OLD RECTORY,

Bolton Gate, Tel: (09657) 647

Dating back all the way to the fifteenth century, the Old Rectory can be found in the village of Bolton Gate, midway between Carlisle and Cockermouth. Fabulous views and a garden orchard will provide glorious memories.

DERBYSHIRE

DALES AND PEAKS HOTEL,
Old Road, Darley Dale, Tel: (0629) 733775
Set in the Derwent valley, the Dales and Peaks is unsurprisingly a great favourite for walkers and riders. Accommodation is both thoughtfully conceived and moderately priced.

DANNAH FARM COUNTRY GUESTHOUSE,
Bowmans Lane, Shottle, Tel: (0773) 550273
If character, atmosphere and quite superb home cooking are your requirements for a suitable abode to stay, then there is absolutely no danger of Dannah Farm failing to live up to your expectations.

LE CHEVALIER BISTRO RESTAURANT,
2 Borough Street, Derby, Tel: (0332) 812005
Although rarely uncomfortably overcrowded, this city centre bistro is sufficiently busy to create an animated and friendly atmosphere. A number of bedrooms are available for those who wish to extend their socialising.

PACKHORSE,
Tansely, Tel: (0629) 582781
A feeling of splendid isolation can be the happy consequence of a stay at this comfortable, secluded farmhouse. Meticulously maintained gardens add a further agreeable dimension.

PEVERIL OF THE PEAK,
Dovedale, Thorpe, Ashbourne, Tel: (033 529) 333
This is a striking country hotel set in eleven acres of grounds below The Thorpe Cloud hill at the gateway to Dovedale. Rooms are spacious and contain every modern amenity.

DEVON

BUCKLEIGH LODGE,
135 Bayview Road, Westward Ho! Tel: (0237) 475988
Golfers are often in evidence at this popular guesthouse which stands on the outskirts of the attractive village of Westward Ho!. However, less active visitors will find the accommodation on offer just as stylish.

CHERRYBROOK HOTEL,
Tavistock, Tel: (0822) 88260
An agreeably furnished lounge bar provides the opportunity for viewing the changing moods of the moors from a position of lazy comfort. The warm and attentive service will not increase any desire to depart.

CRESTA,
26 Sticklepath Hill, Barnstaple, Tel: (0271) 74022
An accommodating and welcoming guesthouse, Cresta is only one mile from the centre of Barnstaple. Features include a colourful lounge and ample parking.

DOCTORS,
Halberton Road, Willand, Tel: (0884) 820525
An intriguingly named property, Doctors is in fact a character-rich farmhouse and visitors should not be deterred by the name. Ninety acres of grounds should provide for plenty of active pursuits.

HEASLEY HOUSE,
Heasley Mill, Devon, Tel: (05984) 213
Overlooking a babbling mill stream, Heasley House is a charming edifice from the outside, and the antique filled interior is equally appealing. Accommodation is clean and well-kept.

HUGHSLADE,
Okehampton, Tel: (0837) 52883
The glories of Dartmoor and the A30 road have little in common but both are located close to this attractive farmhouse. In the event of anybody tiring of the former, a full-sized snooker table provides indoor recreation.

HUXTABLE FARM,
West Buckland, Barnstaple, North Devon, Tel: (05986) 254
Huxtable Farm is a listed medieval longhouse and features a barn furnished with antiques. It is ideally situated for Saunton, Royal North Devon and other golf courses, and various Stately Homes and gardens can be explored by non-playing escorts.

LODGE HILL,
Ashley, Tiverton, Tel: (0884) 252907
The town of Tiverton is easily reached from this spacious farmhouse that sits astride a hilltop in The Exe Valley. Nine rooms are generally available.

MERTON HOUSE,
Beaford, Tel: (08053) 364
This charming Georgian residence offers unobtrusive comfort from April to October, although prospective guests may be advised to visit during the summer months when the grass tennis court is most likely to be in use.

ROWDEN BARTON,
Roundswell, Barnstaple, Tel: (0271) 44365
Friendliness and genuine attention to every detail make this farmhouse a tourist's favourite. Good food and splendid bedrooms confirm the opinion.

SUNNYMEDE,
24 New North Road, Exeter, Tel: (0392) 73844
Yet another Georgian property, this one with the advantage of being located in the neighbourhood of extensive shopping facilities. Exeter offers an abundance of other amenities.

THATCHED COTTAGE RESTAURANT AND HOTEL,
9 Crossley Moor Road, Kingsteignton, Newton Abbot, Tel: (0626) 65650
A host of modern comforts, including ensuite bedrooms, make this sixteenth century cottage an engaging mix of the new and the old. The cuisine is imaginative and often quite adventurous.

THE BLENHEIM HOTEL,
Bovey Tracey, South Devon, Tel: (0626) 832422
This is a family run hotel on the edge of the Dartmoor National Park. Local attractions are many – The Manor House Morehampstead is six miles away, Stover is only one mile away and Teignmouth, Chelston and Torquay golf courses are within ten miles.

WIGHAM,
Morchard Bishop, Tel: (03637) 350
Extensive and sympathetic restoration has made this one of the county's most acclaimed guesthouses. Patrons will not be disappointed, staying in a four poster bed in a sixteenth century thatched longhouse should be somewhere near most people's idea of fun!

WOOLSGROVE,
Sandford, Crediton, Tel: (0363) 84246
The majority of moderately-priced accommodation in Devon seems to be in farmhouses and no-one should bemoan that fact. This is another fine example with yet more spectacular views.

DORSET

CRANSTON COTTAGE,
25 Church Street, Bridport, Tel: (0308) 56240
The sandy beaches and ice-cream sellers of West Bay are only a stroll away from Cranston Cottage. In case more secluded sunbathing is preferred, a patio complete with sun loungers awaits all lazy guests!

OLD RECTORY,
St Johns Hill, St James, Shaftsbury, Tel: (0747) 2003
The most succulent Cordon Bleu cuisine is a feature of this highly recommended guesthouse. Elegant furnishings and a friendly ambiance simply make the food taste even better.

ENGLAND
GOURMET GOLF

PARKLANDS HOTEL,
4 Rushton Crescent, Bournemouth, Tel: (0202) 552529
Parklands Hotel is situated on the edge of lovely Meyrick Park with its fine golf course and facilities for tennis, bowls and squash. Bournemouth, with its shops, woods and golden sands is only minutes away. Parklands also specialises in arranging tailored golfing packages.

VARTREES HOUSE,
Moreton, Crossways, Dorchester, Tel: (0305) 852704
The burial place of Lawrence of Arabia is contained within the pretty village of Moreton. The surrounding countryside is just as scenic and nobody will regret a visit to Vartrees House.

DURHAM

BURNBRAE,
Leazes Villas, Burnopfield, Tel: (0207) 70432
Burnbrae is pleasantly situated in the heart of Burnopfield village and is surrounded by country parks, bowling greens, tennis courts and golf courses. Newcastle and Hexham racecourses are within striking distance, as are Durham, Beamish Museum and Hadrians Wall.

COURT PRIVATE HOTEL,
Yarm Road, Stockton-on-Tees, Tel: (0642) 604483
This impressive edifice is conveniently located for the busy town centre and provides spotless accommodation at reasonable prices. A pleasant dining room serves up tasty fare.

CROXDALE,
Spennymoor, Tel: (0388) 815727
A roadside inn with an agreeable lounge bar, the Croxdale also possesses a number of pleasantly furnished bedrooms which make for a refreshing stopover.

DUN COW,
High Street, Sedgefield, Tel: (0740) 20894
Excellent cuisine and a warm welcome are the trademarks of this popular and well-established inn. Bedrooms lack for nothing and Sedgewick racecourse is a nearby attraction.

GABLES,
Front Street, Haswell Plough, Tel: 091-526 2982
The cathedral city of Durham provides a wealth of things to do and see, and The Gables makes a pleasant headquarters for all types of stay. Rooms are well appointed and a dining room of real character adds extra ambiance.

ESSEX

BOVILLS HALL,
Ardleigh, Colchester, Tel: (0206) 230217
Accommodation at this splendid manor house is both well appointed and equipped to a high standard. The proprietor obviously takes a great pride in her establishment, and equally so in her guests.

NEWHOUSE FARM,
Radwinter, Saffron Walden, Tel: (079987)211
This grade II listed farmhouse is truly a pleasure to behold, with Georgian and Tudor features blending serenely into gardens, lake and moat. Renowned local fare will not take long to seek out.

SWAN HOTEL,
Maldon High Street, Maldon, Tel: (0621) 53170
This hotel is far from opulent, but it does offer clean accommodation in a friendly atmosphere, and food that will satisfy the most ravenous of diners.

WHITE HART,
Bocking End, Braintree, Tel: (0376) 21401
For those wishing a high-standard, bustling hotel close to the city-centre, the White Hart may prove an irresistible choice. Architecture – for the enthusiasts – is part Tudor and part Georgian.

GLOUCESTERSHIRE

HILL FARM GUESTHOUSE,
Bishops Norton, Nr. Gloucester, Tel: (0452) 730351
Cream teas on a sun terrace is an idyllic situation for most holidaymakers. Add to this a thatched, oak timbered farmhouse dating back to the fifteenth century and you have Hill Farm – an excellent guesthouse.

Artist: **Gilroy** **THE HATTRICK** *Courtesy of:* **Burlington Gallery**

ENGLAND
GOURMET GOLF

SEVERN BANK,
Minsterworth, Tel: (0452) 750357
Severn Bank enjoys a picturesque location some four miles west of Gloucester. A fine country house set in six acres of grounds on the banks of the Severn, the Forest of Dean, the Wye Valley and the Cotswolds are easily reachable. This is bed and breakfast at its best.

MILTON HOUSE HOTEL,
12 Royal Parade, Bayshill Road, Cheltenham, Tel: (0242) 582601
Set in a quiet residential area, Milton House is close to both golf courses and racecourses, as well as a wide range of local amenities.

NORTHFIELD,
Cirencester Road, Northleach, Cheltenham, Tel: (0451) 60427
The small market town of Northleach is an attractive and convenient backdrop for this well-established guesthouse. Three comfortable bedrooms guarantee a restful nights sleep.

WOODLEYS,
Toddington, Nr. Winchcombe, Cheltenham, Tel: (0242) 621313
An ideal centre for touring the Cotswolds and surrounding areas, the Woodleys has undergone extensive refurbishment and is one of the areas most distinguished guesthouses. Moderate prices make it too good to miss!

GUERNSEY

ANN-DAWN PRIVATE HOTEL,
Route des Capelles, St Sampson, Tel: (0481) 725606
This hotel will find approval with guests who are seeking traditional comforts and a dignified atmosphere. Elegant accommodation gives way to splendid lawned and landsaped gardens.

LA GIROUETTE COUNTRY HOTEL,
Perelle, Tel: (0481) 63269
Perrelle Bay is only minutes away from this comfortable and accommodating guesthouse. Both bedrooms and public rooms are spacious and well-appointed.

LES OZOUETS LODGE,
Ozouets Road, St Peters Port, Tel: (0481) 21288
Outstanding cuisine is prepared and served by the chef patron, complemented by an extensive wine list. Impressive gardens feature putting and bowling greens, and a tennis court.

MIDHURST HOUSE,
Candie Road, St Peter Port, Tel: (0481) 724391
It is difficult to know what to highlight most in this attractive cottage – all round excellence is the order of the day. Bedrooms, cooking, surroundings and service are all of the highest order.

HAMPSHIRE

CEDAR LODGE,
100 Cedar Road, Portswood, Tel: (0703) 226761
Cedar Lodge is the perfect base for either a shopping trip to Southampton or a picnic in the New Forest. The bedrooms at this popular guesthouse are spacious and the service uncommonly attentive.

CHURCH FARM HOUSE,
Barton Stacey, Winchester, Tel: (0962) 760268
Winchester is one of England's most celebrated towns, with its medieval cathedral a crowning glory. Lucky guests have the choice between staying in the main house and an adjacent coach house.

COCKLE WARREN GUESTHOUSE,
36 Seafront, Hayling Island, Tel: (0705) 464961 Such a picturesque name risks being slightly over-ambitious but in this case the reality does not disappoint. Ensuite bedrooms look out onto hens and ducks, enclosed by a white picket fence, and to the sea beyond.

KINGS HEAD HOTEL,
Hursley, Tel: (0962) 75208
An excellent place for a roadside drink, the Kings Head also offers a number of spacious bedrooms and some extremely tasty food.

NIRVANA HOTEL,
384-386 Winchester Road, Bassett, Southampton, Tel: (0703) 760474
Personally run by the proprietors Douglas and Eileen Dawson, guests are assured of a warm and friendly welcome at this comfortable hotel. As well as the extensive facilities, a superb conference room is a recent addition.

PLUM TREE COTTAGE,
Sandleheath, Fordingbridge, Tel: (0425) 53032
Only a few minutes from the new forest, Plum Tree is a fairytale thatched cottage that offers such charming features as an inglenook fireplace and a wood stove. The cottage may be rented for self catering holidays.

WHEATSHEAF HOUSE,
25 Gosport Street, Lymington, Tel: (05906) 79208
Once a seventeenth century tavern, Wheatsheaf House is now a twentieth century guesthouse of some distinction. The market town of Lymington is most attractive and is convenient for The New Forest.

YEW TREE COTTAGE,
Lower Baybridge Lane, Baybridge, Owslebury, Tel: (096274) 254
A secluded setting some six miles out of Winchester are the tempting credentials of Yew Tree Cottage. Antique furniture and oak beams add an air of authenticity, and are almost as impressive as the home cooking.

HEREFORDSHIRE

LEIGH COURT,
Leigh Sinton, Tel: (0886) 32275
Superb countryside makes this an ideal base for active-minded tourists, whilst those in search of more tranquility will be equally impressed by a billiards room, tithe barn and library.

LION,
Clifton upon Teme, Tel: (08865) 617
One of the county's oldest coaching inns, the Lion offers traditional and well maintained bedrooms, and a menu of some style.

PARK LODGE,
Eye, Leominster, Tel: (0568) 5711
A popular retreat with visitors who appreciate simple, clean accommodation and friendly service, Park Lodge enjoys a quiet location, yet is within easy reach of civilisation, for those who wish it.

PETERSTOW COUNTRY HOUSE
Peterstow, Ross-on-Wye, Herefordshire, Tel: (0989) 62826
An award winning restaurant of local prestige graces this elegantly restored Georgian rectory, which is set in 28 acres of woodlands and pasture and offers individually designed, en-suite accommodation.

THE RED LION,
The Red Lion, Herefordshire, Tel: (09817) 303
This is one of the leading fishing hotels on the Wye, controlling its own water and offering one of the longest privately owned stretches in the country. Accommodation is pleasant and the food delicious.

HERTFORDSHIRE

ARDMORE HOUSE,
54 Lesford Road, St. Albans, Tel: (0727) 59313
This is a large, detached house that dates from the Edwardian era and has retained much of the tradition and elegance from that age. Both Clarence Park and the city-centre are within walking distance.

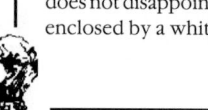

ENGLAND
GOURMET GOLF

BRIGGENS HOUSE HOTEL,
Stanstead Abbots, Nr. Ware, Tel: (027 979) 2416
Briggens House is an extremely comfortable and cultivated country house hotel. Set in its own beautiful grounds, golf, tennis and swimming can all be enjoyed by guests.

VENUS HILL FARM,
Venus Hill, Bovingdon, Tel: (0442) 833396
Three bedrooms all offer modern amenities at this three hundred year old converted farmhouse. An outdoor swimming pool provides the perfect early morning prelude to a short drive to Heathrow.

VINTAGE CORNER HOTEL,
Old Cambridge Road, Puckeridge, Tel: (0920) 822722
A modern hotel in the pretty village of Puckeridge may seem an incongruous idea; however the Vintage Corner sits easily into its environment and provides more than adequate accommodation.

HUMBERSIDE

BARMBY MOOR,
Hull Road, Barmby Moor, Tel: (0759) 302700
Accommodation and cuisine are both excellent in this immensely popular hotel. Bedrooms contain every conceivable convenience and the elegant Honeysuckle restaurant overlooks a courtyard containing a heated swimming pool.

LANGDON HOTEL,
Pembroke Terrace, Bridlington, Tel: (0262) 673065
Bridlington is mostly about the sea and there is certainly plenty of it on view from the Langdon Hotel. The public rooms are particularly alluring.

PARKWOOD HOTEL,
113 Princes' Avenue, Hull, Tel: (0482) 445610
Hull city centre is only a short bus or car journey from this well-appointed guesthouse. Rooms are well furnished and the cuisine carefully prepared.

SOUTHDOWNE HOTEL,
South Marine Drive, Bridlington, Tel: (0262) 673270
Twelve comfortable bedrooms are of a standard that will satisfy the most uncompromising of guests. The sea is constantly in view, always an important consideration in seaside resorts!

TRITON INN,
Sledmere, Tel: (0377) 86644,
Sledmere is an engaging and attractive village that proves an excellent base for a touring holiday. Food and bedrooms are both worth sampling.

ISLE OF MAN

EDELWEISS,
Queens Promenade, Douglas, Tel: (0624) 675115
Set just behind the main promenade, Edelweiss makes a relaxing and agreeable base. All bedrooms are ensuite and the lounge is equally well-appointed.

REGENT HOUSE,
The Promenade, Port Erin, Tel: (0624) 833454
This well-established hotel is a firm favourite with discerning visitors who appreciate home comforts and imaginative cooking. The hotel affords fine views of the bay.

ROSSLYN GUESTHOUSE,
3 Empire Terrace, Central Promenade, Douglas, Tel: (0624) 676056
In case the many and varied attractions of the Isle of Man become too much for the travel-weary, Rosslyn Guesthouses offers a relaxing bar and first floor television lounge.

RUTLAND HOTEL,
Queens Promenade, Douglas, Tel: (0624) 621218
The owners of this hotel take a great deal of pride in their establishment and this is reflected in a smooth running hostelry where every guest is made to feel one of the family.

JERSEY

ALMORAH HOTEL,
Lower Kings Cliff, St Helier, Tel: (0534) 21648
Virtually every bedroom at the Almorah has ensuite facilities and the furnishings are well chosen and stylish. A Breton-style dining room adds further flavour to some delicious cuisine.

CLIFF COURT HOTEL,
St Andrews Road, First Tower, Tel: (0534) 34919
An enviable position overlooking St Aubins Bay makes this quiet property a favourite with discerning holidaymakers. A lounge, bar and dining rooms will all contribute to a comfortable stay.

LAVENDER VILLA HOTEL,
Rue A Don, Grouville, Tel: (0534) 54937
The Lavender Villa is a popular venue for both locals and visitors; both are no doubt drawn by a pleasant setting, friendly atmosphere and wide selection of food and drink.

PANORAMA,
St Aubin, Tel: (0534) 45940
A highly acclaimed establishment with stunning sea views, the Panorama is in the capable hands of owners John and Jill Squinks. Guests are particularly appreciative of afternoon tea served in a silver pot on a silver tray.

KENT

CARVAL HOTEL,
56/58 London Road, Maidstone, Tel: (0622) 762100
A garden and car park are among the amenities at the Carval, a pleasant and welcoming hotel in a quiet residential setting. A well stocked bar also contains useful tourist information.

CHEQUERS INN,
Smarden, Nr. Ashford, Tel: (023377) 217
Chequers dates back to 1450 and has been inhabited since that time by a resident ghost. Walking, golf and fishing are among a multitude of local pursuits on offer.

CROMER,
194 Parrock Street, Gravesend, Tel: (0474) 361935
Gravesend appears unusually well blessed with guesthouses of fine quality, and this is a particularly notable example. All rooms are well appointed and well equipped, and public rooms are tasteful and relaxing.

DELL GUESTHOUSE,
233 Folkstone Road, Dover, Tel: (0304) 202422
Dover is a splendid place and the Dell Guesthouse is an ideal base. Rooms and service can not be faulted and breakfast is even served from 7.00am for the benefit of those wishing to catch the early morning cross-channel ferries.

DOLPHINS HOTEL AND RESTAURANT,
Dymchurch Road, New Romney, Tel: (0679) 63224
The glorious coastline of Kent can be absorbed at your own pace by staying at this popular establishment. The surrounding countryside is equally appealing and is dotted with opportunities for golf, walking and fishing.

FRITH FARM HOUSE,
Otterden, Faversham, Tel: (079589) 701
An immaculately restored Georgian farmhouse, Frith farm is pleasantly set in an area of outstanding natural beauty. The whole of magnificent Kent awaits the avid explorer.

ENGLAND
GOURMET GOLF

GREYSWOLDE HOTEL,
20 Surrey Road, Cliftonville, Margate, Tel: (0843) 223956
Only yards from the promenade, Greyswolde is an imposing Victorian Hotel whose appearance has remained largely unaltered over the last hundred years. Many of the bedrooms are ensuite.

NUMBER ONE GUESTHOUSE,
1 Castle Street, Dover, Tel: (0304) 212007
Looking out onto the majestic castle, Number One guesthouse actually dates back to 1800. Six bedrooms all possess modern amenities and tea/coffee making facilities.

OVERCLIFFE HOTEL,
15-16 The Overcliffe, Gravesend, Tel: (0474) 322131
Both bedrooms and public rooms are of a uniformly excellent standard and the level of service is no less outstanding. Amenities and facilities are within easy reach.

SUTHERLAND HOUSE,
186 London Road, Deal, Tel: (0304) 362853
This is a guesthouse of unusually high quality, offering a level of comfort and cuisine on a par with hotels of much higher aspiration. Royal St Georges, Royal Cinque Ports and Princes will entertain and test all golfing enthusiasts.

WALLETS COURT MANOR,
West Cliffe, St. Margarets, Dover, Tel: (0304) 852424
Once a home of William Pitt the Younger, this 17th century manor house enjoys a spectacular setting, looking down proudly over the White Cliffs of Dover. Oak beams and inglenook fireplaces add further charm.

WALNUT TREE FARM,
Lynsore Bottom, Upper Hardes, Nr. Canterbury, Tel: (022787) 375
Walnut Tree excels in all the things for which farmhouses are renowned – breakfast, fresh eggs, home-made bread and comfortable accommodation.

WINDYRIDGE GUESTHOUSE,
Wraik Hill, Whitstable, Tel: (0227) 263506
The benefits of a family-run guesthouse are only too obvious here – attentive and friendly service, home cooking, clean and comfortable rooms. Vegetarians are also catered for.

YORKE LODGE GUESTHOUSE,
50 London Road, Canterbury, Tel: (0227) 451243
Six nicely furnished bedrooms are at the disposal of guests at this agreeable guesthouse. A library with extensive tourist information is a thoughtful and invaluable extra.

LANCASHIRE

CULLERNE HOTEL,
55 Lightburne Avenue, St. Annes on Sea, Tel: (0253) 721753
Close to the town centre and to every facility that a visitor could wish, the Cullerne is a typically good Lancastrian guesthouse and will undoubtedly receive many return visits from satisfied guests.

FALICON FARM,
Fleet Street Lane, Hothersall, Longridge, Preston, Tel: (025484) 583
A sandstone farmhouse in an enviable setting, Falicon Farm offers modern conveniences in a traditional ambiance. All three bedrooms are ensuite and have an array of other, thoughtful facilities.

HOTEL PROSPECT,
363 Marine Road East, Morecombe, Tel: (0524) 417876
Ensuite bedrooms and a seafront location make this a favourite haunt for visitors to the region. No doubt a fair proportion of them are golfers, enticed by the areas wealth of championship courses.

HOTEL WARWICK,
394 Marine Road East, Morecombe, Tel: (0524) 418151
Morecombe still has much to offer in the way of family holidays and all guests will find that this pleasant guesthouse makes a good and practical headquarters. Added pluses are the friendly atmosphere and attentive service.

LYNSTEAD PRIVATE HOTEL,
40 King Edward Avenue, Blackpool, Tel: (0253) 51050
The challenging Blackpool North Shore Golf Club is almost within putting distance of this quiet, relaxing establishment. Away from the bright lights of town, guests appreciate the peaceful, friendly atmosphere.

Pimm PUTTING Rosenstiel's

ENGLAND
GOURMET GOLF

MAINS HALL,

Mains Lane, Little Singleton, Blackpool, Lancashire, Tel: (0253) 885130

This elegant country house hotel is a sixteenth century manor house and is steeped in history. Situated on the banks of the river Wyre, Mains Hall retains many of its original antique fittings and is convenient for golfers and many Stately Homes.

NEW CAPERNWRAY FARM,

Capernwray, Carnforth, Tel: (0524) 734 284

This is a remote location that is well worth searching for. An imposing, stone built house, New Capernwray Farm provides award-winning accommodation at reasonable prices. The food on offer has to be seen to be believed.

NORTH EUSTON HOTEL,

Esplanade, Fleetwood, Tel: (039 17) 6525

Travellers wishing to treat themselves without spending their entire holiday budget should seriously consider this fine hotel. The Lakeland Hills are distantly visible, although golfers and anglers will probably not have time to enjoy the spectacle!

ROSENEATH,

Preston road, Charnock Richard, Nr. Chorley, Tel: (0257) 791772

Roseneath can virtually guarantee a good night's sleep – unless visitors are distracted by striking views of The Pennines. Extensive grounds allow the opportunity for walking and jogging.

STRATHMORE,

305 Clifton Drive South, Lytham St Annes, Tel: (0253) 725478

Conscientous owners ensure that this guesthouse moves from strength to strength, with its central location a particular advantage. Bedrooms are spacious and well-furnished.

WYTHA FARM,

Rimington, Clitheroe, Lancaster, Tel: (0200) 445295

Panoramic views over the Ribble Valley give added appeal to this well-established and welcoming farm. Walkers would do worse than to start their journey here.

LINCOLNSHIRE

BOURNE EAU HOUSE,

30 South Street, Bourne, Tel: (0778) 423621

Bourne Eau is a handsome country home that dates back to Georgian/Elizabethan times. The friendly welcome is matched only by the superb standard of accommodation which would put many aspiring hotels to shame.

DUNS,

The Broadway, Woodhall Spa, Tel: (0526) 52969

The nearby championship golf course provides this hotel with a fair proportion of its custom although businessmen and tourists find it equally congenial. Service is particularly attentive.

DUNSTON MANOR,

Dunston, Lincoln, Tel: (0526) 20463

The small village of Dunston has ceded little to modern civilisation and Dunston Manor retains an elegant atmosphere that has little to do with urban hotels. Bedrooms are quaint and splendidly furnished but should be temporaily abandoned to taste the admirable home cooking.

MANOR HOUSE,

Nocton Road, Potterhanworth, Tel: (0522) 791288

Proudly standing in some ten acres of gardens, this elegant nineteenth century manor house contains four agreeably furnished rooms, each with radio, TV and tea/coffee making facilities. An outdoor swimming pool and summer house distinguish this establishment from the crowd.

LONDON

ABER HOTEL,

89 Crouch Hill, Hornsey, Tel: 081-340 2847

A medium-sized, family-run hotel, the Aber offers a peaceful night's sleep within easy reach of the bright lights and loud noises of central London.

BELGRAVE HOUSE HOTEL,

28-32 Belgrave Road, Tel: 071-828 1563

The Belgrave House is centrally located with easy access to Victoria stations, Buckingham Palace and the West End. All bedrooms are centrally heated and some have private facilities.

BYRON HOTEL,

36-38 Queensborough Terrace, Tel: 071-243 0987

Opposite Kensington Gardens, this acclaimed hotel aims to recapture some of the charm and elegance of Victorian England. Whatever the objectives, the results are excellent, with the interior decor particularly fine.

CHASE LODGE,

10 Park Road, Hampton Wick, Kingston-upon-Thames, Tel: 081-943 1862

This excellent and high-quality establishment, close to Kempton and Sandown racecourses, is a perfect base for avid tourists. A multitude of places of interest are within easy travelling distance, including Syon Park, Kew Gardens, Wisley, Hampton Court Palace, Windsor Castle, Osterley House and Royal Bushy Park.

CHESHAM HOUSE HOTEL,

64-66 Ebury Street, Tel: 071-730 8513

The Chesham has undergone recent and extensive refurbishment, and looks set to reap immense benefits. Service, too, is consistently courteous and helps to create an atmosphere of well-being.

CLEARVIEW HOUSE,

161 Fordwych Road, Cricklewood, Tel: 081-452 9773

Guesthouses in the capital that are set in quiet residential areas are not always over-easy to find, but this example is well worth seeking out. Accommodation is both modern and tasteful.

CRANBROOK HOTEL,

24 Coventry Road, Ilford, Essex, Tel: 081-554 6544

The occasion to pamper oneself without spending a small fortune does not arise frequently. However, this extremely comfortable suburban hotel offers some rooms with ensuite facilities and jacuzzi and, most importantly, is not excessively priced.

KNIGHTSBRIDGE HOTEL,

10 Beaufort Gardens, Knightsbridge, Tel: 071-589 9271

The first time visitor to the Knightsbridge will immediately be impressed by its elegant facade. Entering the hotel will most definitely not prove a let down, with stylish and appropriate furnishings the order of the day.

STONEHALL HOUSE,

35-37 Westcombe Park, Blackheath, Tel: 081-858 8706

Stonehall is a traditional guesthouse that will make its visitors more than welcome. A TV lounge and garden are both well used and well thought of.

WIMBLEDON HOTEL,

78 Worple Road, Wimbledon, Tel: 081-946 9265

Cosy and family run, this popular hotel is always highly praised by previous residents. Local amenities are within walking distance.

WINCHESTER HOTEL,

12 Belgravia Road, Westminster, Tel: 071-8282972

The elegance of the area is matched by this well-appointed and furnished hotel. Rooms are of a uniformly high standard and guests will leave feeling refreshed and invigorated.

NORFOLK

ABBEY HOTEL,
Church street, Wymondham, Tel: (0953) 602148
Overlooking an ancient abbey, this hotel has a reputation of combining yesterday's charm with today's comforts. For the business community there is an excellent Conference Suite and three syndicate rooms.

AMBERLEY HOUSE,
24 Eaton Road, Norwich, Tel: (0603) 57115
Although pleasantly located in a quiet residential area, Amberley House is within easy reach of the town centre, university and a challenging 18-hole golf course. All rooms have radio, TV and tea/coffee making facilities.

BARNHAM BROOM HOTEL,
Barnham Broom, Norwich, Tel: (060545) 393
Set in the beautiful valley of the river Yare, this modern hotel and sports complex has 52 luxury bedrooms plus a host of leisure facilities including two 18 hole golf courses, squash, tennis, sauna, fitness centre and indoor swimming pool.

FIELDSEND HOUSE,
Homefields Road, Hunstanton, Tel: (0485) 532593
Golf and fishing are only two of the attractions of Hunstanton, and both can be found within a short distance of this highly-recommended guesthouse. Sea views from every bedroom are certainly partly responsible for its perennial popularity.

STAITHEWAY HOUSE,
Staitheway Road, Wroxham, Tel: (06053) 3347
Welcome, bedrooms, cooking and general ambiance are all consistently high at this popular guesthouse. Needless to say, this part of the country is ideal for boat lovers and walkers.

NORTHUMBERLAND

BILTON BARNS,
Alnmouth, Tel: (0665) 830427
Set in the glorious Northumbrian countryside, this well-furnished and spacious farmhouse is only minutes away from the picturesque fishing village of Alnwick. The farmhouse food is truly excellent.

CLIVE COTTAGE,
Appletree Lane, Corbridge, Tel: (0434) 632617
A warm welcome is accompanied by pleasant accommodation and personal attention at this charming period cottage. Two bedrooms feature 4-poster beds and all rooms have tea/coffee facilities, hair dryers, and electric blankets.

HOLMHEAD FARM,
Hadrians Wall, Greenhead, via Carlisle, Tel: (06972) 402
This a truly excellent licensed guesthouse and is immensely popular with visitors to Hadrians Wall, venue of some of Britain's bloodiest history. Fabulous walks and opportunities for sightseeing abound.

KITTY FRISK HOUSE,
Corbridge Road, Hexham, Tel: (0434) 606850
The bustling and attractive market town of Hexham is only a short distance from this pleasant and welcoming establishment. Large stylish gardens and three acres of woodland offer the opportunity for some relaxing escapism.

NOTTINGHAMSHIRE

BALMORAL HOTEL,
55-57 Loughborough Street, West Bridgeford, Tel: (0602) 455020
Ardent cricket and football followers will find that this modern, efficient hotel has much to recommend it. Both The Nottingham Forest football ground and Trent Bridge cricket ground are within walking distance and the city centre is also in the close vicinity.

PARK HOTEL,
7 Waverley Street, Nottingham, Tel: (0602) 786229
A Georgian period house that still exudes an air of elegance, this city centre hotel has much to commend it, including a high proportion of ensuite bedrooms.

TITCHFIELD GUESTHOUSE,
300/302 Chesterfield Road North, Mansfield, Notts, Tel: (0623) 810356
Two large houses converted into one, Titchfield is a family run guesthouse offering eight bedrooms, a T.V. lounge and drinks facilities. A warm and friendly welcome is extended to all guests.

UPTON FIELDS HOTEL,
Southwell, Tel: (0636) 812303
Conveniently located for visitors to both Southwell and Upton, the Upton Fields Hotel comes highly recommended for a number of reasons, not least excellent bedrooms and highly-edible food.

OXON

COURTFIELD PRIVATE HOTEL,
367 Iffley Road, Oxford, Tel: (00865) 242991
Conveniently and pleasantly located in a central residential area, the Courtfield is within easy reach of the city centre and its many attractions. Excellent service is always provided.

CRAVEN,
Fernham Road, Ufington, Tel: (036782) 449
Half-way between Oxford and Swindon, this seventeenth century thatched and beamed house offers an extremely relaxed atmosphere. Choose between open log fires in the winter and an attractive terrace and gardens in the summer.

FALLOWFIELDS,
Southmoor with Kingston Bagpuize, Abingdon, Tel: (0865) 820416
Only ten miles from Oxford, this lovely country house is set in twelve acres and offers an outdoor pool, croquet and tennis. Golfers are spoilt for choice with various courses in the proximity including a splendid 36 holes at Frilford Heath.

FELDON HOUSE,
Lower Brailes, Nr. Banbury, Tel: (0060885) 580
Set in beautiful grounds, this imposing house dates back to the seventeenth century and has retained much of its original charm. Rooms are spacious and tidy and the food prepared by the owners is quite superb.

FULFORD HOUSE,
The Green, Culworth, Nr. Banbury, Tel: (029576) 355
Personal attention and service are the hallmarks of this highly recommended guesthouse. Guests will be made to feel quite at home and should find time to explore the delightful gardens.

THREE PIGEONS,
Great Milton, Tel: (0844) 279247
This country inn makes a friendly and enjoyable stopping place for travellers. Three comfortable bedrooms are all well equipped and home cooking is also worth sampling.

DEVELOPING FOR THE FUTURE

Peterstone Golf Course, South Wales marketed in 1992/3 by Savills Leisure

Chartered surveyors within Savills Rural Leisure Division have provided specialist property advice to many of the UK's golf and hotel enterprises, including a number in this book.

We are experienced in the valuation, purchase and sale of a wide range of leisure facilities.

Our Rural Leisure Division operates from our London Head Office as well as from regional bases in Banbury, Bath, Chelmsford, Edinburgh, Stamford and Salisbury. We have access to detailed local property knowledge through our numerous country offices spread through England and Scotland.

Our international contacts are extensive, through associates in Spain, France, Austria, Italy, Germany, Portugal and Hong Kong. We are currently involved in leisure work in France, Spain, Portugal, the Caribbean and Madeira. We also anticipate involvement in leisure development in Eastern Block countries in 1993.

'Following the Fairways' identifies some of the finest golf courses and hotels in the country, a number of which are sensitive conversions of prestigious country properties. Savills are highly experienced in dealing with such properties and we are able to combine our leisure expertise with this knowledge to provide a first class service.

Savills Leisure are also extensively involved in advice on new golf and hotel development projects, ranging from small golf driving ranges to some of the largest golf, hotel and country club complexes in the country. Many of these are likely to be completed during 1993, and we would hope to see the best of them included in the 1994 edition of this book.

Savills Leisure also offer a Building Consultancy and Project Management Service for buildings associated with leisure developments. We have extensive experience in the design and construction of new buildings from golf driving ranges to golf clubhouses to new hotels with ancillary leisure facilities. In conjunction with our specialist planning team we are able to provide advice from the conception of a development, through obtaining detailed planning permission, to construction and fitting out of the property. These skills are similarly applied to alteration and refurbishment projects to upgrade existing buildings of character, so as to ensure that the quality of facilities is maintained in the increasingly competitive leisure market.

Our experience in the marketing and sale of a wide range of leisure properties enables us to provide detailed advice on the valuation and purchase of leisure facilities.

Savills Marketing Department, based in London, provides detailed advice on brochure design and effective media purchasing, so as to ensure high quality presentation of all properties offered for sale on behalf of clients, by Savills Leisure.

For further information on Savills Rural Leisure services, or for informal advice in the first instance, contact:

Alan Plumb Bsc. FRICS, Savills, Banbury (0295 263535)
Henry Richards ARICS, Savills, London (071 499 8644)
Ian Simpson Bsc. ARICS, Savills, Chelmsford (0245 269311)

L E I S U R E

DEVELOPING FOR THE FUTURE

Orchardleigh Park, Nr Bath, a golf and hotel project under development

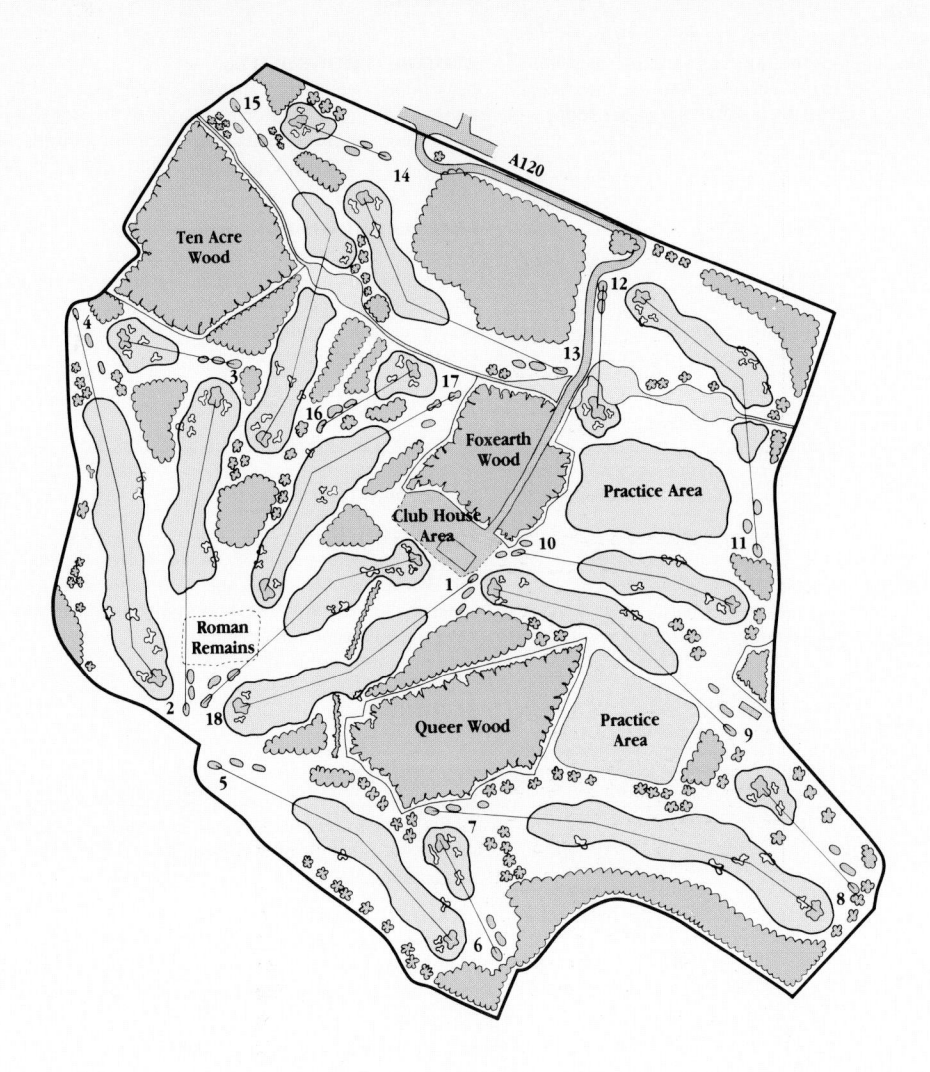

Illustrative layout of proposed golf course at Albury End; designed by Howard Swan, marketed by Savills Leisure in 1992

ENGLAND
GOURMET GOLF

SHROPSHIRE

BELDEVERE GUESTHOUSE,
Burway Road, Church Stretton, Tel: (0694) 722232
Church Stretton is a delightful village and Beldevere is an integral and much admired part of it. Guests risk spending little time there, however, as Shopshire has much to offer.

NEW FARM,
Muckleton, Nr. Shawbury, Telford, Tel: (0939) 250358
The tranquillity and beauty of the Shropshire-Welsh border – not that it has always been so peaceful-is the setting for this splendid farmhouse. Hawkstone Park is close by and the historic towns of Chester and Ludlow are equally convenient.

OLD POST OFFICE RESTAURANT,
9 The Square, Clun, Nr. Craven Arms, Tel: (05884) 687
Careful restoration has resulted in an imaginative and attractive restaurant whose fare is quite delicious. Accommodation is provided for those who really over-indulge.

SANDFORD HOUSE HOTEL,
St Julian's Friars, Shrewsbury, Tel: (0743) 343829
Only a short distance from the town centre, Sandford House occupies a quiet setting and has many pleasant country walks within easy reach. Bedrooms are tastefully decorated and the public rooms are no less agreeable.

TANKERVILLE LODGE,
Stiperstones, Nr. Minsterley, Shrewsbury, Tel: (0743) 791401
This is surely one of the area's most friendly and welcoming establishments. Guests are made to feel totally at home and are provided plenty of sustenance with which to tackle the nearby Stiperstone Ridge and Devils Chair.

STAFFORDSHIRE

HILLCREST,
3 Leighton Road, Uttoxeter, Tel: (0889) 564627
A hilltop location provides guests with extensive and impressive views of the surrounding countryside. Most rooms are ensuite and all are comfortably furnished.

LARKSFIELD COUNTRY ACCOMMODATION,
Stoniford Lane, Aston, Tel: (063081) 7069
This will prove an ideal base for visitors envisaging golfing, fishing, walking or simply sightseeing. Expert gun tuition is even available for the really ambitious.

LEONARDS CROFT HOTEL,
80 Lichfield Road, Stafford, Tel: (0785) 223676
Set pleasantly on the outskirts of Stafford, Leonards Croft Hotel is a well-appointed, impressive detached house. First appearances are not at all deceiving.

MARSH,
Abbots Bromley, Tel: (0283) 840323
Hospitality that always aims – and invariably succeeds – to please is the hallmark of this friendly and well run farmhouse accommodation. The surrounding farmland makes impressive viewing.

WHITE GABLES HOTEL,
Trentham Road, Blurton, Stoke-on-Trent, Tel: (0782) 324882
The White Gables has earned a formidable reputation among battle-hardened travellers, with a relaxing and friendly atmosphere making for an enjoyable stay.

SOMERSET

BINCOMBE HOUSE,
Bincombe, Overstowey, Tel: (0278) 732386
Set in secluded woodland at the foot of the Quantock Hills, this is a picturesque farmhouse that really is a scenic delight. The interior is no less engaging and the bedrooms are unsurprisingly comfortable.

MANOR FARM,
Chiselborough, Stoke-sub-Hamdon, Tel: (093588) 203
In addition to accommodation that will never provoke the slightest disatisfaction, the food at Manor Farm is quite something to behold. Home baked rolls and jugs of cider all make for a cheery stay.

OLD STOWEY FARM,
Wheddon Cross, Minehead, Tel: (064384) 268
A delightful sixteenth century farmhouse, imposingly set in eighty acres of land within the boundaries of Exmoor National Park. Log fires and woodburning stoves all make for a most congenial atmosphere.

WARREN GUESTHOUSE,
29 Berrow Road, Burnham-on-Sea, Tel: (0278) 786726
This an ideal centre for both family and activity-based holidays. Within a short distance of this pleasant guesthouse can be found the town centre, swimming pool and championship golf course.

SUFFOLK

BEDFORD LODGE HOTEL,
Bury Road, Newmarket, Suffolk, Tel: (0638) 663175
Renowned among the horseracing fraternity for its hospitality, this listed Georgian House is set in four acres of grounds, surrounded by mature trees. With its restaurant, bar and conference facilities, guests find the relaxing atmosphere of a bygone era.

LIMES FARMHOUSE,
Saxtead Green, Framlingham, Suffolk, Tel: (0728) 685303
The Limes Farmhouse, a listed Grade 2 building, dates from the fifteenth century and is situated opposite Saxtead Mill. Historic places nearby include Famlingham Castle and Church, Otley Hall, Orford Castle and Dunwich museum.

OTLEY HOUSE,
Otley, Ipswich, Tel: (047339) 253
Golf, sailing and riding are all pastimes that can easily be enjoyed from this splendid guesthouse. Other local places of interest include Woodbridge, Orford and Dunwich.

TUDOR HOUSE,
34 Guildhall Street, Bury St. Edmunds, Tel: (0284) 703677
Bed & Breakfast of an agreeable nature are provided at this pleasant, sixteenth century dwelling. Rooms are thoughtfully furnished and the food is wholesome and imaginative.

SURREY

BULMER FARM,
Holmbury St. Mary, Dorking, Tel: (0306) 730210
Convenient for the varied and interesting scenery of Sussex and Surrey, Bulmer Farm offers a taste of authentic countryside. The farm produce is delicious.

CRANLEIGH HOTEL,
41 West Street, Reigate, Tel: (0737) 223417
An outdoor heated swimming pool will provide summer relaxation for residents. In the colder months, the interior of this hotel is just as appealing.

ENGLAND
GOURMET GOLF

DEERFELL,
Blackdown Park, Fernden Lane, Haslemere, Tel: (0428) 53409
Sussex, rather than Surrey is the county in focus here, as Deerfell offers splendid views of the Sussex hills. Walking, riding, fishing and golfing can all be easily found.

IELD HOUSE,
Babylon Lane, Lower Kingswood, Tadworth, Tel: (0737) 221745
Strange though it may seem, this guesthouse is only fifteen minutes from Gatwick Airport yet occupies a secluded and attractive setting. A guests' lounge and gym provide different types of indoor relaxation.

GLENCOURT,
St Johns Hill Road, Woking, Tel: (04862) 64154
This hotel can be recommended without reservation. The reasons? One is tempted to say, go and find out:- suffice to say that surroundings, service and food are all top-notch.

KNAPHILL MANOR,
Woking, Surrey, Tel: (0276) 857962
Dating from the 18th century this family home is set in 6 acres of pretty grounds, with a tennis court and croquet lawn. Situated in close proximity to many golf courses including Sunningdale and Wentworth.

QUINNS HOTEL,
78 Epsom Road, Guildford, Tel: (0483) 60422
Guildford is near enough to London to be convenient and suufficiently far away to be relatively relaxing. Quinns Hotel is proud of its location and equally so of its service and style.

SUSSEX

BOLEBROKE MILL,
Perry Hill, Edenbridge Road, Hartfield, Tel: (089277) 425
An entry in the Doomsday book is only one of the claims to fame of this excellent hostelry. Originally a watermill, Bolebrook has been caringly converted and provides a scenic retreat for those in search of relaxing escapism.

CLEAVERS LYNG,
Church Road, Herstmonceux, Tel: (0323) 833131
Situated beside Herstmonceux Castle, Cleavers Lyng itself has the aura of times past, with inglenook fireplaces and exposed oak beams giving an air of solidity and dependability. The high standard of care will more than bear this out.

CROUCHERS BOTTOM,
Birdham Road, Appledram, Chichester, Tel: (0243) 784995
A converted farmhouse, set in extensive grounds, the imaginatively named Crouchers Bottom possesses four ensuite bedrooms and an attractive guests lounge. Chichester Cathedral and the South Downs are distantly visible.

GLEBE END,
Church Street, Warnham, Horsham, Tel: (0403) 61711
Visitors are spoilt for choice at this agreeable guesthouse. On one hand, guests may be tempted to take advantage of nearby opportunities for golf and tennis. Alternatively, with mediaeval architecture, log-burning stove, Tudor dining room and a beautiful walled garden, there are good grounds for staying put!

HATPINS,
Bosham Lane, Old Bosham, Tel: (0243) 572644
The weary traveller in search of a soft pillow for the night would do a lot worse than to seek out Hatpins. All rooms are ensuite and beds can even be made up with French linen.

HOOKE HALL,
250 High Street, Uckfield, Tel: (0825) 61578
The attractive and bustling market town of Uckfield is the setting for Hooke Hall, an elegant and popular guesthouse. Leeds and Hever Castles are easily accessible and Glyndebourne is only fifteen minutes distant by car.

JEAKES HOUSE,
Mermaid Street, Rye, Tel: (0797) 222828
Jeakes is a listed building, dating from the seventeenth century and guests will enjoy a tranquil and dignified atmosphere. All bedrooms are either ensuite or have private facilities.

LITTLE ORCHARD HOUSE,
West Street, Rye, East Sussex, Tel: (0797) 223831
This Georgian townhouse and garden stands at the very heart of the unique Conservation Area that is ancient Rye. Although recently renovated to provide central heating and bathrooms, the house retains an inherently Georgian character.

OLD RECTORY,
Cot Lane, Chidham, Nr. Chichester, Tel: (0243) 572088
This is an old, period house that proudly stands in the village of Chidham. Bedrooms are more than adequate and a large garden and swimming pool provide outdoor amusement.

POWDERMILL HOUSE,
Powdermill Lane, Battle, Tel: (04246) 2035
As far as sportsmen's paradises go, this must rank highly. In addition to well-appointed accommodation, also available are walks, fishing, swimming, croquet, golf and riding.

RACECOURSE COTTAGE,
Nepcote, Findon, Tel: (090671) 3783
Both the accommodation and the welcome are to be applauded here. If that does not suffice, then a wealth of nearby attractions and amenities surely will.

TAPLOW COTTAGE,
81 Nyewood Lane, Bognor Regis, Tel: (0243) 821398
Racing and Stately Home enthusiasts will find this a convenient and pleasant base for Arundel Castle and Goodwood racecourse. For really hardy souls, the sea is almost within touching distance.

WESTERN HOUSE,
113 Winchelsea Road, Rye, Tel: (0797) 223419
An insight into the past is on offer for guests at Western House, with the owner's propensity for antiques everywhere apparent. The town of Rye and the Brede valley provide further historical interest. All rooms are ensuite.

WESTLANDS,
Brighton Road, Monks Gate, Nr Horsham, Tel: (0403) 76383
Three large bedrooms with modern amenities are the important feature of this large, conveniently situated guesthouse. Gatwick, Brighton, Horsham and the Sussex coast are all easily reached, and with the exception of Gatwick, are all worth a visit.

TYNE AND WEAR

CHIRTON HOUSE HOTEL,
46 Clifton Road, Newcastle-upon-Tyne, Tel: 091-273 0407
The pleasant and cosmopolitan city of Newcastle houses the equally pleasant Chirton House Hotel. Bedrooms and public rooms are decorated with style and panache.

DENE HOTEL,
40-42 Grovenor Road, Newcastle-upon-Tyne, Tel: 091-281 1502
This is a well-established and conscientiously run hotel that makes a point of ensuring the well-being of its guests. Nearby Jesmond offers tranquillity, a taste of the countryside and even a children's zoo.

LINDISFARNE HOTEL,
11 Holly Avenue, Whitley Bay, Tel: 091-2513628
A family run hotel with the accent on care and friendliness, the Lindisfarne hotel is the perfect base for the seaside resort of Whitley Bay. The wider delights of the region provide endless opportunities for all ages and persuasions.

ENGLAND
GOURMET GOLF

PARKHOLME GUESTHOUSE,
8 Ocean View, Whitley Bay, Tel: 091-253 0370
Only one hundred yards separate this attractively proportioned Edwardian house and the shimmering (sometimes!) North Sea. Bedrooms include central heating and colour TV.

WARWICKSHIRE AND THE MIDLANDS

ASHLEIGH HOUSE
Whitley Hill, Henley-in-Arden, Tel: (05642) 2315
The Cotswold Hills provide some memorable scenery and this elegant guesthouse provides splendid views of the said range. Most bedrooms are ensuite and all have colour TV and tea/coffee making facilities.

AVONDALE,
16 Elsee Road, Rugby, Tel: (0788) 578639
Close to the town centre and Rugby School, Avondale is popular with business and holiday guests. All appreciate the personal touches that are given a high priority by the attentive and conscientious proprietors.

BEARWOOD COURT HOTEL,
360-366 Bearwood Road, Bearwood, Warley, Tel: 021-429 9731
This medium sized hotel can offer guests all that they require in terms of a restful night and attentive service. The benefits of a family-run hotel are clearly demonstrated.

CAPE RACE HOTEL,
929 Chester Road, Erdington, Birmingham, 021-373 3085
Cape Race is a popular stopover for business travellers. However those with a little more time to spare will no doubt appreciate the outdoor swimming pool and tennis courts.

CHURCH FARM,
Tysoe, Tel: (029588) 385
If the world isn't exactly your oyster when saying at this popular farm, then a sizable part of Warwickshire certainly is. The Cotswolds, Oxford, Warwick Castle and Stratford all make for exhilarating exploration.

CRAIG HOUSE,
67/69 Shipston Road, Stratford-upon-Avon, Tel: (0789) 293313
As well as the well-documented historical attractions and associations, Stratford – and more especially Craig House – also makes a practical base for the walking, angling and golfing communities.

CRANDON HOUSE,
Avon Dassett, Leamington Spa, Tel: (0295) 770652
Set in twenty acres of picturesque ground, Crandon House is actually a working farm and the fresh produce is used to prepare some excellent dishes.

HALFORD BRIDGE INN,
Fosse Way, Stratford on Avon, Tel: (0789) 740382
Halford Bridge happily specialises in excellent value, immaculate bedrooms and helpful service. The food is good too!

HEATH LODGE HOTEL,
Coleshill Road, Marston Green, Tel: 021-779 2218
What the rooms may lack in size at this highly recommended hotel, they certainly make up for in comfort and style. A bar and television lounge provide further relaxation.

HIGHFIELD HOUSE,
Holly Road, Rowley Regis, Tel: 021-559 1066
Comfort and convenience contribute to a happy, friendly atmosphere at this family run hotel. Although mainly populated by commercial visitors, amenities and golf courses can be found in the locality.

KAWARTHA GUESTHOUSE,
39 Grove Road, Stratford-upon-Avon, Tel: (0789) 204469
Stratford is one of the country's most visited places, and the Kawartha guesthouse constitutes a convenient headquarters for a thorough exploration. Guests are likely to leave later rather than sooner.

LYNDHURST HOTEL,
135 Kingsbury Road, Erdington, Birmingham, Tel: 021-373 5695
This is a perennial favourite with the business community, due partly to the unobtrusive comfort and service and partly to its proximity to the motorway network.

MALT HOUSE,
Broad Campden, Chipping Campden, Tel: (0386) 840295
An unusually striking property, the Malthouse has been converted from Cotswold stone cottages and little expense has been spared either outside or inside. A combination of French and English cuisine can contribute to a memorable stay.

MELITA PRIVATE HOTEL,
37 Shipston Road, Stratford-upon-Avon, Tel: (0789) 292432
As well as the delights of Stratford, the Melita is within relatively rapid access of Warwick, Coventry and the Cotswolds. Attentive staff are only too pleased to offer advice and assistance.

STANDBRIDGE HOTEL,
138 Birmingham Road, Sutton Coldfield, Tel: 021-354 3007
Accommodation here is simple but perfectly acceptable. Particularly in the Standbridges favour is its location – convenient for The Belfry, Birmingham and the Midlands motorway network.

WILLOW TREE HOTEL,
759 Chester Road, Erdington, Birmingham, Tel: 021-373 6388
The majority of rooms at the Willow Tree Hotel have ensuite facilities and all are fitted out with direct dial telephone, colour television, video channel, hostess trays and radio. A quiet, residential setting should make for a restful stay.

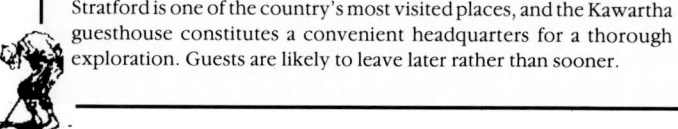

J. Barrow **THE BERKSHIRE** *Burlington Gallery*

ENGLAND
GOURMET GOLF

WILTSHIRE

BAYLYS ALE HOUSE,
High Street, Box, Tel: (0225) 743622
As befits its name, Baylys is celebrated for a mouth-watering range of beers and spirits. However three bedrooms are also available – all are ensuite and have colour TV.

OXFORD HOTEL,
32/36 Langley Road, Chippenham, Tel: (0249) 652542
For travellers passing through and for those wishing to stay awhile, the Oxford offers a refreshing combination of modern amenities and traditional standards of service.

RATHLIN,
Wick Lane, Devizes, Tel: (0380) 721999
A number of tasteful antiques adorn this comfortable guesthouse and make for a dignified and elegant atmosphere. The accommodation is immaculate and comfortable.

WIDBROOK GRANGE,
Trowbridge Road, Bradford-on-Avon, Tel: (02216) 31
Only a short drive away from the glories of Bath, Widbrook is a Georgian listed house and provides a warm and sincere welcome to all guests. Bedrooms are all ensuite.

WORCESTERSHIRE

BARBOURNE,
Worcester, Tel: (0905) 27507
A frequent and much appreciated resting place with the commercial community, the Barbourne is unpretentious but extremely comfortable. Bedrooms all have colour TV.

COTTAGE IN THE WOOD HOTEL,
Holywell Road, Malvern Wells, Worcestershire, Tel:(0684) 573487
Following recent refurbishment, The Cottage in the Wood, a three star country House Hotel, offers a high level of comfort and service. Perched high in the Malvern Hills and with a truly spectacular view, the hotel offers 20 ensuite luxury bedrooms. Extremely convenient for Cheltenham Races.

OLD PARSONAGE FARM,
Hanley Swan, Tel: (0684) 310124
This is a truly excellent establishment where the standard of accommodation is matched only by the warmth of the welcome. A copious range of wines and foods are certain to cap an extremely enjoyable stay.

PHEPSON,
Himbleton, Tel: (090569) 205
This is a seventeenth century farmhouse, whose decor and furnishings are of a tasteful simplicity. An annexe provides bedrooms that are spacious and relaxing.

YORKSHIRE

ALEXA HOUSE HOTEL,
26 Ripon Road, Harrogate, Tel: (0423) 501988
This splendid hotel is a previous award winner, and standards have not been allowed to slip. Originally built in 1830 for Baron de Ferrier, Alexa is now in the capable hands of Roberta and John Black. Twelve bedrooms are all ensuite.

CARLTON HOTEL,
Albert Street, Hebden Bridge, West Yorkshire, Tel: (0422) 844400
Visitors will find a warm and friendly atmosphere at this splendid hotel, typical of the town and of Yorkshire. Guests will find the perfect setting to relax and recover, be it from the rigours of business or country pursuits.

ELMFIELD HOUSE,
Arrathorne, Bedale, North Yorkshire, Tel: (0677) 50558
Nestled in the heart of Herriot Country, Elmfield House sits in its own secluded grounds with uninterrupted views. Golf, riding, fishing, hang gliding are all within easy reach, as are York and Rippon racecourses.

GRASMEAD HOUSE HOTEL,
1 Scarcroft Hill, The Mount, York, Tel: (0904) 629996
The splendours of York ensure that time spent indoors is usually minimal but this hotel will do its best to change your mind. The standard of every aspect – rooms, service, food and character – is absolutely and consistently first-rate.

HEATHER COTTAGE
12 Chapel Street, Flamborough, Tel: (0262) 851036
This homely cottage is set in the midst of a typically picturesque Yorkshire village and is within comfortable striking distance of Danes Dyke, Bempton Bird Reserve and the Heritage Coast.

INGLEWOOD GUESTHOUSE,
7 Clifton Green, York, Tel: (0904) 653523
A charming Victorian House, guests will instantly feel at home at Inglenook. Some bedrooms are ensuite and all have colour TV and amenities.

KNOX MILL HOUSE,
Knox Mill Lane, Harrogate, Tel: (0423) 560650
The centre of Harrogate lies only a few minutes drive from this beautiful old millhouse. The bedrooms are all equipped with modern amenities but retain an olde-worlde graciousness that captivate the visitor of today.

LANGHAM HOTEL
21027 Valley Drive, Harrogate, Tel: (0423) 502179
Family owned Victorian hotel, beautifully restored. 50 bedrooms and excellent restaurant. Courses and tee times can be arranged for golfers, contact Stephen Ward.

MANOR HOUSE FARM,
Ingleby Greenhow, Great Ayton, Tel: (0642) 722384
This is truly a farm well worth visiting, both for the quality of accommodation and its splendid setting. Horse riding, fishing and golf are among a wide variety of pursuits that can be locally enjoyed.

PARAGON HOTEL,
123 Queens Parade, Scarborough, Tel: (0723) 372676
Splendidly located overlooking the North Bay, the Paragon offers good old fashioned value and good old-fashioned service. Scarborough has something to please everyone.

RUSKIN HOTEL AND RESTAURANT,
1 Swan Road, Harrogate, Tel: (0423) 66630
The Dales and stately homes of Yorkshire do not involve an inordinate amount of travelling using Ruskins as a base. For those more interested in home comforts, the hotel is attractively laid out and takes good care of its guests.

WHITE HORSE FARM HOTEL,
Rosedale Abbey, Nr. Pickering, Tel: (07515) 312
Seclusion and splendid isolation are two words used frequently to describe the North Yorkshire Moors, and the White Horse is set right in their midst. Riding and Golf can be practised nearby, in addition to the innumerable places of interest in the locality.

WALES

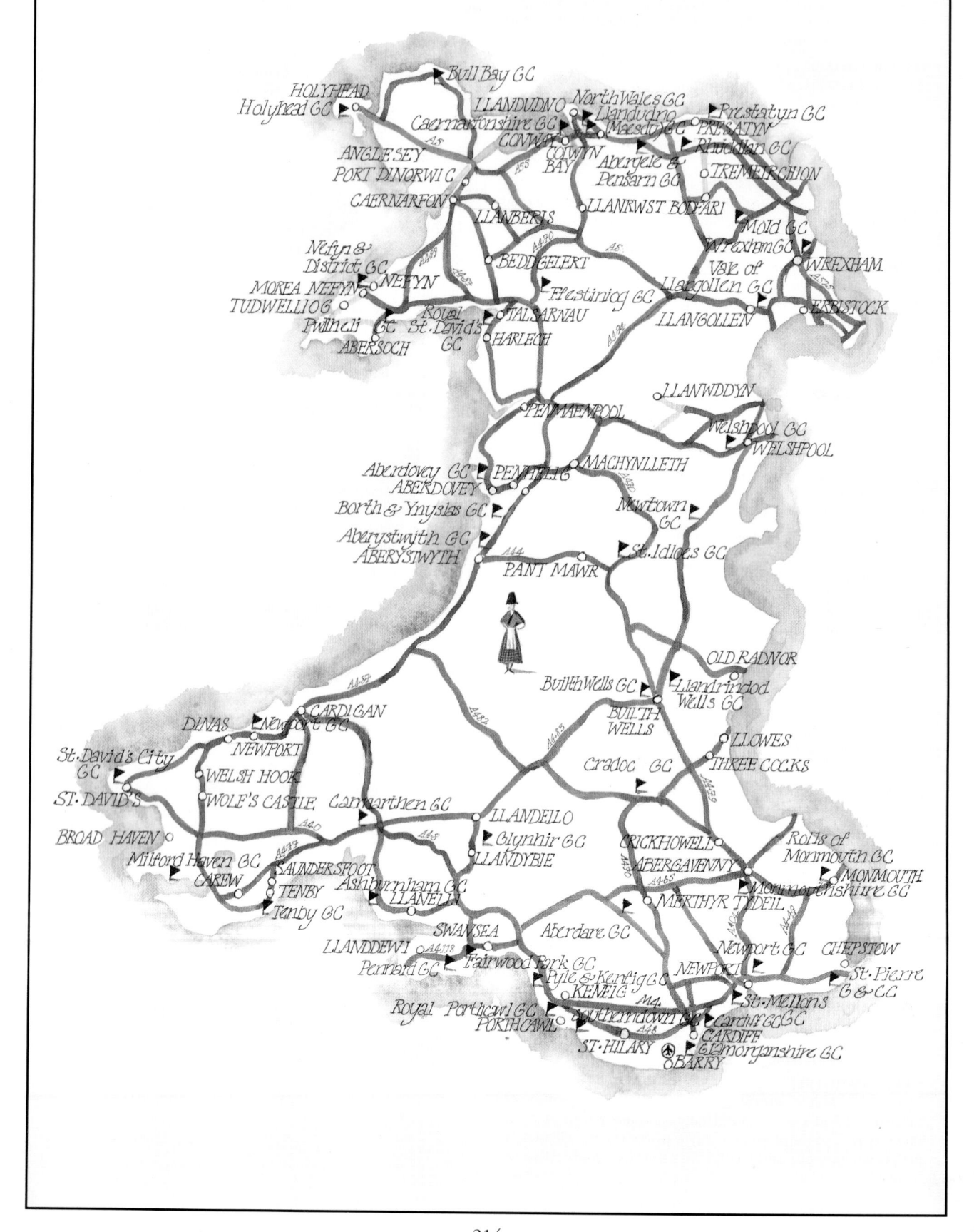

Balls in South Wales are often large, oval-shaped and made of leather. However, those belonging to the much smaller dimpled breed – usually white, though these days sometimes shocking yellow – are to be found in some particularly pleasant spots, and in a great variety of places between the Wye Valley and the Gower Peninsula.

In addition to 'The Glamorgans' and Gwent our region takes in Mid Wales as well, that is the larger, less inhabited counties of Dyfed and Powys – 'the real Wales', they'll tell you there.

GWENT

For many travellers their first sample of golf in South Wales will be the impressive **St Pierre** Golf and Country Club at Chepstow (see feature page). Unfortunately, far too great a number make St Pierre their one and only stop. Further up the Wye Valley both **Monmouthshire** and **The Rolls of Monmouth** offer an outstanding game in delightful surroundings. Bounded by the River Usk, the Monmouthshire Golf Club lies half a mile west of Abergavenny at Llanfoist. In 1992 the Club celebrated its centenary – quite an achievement when one considers its unusual beginnings. Laid out on ground formerly used for polo and later for horseracing, golf was started here in 1892, as the Club handbook tells you, 'the result of a bet as to whether such a venture could be run successfully at Abergavenny!' Clearly the golfers backed a winner. Golf at 'The Rolls' is explored on a later page.

The St Pierre Hotel (0291) 625261 is a 14th Century mansion providing a whole range of facilities. However, those not wishing to wake up next to the famous 18th green should note the Castle View Hotel (02912) 70349, also in Chepstow and very comfortable. In Abergavenny, The Walnut Tree (0873) 2797 is without doubt one of the finest restaurants in Wales and Monmouth provides The Kings Head Hotel (0600) 2177.

One other golf course in Gwent which is well worth a visit is **Newport** at Rogerstone. It is a very fine downland course and decidedly handy when travelling along the M4 (junction 27) – en route to Porthcawl perhaps?

'THE GLAMORGANS'

Golfers in Cardiff (or Caerdydd) are quite fortunate having a number of well-established courses close at hand. Not surprisingly they tend to be busier than the majority of Welsh courses and therefore before setting off it is especially important to contact the particular Club in question. The **Cardiff** Golf Club is a superior parkland course situated some 3 miles from the city centre at Cyncoed. **St Mellons**, north east of the city, within easy access of the M4, is another popular parkland course – quite challenging, with several interesting holes. To the south west of Cardiff, **Wenvoe Castle**, one of the more hilly courses in South Glamorgan can be recommended as can the **Glamorganshire** course, located to the west of Penarth.

Perhaps the best three hotels in Cardiff are the Park Hotel (0222) 383471, the Angel Hotel (0222) 232633 and the very modern Cardiff Moat House (0222) 732520. Among the better restaurants, Noble House (0222) 388430 is well thought of, while the Blas-Ar Cymru (0222) 382132 offers a delightful taste of Wales. Another good eating place is found in Penarth, The Caprice (0222) 702424 where excellent sea food accompanies fine views over the Bristol Channel. Also in Penarth, The Captain's

Wife is recommended (a pub it should be added!) More pubs, and to the north and south of Cardiff are The Maenllwyd at Rudry and the beautifully thatched Bush at St Hilary. Still further south is the popular Blue Anchor at East Aberthan (superb lunches).

A short distance to the north of Cardiff, the town of Caerphilly is more famous for its castle and its cheese than for its golf; however there is some good golf in the area, **Mountain Lakes** Golf and Country Club being particularly noteworthy.

Before heading off to the glorious coastal strip around Porthcawl a course certainly deserving a mention is **Aberdare** – and not merely because the professional goes by the impressive name of Mr A Palmer! (Incidentally, I heard recently that Mr Palmer once had an assistant called Mr Nicholas!) Aberdare is an excellent woodland course, undoubtedly the finest in 'the Valleys'.

One would have to travel many a mile to find a course the equal of **Royal Porthcawl** (also featured later this chapter) but its near neighbour to the east, **Southerndown** gets closer than most. Situated on high ground it is an outstandingly scenic downland type course measuring a little over 6600 yards (par 70). Even closer to Porthcawl is the fine links of **Pyle and Kenfig**, on more than one occasion the venue for the Welsh Amateur Stroke Play Championship. It is a very tough challenge, being open to the elements, and boasts some very large sand dunes.

Some ideas for a well-earned night's rest in the area include in Porthcawl, The Atlantic Hotel (0656) 785011 and The Fairways (0656) 782085. In Nottage, The Rose and Crown (0656) 784850 is an excellent pub serving good food and with some accommodation while another notable drinking establishment is The Prince of Wales in Kenfig.

Beyond Pyle and Kenfig the M4 heads into West Glamorgan passing through Port Talbot towards Swansea, and beyond Swansea is the beautifully secluded Gower Peninsula. If you are fortunate enough to be visiting these parts, three courses that can be strongly recommended are **Fairwood Park, Clyne** and **Pennard**. Fairwood park, situated close to Swansea Airport, is a second course over which racehorses once galloped. It is a much improved course and has several long par fours. Clyne offers a moorland challenge while from Pennard's cliff-top course there are some splendid views out across the Bristol Channel.

A hotel for the night? In Swansea, the Dragon Hotel (0792) 651074 is very good and in nearby Mumbles The Norton House Hotel (0792) 404891 is most relaxing. On the Gower, Fairyhill Country House (0792) 390139 is recommended, especially for its cuisine. No less restful is Langrove Lodge. As for a drink there are numerous pubs, here are two suggestions; The Joiners Arms in Bishopston and the Welcome to Town in Lanrhidian.

DYFED

For every person in New Zealand there are twenty sheep. Regrettably, I don't have the figures for Dyfed and Powys but I suspect they're fairly similar. The bad news is that the lack of human beings is unfortunately reflected by a low number of top class golf courses (unlike in New Zealand it should be said). However, the good news is that even during the summer months most of the courses remain relatively uncrowded,

visitors are made very welcome and the green fees tend to be a lot cheaper than in most parts of Britain.

The two Championship courses in this region lie on Dyfed's southern coast, some 30 miles apart. Both **Ashburnham** and **Tenby** were founded before the turn of the century and each has staged more than one Welsh Amateur Championship, Ashburnham in fact being a regular venue.

Located one mile west of Burry Port, Ashburnham's links is fairly close to industrial South Wales which, I suppose, extends as far as Llanelli, or at least to where the M4 from London fizzles out. The course measures 7,000 yards from the Championship tees and 6,686 yards from the medal tees – certainly not a course for the inexperienced! Connoisseurs of the game, however, should find it an excellent challenge.

There are more glorious sandy beaches around Tenby than one could care to count. There is a story of one five year old boy who raced on to one of these golden stretches arms aloft shouting, 'This is the sixth beach I've been on today!' Anyway as well as being a haven for the bucket and spade it is also a wonderful place for a round of golf. Tenby is a true links course with natural sand hazards and fast greens.

In Llanelli, The Diplomat (0554) 756156 is convenient for Ashburnham, for a relaxing 19th hole, however, golfers may prefer to stay in Tenby with its stylish Georgian harbour. Here, The Imperial (0834) 3737 is recommended. The Tall Ships (0834) 2055 also enjoys a suitably convenient location. A local favourite is the St Brides Hotel (0834) 812304 which enjoys superb views of Carmarthen Bay and its restaurant makes the best use of locally captured lobster. To the north, nestling in the foothills of the Black Mountains, is the town of Llandeilo and a stay at the delightful eighteenth century coaching inn of the Cawdor Arms Hotel (0558) 823500 is highly recommended. Another good hotel which also offers excellent sea food can be found in Broadhaven – The Druidstone Hotel (0437) 781221. Crab is the order of the day here.

Moving westwards along the Dyfed coast the next 18 holes are to be found at **Milford Haven**, a medium-length parkland course to the west of the town. In days of old the former whaling town may well have been a haven but the present day 'landscape in oils' isn't everyone's cup of tea. More attractive is **St Davids** with its beautiful Cathedral making it the smallest city in Britain. Unfortunately for golfing visitors there is only a modest 9 hole golf course. 20 miles away at **Newport**, although again only a 9 holer, there is a very fine golf course, and one which offers some tremendous sea views.

St Davids has many pleasing hotels, and Warpool Court (0437) 720300 is particularly good. Should one tire of the coast (unlikely) then The Wolfscastle Country Hotel (043 787) 225, in Wolfscastle is very welcoming (even though it may not sound like it) and Penally Abbey (0834) 3033 makes for an equally pleasant stay. The 17th Century Hotel Merineth (0437) 763353 in Haverford West is another comfortable hotel in this area. Perhaps the most appropriate place for golfers who have played somewhat waywardly is the village of Welsh Hook. Stone Hall (0348) 840212 is the establishment recommended. Good places for a drink include the contradictory Sailors Safety and The Ship Aground, both at Dinas and The Golden Lion in Newport. If you are still hungry then the best tip is to

visit Cardigan and The Pantry (0239) 820420. Failing the Pantry, try the kitchen – The Castle Kitchen (0239) 615055, an informal but well-run restaurant nearby.

Leaving 'Little England beyond Wales' and heading still further up the coast, the University town of **Aberystwyth** has an 18 hole course that looks out over Cardigan Bay. Try the Belle Vue Royal Hotel (0970) 617558 for a 19th hole here – a lovely hotel with seafront views over Cardigan Bay. A more impressive golf course though is **Borth and Ynyslas** one of the oldest Clubs in Wales. Borth is a superbly-maintained seaside links. The B4353 road runs right alongside much of the course and is often peppered by golf balls. Taking out insurance before playing Borth is recommended.

Whether you've peppered the road or the flagsticks the Cliff Haven Hotel (0970) 871659 in Borth may be the most convenient place for a good sleep, however, further north at Eglwysfach, 16th Century Ynyshir Hall (0654) 781209 is well worth inspecting (note the nearby bird sanctuary) and in Machynlleth, The Wynnstay Arms (0654) 70294 is a cosy former coaching inn. Back in Borth the Victoria Inn is a good pub and finally a great example of friendly local hospitality in an elegant setting is The Conrah Country Hotel (0970) 617941.

Inland, there is precious little golf to speak of in Dyfed, though there is a fairly testing hilltop course at **Carmarthen** – one which is decidedly better in summer than in winter and an attractive parkland course, **Glynhir**, near the foothills of the Black Mountain Range. The latter is a particularly friendly club situated close to the Glynhir Mansion where the first news of Wellington's victory at Waterloo is reputed to have been received by carrier pigeon. (Must have been a pretty sharp pigeon!) One doesn't have to look far for a night's stay either; in Llandybie, the Mill at Glynhir (0269) 850672 overlooks the 14th green.

POWYS

The golf courses in Powys are few and far between, but those that there are tend to be set amidst some splendid scenery. There is an 18 hole course at **Welshpool** up in the hills near the English border (do try to visit Powis Castle and its superb gardens if you're in the area) and two interesting 9 hole courses at Newton (**St Giles**) and at Llanidloes (**St Idloes**) in the quiet of the Cambrian Mountains (note the very fine Glansevern Arms (05515) 240 in Pant Mawr). Two of the best courses are situated right in the centre of Wales, **Llandrindod Wells** and **Builth Wells**. Both are attractive courses, Llandrindod in particular offers spectacular views, situated as it is on a plateau 1,000 feet above sea level. In Builth Wells, The Lion Hotel (0982) 553670 is an historic inn in the centre of town, very pleasant too, while in Llandrindod the large Metropole Hotel (0597) 82881 is very convenient. The Harp at Old Radnor is an ideal place for a drink and a snack after a round at Llandrindod, while for a real overnight treat a visit to a Welsh Rarebits property (0686) 668030 is recommended.

One final course to mention, and one good enough to have held the Welsh Amateur Stroke Play Championship is **Cradoc** near Brecon. A lovely course this, again, very scenic being within the Brecon Beacons National park. This may be one's last night in mid Wales; if so here's another tip: a drink at The White Swan in Llanfrynach followed by dinner and a relaxing stay at Gliffaes (0874) 730371 in Crickhowell, and I'll guarantee you'll not want to leave!

PENALLY ABBEY

Penally Abbey is an eleven bedroom, gothic style, stone built mansion, situated in an elevated position, adjacent to the church, on the village green in the picturesque floral village of Penally, two miles from Tenby.

Penally is, quite simply, one of Pembrokeshire's loveliest country houses. Elegant but not imposing, its very name conjures up an air of tranquillity where time stands still and the emphasis is on relaxation.

For our active guests, every season brings with it a variety of outdoor pursuits. Spring and Autumn are the perfect time for horse-riding, sailing, or playing golf. Summer brings surfing and swimming and Eisteddfods, pageants, concerts and county shows galore. In winter you can walk the coastal park in appreciation of Pembrokeshire's incomparable, savagely beautiful coastline.

Whatever the weather Penally Abbey is a haven of comfort and cheerful ambience, with crackling log fires and the warmest of welcomes.

Set in five acres of gardens and woodland, Penally Abbey boasts its own flemish chimney wishing well and ruined chapel, the last surviving link with its monastic past.

The elegant lounge and dining room overlook the gardens and terrace and enjoy spectacular sea views across the golf course and Camarthen Bay.

Dinner is a candle-lit affair with mouthwatering dishes of fresh seasonal delicacies, complemented by excellent wines from our cellar. Vegetarian and special diets are cared for. Each meal is a celebration especially prepared for you.

The bedrooms are perfect for that special occasion, anniversary or honeymoon. Exquisitely furnished and decorated with antiques and period furniture, many have four poster beds. All are centrally heated, have en suite bathrooms, tea and coffee-making facilities, telephones, colour television and hairdriers. Whether in the main building or in the adjoining converted coach house you will be delighted with their old world charm.

Penally Abbey
Penally
Pembrokeshire
Tel: (0834) 843033
Fax: (0834) 844714

ST PIERRE
CHAMPIONSHIP GOLF

One of the first jokes that an English Schoolboy learns is, 'How do you get two whales in a mini?' – (Answer) 'Cross the Severn Bridge!' For golfers the act of crossing the famous bridge usually means one thing – **The St Pierre Golf and Country Club** at **Chepstow**.

St. Pierre has been in existence for over thirty years. **Mr. Bill Graham** founded the Club in 1961 and the **Ken Cotton** designed **Old Course** opened the following May. The first thing to strike one at St. Pierre is the setting: quite simply, magnificent. The golf course occupies land that was originally a deer park and it has an abundance and great variety of mature trees. There is also a lake covering eleven acres situated in the heart of the course. Whilst the Old Course is understandably St. Pierre's pride and joy, there are in fact 36 holes, since a second eighteen, the **Mathern Course** opened in 1975.

Mr. Thomas Davidson is the Golf Manager at St. Pierre, he may be contacted by telephone on **(0291) 625261**. All written correspondence should be addressed to: **The St. Pierre Hotel, Golf and Country Club, St. Pierre Park, Chepstow, Gwent NP6 6YA**. The Club's professional, **Renton Doig**, can also be contacted via the above telephone number.

Visitors wishing to arrange a game at St. Pierre must book starting times in advance. Other than proof of handicap there are no general restrictions on times of play. The 1992 Summer green fees are as follows: £32 for a round over the Old Course during the week, £40 at the weekend, with £20 and £25 payable for a game on the Mathern Course at similar periods. For those wishing to play a round over both courses the fees are £45 between Monday and Friday, or £55 at the weekend. For junior golfers a single round on the Old Course is priced at £20 with £15 purchasing a game on the Mathern. Both courses are extremely popular with Golfing Societies and prior arrangements can be made with the Secretary. Societies are normally only received during the week unless they are resident at the hotel, in which case they may also play at week-ends.

Travelling to St. Pierre ought to present few problems. The Golf Club is located to the South of Chepstow off the A48. The M4 links Chepstow to Cardiff and Swansea in the west and to London and Bristol in the east. The M4 should be left at exit 22, the A446 then taken into Chepstow where the A48 can be joined and followed to St. Pierre. The best route for those approaching from Birmingham and the north of England is probably to travel south on the M5 leaving at exit 8, thereafter picking up the M50 to Ross-on-Wye. From Ross-on-Wye a combination of the A40 and A466 provides a pleasant drive through the Wye Valley to Chepstow.

The Old and the Mathern Course differ quite considerably in length. The Old is the Championship Course and from the back tees it measures 6748 yards (par 71). The forward tees reduce the length to 6492 yards, while for the ladies it measures 5950 yards (par 75). The respective distances for the Mathern Course are 5762 yards (par 68), 5593 yards and 5204 yards (par 70).

Despite its relative youth, the Old Course has been the venue for a remarkable number of professional events. The Dunlop Masters and Silk Cut Masters were staged regularly here; illustrious winners included **Tony Jacklin, Bernhard Langer** and **Greg Norman**. The latter on his way to a seven stroke victory in 1982 drove the 362 yard **10th** with a three wood. In recent years the Epson Grand Prix tournament was also held at St. Pierre. In 1989 **Seve Ballesteros** produced easily his best golf of the year to win his first title in Wales; in 1990 the tournament changed its format from match play to stroke play and resulted in a popular home victory for the Welsh Wizard **Ian Woosnam** and a year later **Jose Maria Olazabal** strolled home nine shots ahead of the field.

Perhaps the most famous hole on the Old Course is the **18th**, surely one of the most dramatic finishing holes in golf. A par three of 237 yards, it requires a brave tee shot across the edge of the lake with large trees lining the left hand side of the fairway. Standing proudly behind the green is the St. Pierre Hotel.

The Hotel is in fact a former 14th century country mansion and it serves the golfer as a particularly impressive 19th. In addition to an excellent restaurant which offers breakfast, lunch and dinner, there are four bars. Celebrating at the end of a round is always to be recommended – particularly if the 18th hole has been tackled successfully. Share a thought though for a person by the name of **Arwyn Griffiths** who came to the 18th needing a three for a gross 63. A few minutes later he walked off the green having taken eleven strokes – but even he found cause for celebration, for Arwyn still won the competition!

Old Course

Hole	Yards	Par	Hole	Yards	Par
1	576	5	10	362	4
2	388	4	11	393	4
3	135	3	12	545	5
4	379	4	13	219	3
5	420	4	14	521	5
6	165	3	15	375	4
7	442	4	16	426	4
8	309	4	17	412	4
9	444	4	18	237	3
Out	3,258	35	In	3,490	36
			Out	3,258	35
			TOTALS	6,748	71

ROYAL PORTHCAWL
CHAMPIONSHIP GOLF

By common consent Royal Porthcawl is not only the finest course in Wales, it is also one of the greatest Championship links in the British Isles; yet like many famous Clubs, Porthcawl's beginnings were rather humble. The Club was founded in June **1891** and the following year a nine hole course was laid out on a patch of common land known as **Lock's Common**, consent having been given by the local parish vestry. Having to share the course with, amongst other things cattle, soon frustrated the Members and a second nine holes were sought. These they found on the present site closer to the shore. By 1898 Lock's Common was abandoned altogether and the 'favoured' second nine holes were extended to a full eighteen. Once settled the Club prospered and in 1909 patronage was bestowed. Royal Porthcawl had well and truly arrived.

The Members were extremely fortunate in finding this new home for today Royal Porthcawl is not only considered to be one of Britain's finest golfing challenges but also one of the most beautifully situated. Every hole on the course provides a sight of the sea and from many points there are spectacular views across the Bristol Channel to the distant hills of Somerset and North Devon.

Presently presiding over the Royal domain is the Club's helpful Secretary, **Mr. Tony Woolcott**. He may be contacted by telephone on **(0656) 782251**. The professional can be reached on **(0656) 786984**. Golfers wishing to visit Royal Porthcawl can expect a warm welcome. Subject to possessing a Golf Club handicap there are no general restrictions; however, being an understandably popular Club prior telephoning is advisable. Those wishing to organise Golf Society Meetings should either telephone or preferably address a written application to the Secretary at **The Royal Porthcawl Golf Club, Porthcawl, Mid Glamorgan, Wales, CF36 3UW**. Tuesdays and Thursdays are the usual Society days.

The green fees at Royal Porthcawl for 1992 were set at £30 per day during the week with £45 payable at weekends. A rather novel and most encouraging policy is adopted towards junior golfers. Junior Members of the Club can introduce an outside junior for a green fee of just £1 during weekdays.

The course is situated approximately 15 miles east of Swansea and about 20 miles west of Cardiff. The M4 makes travelling to Porthcawl fairly straightforward. Approaching from either east or west the motorway should be left at junction 37; thereafter the A4229 can be followed into Porthcawl. The course's precise location is towards the northern end of the town.

In the opening paragraph Porthcawl was described as a 'links'. This isn't perhaps entirely accurate for although much of the course is certainly of a links nature, some parts are more strictly downland and heathland in character and there aren't the massive sandhills that feature so prominently on the great Championship links of Lancashire, and which are indeed to be found at neighbouring Pyle and Kenfig. The absence of sandhills means there is no real protection from the elements on stormy days and when the winds blow fiercely Porthcawl can be as tough a challenge as one is likely to meet.

From its Championship tees the course stretches to 6691 yards (par 72 s.s.s. 74) while from the medal tees it measures 6409 yards (par 72) with the ladies playing over 5714 yards (par 75). Good scores at Porthcawl (the course record stands at 65) are likely to be fashioned on the first ten holes; from the tough par three **11th** inwards there are some very difficult holes. The second shot from the fairway on the dog-leg **13th** is one not to be hurried though, the views out across the course are quite breathtaking. The **15th** and **16th** are two quite lengthy par fours and the round ends with a glorious downhill finishing hole.

As for its 19th Porthcawl has a splendid Clubhouse. There is an informal Men's Bar where spikes may be worn, a mixed lounge (jacket and tie after 7pm) and a Dining Room (jacket and tie at all times). Both lunches and dinners can be arranged with prior notice, and light snacks are offered at all times except on Sundays.

One final thought for those wishing to explore the delights of Royal Porthcawl, I beg you to consider carefully before deciding to visit late on a November's afternoon for as the light fades and a mist starts to descend upon the links the ghost of the **Maid of Sker** walks the **17th** fairway – don't say you haven't been warned!

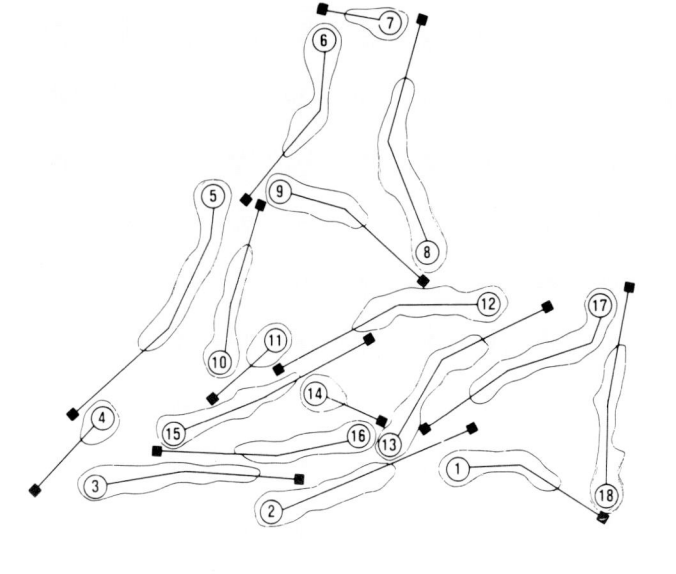

Hole	Yards	Par	Hole	Yards	Par
1	326	4	10	337	4
2	436	4	11	187	3
3	420	4	12	476	5
4	197	3	13	426	4
5	485	5	14	152	3
6	394	4	15	421	4
7	116	3	16	420	4
8	480	5	17	489	5
9	371	4	18	385	4
Out	3,225	36	In	3,380	36
			Out	3,225	36
			TOTALS	6,605	72

THE ROLLS OF MONMOUTH
CHAMPIONSHIP GOLF

If this golf course didn't already have such a splendid name it would be necessary to invent one. 'Tranquillity Golf Club' might suffice. O.K. maybe that's a bit naff, but it wouldn't be in breach of the Trade Descriptions Act. The Rolls of Monmouth enjoys one of the most peaceful and secluded settings in Britain. The golf course is relatively young – it opened in 1982 – but the accompanying countryside of gentle, circling hills and far off mountains cannot have altered greatly in hundreds of years. Indeed the 20th century seems strangely to have passed it by.

The actual name is no mystery at all for the golf course lies within the grounds of the Rolls Estate, the former country home of **Charles Stuart Rolls**, who, together with Henry Royce, founded the famous Rolls Royce company. The imposing mansion which dominates the grounds and is visible from several parts of the course was largely built in the 18th century. Fortunately for we present day golfers the Rolls family were rather keen on landscaping and the grounds are blessed with a wonderful variety of trees and shrubs. Given such a setting and the fact that the Rolls course was laid out to championship specifications, incorporating several small lakes and streams, it isn't difficult to see why it has quickly established itself as one of the finest parkland tests in Britain.

Individual visitors and societies are equally welcome at The Rolls and can make bookings seven days per week. Tee reservations should be made by contacting the secretary, **Mr J.D.Ross**, or his staff by telephone on **(0600) 715353** or by fax on (0600) 713115. The Club's full address is **The Rolls of Monmouth Golf Club, The Hendre, Monmouth, Gwent NP5 4HG**. Handicap certificates are not essential but as this is a serious test of golf, all players should have attained a reasonable level of competence. The green fees in 1992 were £25 per day during the week with £30 payable at weekends. Both the clubhouse and golf shop are adjacent to the mansion and full catering is available in the former throughout the week.

The precise location of the club is 4 miles west of Monmouth, immediately off the B4233 Monmouth to Abergavenny road. The attractive market town is itself linked to Chepstow and Hereford by the scenic A466 and to Ross-on-Wye by the A40.

From its back markers the course measures a lengthy 6733 yards, par 72, although many are likely to play from the forward tees which reduce the length to a more modest 6283 yards. The Rolls is very much a course of two halves, the two nines being laid out on opposite sides of the estate (this of course enables groups to start from either the 1st or the 10th tee with minimal fuss).

The front nine opens fairly tamely (though prettily enough) with three gentle par fours all requiring slightly downhill approaches and the short **4th** which has an attractive lake just behind the green and a semi-concealed bunker to the left. Then comes probably the most difficult series of holes in the round. The **5th** has a deep ravine in front of the green and the only saving grace for the golfer is that it is a par five; the **6th** is the stroke one hole and requires two very accurate shots across a severley contoured fairway and the **7th** dramatically curls, tumbles and twists its way downhill for all of 500 yards until it meets a lake and a little stream – as for the green it's still another thirty yards the other side of the stream. The **8th** is one of four very good par three holes at The Rolls, and the **9th**, a short par four played from a spectacular high tee is a real 'open the shoulders' type!

Among the more memorable holes on the back nine are the **11th**, a lovely sweeping downhill par four, the sharply dog-legging **15th** at the far end of the course (some splendid mountain views here) and the two par threes, the **13th** and the **18th**. The former has been described as 'an absolute beauty' and the latter 'an absolute horror'! Water features on both holes, but while it merely helps to shape the 13th and make it a very picturesque one-shotter, it turns the 18th into a very intimidating closing hole. 'Tranquillity'? Tell that to the match waiting on the 18th tee with all bets in the balance!

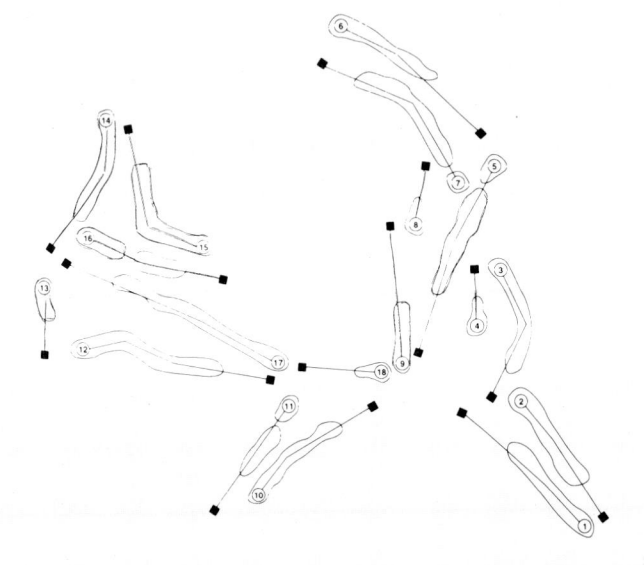

Hole	Yards	Par	Hole	Yards	Par
1	401	4	10	406	4
2	353	4	11	328	4
3	382	4	12	533	5
4	167	3	13	184	3
5	519	5	14	364	4
6	435	4	15	437	4
7	526	5	16	391	4
8	176	3	17	552	5
9	343	4	18	226	3
Out	**3,302**	**36**	**In**	**3,421**	**38**
			Out	**3,302**	**36**
			TOTALS	**6,723**	**72**

THE LAKE COUNTRY HOUSE

The Lake is a riverside country house set in 50 acres of beautiful grounds with sweeping lawns, woods, riverside walks and a large well stocked lake. The hotel offers spacious and luxurious accommodation, enhanced by log fires and antiques. Excellent imaginative food, prepared from fresh local produce, is served in the elegant dining room, accompanied by one of the finest wine lists in Wales. The Lake has been awarded the Restaurant of the Year by Johansens for 1991 and has also received a Rosette for food from the AA for the last two years. The Lake offers all that is best in country house hospitality and satisfied guests return again and again.

For the golf enthusiast there are four full size courses in close proximity, with Builth Wells Course only 10 minutes away, an attractive parkland course of 5386 yards, par 66, the hotel can organise concessionary tickets here.

It is a fisherman's paradise with a lake covering 2 1/2 acres, within the grounds and a 4 1/2 mile stretch of the River Irfon running through the extensive parkland of the hotel. The trout in the river are mostly wild fish and run up to 5lb, with some larger. Our water is divided into six beats, a maximum of two rods being allowed on each. **The Wye** provides good trout fishing, specimens up to and over 1lb are not uncommon. The number of rods per beat is restricted. **The Irfon** is likely to produce salmon almost anytime in the season, but really comes into its own in the latter part. There are also a number of Welsh Water Authorities Reservoirs within easy reach. Our gillie is on hand to give fishing instruction at a very reasonable charge.

The region is well known to birdwatchers and is an ideal centre for walkers and also a haven for wildlife, including badgers and red kite. There are spectacular drives in all directions. Clay pigeon shooting and horse riding are available. AA and RAC 3 Stars and Merit Award. Children welcome. Dogs by arrangement.

The Lake Country House
Llangammarch Wells
Powys
Wales LD4 4BS
Tel: (05912) 202/474
Fax: (05912) 457

NORTH WALES
CHOICE GOLF

One's first thoughts of North Wales are often of lakes, great castles and even greater mountains, or as a fine fellow by the name of Hywell ap Owain, 12th Century Prince of Gwynedd, put it (I offer it in translation):

I love its sea-marsh and its mountains,
And its fortress by its forest and its bright lands,
And its meadows and its water and its valleys,
And its white seagulls and its lovely women.

A man who had obviously seen much of the world! Of course in the 12th Century the Welsh didn't play golf, or at least if they did they kept it pretty quiet and in any case you can be pretty confident that Hywell ap Owain would have told us about it. Well, what about the golf in North Wales then? In a word, marvellous. Inland it tends to get hilly to put it mildly, and should you wish to venture up into 'them thar hills' as well as the climbing gear, don't forget to bring the waterproofs! But there again, leave room for the camera (hope you've got a large golf bag).

In the main though, it is to the coast that the travelling golfer will wish to head. Between Flint to the east of Clwyd and Aberdovey in southern Gwynedd are the impressive Championship links of Prestatyn, Maesdu, North Wales, Conwy, Royal St Davids and of course Aberdovey itself. In addition, there are several with spectacular locations, Nefyn on the Lleyn Peninsula being an outstanding example.

CLWYD

Before journeying around the coast though, a brief mention for some of the inland courses, with a few thoughts as to where one might stop off in order to eat, drink, be merry or simply rest the weary golf clubs. Away from the sea and sand probably the best two challenges are to be found at Wrexham and Llangollen. **Wrexham**, located just off the A53, is fairly close to the English border and indeed the views here are across the Cheshire Plain. Two good holes to look out for are the 4th and 14th. Llangollen's splendid course, **The Vale of Llangollen**, is set out alongside the banks of the River Dee. There are some truly excellent holes, notably the 9th. Appropriately named the River Hole it is a really tough par four of 425 yards. The golfer who likes a spot of fishing (or perhaps even the golfing fisherman) would be in his element here and on a good day should see a few of the famous Dee Salmon being landed – probably easier than netting a birdie. One name to watch in the future is the spectacular new **Chirk Golf and Country Club**, south of Wrexham on the A483. Over seven thousand yards of manicured fairways are complemented by a much less taxing par three course and driving range.

As host to the famous International Eisteddfod Festival Llangollen has long been a popular tourist centre and there are a number of fine hotels in the town including the Hand (0978) 860303 and the Royal (0978) 860202. Also in Llangollen, Gales Wine Bar is well recommended as is Caesars restaurant (0978) 860133 with its enterprising menu. Practically midway between Llangollen and Wrexham with a beautiful Deeside setting is the Boat Inn (0978) 780143 at Erbistock – not quite the first (or is it the last) inn in Wales, but one of the best – especially appealing when floodlit at night. In Wrexham itself, the Crest Hotel offers a comfortable forty winks.

Remaining in Clwyd and the unfortunately named town of

Mold. A pleasant parkland challenge here, while still further north and getting nearer the coast is the **Rhuddlan** Golf Club. They say you should never rush a round at Rhuddlan. If you are heading for the tougher links courses on the coast then this is the ideal place to groove the swing. The course is laid out close to one of North Wales' famous massive fortresses in the grounds of Bodrhydden estate and overlooks the Vale of Clwyd. Just a couple of thoughts for golfers wishing to wet the whistle; The Dinorben Arms at Bodfari and the Salisbury Arms at Tremeirchion – two fine hostelries.

Golfwise there is not a great deal more in the deeper realms of North Wales. **Ffestiniog**, (in Gwynedd) famed for its mountain railway, has a short nine holes of the moorland variety but the scenery in these parts may prove a little too distracting. Ffestiniog nestles in the heart of Snowdonia and the encircling mountains are quite awe-inspiring. Exploring the countryside is a delight and there is a plentiful supply of country houses and inns to entice the traveller. Somewhat isolated, though quite outstanding, is Pale Hall (06783) 285 at Llandderfel near Bala (off the B4401). Lake Bala is actually not that far away and those who enjoy watersports should take note. Another charming place to rest is the 16th Century Hand Hotel (069176) 666 at Llanarmon Dyffryn Ceiriog – all wooden beams and roaring fires – wonderful! Time to tear oneself away; the coast beckons and its time to put that grooved swing into practise.

Prestatyn warrants first attention. Close to Pontin's holiday camp (or is it village nowadays?) it is a genuine links and when the prevailing westerly blows, can play very long (the Championship tees stretch the course to 6714 yards). If a day at Pontin's isn't your cup of tea then the Sands Hotel located in the town is convenient. Thirsty golfers might also find the time to drive over the hill to the village of Gwaenysgor and the Eagle and Child pub – good food and good ale.

The A55 is the coastal road that should be followed to find our next port of call, the **Abergele and Pensarn** Golf Club, just west of Abergele. This course is a fairly new parkland layout (the bulldozer having removed the former) and it lies beneath the walls of fairytale Gwyrch Castle. Games are often won or lost on the last three holes at Abergele. The round is supposed to finish five, three, five – but not many scorecards seem to!

GWYNEDD

A trio of Championship courses are to be found a little further along the coast and just over the county border in Gwynedd. Golfers in Llandudno are more fortunate than most, having two fine courses to choose from: **North Wales** and **Llandudno (Maesdu)**. The latter is perhaps the better known of the two but both are of a high standard and each offers superb views across the Conwy estuary towards Anglesey.

The **Caernarvonshire** Golf Club lies the other side of the estuary close to the old walled town of Conwy – yet another spectacular siting between the sea and mountains and another course where the wind can blow fiercely. A regular venue for the important Welsh Championships, Conwy is a long course and is generally considered second only to Royal St. Davids in terms of golfing challenges in North Wales. It possesses everything that makes links golf so difficult – gorse, rushes, sandhills and more gorse, rushes and sandhills – quite frightening!

NORTH WALES
CHOICE GOLF

The Llandudno-Conwy-Colwyn Bay area is riddled with places of interest and places to stay; indeed it offers a veritable feast for the golfing gourmet. Here are a few thoughts. In Llandudno, famed for its Great Orme, are four excellent hotels, the Empire (0492) 860555, St Tudno (0492) 874411, St. Georges (0492) 877544 and the Marine Hotel (0492) 77521, while slightly inland at Deganwy is the renowned 17th Century Bodysgallen Hall (0492) 584466. Set amid quite idyllic grounds, the hotel offers great style as well as sumptuous cuisine. Less expensive accommodation can be found at the Bryn Cregin Garden Hotel (0492) 585266 also in Deganwy and very highly recommended. Returning to Llandudno the Floral restaurant (0492) 75735 has a gregarious atmosphere and is most pleasing while a pair of pubs whose names you should have little difficulty in remembering are the Kings Head and The Queens Head, the latter a little to the south of the town at Llandudno Junction. Nearby in Conwy a liquid round can be enjoyed at The Liverpool Arms on the quay. There are many attractions in the area: the great castle of course and the town walls, Bodnant Gardens in the Conwy Valley and even the smallest house in Great Britain. Finally in Colwyn Bay among the many hotels two that merit attention are The Norfolk House Motel (0492) 531757 and the interestingly named Hotel Seventy Degrees (0492) 516555.

Heading for the golf courses of the Lleyn Peninsular, many may wish to break their journey at Caernarfon. The castle is splendid and well worth inspecting. Those staying in the area might note that one of the best restaurants in Wales is to be found here – The Seahorse (0248) 670546 at Port Dinorwic.

I suppose every golfer has at one time or another drawn up a mental listing of favourite golf courses. Anyone who has made the trip to **Nefyn** is almost certain to have the course high on such a list. A sheer delight to play on (see feature page), Nefyn was a regular haunt of Lloyd-George as was neighbouring **Pwllheli**, which was in fact opened by him in 1909 when he was the Chancellor of the Exchequer. Not far from Pwllheli there is a good nine hole course at **Aberscoch**, soon to be extended to the full 18.

Handy hotels for Nefyn include the Linksway (0758) 720258, Woodland Hall (0758) 720425 and the Caeau Capel Hotel (0758) 720240. There are numerous pubs, including the Ty Coch Inn (almost on the course itself), and the Sportsman. Close by, situated right on the cliffs is the Dive Inn (0758) 7246 at Tudweilog, which has an excellent restaurant. Another pleasant establishment is the lively Bryncyann Inn (0758) 720879 in Morfa Nefyn. In Pwllheli The Tower Hotel (0758) 612822, the Bel-Air Restaurant (0758) 613198 and Porth Tocyn Hotel (0758) 813303 can also be thoroughly recommended.

A trip to the north west of Wales wouldn't be complete without a visit to Harlech, another great castle and certainly a great golf links, home of course, of the **Royal St. Davids** Golf Club (it too is explored on a later page). On the culinary side in Harlech there are two good restaurants, the Castle Cottage (0766) 780479 (some accommodation) and the Cemlyn (0766) 780425, while not far off in Talsarnau is the excellent Maes-y-Neuadd (0766) 780200 Hotel and restaurant, extremely convenient for Royal St Davids, as is St Davids Hotel (0766) 780366. Finally in Harlech, Alexa House and StableCottages offer charming accommodation at a charming price. In Porthmadoc is another good hotel, the Royal Sportsman (0766) 512015. Lastly, you cannot miss out on visiting Portmeir-ion, Cluff Williams Ellis attempt at creating the Italian Riviera on the coast of Wales. We recommend you stay at the Hotel Portmeirion (0766) 770228.

Heading further south and passing the George III Hotel (0341) 422525 at Penmaenpool, **Aberdovey** is soon reached. The subject of favourite courses has been raised and Aberdovey was the choice of the celebrated golf writer Bernard Darwin, 'the course that my soul loves best of all the courses in the world.' It has an interesting layout, sandwiched between the sand dunes on the one side and a railway line on the other, (the railway line in fact links Aberdovey to Harlech and is a pretty good service).

Golfers ending their journey in Aberdovey will find that the superb Trefeddian Hotel (0654) 72213 is exceptionally convenient for the course. As an alternative though, there is the attractive Hotel Plas Penhelig (0654) 767676 which overlooks the Dovey estuary.

ISLE OF ANGLESEY

The Isle of Anglesey is linked by a road bridge to the mainland across the Menai Straits. There is a choice of four golf courses with plans in the pipeline for extending this number. Perhaps the best two games to be found are at **Bull Bay**, near Amlwch, and at **Holyhead** on Holy Island. Both courses are very scenic and we have featured Holyhead separately. Bull Bay enjoys a fairly remote, and certainly spectacular setting on the island's northern coast. It is a hilly course with much gorse and several rocks to confront and when the wind blows it can be very tricky. The Club handbook relates how, in an exhibition match to mark the opening of the course, featuring John H. Taylor and James Braid, the latter tangled with the gorse on the short third hole and finished up with an eight! There's hope for us all. Two convenient resting places are the Bull Bay Hotel (0407) 830223 at Amlwch and the impressive Trearddur Bay Hotel (0407) 860301 which lies adjacent to the Holyhead Golf Club. In addition there are not surprisingly a vast number of reasonably priced guest houses on Anglesey – contact the Welsh Tourist Board for details – and for a real treat we recommend the Tre-Ysgawen Country House (0248) 750750 at Capel Coch near Llangefni.

Lance Thackeray   A LONG DRIVE   Burlington Gallery

HOTEL MAES-Y-NEUADD

Maes-y-Neuadd, an ancient Welsh Manor House, built between 1350 and 1720, was home to the Nanney Wynn family for several centuries. Since 1981 it has been owned and personally run by the Slatter and Horsfall families.

The hotel setting is superb, Maes-y-Neuadd - "The Mansion in the meadow" stands in eight acres of landscaped lawns, orchards and paddock on a wooded mountain side high above the waters of Tremadog Bay, perfect for exhilarating walks.

All modern comforts have been blended into this historic house, with its inglenook fireplace, decorated plaster work and oak beams. Each bedroom is imaginatively designed and furnished, each with its own very individual style, and many have fabulous views of the mountains or Tremadoc Bay and the distant Lleyn Peninsular. Some have antiques collected over the years, and others contain examples of the very best work of some of our contemporary crafts people.

A Boardroom facility has been created for the small, important meeting and clay pigeon shooting, riding, golf and gun dog demonstrations can be arranged.

Snowdonia's grandeur is right on the doorstep, with some of the most stunning scenery in Britain. Harlech, with its mighty Castle and famous Golf Links if but 3 miles away. There are beautiful beaches, the Italianate village of Portmerion, world famous slate caverns and many of the great little trains of Wales, all within easy reach.

Hotel Maes-y-Neuadd
Talsarnau
Nr. Harlech
Gwynedd
North Wales
LL47 6YA
Tel: (0766) 780200
Fax: (0766) 780211

PLAS PENHELIG COUNTRY HOUSE HOTEL
& RESTAURANT

In the tranquil beauty of the Welsh hillside, the secluded grounds of the Plas Penhelig offer peace amidst peace. Surrounded by seven acres of award winning landscaped gardens and enjoying glorious views across the Dovey estuary and Cardigan Bay, the hotel has an air of welcome about it, comfortable armchairs, open log fires and friendly staff give a charming atmosphere.

The beauty of the gardens can be seen from the delightful terrace, inviting the visitor to take a stroll of gentle exploration. For the more energetic, there is a manicured putting green and perfectly maintained croquet lawn.

Inside, the oak-panelled entrance hall and lounge provide a relaxing setting for afternoon coffee or tea, whilst the dining room is a world unto itself. Decorated with beautifully arranged flowers collected from the hotel gardens, the restaurant prides itself on its fresh, locally-produced fare. Fresh fruit, seasonal vegetables and crisp salads are a speciality, carefully grown in the hotel's own greenhouses, orchards and walled kitchen garden, and used to creatively complement both the imaginative and more traditional daily menus that the chef presents. For a lighter lunch or snack, smaller meals may be taken in the cocktail bar or beneath a sun-shade out on the terrace, to the accompaniment of a cool, refreshing drink.

The area around the hotel provides a wealth of relaxation. Sailing is a popular pursuit and walking around the natural beauty of the surrounding countryside is wonderfully satisfying and you will be refreshed still further by the pure Welsh air. For the golfer, the hotel has arranged reduced fees at the Aberdovey Golf Club.

The Plas Penhelig has 12 rooms, all with bath or shower ensuite, colour television, radio and self-dialling telephones. The staff have experience at accommodating meetings, seminars or small private parties and are renowned for the extra care and attention devoted to these successful receptions.

Plas Penhelig
Country House Hotel and Restaurant
Aberdovey
Gwynedd LL35 0NA
Tel: (0654) 767 676
Fax: (0654) 767 783

ROYAL ST DAVID'S (HARLECH)
CHAMPIONSHIP GOLF

With a **St. Andrews** in Scotland and a **St. Georges** in England, it seems only right that there should be a **St. David's** in Wales. Along with Royal Porthcawl in the South, the Royal St. David's Golf Club at Harlech is one of the Principality's two greatest Championship links.

The Club was founded in 1894 by **the Hon. Harold Finch-Hatton** together with **Mr. W.H. More** who for twenty years acted as Honourary Secretary. The course itself was open for play at the end of 1894 and the opening competition was fittingly won by the greatest golfer of the day and the then reigning Amateur Champion, **John Ball**. St. David's became Royal St David's early this century and in 1935 **The Duke of Windsor** (then Prince of Wales) became the Club's captain.

Of its many attributes St David's is perhaps best known for its glorious setting: on the one side stretch the blue waters of Tremedog Bay, and on the other the imperious Snowdon and the other great mountains of Snowdonia National Park; while surveying all from its lofty perch is the almost forbidding presence of Harlech Castle. The massive fortress built by Edward I has known a particularly turbulent past. It played a prominent role in the War of the Roses when a great seige took place eventually ending in surrender. The seige is commemorated in the famous song 'Men of Harlech'.

The present 'Men of Harlech' to whom I should introduce you are the Secretary, **Mr R I Jones** (tel. **(0766) 780361** and the Club's professional **John Barnett** who may be contacted by telephone on **(0766) 780857**. The Club has the simple address of **Royal St David's Golf Club, Harlech, Gwynedd, LL46 2UB**.

St David's has a reputation for being one of Britain's friendliest Clubs; subject to being Members of Golf Clubs visitors and Golfing Societies are welcome at all times although those wishing to make party bookings must do so by written application to the Secretary. The cost of a day's golf in 1992 was set at £20 during the week with £25 payable at the weekend and on Bank Holidays. For junior golfers, the corresponding figures were £10 and £12 respectively.

The setting is indeed superb but the journey to get there can be a lengthy one – Harlech alas isn't like the proverbial Rome and there is just one road that travellers must join, namely the A496. From the North this road approaches from Blaenau Ffestiniog via Maentwrog (east of Porthmadog) and from the South via Dolgellau and Barmouth. Those coming from further afield may find Bala (if travelling from the north) and Welshpool (if motoring from the south) useful towns to head for. Bala links with Maentwrog by way of the A4212 and the A487, while the A458 and A470 link Welshpool to Barmouth. Finally, for those not travelling by car, the train station at Harlech may prove of assistance.

Measuring 6427 yards from the Championship tees, St David's may not at first glance seem overly testing. However the general consensus is that the course, to adopt golfers' terminology, 'plays long'. Par is a very tight 69 and there are only two par fives on the card. Furthermore the rough can be very punishing (not to mention frustrating) and it is very rare for there not to be a stiff westerly wind. It is interesting to note that despite countless Championships the course record stands at only three under par.

Perhaps the most difficult holes on the course are the **10th**, a long par four into the prevailing wind, and the classic **15th** which requires a lengthy, angled drive followed by a precise approach. The round finishes with, to adopt another curious golfing expression, 'a nasty long short hole.'

The nineteenth at St David's matches the high standards set by the previous eighteen. There is an excellent bar for celebration or recuperation and light snacks, lunches and dinners are all offered. With prior warning a full Anglo/Welsh breakfast can also be arranged.

As one might imagine, each of the major Welsh Championships is staged regularly at St David's; in addition the British Ladies Championship, (won for the fourth time by Cecil Leitch in 1926) and both Mens and Ladies Home International Matches have also been played at Harlech.

The conviviality of the Club atmosphere has already been mentioned; unfortunately there are some English who consider the Welsh a little insular – a visit to Royal St David's makes one realise that Welsh Golf Clubs could teach many of their English counterparts a thing or two about hospitality...and on that controversial note, I wish you good golfing!

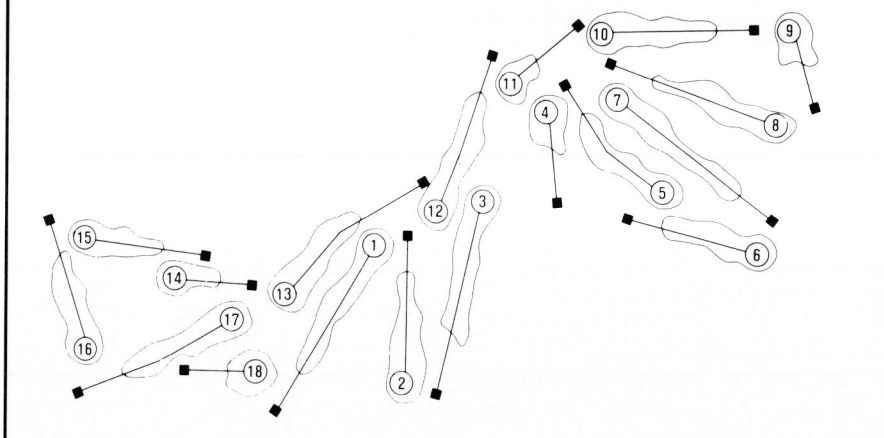

Hole	Yards	Par	Hole	Yards	Par
1	436	4	10	458	4
2	373	4	11	144	3
3	463	4	12	437	4
4	188	3	13	451	4
5	393	4	14	218	3
6	371	4	15	427	4
7	481	5	16	354	4
8	499	5	17	427	4
9	173	3	18	202	3
Out	**3,377**	**36**	**In**	**3,118**	**33**
			Out	**3,377**	**36**
			TOTALS	**6,495**	**69**

NEFYN
CHAMPIONSHIP GOLF

We golfers in Britain are doubly fortunate – not only do we have an infinite variety of courses to play upon (contrast for instance the Surrey heathland with the Scottish links), but we also possess a wealth of outstandingly scenic courses. Perhaps one of our lesser known treasures is perched on the cliffs of North Wales' western tip. Nefyn, or more precisely Nefyn and District, was founded in 1907, although the course really came into its own in 1920 when an extension was opened by **James Braid** and **John H. Taylor** (where was Harry you ask!)

I suppose Nefyn could be described as a classic holiday course: there is a very pleasant drive to the Club (which is probably just as well as it is quite a way off the beaten track). The course is always well maintained with particularly pleasing fairways; whilst the golf is by no means easy, it is never too severe or unfair (indeed, unless the wind blows fiercely, good scores should definitely appear on the cards); the views as mentioned are quite stupendous and Good Lord to cap it all, there is even a pub two thirds of the way round! Well, what more could a golfer ask for?

Visitors to Nefyn must be prepared to produce a handicap certificate and be a member of a recognised Club. Should there be a wish to contact the Club before setting off then the Secretary, **Lt. Col. R.W. Parry** can be reached via **The Nefyn & District Golf Club, Morfa Nefyn, Pwllheli, Gwynedd LL53 6DA** tel. **(0758) 720966** and the professional, **John Pilkington** on **(0758) 720218)**. Green fees for 1992 were priced at £16 per round, £20 per day for weekdays with £22.50 (£30) payable at weekends and on Bank Holidays. Those holidaying close by may well be interested in a weekly ticket (please telephone for details). Keen competitors should be pleased to hear that the Club stages open events annually during the first fortnight in August. Societies are welcome at Nefyn although prior arrangement with the secretary is necessary. One final thing to note is that two motorised buggies can be hired from the pro-shop.

A glance at the map tells you that this part of the world is not particularly well served with major roads (although this doubtless contributes to the area's natural beauty). Visitors

from afar are more than likely to have planned some kind of golfing holiday and so it is to be assumed that the traveller is already in North Wales. Coming from the Colwyn Bay, Llandudno area one should take the A55 towards Bangor. Then from Bangor head for Caernafon on the A487 and just beyond Caernafon take the A499 and the B4417 roads through Nefyn to Morfa Nefyn. From the South the A497 connects Pwllheli with Nefyn.

From the back markers Nefyn stretches to 6301 yards and has a par of 72. **Ian Woosnam**, the 1991 US Masters Champion, holds the professional course record of 67. I am reliably informed that another model of Welsh consistency, **Lloyd-George**, was a frequent visitor to Nefyn and that this trend was in turn followed by **Clement Attlee** – who doubtless found the golf here a welcome diversion from the pressures of No. 10.

After a lengthy opener which certainly invites a hearty belt from the tee (sorry, controlled power) the course moves out along by the cliff edges for a number of spectacular holes. It then turns back on itself before heading in a different direction out on to a headland where arguably the best holes on the course, numbers **11** to **18** are found.

There is no real place on the course where you lose sight of the sea and you may just encounter the occasional sunbather who has lost his or her way. If the holiday mood really takes you, then down in a cove by the **12th** green is the **Ty Coch Inn**. Yes, it is accessible from the course and on a really hot summer's day can doubtless be mistaken for a heavenly mirage. One cannot help wondering how many steady score cards have suddenly taken on erratic proportions from the 13th hole in! Staying sober may take on even greater relevance after 1992 when a further nine holes should be ready for play.

Returning to the Clubhouse you will find that full catering facilities are offered. There is a snooker room and a genuinely pleasant atmosphere in which to relax and reflect on your day. Well, if you have not enjoyed your golf at Nefyn then I must venture to suggest that you are an extremely difficult person to please!

Hole	Yards	Par	Hole	Yards	Par
1	458	4	10	415	4
2	361	4	11	323	4
3	380	4	12	478	5
4	486	5	13	415	4
5	156	3	14	165	3
6	330	4	15	328	4
7	532	5	16	172	3
8	322	4	17	526	5
9	163	3	18	325	4
Out	3,188	36	In	3,147	36
			Out	3,188	36
			TOTALS	6,335	72

HOLYHEAD (TREARDDUR BAY)
CHAMPIONSHIP GOLF

'Which do you reckon are the best holes at Holyhead?' I asked a Mancunian friend who plays the course every summer without fail. 'They're all real crackers down there' he replied. In fact, its a cracking course full stop. And he's right.

Holyhead, or Trearddur Bay as many people call it, is one of two superb golf courses on the Isle of Anglesey, the other being Bull Bay on the island's northerly tip at Amlwch. There are other courses on Anglesey, making it an ideal place for a week's golfing holiday, but these two are the best – a couple of crackers in fact! Arguments as to which is the better frequently dominate 19th hole discussions in pubs around the island. Bull Bay's cliff top setting is certainly spectacular and the course provides a real test, but maybe Trearddur Bay offers the greater variety of challenge and its location on Holy Island, if not quite as stunning as Bull Bay, is sufficiently invigorating for most golfing souls.

A glance at the scorecard tells you that the course measures only just over 6000 yards in length from the back tees (6058 yards, par 70; 5321 yards par 72 for the ladies.) Moreover, from a distance, it looks relatively tame with only one serious hill to negotiate. Look a little closer however, and you will soon realise that not only are the fairways extremely narrow and quite undulating but the rough comprises much gorse, heather, bracken and, as my friend puts it, 'all kinds of horror stories' – the words of one who has been thrilled too often – and then there is the wind which whips across from the Irish Sea. Yes, a real challenge, and thanks to architect **James Braid,** 18 very different holes to savour.

The course can get fairly busy during the peak summer months but the Club is very welcoming and does its best to cater for parties of all sizes. The Secretary at Trearddur Bay is **David Entwistle**; visitors should make prior arrangements with him, either by telephone on **(0407) 763279** or in writing to **The Secretary, Holyhead Golf Club, Lon Garreg Fawr, Trearddur Bay, Anglesey, LL65 2YG**. Also very helpful is the Club's professional **Paul Capper** who can be reached on **(0407) 762022**.

In 1992 the green fees were set at £17 per day during the week with £20 payable at weekends and Bank Holidays. Juniors pay half the above rates. There is a very relaxed atmosphere in the Clubhouse and some fine refreshment is usually available throughout the day. Visitors might also note that between the months of March and September full board facilities are offered in the club's Dormy House.

Being wide awake on the **1st** tee is strongly recommended. You had been licking your lips contemplating a very short, straightforward par four to open proceedings but you survey the scene ahead and suddenly you get the feeling you are looking down a gun barrel. The fearless big hitter will hope to fire one up the middle and perhaps even reach the green; most golfers however, could only feel really comfortable playing this and the next few holes wearing blinkers.

The **2nd** is a very tricky par three. Clammy hands is the sensation here: go left and you must visit the local farmer (not recommended) – stray right and you may tumble down the edge of a cliff on to an adjacent fairway from which the pitch to the green is less than inviting. Much less! The next is a tremendous hole – a par four from the front tees but the **3rd** is a genuine five from the back markers. Here the drive is hit straight into the crest of a hill. Once over the hill, there is then a gentle climb to the green; two good straight hits – usually into the wind – will be needed to set up any chance of a birdie. Then comes the shortest hole on the course, the **4th**, played directly towards the sea. Very exposed to the elements, this hole can play anything from a long iron to a sand iron. If the wind is against you, as it usually is, the only good news is that it's going to be at your back for the next few holes.

Whether the wind is with you or against you, the challenge continues throughout the round with the Stroke One **9th** and the **10th** being two especially memorable holes. It also culminates with a glorious, if fiendish finishing hole where to the right of the fairway the gorse and bracken have been permitted to run rampant. 'Can't remember the last time I hit the **18th** green in two' my friend tells me, 'in fact, I can't remember the last time I parred it – it's far too tough for me' he says. Perhaps you should give Anglesey a miss this summer, I dare to suggest. Go to Spain perhaps? 'What! Five hours for a round under a blazing hot sun instead of playing golf here... you must be crackers. Absolute crackers.'

Hole	Yards	Par	Hole	Yards	Par
1	277	4	10	478	5
2	180	3	11	226	3
3	479	5	12	517	5
4	124	3	13	177	3
5	391	4	14	268	4
6	154	3	15	416	4
7	376	4	16	448	4
8	337	4	17	343	4
9	454	4	18	413	4
Out	**2,772**	**34**	**In**	**3,286**	**36**
			Out	**2,772**	**34**
			Totals	**6,058**	**70**

WALES
COMPLETE GOLF

KEY

*** Visitors welcome at most times
** Visitors usually allowed on
weekdays only
* Visitors not normally permitted
(Mon, Wed) No visitors on
specified days

APPROXIMATE GREEN FEES
A – £30 plus
B – £20 – £30
C – £15 – £25
D – £10 – £20
E – Under £10
F – Green fees on application

RESTRICTIONS
G – Guests only
H – Handicap certificate required
H(24) – Handicap of 24 or less
required
L – Letter of introduction required
M – Visitor must be a member of
another recognised club.

SOUTH & MID WALES

GWENT
Caerleon G.C
(0633) 420342
Broadway, Caerleon
Leave M4 at junction 25 for Caerleon
(9) 3092 yards/***/E

Greenmeadow G.C
(06333) 62626
Treherbert Road, Croesyceiliog, Cwmbran
Leave M4 at junction 26, take A4042 N. for
Cwmbran
(18) 5587 yards/***/E

Llanwern G.C
(0633) 412029
Golf House, Tennyson Avenue, Llanwern
Leave M4 at junction 24, take A455 to Llanwern
(18) 6206 yards/**/F/M

Monmouth G.C
(0600) 712212
Leesebrook Lane, Monmouth
N. of town on A40
(9) 5454 yards/***/D

Monmouthshire G.C
(0873) 2606
Llanfoist, Abergavenny
S. of Abergavenny on B4269
(18) 6054 yards/***/C/H

Newport G.C
(0633) 892643
Great Oak, Rogerstone, Newport
Leave M4 at junction 27, take B451 towards
Highcross
(18) 6370 yards/**/C/M

Pontnewydd G.C
(06333) 2170West Pontnewydd, Upper
Cwmbran
Leave M4 at junction 26, take A4042 then A4057
to Cwmbran
(18) 5340 yards/**/E

Pontypool G.C
(0495) 5763655
Trevethyn, Pontypool
Leave M4 at junction 26, take A4042 to
Pontypool
(18) 6058 yards/***/D/H

The Rolls of Monmouth G.C
(0600) 715353
The Hendre, Monmouth
Take B4233 E. from Abergavenny
(18) 6733 yards/***/B

St. Mellons G.C
(0633) 680401
St. Mellons, Cardiff
On A48 between Newport and Cardiff
(18) 6275 yards/**/D/H

St. Pierre G & C C
(0291) 625261
St. Pierre Park, Chepstow
On A48 near Severn Bridge
(18) 6700 yards/***/F/H
(18) 5762 yards/***/F/H

Tredegar Park G.C
(0633) 894433
Bassaleg Road, Newport
Leave M4 at junction 28, from A48 take A4072 N.
(18) 5575 yards/***/D/H

West Monmouthshire G.C
(0495) 310233
Pond Road, Nantyglo
Leave M4 at junction 28, take A467 to Nantyglo
(18) 6097 yards/***/F

THE GLAMORGANS

Aberdare G.C
(0685) 871188
Abernant, Aberdare, Mid
N.E of Aberdare off A4059
(18) 5874 yards/**/D

Bargoed G.C
(0443) 830143
Heolddu, Bargoed, Mid
17 miles N. of Cardiff on A469
(18) 6213 yards/**/D

Bryn Meadows G.C & Hotel
(0495) 225590
The Bryn, Hengoed, Mid
15 miles N. of Cardiff on A469
(18)5 963 yards/**/D

Brynhill G.C
(0446) 720277
Port Road, Barry, South
Take A48 from Cardiff to Wenvoe and Port Road
(18) 6000 yards/** (also Sat)/F

Caerphilly G.C
(0222) 883481
Pencapel, Mountain Road, Caerphilly, Mid
7 miles N. of Cardiff on A469
(18) 5819 yards/**/E

Cardiff G.C
(0222) 753320
Sherborne Avenue, Cyncoed, South
2 miles N. of Cardiff centre
(18) 6016 yards/**/B

Castell Heights G.C
(0222) 861128
Blaengwynlais, Caerphilly, South
4 miles N. of Cardiff on Tongwynlais-Caerphilly
Road
(18) 7000 yards/***/D/H
(9) 2670 yards/***/E

Clyne G.C
(0792) 401989
120 Owls Lodge Lane, Mayals, Black Pill,
Swansea
Leave Swansea by A4067
(18) 6312 yards/***/D/H

Creigiau G.C
(0222) 890263 5955
Creigiau, Cardiff, South
Leave M4 at junction 34, Take A4119 to
Llantrisant
(18) 5786 yards/**/D

Dinas Powis G.C
(0222) 512727
Old Highwalls, Dinas Powis, South
Leave Cardiff on A4055 to Dinas Powis
(18) 5377 yards/**/D

Fairwood Park G.C
(0792) 203648Upper Killay, Swansea
Leave Swansea on A4118 to Upper Killay
(18) 6606 yards/***/F

Glamorganshire G.C
(0222) 701185
Lavernock Road, Penarth, South
Leave Cardiff on A4160, take B4267 to
Lavernock
(18) 6150 yards/***/D/H

Glynneath G.C
(0639) 720452
Penycraig, Pontneathvaughan, Neath, West
North of Neath off A465
(18) 5499 yards/***/F

Inco G.C
(0792) 844216
Clydach, Swansea, West
Situated in the Swansea Valley
(12) 6230 yards/***/E

Langland Bay G.C
(0792) 366023
Llangland Bay, Swansea, West
Take A4067 coast road from Swansea to
Mumbles Head
(18) 5812 yards/***/D/H

Llanishen G.C
(0222) 752205
Cwm, Lisvane, Cardiff
5 miles N. of Cardiff via Heol Hir
(18) 5296 yards/***/F/H

Llantrisant and Ponty Clun G.C
(0443) 22148
Lanelay Road, Talbot Green, Ponty Clun
N. of Cardiff on A4119 to Llantrisant
(12) 5712 yards/**/D/H

Maesteg G.C
(0656) 732037
Mount Pleasant, Neath Road, Maesteg, Mid
Leave A4107 for B4282 to Maesteg
(18) 5845 yards/***/D

Merthyr Tydfil G.C
(0685) 3308
Cilsanws Mt, Cefn Coed, Nr Merthyr Tydfil, Mid
Take A465 N. at Cefn Coed
(9) 5794 yards/***/F

Morlais Castle G.C
(0685) 2822Pant, Dowlais, Merthyr Tydfil, Mid
N. of Merthyr Tydfil toward Brecon Railway
(9) 6255 yards/***(not Sat)/F

Morriston G.C
(0792) 771079
160 Clasemont Road, Morriston, Swansea, West
3 miles N. of Swansea on A4067
(18) 5734 yards/***/D

Mountain Ash G.C
(0443) 472265
Cefnpennar, Mountain Ash, Mid
From A470 take A4059 to Mountain Ash
(18) 5485 yards/***/D

Mountain Lakes G.C
(0222) 861128
Blaengwynlais, Caerphilly
Leave M4 at junction 32. 4 miles N. of Cardiff
(18) 6851 yards/***/D/H

Neath G.C
(0639) 643615
Cadoxton, Neath, West
Take A48 to Neath, E. to Cadoxton
(18) 6465 yards/***/D

Palleg G.C
(0639) 842193
Palleg Road, Lower Cwmtwrch, Swansea
15 miles N. of Swansea on A4067 Brecon road
(9) 3260 yards/***/D

Pennard G.C
(0441) 283131
2 Southgate Road, Southgate, Swansea, West
(18) 6266 yards/***/F/H

Pontardawe G.C
(0792) 863118
Cefn Llan, Pontardawe, Swansea
N. of Swansea on A4067 to Pontardawe
(18) 6061 yards/E/M

Pontypridd G.C
(0443) 402539
Ty Gywn, The Common, Pontypridd, Mid
N. of Cardiff on A470 to Pontypridd
(18) 5650 yards/***/E

Pyle and Kenfig G.C
(065 671) 3093
Waun-y-Mer, Kenfig, MidW. of Cardiff on M4,
take junction 37 to Porthcawl
(18) 6640 yards/**/C/H

Raf St Athan G.C
(0446) 751043
Barry
2 miles E. of Llanwit Major on B4265
(9) 5957 yards/***(not Sun am)/E

Radyr G.C
(0222) 842408
Drysgolf Road, Radyr, Cardiff
Turn off A470 N. at Taffs Well
(18) 6031 yards/**/D/H

Rhondda G.C
(0443) 433204
Ponygwaith, Ferndale, Rhondda
3 miles past Porth on A4058
(18) 6428 yards/**/F/M

Royal Porthcawl G.C
(065 671) 2251
Porthcawl, Mid
Leave M4 at junction 37 for A4229 to Porthcawl
(18) 6605 yards/***/F/H

Southerndown G.C
(0656) 880474
Ewenny, Bridgend, Mid
Leave M4 at junction 36 for A4061, then B4524
for Ogmore
(18) 6613 yards/**/C/H

Swansea Bay G.C
(0792) 814153
Jersey Marine, Neath, West
Off A48 between Neath and Swansea
(18) 6302 yards/***/F

Tredegar and Rhymney G.C
(0685) 840743
Cwmtysswg, Rhymney, Gwent
2 miles from Rhymney on B4256
(9) 2788 yards/***/E

Wenvoe Castle G.C
(0222) 594371
Wenvoe, Cardiff
2 miles from Wenvoe on A4050
(18) 6411 yards/***/F/H

Whitchurch G.C
(0222) 620125
Pontmawr Road, Whitchurch, CardiffLeave M4
at junction 32, take A470 S.
(18) 6245 yards/**/C/H

Whitehall G.C
(0443) 740245
Nelson, Treharris, Mid
Take A470 N. of Cardiff for Treharris
(9) 5750 yards/**/F

DYFED

Aberystwyth G.C
(0970) 615104
Brynmor, Aberystwyth
At north end of promenade
(18) 5735 yards/***/F

Ashburnham G.C
(05546) 2269
Cliffe Terrace, Burry Port
On coast side of Burry Port off A484
(18) 6916 yards/**/C

Borth and Ynyslas G.C
(097 081) 202
Borth
Off B4353 to Borth
(18) 6094 yards/***/F

Cardigan G.C
(0293) 612035
Gwbert on Sea, Cardigan
From A487 take B4548 N.W to Gwbert
(18) 6207 yards/***/F

Carmarthen G.C
(0267) 87214
Blaen-y-coed Road, Carmarthen
Take A40, N. to A485 then onto A484
(18) 6212 yards/***/F

Cilgwyn G.C
(0570) 45286
Llangybi, Lampeter
Take A485 N.E for 4 miles to Llangybi
(9) 5318 yards/***/T

Glynhir G.C
(0269) 850472
Glynhir Road, Llandybie, Ammanford
From M4 junction 49 take A483 to Llandybie
(18) 6090 yards/***/F

Haverfordwest G.C(0437) 764523
Arnolds Down, Narberth Road, Haverfordwest
N. of A40, 1 mile E. of the town
(18) 5908 yards/**/E

Milford Haven G.C
(0646) 692368
Woodbine House, Hubberston, Milford Haven
W. of the town at Hubberston
(18) 6071 yards/***/F

Newport (Pembs) G.C
(0239) 820244
Newport
On bayside, follow Newport Sands signs
(9) 6179 yards/***/F

St. Davids City G.C
(0437) 720392 (tourist office)
Whitesands Bay, St. Davids
Take A487 from Haverfordwest to St. Davids
(9) 5693 yards/***/F

South Pembrokeshire G.C
(0646) 682817
Defensible Barracks, Pembroke Dock
Take A477 to Pembroke and Pembroke Docks
(9) 5804 yards/***/E

Teny G.C
(0834) 2978
The Burrows, Tenby
Through town on A4139
(18) 6232 yards/***/D

POWYS

Brecon G.C
(0874) 2004
Newton Park, Llanfaes, Brecon
S. of town on A40 from Abergavenny
(9) 5218 yards/***/E

Builth Wells G.C
(0982) 553296
Builth Wells
W. of town on A483
(18) 5760 yards/***/E

Cradoc G.C
(0874) 3658
Penoyre Park, Cradoc, Brecon
Through Brecon and N. on B4520
(18) 6318 yards/***/F

Llandrindod Wells G.C
(0597) 823873
Llandrindod Wells
Take A483 from Brecon to Llandrindod Wells
(18) 5749 yards/***/F

Old Rectory G.C
(0873) 810373
Llangattock, Crickhowell
Take A40 W. from Abergavenny to Crickhowell
(9) 2878 yards/***/E

Welshpool G.C
(0938) 83249
Golfa Hill, Welshpool
W. of the town on the A458
(18) 5708 yards/***/E

LLANGOED HALL

On this site, fourteen hundred years ago, the Welsh Parliament stood; at least according to legend. Inspired by this, the celebrated architect, Sir Clough Williams-Ellis transformed the largely Jacobean mansion he found here into the great country house it is today. Llangoed Hall was completed in 1918 although parts of the South facing wing, including the panelled library date, from 1632. Inside it is the Laura Ashley genius that is most striking, that ability of interpreting the past to bring comfort and beauty to the present.

The intention of Sir Bernard Ashley, when he decided to convert the hall, was never that of the usual hotelier. Having decided to return to the idea of entertaining guests, rather than patrons, he worked hard to re-create the style and atmosphere of what it once was, a great Edwardian country house where visitors could stay and enjoy the way of life it once stood for. Thoughtful luxuries abound, personal touches make all the difference; fresh fruit; a decanter of sherry or mineral water ready to pour; plenty of books in the bedrooms fleecy robes and luxurious oils in the bathrooms a tray of famous Welsh afternoon tea of scones and home-made jam, shortbread and cream-filled meringues and local Bara Brith served in the Morning Room to welcome you on arrival.

The dining room is handsome with yellow and cornflower blue, a perfect complement to the menu of one the finest young chefs in Britain; always insisting on fresh local produce; Welsh lamb, Wye salmon and traditional laverbread; vegetables and herbs collected from the hotel's own gardens. All to be enjoyed with a choice from some of the 300 superb wines assembled from the greatest wine regions of the world.

For the sportsman, three superb golf courses are within easy driving distance; all 18-hole with breathtaking scenery. In addition to the hotel's own all-weather tennis court and croquet lawn guests may fish for salmon and trout on the Upper Wye and River Irfon. The countryside, rich in wildlife, offers a variety of rough shooting and bird-watching. Riding can be easily arranged and the magnificent Brecon Beacons have much to offer both the serious and casual walker; not to mention the fascinating surrounding countryside, from Wordsworth's beloved Tintern Abbey to the ancient castles of Raglan and Caerphilly.

Conference facilities are, naturally, extensive, with a variety of rooms available, from the panelled, book-lined library to separate dining room, the Flower Room. For all guests a chauffeur-driven car is available for day-to-day touring or collection from rail and air terminals, and helicopters may use the south lawn by prior arrangement.

Llangoed Hall
Llyswen
Brecon
Powys
Wales
LD3 0YP
Tel: (0874) 754525
Fax: (0874) 754545

WALES
COMPLETE GOLF

NORTH WALES

CLWYD

Abergele & Pensarn G.C
(0745) 824034
Tan-y-Goppa Road, Abergele
Through town on the A547
(18) 6086 yards/***/D/H

Bryn Morfydd G.C
(074 578) 280
The Princess Course, Bryn Morfydd Hotel,
Llanrhaedr
From A55 take A525 to Llanrhaedr
(9) 1190 yards/***/E

Chirk G. & C.C
(0691) 774407
Chirk, nr Wrexham
(18)/**/F

Denbigh G.C
(074 581) 4159
Henllan Road, Denbigh
On the B5382 to Henllan
(18) 5650 yard/***/F/H

Hoywell G.C
(0352) 710040
Brynford, Holywell
Take A55 to Holywell
(9) 6484 yards/***/F

Mold G.C(0352) 740318
Clicain Road, Pantymwyn, Mold
Take A494 to Mold, turn onto Denbigh Road
(18) 5545 yards/***/H

Old Colwyn G.C
(0492) 515581
Woodland Avenue, Old Colwyn
Take A55 to Old Colwyn
(9) 5800 yards/***(not Tues, Wed, Sat, pm)/E

Old Padeswood G.C
(0244) 547401
Station Road, Padeswood, Mold
Take A541 E from Mold for 1 mile, then A5118
(18) 6639 yards/***/F

Padeswood and Buckley G.C
(0244) 550537
The Cala, Station Lane, Padeswood, Mold
Take A541 E. from Mold for 1 mile, then take
A5118
(18) 5775 yards/***/D/H

Prestatyn G.C
(0745) 888353
Marine Road East, Prestatyn
Take A548 to Prestatyn and Prestatyn Sands
(18) 6764 yards/***(not Sat & Tues am)/D/H

Rhuddlan G.C
(0745) 590271
Meliden Road
Rhuddlan
Nr. Bodrhyddan Hall on A5151
(18) 6045 yards/***(not Sun)/F/H

Rhyl G.C
(0745) 35317
Coast Road, Rhyl
On A548 E. of Rhyl
(9) 6185 yards/***/E/H

Ruthin Pwllglas G.C
(082 42) 2296
Ruthin Pwllglas, Ruthin
S. of the town off the A494
(9) 5418 yards/***/E/H

Vale Of Llangollen G.C
(0978) 860040
Llangollen
1 mile E. of town off A5 to Llangollen
(18) 6461 yards/***/D/H

Wrexham G.C
(0978) 364268
Holt Road, Wrexham
E. of the town off the A534
(18) 6078 yards/***/F/H

GWYNEDD

Aberdovey G.C
(0654) 72493
Aberdovey
Take A493 from Machynlleth to Aberdovey
(18) 6445 yards/***/D/H

Abersoch G.C
(075 881) 2622
Abersoch
Take A499 from Pwllheli to Abersoch
(9) 5910 yards/***/F

Betws-Y-Coed G.C
(069 02) 556
Betws-y-coed
Take A470 S. from Llandudno to Betws-y-coed
(18) 4996 yards/***/F

Caernarfon G.C
(0286) 3783
Llanfaglan, Caernarfon
Half-mile S. of Caernarfon off A487
(18) 5860 yards/***/E

Conwy G.C
(0492) 5592423
Morfa, Conwy
Take A55 from Conwy to Bangor
(18) 6901 yards/**/F/H

Criccieth G.C
(0776) 522154
Ednyfed Hill, Criccieth
N. of the town off B4411 or A497
(18) 5787 yards/***/F

Dolgellau G.C
(0341) 422603
Pencefn, Golfdown, Dolgellau
Leave A5 at A494 at Druid for Dolgellau
(9) 4512 yards/***/E

Llandudno (Maesdu) G.C
(0492) 76450
Hospital Road, Llandudno
1 mile from town centre
(18) 6513 yards/***/D/H

Nefyn and District G.C
(0758) 720218
Morfa Nefyn, Pwlheli
Leave A499 for B4417 to Nefyn
(18) 6335 yards/***/D

North Wales G.C
(0492) 75325
72 Brymau Road, West Shore, Llandudno
Leave AA55 for B5115 out to West Shore
(18) 6132 yards/***/D/H

Penmaenmawr G.C
(0492) 623330
Conwy Old Road, Penmaenmawr
Take A55 W. from Conwy
(9) 5031 yards/***/E

Portmadog G.C
(0766) 512037
Morfa Bychau, Portmadog
Take A487 to Portmadog
(18) 5838 yards/***/F/H

Pwllheli G.C
(0758) 612520
Golf Road, Pwllheli
Take A497 from Portmadog to Pwllheli
(18) 6110 yards/***/F

Rhos-On-Sea G.C
(0492) 49641
Penrhyn Bay, Llandudno
Take B5115 from A55 to Rhos-On-Sea
(18) 6064 yards/***/E

Royal St. Davids G.C
(0766) 780361
Harlech
Take A496 from Portmadog to Barmouth
(18) 6427 yards/***/F/H

St Deniol G.C
(0248) 353098
Penybryn, Bangor
E. of Bangor off A55
(18) 5500 yards/***/E

ANGLESEY

Anglesey G.C
(0407) 810219Station Road, Rhosneigr
Leave A5 for A4080 to Rhosneigr
(18) 5713 yards/***/F

Baron Hills G.C
(0248) 810231
Beaumaris
(9) 5564 yards/***/E

Bull Bay G.C
(0407) 830960
Bull Bay Road, Amlwch
Through Amlwch on A5025
(18) 6160 yards/**/F/H

Holyhead G.C
(0407) 763179
Trearddur Bay, Holyhead, Gwynedd
On A5 over Menai bridge to Holyhead
(18) 6058 yards/***/D/H

Llangefni G.C
(0248) 722193
Llangefni
W. on A5 then onto A5114 to Llangefni
(9) 1467 yards/***/E

ST. TUDNO HOTEL

Without doubt the St Tudno is one of the most delightful small hotels to be found on the coast of Great Britain. The Hotel has won a host of awards in recent years from 'Best Seaside Resort Hotel in Great Britain' through to the 'Johansens Hotel of the Year Award for Excellence 1992'. It was the National winner of the AA's 'Warmest Welcome Award' and has even won an accolade for having the best hotel loos in Britain!

Situated on Llandudno's fine promenade opposite the Pier and Gardens the St Tudno epitomises all that is best of a quality hotel. Not only is it elegant, beautifully and lovingly furnished with meticulous attention to detail, but the warmth of the welcome that owners Martin and Janette Bland and their team of friendly young staff extend to their guests is both remarkable and sincere.

The twenty one bedrooms are all individually designed and beautifully co-ordinated having many thoughtful extras. The air-conditioned Garden Room Restaurant which is regarded as one of the best in Wales has won two AA Rosettes for its excellent cuisine.

St Tudno is ideally situated for visits to Snowdonia, Conway and Caernarvon Castles, Bodnant Gardens and Anglesey. There are three championship golf courses all within a radius of five miles, two of which are on the doorsteps at Llandudno (Maesdu) and North Wales and the third, Conway is situated just over the estuary.

St Tudno Hotel
Promenade
Llandudno
Gwynedd LL30 2LP
Tel: (0492) 874411
Fax: (0492) 860407

GLIFFAES COUNTRY HOUSE

A thoroughly charming Victorian country house hotel, Gliffaes boasts fine gardens and parkland, situated in the National Park yet only one mile off the main A40 road. It offers peace and tranquillity as well as being easily accessible.

The house, which faces due south, stands in its own 29 acres in the beautiful valley of the River Usk, midway between the Brecon Beacons and the Black Mountains. Built in 1885 as a private residence, it has been ideally adapted to provide spacious comfort in the country house tradition. There are 22 bedrooms with private bathrooms or showers and all are individual in decor and furnishings, including three in the converted lodge.

The downstairs rooms include a large, comfortable, panelled sitting-room which leads into an elegant regency style drawing-room. From here, french windows open into a large conservatory with double doors on to the terrace. The dining-room and comfortable bar also open on to the terrace, with the glorious views of the surrounding hills and River Usk one hundred and fifty feet below. The billiard room has a full sized table and provides an additional sitting-room with something of a club atmosphere.

Breakfast is served from a sideboard, lunch is a cold buffet with soup and a hot dish. Dinner is either table d'hote or a la carte. In fact, country house standards of the old order are carefully maintained by the resident owners; the Brabner family have held sway here since 1948.

External facilities include fishing for salmon and trout in the part of the Usk which the hotel overlooks, tennis, bowls, putting and croquet. There is an extensive range of short walks in the vicinity and a nearby riding and pony trekking establishment where horses and ponies can be hired.

The hotel is justly proud of its in-house cooking and remains open from the middle of March to the end of the year.

Gliffaes Country House Hotel
Crickhowell
Powys
Wales NP8 1RH
Tel: (0874) 730371 Fax: (0874) 730463

WALES
GOURMET GOLF

SOUTH AND MID WALES

ANGEL HOTEL ,
Castle Street, Cardiff, Tel: (0222) 232633
Few hotels can boast of such a location – in the heart of the Welsh Capital between the world famous Cardiff Arms Park and Cardiff Castle, minutes from the business centre and St. Davids Hall. Restored with care, the Angel is again in its place as Cardiff's premier hotel.

AUSTINS,
11 Coldstream Terrace, Cardiff, Tel: (0222) 377148
Austins is a small, friendly hotel situated in the centre of Cardiff, 200 yards from the castle. Most rooms are ensuite and the reasonable rates include a full English breakfast.

BIKEREHYD FARM,
Pennant, Llanon Dyfed, Tel: (0974) 272365
This highly recommended guesthouse is peacefully set in its own farmland. Guests are comfortably housed in either the main house or in three adjacent cottages. A beautiful restaurant offers first-class food, and paves the way for a visit to one of many places of scenic and historical interest.

CASTLE VIEW HOTEL,
16 Bridge Street, Chepstow, Tel: (0291) 270349
Golf and racing enthusiasts staying at this hotel are really spoilt for choice. Chepstow racecourse is a mere stones throw away and the championship links of St Pierre only three miles distant. The Castle View is open all year round.

COURT HOTEL,
Lamphey, Pembroke, Tel: (0646) 672273
A huge range of sporting and leisure opportunities are offered at this excellent hotel. As well as special golfing breaks, guests can enjoy swimming, yachting, sauna, solarium and gym. Conference and wedding facilities are also available.

CROWN AT WHITEBROOK,
Whitebrook, Monmouth, Gwent, Tel: (0600) 860254
Award winning cuisine is one feature of this comfortable hotel. Accommodation is also of a high standard and guests are always assured of a warm welcome. Racing and golf are among the many local attractions.

DRAGON HOTEL,
Montgomery, Powys, Tel: (0686) 668359
This popular hotel can provide both active and relaxing holidays to suit every taste. A wide range of facilities are available, including swimming, tennis and a well-equipped gym, whilst the surrounding countryside offers many scenic and historic attractions.

FLEECE HOUSE,
Market Street, Knighton, Powys, Tel: (0547) 520168
Originally an eighteenth century coaching inn, Fleece offers a genuine olde worlde atmosphere that has been maintained despite extensive modernisation. Weekly and weekend golfing breaks can be arranged.

FOUNTAIN INN,
Trellech Grange, Chepstow, Gwent. Tel: (0291) 689303
The Fountain is a lovely old inn situated just off the Wye Valley in a designated Area of Outstanding Natural Beauty. Simple but comfortable accommodation is available, as well as excellent food and a fine selection of wines and beers.

GLASFRYN HOUSE,
Church Street, Llanfaes, Brecon, Powys, Tel: (0874) 623014
Guests are always welcome at this small, clean and friendly hotel that provides excellent value and personal attention. Set in the heart of The Brecon Beacons National Park, the surroundings are unforgettable.

HAMMONDS PARK HOTEL,
Narberth Road, Tenby, Dyfed, Tel: (0834) 2696
This family run hotel provides accommodation and service of a high standard. All rooms have TV and hospitality trays, and parking is available within the hotel grounds.

HIGH HOUSE FARM,
Bryngwyn, Raglan, Gwent, Tel: (0291) 690529
Comfortable accommodation is available on this working farm. A convenient location makes it easy to reach and the surrounding countryside is quite delightful. Golf and fishing can be found nearby.

HIGH NOON GUESTHOUSE,
Lower Lamphey Road, Pembroke, Dyfed, Tel: (0646) 683736
This modern guesthouse is highly recommended and can offer several ensuite rooms. Golf and fishing are available nearby, as is the magnificent Pembrokeshire coastal path and beaches. A restaurant provides excellent fare.

HILDERBRAND HOTEL,
Victoria Street, Tenby, Dyfed, Tel: (0834) 2403
Tenby's championship golf course is only a short distance from this friendly hotel. Most bedrooms have private bathrooms and a dining room and lounge make for a comfortable and relaxing stay.

PARC LE BROS HOUSE,
Parkmill, Gower, Swansea, Tel: (0792)-371636
A secluded and picturesque nineteenth century farmhouse, Parc le Breos offers an opportunity to enjoy local riding, ponytrekking, walking, golf, and the many facilities of nearby Swansea. A lounge and games room are at the disposal of residents.

PENBONTBREN HOTEL,
Glynarthen, Cardigan, Dyfed, Tel: (0239) 810248
This comfortable hotel provides a range of comfortable accommodation and a high level of service. Disabled guests are welcome and the hotel can also be hired for weddings and conferences.

ROYAL OAK HOTEL,
The Cross, Welshpool, Powys , Tel: (0938) 552217
Accommodation is well-appointed and extremely comfortable at this highly recommended medium-size hotel. A restaurant serves fine cuisine and can also cater for weddings and conferences.

ST-Y-NYLL HOUSE,
St Brides, Super Ely, South Glamorgan, Tel: (0446) 760209
The comfort and elegance of a country house combine with first-rate service at St-Y-Nyll. Set in the vale of Glamorgan, it is surrounded by many places of interest, including its own extensive grounds. A beauty clinic is located on the premises.

STARCROSS GUESTHOUSE
Starcross Guesthouse, 1 Archer Road Penarth, Nr Cardiff Tel: (0222) 702718
The Starcross is an attractive Victorian house located in a quiet residential area. Excellent food includes the availability of vegetarian meals and home made bread. The atmosphere is always friendly and welcoming.

NORTH WALES

DEUCOCH HOTEL,
Abersoch, Pwllheli, Gwynedd, Tel: (075) 881 2680
This highly recommended hotel features panoramic views, an excellent restaurant and a fine collection of malt whiskies. Golfing breaks can be arranged, including DBB and green fees at various local courses.

DOLMELYNLLYN HALL,
Ganllywd, Dolgellau, Gwynedd, Tel: (034) 140273
Golf, fishing and Stately Home fans are well catered for at this elegant Country House Hotel. Of particular local note are the castles of Erdigg and Powis, whilst the rivers Mawddach and Wnion are sure to keep eager anglers occupied.

WALES
GOURMET GOLF

EDELWEISS HOTEL,
Off Lawson Road, Colwyn Bay, Tel: (0492) 532314
A multitude of facilities are provided to suit all tastes at this well-established hotel. Features include swimming, tennis, sauna, solarium and squash. Disabled guests are also welcomed.

THE FAIRBOURNE HOTEL,
Fairbourne, Gwynedd, Tel: (0341) 250203
Good food is the order of the day at this popular hotel. Thoughtful service and a friendly atmosphere are always present, leaving ample time for golf, fishing, pony-trekking, climbing and canoeing. Pets are welcome.

HAFOTY,
Rhostryfan, Caernarfon, Gwynedd, Tel: (0286) 830144
Hafoty is a comfortable farmhouse set in seventeen acres, overlooking Caernarfon with the nearest golf course only a ten minutes drive. An oak-beamed lounge with an open fire provides a warm welcome and is complemented by excellent food.

LLYS LLYWELYN,
Trefriw, Nr Llanrwst, Gwynedd, Tel: (0492) 640625
Relax and enjoy an idyllic break in this comfortable old house, nestling in a pretty, village location at the foot of the Carneddau Mountains. The food here is renowned and is prepared using many local ingredients.

THE OLD RECTORY,
Llanrwst Road, Llansnffraid, Glan Conwy, Tel: (0492) 580611
Tourists wishing an enjoyable holiday in a relaxing atmosphere will find this the perfect solution. The Georgian Country House offers panoramic vistas and a host of local facilities. Penrhyn Castle is a particular local favourite.

PLAS COCH HOTEL,
Bala, Gwynedd, Tel: (0678) 520
This hotel is popular with both locals and holidaymakers, offering as it does comfortable accommodation and a convivial atmosphere. An added enticement is free golf at the nearby Bala Club.

STANTON HOUSE HOTEL,
Whitehall Road, Rhos-on-Sea, Tel: (0492) 44363
Colwyn Bay is an ideal centre for touring the wonderful scenery of North Wales and The Stanton House Hotel makes the ideal base. Facilities are agreeable and only a short walk away from the Promenade, shops, squash club and other amenities.

ST TUDNO HOTEL,
Promenade, Llandudno, Gwynedd, Tel: (0492) 874411
This award-winning hotel provides accommodation of the very highest calibre and is equally renowned for its fine cuisine. Golf, fishing and various castles and homes are all within easy travelling distance.

TYDDN PERTHI FARM,
Portdinorwic, Gwynedd, Tel: (0248) 670336
Tyddyn Perthi is a family-run, working dairy farm situated between the historic town of Caernarfon and the University City of Bangor. There is much to see and do in this beautiful part of North Wales and guests will be made extremely welcome.

CONRAH COUNTRY HOUSE HOTEL

Resting in 22 acres of rolling landscaped grounds and woods the Conrah Country House Hotel is a delightful Mid Wales retreat. Tucked away at the end of a long rhododendron-lined driveway, only minutes from the Cambrian Coast, it commands magnificent views as far north as the Cader Idris mountain range. Originally the Mansion House to the old Welsh 'Ffosrhydgaled Estate' it now takes pride of place amidst spectacular scenery as a first class hotel.

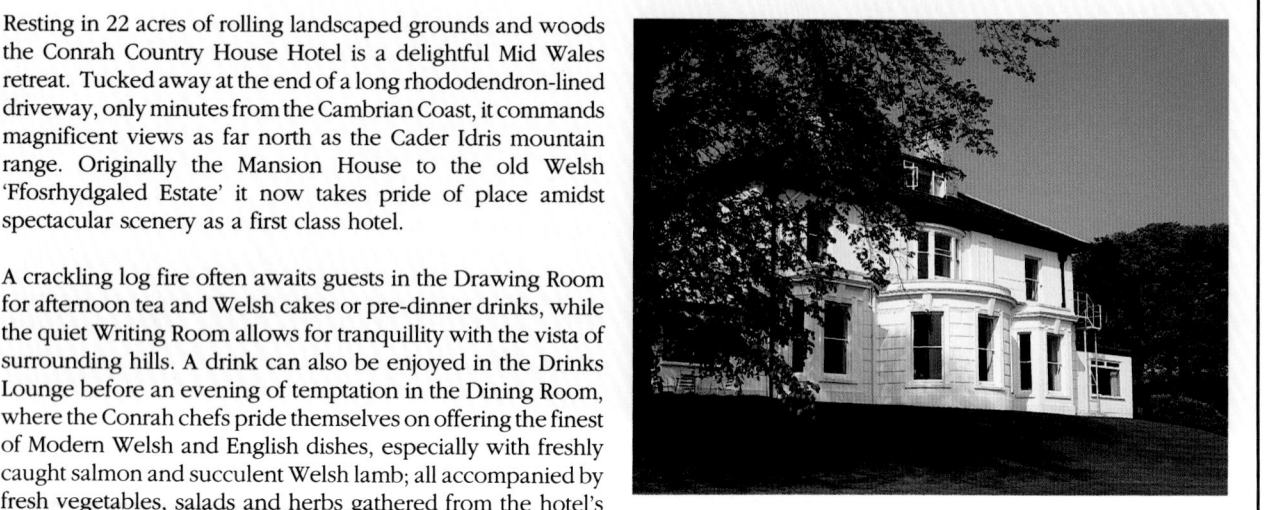

A crackling log fire often awaits guests in the Drawing Room for afternoon tea and Welsh cakes or pre-dinner drinks, while the quiet Writing Room allows for tranquillity with the vista of surrounding hills. A drink can also be enjoyed in the Drinks Lounge before an evening of temptation in the Dining Room, where the Conrah chefs pride themselves on offering the finest of Modern Welsh and English dishes, especially with freshly caught salmon and succulent Welsh lamb; all accompanied by fresh vegetables, salads and herbs gathered from the hotel's own kitchen garden, along with the perfect wine from a carefully selected list. There is always an extensive choice for vegetarians, while on good days hampers are available for delicious picnics in the country.

All of the twenty bedrooms have en suite bath or shower rooms, colour television and tea and coffee making facilities.

For the golfing enthusiast details of the ideal mini break golfing packages are available on request. For a different sporting pursuit try tennis, sea fishing or pony trekking - all available locally, while table tennis and croquet are to be enjoyed in the hotel itself. The area abounds in sites of historic interest, along with museums, galleries and superb walking. On your return why not relax with a sauna and cool off with a swim in the private pool, heated as a matter of course, with the addition of roaring log fire in winter.

The Conrah Country House Hotel
Rhydgaled
Chancery
Aberystwyth
Dyfed SY3 4DF
Tel: (0970) 617941
Fax: (0970) 624546

DUMFRIES, GALLOWAY & BORDERS

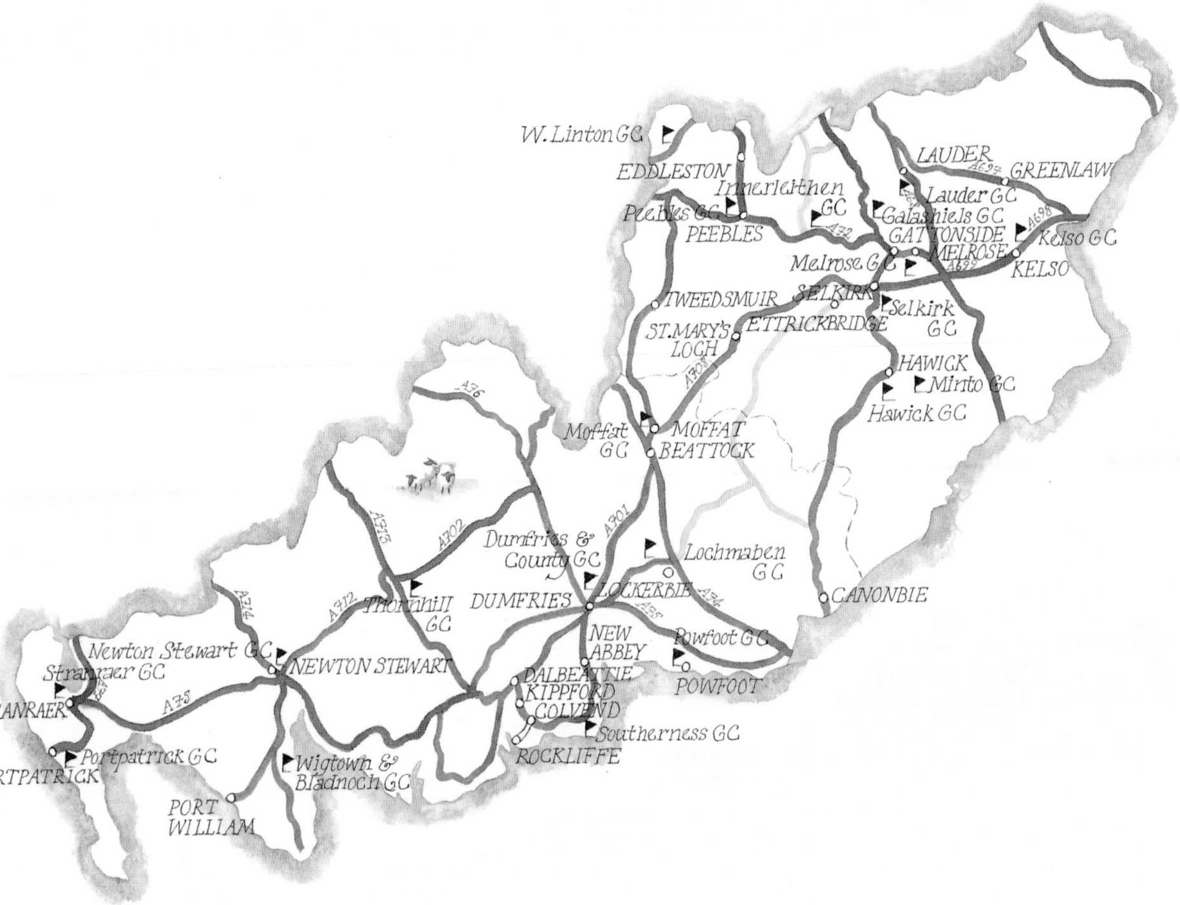
W. Linton GC
EDDLESTON
Innerleithen GC
Peebles GC
PEEBLES
LAUDER
GREENLAW
Lauder GC
Galashiels GC
GATTONSIDE
MELROSE
Kelso GC
Melrose GC
KELSO
TWEEDSMUIR
SELKIRK
Selkirk GC
ST. MARY'S LOCH
ETTRICKBRIDGE
HAWICK
Minto GC
Hawick GC
Moffat GC
MOFFAT
BEATTOCK
Dumfries & County GC
Lochmaben GC
DUMFRIES
LOCKERBIE
CANONBIE
Thornhill GC
Newton Stewart GC
NEWTON STEWART
Stranraer GC
STRANRAER
NEW ABBEY
Powfoot GC
POWFOOT
DALBEATTIE
KIPPFORD
COLVEND
Southerness GC
ROCKLIFFE
Portpatrick GC
PORTPATRICK
Wigtown & Bladnoch GC
PORT WILLIAM
A76
A701
A702
A713
A712
A714
A75
A74
A708
A697
A698
A699
A72

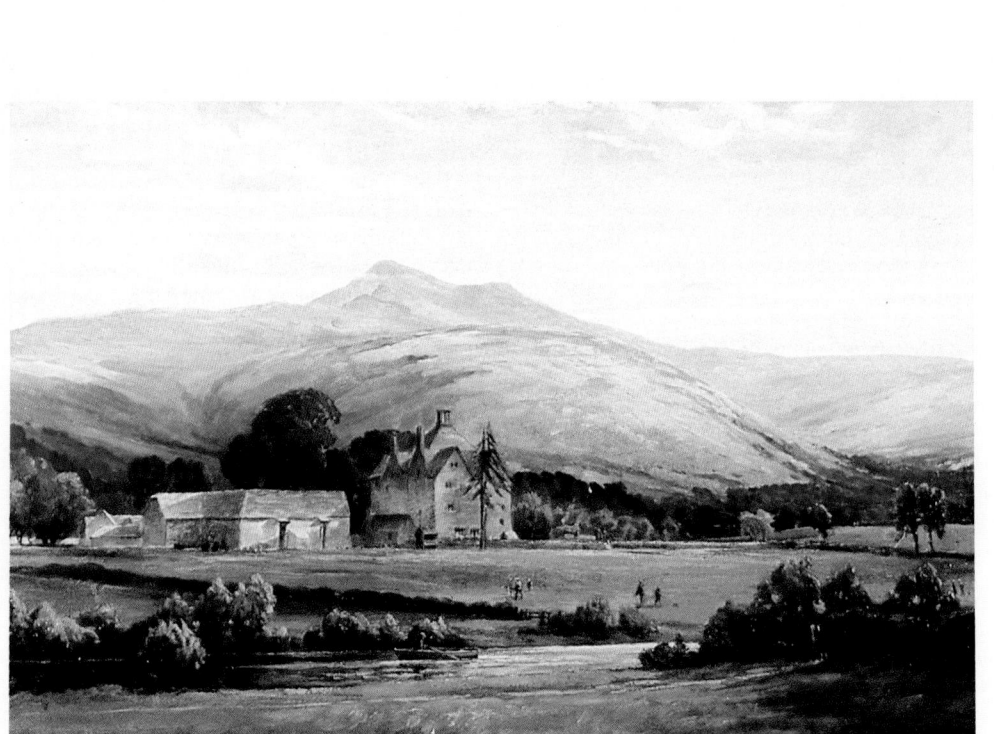

Sam Garratt PEEBLES Burlington Gallery

DUMFRIES, GALLOWAY & BORDERS
CHOICE GOLF

The two modern counties of Dumfries & Galloway and Borders (bit of a mouthful? – try the old Dumfrieshire, Kirkudbrightshire, Wigtownshire, Berwickshire, Peebleshire, Roxburghshire and Selkirkshire) encompass most of the Scottish Lowlands. A beautiful area of Britain – as of course is most of Scotland – but surely not one terribly renowned for its golf? It may not be renowned but there is still certainly no shortage of exciting and challenging courses in the area. Indeed, the very fact that the great hordes head for the more famous venues further north means that Scotland's southerly golfing gems remain by and large marvellously uncrowded.

DUMFRIES & GALLOWAY

The one true Championship test in this region is found at **Southerness**. Of all Scotland's great links courses this is perhaps the least widely known. We have featured MacKenzie Ross's masterpiece on a separate page.

Powfoot is a fairly close neighbour of Southerness (though not as the crow flies) the course lying 5 miles west of Annan off the B724. A semi-links with plenty of heather and gorse it offers a tremendous test of golf and is an admirable companion to Southerness. Adding to the enjoyment of a round at Powfoot is the setting – the course provides extensive views towards the Cumberland Hills to the south and the Galloway Hills to the west. The Isle of Man is also visible on a clear day.

Two convenient resting places after a game at Southerness are in Rockliffe, The Baron's Craig Hotel (055663) 225 and a little closer in Colvend, The Clonyard House (055663) 372. Good eating places include, The Abbey Arms (038785) 215 and The Criffel Inn (038785) 244, both in New Abbey, and The Pheasant in Dalbeattie. Powfoot has The Golf Hotel (04617) 254 whilst a little further away is Canonbie and an exceptional restaurant at the Riverside Inn (03873) 71512.

Nearby there are two good eighteen hole courses at Dumfries, **Dumfries and County**, to the north of the town being the pick of the two, but golfers travelling north would do well to pay **Lochmaben** a visit as well. It is a very friendly Club with an interesting nine hole course designed by James Braid. The setting around the Kirk Loch is most picturesque and the course is famed for its many beautiful old trees.

When inspecting any of the above courses, Dumfries, the county's largest town is a likely base and here The Cairndale Hotel (0387) 54111 is most pleasant. Other recommended establishments in the area include The Dryfesdale (05762) 2427 in Lockerbie, The Lockerbie House Country Hotel (05762) 2610, 14th century Comlongon Castle (038 787) 283 and Allanton House (038774) 509 with its resident farm. Also note the Barjarg Tower (0848) 31545 at Auldgirth, a first class 16th century country house hotel.

Towards the western corner of Dumfries and Galloway there is some fine golf. Two nine hole courses well worth playing are at Wigtown, **Wigtown and Bladnoch** to be precise, and at **Newton Stewart**. Still further west, **Stranraer**, the ferry terminal for Larne, has a fine parkland course north of the town overlooking Loch Ryan. But the cliff top course at **Portpatrick** is surely the major golfing attraction; it is rated by many to be one of the most beautiful courses in Britain. Apparently Portpatrick for

many years in the last century was Ireland's Gretna Green – couples sailing across the Irish Sea to get hitched in Portpatrick's tiny church. The golf course provides some breathtaking scenery, particularly outstanding is the view from the 13th fairway. It can often get quite breezy and although only 5,644 yards in length, the course is certainly no pushover.

Superb golf is accompanied by an exceptionally high number of first rate hotels. In Castle Douglas, Milton Park (06443) 286 is a recurring favourite whilst in Newton Stewart, the Kirroughtree Hotel (0671) 2141 is excellent. More modest but still welcoming is The Bruce (0671) 2294. Port William offers the very fine Corsemalzie House Hotel (09886) 254 while a number of alternatives are found at Portpatrick. Pick of the bunch is The Knockinaam Lodge Hotel (077681) 471 which has a glorious setting and a tremendous restaurant. Others to note here are The Fernhill (0877681) 220 and The Portpatrick Hotel (077681) 333.

Having sampled the delights of the coast of Southern Scotland one may head inland to the delights of the Border towns. En route one could slip 18 holes in at **Thornhill** or perhaps visit **Moffat**. The town has a very enjoyable moorland course with a marvellous setting in the valley of Annandale. The Black Bull is well worth a visit after a round and a recommended place to spend an evening is the Beechwood Country House Hotel (0683) 20210.

BORDERS

The Border towns offer castles aplenty, some superb woollens and some excellent rugby. Golfwise, no course here could claim to be of Championship proportions, however, the majority can boast spectacular settings, visitors are always encouraged and the green fees in these parts are just about the cheapest in Britain.

A cluster of courses are to be found in the centre of the county. The town of **Melrose** is famed for its ruined Abbey where the heart of Robert The Bruce is said to have been buried (gruesome stuff!) It has a fine nine hole course and there are others equally pleasant at **Selkirk, Hawick, Lauder**, **St. Boswells**, **Innerliethen** and **West Linton**. **Kelso** has an interesting layout being inside Kelso racecourse. Finally well worth noting are **Peebles** and **Galashiels** – both are public courses, very well maintained and true to form set amidst magnificent countryside.

Walter Scott's land really does deserve a lengthy inspection. This alas isn't the place but whether one is golfing in the Borders or simply breaking a journey, here are some ideas for places to stay. In Peebles, two choice hotels can be found; Cringletie House Hotel (0721) 3233 and The Peebles Hotel Hydro (0721) 20602. Good guesthouses are also plentiful, with Lindores (0721) 20441 and Whitestone House (0721) 20337 among the best. Golfers who like a spot of fishing should also note The Tweed Valley Hotel (089687) 636 in nearby Walkerburn. St Mary's Loch offers The Tibbie Shiels Inn (0750) 42231, Selkirk the Woodburn House Hotel (0750) 20815 and Tweedsmuir the cosy Crook Inn (08997) 272. Ettrickshaws Hotel (0750) 52229 in Ettrickbridge, Sunlaws House Hotel (05735) 331 and the Cross Keys Hotel (0573) 223303 in Kelso are three outstanding places to conclude our journey.

SUNLAWS HOUSE

Sunlaws House stands in the heart of Scotland's beautiful Border country, in 200 acres of gardens and mature parkland along the banks of the Teviot, three miles from the historic town of Kelso.There has been a house on the same site at Sunlaws for nearly 500 years and from its beginnings it has always been a Scottish family house – and that, to all intents and purposes, is how it will stay!

Sunlaws has a place in history, from the faint echoes of ancient strife when English armies of the 15th and 16th centuries came marauding through Roxburghshire and the Borders, to the Jacobite rebellion of 1745. Indeed Prince Charles Edward Stuart is reputed to have stayed on November 5th 1745 and to have planted a white rose bush in the grounds.

Sunlaws hope that their guests will find that in the intervening year there have been some welcome changes. Its owner, the Duke of Roxburghe, has carefully converted Sunlaws into the small, welcoming but unpretentious hotel of comfort and character that it is.

There are 22 bedrooms, which include the splendid Bowmont Suite and six delightful rooms in the stable courtyard, all furnished with care to His Graces' own taste and all with private bathroom or shower, colour television, radio and direct-dial telephone. Disabled guests too are provided with the amenities they need.

The spacious public rooms are furnished with the same care and elegance, which adds to the overall atmosphere of warmth and welcome with log fires burning in the main and inner hall, drawing room, library bar and dining room, throughout the winter and on cold summer evenings.

Flowers and plants, from the gardens and the conservatory, will be found all over the house; herbs too are grown for the kitchen and will be found in many of the traditional dishes that are prepared for the dining room. Not only is Sunlaws right in the heart of Scotland's beautiful Border Country, it is also the perfect centre for a host of holiday activities. Sporting and cultural interests are well served, too.

Salmon and trout fishing, and a complete range of shooting are available at the Hotel, with golf, horse-riding, racing and fox hunting all nearby.

Sunlaws is the perfect location for touring the Borders, with great country houses including Abbotsford, the home of Sir Walter Scott, and a number of abbeys and museums all within easy reach.

Sunlaws House Hotel
Kelso
Roxburghshire
Scotland
Tel: (05735) 331 Fax: (05735) 611

SOUTHERNESS
CHAMPIONSHIP GOLF

Two of Britain's greatest (and least explored) links courses stare at one another across the Solway Firth – one is on the English side at Silloth and the other lies north of the border at Southerness. As close as they appear on the map, the only way of travelling from one to the other is by a fairly lengthy drive around the coast via Gretna Green. Before the War a bridge crossed the Solway, but before the War Southerness didn't have a golf course.

Situated 16 miles south of Dumfries, in an almost forgotten corner of southern Scotland, Southerness is the only true Championship links in Great Britain to have been built since 1945. (Quite a contrast to Ireland where the likes of Waterville, Tralee, Connemara and Ballybunion New have all been constructed within the last 20 years.)

So golf came to Southerness about 500 years after it came to St. Andrews but one cannot help wondering why it took so long – after all – the much more remote golfing outposts of Dornoch and Machrihanish took root in the dim and distant past and a more natural and pleasanter site for the links it is hard to imagine. Wild dunes, rampant heather, dense bracken and prickly golden gorse all present themselves in abundance here; as for that matter do twisting, tumbling fairways and firm, fast greens – yes, Southerness is as every truly traditional Scottish links should be, terrifyingly wonderful! In fact the golf at Southerness is probably more terrifying and more wonderful than at most.

If Mother Nature created the wonder of the setting then Mackenzie Ross (the architect of modern Turnberry) must be credited with the production of a genuine thriller. Golf at Southerness is nothing if not exhilarating. From the Championship tees the links can be stretched to 7000 yards; most mortal golfers will still find the 6564 yards, par 71 from the white tees (or 6093 yards, par 69 from the yellow tees) an awesome challenge; several of the par fours measure in excess of 400 yards (with prodigious carries to match) and two of the par threes are well over 200 yards long. A visit to Southerness is certainly recommended but pray that your long game is in fine fettle!

Before approaching the 1st tee, consultation with the Club's Secretary, **Mr W.D. Ramage** is advisable. Visitors can book tee times beween 10.00 – 12.00 and 2.00 – 5.00 midweek and between 10.30 – 12.00 and 2.30 – 5.00 at weekends. Mr Ramage can be contacted by telephone on **(0387) 88677** or by addressing a letter to **The Secretary, Southerness Golf Club, Southerness, Dumfries DG2 8AZ.** Golfing Societies are equally welcome but must contact the Secretary in advance. Southerness does not have a golf professional.

The green fees at Southerness compare very favourably with those at many of Scotland's more celebrated Championship courses. A full day's golf in 1992 cost £20 per day during the week and £26 at weekends. Junior visitors can play midweek for a green fee of just £6.

Southerness's situation is quiet rather than remote. Golfers from England, heading to or from Turnberry, Troon and Prestwick will likely drive through the town of Dumfries on the A75/A76 and Southerness is just half an hour's detour from Dumfries along the A710; a pretty drive via New Abbey. From the west the A710 approaches via Dalbeattie while Dumfries is linked to Glasgow by the A710 and the A74/M74, and to Edinburgh by the A702 and the A74.

Unless the weather is frightful we will not regret making that detour. Catch Southerness on a glorious morning with the sun reflecting off the dancing waters of the Solway Firth and we may just wonder why we were heading for the Ayrshire coast in the first place!

Southerness opens with three dog-legged holes, the **2nd** being a classic par four and a half hole – in length strictly a par four but into the prevailing wind, in reality a par five; certainly a 4-5-4 start at Southerness is an accomplishment. After the short **4th** the course doubles back on itself, then turns towards the sea. The views become more distracting but the challenge in no way diminishes. The **7th** is the first of two long par threes and you aim your tee shot directly at the Solway but the best run of holes are arguably those between the **10th**, a par three surrounded by a sea of heather and the **13th**, the longest par four on the card. The **12th** is generally considered to be the best hole of all; here a well positioned drive (avoiding the deviously positioned fairway bunkers) is essential as the second shot must be fired towards a narrow green which sits on a plateau and looks down over a beautiful beach; deep bunkers guard the green front right and a pond will gleefully swallow any shot that strays left of centre.

The toughest hole on the closing stretch is yet another of Southerness's cunning dog-legs, the **16th** which is normally played into the teeth of the wind; a four here may prove more illusive than at the par five **18th**, where with the wind finally at our backs we have the chance of finding the green with two good blows. Shall we go for it? Why not, Southerness is that kind of course.

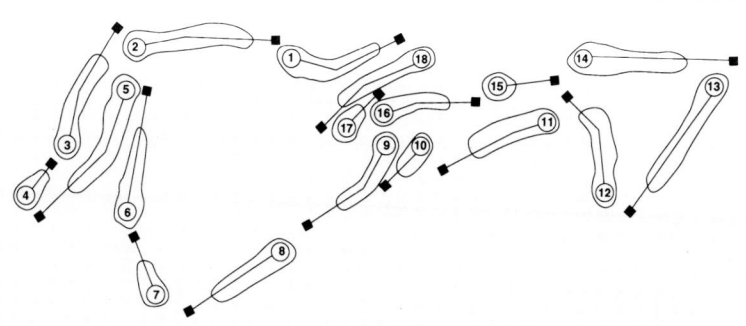

Hole	Yards	Par	Hole	Yards	Par
1	393	4	10	168	3
2	450	5	11	390	4
3	408	4	12	421	4
4	169	3	13	467	4
5	494	5	14	458	5
6	405	4	15	217	3
7	215	3	16	433	4
8	371	4	17	175	3
9	435	4	18	485	5
Out	**3,340**	**36**	**In**	**3,214**	**35**
			Out	**3,340**	**36**
			Totals	**6,554**	**71**

CRINGLETIE HOUSE HOTEL

Cringletie is a distinguished mansion which has retained the warm atmosphere of a private country house. It is set well back from the Peebles/Edinburgh road (A703) in 28 acres of garden and woodland, in peaceful surroundings. Only 20 miles from Edinburgh, it is an excellent centre.

All rooms are tastefully decorated and furnished to a high standard of comfort, with colour televisions, direct dial telephones and en-suite facilities. There are magnificent views from all rooms. The restaurant has been consistently recommended since 1971.

Recommended by Johansen; Egon Ronay; The A.A.; The R.A.C.; Signpost; Ashley Courtenay and other guidebooks.

Cringletie House Hotel
Peebles EH45 8PL
Tel: (07213) 233
Fax: (07213) 244

LOCKERBIE MANOR COUNTRY HOTEL

Set amidst 78 acres of tranquil park and woodland, Lockerbie Country Manor is a haven of peace and relaxation, yet it is situated only a mile off the A74. Built in 1814 for Sir William Douglas and Dame Grace Johnstone, whose great-grandson, the Marquis of Queensbury formulated the present day boxing rules, it became the smart country hotel it is today in 1920.

Guests can enjoy the traditions of a bygone era at Lockerbie Manor. The long tree-lined driveway gives a taste of the luxury that lies ahead. Both of the public lounges are furnished in authentic period style with an Adam fireplace amidst period furniture and walls lined with oil paintings. The atmosphere exudes warmth and hospitality; a home away from home for the traveller.

All the 29 bedrooms are individually decorated with private bathrooms, colour T.V. and every comfort. There are three four-poster bedded suites, with front-facing views over the fields and surrounding countryside. The Queensbury Dining Room, with its wood panelled wall, ornate chandeliers and magnificent views, is the ideal setting for a delectable meal. The cuisine is of an international nature, where Eastern flavours and cooking subtly blend with Western recipes.

Golfers will love the courses in the area, offering challenges of varying degrees of difficulty. Lockerbie, Dumfries, Lochmaben, Powfoot and Moffat are all near by. If shooting is more your scene, there are numerous large estates around Lockerbie offering facilities. For the fisherman, the Rivers Annan, Milk, Cree, Blanock and Penkiln all beckon. Within the space of a short drive you can visit the beautiful Galloway coast, Drumlanrigg Castle, Maxwellton House in Monaive, Threave Gardens and Castle near Castle Douglas, and Thomas Carlyle's birthplace at Ecclefechan.

Lockerbie Manor Country Hotel
Boreland Road
Lockerbie
Dumfries and Galloway
DG11 2RG
Tel: (05762) 2610
Fax: (05762) 3046

CORSEMALZIE HOUSE HOTEL

Corsemalzie House Hotel, a secluded country mansion is set in the heart of the picturesque countryside of the Machars (moors) of Wigtownshire, away from the rigours of city life. Relax in a setting which is hard to beat, the only noise to upset the tranquillity are the cries of the whaup (curlew) and the babbling burn. The seasonal changes create a different backdrop for the hotel, making Corsemalzie a delight to stay at whatever time of year is your preference.

The gastronome will find Corsemalzie has a great deal to offer, with dishes created using only the finest ingredients carefully and enthusiastically supervised by the proprietor Mr Peter McDougall. Fresh and local produce is used whenever possible.

This attention to detail is carried throughout the hotel with Mr and Mrs McDougall ensuring that your stay will not only be memorable for the cuisine but also for the little things that make the difference between a good hotel and a great hotel.

If you can drag yourself away from this comfort, the surrounding area has much to offer, with riding pony trekking and walking, some superb golf on your doorstep, a whole host of 9 hole courses, with 18 hole courses at Portpatrick, Glenluce where the hotel pays half your green fees, Stranraer and a little further afield at the famous Turnberry Links course.

For the game sportsmen, shooting and fishing are here in an abundance, Mr McDougall will personally organise and assist you shooting for pheasant, grouse, partridge, duck geese, snipe woodcock, rabbits and hares in the hotel grounds and neighbouring estates amounting to some 8,000 acres. The hotel has exclusive salmon and trout fishing rights on four and a half miles of the River Bladnoch and five miles on the River Tarff. Fishing can also be organised in the Mazie Burn. A gillie is available for most of the season to advise and assist wherever needed.

Corsemalzie House Hotel
Port William
Newton Stewart
Wigtownshire
Scotland DG8 9RL
Tel: (098 886) 254
Fax: (098 886) 213

DUMFRIES & GALLOWAY AND BORDERS
COMPLETE GOLF

BORDERS

Duns G.C
(0361) 83327
Hardens Road, Duns, Berwickshire
1 mile W. of Duns on A6105
(9) 5754 yards/***/E

Eyemouth G.C
(08907) 50551
Gunsgreen House, Eyemouth
3 miles N. of Burnmouth on A1107
(9) 5446 yards/***/E

Galashiels G.C
(0896) 3724
Ladhope Recreation Ground, Galashiels,
Selkirkshire
N.E of town, off A7
(18) 5309 yards/***/E

Gatehouse G.C
(055 74) 654
Laurieston Road, Gatehouse
Quarter of a mile off A75
(9) 4796 yards/***/E

Hawick G.C
(0450) 72293
Vertish Hill, Hawick, Roxburghshire
S. of Hawick on A7
(18) 5929 yards/***/E

Hirsel G.C
(0890) 2678
Kelso Road, Coldstream
At west end of Coldstream on A697
(9) 2828 yards/***/E

Jedburgh G.C
(0835) 63587
Dunion Road, Jedburgh, Roxburghshire
Half mile out of town
(9) 5522 yards/***/F

Kelso G.C
(0573) 23009
Racecourse Road, Kelso, Roxburghshire
1 mile from town centre within National Hunt
Racecourse
(18) 6066 yards/***/F

Lauder G.C
(057) 82409
Galashiels Road, Lauder
Half mile from Lauder off A68
(9) 6003 yards/***/F

Melrose G.C
(089682) 2855
Dingleton, Melrose, Roxburghshire
Half mile S. of Melrose town centre
(9) 5464 yards/**/F

Minto G.C
(0450) 87220
Minto Village, by Denholme, Hawick,
Roxburghshire
5 miles N.E. of Hawick off A698
(18) 5460 yards/***/E

Peebles G.C
(0721) 20197
Kirkland Street, Peebles
N.W. of town off the A72
(18) 6137 yards/***/E

St. Boswells G.C
(0835) 22359
St Boswells, Roxburghshire
At junction of A68 and B6404
(9) 2625 yards/***/E

Selkirk G.C
(0750) 20621
The Hill, Selkirk
1 mile S. of Selkirk on the A7 to Hawick
(9) 5640 yards/***/E

Torwoodlee G.C
(0896) 2260
Edinburgh Road, Galashiels, Selkirkshire
1 mile from Galashiels on A7 to Edinburgh
(9) 5800 yards/***(not Sat)/F

West Linton G.C
(0968) 60256
West Linton, Peeblshire
17 miles S.W. of Edinburgh on the A702
(18) 6024 yards/***/D

DUMFRIES & GALLOWAY

Castle Douglas G.C
(0556) 2801Abercromby Road, Castle Douglas,
Kirkcudbrightshire
In the centre of the town
(9) 5400 yards/***(not Thurs pm)/F

Colvend G.C
(055663) 398
Sandyhills, By Dalbeattie, Kirkcudbrightshire
6 miles from Dalbeattie on A710
(9) 2322 yards/***/F

Dumfries & County G.C
(0387) 53585
Edinburgh Road, Dumfries
1 mile N. of Dumfries on the A701
(18) 5928 yards/***(not Sat)/D

Dumfries & Galloway G.C
(0387) 63582
Laurieston Avenue, Dumfries
W. of Dumfries on the A75
(18) 5782 yards/***/D

Kircudbright G.C
(0567) 30542
Stirling Crescent, Kirkcudbright
Near centre of town, off B727
(18) 5598 yards/***/E

Langholm G.C
(0541) 80559
Langholm, Dumfriesshire
Between Carlisle and Hawick on the A7
(9) 5246 yards/***/E

Lochmaben G.C
(0387) 810552
Castlehill Gate, Lochmaben, Dumfriesshire
Leave A74 at Lockerbie for A709 for Dumfries
(9) 5304 yards/***/F

Lockerbie
(05762) 3363
Currie Road, Lockerbie, Dumfriesshir
Take A74 to Lockerbie
(18) 5228 yards/***(not Sat)/F

Moffat G.C
(0683) 20020
Coatshill, Moffat
Take A701 for 1 mile off the A74
(18) 5218 yards/***(not Wed pm)/D

New Galloway G.C
(06442) 239Castle Douglas, Kirkcudbrightshire
Just out of Village on the A762
(9) 5058 yards/***/E

Newton Stewart G.C
(0671) 2172
Kirroughtree Avenue, Minnigaff, Newton
Stewart
Leave the A75 at sign for Minnigaff Village
(9) 5500 yards/***/E

Portpatrick (Dunskey) G.C
(077681) 273
Portpatrick, Stranraer, Wigtownshire
Signposted on the A77 to Portpatrick
(18) 5644 yards/***/D/H

Powfoot G.C
(04612) 2866
Cummertrees, Annan, Dumfriesshire
3 miles from Annan on the B724
(18) 6266 yards/**/F

St Medan G.C
(098 87) 358
Monreith, Port William, Wigtownshire
3 miles S. of Port William on the A747
(9) 4454 yards/***/E

Sanquhar G.C
(0659) 50577
Old Barr Road, Sanquhar, Dumfriesshire
mile from Sanquhar off the A76
(9) 2572 yards/***/E

Southerness G.C
(038 788) 677
Southerness, Dumfries
16 miles S.W of Dumfries off the A710
(18) 6554 yards/***/D

Stranraer G.C
(0776) 3539
Creachmore, Stranraer
Take the A718 from Stranraer towards Leswalt
(18) 6300 yards/***/D

Thornhill G.C
(0848) 30546
Blacknest, Thornhill, Dumfries
14 miles N. of Dumfries on the A76 to Thornhill
(18) 6011 yards/***/F

Wigtown and Bladnoch
(098 84) 3354Lightlands Avenue, Wigtown,
Wigtownshire
Right at town square, left at Agnew Crescent
(9) 2732 yards/***/E

Wigtownshire County G.C
(05813)420
Mains of Park, Glenluce, Newton Stewart,
Wigtownshire
8 miles E. of Stranraer on the A75
(18) 5715 yards/***/D

LOTHIAN

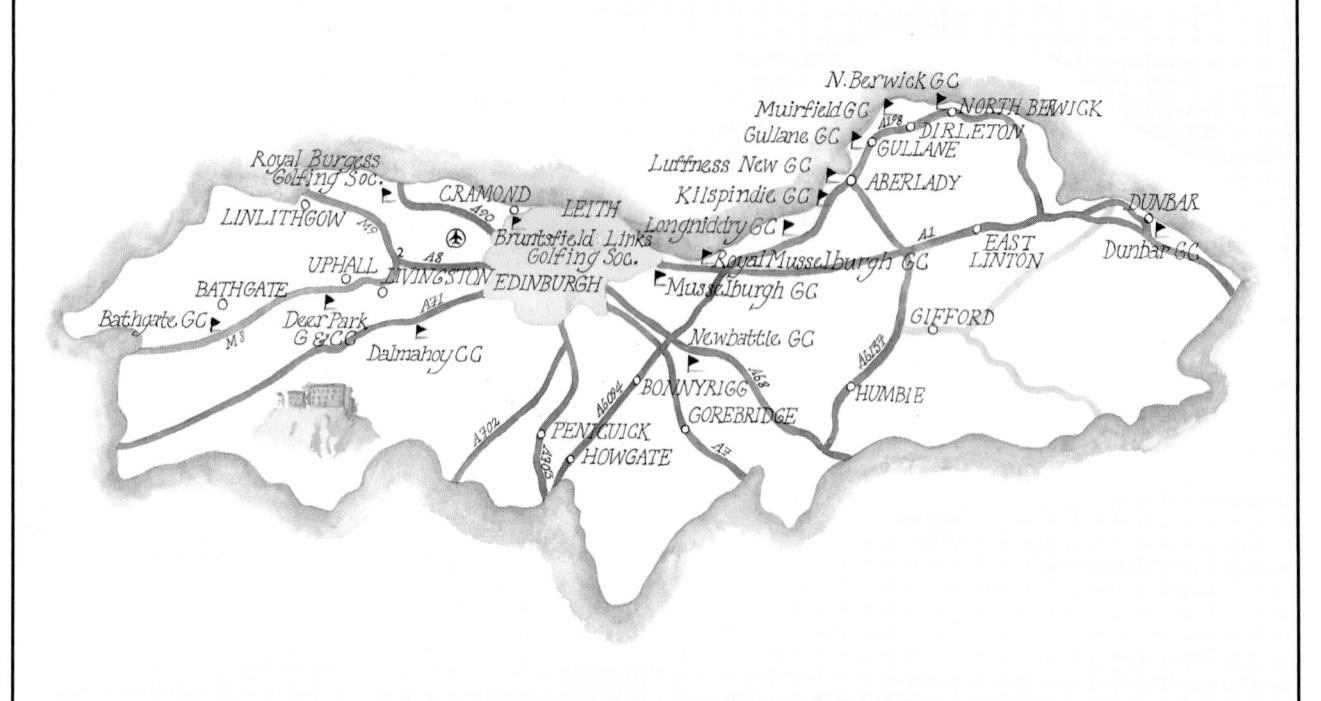

John Lavery   NORTH BERWICK   Sotheby's

'Hard by in the fields called the links, the citizens of Edinburgh divert themselves at a game called golf, in which they use a curious kind of bat tipt with horn and a small elastic ball of leather stuffed with feathers rather less than tennis balls, but out of a much harder consistency and this they strike with such force and dexterity that it will fly to an incredible distance'.

When Tobias Smollett wrote these words in 1771 golf had already been played in the 'fields' around Edinburgh for at least three hundred years. The seemingly harmless pastime wasn't always popular with the authorities. In 1593 the Town Council of Edinburgh deplored the fact that a great number of its inhabitants chose to spend the Sabbath in the town of Leith where 'in tyme of sermons' many were 'sene in the streets, drynking in taverns, or otherwise at Golf'. Shame on them!

Today the east coast of Scotland is famous the world over, not only because it was here that it all began, but also because its many courses remain among the very finest the game has to offer. In a 30 mile coastal stretch between the courses of **Royal Burgess** and **Dunbar** lie the likes of **Muirfield, Gullane, North Berwick, Luffness New** and **Longniddry** – truly a magnificent seven and there are many others.

EDINBURGH

Visitors to the beautiful city of Edinburgh, the so called 'Athens of the North', should have little trouble getting a game. There are numerous first class courses in and around the capital; regrettably we only have space to mention a handful of the best. To the west of the city lie a particularly historic pair – **Bruntsfield Links** and **Royal Burgess**: between them they have witnessed nearly 500 years of golfing history. The latter Club in fact claims to be the world's oldest. (A claim hotly disputed I might add by Muirfield's 'Honourable Company'!) These more prestigious courses are of course difficult to play, but with advance preparation it is possible; another Edinburgh gem not to be missed is **Braid Hills**; in fact two fine public courses here, just south of the city. The **Dalmahoy** Hotel Golf and Country Club situated to the south west of the city nestles at the base of the Pentland Hills and has two excellent 18 hole courses. Dalmahoy, like **Muirfield** and **Dunbar** is featured ahead. Towards the east side of Edinburgh is Musselburgh. The old Open links is not what it was, alas, although you can still play the nine holes adjacent to Musselburgh racecourse for history's sake; however, perhaps the best place for a game is at **Royal Musselburgh**, a beautiful parkland course and a little further out of the city the course at **Newbattle** can be recommended.

Spending a few days in Edinburgh is a real treat whether one is a golfer or not. The city's leading hotels include the magnificent Balmoral Hotel (031) 556 2414, re-opened in 1991 to great acclaim and the Caledonian Hotel (031) 225 2433. The latter's Pompadour Restaurant is quite superb. Among the many other hotels, The Sheraton (031) 229 9131 is on a par with the city's best while The George (031) 225 1251 has a most impressive edifice and is a great favourite for post-rugby celebrations. Johnstounburn House (087533) 696, at nearby Humbie, offers an out-of-town alternative.

Edinburgh is as well blessed with restaurants as it is with hotels. These are some of the many worth considering (or sampling if you have the time and resources!) to consider: La Caveau (031) 556 5707 and L'Auberge (031) 556 5888 will delight lovers of French food, while those who prefer pasta should sample Cos-

mo (031) 226 6743 or for an Indian, try the Kalpna (031) 667 9890 which offers some mouth-watering Indian cuisine. In Leith two noted restaurants are Oysters (031) 553 6363 and Skippers (031) 554 1018. To work off the excesses caused by such culinary delights, Channings (031) 315 2226 is a sophisticated and elegant hotel with excellent leisure facilities.

The courses of West Lothian are not as well known as their eastern counterparts, however, two are particularly worth considering, **Bathgate**, a fine moorland course and the **Deer Park** Golf and Country Club at Livingston. Both lie within easy access of Edinburgh. The Bathgate Club which recently celebrated its centenary can lay claim to having produced two Ryder Cup players – Eric Brown and Bernard Gallacher, both of whom were members of the 1969 and 1971 sides.

LINKS GOLF

Travellers wishing to explore the delights of the East Coast should aim to pick up the A198 at Prestonpans near Musselburgh. Before it reaches Longniddry the road passes through Seton, where Mary Queen of Scots is known to have sharpened up her golf swing more than 400 years ago. 13 miles East of Edinburgh, **Longniddry** ought not to be considered as merely a stopping place en route to Muirfield. It is a superb course, part links part parkland with every hole having a view of the sea. **Kilspindie Golf Club** is also worth a little detour while **Luffness New** and the three neighbouring courses of **Gullane**, lie only a short distance further along the coast. Each is outstanding in its way though if you only have time to play two then Luffness New and Gullane Number One are probably the pick, although the former can be difficult to get on! The panoramic view from the top of Gullane Hill on the latter's 7th hole is one of the most famous in golf.

The West Links at **North Berwick** has a wealth of charm and tradition; it is one of the most natural courses one is likely to come across and several blind shots must be encountered. Two of its holes, the 14th 'Perfection' and the 15th 'Redan' have been imitated by golf architects all over the world. As at Dunbar there are some splendid views across to Bass Rock.

Time for a 19th hole. Hotels are numerous, as indeed are good restaurants. In Gullane, Greywalls (0620) 842144 has gained an enviable reputation and is literally on the doorstep of Muirfield and the three links of Gullane, while La Potiniere (0620) 843214 is a restaurant to savour when in these parts. Gullane is also resplendent with guest houses; The Golf Tavern (0620) 843259 is but one recommended illustration. In Aberlady the Kilspindie House Hotel (08757) 682 and The Wagon (08757) 319 are both welcoming as is clearly The Open Arms (062085) 241 in the pretty village of Dirleton. The Marine Hotel (0620) 2406 is convenient for North Berwick while other well priced alternatives include The Mallard (0620) 843228, The Royal (0620) 2401, The Point Garry Hotel (0620) 2380 and the Golf Hotel (0620) 2202. Towards Dunbar, in the town itself, The Bellevue (0368) 62322 and The Bayswell (0368) 62225 are both comfortable hotels but many super establishments are found a little inland. Note especially The Harvesters Hotel (0620) 860395 at East Linton and The Tweedale Arms (0620) 81240 at Gifford. Travelling back westwards, 15th century Borthwick Castle (0875) 20514 at Gorebridge is a first class establishment. For the touring golfer in Scotland, a country cottage can serve as an ideal base, and both Blakes Country Cottages (0603) 783227 and Mackays (031) 225 3539 offer an enticing range of self-catering accommodation.

MUIRFIELD
CHAMPIONSHIP GOLF

Muirfield is of course much more than one of the world's greatest golf links, it is also the home of the world's oldest Golf Club. **The Honourable Company of Edinburgh Golfers** are the direct descendants of the Gentlemen Golfers who played at **Leith Links** from at least as early as the fifteenth century. On **7th March 1744** several Gentlemen of Honour, skilful in the ancient and healthful exercise of Golf, petitioned the city fathers of Edinburgh to provide a silver club to be played for annually on the links at Leith. The winner of this competition became Captain of Golf and the club was paraded through the city. In 1744 the Edinburgh Golfers formulated the game's first code of rules, **The Thirteen Articles**, which were adopted almost word for word ten years later by the Royal and Ancient Club at St Andrews.

The Company played over the five holes at Leith for almost a hundred years before overcrowding forced the decision to move to the nine hole course at **Musselburgh**, to the east of the city. Long before they had left Leith the Members had begun to dine and play in the famous red uniform; failure to wear this usually resulted in a fine. A minute from the 1830's records how one member was fined two tappit hens for playing golf without his red coat! The **Open Championship** first came to Musselburgh in 1874 and was held there every third year until 1889. Meanwhile Musselburgh, like Leith, had become terribly crowded and the Company decided that the time had come for a second move. Again, they looked to the east and almost twenty miles from Edinburgh, under the lee of Gullane Hill, they discovered Muirfield. The course was designed by **'Old' Tom Morris** and opened for play on 3rd May 1891. In its early years the course received much criticism. One professional described it as 'nothing but an auld watter meddie' but it appears that this had more to do with jealousy, owing to the fact that when the Honourable Company left Musselburgh they took the Open Championship with them. It was held at Muirfield in 1892 and it never again returned to Musselburgh. Following the success of the 1892 Championship, Muirfield's reputation grew rapidly and today it is widely considered to be the fairest, if not the finest test in golf.

Visitors wishing to play at Muirfield must make prior arrangements with the Secretry, **Group Captain J A Prideaux**, who may be contacted by telephone on **(0620) 842123**. For gentlemen golfers there is a requirement that they belong to a recognised Golf Club and carry a handicap of 18 or less, while for lady golfers (who may only play if accompanied by a gentleman player) the handicap limit is 24.

The days on which visitors are welcome are Tuesdays, Thursdays and, with the exception of July and August, on Friday mornings. It should also be noted that by tradition foursome matches are strongly favoured at Muirfield and four ball games will only be permitted in the mornings. Golfing Societies (limited to 40 players) are also received on the usual visiting days and arrangements may be made with the Secretary. All written correspondence should be addressed to **The Secretary, The Honourable Company of Edinburgh Golfers, Muirfield, Gullane, East Lothian, EH31 2EG**. The green fees for 1992 were set at £45 for a single round with £60 entitling the visitor to a full day's golf. All fees should be paid to the cashier in the Clubhouse Dining Room.

Travelling to Muirfield (or Gullane) will often be by way of Edinburgh. Gullane is connected to the capital city by the A198. Northbound travellers can avoid Edinburgh by approaching on the A1 which runs to Dunbar to the east of Gullane. From Dunbar the A198 can be picked up. Those coming from the north and west of Scotland will need to travel via Edinburgh. The M8 links Glasgow to Edinburgh, whilst the M9 should be taken from Stirling and the M90 from Perth.

One of the unique features of Muirfield (or at least unique in terms of Scottish Championship links) is its layout of two separate loops, an outer and an inner. This ensures that the golfer will not have to play several successive holes into or against the same wind direction. Although quite undulating, the course doesn't require blind shots and this contributes much to Muirfields fairness tag. From the Championship tees the links stretch to 6941 yards, and with the often prodigiously thick rough and deep, cavernous bunkers, it can be a very severe test of golf. From the Medal tees Muirfield still measures a fairly lengthy 6601 yards, par 70.

Since 1892 the Open Championship has been played at Muirfield on 13 occasions. Before the last War winners included **Harry Vardon, James Braid** and **Walter Hagen**. The first Open to be held at Muirfield after the War was in 1948, when **Henry Cotton** won his third title. Cotton's second round of 66 was achieved in front of the watching King George VI. **Gary Player** won in 1959 and **Jack Nicklaus** in 1966. Perhaps the most dramatic Open in Muirfield's history came in 1972 when **Lee Trevino** holed his famous chip shot from the edge of the 17th green and in the process stole the title from Tony Jacklin. The Open was last played at Muirfield in 1987, **Nick Faldo** securing a memorable victory for Britain, and it returns once again in 1992.

Hole	Yards	Par	Hole	Yards	Par
1	449	4	10	475	5
2	349	4	11	386	4
3	379	4	12	381	4
4	181	3	13	153	3
5	558	5	14	447	4
6	471	4	15	396	4
7	185	3	16	188	3
8	444	4	17	542	5
9	510	5	18	447	4
Out	3.526	36	In	3.415	36
			Out	3.526	36
			TOTALS	6.941	72

CHANNINGS

Walk through the quiet cobbled streets of Edinburgh's city centre, just a little way from the castle and push open the door of a row of five beautifully maintained Edwardian townhouses. These, together, make up Channings, a privately owned hotel with cosy, old-fashioned clublike atmosphere right in heart of historic Edinburgh. The style of Channings is rarely found today; a feeling of classic care from the peaceful, fire-lit lounges to any of the 45 individually designed guest rooms, several of which offer wonderful panoramic views over the Firth of Forth to the hills of Fife.

The Brasserie is one of the popular haunts of the city. A restaurant that prides itself on honest food and personable service. After dinner, the bar welcomes you with an interesting and highly tempting range of malt whiskies and the odd game of chess. In the warmer months, take your lunch outside where the hotel's terraced garden captures the heat of the sun.

The quiet, classical feel of the hotel makes it the ideal venue for a corporate dinner or small conference but it is more than homely enough for any private meeting too. Any such gathering can be held in one of seven different rooms, including the oak-panelled Library and the Kingsleigh Suite.

For a rewarding afternoon's browsing through local and not-so-local history, the hotel has an absorbing collection of antique prints, furniture, object d'art, periodicals and books, or wander through the streets of the Edinburgh itself and soak up the atmosphere and culture of this beautiful city.

Take a short trip into the surrounding countryside to the famous golf clubs of Scotland. It was at nearby Muirfield where the Honourable Company of Edinburgh Golfers was founded in 1744, on the southern tip of the Firth of Forth, the oldest golf club in history.

Channings
South Learmonth Gardens
Edinburgh
Scotland EH4 1EZ
Tel: 031-315 2226
Fax: 031-332 9631

DUNBAR
CHAMPIONSHIP GOLF

In common with much of Eastern Scotland it isn't entirely clear when golf was first played at Dunbar. Whilst the Dunbar Golf Club was founded in 1856 following a meeting in the Town Hall, **The Dunbar Golfing Society** had been instituted in **1794**. Furthermore, records suggest that some cruder form of golf had been played in the area at least as early as the beginning of the 17th century. In **1616** two men of the parish of Tyninghame were censured by the Kirk Session for 'playing at ye nyneholis' on the Lord's Day and in **1640** an Assistant Minister of Dunbar was disgraced 'for playing at gouff'.

Times, as they say, change and three hundred and fifty years later 'gouff' is still played at Dunbar, although no one is likely to be censured or disgraced for doing so and there are now eighteen splendid holes.

Presently in charge of the famous links is the Club's Secretary, **Mr. Don Thompson**. He may be contacted on **(0368) 62317**. Very much a welcoming golf club, Dunbar receives visitors at all times. Societies are equally catered for although pre-booking is not surprisingly required. Those organising Societies should write to Mr. Thompson at **The Dunbar Golf Club, East Links, Dunbar, East Lothian.** In 1992 the green fee for either a single round or a full day's golf was priced at £20 during the week and £35 at weekends. One final introduction; **Derek Small** is the Club's Professional, he may be reached on **(0368) 62086**.

Having spent countless hours poring over maps trying to work out the best routes to a particular Golf Club it is with great pleasure that I turn to Dunbar: from the west, approach via the A1; from the south east approach via the A1! Less flippantly, the A1 runs from Berwick upon-Tweed to Edinburgh and passes through Dunbar. Those travelling from the Borders region of Melrose and Galashiels may find helpful a combination of the A68 and the A6137 to Haddington, thereafter picking up the A1 to Dunbar.

Dunbar is very much a natural links, laid out on a fairly narrow tract of land closely following the contours of the shoreline. It is bounded by a stone wall which runs the full length of the course. While Dunbar is by no means the longest of Scottish links, when the winds blow it can prove to be one of the most difficult – this may have something to do with the fact that there is an 'out of bounds' on the **3rd, 4th, 5th, 6th, 7th, 8th, 9th, 16th, 17th** and **18th** holes, and the beach can come in to play on the **4th, 5th, 6th, 7th, 12th, 14th, 15th, 16th** and **17th** – straight hitting would appear to be called for!

Dunbar is without doubt one of the East Coast's most attractive links with some splendid views out across the sea towards **Bass Rock**. The first three holes are played fairly close to the Clubhouse, the opening two being relatively tame par fives and the **3rd** a spectacular short hole played from an elevated tee. The **4th** then takes you alongside the beach as the course begins to move away from the Clubhouse. Perhaps the most testing holes occur around the turn, the **9th** to the **12th**, and there is no let-up either on the closing stretch with the beach readily receiving the mildest of slices. The **18th** can also be a card-wrecker with the stone wall out of bounds running the entire length of the fairway to the right.

All the major Scottish Championships have been played at Dunbar, including the Scottish Amateur and Scottish Professional Championships. The Club has also staged the British Boys Championship and has become something of a home in recent years for the Scottish Boys title. The course record stands at an impressive 66.

Dunbar's 19th is a comfortable building with views from the lounge across much of the course. Lunches and snacks are available seven days a week and with prior arrangement both breakfasts and dinners are also offered. A jacket and tie should be worn after 7.30pm. One final thought as you relax in the Clubhouse – one of the Regulations of the Dunbar Golfing Society dated 1794 reads as follows: '**When the expense of each Member for dinner amounts to two shillings and sixpence, the Club shall be dissolved**' – times, as they say, change!

Hole	Yards	Par	Hole	Yards	Par
1	477	5	10	202	3
2	494	5	11	417	4
3	172	3	12	459	4
4	349	4	13	378	4
5	148	3	14	433	4
6	350	4	15	343	4
7	386	4	16	166	3
8	369	4	17	339	4
9	507	5	18	437	4
Out	**3,252**	**37**	**In**	**3,174**	**34**
			Out	**3,252**	**37**
			TOTALS	**6,426**	**71**

DALMAHOY
CHAMPIONSHIP GOLF

Dalmahoy near Edinburgh – the venue for the 1992 **Solheim Cup** – has a lot in common with Moor Park, near London. Apart from being an easy drive from its country's capital (although it is much easier to escape from central Edinburgh than central London) both have two parkland courses – the one being much more testing than the other; both have staged televised professional tournaments over their championship course and most immediately striking of all is that the courses of Dalmahoy and Moor park are each overlooked by magnificent mansion houses which act as extraordinarily elegant 19th holes.

Dalmahoy's mansion is a three storey Georgian building, originally designed for the **Earl of Morton** in **1735**. To wander around its interior is an experience itself; many magnificent paintings adorn the walls and a wonderful sense of well being pervades throughout the building. The mansion has in fact been the focal point of a considerable amount of activity in recent times. The Georgian building has been sympathetically restored and is now the centrepiece of a 116 bedroomed luxury hotel and country club. The whole development plan comprised an investment of some £14 million. Lord knows what the Earl of Morton would have thought of it all! It certainly gives Dalmahoy an advantage over Moor Park where it has never been possible to stay overnight immediately behind the 18th green.

Golf has been played at Dalmahoy since the 1920s, five times Open Champion **James Braid** designing both courses, the championship **East** and the **West**, in 1927. From the day the very first ball was struck they have been held in extremely high esteem. The courses personify all that is best in parkland golf and offer a very real contrast to the nearby challenges of Muirfield, Gullane, Dunbar and the other great links courses that lie like a string of pearls along Lothian's coast. Again, like Moor Park, Dalmahoy's fairways are quite undulating and provide some far reaching views; Edinburgh Castle sits proudly on the horizon.

Casual visitors are normally only received at Dalmahoy on weekdays, the courses being reserved at weekends for members and hotel residents. There are some exceptions to the rule however, and it is always best to check with the Club. Bookings can be made through the **Reservations Centre**. The Director of Golf at Dalmahoy is **Mr Brian Anderson** and he can be contacted by telephone on **(031) 333 4105**. The Club's full address is; **The Dalmahoy Hotel, Golf and Country Club, Kirknewton, Midlothian EH27 8EB**. All golfing enquiries are best addressed to Mr Anderson. Equally helpful is the professional **Scott Maxwell** and he can also be reached on **(031) 333 4105**.

In 1992 green fees at Dalmahoy were as follows: £20 to play a round on the West Course midweek, £30 at weekends and £30 for a midweek round on the East Course and £40 at weekends. Reduced fees are available for junior golfers. A current handicap certificate is preferred.

Dalmahoy's precise location is 7 miles south west of Edinburgh off the A71 Kilmarnock Road. It is approximately 3 miles from the City's ring road. Travelling from the Glasgow region the M8 should be left at junction 3, the A899 linking the M8 with the A71. South of Glasgow the A71 itself is a fairly quick route while travellers approaching from the north are likely to find the M9 of most assistance. Finally, it is worth noting that Edinburgh's airport is only about 6 miles from Dalmahoy and is on the 'right side' of the city.

Measuring 6664 yards, par 72, the East Course is considerably longer than the West at 5317 yards, par 69. Both however are maintained in the same superb condition all year round. Due to the recent works at Dalmahoy the East Course front and back nines have been reversed, in other words, what was formerly the 10th is now being played as the opening hole. This isn't the first time this has happened. The course was played 'this way round' in 1981 during the televised Haig Tournament Players Championship.

That 1981 Tournament Players Championship witnessed some outstanding golf. On the final day, Scotland's **Brian Barnes,** cheered on by a partisan crowd, stormed around the course in an unbelievable 62 strokes; most unbelievable was his inward nine of just 28. This score enabled him to catch Brian Waites and inevitably, Barnes went on to win the play off. It was perhaps the giant Scot's greatest hour, although history will doubtless remember him as the man who twice defeated Jack Nicklaus on the same day during the 1975 Ryder Cup matches in America. That day, as at Dalmahoy in 1981, Barnes, one of the game's most outspoken characters, simply puffed his pipe and left his clubs to do the talking. Barnes' Ryder Cup partner for many years was fellow Scot **Bernard Gallacher;** and that takes us nicely back to Dalmahoy for it was on its splendid East and West Courses that our current Ryder Cup captain fashioned many of his skills as a boy.

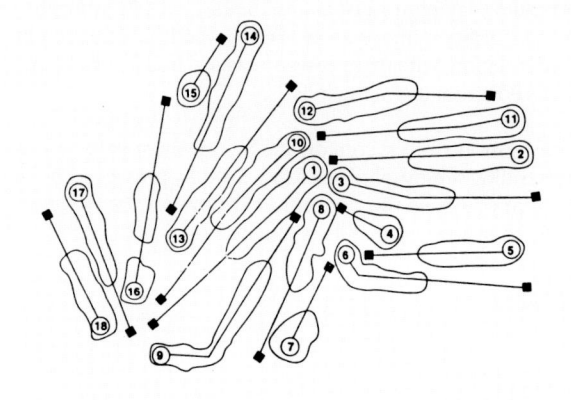

East Course

Hole	Yards	Par	Hole	Yards	Par
1	495	5	10	505	5
2	406	4	11	435	4
3	431	4	12	416	4
4	145	3	13	430	4
5	306	4	14	461	4
6	390	4	15	149	3
7	206	3	16	423	4
8	356	4	17	309	4
9	480	5	18	321	4
Out	3,215	36	In	3,449	36
			Out	3,215	36
			TOTALS	6,664	72

THE JOHNSTOUNBURN HOUSE HOTEL

Scotland is the home of golf, and Johnstounburn offers the golfer an opportunity of staying in one of Scotland's original homes. The earliest reference to the estate goes back to 1260, and the house dates to certainly the early 17th century. Since those distant days, Johnstounburn has been cared for and enhanced by influential Scottish families - Borthwick, Broun and Usher - with most of the building on the estate having been effected in the nineteenth century.

The house sits proudly, surrounded by spacious lawns, gardens and unspoilt countryside overlooking the Lammermuir hills. The eleven bedrooms in the main house are rich in individuality and have been decorated to achieve the standard of comfort required by discerning travellers. Each has a private bathroom (only one is not ensuite), colour television and direct dial telephone. A further nine bedrooms were added when the coach house (circa 1840), some 300 yards through the gardens, was converted in 1986.

The 'Piece De Resistance' is the dining room with ornate hand carved wood panelling from floor to ceiling, created in the mid eighteenth century. After a sumptuous meal from the table d'hote menu featuring the finest fresh local produce, and served by candlelight in traditional style, you can retire to the Cedar lounge and enjoy your coffee in front of an open hearth. Or, if the night is kind, you can stroll in the gardens and experience the tranquillity of the surrounds.

The famous golf courses of East Lothian - Muirfield, Gullane, North Berwick, Dunbar - are all within thirty minutes drive. There are more than a dozen courses from which to choose. For those not playing (or just taking the day off), Edinburgh City centre is thirty minutes away. To the south lies the beautiful Border region, with many historic castles, houses and gardens scattered about its rolling hills.

Johnstounburn offers comfort and friendly hospitality in a truly outstanding setting, with fine food carefully presented. Most of all, here you have the opportunity to savour the tradition of Scotland in a house that feels like home.

Johnstounburn House
Humbie
Nr. Edinburgh
East Lothian EH36 5PL
Tel: (087533) 696
Fax: (087533) 626

LOTHIAN
COMPLETE GOLF

Baberton G.C
031-453 4911
Baberton Avenue, Juniper Green, Edinburgh
W. of Edinburgh on the Lanark Road
(18) 6098 yards/*(intro by member)/F

Bathgate G.C
(0506) 630505
Edinburgh Road, Bathgate, West Lothian
400 yards E. of George Square
(18) 6328 yards/***/D

Braids United G.C
031-447 3327
22 Braids Hill Approach, Edinburgh
At Braids Hill, S. of Edinburgh
(18) 5731 yards/***/E
(18) 4832 yards/***/E

Broomieknowe G.C
031-663 9317
36 Golf Course Road, Bonnyrigg, Midlothian
S. of Edinburgh on the A6094 from Dalkeith
(18) 6046 yards/**/F

Bruntsfield Links G.C
031-336 1479
32 Barton Avenue, Davidsons Mains, Edinburgh
2-3 miles W. of Edinburgh on A90
(18) 6407 yards/**/F/H

Carrickvale G.C
031-337 1932
Glendevon Park, Edinburgh
Opposite Post House Hotel on Balgreen Road
(18) 6299 yards/***/F/H

Craigmillar Park G.C
031-667 2837
1 Observatory Road, Edinburgh
3 miles from City centre
(18) 5846 yards/***/D/H or M or L

Dalmahoy G.C
031-333 1845
Dalmahoy, Kirknewton, Midlothian 7 miles W. of Edinburgh on the A71
(18) 6664 yards/***/F
(18) 5121 yards/***/F

Duddingston G.C
031-661 7688 4301
Duddingston Road, Edinburgh
E. of city centre, adjacent to the A1
(18) 6647 yards/**/D/H

Dunbar G.C
(0368) 62317
East Links, Dunbar
Half mile from Dunbar centre on sea side
(18) 6426 yards/***/C

Gifford G.C
(062 081) 267
Gifford
5 miles S. of Haddington off the A6137
(9) 5613 yards/***(not Tues, Wed, weekend pm)/E

Glen G.C
(0620) 2221
Tantallon Terrace, North Berwick, East Lothian
22 miles N.E. of Edinburgh on the A198
(18) 6098 yards/***/E

Glencorse G.C
(0968) 77189
Milton Bridge, Penicuik, Midlothian
9 miles S. of Edinburgh on the A701
(18) 5205 yards/***/D/H

Greenburn G.C
(0501) 70292
Fauldhouse, West Lothian
Midway between Glasgow and Edinburgh
(18) 6210 yards/**/E/H

Gullane G.C
(0620) 842255
Gullane, East Lothian
Off the A198 on the A198 to Gullane
(18)6466 yards/**/F/H
(18)6127 yards/***/F/H
(18)5128 yards/***/F/H

Haddington G.C
(062 082) 3627
Amisfield Park, Haddington, East Lothian
17 miles E. of Edinburgh on the A1
(18) 6280 yards/**(not pm)/E

Harburn G.C
(0506) 871256
West Calder, West Lothian
S. off the A70, 2 miles S. of West Calder
(18) 5843 yards/***/E

Honourable Company Of
Edinburgh Golfers
(0620) 842123
Muirfield, Gullane, East Lothian
Off the A198 from Gullane to North Berwick
(18) 6601 yards/(Tues, Thurs, Fri am only)/A/H
(18)/M/L

Kilspindie G.C
(087 57) 358
Aberlady, East Lothian
On the South bank of the Forth Estuary
(18) 5410 yards/***/F

Kingsknowe G.C
031-441 4030
326 Lanark Road, Edinburgh
W. of Edinburgh on the A71
(18) 5979 yards/**/E/H

Liberton G.C
031-664 8580
297 Gilmerton Road, Edinburgh
S. of Edinburgh on the A7
(18) 5299 yards/***/F/H

Linlithgow G.C
(0506) 842585
Braehead, Linlithgow, West Lothian
20 miles from Edinburgh off the M9
(18) 5858 yards/***(not Wed, Sat)/E

Deer Park G.C
(0506) 38843
Carmondean, Livingston, West Lothian
Signposted from Knightsridge from the M8
(18) 6636 yards/***/D

Longniddry G.C
(0875) 52141
Links Road, Longniddry, East Lothian
(18) 6210 yards/***/F

Luffness New G.C
(0620) 843114
Aberlady, East Lothian E. of Edinburgh along the A198
(18) 6122 yards/***/F/H

Merchants of Edinburgh G.C
031-447 219
10 Craighill Gardens, Edinburgh
South side of Edinburgh off the A701
(18) 4889 yards/(intro by member)/E

Mortonhall G.C
031-447 6974
231 Braid Road, Edinburgh
2 miles S. of city centre
(18) 6557 yards/**/F/M

Murrayfield G.C
031-337 3478
43 Murrayfield Road, Edinburgh
2 miles W. of the city centre
(18) 5727 yards/***/E/L/H

Musselburgh G.C
031-665 2005
Monktonhall, Musselburgh, Midlothian
1 mile S. of Musselburgh off the A1
(18) 6623 yards/***/F/H

Newbattle G.C
031-663 2123
Abbey Road, Dalkeith, Midlothian
7 miles S.W. of Edinburgh on the A7
(18) 6012 yards/**/D

North Berwick
(0620) 2135
West Links, Beach Road
North Berwick
(18) 6317 yards/***/D

Portobello G.C
031-669 4361
Stanley Road, Portobello, Edinburgh
(9) 2400 yards/***/E

Prestonfield G.C
031-667 1273
6 Prestonfield Road North, Edinburgh
Just off Dalkeith Road, nr Commonwealth Pool
(18) 6216 yards/**(+ Sat, Sun pm)/E

Pumpherston G.C
(0506) 32869
Drumshoreland Road, Pumpherston, Livingston
1 mile S. of Uphall, off the A89(9) 5154 yards/
*(with member only)/F

Ratho Park G.C
031-333 1752
Ratho, Newbridge, Midlothian
8 miles W. of Edinburgh via A71 or A8
(18) 6028 yards/***/D

Ravelston G.C
031-315 2486
24 Ravelston Dykes Road, Blackhall, Edinburgh
Take A90 Queensferry Road to Blackhall
(9) 5200 yards/*(with member)/F

Royal Burgess G.C
031-339 2075
181 Whitehouse Road, Edinburgh
Take A90 to Queensferry, behind Barnton
Thistle Hotel
(18) 6604 yards/**/F/L

Royal Musselburgh G.C
(0875) 810276
Preston Grange House, Prestonpans, East Lothian
(18) 6237 yards/***/D/H

Silverknowes G.C
031-336 5359
Silverknowes, Parkway, Edinburgh
On coast overlooking Firth of Forth
(18) 6210 yards/***/F

Swanston G.C
031-445 2239
111 Swanston Road, Edinburgh
5 miles from Edinburgh centre
(18) 5024 yards/**/F

Torphin Hill
031-441 1100
Torphin Road, Colinton, Edinburgh
On S.W side of Colinton
(18) 5024 yards/***/E

Turnhouse G.C
031-339 1014
154 Turnhouse Road, Edinburgh
(18) 6171 yards/**/D

Uphall G.C
(0506) 856404
Uphall, West Lothian
On outskirts of Uphall adjacent to the A8
(18)6250 yards/***/E

West Lothian G.C
(0506) 826030
Airngarth Hill, Linlithgow, West Lothian
On hill, marked by the Hope Monument
(18) 6578 yards/**/D

E.A. Pettitt   THE MARINE, NORTH BERWICK   Burlington Gallery

STRATHCLYDE

POKT APPIN

OBAN

KILCHRENAN

ARDUAINE   INVERARAY

CRINAN   TAKPET

BINACHUR   LOCHGOILHEAD

ARGYLL

JURA   Blairmore & Strone GC

                        Cowal G C   GOUROCK   Dullatur GC

                        DUNOON   Inchbriggs GC   Westerwood

                Kyles of Bute   HOUSE & GC

                        GC   Innellan GC   LANGBANK

PORT ASKAIG   Port   Renfrew GC

ISLE OF   Bannatyne   Cleddoch G & GC

ISLAY   KENNACRAIG   WEMYSS BAY   Haggs Castle GC

                        ISLE OF   GLASGOW

Islay GC   BUTE Rothesay GC   Pollok GC

(Machrie)   BARRHEAD

                        Kingarth GC   Largs GC   East Renfrewshire GC

PORT ELLEN   FAIRLIE

                        W. Kilbride GC   Tarrarine House GC

                ISLE OF   KILWINNING   STEWARTON

                ARRAN   ARDROSSAN   Strathaven GC   LANARK

                        Glasgow Gailes GC Irvine GC IRVINE

        Brodick GC   Kilmarnock GC   KILMARNOCK

                Lamlash GC   Western Gailes GC Royal Troon GC

                        Blackwaterfoot TROON Prestwick St. Nicholas GC

        CAMBELTOWN   Prestwick GC PRESTWICK Ballochmyle GC

Machrihanish GC   Whiting Bay   ALLOWAY AYR

                                                Belleisle GC

                CULZEAN CASTLE   AYRSHIRE

                Turnberry Hotel

                & GC

        AILSA CRAIG   GIRVAN

STRATHCLYDE
CHOICE GOLF

An ancient golfing rhyme from the land of Burns runs:

'Troon and Prestwick, old and classy,
Bogside, Dundonald, Glasgow Gailes, Barassie,
Prestwick St. Nicholas, Western Gailes,
St. Cuthbert, Portland – memory fails,
Troon Municipal (three links there)
Prestwick Municipal, Irvine, Ayr,
They faced the list with delighted smiles -
Sixteen courses within ten miles'.

Even without Turnberry, that 'little corner of heaven on earth', some fifteen miles south of Ayr, an extraordinarily impressive list, and little wonder that this small region of Scotland's coast has become nothing short of a mecca for golfers the world over.

Prestwick, Troon and **Turnberry** have of course each staged the Open Championship. Prestwick was the birthplace of the event back in 1860 and is probably the most classical test of traditional links golf – penal the American architects would describe it, on account of the many blind shots. The Open is no longer held at Prestwick but the history of the place is overwhelming and quite magnetic. Troon and Turnberry are both firmly on the 'Open' rota. It was last played over the latter's Ailsa course in 1986 (Norman's great victory) and was last held at Troon in 1989 (Norman's near victory). Understandably the golfer making a pilgrimage to the Ayrshire coast will be drawn towards this famous trio. However, if time isn't, as they say, of the essence it would be bordering on a disgrace not to sample as many of the nearby delights as possible. As the old rhyme relates, within short distance of one another lie a number of outstanding courses and where at any of which it may be easier to arrange a game.

While not all roads lead to Ayr, as the largest town on the coast, it's probably as good a starting point as any. Here we find a belle – **Belleisle** to be precise and a most attractive parkland course. Considered by many to be the finest public course outside of St Andrews and Carnoustie and, being somewhat sheltered it's an admirable retreat from the more windswept links nearby. Furthermore as a municipal course the green fees are very cheap.

Just north of Ayr lie a series of outstanding links courses, all within a mile or two of one another. Prestwick and Troon are featured on later pages (as is Turnberry) but also in this area one finds first class courses at **Prestwick St Nicholas, Barassie, Western Gailes, Glasgow (Gailes)** and **Irvine** (also known somewhat unfortunately as Bogside). Each warmly welcome visitors and although less busy than the big three prior telephoning is strongly recommended, especially during the peak summer months. Weekdays are inevitably the best times for a visit.

Just as there is a proliferation of golf courses so the area is inundated with all manner of hotels, guest houses, pubs and restaurants. A few thoughts follow. To start at a pinnacle, undoubtedly one of the best hotels in Britain is The Turnberry Hotel (0655) 31000, the first ever purpose built Hotel and Golf Course. Both Hotel and restaurant are truly outstanding in every way. Guests enjoy reduced green fees and more importantly have priority on the golf courses. For beautiful views over the Isle of Arran, we also recommend Malin Court (0655) 31457. If staying in this area, Culzean Castle (open between April and October) is well worth a visit and in nearby **Girvan** where there is an underrated municipal course, an excellent place for liquid

refreshment is the King's Arms (0465) 3322. If you've food on your mind we suggest you forget about calories and go for a slap up meal in Splinters (0465) 3481. Perhaps the most popular, and certainly the most convenient hotel for Royal Troon is The Marine Highland (0292) 314444. It proudly overlooks the Old Course Championship links. Two other splendid hotels in Troon are Piersland House (0292) 314747 and The Ardneil (0292) 311611. The two best known hotels in Ayr are The Caledonian (0292) 269331 and the Pickwick (0292) 260111 while close by in Alloway is the excellent Balgarth Hotel (0292) 42441 and in Maybole, The Ladyburn Hotel (06554) 585 is good value. On to Prestwick, which if you've arrived by plane may well be your first port of call. Here, The Carlton (0292) 76811 and the Parkstone (0292) 77286 stand out from the crowd although there are numerous B&B's and small hotels. The Fairways Hotel (0292) 70396 and Fernbank Guest House (0292) 75027 are always popular retreats. Kilmarnock is now a busy industrial centre yet it was here that Robbie Burns' first collection of poems was published. Just to the north of the town at Irvine is The Hospitality Inn (0294) 74272 which in keeping with its name is most welcoming. If an escape to the countryside is sought then a trip to Stewarton is highly recommended. Here, set in glorious surroundings, is the redoubtable Chapeltoun House (0560) 82696 – quiet and very comfortable with a first class restaurant. Kilwinning is a final recommendation for this area. It is somewhat off the beaten track perhaps but the Montgreenan Mansion House (0294) 57733 is superbly comfortable.

To the north of the famous golfing stretch there is plenty of less testing golf to be found. This may well be necessary in order to restore battered pride! **West Kilbride** (another links type) and **Largs** (a well-wooded parkland course) should suit admirably. Both also offer some magnificent views across to Argyle and the Isle of Arran where there are no fewer than seven golf courses! Also roughly due east of Ayr, close to the A76 there is a very good course at **Ballochmyle.**

Glasgow is Britain's third largest city after London and Birmingham and, being Scottish-to-boot, not surprisingly has a huge number of golf courses. Indeed some wag once said of Glasgow that there was a pub in every street with a Golf Club around each corner. One interesting statistic is that between 1880 and 1910 more than 80 golf courses were built in the Greater Glasgow area – so much for today's golf boom! Unfortunately the problem for the golfing stranger to Glasgow is that many of the city's leading Clubs only permit visitors to play if accompanied by a Member. Among the city's more traditional courses – and where arranging a game can be difficult – are **Haggs Castle, Pollok** and **Glasgow Killermont**. Other suggestions include **Renfrew** and **East Renfrewshire,** to the north west and south west respectively and **Bishopriggs** to the north of Glasgow. There are a number of public courses in Glasgow so the golfer confined to the city need not get too depressed. The pick of the municipals is probably **Lethamhill** and **Little Hill** – a game on either is remarkably inexpensive.

Forgetting the golf for a moment, it came as something of a surprise for many south of the border when Glasgow was chosen as European City of Culture for 1990, in succession to Athens and Paris, among other cities. Of course those familiar with the city will know that it has changed out of all recognition in the past decade or so. Good hotels are not as prolific as golf courses but a list of the best might include The Holiday Inn (041) 226 5577, the Hospitality Inn (041) 332 3311 and the less modern (and with a

STRATHCLYDE
CHOICE GOLF

much more attractive exterior) Stakis Grosvenor (041) 339 8811. One Devonshire Gardens (041) 339 2001 also combines old-fashioned elegance and service. Glasgow Airport, actually situated 8 miles away in Paisley, offers a choice between the Stakis Normandy Hotel, complete with driving range (041) 886 4100 and the Forte Crest (041) 887 1212. As for restaurants, Glasgow is pretty well endowed. Fish lovers will adore Rogano's Oyster Bar (041) 248 4055 in Exchange Square while those seeking first class French cuisine should head for The Buttery (041) 221 8188 on Argyle Street. High quality Chinese and Indian restaurants also abound, with the Amber (041) 339 6121 and Balbir's Ashoka Tandoori (041) 221 1761 both well worth seeking out. For a sample of Glasgow's culture the Theatre Royal (041) 332 9000 offers distinguished ballet, opera and drama and the Burrell Collection in Pollok Park is Scotland's leading Art Gallery.

Time for a spot more golf, and the **Gleddoch House** Hotel Golf and Country Club (047554) 711 provides the solution. Located at Langbank it is close to the Clyde Estuary and offers views of the Lombard Hills. It is easily accessible from Glasgow by way of the M8 and in a nutshell could be described as a darn good hotel with a darn good restaurant and a darn good golf course! Further north, the course at **Helensburgh** is also worth a visit and on the shores of **Loch Lomond** Tom Weiskopf has designed two courses which promise to be something rather special – that is if the project is ever successfully financed and thus finished.

From Glasgow, the great challenges of Troon, Turnberry and Prestwick lie to the south West (the A77 is incidentally the most convenient route), but Championship golf can also be found to the north and east; **Dullatur** is one such venue, **Lanark** another. The former is a parkland course whereas Lanark is essentially moorland. For Dullatur a hotel to note is Crow Wood House (041779) 3861 and an excellent restaurant, La Campagnola (041779) 3405 – both are in Muirhead. The Cartland Bridge Hotel (0555) 4426 is recommended for the course at Lanark. 20 miles or so east of Glasgow near Cumbernauld **The Westerwood Hotel** (0236) 457171 and its golf course have only recently appeared on the map. An inspection is strongly recommended; the golf course is very challenging and calls for many daring shots – this is not altogether surprising since Seve Ballesteros had a hand in its design (Westerwood is featured later in this section).

Before heading for the more distant corners of Strathclyde a quick mention for two courses lying due south of Glasgow; **Torrance House** and **Strathaven** are the pair in question. Both are very easily reached by way of the A726, although Strathaven is quite a bit of a way from the city and by the time you arrive at the course you'll have climbed 700 feet above sea level. But a lovely setting, and a most convenient hotel, The Strathaven (0357) 20421 await.

What of the more remote outposts then? Strathclyde is a vast region extending well into the Highlands. There's not a great deal in the way of golfing challenges here – the landscape precludes it – but the countryside is quite glorious and there are some extremely fine hotels and country houses nestling in and around the hills, all making splendid bases for exploring the magnificent scenery of these parts. North of Loch Lomond one finds Stonefield Castle (0880 820) 836 at Tarbet alongside Loch Fyne. If inspecting the delights of Oban a detour to Kilchrenan is highly recommended; The Ardanaiseig (08663) 333 is the place – outstandingly relaxing. Still nearer

to Oban at Knipoch, the Knipoch Hotel (08526) 251 offers great comfort together with all manner of country pursuits.

Two great courses still remain to be charted – those magical 'M's' – **Machrie** and **Machrihanish**. Each enjoys a kind of splendid isolation and is a superb test of traditional links golf. Machrie is to be found on the distant Isle of Islay at Port Ellen. As it can now be reached by plane from Glasgow there can be no excuse for not making the trip; besides right on the course is the excellent Machrie Hotel (0496) 2085, where host Murdo McDonald is only too happy to arrange golf competitions and visits to local distilleries (in that order!) Many have already made the pilgrimage to Machrihanish and as it too is reachable by air a large number are certain to follow. Following The Fairways has also succumbed to its charms and Machrihanish is explored on a later page. There are a number of hotels nearby, both in Machrihanish itself and in Campbeltown, and its well worth spending a few days here. Before you leave the area a mellow tune may come to mind – Mull of Kintyre by one Paul McCartney. The music inspired millions, the golf course and its surrounds will almost certainly give equal satisfaction.

Arthur Weaver **WILLIE PARK JNR** *Burlington Gallery*

ROYAL TROON
CHAMPIONSHIP GOLF

O'a the links where I hae golfed
Frae Ayr to Aberdeen,
On Prestwick or Carnoustie and mony mair I ween
What tho' the bents are rough and bunkers yawn aroun'
I dearly lo'e the breezy links, the breezy links o' Troon.

(Gilmour)

When the golfing mind focuses on Troon it invariably thinks of the **Postage Stamp**, the par three **8th** on the **Old Course**. Unquestionably the world's most celebrated short hole. During the **1973 Open Championship, Gene Sarazen**, then at the mature age of 71, holed out with his punched five iron shot in front of the watching television cameras. Sarazen declared that he would take with him to heaven a copy of the film to show to Walter Hagen and Co. Legend has it, that on hearing of Sarazen's feat, an American flew to Britain and travelled to Troon. He strode to the 8th tee and proceeded to strike 500 balls in succession towards the green. Not surprisingly he failed to equal Sarazen's achievement whereupon he left the course and duly flew home to America. Who said it was only mad dogs and Englishmen?

Anyone contemplating the above ought at least to consult the Secretary first, **Mr. J.D. Montgomerie** being the gentleman in question. He can be contacted at the **Royal Troon Golf Club, Craigend Road, Troon, Ayrshire KA10 6EP**. Tel. **(0292) 311555**. (Fax. (0292) 318204.)

The Royal Troon Club Golf possesses two 18 hole courses; **The Old** and **The Portland**. Gentlemen visitors are welcome to play both courses between Mondays and Thursdays provided prior arrangement is made with the Secretary. Lady golfers are also welcome, although they are limited to playing on the Portland Course. All visitors must be members of a recognised club and be able to produce a certificate of handicap (maximum 18). Society games may be arranged but organisers should note that their numbers must not exceed 24. In 1992 a green fee of £65 entitled the visitor to a round on each course, while a fee of £40 secured a full day's golf on the Portland Course; both fees are inclusive of lunch or high tea. There are no concessionary rates for junior golfers who, in any event, must have attained the age of eighteen before they will be permitted to play over the Old Course. Sets of clubs and trolleys may be hired from the Club's professional, **Brian Anderson** (tel. **0292 313281**). A caddy can also usually be obtained.

Troon lies just to the north of Prestwick and Ayr. The town can be reached from Glasgow and the north via the A77, which also runs from near Stranraer in the south. The A78 is the coastal road, running from Largs through Irvine to Loans just east of Troon. Travelling from Edinburgh, the A71 should be taken, whilst from the North of England the best route is probably via the A74 and the A71. Finally, Prestwick Airport is no more than two miles away. Located as it is, bordering the Firth of Clyde, the wind often blows very fiercely across the links and Troon is hardly a place for the faint-hearted golfer.

The Old Course at Troon has both the longest hole of any Open Championship course – the **6th** at 577 yards and the shortest – the Postage Stamp, which measures a mere 126 yards. In the **11th** it also possesses one of the toughest, with its railway out-of-bounds, thick gorse and painfully narrow fairway. At 6274 yards the Portland Course represents a more modest test but it is none-the-less a very fine course and although in parts closely resembles a moorland-type course, has all the challenges of traditional links golf.

The Club is naturally proud of its great history. When it was founded in 1878 by twenty-four local enthusiasts there were originally only five holes – by 1923 it had staged its first **Open Championship**. Since then the Club has held five Opens; in 1950, 1962 (when a rampant **Palmer** stormed to a six stroke victory), 1973 and 1982 (bringing popular triumphs for Americans **Weiskopf** and **Watson**) and of course most recently the Championship of 1989 and that unforgettable final day's play.

Mark Calcavecchia had the luck of a Sarazen to hole out from the deep rough on the **12th** during the final round. It helped him catch **Greg Norman** whose **64**, highlighted by six straight birdies from the 1st, is likely to stand as the course record for a long time. The Gods of Troon seem to have little difficulty in smiling on an American golfer, but we shouldn't take anything away from Calcavecchia for it takes more than just a little skill to birdie the **18th** hole twice in an afternoon.

If you have played all 36 holes at Troon and waged a successful war against the elements you will have earned your drink at the 19th. The Clubhouse provides all the usual facilities and the catering has a very good reputation. When you leave you will probably not have a video to take to heaven, but you will at least know that you have visited one of the earth's greatest golfing shrines.

Old Course

Hole	Yards	Par	Hole	Yards	Par
1	364	4	10	438	4
2	391	4	11	481	4
3	379	4	12	431	4
4	557	5	13	465	4
5	210	3	14	179	3
6	577	5	15	457	4
7	402	4	16	542	5
8	126	3	17	223	3
9	423	4	18	452	4
Out	3,429	36	In	3,668	35
			Out	3,429	36
			TOTALS	7,097	71

TURNBERRY HOTEL GOLF COURSES & SPA

Voted Britain's 5 Star Hotel of the Year in 1990, and perhaps best known for its two championship links golf courses, Turnberry is located on the west coast of Scotland, set in 360 acres overlooking the islands of Arran and Ailsa Craig.

The two golf courses, owned and managed by the hotel, make it a year round Mecca for golfers and the Ailsa Course will again host the British Open in 1994. A superb new Clubhouse will open in Spring 1993.

The new Turnberry Spa and Leisure is an additional amenity for our guests. The leisure facilities include a 20 metre deck level pool, poolside spa bath and bio-sauna, 2 squash courts, cardiovascular and muscular gymnasium and planned aqua and floor aerobics. The nine treatment rooms offer a complete range of treatments, including aromatherapy and hydrotherapy.

Nearby are riding stables, and fishing, rough shooting, clay pigeon shooting can be arranged. Culzean Castle, Robert Burns country and the Burrell Collection are also of interest in the area.

The hotel was built at the turn of the century and the tradition of elegance and comfort is retained in the bedrooms. At Turnberry, living is indeed comfortable and relaxed; every bedroom has its individual character.

The Turnberry Restaurant, under the direction of Executive Chef, Stewart Cameron, specialises in an alliance of traditional Scottish and French cooking. Entertainment is provided each evening by resident musicians and the atmosphere is very much that of the grand Country House.

The Bay at Turnberry Restaurant enjoys spectacular views of Turnberry Bay towards Arran and Ailsa Craig. The focus is on a lighter style of cooking both at lunch and dinner, in an informal setting.

Whilst staying at Turnberry, guests will enjoy warm hospitality, the constant concern and those little formalities and gracious touches that make all the difference. Perhaps it is because of this that so many guests and their families choose to return year after year.

Turnberry Hotel, Golf Courses and Spa
Ayrshire
Scotland KA26 9LT
Tel: (0655) 31000
Fax: (0655) 31706

TURNBERRY
CHAMPIONSHIP GOLF

Not so many years ago it was said that the golfing visitor to Scotland journeyed to **St. Andrews** for the history and to **Turnberry** for the beauty. Incomparable is a word often used to describe Turnberry's setting, magnificent and majestic are two others. Quite what causes **Ailsa Craig** to be so mesmerising is a mystery, but mesmerising it is and the views towards the distant **Isle of Arran** and the **Mull of Kintyre** can be equally captivating and enchanting. Since 1977, Turnberry has possessed history as well as beauty.

The **Open Championship** of **1977**, Turnberry's first, is generally considered to have been the greatest of all Championships. **Nicklaus** and **Watson**, the two finest golfers of the day, turned the tournament into a titanic, head-to-head confrontation – the 'Duel in the Sun' as it came to be known. On the final day, both having pulled along way clear of the field, Nicklaus held a two stroke advantage as they left the 12th green. Who in the world can give Jack Nicklaus two shots over six holes and beat him? asked Peter Alliss – the rest, as they say, is history.

There are two Championship courses at Turnberry; the better known **Ailsa Course** to which the Open returns in 1994 and the **Arran Course**. Both are owned and run by the Turnberry Hotel. Visitors with handicaps are welcome to play on either course although written prior arrangements must be made with the Golf Club Manager **Mr. R. Hamblett**. Mr. Hamblett can be contacted via **The Turnberry Hotel, Turnberry, Strathclyde, KA26 9LT**, telephone **(0655) 31000 Ext. 424**.

In 1992 the summer green fees were set at £65 for a day's golf consisting of one round on each course. A single round on the Arran is priced at £25. Reduced rates of £35 for a round on both courses are available to Hotel residents and further reductions are available to all golfers during the winter months. Turnberry's professional **Bob Jamieson** can also be contacted on **(0655) 31000**. Caddies and hire of clubs are best arranged in advance by telephone.

The Hotel and golf courses lie approximately 17 miles south of the town of Ayr off the A77. For those travelling from the Glasgow region, the A77 runs direct from Glasgow to Turnberry and is dual carriageway for much of the journey. Motoring from Edinburgh the A71 is the best route, picking up the A77 at Kilmarnock. Approaching from England, Carlisle is likely to be a starting point (M6 to Carlisle). The distance from Carlisle to Turnberry is one of just under 120 miles, and although there are two choices, the quickest route is to head north on the A74 leaving (in what appears to be no man's land) and joining the A70 towards Ayr. Finally, Prestwick Airport is situated just to the north of Ayr.

From its elevated perch, the red-roofed Turnberry Hotel enjoys a commanding view over both courses. It will have witnessed much of Turnberry's rather turbulent past. During the War the rolling expanse of links had been used as an air base and a vast runway had been constructed. Much levelling of the ground had also taken place and in 1945 the last thing Turnberry must have looked was the setting for two Championship courses. **Mackenzie Ross** is the architect we all have to thank. From its medal tees, the Ailsa course isn't a great deal longer than the Arran, their respective distances being 6408 yards, par 70, and 6249 yards, par 69. The same from the ladies tees are 5836 yards, par 75 and 5732 yards par 73. When Turnberry's second Open was staged in 1986 the Ailsa course weighed in at 6950 yards, par 70 and the fairways had been narrowed to alarming proportions. **Greg Norman's** second round **63** achieved in far from perfect weather conditions was a remarkable feat, indeed many writers and players (Tom Watson included) regard it as the finest Championship round the world has ever seen.

After three holes 'inland' as it were, the Ailsa course hugs the shore tightly for a series of dramatic holes between the **4th** and the **11th**. The **6th**, named Tappie Toorie, is possibly the most difficult par three on the course; the shot is to a heavily guarded green across a valley (play it into the wind and you may be short with a driver). The **9th** and the **10th** though are the holes most likely to be remembered. The 9th 'Bruce's Castle', is played alongside the famous Turnberry lighthouse, built over the remains of Turnberry Castle, birthplace of Robert the Bruce. The Championship tee for this hole is perched on a pinnacle of rock with the sea crashing below. Stand on this tee and you can appreciate why parallels have often been drawn between Turnberry and Pebble Beach. Following the par three 11th, the holes turn inland and if the scenery is a little less spectacular the challenge in no way diminishes.

The closing holes will invariably invoke thoughts of the Nicklaus-Watson battle. To complete 'the history' Nicklaus played the final six holes in one under par yet was still beaten. The end of an era suggested many – Jack's response was delivered 12 months later at St. Andrews.

Ailsa Course

Hole	Yards	Par	Hole	Yards	Par
1	350	4	10	452	4
2	428	4	11	177	3
3	462	4	12	448	4
4	167	3	13	411	4
5	441	4	14	440	4
6	222	3	15	209	3
7	528	5	16	409	4
8	427	4	17	500	5
9	455	4	18	431	4
Out	**3,480**	**35**	**In**	**3,477**	**35**
			Out	**3,480**	**35**
			TOTALS	**6,957**	**70**

PRESTWICK
CHAMPIONSHIP GOLF

One could be forgiven for thinking that they take their golf a little too seriously at Prestwick – especially when one hears of such apparently true stories like the one about the monk from a nearby monastery who played a match against the Lord of Culzean to settle a deadly feud: at stake was the monk's nose!

The truth more likely is that Prestwick folk are a competitive breed. Only nine years after the formation of their Club in 1851 the Members got together and decided to stage an annual Open competition. The winner of the event was to receive an elegant red belt subscribed for by the Members. Whilst there may have been only eight entrants, the **1860 Open** marks the birth of the world's most prestigious Championship.

Willie Park of Musselburgh (a 'foreigner from the east coast') won the 1860 Open and it was decided that if anyone should win the event three years in succession they would win the Belt outright. **'Young' Tom Morris** (somehow Tom Morris Junior doesn't seem quite appropriate) was the greatest player of his day and fittingly enough in 1870 won his third title in as many years. Whereas Tom may have kept the Belt, Prestwick didn't keep the Open, or at least not the sole rights, as St. Andrews and Muirfield now joined Prestwick in the dawning of a new era.

In those early days the combatants played over a twelve hole course; today there are eighteen holes though the distinctive flavour remains (in fact seven of the original greens are in the same place). The modern day golfer must still play over the humps and hillocks, face blind shots and tackle the numerous deep sleeper-faced bunkers that are so much the charm of Prestwick.

Visitors wishing to play the historic course are advised to approach **Mr. D. E. Donaldson**, the Club's Secretary, in order to book a starting time. Mr. Donaldson can be contacted at **The Prestwick Golf Club, 2 Links Road, Prestwick, Ayrshire, KA9 1QG**, Tel. **(0292) 77404.** Visitors should note that they will not be permitted to play at weekends or after 11am on Thursdays, and that the first tee will usually be reserved for Members between the hours of 9am-10am and 12.30pm and 2.45pm. Furthermore, three ball and four ball matches are not allowed prior to 9.00 am.

In 1992 the summer green fee was set at £45 per day; however, for those arriving after 2.45pm the green fee is reduced to £30. The winter green fee is also £30 per day. Sets of golf clubs and caddies can be hired through the professional, **Frank Rennie**, Tel. **(0292) 79483**.

I suppose, like most things at Prestwick, the Clubhouse could be described as having a traditional atmosphere. Ladies are not permitted in the Dining and Smoking Rooms where jackets and ties must be worn at all times, but all may enter the Cardinal Room where some fine light lunches are offered. Dinners can also be arranged though some prior warning is necessary.

At one time Prestwick was a fairly remote place. However, improved roads and the opening of an International Airport has made the area much more accessible from all directions. More immediately, the A77 runs directly from Glasgow in the North and along the coast from Stranraer in the South. Those travelling from Edinburgh should use the A71, before joining the A77 at Kilmarnock.

From the back markers Prestwick measures 6544 yards and has a par of 71. Perhaps not overly long by modern Championship standards it is nonetheless extremely challenging and local knowledge (not to mention rub of the green) can make a considerable difference. At 346 yards the opening hole is small beer in comparison to the first on the original twelve hole layout – that one measured a lengthy 578 yards and in an age of hickory shafts and gutty balls no doubt proved a stiff bogey six. One can only wonder as to how in the 1870 Open, en route to his aforementioned hat trick, 'Young' Tom Morris managed to hole out in three strokes! Another of Tom's notable achievements at Prestwick occurred in the 1868 Open when he scored the first ever recorded hole in one. The **3rd** hole at Prestwick is probably the most famous; here the golfer must carry the vast **Cardinal Bunker** which stretches the entire width of the fairway right at the point of the dog-leg. Later on in his round he must also confront the legendary **'Himalayas' (5th)** and the **'Alps' (17th)**. The course is not actually quite so mountainous as some of the names suggest and the American who arrived at the Airport saying he was going to take thirteen clubs and a pick-axe was himself going a little 'over the top'. If the golfer does find himself getting frustrated with his game he should at least enjoy the marvellous views of Ailsa Craig and the Isle of Arran.

Hole	Yards	Par	Hole	Yards	Par
1	346	4	10	454	4
2	167	3	11	195	3
3	482	5	12	513	5
4	382	4	13	460	4
5	206	3	14	362	4
6	362	4	15	347	4
7	430	4	16	288	4
8	431	4	17	391	4
9	444	4	18	284	4
Out	**3,250**	**35**	**In**	**3,294**	**36**
			Out	**3,250**	**35**
			TOTALS	**6,544**	**71**

LADYBURN

Ladyburn, the home of David and Jane Hepburn, lies in the heart of 'the most beautiful valley in Ayrshire' on the edge of the magnificent estate of Kilkerran surrounded by the most intriguing pattern of woods and fields. Ladyburn was acquired in the late 17th century by the Fergussons of Kilkerran and remained in their hands until the death of Francis, widow of Sir James Fergusson.

Visitors are welcomed to Ladyburn by the friendly atmosphere of gracious living enjoyed by former generations of Hepburns. The house is furnished with antiques inherited by the family. All the bedrooms are different, each with its own character and style of furniture and furnishings.

The cuisine is traditional using only local fresh produce, much of which is grown in the gardens, and is prepared by Jane.

For those who are 'Following the Fairways', Ladyburn is situated only a short drive from the world famous Turnberry courses, within 45 minutes are the excellent and equally renowned courses of Troon and Prestwick. However, most excitingly, a new International Standard Course is to open in the Spring of 1992 at Brunston Castle only 3 miles away. This untried course (par 72, 6790 yards/6195 metres) has been laid out in the same beautiful valley in which Ladyburn lies and is likely to prove challenging to both amateur and professional alike.

Staying at Ladyburn is being a guest in a beautiful country house where the welcome and attention given by David and Jane Hepburn is reminiscent of a bygone era.

Ladyburn
By Maybole
Ayrshire
KA19 7SG
Tel: (06554) 585
Fax: (06554) 580

AA★★   RAC ★★★

WESTERWOOD
CHAMPIONSHIP GOLF

If your regular golfing partner is getting a bit cocky, a little bit too big for his golf shoes then it may be an idea to take him to Westerwood on a cold and blustery day and make him play off the back tees. If he scores under his handicap then you have every justification for shooting him or at least drowning him in the pond beside the 18th green. You see, Westerwood is a golf course that doesn't take prisoners.

Less than 20 miles to the east of Glasgow and 30 miles west of Edinburgh at Cumbernauld, Westerwood is a new Championship golf course designed by **Seve Ballesteros** with help from **Dave Thomas,** and, to a lesser extent, **Laura Davies**. Ballesteros, Thomas and Davies have at least two things in common: firstly, each hits the ball the proverbial country mile and secondly each has a reputation for playing attacking, devil-may-care golf. Westerwood was never destined to be a tame golf course! Of course one doesn't have to play Westerwood from the back tees (nor pick a cold and blustery day) but anyone who does, and scores below their handicap, is a bigger bandit than Ned Kelly. This course is one of the most challenging one is likely to come across. It is also one of the most thrilling.

Westerwood is set amid pretty countryside, with three distinct ranges of hills, the Kilsyth, Ochil and Campsie Hills forming the backdrop to the golf course. It is the first course in Britain that Seve has put his signature to and like Jack Nicklaus and Johnny Miller's first designs in England it has opened to great acclaim and reflects the personality and philosophy of its architect.

The golf course is the centre piece attraction of an impressive hotel and leisure complex, however, as with the Club's sister course in Scotland, Murrayshall, and unlike many new grand schemes in Great Britain, there is nothing exclusive about Westerwood. Non resident golfing visitors are very welcome to play the course although they do pay higher green fees. Tee reservations can be made by telephoning the Club's professional, **Anthony Smith** on **(0236 725281)**. The Club's full address is **The Westerwood Hotel, Golf and Country Club, St. Andrews Drive, Cumbernauld G68 0EW**, tel: **(0236) 457171**. Green fees for 1992 were, for non residents, £22.50 per round, £35 per day midweek and £27.50 per round, £45 per day at weekends. Hotel guests paid just £12.50 (between 1st April and 31st October 1992). Golf societies and company days are encouraged and details of special golfing breaks can be obtained by telephoning the hotel. It is not essential for visitors to have a golf handicap but

they should be of a reasonable standard.

The possibility of playing golf on a Championship course at the weekend is extremely attractive to nomadic golfers from Glasgow and Edinburgh in particular where it can prove difficult to arrange a game on the more traditional, established courses. Travelling from both cities is very straightforward (and quick). Westerwood is located just off the A80 which runs through Cumbernauld; in Cumbernauld the Dullatur road should be taken and Westerwood is off to the right. The A80 links Cumbernauld to Glasgow. Those approaching from Perth and further north should travel on the M9 before joining the M80 just south of Stirling; the M80 becomes the A80 only 3 miles from Cumbernauld. A combination of motorways (M9, M876, M80) should also prove the best bet from the Edinburgh region.

What makes Westerwood such a demanding course? First of all it is pretty long – 6721 yards from the back tees (6429 from the forward tees and 5883 yards from the ladies tees – many of which were positioned on the advice of Laura Davies). Secondly, the terrain is fairly rugged: there are some steep climbs and several very undulating, twisting fairways, often creating blind shots. Then there are the natural hazards – heather, bracken, firs and silver birch trees – all very pretty and colourful but they haven't exactly been asked to make way for the golf course. And finally, there are the many water hazards, the cunningly placed bunkers and the often severely contoured greens.

The challenge is present from the outset: stand on the **1st** tee and you are confronted by a swinging, tumbling dog-leg of 500 yards – a very good opening hole. The **2nd** is an enormously long par three; 231 yards from the tiger tees! And so it continues. Other memorable holes on the front nine include the **6th**, called Seve's Trap because of the bunker fronting the green which even the maestro might find difficult to get up and down from, and the par five **9th**.

On the back nine, the **13th**, **14th** and **15th** provide a spectacular sequence of holes with the 15th, 'Waterfall' being easily the most dramatic on the course. The waterfall itself doesn't actually come into play (or shouldn't!) but it does provide a charming backdrop and in any event a brook runs in front of the green and meets up with the waterfall in a pond beside the green! The round ends as it began, with an excellent par five, one of half a dozen in total at Westerwood, and I bet even your cocky friend won't be able to keep a six off his card.

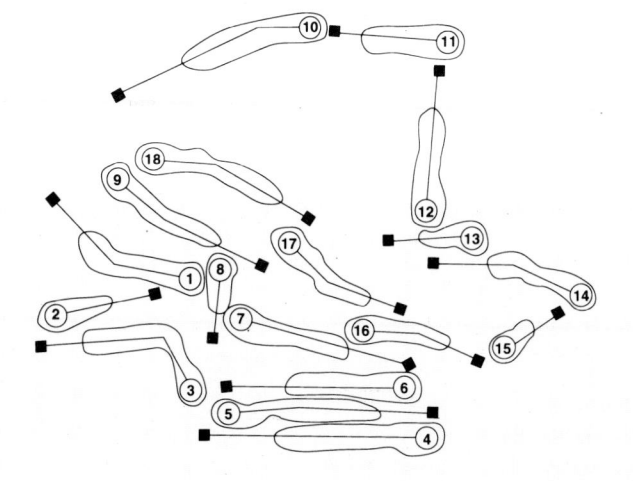

Hole	Yards	Par	Hole	Yards	Par
1	505	5	10	362	4
2	231	3	11	187	3
3	329	4	12	485	5
4	470	5	13	197	3
5	383	4	14	518	5
6	368	4	15	170	3
7	428	4	16	414	4
8	176	3	17	403	4
9	548	5	18	547	5
Out	3,438	37	In	3,283	36
			Out	3,438	37
			Totals	6,721	73

WESTERWOOD HOTEL, GOLF & COUNTRY CLUB

Westerwood Hotel, Golf and Country Club is located in Cumbernauld 13 miles from Glasgow City Centre. Its location on the A80 makes Westerwood within easy access of the key road networks and both Glasgow and Edinburgh Airports.

The hotel has 47 bedrooms, comprising of standard and executive rooms and both one and two bedroomed suites. All rooms are furnished in a traditional style with modern fabrics, many of which have scenic views over the golf course to the Campsie Hills.

Dining at Westerwood offers a choice of a light snack, an informal meal in our Club House overlooking the course or an a la carte menu in the Old Masters Restaurant where a pianist plays nightly.

Set in ideal golfing country the 18 hole par 73 course designed by Seve Ballesteros and Dave Thomas offers an exciting challenge to all golfers. The most spectacular hole is the 15th aptly named the Waterfall, set against a 40 foot rock face.

Each hole meanders through the silver birches, firs, heaths and heathers which are natural to this area of countryside, each offering a different and exciting challenge to every class of golfer.

Standing on the first tee, the player sees the fairway sweep away to the left and two very well struck shots will be required to reach the well guarded green tucked away amongst the trees. This sets the scene for the round and before the majestic 18th is reached there are another 16 golfing delights to savour. These include the difficult 4th with its two water hazards. Seve's trap, the 6th with Seve's cunningly placed bunker in front of the green, the tantalising 9th with its small undulating green, the 15th aptly named the waterfall - a fabulous par 3 and finally the 18th, possibly one of the finest finishing holes in golf.

The round is over, but not the memories. These will linger with you for many a day and entice you back to once again tackle this superb test of golf.

Westerwood is one of a group of three courses, the other two are Murrayshall and Fernfell. Murrayshall is at Scone, Perth and boasts a Country House Hotel with award winning cuisine. Fernfell Golf and Country Club is located just out of Cranleigh, 8 miles from Guildford, Surrey. For details of these courses please refer to their entries in this guide. Corporate golf packages are offered at all three courses with the opportunity to place your company name and logo on a tee, and reserve the course for your company golf day. Golf societies and Green Fee Players are welcome.

Westerwood Hotel
Golf and Country Club
St Andrews Drive
Cumbernauld
Glasgow
G68 OEW
Tel: (0236) 457171
Fax: (0236) 738478
Pro-shop (0236) 725281

MACHRIHANISH
CHAMPIONSHIP GOLF

The chief purpose of **Following the Fairways** is to guide the golfer around the counties of Great Britain and Ireland seeking out the finest golfing challenges (not to mention some of the most welcoming 19th hole establishments). Let us imagine, for once, that we are only allowed to play 18 holes but that we may assemble these 18 from any course in Great Britain and Ireland – a dream round if you like.

If there is any romance in our souls we will conclude this round on the 18th green of the Mahony's Point Course at Killarney, no doubt lining up a twenty footer for a two in the lengthening shadows of the encircling pines, and with the gentle lapping of Lough Leane in the background. And if we are bold we will step on to the 18th tee after tackling the Road Hole 17th at St. Andrews. But what do we choose for our opening hole? Well, if we are both romantic and bold we will select the 1st at Machrihanish. Let us hope that we have picked a mild day and that any wind is at our backs .....

Machrihanish – the very name borders on the mystical – was founded in 1876 (although it was in fact originally named the Kintyre Golf Club). Situated on the south western tip of the Mull of Kintyre, Machrihanish is perhaps the most geographically remote of all the great courses in the British Isles. Fortunately for golfers however, Machrihanish is actually only half an hour's flying time from Glasgow; there is an alternative – a three hour drive (each way) along the A82 A83 which admittedly passes through some magnificent countryside. **Loganair (041) 889 3181** are the people to talk to for anyone contemplating the aerial route.

Pilgrims have always been made very welcome at Machrihanish though one shouldn't assume that the course will be deserted. Machrihanish has never been golf's greatest secret. **Old Tom Morris** first let the cat out of the bag when he visited the links to advise on any alterations to the layout. Old Tom declared that 'The Almighty had designed Machrihanish for playing golf'. Before the First World War Machrihanish had already hosted a number of important amateur events. In those pre-1914 days a journey to Machrihanish must have been quite a trek, but then every Briton fancied himself as an intrepid explorer and on arrival doubtless some approached the first elderly bearded man they came across with the greeting, 'Tom Morris, I presume.'

Today, visitors are requested to book starting times with the Club's professional, **Ken Campbell**. The address for written correspondence is **The Machrihanish Golf Club, Machrihanish by Campbeltown, Argyl PA28 6PT**. Mr Campbell can also be contacted by telephone on **(058681) 277**. The Club's Secretary, **Mrs Anderson** can be reached on **(058681) 213**.

The green fees for 1992 are £13.50 per round, £18 per day midweek with a weekend green fee of £18. Anyone planning to spend a few days in the area – there are plenty of convenient guest houses and hotels nearby, many offering golfing packages – might consider a weekly ticket, available for £75 in 1992 or a fortnightly ticket (£130).

If the situation is exhilarating and invigorating in itself the golf course will in no way disappoint; certainly for the lover of traditional links golf, Machrihanish has everything. The layout has altered quite a bit since Tom Morris' day but the natural character of the course remains: awkward stances and blind shots are very much a feature of Machrihanish.

There is nothing blind however about the **1st** hole; from the tee the challenge ahead is a very visible one. It is a long par four of 423 yards and the only way of ensuring that the green can be reached in two shots is by hitting a full-blooded drive across the waters of Machrihanish Bay. From the back tees a 200 yard carry is called for. 'Intimidating' is the description; 'Death or Glory' is the result.

After the 1st the rest must be easy? Not a chance! If the opening hole tests the drive, several of the following holes will test the approach shot, particularly perhaps at the **3rd, 6th,** and **7th**. Machrihanish has its own 'Postage Stamp' hole, the **4th** which measures just 123 yards, and on the back nine there are successive short holes at the **15th** and **16th**, although the latter is hardly short being almost twice the length of the 4th. The course starts to wind down at the **17th** and pars here are frequently followed by birdies at the **18th** and considerable celebration at the 19th.

.... So there we are, on our dream round, standing bewitched on the 1st tee at Machrihanish. The Atlantic rollers are crashing below and, just as the song told us it would, the mist is about to roll in from the sea. Dare we smash one across the Bay? Or do we play safe out to the right? A famous golfing phrase is whispered in our ear: 'If you can't take golf you can't take life'. Of course we have no option ....

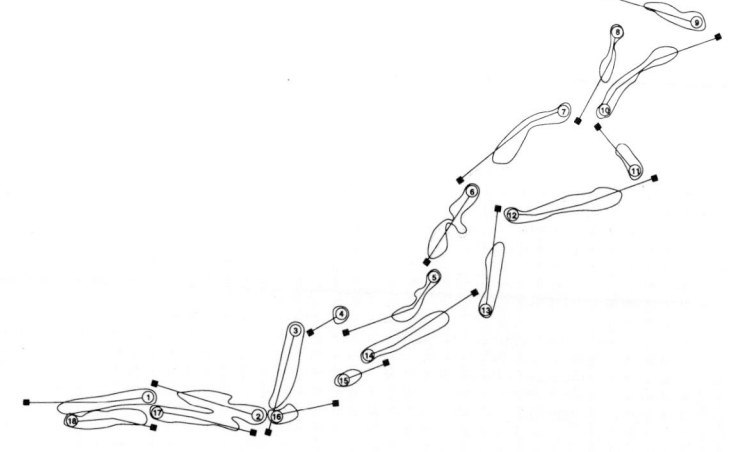

Hole	Yards	Par	Hole	Yards	Par
1	423	4	10	497	5
2	395	4	11	197	3
3	376	4	12	505	5
4	123	3	13	370	4
5	385	4	14	442	4
6	315	4	15	167	3
7	432	4	16	233	3
8	337	4	17	362	4
9	354	4	18	315	4
Out	**3,140**	**35**	**In**	**3,088**	**35**
			Out	**3,140**	**35**
			Totals	**6,228**	**70**

KEY

*** Visitors welcome at most times
** Visitors usually allowed on
weekdays only
* Visitors not normally permitted
(Mon, Wed) No visitors on
specified days

APPROXIMATE GREEN FEES

A – £30 plus
B – £20 – £30
C – £15 – £25
D – £10 – £20
E – Under £10
F – Green fees on application

RESTRICTIONS

G – Guests only
H – Handicap certificate required
H(24) – Handicap of 24 or less
required
L – Letter of introduction required
M – Visitor must be a member of
another recognised club.

Airdrie G.C
(0236) 62195
Rochsoles, Airdrie
1 mile N. from Airdrie Cross (town centre)
(18) 6004 yards/***/F/L

Alexandra G.C
041-556 3711
Sannox Gardens, Alexandra Parade, Glasgow
Half mile E. of city centre
(9) 1968 yards/***/E

Annanhill G.C
(0563) 21644
Irvine Road, Kilmarnock
On the main Kilmarnock-Irvine Road
(18) 6270 yards/***/(not Sat)/F

Ardeer G.C
(0294) 64542
Greenhead, Stevenston, Ayrshire
Turn into Kerelaw Road off the A78
(18) 6630 yards/***/(not Sat)/E/H

Ayr Belleisle G.C
(0292) 41258
Belleisle Park, Doonfoot Road, Ayr
2 miles S.W of the town centre on the A719
(18) 6550 yards/***/F

Ayr Dalmilling G.C
(0292) 263893
Westwood Avenue, Ayr
2 miles from town centre, off the A77
(18) 5401 yards/***/E

Ayr Seafield G.C
(0292) 41258
Ayr
2 miles from town centre in Belleisle Park
on the A719
(18) 5244 yards/***/F/H

Ballochmyle G.C
(0290) 50469
Ballochmyle, Mauchline, Ayrshire
1 mile from Mauchline village
(18) 5952 yards/**/D/H

Balmore G.C
(0360) 2120240
2 miles N. of Glasgow, 7 miles from city centre
(18) 5736 yards/***/F

Barshaw G.C
041-889 2908
Barshaw Park, Glasgow Road, Paisley,
Renfrewshire
Take A737 from Glasgow West to Paisley.
(18) 5673 yards/***/E

Bearsden G.C
041-942 2351
Thorn Road, Bearsden, Glasgow
1 mile from Bearsden Cross on Thorn Road
(9) 5569 yards/***/F/L

Beith G.C
(05055) 3166
Bigholm Road, Beith
1 mile E. of Beith
(9) 5600 yards/**/E/H

Bellshill G.C
(0698) 745124
Orbiston, Bellshill
10 miles S. of Glasgow on Bellshill to
Motherwell road
(18) 6605 yards/***/D/H

Biggar G.C
(0899) 20618
The Park, Broughton Road, Biggar, Lanarkshire
1 mile E. of Biggar on the Broughton Road
(18) 5416 yards/***/E

Bishopbriggs G.C
041-772 1810
Brackanbrae Road, Bishopbriggs, Glasgow
Take A803 from Glasgow North for 4 miles to
Bishopbriggs
(18) 6041 yards/*(intro only)/D/H

Blairbeth G.C
041-634 3355
Burnside, Rutherglen, Glasgow
1 mile S. of Rutherglen via Stonelaw Road, off
the A749
(18) 5448 yards/*(with member)/F

Blairmore & Strone
(036984) 217
Strone, By Dunoon, Argyll
9 miles N. of Dunoon on the A880
(9) 2112 yards/***/E

Bonnyton G.C(035 53)2781
Eaglesham, Glasgow
(18) 6252 yards/***/F

Bothwell Castle G.C
(0698) 853177
Blantyre Road, Bothwell, Glasgow
Adjacent to the M74, 3 miles N. of Hamilton
(18) 6426 yards/***/D/H

Brodick G.C
(0770) 2349
Brodick, Isle of Arran
By ferry from Androssan
(18) 4404 yards/***/E

Calderbraes G.C
(0698) 813425
57 Roundknowe Road, Uddingston,
Lanarkshire
At start of M74, 4 miles from Glasgow
(9) 5046 yards/*(intro by member)/F

Caldwell G.C
(050585) 616
Uplawmoor, Renfrewshire
15 miles from Glasgow off the A736
(18) 6102 yards/**/D

Cambuslang G.C
041-641 3130
30 Westburn Drive, Cambuslang, Glasgow
1 mile from the station in Cambuslang
(9) 6072 yards/*(intro by member)/E

Campsie G.C
(0360) 310244
Crow Road, Lennoxtown, Glasgow
N. of Lennoxtown on the B822
(18 5517 yards/**/E

Caprington G.C
(0563) 21915
Ayr Road, Kilmarnock
S. of Kilmarnock on the Ayr Road
(18) 5718 yards/***/F

Cardross G.C
(0389) 841754
Main Road, Cardross, Dumbarton
Between Dumbarton and Helensburgh on
the A814
(18) 6466 yards/**/D

Carluke G.C
(0555) 71070Hallcraig, Mauldslie Road, Carluke
2 miles from town centre on the road to
Hamilton
(18) 5805 yards/**(not Tues)/E/H

Carnwath G.C
(0555) 840251
Main Street, Carnwath
5 miles N.E of Lanark
(18) 5855 yards/***(not Tues, Thurs, Sat)/D/H

Carradale G.C
(05833) 387
Carradale, Campbeltown, Argyll
Off the B842 from Campbeltown to Carradale
(9) 2387 yards/**/E/H

Cathcart Castle G.C
041-638 9449
Mearns Road, Clarkston, Glasgow
7 miles from Glasgow on the A77
(18) 5832 yards/*(intro by member)/F/H

Cathkin Braes G.C
041-634 6605
Cathkin Road, Rutherglen, Glasgow
S.E of Glasgow on the road to East Kilbride
(18) 6266/**/D/H

Cawder G.C
041-772 5167
Cawder Road, Bishopbriggs, Glasgow
Half mile E. of Bishopbriggs off the A803
(18) 6229 yards/**(prior arrangement)/F/H
(18) 5877 yards/**(prior arrangement)/F/H

Clober G.C
041-956 1685
Craigton Road, Milngavie
7 miles N.W of Glasgow
(18) 5068 yards/**/E

Clydebank & District G.C
(0389) 73289
Hardgate, Clydebank, Dunbartonshire
8 miles N.W of Glasgow off Great
Western Road
(18) 5825 yards/**/D/H

Clydebank Overtoun G.C
041-952 6372
Overtoun Road, Clydebank, Dunbartonshire
Turn right at Dalmuir station, 5 minutes from
there
(18) 5643 yards/***/D(B on Sun)

Cochran Castle G.C(0505) 20146
Craigston, Scott Avenue, Johnstone
Quarter mile off the Johnstone-Beith Road,
S. of the town
(18) 6226 yards/**/D/H

Colville Park G.C
(0698) 63017
Jerviston Estate, Motherwell
1 mile N. of Motherwell on the A723
(18) 6208 yards/**/D

Corrie G.C
(077081) 223
Sannox, Isle of Arran
By ferry to Brodick, then 7 miles N. on
the A84
(9) 3896 yards/***/E/H

Cowal G.C
(0369) 5673
Ardenslate Road, Kirn, Dunoon
Quarter mile from A815 at Kirn
(18) 6250 yards/***/D

Cowglen G.C
041-632 0556
301 Barrhead Road, Glasgow
On S. side of Glasgow
(18) 6006 yards/***/E/L/H

Crow Wood G.C
041-779 1943
Garnkirk Estate, Muirhead, Chryston, Glasgow
1 mile N. of Stepps on the A80
(18) 6209 yards/*(with member)/D/H

Cumbernauld G.C
(0236) 734969
Palacerigg Country Park, Cumbernauld
Take A80 to Cumbernauld, follow signs to
Country park
(18) 6800 yards/**/E

Douglas Park G.C
041-942 2220
Hillfoot, Bearsden, Glasgow
Next to Hillfoot station on the east side
of town
(18) 5957 yards/*(with member)/F

Douglas Water G.C
(0555) 2295
Ayr Road, Rigside, Lanark
7 miles S.W of Lanark on A70
(9) 2947 yards/***/E

Douglaston G.C041-956 5750
Strathblane Road, Milngavie, Glasgow
7 miles N. of Glasgow on A81
(18) 6683 yards/***/E

Drumpellier G.C
(0236) 24139
Drumpellier Avenue, Coatbridge
1 mile from Coatbridge off A89
(18) 6227 yards/**/D

Dullatur G.C
(023 67) 27847
Dullatur, Glasgow
12 miles E. of Glasgow on Kilsyth road
(18) 6195 yards/**/F

Dumbarton G.C
(0389) 32830
Broadmeadows, Dumbarton, Dunbartonshire
Quarter mile N. of Dumbarton off A814
(18) 5654 yards/**/D

Dunaverty G.C
Southend, Campbeltown, Argyll
10 miles S. of Campbeltown on B842
(18)4597 yards/***/F

Easter Moffat G.C
(0236) 842289
Mansion House, Plains, By Airdrie, Lanarkshire
(18) 6221 yards/***/D/H

East Kilbride G.C
(035 52) 20913
Chapelside Road, Nerston, East Kilbride
Leave Glasgow by A7 and turn off at Nerston
village
(18) 6419 yards/*(with member)/F

East Renfrewshire G.C
(035 55) 206
Loganswell, Pilmuir, Newton Mearns, Glasgow
1 mile from Mearns Cross off the A77
(18) 6100 yards/***/C

Eastwood G.C
(035 55)261
Muirshield, Loganswell, Newton Mearns,
Glasgow
3 miles S. of Newton Mearns Cross on A77 from
Glasgow
(18) 5886 yards/***/D

Elderslie G.C
(0505) 22835
63 Main Road, Elderslie, Renfrewshire
Leave M8 for Linwood road to traffic lights
(18) 6004 yards/**/D

Erskine G.C
(0505) 863327
Bishopston, Renfrewshire
Leave M8 for B815 for 1 mile
(18) 6287 yards/*(with member)/F

Girvan G.C
(0465) 4346
Girvan, Ayrshire
Off the A77 from Glasgow to Ayr
(18) 5078 yards/***/E

Glasgow (Gailes) G.C
(0294) 311347
Gailes, By Irvine, Ayrshire
2 miles S. of Irvine on the road to Troon
(18) 6500 yards/***/(on application)/B/H

Glasgow (Killermont) G.C
041-942 2340
Killermont, Bearsden, Glasgow
6 miles N.W of Glasgow off the A81
(18) 5968 yards/***/(on application)/C/H

Gleddoch G.& C.C
(047554) 711
Langbank, Renfrewshire
Langbank signposted on M8 W. of Glasgow
(18) 6333 yards/***/(by arrangement)/C

Glencruitten G.C
(0631) 62868
Glencruitten Road, Oban
1 mile from town centre off the A816
(18) 4452 yards/***/F/M

Gourock G.C
(0475) 31001
Cowal View, Gourock, Renfrewshire
2 miles W. of Gourock Station via Victoria Road
(18) 6492 yards/**/E/H

Greenock G.C
(0475) 20793
Forsyth Street, Greenock, Renfrewshire
1 mile S.W of the town on the main road to
Gourock
(18) 5838 yards/***/(not Sat)/F/H

Haggs Castle G.C
041-427 1157
70 Drumbreck Road, GlasgowS.W of Glasgow
nr Ibrox Stadium
(18) 6464 yards/*/F

Hamilton G.C
(0698) 282872
Riccarton, Ferniegair, Hamilton, Lanarkshire
2 miles up Larkhall Road off the M74
(18) 6264 yards/*(with member)/F

Hayston G.C
041-776 1244
Campsie Road, Kirkintilloch, Glasgow
10 miles N.E of Glasgow off the A803
(18) 6042 yards/**/D

Helensburgh G.C
(0436) 74173
15 Abercromby Street, Helensburgh,
Dunbartonshire
Off Sinclair Street on N.E side of town
(18) 6053 yards/**/D/H

Hollandbush G.C
(0555) 893484
Acretophead, Lesmahagow
Leave M74 or A74 between Lesmahagow and
Coalburn
(18) 6100 yards/***/E

Innellan G.C
(0369) 3546
Knockamillie Road, Innellan, Argyll
4 miles from Dunoon
(9) 4878 yards/***/E

Irvine G.C
(0294) 75626
Bogside, Irvine
Through Irvine to Kilwinning and Ravenspark
Academy
(18) 6434 yards/***/(not Sat)/F

Irvine Ravenspark G.C
(0294) 76983
Kidsneuk, Irvine, Ayrshire
On the A78 between Irvine and Kilwinning
(18) 6429 yards/***/F

Kilbirnie Place G.C
(0505) 683398
Largs Road, Kilbirnie, Ayrshire
On the outskirts of Kilbirnie
(18) 5411 yards/***/(not Sat)/F

STRATHCLYDE
COMPLETE GOLF

Kilmalcolm G.C
(050587) 2139
Porterfield Road, Kilmalcolm,
RenfrewshireTake A740 to Linwood, then A761
to Bridge of weir
(18) 5890 yards/**/D

Kilmarnock (Barassie) G.C
(0292) 311077
29 Hillhouse Road, Barassie, Troon, Ayrshire
(18) 6473 yards/**(not Wed)/B

Kilsyth Lennox G.C
(0236) 822190
Tak-Ma-Doon Road, Kilsyth, Glasgow
12 N.E of Glasgow on the A80
(9) 5944 yards/***(not weekend am)/E/H

Kirkhill G.C
041-641 3083
Greenless Road, Cambuslang, Glasgow
Take the East Kilbride Road from Burnside
(18) 5862 yards/***/F

Kirkintilloch G.C
041-776 1256
Todhill, Campsie Road, Kirkintilloch, Glasgow
1 mile from Kirkintilloch on road to
Lennoxtown
(18) 5269 yards/*(with member)/F/H

Knightswood G.C
041-959 2131
Lincoln Avenue, Knightswood, Glasgow
Off Dumbarton Road from city centre
(9) 2717 yards/***/E

Kyles of Bute G.C
(0700) 811355
Tighnabruaich, Argyll
Take A885 from Dunoon, then B836 to
Tighnabruaich
(9) 2389 yards/***(not Sun am)/E

Lamlash G.C
(07706) 296
Lamlash, Brodick, Isle of Arran
On A841, 3 miles S. of ferry terminal
(18) 4681 yards/***/F

Lanark G.C
(0555) 3219
The Moor, Whitelees Road, Lanark
Leave A73 or A72 at Lanark, take Whitelees Road
(18) 6423 yards/**/F/H

Largs G.C
(0475) 673594
Irvine Road, Largs, Ayrshire
1 mile S. of Largs on the A78
(18) 6220 yards/***/D/H

Larkhall G.C
(0698) 88113
Burnhead Road, Larkhall, Lanarkshire
On east side of town, on B7019
(9) 6236 yards/***/F

Leadhills G.C
(0659) 74222
Leadhills, Biggar, Lanarkshire
Within the village, 6 miles from A74 at Abington
(9) 2400 yards/***/E

Lenzie G.C
041-776 1535
19 Crosshill Road, Lenzie, Glasgow
Take A80 to Stepps and into Lenzie Road
(18) 5982 yards/*(with member)/F

Lethamhill G.C
041-770 6220
Cumbernauld Road, Glasgow
On A80 adjacent to Hogganfield Loch
(18) 6073 yards/***/E

Linn Park G.C
041-637 5871
Simshill Road, Glasgow
Off the B766, 5 miles S. of Glasgow
(18) 4848 yards/***/F/H

Littlehill G.C
041-772 1916
Auchinairn Road, Bishopbriggs, Glasgow
3 miles N. of city centre
(18) 6228 yards/***/E

Lochranza G.C
(077 083) 273
Lochranza, Isle of Arran
(9) 1815 yards/***/E

Lochwinnoch G.C
Burnfoot Road, Lochwinnoch, Renfrewshire
On A760, 10 miles W. of Paisley
(18) 6202 yards/**/E/H

Loudoun G.C
(0563) 821993
Galston, Ayrshire
From Kilmarnock, take A71 towards Galston
(18) 5854 yards/**/F

Machrie G.C
(0496) 2310
Machrie Hotel, Port Ellen, Isle of Islay, Argyll
On A846 adjacent to airport
(18) 6226 yards/***/D/H

Machrie Bay G.C
(077084) 267
Machrie, by Brodick, Isle of Arran
Take ferry to Brodick, take String Road to
Machrie
(9) 2123 yards/***/E

Machrihanish G.C
(058 681) 213
Machrihanish, Campbeltown, Argyll
5 miles W. of Campbeltown on the B843
(18) 6228 yards/***/D/H
(9) 2395 yards/***/D/H

Millport G.C
(0475) 530311
Golf Road, Millport, Isle of Cumbrae
Take McBrayne ferry from Largs to Cumbrae
(18) 5831 yards/***/F/H

Milngavie G.C
041-956 1619
Laighpark, Milngavie, Glasgow
Off the A809, N.W of Glasgow
(18) 5818 yards/*(with member)/D

Mount Ellen G.C
(0236) 872277
Johnston House, Johnston Road, Gartcosh,
Glasgow
1 mile S. of the A80
(18) 5526 yards/***/E

Old Ranfurly G.C
(0505) 613612
Ranfurly Place, Bridge of Weir, Renfrewshire
7 miles W. of Paisley
(18) 6266 yards/**/D/L/H

Paisley G.C
041-884 3903
Braehead, Paisley
From Glasgow take the A737 to Paisley
(18) 6424 yards/***/D/L

Pollok G.C
041-632 1080
90 Barrhead Road, Glasgow
On A762, 4 miles S. of Glasgow
(18) 6257 yards/**(male only)/C/H

Port Bannatyne G.C
(0700) 2009
Bannatyne Mains Road, Port Bannatyne,
Isle of Bute
2 miles N. of Rothesay ferry terminal
(13) 4654 yards/***/E

Port Glasgow G.C
(0475) 704181
Devol Farm Industrial Estate, Port Glasgow,
Renfrewshire
(18) 5712 yards/**/E

Prestwick G.C
(0292) 77404
2 Links Road, Prestwick, Ayrshire
1 mile from Prestwick airport
(18) 6544 yards/***/F/M/L

Prestwick St Cuthbert G.C
(0292) 77101
East Road, Prestwick, Ayrshire
Off the A77, nr the irport
(18) 6470 yards/**/E

Prestwick St Nicholas G.C
(0292) 77608
Grangemuir Road, Prestwick, Ayrshire
On the seafront, off the A79
(18) 5926 yards/**/D/H

Ralston G.C
041-882 1349
Strathmore Avenue, Ralston, Paisley
To the E. of Paisley, off main road
(18) 6100 yards/*(by arrangement)/F

Ranfurly Castle G.C
(0505) 612609
Golf Road, Bridge of Weir, Renfrewshire
Leave M8 ta junction 29, take A240 and A761
(18) 6284 yards/**/F/L

Renfrew G.C
041-886 6692
Blythswood Estate, Inchinnan Road, Renfrew
Take A8 to Renfrew
(18) 6818 yards/*(with member)/D/H

Rothesay G.C
(0700) 2244
Canada Hill, Rothesay, Isle of Bute
Take hourly steamer from Wemyss Bay
(18) 5440 yards/***/E/H

Routenburn G.C
(0475) 673230
Largs, Ayrshire
1 mile N. of Largs off A78
(18) 5650 yards/**/E/H

Royal Troon G.C
(0292) 311555
Craigend Road, Troon, Ayrshire
3 miles from Prestwick airport on B749
(18) 6641 yards/**/A/H (18 max)
(18) 6274 yards/**/B/H

Sandyhills G.C
041-778 1179
223 Sandyhills Road, Glasgow
Sandyhills Rd on E. of city
(18) 6253 yards/***/E/H

Shiskine G.C
(077086) 293
Blackwaterfoot, Isle of Arran
(12) 3000 yards/***/E

Shotts G.C
(0501) 20431
Blairhead, Shotts
Between Edinburgh and Glasgow, 2 miles off
M8
(18) 6125 yards/***/E

Skelmorlie G.C
(0475) 520152
Skelmorlie, Ayrshire
5 miles N. of Largs
(13) 5104 yards/***(not Sat)/E

Strathaven G.C
(0357) 20421
Overton Avenue, Glasgow Road, Strathaven
On outskirts of town, on A726
(18) 6226 yards/**/F

Tarbert G.C
(088 02) 565
Kilberry Road, Tarbert, Argyll
Leave A83 from Tarbert for B8024
(9) 2230 yards/***/E

Torrance House G.C
(035 52) 33451
Strathaven Road, East Kilbride, Glasgow
(18) 6640 yards/***/F/H

Troon Municipal G.C(0292) 312464
Harling Drive, Troon, Ayrshire
Take A77 from Glasgow, follow signs for Troon
(18) 6687 yards/***/E
(18) 6327 yards/***/E
(18) 4784 yards/***/E

Turnberry Hotel G.C
(0655) 31000
Turnberry Hotel, Turnberry, Ayrshire
Off A77 from Glasgow
(18) 6950 yards/***/A/H
(18) 6276 yards/***/B/H
(less for Hotel guests)

Vale of Leven G.C
(0389) 52351
Northfield Course, Bonfield, Alexandria,
Dunbartonshire
Leave A82 at Bonhill
(18) 5156 yards/**/E

Vaul G.C
(087 92) 566
Scarinish, Isle of Tiree, Argyll
(9) 6246 yards/***/E

Westerwood Hotel & G.C
(0236) 725281
St Andrews Drive, Cumbernauld
(18) 6800 yards/***/F

Western Gailes G.C
(0294) 311649
Gailes, By Irvine, Ayrshire
5 miles N. of Troon on A78
(18) 6664 yards/***(not Thurs or Sat)/F/H

West Kilbride G.C
(0294) 823911
33-35 Fullerton Drive, Seamill, West Kilbride,
Ayrshire
Leave A78 at Seamill
6247 yards/**/F/L/H

Whitecraigs G.C
041-639 4530
72 Ayr Road, Giffnock, Glasgow
7 miles S. of Glasgow on the A77
(18) 6230 yards/*(intro only)/F

Williamwood G.C
041-637 2715
Clarkston Road, Netherlee, Glasgow
5 miles S. of city centre on the B767
(18) 5808 yards/***/H

Windyhill G.C
041-942 7157
Bal Jaffray Road, Bearsden, Glasgow
Take A809 for 1 mile to A810 to club
(18) 6254 yards/**/F

Wishaw G.C
(0698) 372869
55 Cleland Road, Wishaw, Lanarkshire
In centre of town, 3 miles S. of Motherwell
(18) 6160 yards/***(not Sat)/D

Arthur Weaver   YOUNG TOM MORRIS
Burlington Gallery

FIFE

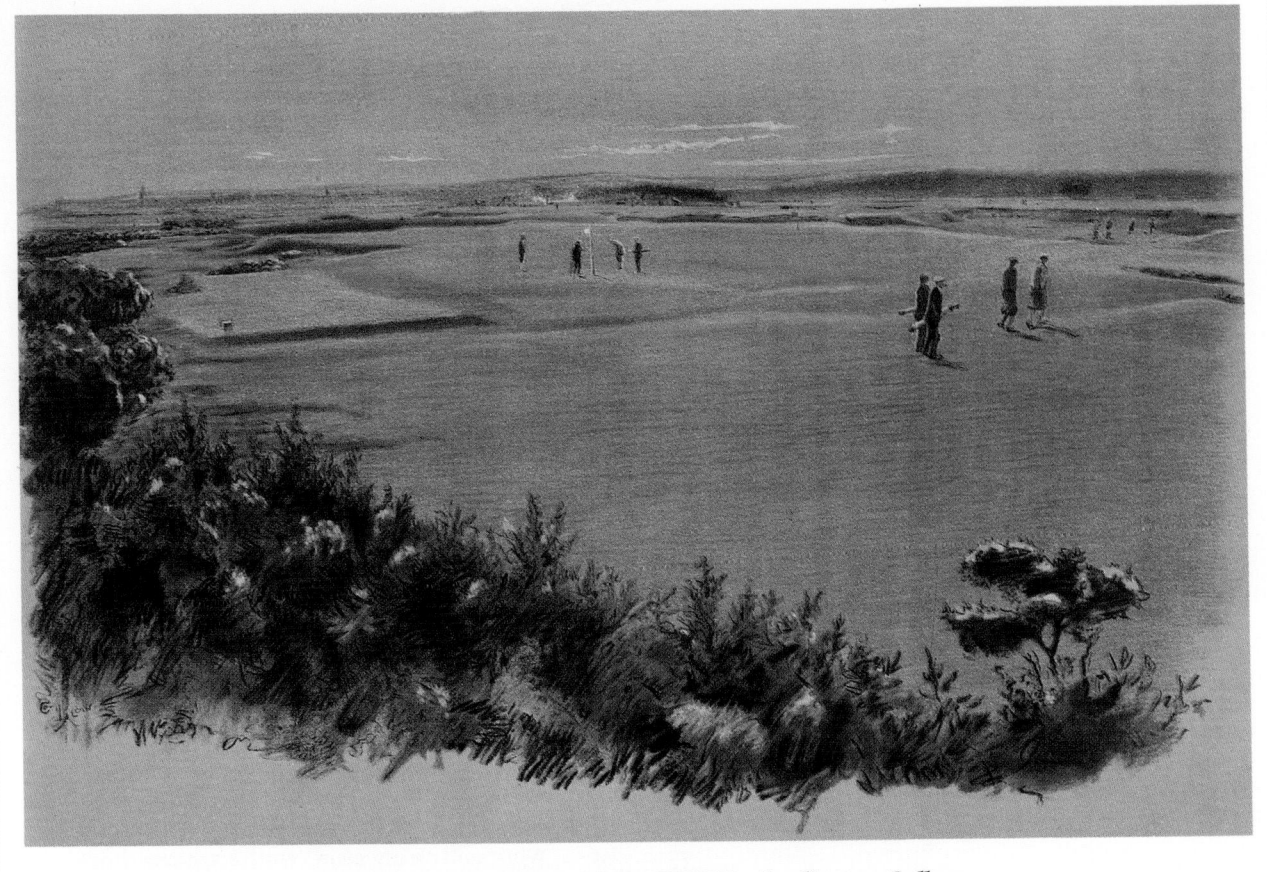

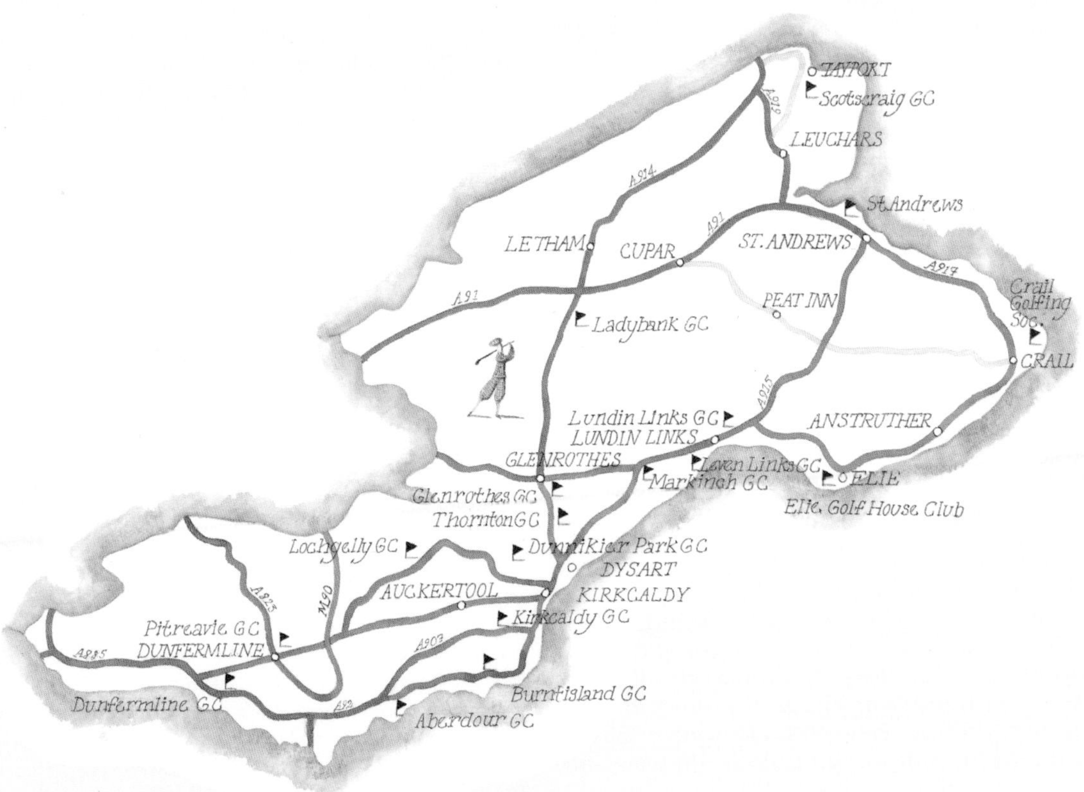
TAYPORT
Scotscraig GC
LEUCHARS
St.Andrews
LETHAM
CUPAR
ST. ANDREWS
PEAT INN
Crail Golfing Soc.
CRAIL
Ladybank GC
Lundin Links GC
LUNDIN LINKS
ANSTRUTHER
GLENROTHES
Leven Links GC
ELIE
Markinch GC
Glenrothes GC
Elie Golf House Club
Thornton GC
Lochgelly GC
Dunnikier Park GC
DYSART
AUCKERTOOL
KIRKCALDY
Kirkcaldy GC
Pitreavie GC
DUNFERMLINE
Dunfermline GC
Burntisland GC
Aberdour GC
A91
A914
A919
A917
A915
A92
A907
A823
M90
A985

Cecil Aldin ***THE 5TH & 13TH GREENS*** ***Burlington Gallery***

FIFE
CHOICE GOLF

Many years ago, watching an England versus Scotland soccer game at Wembley, I remember being amused by one of the banners carried by a group of Scottish supporters which boldly declared, 'Remember Bannockburn'. Being a pigheaded Englishman I thought to myself, they ought to remember it – it was just about the only battle they won in centuries. Of course, all is now abundantly clear – the Scots were far too busy priming their golfing skills to bother themselves fighting the Sassenachs.

As long ago as 1457 the Scottish Parliament, unimpressed by the performance of its sharp shooters, felt that too much golf and football were to blame for the lack-lustre performances on the battlefields. An Act was passed stating that because of their interference with the practice of archery, the 'fute-ball and golf be utterly cryit down and nocht usit'. History would seem to suggest that the Scots didn't take a blind bit of notice, and golf steadily grew in popularity. Juggle the figures that make up 1457 and we have 1754, perhaps the most significant date in golf's history – the year the Society of St Andrews golfers drew up its written rules of golf.

Today **St Andrews**, deep in the Kingdom of Fife, is the place every golfer in the world wants to visit. Even if you have only swung a club at the local municipal you'll be itching to do the same at St Andrews. However, for those contemplating a pilgrimage to the centre of the golfing world it should be said that St Andrews has several near neighbours that warrant the most discerning attention. Between Dunfermline, to the west of Fife, and St Andrews, lie what are undoubtedly some of the finest courses in Scotland.

AROUND THE COAST

For six hundred years Dunfermline was the country's capital and the body of its most famous king, Robert the Bruce, lies buried in Dunfermline Abbey (minus his heart which is in Melrose Abbey). The town has two courses, **Dunfermline** and **Pitreavie**. Both are parkland courses at which visitors are welcome provided some prior arrangement is made. Neither is unduly hard on the pocket. For those wishing to spend a day or two in the old royal town, the appropriately named King Malcolm Thistle Hotel (0383) 722611 provides convenient comfort.

East of Dunfermline there is a testing links at **Burntisland** with fine views over the Firth of Forth and there are again two courses in Kirkcaldy, the **Dunnikier Park** and **Kirkcaldy** Golf Clubs, (and make sure you pronounce it Ker-coddy!) Dunnikier Park is a public course. One other good golf club to note in the area is **Aberdour**. A peaceful night's sleep can be found at the Long Boat (0592) 890625 in Kinghorn and good fare is abundantly available at the Old Rectory Inn (0592) 51211 in Dysart.

Beyond Kirkcaldy, out along a glorious stretch of spectacular coast are Fife's famous five – **Leven Links, Lundin Links, Elie, Balcomie** and of course **St Andrews**. The first two are often considered as a pair probably on account of there being very little land in between (an old stone wall serves as the boundary). Two proud clubs share the 6,433 yards links at Leven, the **Leven Golfing Society** and **Leven Thistle** however, the visitor is always made to feel welcome – as indeed he, or she is at the more hilly **Lundin** – an excellent course, which although very much a links has an abundance of trees on the back nine.

Elie, or the **Golf House Club**, lies a short distance from the two across Largo Bay, the A917 linking the town with Leven. Elie is famed for its unique periscope by the first tee and for the fact that it was here that James Braid fashioned many of the skills that won him five Open Championships. A charming and very natural links – you won't see trees anywhere here – and not too demanding in length, several of the holes are laid out right alongside a rocky shoreline. A ballot system operates at Elie during the summer but otherwise there are no general restrictions on times visitors can play.

Following the aforementioned A917 eastwards from Elie, the town of Crail is soon reached. Just beyond the town at Fife Ness is the magnificent **Balcomie** links, home of the two hundred year old **Crail Golfing Society**. Together with St Andrews it is featured a few pages on. Incidentally, when visiting St. Andrews, or if just passing by, try to visit the British Golf Museum – it's right next to the 1st tee on the Old Course.

In addition to the large hotels in St Andrews, accommodation near to the great links courses of Fife is generally inexpensive. A great number are geared almost solely towards the interests of the golfing community and are situated within pitching distance of the nearest fairway. Here are a few thoughts; In Lundin Links, the Old Manor Hotel (0333) 320368 is highly thought of with a particularly good restaurant while less expensive accommodation can be enjoyed at the Lundin Links Hotel (0333) 320207, an especially popular retreat for golfers. The Golf Hotel (0333) 330209 in Elie is self explanatory, and just a short distance away in Anstruther is the popular Craws Nest Hotel (0333) 310691 – located midway between Elie and Crail it's an excellent base. In Anstruther one might also visit the Smugglers Inn, a cosy 300 year old tavern. Crail is a delightful fishing village and here the Golf Hotel (0333) 50206 is another obvious choice, it's a place of great character and is one of Scotland's oldest licensed inns. Still in Crail, the Caiplie Guest House (0333) 50564 is good value. Two restaurants that can be strongly recommended are found a little inland, they are; Ostlers Close (0334) 55574 at Cupar and the exceptional Peat Inn (0334) 84206 on the road to Cupar.

It isn't an overstatement to say that **St Andrews** is the centre of the golfing world. As early as 1691 it was described as the 'Metropolis of Golfing'. With pilgrims today making the trip from all corners of the globe (and especially from America and Japan) the number of hotels and guest houses is understandably considerable. The St. Andrews Old Course Hotel (0334) 74371, sumptuously refurbished, is unquestionably one of Scotland's leading hotels, and overlooking the most famous hole in golf, The Road Hole 17th on the Old Course, couldn't be better positioned. More aesthetically pleasing than prior to its restoration, it now oozes class both within and without. St Andrews does have several other hotels of note; Rufflets Hotel (0334) 72594 just outside the town is an excellent base while another room with a view can be booked at the Rusacks Marine Hotel (0334) 74321, formerly the Golf Inn, and which oozes golfing history (the restaurant is also good and rather appropriately named the Niblick). The other hotels which might just hint at a round of the good old game include the St Andrews Golf Hotel (0334) 72611 and the Scores Hotel (0334) 72451, both good value and pleasant. There is also any number of comfortable guesthouses and B&B's to be found; noteworthy examples include the Albany (0334) 77737, Arran House (0334) 74724 and the Amberside (0334) 74644. While golf clearly takes centre stage one should not forget the pleasant coastline nearby (scenes from Chariots Of

FIFE
CHOICE GOLF

Fire were filmed on St. Andrews' vast sands), nor the twelfth century Cathedral or Scotland's oldest university. One final thought for hungry souls is the popular Grange Inn (0334) 72670 in Grange Village – an excellent eating place.

INLAND GOLF

Just as the leading courses of Surrey aren't all heathland and heather neither are those of Fife all seaviews and sandhills.

Ladybank is actually only a few miles north of Leven but is completely different in character with heathland fairways and much pine and heather – a very beautiful course and well worth a visit. North of Ladybank lies **Cupar**, one of the oldest nine-hole golf courses in Scotland and a clubhouse that has to be approached through a cemetery (slightly older even than the golf course!)

In an area steeped in history **Glenrothes** is a relative newcomer to the scene. Young, perhaps, but an excellent course nonetheless. Situated to the west of the town it is a fairly hilly parkland type, offering many superb views. A friendly welcome awaits but the names of two of the holes worry me a little – the 11th, titled 'Satan's Gateway' and the 18th, 'Hells End'!

A restful 19th is clearly in order. In Glenrothes quality places abound. The Balgeddie House (0592) 742511 is superbly secluded and most relaxing, while the Rescobie Hotel (0592) 742143 and the Rothes Arms (0592) 753701 should also placate the soul. Letham is only a short distance from Ladybank and here Fernie Castle (033781) 381 is decidedly recommended. Equally convenient and comfortable is the Lomond Hills Hotel at Freuchie (0337) 57329.

Two other courses that are well worth visiting if journeying inland in Fife are at **Thornton,** where the River Ore makes for some challenging holes and at **Lochgelly** – convenient if travelling between Dunfermline and Kirkcaldy. The final mention though goes to **Scotscraig**, an Open Championship qualifying course at Tayport. Although close to the sea its actually a downland type course rather than a true links, and its an admirable test of golf.

Following that testing game at Scotscraig one is likely to be left with a difficult decision. To the north, Carnoustie and many other great challenges await; but then no golfer who experienced the pleasures of the Kingdom of Fife ever left easily.

Robert Turnbull   ST. ANDREWS   Private Collection

ST ANDREWS
CHAMPIONSHIP GOLF

If there is such a thing as a truly global sport then it has to be golf. From parochial beginnings on the east coast of Scotland it is now played on every continent, in every conceivable corner. Not only are there golf courses on the exotic islands of Tahiti and Bali but there is one in the Himalayas and there is one in the Arctic; golf has even been played on the Moon. For all this there remains but one home – St. Andrews.

Whilst we will never be able to put an exact date on the time golf was first played on the famous links, several documents refer to a crude form of the game being played as early as the **mid 1400s.** As for the right to play at St. Andrews, which of course, the whole world enjoys, the origins are embodied in a licence dated **1552** drawn up by the **Archbishop** of **St. Andrews**. It permitted the community to breed rabbits on the links and to 'play at golf, futeball, schueting, at all gamis with all uther, as ever they pleis and in ony time'. Furthermore the proprietor was bound 'not to plough up any part of the said golf links in all time coming.' Organised golf came to St. Andrews in **1754** when twenty-two Noblemen and Gentlemen formed the **St. Andrews Society of Golfers**. In **1834** the Society became the **Royal and Ancient Golf Club**.

Not only can all the world play at St. Andrews, but all the world wants to and arranging a game on the **Old Course** can be a little difficult. The **St. Andrews Links Management Committee** handles all matters relating to times of play and they should be contacted well in advance. The summer months are naturally the busiest period and it is best to write to the Committee two to three months prior to intended play, offering if possible a number of alternative dates. The address to write to is **The St. Andrews Links Management Committee, Golf Place, St. Andrews, Fife, KY16 9JA.** The Secretary, **Mr. Alec Beveridge** and his staff can be contacted by telephone on **(0334) 75757** and by fax on (0334) 77036. There are no handicap limits to play over the Old Course. However a handicap certificate or letter of introduction is required. It should also be noted that there is no Sunday golf on the Old Course. In 1992 the green fee for a round was priced at £34.

In addition to the Old Course there are four other eighteen hole links at St. Andrews, the **New Course**, which dates from 1896, the **Jubilee** (1897) – recently lengthened and improved by Donald Steel – the **Eden** (1914) and the new **Strathyrum**

Course. No handicap certificate is required to play over any of the above four courses and the green fees for 1992 on each were £14, £14, £12 and £10 respectively. A 9 hole course, the **Balgove**, is also available together with a driving range and extensive practice facilities.

St. Andrews is situated 57 miles north east of Edinburgh. For northbound travellers the most direct route to take is the M90 after crossing the Forth Road Bridge. The A91 should be joined at junction 8. This road can be followed to St. Andrews. Southbound travellers should head for Perth which is linked in turn to Dundee by the A85 and to the north of Scotland by the A9. From Perth a combination of the A90 and the A913 takes one to Cupar where the A91 can be picked up.

It was nature that fashioned St. Andrews and over the centuries the Old Course has seen little change. Its myriad tiny pot bunkers remain both a fascination and a frustration – providing just enough room as **Bernard Darwin** put it 'for an angry man and his niblick'. Laid out on a narrow strip of land ranging from 50 to 100 yards in width, St. Andrews is famed for its enormous double greens. There are seven in all and some are more than an acre in size. With little definition between the fairways there tends to be no standard way of playing a particular hole and as a rule the wind direction will determine the preferred line. Individual holes are not likely to be easily remembered the first time of playing, especially as one will probably be walking the course in a semi-trance. History is everywhere and on the first hole as you cross the bridge over the **Swilcan Burn** a voice from somewhere says 'they've all walked this bridge' – and of course they have, just as they've all passed through the **Elysian Fields**, tackled **Hell's Bunker**, **the Beardies** and the **Principal's Nose**. And then of course they've all faced **the Road Hole** with its desperate drive and even more desperate approach and then finally strolled over the great expanse of the **18th** fairway towards the **Valley of Sin** and the famous R & A Clubhouse beyond.

It isn't always love at first sight with St. Andrews and **Bobby Jones** tore up his card on the 11th when he first played. Jones went on to meet great triumph at St. Andrews and it is perhaps fitting to end with a few words from the great man: 'the more I studied the Old Course the more I loved it, and the more I loved it the more I studied it, so that I came to feel that it was for me the most favourable meeting ground possible for an important contest'.

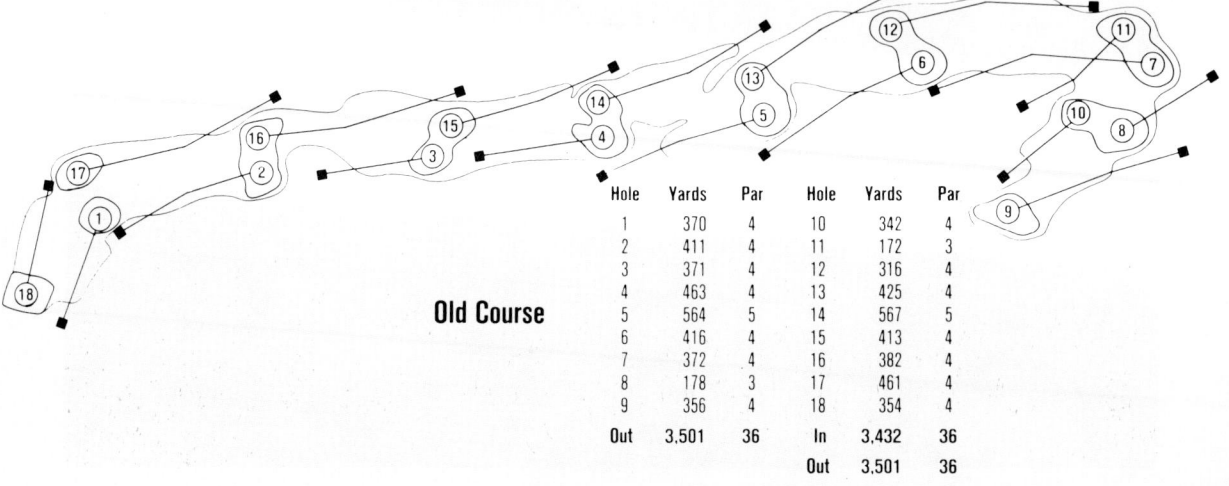

Old Course

Hole	Yards	Par	Hole	Yards	Par
1	370	4	10	342	4
2	411	4	11	172	3
3	371	4	12	316	4
4	463	4	13	425	4
5	564	5	14	567	5
6	416	4	15	413	4
7	372	4	16	382	4
8	178	3	17	461	4
9	356	4	18	354	4
Out	3,501	36	In	3,432	36
			Out	3,501	36
			TOTALS	6,933	72

ST. ANDREWS GOLF HOTEL

St. Andrews Golf Hotel is a tastefully modernised Victorian House situated on the cliffs above St. Andrews Bay, some 200 yards from the 18th tee of the 'Old Course'.

There are 23 bedrooms all with private bath and shower, and all furnished individually to a high degree of comfort, with telephone, radio, T.V., tea/coffee maker, trouser press and hair-dryer. A nice touch is the fresh flowers and welcoming fruit basket.

There is a quiet front lounge for residents and a most interesting golfer's cocktail bar featuring pictures and photographs of Open Champions past and present. This gives onto a small south facing patio garden.

With a separate entrance is 'Ma Bell's' Bar and day time restaurant, popular with students and visitors alike. Tasty food, hot and cold and reasonably priced is served from noon to 6.00 pm. A main attraction is the selection of more than 80 bottled beers from all over the world, and no fewer than 14 on draught, including cask-conditioned ales.

The central feature of the hotel is the candle-lit oak-panelled restaurant with its magnificent sea view. A la carte and table d'hote menus both feature the best of local produce – fish, shell-fish, beef, lamb, game and vegetables – conjured into delightful dishes by chef Adam Harrow. The food is well complemented by an interesting and comprehensive list of wines selected personally by owner, Brian Hughes.

Golf of course, is the speciality of the hotel, and you can find either prepared golf packages and golf weeks or have something tailored to your particular requirements, using any of the thirty or so courses within 45 minutes of St. Andrews.

St. Andrews Golf Hotel
40 The Scores
St. Andrews
KY16 9AS
Tel: (0334) 72611
Fax: (0334) 72188

CRAIL GOLFING SOCIETY
CHAMPIONSHIP GOLF

On 23rd February 1986 the seventh oldest Golf Club in the world celebrated its bicentenary. Some three years before the Bastille was stormed a group of eleven gentlemen met at the Golf Inn in Crail and together formed the **Crail Golfing Society.** The records of that historic day are still preserved; indeed remarkably the Society possesses a complete set of minutes from the date of its inception. In those early days the Society members wore scarlet jackets with yellow buttons and dined at the Golf Inn after a day on the links. The local punch flowed and a good time was doubtless had by all – now those were the days!

Since 1895 the Club has played over the **Balcomie Links** which is located approximately two miles north east of Crail at Fifeness. Earlier the Society had used a narrow strip of land at Sauchope, slightly closer to Crail (and of course to the Golf Inn).

The atmosphere is still jovial and visitors are made most welcome. With the exception of a few competition days there are no general restrictions on times of play. However, individual visitors are advised to telephone the Professional, **Graeme Lennie** the day before playing. He can be contacted on **(0333) 50278** or **(0333) 50960**. Societies, or golfing parties, are equally welcome and advance bookings can be made at all times apart from during the peak summer period. Written enquiries should be addressed to **The Secretary, Crail Golfing Society, Balcomie Clubhouse, Crail, Fife KY10 3XN.** The Secretary, **Mrs Cynthia Penhale**, can be reached by telephone on **(0333) 50686.**

The green fees for 1992 are pitched at £16 per round, £24 per day during weekdays or £20 per round and £30 per day at weekends. Juniors can obtain a weekday round for £8 though at other times full fees are charged. In addition short Temporary Membership is offered: examples include £48 for 3 consecutive weekdays and £128 for a fortnightly ticket (excluding Sundays).

The Balcomie Links is in fact ideal for 'holiday golf'. Without being overly long (5,720 yards, par 69) – though the wind can affect distances greatly – it offers some exceptionally spectacular scenery and similar to Cruden Bay further north, a nearby Castle casts a watchful eye. **Balcomie Castle**, where Mary of Guies, mother-to-be of Mary Queen of Scots, spent her first few days in Scotland, comes complete with ghost. The course is always well maintained and the greens especially, have acquired an enviable reputation. The holes have been laid out so that each provides a view of the sea. There is an unusual balance to the round with the front nine containing seven par fours and the back nine only two; as for par three holes, there are none on the front nine after the 3rd but the second nine boasts five short holes including the 18th. There are some rather interesting names too: 'Fluke Dub' **(4th)** 'Hell's Hole' **(5th)** 'Castle Yetts' **(9th)** and 'Lang Whang' **(11th).**

From all points south, travelling to Crail will be by way of the Forth Road Bridge and thereafter following a combination of 'A' roads. However, the M90 may also be used if St. Andrews is to be taken in en route. The A915/A917 approaches Crail from along the coast via Lundin Links and Elie, while from Cupar and St Andrews the A91/A917 should be taken. As stated the course is situated two miles from Crail in the direction of Fifeness and is well-signposted.

The 19th at Crail is as it should be, right next to the 18th green and provides commanding views over much of the course and out across the North Sea. Smart casual dress is acceptable in the Clubhouse, though presumably today if you strolled in wearing a bright scarlet jacket with yellow buttons you might raise a few eyebrows! A full complement of catering is offered at all times but for those wishing to make advanced arrangements, a quick telephone call to the Steward is never a bad idea. **Mr New** is the gentleman in question and he can be contacted on **(0333) 50278.**

The temptation for many on crossing the Forth Road Bridge is of course to head straight for the Royal and Ancient. Although St. Andrews may be the undisputed sovereign in the so-called Kingdom of Fife, there are also a number of handsome Princes. Balcomie stands comparison with the best and is a course of which the two hundred year old Society can justifiably be proud.

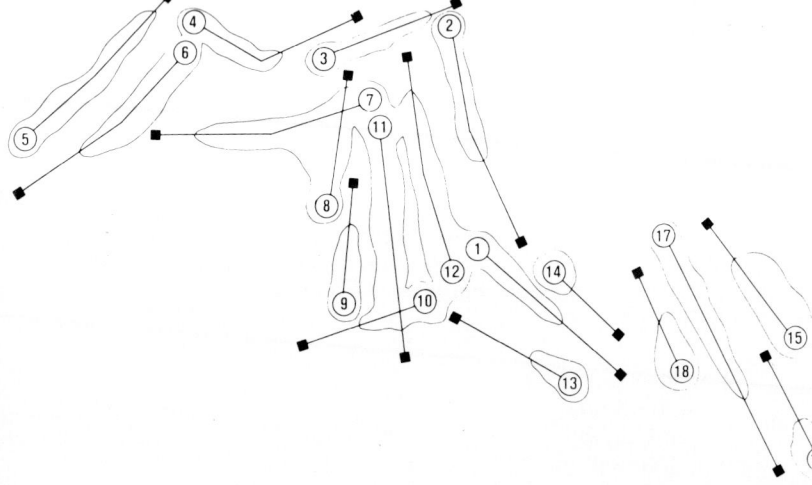

Hole	Yards	Par	Hole	Yards	Par
1	312	4	10	209	3
2	480	5	11	500	5
3	179	3	12	489	5
4	348	4	13	215	3
5	346	4	14	149	3
6	334	4	15	265	4
7	421	4	16	163	3
8	306	4	17	461	4
9	334	4	18	209	3
Out	3.060	36	In	2.660	33
			Out	3.060	36
			TOTALS	5.720	69

RESCOBIE HOTEL AND RESTAURANT

Rescobie is a 1920s country house set in two acres of grounds on the edge of the old village of Leslie, which adjoins the new industrial town of Glenrothes. The house, whose gardens contain a functional herb garden and a wild flower meadow, was converted in the 70s and 80s to a fully licensed hotel; all of its ten individually decorated bedrooms now have private bath or shower, direct dial telephone, colour television, radio/alarm, room bar, etc. The furnishings are comfortable, old village photographs adorn the walls of the bar and in cooler months a log fire burns in the lounge.

Perfectly positioned for golfers in the heart of an area rich in golf courses - St Andrews, Dalmahoy, Carnoustie and Gleneagles to name but a few - Rescobie is only half an hour's drive away from Perth and Dundee and forty five minutes from the centre of Edinburgh.

The owners take great pains to run the hotel as a traditional country house. There is no formal reception area; guests will find a bell in the hall and other public rooms to summon waitresses, who are dressed smartly but informally in tartan skirt and blouse in preference to the customary black and white. The owners, Tony and Wendy Hughes-Lewis, make a point of meeting all of their guests, and if Wendy does not actually welcome you into hotel one of them will meet you later on.

There are four full-time chefs, which is a large brigade for a small hotel, but they make by hand what most other catering establishments buy in. In addition to producing stocks, soups and sauces, the chefs make all of the sweets and petits fours, roll their own pasta and even cut their own chips. Tony himself makes marmalade with Seville oranges in the spring and jellies with crab apples and elderberries in the Autunm, and tends the herb garden, where the chefs can be seen in the summer gathering their daily requirements.

The effort the owners make to preserve the atmosphere of a country house is reflected in their personal attention to the well-being of their guests, the conduct of their staff and the quality of their cuisine. Such high standards are expected in a four star establishment; to find them at two star level makes the Rescobie Hotel a rare find and excellent value for money.

The Rescobie Hotel and Restaurant
Valley Drive
Leslie
Fife
KY6 3BQ
Tel: (0592) 742143
Fax: (0592) 620231

FERNIE CASTLE HOTEL

Located in the heart of the historic Kingdom of Fife, Fernie Castle Hotel is the ideal base for a golfing holiday. With more than 30 Championship courses within 25 miles of the hotel, there can't be many places which offer such a choice.

The golfer's mecca - St Andrews - is within 30 minutes drive, and the famous courses at Carnoustie and Gleneagles are within easy striking distance. Ladybank, used as an Open Championship Qualifying Course, and loved by all who play it, is only 2 miles away. Complete golf holiday packages can be arranged and staff at the hotel will be delighted to discuss your requirements.

Fernie Castle is a small luxury hotel specialising in the care of its guests and the quality of food offered. Steeped in history, the Castle was first recorded in 1353 when it belonged to the Earl of Fife. By the fifteenth century, Fernie was held by a family known as Fernie of that Ilk, and then, in the sixteenth century by the Arnotts who kept it for a century. In 1680 the Balfours of Burleigh became the owners and their descendants

retained the tenture until 1965. In 1967 the house was converted into a hotel and entered the 'family' of Scottish Country Castle Hotels which have emerged, offering a balance of historic antiquity with modern comfort.

All the bedrooms are equipped with television, telephone, tea and coffee making facilities, private bath or shower and central heating. Guests can relax in the historic Keep Bar or enjoy coffee in the comfortable drawing room. The dining room, with its crystal glass, candlelight and elegance can only add to your delight in your visit. Menus which change daily use only the best fresh produce including mussels from Orkney and salmon from Shetland.

The grounds surrounding the Castle are comprised of formal lawns, mature woodlands, paddocks and a small loch with swans and ducks.

Totally committed to the guests' enjoyment of this splendid part of Scotland, Fernie Castle Hotel will delight and surprise.

Fernie Castle Hotel
Letham
Near Cupar
Fife KY7 7RU
Tel: (033781) 381
Fax: (033781) 422

THE LOMOND HILLS HOTEL

The Lomond Hills Hotel is situated in the picturesque village of Freuchie in the heart of Fife. Years ago it was the place to which courtiers out of favour at nearby Falkland Palace were banished. Even today the derisory saying 'Awa tae Freuchie and eat mice' is used in some parts of Scotland!

The Kingdom of Fife is rich farming country, and although noblemen in the last century used to hunt wild boar, today the area lends itself to the more relaxing pursuits of hill or forest walking. Visitors may prefer to visit the numerous museums, castles and National Trust properties in the area, or enjoy the sporting delights that Fife can offer, sailing, gliding, and pony-trekking and some thirty golf courses are all within easy reach. Fishermen will find a wealth of rivers and reservoirs: there is truly something for everyone.

Atmosphere and comfort are two features of the Lomond Hills Hotel which make every guest's stay so enjoyable. Candlelight and simple but courteous service will enhance every meal, with a large choice of wines, sherries and liqueurs. A small selection of Scottish specialities, together with popular French Flambe dishes create at appetising 'a la carte' menu and fresh produce is used wherever possible.

All bedrooms have en suite facilities, plus all the usual refinements expected of a 4 crown hotel.

Start the day pleasantly with a traditional Scottish breakfast and relax in the well-appointed resident's lounge after a busy day, or perhaps pay a visit to the swimming pool, leisure centre or roof terrace.

The Lomond Hills Hotel
Freuchie
Fife
Tel: (0337) 57329/57498

FIFE
COMPLETE GOLF

KEY

*** Visitors welcome at most times
** Visitors usually allowed on
weekdays only
* Visitors not normally permitted
(Mon, Wed) No visitors on
specified days

APPROXIMATE GREEN FEES
A – £30 plus
B – £20 – £30
C – £15 – £25
D – £10 – £20
E – Under £10
F – Green fees on application

RESTRICTIONS
G – Guests only
H – Handicap certificate required
H(24) – Handicap of 24 or less
required
L – Letter of introduction required
M – Visitor must be a member of
another recognised club.

Aberdour G.C
(0383) 860256
Seaside Place, Aberdour
From Inverkeithing, turn off A92 to Aberdour
village
(18) 5469 yards/**/E

Anstruther G.C
(0333) 312055
Marsfield, Shore Road, Anstruther
4 miles S. of St Andrews
(9) 4120 yards/***/E

Auchterderran G.C
(0592) 721579
Woodend Road, Cardenden
On the Glenrothes-Cardenden road
(9) 5400 yards/***/F

Burntisland G.C
(0592) 874093
Dodhead, Burntisland
1 miles N.E of town on the B923
(18) 5871 yards/***/F/H

Canmore G.C
(0383) 724969
Venturefair Avenue, Dunfermline
1 mile N. of Dunfermline on the A823
(18) 5474 yards/**/C

Crail G.S
(0333) 50960
Balcomie Clubhouse, Fifeness, Crail
2 miles E. of Crail
(18) 5720 yards/***/D/H

Cupar G.C
(0334) 53549
Hilltarvit, Cupar
10 miles from St Andrew off the A91
(9) 5300 yards/***(not Sat)/F/H

Dunfermline G.C
(0383) 723534
Pitfirrane, Crossford, Dunfermline
4 miles W. of town on Kincardine Bridge road
(18) 6244 yards/**/D

Dunnikier Park G.C
(0592) 261599
Dunnikier Way, Kirkcaldy
(18) 6601 yards/***/D/H

Elie G.C
(0333) 330301
Golf Club House, Elie, Leven
6 miles from Leven on the A917
(18) 6241 yards/***/F

Glenrothes G.C
(0592) 754561
Golf Course Road, Glenrothes
At W. of town, 8 miles from M90
(18) 6449 yards/***/E

Kinghorn G.C
(0592) 890345
Macduff Crescent, Kinghorn
3 miles W. of Kircaldy, off the A92
(18) 5246 yards/***/E

Kirkcaldy G.C
(0592) 260370
Balwearie Road, Kirkcaldy
W. of town on the A907
(18) 6004 yards/***(not Sat)/D

Ladybank G.C
(0337) 30814
Annsmuir, Ladybank
6 miles S. of Cupar on Edinburgh-Dunbar road
(18) 6617 yards/***/C

Leslie G.C
(0592) 741 449
Balsillie, Leslie
W. of Glenrothes on the A911
(9) 4940 yards/***/E

Leven Thistle G.C
(0333) 26397
Balfourst, Leven
In Links Road, off Church Road from the
Promenade
(18) 6434 yards/***/D

Lochgelly G.C
(0592) 80174
Cartmore Road, Lochgelly
W. of town, off the A910
(18) 5491 yards/***/F

Lundin Links G.C
(0333) 320202Golf Road, Lundin Links
3 miles E. of Leven on the A915
(18) 6377 yards/**(+ Sat pm)/F/H

Pitreavie (Dunfermline) G.C
(0383) 722591
Queensferry Road, Dunfermline
Leave A90 for the A823 to Dunfermline
(18) 6086 yards/***/D

St Andrews
(0334) 75757
St Andrews
(9) 1754 yards/***/F (Balgove)
(18) 5971 yards/***/F (Eden)
(18) 6284 yards/***/F (Jubilee)
(18) 6500 yards/***/F (Strathyrum)
(18) 6604 yards/***/F (New)
(18) 6933 yards/***(not Sun)/F/H/L (Old)

St Michaels G.C
(033 483) 365
Leuchars, St Andrews
200 yards W. of the village on the A919
(9) 5510 yards/***(not Sun am)/E

Saline G.C
(0383) 852591
Kinneddar Hill, Saline
5 miles N.W of Dunfermline, off the A907
(9) 5302 yards/***(not Sat)/E

Scoonie G.C
(033) 27057
North Links, Leven
10 miles S.W of St Andrews
(18) 5500 yards/***/F

Scotscraig G.C
(0382) 552515
Golf Road, Tayport
S. of the Tay Bridge, off the B946
(18) 6496 yards/***/F/M

Thornton G.C
(0592) 77111
Station Road, Thornton
In centre of village, 1 mile E. of A92
(18) 6177 yards/***/F

Arthur Weaver   TEEING OFF   Burlington Gallery

TAYSIDE & CENTRAL

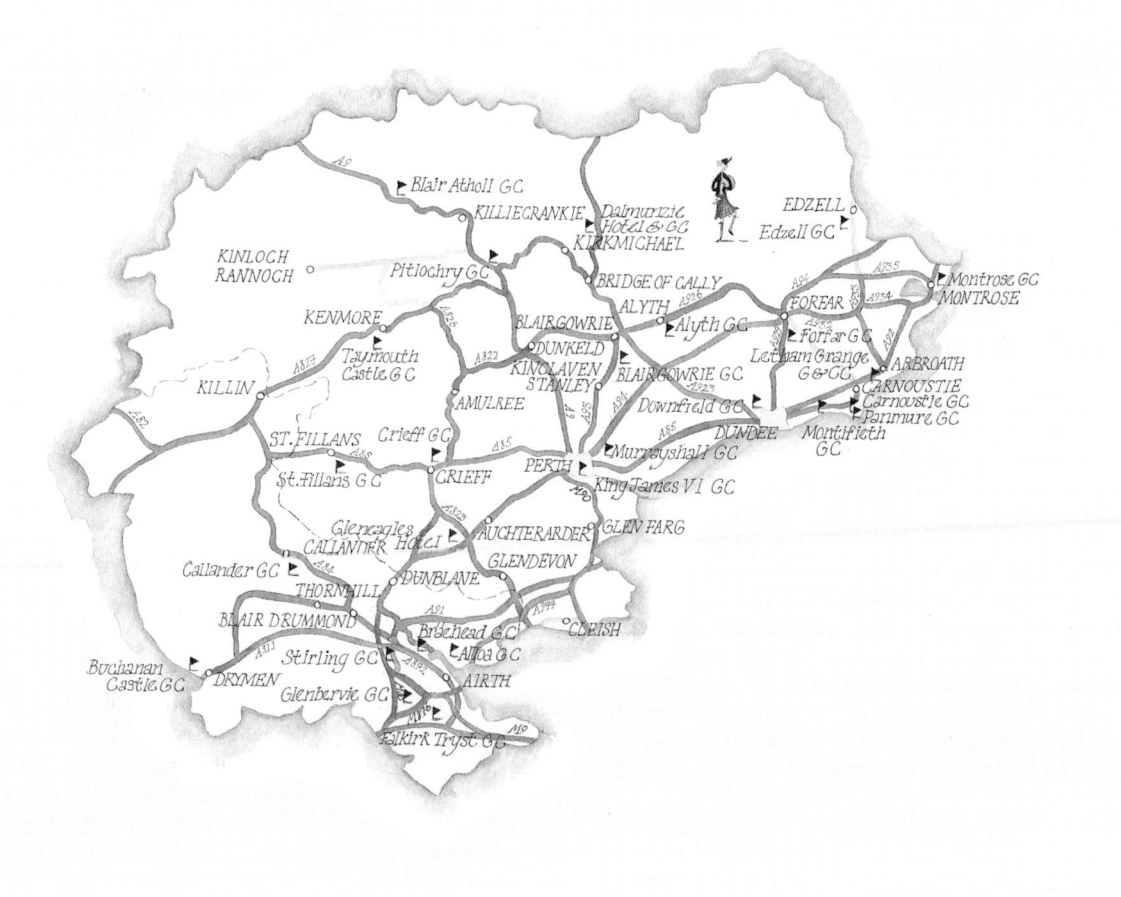

Arthur Weaver **GLENEAGLES** *Burlington Gallery*

If, as the song says, the streams of the mountains please you more than the sea then it is to the likes of **Gleneagles, Pitlochry** and **Murrayshall** you will head; if you are one of the diehards who think there is but one form of golf then you will probably set course for **Carnoustie, Monifieth** and **Montrose**. Then again if it is felt that variety is the spice of golf a nice combination of the two can be devised. The heart of Scotland has much to offer of everything.

While there is an inevitable temptation to head for the 'bigger Clubs', the Gleneagles and the Carnousties, the region boasts a staggering number of smaller Clubs where golf can be equally enjoyable. **Taymouth Castle** and **Callander** are perhaps two of Scotland's lesser known courses, at least to many south of the border, yet they are two of the most scenic courses one is likely to find anywhere. At Callander in early spring the deer come down from the Perthshire hills to forage, a glorious sight, while the course at Taymouth Castle is situated in a conservation area surrounded by beautiful woods.

For golfers travelling northwards, before Gleneagles is reached some excellent golf is to be found at **Falkirk Tryst, Glenbervie** (Larbert), **Braehead** and **Alloa**, while over to the west of the Central region and somewhat isolated is picturesque **Buchanan Castle** – well worth the drive. The town of Stirling is known as the 'Gateway to the Highlands' and **Stirling's** golf course has a beautiful setting beneath the Ochil Hills and in the shadows of Stirling Castle.

The world renowned Gleneagles Hotel (0764) 62231 near Auchterarder is a superb base, not only to secure a game on one or more of its own magnificent courses (see feature page) but also for exploring the many fine golf courses nearby. However, there is certainly no shortage of very good alternatives for a night's stay. Three miles away The Auchterarder House Hotel (0764) 63646 is excellent and is set amid beautiful gardens. In Cleish, Nivingston House (05775) 216 is a small, very pleasant family-run hotel – ideal for the M90 (exit 5), while at Dunblane set in its own 5,000 acre estate is the celebrated Cromlix House (0786) 822125 (note especially the marvellous restaurant). Stirling, with its splendid castle offers The Park Lodge (0786) 74862, Callander, The Roman Camp Hotel (0877) 30003 and Drymen The Buchanan Arms (0360) 60588 (perfect for The Buchanan Castle course). Finally near Falkirk, Airth Castle (032483) 411 at Airth provides a wonderfully relaxing environment.

After Gleneagles, **Blairgowrie** is probably the best known inland course and it too is featured on a later page. However, the golfer should undoubtedly pay a visit to the 'fair city of Perth'. The **King James VI** Golf Club on Moncrieffe Island is steeped in history while nearby at Scone – former crowning place of Kings – is the **Murrayshall** Country House Hotel and its superb golf course (see ahead). A round at each is strongly recommended, and the above mentioned hotel (0738) 51171 offers some of Scotland's best accommodation and cuisine. To the south of Perth at Glenfarg is the popular Bein Inn (05773) 216, set in the most beautiful surroundings and ideal for Carnoustie, Gleneagles or even St Andrews. Visitors tackling Blairgowrie, meanwhile, should seriously consider the popular Merryburn Hotel (0350) 727216 in nearby Birnam.

Those wishing to stay close to Blairgowrie should note the Rosemount Golf Hotel (0250) 2604. A little distance to the west of Perth there is more fine golf at **Crieff** where there are 27 holes

(note the Crieff Hydro (0764) 2401 and Galvelmore House (0764) 2277) and a very pretty nine hole course even further west at **St Fillans** and where The Four Seasons (076485) 333 is a charming place to stay. To the north of our region and tucked away amid some breathtaking scenery, **Dalmunzie House** (0250885) 224 should not be forgotten either; situated at Spittal O'Glenshee, the hotel has its own spectacular nine hole golf course where drives are said to travel further in the rarefied atmosphere! Finally, the Ardeonaig Hotel (05672) 400 in Killin combines splendid views with distinguished accommodation.

Returning to Blairgowrie, if a game cannot be arranged on either of the Club's outstanding courses, then the heathland course at **Alyth** is very nearby and certainly won't disappoint. The Lands Of Loyal (08283) 3151 is a comfortable hotel close to the course, the nearby Losset Inn (08283) 2393 is more modest but equally accommodating. Perth's delights as mentioned are at hand to the south, while to the west is **Taymouth Castle** and to the north along the A9 stands **Pitlochry**. The latter is another course many will choose to play, for this is one of the most attractive in Britain – a veritable 'theatre in the hills'. Green fees at all these courses are relatively inexpensive and certainly very good value. Still further north the scenic 9 holer at **Blair Atholl** is also worth a visit. In Strathtay, near Pitlochry a recommended 19th hole is the Grantully Hotel (08874) 207.

More ideas for a relaxing stay include the Kenmore Hotel (08873) 205 in Kenmore, Scotland's oldest inn, and very near Taymouth Castle, Killiecrankie Hotel (0796) 3220 in Killiecrankie (north of Pitlochry), the sporty Ballathie House (025083) 268 at Kinclave by Stanley, Kinloch House (04713) 214 at Kinloch Rannoch and The Log Cabin (025081) 288 at Kirkmichael. Indeed, the list is almost endless, such is the popularity of this magnificent area.

Some of Scotland's greatest links courses are to be found between Dundee and Montrose on the Tayside coast. However, to the north west of Dundee lies **Downfield** one of the country's finest inland courses. Indeed five times Open Champion Peter Thomson rates this heavily wooded parkland course as one of the best inland courses in the world. It is said that Downfield is very popular with American visitors because it reminds them of some of their better courses 'back home'.

East of Dundee The Medal Course at **Monifieth** has staged the Scottish Amateur Championship, while **Panmure** at Barry has in the past hosted the Seniors Championship. Both are classic links courses and fairly inexpensive to play over. **Carnoustie** is, of course, one of Scotland's greatest golfing shrines and along with Montrose, Gleneagles, Letham Grange, Murrayshall and Blairgowrie is featured ahead. **Montrose** like Monifeith is a public links (two courses at each in fact) and when the winds blow can be extremely difficult. As earlier noted, fees along this great coastal stretch are relatively cheap and provided some forward planning is done a game is possible at most times.

A brief word on staying in the area. In Carnoustie, The Glencoe Hotel (0241) 53273 is very convenient as are The Park Hotel (0674) 73415 and The George Hotel (0674) 75050, both in Montrose. Perhaps the pick of the many hotels in Dundee is The Angus Thistle Hotel (0382) 26874 and in nearby Broughty Ferry, L'Auberge (0382) 730890 is a fine restaurant. For those seeking excellent value, the Kingsley Guesthouse (0241) 73933 in Arbroath provides exactly that. Moorfield House (0828) 27303 in Cupar Angus is also well worth trying. There

are plans underfoot to build a major new hotel in Carnoustie, and if these finally come to fruition there are hopes that the Open might one day return to the great links.

Two inland courses to the north east of Tayside which strongly merit attention are **Edzell** and **Letham Grange**. The former, just north of Brechin, and in a charming village is a beautiful heathland course where some marvellous mountain views can be enjoyed. The Glenesk Hotel (03564) 319 is but a par four away. Letham Grange is in fact a Hotel and Country Club (024189) 373 and is situated at Colliston near Arbroath. The hotel is a splendidly restored Victorian Mansion, and with 36 holes of golf now on offer is well worth a visit; we make such an inspection later in this chapter.

*Robert Turnbull **GLENEAGLES** Private Collection*

THE ROMAN CAMP

The Roman Camp Hotel sits on the North Bank of the River Tieth amongst twenty acres of mature and secluded gardens, which nestle by the picturesque village of Callandar, the Gateway to the Trossachs and the Highlands of Scotland.

The House was originally built as a Hunting Lodge for the Dukes of Perth in 1625 and was given its name from the conspicuous earth mounds, believed to be the site of a Roman Fort, which are visible across the meadow to the east of the walled garden.

The building has grown over many years as each consecutive family has added their own embellishments to this lovely home. The most obvious of these are the towers, one of which contains a tiny Chapel.

Today under the guidance of Eric and Marion Brown the traditional country house atmosphere still evokes its alluring charm. As you enter you will notice the abundance of freshly cut flowers, their scent lingering in the air, and be greeted to this peaceful retreat by great log fires.

Our Library and Drawing Room are of grand proportions, with an atmosphere of warmth and relaxation and are places to enjoy and reflect on the days sport, especially after dinner in the company of friends and a fine malt.

The tapestry hung Dining Room is crowned by a richly painted 16th century style ceiling. Here dinner is served at candle lit tables, laid with fine silver and crystal, while you choose from menus of local game and fish, prepared by our chef and accompanied by vegetables and herbs from our own gardens.

Each of our bedrooms has its own distinctive style and character, and is equipped with all the little thoughtful extras to make your stay as comfortable as possible.

At the Roman Camp Country House you are within easy reach of many Championship and picturesque Golf Courses, and we are able to arrange and book tee times at the local course, only two minutes walk from the hotel.

We have three-quarters of a mile of river running through our gardens, enablng guests to fish complementary for Wild Brown Trout and Salmon on our private beat. There is also the opportunity for the hotel to arrange fishing on the many lochs and other private beats surrounding Callander.

We hope that you will be able to make the Roman Camp your favourite country retreat.

The Roman Camp Country House Hotel
Callander
Scotland FK17 8BG
Tel: (0877) 30003
Fax: (0877) 31533

GLENEAGLES
CHAMPIONSHIP GOLF

There is a vast oil painting that hangs in the Tate Gallery in London, the artist is John Martin and the painting is titled 'The Plains Of Heaven'. Some may know it well, others will wonder what on earth I'm gibbering on about – suffice to say that it depicts in the most vivid colours imaginable the artist's impression of Paradise. I suspect that John Martin wasn't a golfer. Blasphemy isn't intended but for many of us who stalk the fairways of the world, Gleneagles is just about our best idea of how heaven might look – give or take a couple of angels.

The Gleneagles Hotel and its golf courses are set in the heart of some of the most glorious Perthshire countryside. Surrounded by the foothills of the Grampian Mountain range everywhere one turns there is a shock of colour. The mountains themselves often appear wrapped in purples and blues. Heather, silver birch and rowan cover the crisp moorland turf. With so much around one could be forgiven for losing a little concentration, yet the golf too is glorious and for those wishing to enjoy their golf in leisurely five star surroundings there really is nothing quite like Gleneagles. The land was first surveyed with a view to designing one or more golf courses before the first World War and **James Braid** was called in to direct affairs. By 1919 the **King's** and **Queen's** courses were both open for play. Braid's work met with instant acclaim and in 1921 the forerunner of the Ryder Cup was staged at Gleneagles, when a team of British professionals played a team from America.

Until quite recently, The Gleneagles Hotel maintained four 18 hole golf courses, the Prince's and Glendevon courses being opened in 1974 and 1980 respectively. Subject to making a booking through the Golf Office all were open to the general public. Golf became so popular at Gleneagles that at times it came close to resembling a fairways version of Piccadilly Circus and since **1st January 1990 golf at Gleneagles has been restricted to Hotel Residents and Gleneagles Golf Club Members**.

Since the above date, play at Gleneagles has also been limited to the King's and Queen's courses; however there is a very good reason. In spring **1993** a third 18 hole Championship Course designed by **Jack Nicklaus** will be ready for play. It is Nicklaus' first course in Scotland and, like his first ventures in England (St Mellion) and Ireland (Mount Juliet), it promises to be something rather special. Laid out on land previously utilised by the Prince's and Glendevon courses, plus adjacent acquired land, the **Monarch's** Course will measure in excess of 7,000 yards from the Championship tees.

Things are certainly happening apace at Gleneagles and a sparkling new clubhouse has recently been constructed. Its architectural style is in keeping with the Edwardian Hotel. In April 1992 the green fee for hotel residents was set at £30 for a day ticket on the King's and Queen's courses. **Billy Marchbank**, Gleneagles' golf professional can be reached on **(0764) 62231.**

Located approximately midway between Perth and Stirling and half a mile west of Auchterarder, Gleneagles is easily reached by road. The A9 which in fact links Perth to Stirling is likely to prove of most assistance. Travelling from the Glasgow region a combination of the A80 and the M80 should be taken to Stirling. Those approaching from further south can avoid Glasgow by following the A74 and the M74/M73 joining the A80 below Stirling. Motoring from Edinburgh the best route is to cross the Forth Road Bridge via the A90 heading for Dunfermline and thereafter taking the A823 road to Auchterarder. Southbound travellers will find the A9 helpful if coming from the Highlands via Blair Atholl and Pitlochry. Motoring from Aberdeen and the North East of Scotland, the A92 links Aberdeen to Dundee and Dundee is in turn linked to Perth by the A85 (dual carriageway all the way). The Gleneagles Hotel can also be reached by rail, with a bus meeting trains from Gleneagles Station.

Measuring 6471 yards, par 70 the King's course is some 500 yards longer that the Queen's at 5965 yards, par 68. Perhaps the best known hole at Gleneagles is **Braid's Brawest**, the **13th** on the King's Course – a tough par four which requires a long straight drive to carry a ridge and a second to a raised and heavily guarded sloping green.

Many will have first viewed the glories of Gleneagles through the medium of television – the BBC Pro-Celebrity series being staged on several occasions over the King's Course during the 1970s. In the mid 1980s Bell's brought the **Scottish Open** to Gleneagles and now golfing addicts have a wonderful prospect to look forward to each July – the Scottish Open at Gleneagles, followed immediately by the Open Championship....... Paradise indeed!

King's Course

Hole	Yards	Par	Hole	Yards	Par
1	362	4	10	445	4
2	405	4	11	230	3
3	377	4	12	387	4
4	465	4	13	446	4
5	160	3	14	260	4
6	476	5	15	457	4
7	439	4	16	133	3
8	158	3	17	376	4
9	351	4	18	525	5
Out	**3,193**	**35**	**In**	**3,259**	**35**
			Out	**3,193**	**35**
			TOTALS	**6,452**	**70**

BLAIRGOWRIE
CHAMPIONSHIP GOLF

With so many outstanding courses to choose from, all within fairly close proximity of one another, even the most blinkered of diehard Englishmen would be forced to concede that Scotland is just about the finest place on earth for a week's golfing holiday. Given seven precious days a large number of would-be travellers on opening their maps of Scotland are likely to plan a trip thus: three days on the west coast playing Prestwick, Turnberry and Troon; a day in the middle visiting Gleneagles, finishing with three on the east coast taking in Carnoustie, St Andrews and Muirfield. Marvellous stuff of course, but many of the golfing sages hold the opinion that such an itinerary misses out the greatest gem of all – the Rosemount course at Blairgowrie.

There are in fact two 18 hole courses at Blairgowrie, the older and more celebrated **Rosemount**, designed by **James Braid** and the **Lansdowne** course, a fairly recent addition, the work of **Peter Alliss** and **Dave Thomas**. On each, golf is played over beautiful moorland fairways, lined by forests of pine, larch and silver birch. A liberal sprinkling of purple heather and gorse add considerable colour to an already majestic setting – as one bewitched observer put it, 'somebody seems to have gone mad with a paint brush!'

Persons wishing to sample the delights of either course are advised to book starting times through the Club's Professional, **Gordon Kinnoch**, tel **(0250) 873116**. Visitors are welcome at Blairgowrie on Mondays, Tuesdays, Thursdays and, to a limited extent, on Fridays and occasionally at weekends. Fourball matches, it should be noted, are not normally allowed before 10 a.m. on the Rosemount course. Furthermore all visitors must be able to provide proof of handicap. Golfing parties are also welcome during the week (except on Wednesdays) though teeing off will not be permitted between 12pm and 2pm nor after 4 pm. Those wishing to organise golfing parties should address written applications to the Club's Secretary, **Mr. J. N. Simpson**, the Club's full address being, **Blairgowrie Golf Club, Golf Course Road, Blairgowrie, Perthshire PH10 6LG**. Mr. Simpson can be contacted by telephone on **(0250) 872622**. In 1992 the midweek green fee for a single round on either course was set at £22 with £33 securing a day ticket. At weekends, when available, a single round green fee cost £30.

Having metaphorically chastised the golfer who doesn't make Blairgowrie a 'must' on any golfing tour I had better detail the best routes to reach it. Hopefully the following will prove of assistance: approaching from the south the A93 Braemar road runs directly from Perth, Perth being linked to Edinburgh by the A90/M90. From easterly directions, Blairgowrie (Rosemount is just south of the town) is connected to Dundee by the A923 and to Forfar by the A926. Anyone motoring down from the north will probably travel either on the A9 (via Aviemore and Pitlochry) or on the A93 passing through Ballater and Braemar. Blairgowrie is 15 miles from Perth and 18 miles from Dundee. Gleneagles (via Perth) and Carnoustie and St Andrews (both via Dundee) are all approximately 30 miles away.

Measuring 6568 yards, par 72 from the medal tees (6239 yards, par 70 from the forward tees) the Rosemount Course may not be the toughest challenge one is likely to face but it must rank among the most enchanting. The course and surrounding landscape abound with wildlife, from pheasants and partridge to deer and winter geese, but the golfer who lifts his head too much is likely to suffer over the closing stretch; **16**, **17** and **18** are all difficult holes, especially the 16th where the golfer must twice confront the infamous Black Loch.

The official course record at Rosemount stands at 66, though in 1973, during a practice round for the Sumrie Better-Ball tournament, Professional **Lionel Platts** achieved an amazing ten consecutive birdies between the **8th** and **17th** – quite obscene don't you think?!

The Lansdowne course is slightly longer than its older brother, and many would say a sterner test – either way a game on each is strongly recommended.

It need hardly be added that Blairgowrie with its two courses – three if one includes the aptly named Wee Course, a short nine-holer – has a more than adequate 19th. Lunches, high teas, dinners and light snacks are all offered. There are also two bars, comfortable places where many will choose to go and celebrate a magnificent day's golfing in one of the most glorious settings the game has to offer. Planning a week's golf? ....

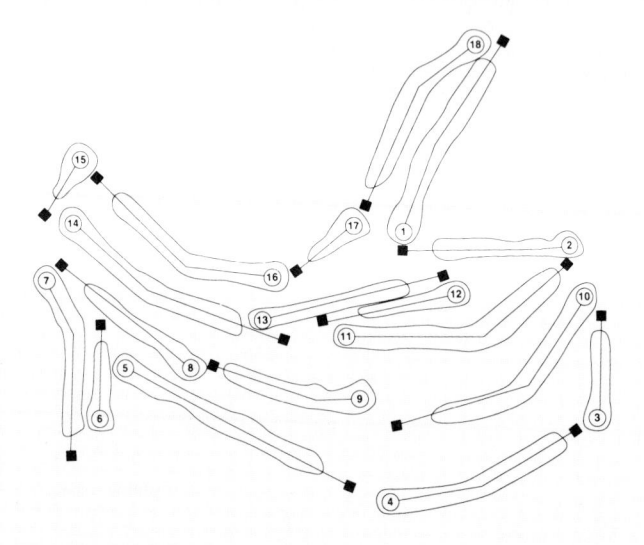

Rosemount Course

Hole	Yards	Par	Hole	Yards	Par
1	444	4	10	507	5
2	339	4	11	500	5
3	220	3	12	293	4
4	408	4	13	401	4
5	551	5	14	512	5
6	189	3	15	129	3
7	371	4	16	475	4
8	368	4	17	165	3
9	326	4	18	390	4
Out	**3,216**	**35**	**In**	**3,372**	**37**
			Out	**3,216**	**35**
			TOTALS	**6,588**	**72**

DALMUNZIE HOUSE

Dalmunzie House enjoys a glorious position in the mountains of the Scottish Highlands. The hotel stands in its own 6,000 acre mountain estate. It is owned and run by the Winton family who have been in the glen for a number of decades and have many years' experience looking after guests. Exacting attention to detail and unobtrusive service ensure a comfortable stay at all times.

As you would expect, the food at Dalmunzie House is fresh from the hills and lochs, cooked with flair and imagination to satisfy the most descerning palates.

Most of the bedrooms have ensuite facilities. Many are of indi-vidual character and all are centrally heated. Their charming decor, restful tranquility and beautiful arrangements of fresh flowers reflect the ambience found elsewhere at Dalmunzie.

Many activities can be pursued here. The hotel has its own private golf course, and in addition there is a tennis court and games room for the family complete with bar billiard table. River and loch fishing as well as shooting and stalking can all be easily arranged. Some of Scotland's finest mountains surround the hotel and for cross country and alpine skiers the Glenshee Ski Centre is only a few minutes' drive away.

For further information, contact:
Dalmunzie House Hotel
Spittal o'Glenshee
Blairgowrie
Perthshire
Scotland PH10 7QG
Tel: (0250) 885224
Fax: (0250) 885225

MURRAYSHALL
CHAMPIONSHIP GOLF

Perth is a legendary place, a city steeped in history and one surrounded by stunning natural beauty. Perthshire the county evokes thoughts of everything Scottish. To North Americans, mention of the very word 'Perthshire' is enough to send them drooling. It is arguably one of the most romantic places in the world and for golfers, whether from the New World or the Old, the contemplation of a game of golf in the heart of Scotland is enough to make us forget a tweaked three footer (well almost.)

It is often said that a person's golfing education is incomplete until he or she has swung a club in Scotland. And how can you visit Scotland without visiting Perth, the ancient crowning place of Kings? To the south west of Perth and half an hour's drive away is Gleneagles which, along with St. Andrews and Augusta, is surely one of the three best known golfing centres in the world. Almost due north of Perth and again about 30 minutes by road is Blairgowrie and the delights of the Rosemount and Lansdowne courses. A little further, but still no more than an hour, are St. Andrews and Carnoustie; Perth cannot be a bad place sitting amidst all this finery! But there is more. Right on the city's doorstep not 4 miles from the town centre is a comparatively modern golfing jewel; Murrayshall, or to give it its full name, The Murrayshall Country House Hotel and Golf Course.

Golfwise, Murrayshall has only been on the map for a dozen years (the course, designed by renowned architect **J Hamilton Stutt**, opened in **1981**.) The country house however, is much older and has that unmistakeable air of Scotchness. A house of great character with wonderful grounds is an ideal setting for a golf course anywhere – but on Perth's doorstep too! Murrayshall is where the peacocks strut, the pheasants call and the deer run freely in the woods. The golf course is set in 300 acres of truly rolling parkland and the holes weave their way in and out of the copses and alongside ponds. In fact, there is quite a lot of water at Murrayshall: little lakes, ponds and streams – but the golfer is guided over and around them via quaint stone bridges. Some 200,000 tulips adorn the hotel grounds and golf course ... yes Murrayshall makes folks drool and perhaps at least smile after that missed three foot putt.

Those wishing to look a little closer should approach the Golf Manager, **Neil MacKintosh.** He and his staff handle all golf enquiries and bookings should be made through him. Mr MacKintosh, who is also Murrayshall's professional can be contacted on **(0738) 52784**. The address to write to is **Murrayshall Country House Hotel and Golf Course, Murrayshall, Scone, Perthshire PH2 7PH**.

Subject to players being of a reasonable golfing standard, visitors are welcome at all times. In 1992, the green fees for 18 holes were £20 midweek and £25 at weekends. A full day ticket could be purchased for £30 midweek and £40 at weekends. Reduced fees are available for Hotel residents (just £10 per round) and junior golfers. Golf societies and corporate golf days are very popular at Murrayshall and all enquiries should be directed to the Golf Manager.

Finding Murrayshall from Perth should not be too difficult. The road to take is the A94 towards New Scone; two miles out of Perth, Murrayshall is signposted off to the right. Perth itself is easily reached from all directions. It is linked to Edinburgh by the M90 and the Forth Road Bridge; to the Highlands via the wonderfully scenic A9 and to Dundee by the A35. To the south west, Perth is joined to Stirling by the A9 and anyone coming from the Glasgow area is likely to travel via Stirling. Finally, the A93 links Perth with Blairgowrie to the north east.

From the back markers, Murrayshall measures 6446 yards, par 73. The forward tees reduce the course to around the 6,000 yards mark. It isn't a long course by any means but is both attractive and challenging and certainly full of interest. Many of the fairways are bordered by magnificent oaks, copper beeches and chestnuts not to mention those marvellous tulips. There are also some wonderful views from the higher parts of the course.

Notable holes include the **3rd**, one of those par four and a half holes; the short **4th** where if you miss-hit you will land in the pond; the severely dog-legged **7th** – so severe that it is known as the 'dog's grave' – and most people's favourite, the short par four **10th** where the approach is played over water to a raised green.

If possible, try to stay overnight in the Hotel. The bedrooms are superbly furnished and most have views over the course and towards the distant Grampian Mountains. Perhaps a final mention for Murrayshall's Old Masters Restaurant; it has won many awards for outstanding cuisine and its name is most fitting. As with everything at Murrayshall, it oozes class.

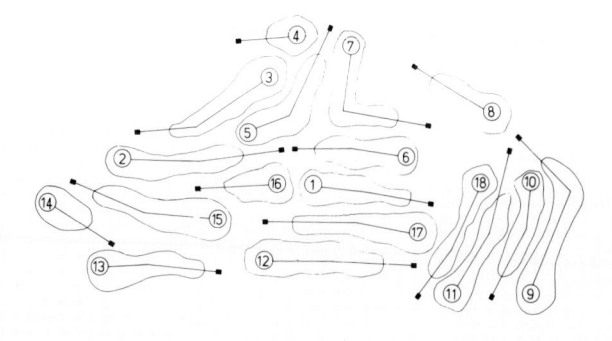

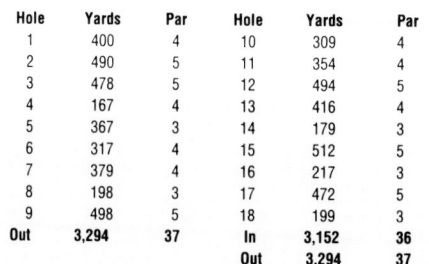

Hole	Yards	Par	Hole	Yards	Par
1	400	4	10	309	4
2	490	5	11	354	4
3	478	5	12	494	5
4	167	4	13	416	4
5	367	3	14	179	3
6	317	4	15	512	5
7	379	4	16	217	3
8	198	3	17	472	5
9	498	5	18	199	3
Out	**3,294**	**37**	**In**	**3,152**	**36**
			Out	**3,294**	**37**
			Totals	**6,446**	**73**

MURRAYSHALL COUNTRY HOUSE HOTEL

The Murrayshall Country House Hotel and Golf Course is only 4 miles from Perth, set in 300 acres of parkland. Deer stroll the wooded hillside, pheasants and peacocks call from the greens. The natural beauty and splashes of colour in the garden are complemented by the mellow stone of the main house with its crow stepped gables.

The hotel, completely refurbished, is elegantly furnished in a traditional style but with the use of the wonderful fabric designs available today. The bedrooms all have en suite facilities, self dial telephone and colour television.

The aptly named Old Masters Restaurant has walls hung with Dutch Masters and table settings befitting the artistry of master chef, Bruce Sangster. The restaurant has received various culinary accolades. Vegetables and herbs from the hotels walled garden and an abundance of local produce form the basis of the menus which have a Scottish flavour with a hint of modern French cuisine. A well balanced wine list is complemented by the finest of rare malt whiskies.

The 6420 yard, 18 hole, par 73 course is interspersed with magnificent specimen trees lining the fairways, water hazards and white sanded bunkers to offer a challenge to all golfers. Buggies and sets of clubs are available for hire. Neil Mackintosh, our resident professional, is pleased to give tuition, from

half an hour to a weeks course. Perth is ideally situated for Scotland's courses. Golfers can relax in the newly refurbished club house which overlooks the course and provides informal dining.

Other sporting activities include tennis, croquet and bowls. However, situated only a few miles from the famous Salmon Waters of the River Tay, even closer to Perth Race Course, Murrayshall is uniquely placed to make it an attractive venue for whatever might bring you to this area of Scotland.

Private dining and conference facilities are available in both the hotel and club house. Conference organisers, requiring the best of service and attention for their senior delegates, will find Murrayshall the ideal conference haven.

Murrayshall is one of three group golf courses, the other two are Westerwood and Fernfell. Westerwood Golf Course was designed by Seve Ballesteros and Dave Thomas and is located at Cumbernauld, near Glasgow. Fernfell Golf and Country Club is located just out of Cranleigh, 8 miles from Guildford in Surrey. Corporate golf packages are offered at all three courses with the opportunity to place your company name and logo on a tee and to reserve the course for your company golf day. Golf Societies and Green Fee Payers are welcome.

Murrayshall Country House Hotel and Golf Course
Scone
Perthshire
PH2 7PH
Tel: (0738) 51171
Fax: (0738) 52595

MONTROSE
CHAMPIONSHIP GOLF

Perhaps there are two things that strike you most when you arrive at one of the famous golfing links on the east coast of Scotland: the first will almost certainly be the thought, 'So this is where it all started' – a feeling that can often leave one slightly numb. The second, and equally numbing is likely to be the thought, 'Will this wretched wind ever die down?' The famous links at Montrose is just such a place.

Golf has been played on Montrose links since the 16th century and according to the best records it is the fifth oldest course in the world. By course is meant the **Medal Course**, for there are two 18 hole links at Montrose, the Medal and the shorter **Broomfield Course**, the former having altered surprisingly little through the ages. One interesting fact is that in the 1800's, at a time when one or two more famous clubs had only 5 holes, The Medal Course at Montrose boasted 25! All of which were played in a unique tournament in 1866 won by a **Mr T Doleman** from Glasgow who played the 25 holes in 112 strokes; **Willie Park**, winner of the first Open Championship in 1860, finished 2nd scoring a 115.

In common with St Andrews and Carnoustie, Montrose is a public links and although three Golf Clubs play over the two courses, namely, the **Royal Montrose, Caledonian** and **Mercantile** Clubs, both are effectively managed by the **Montrose Links Trust** who handle all administrative matters. Any written correspondence should be addressed to this body care of **The Secretary, Traill Drive, Montrose, Angus DD10 8SW**. **Mrs Margaret Stewart** is in fact the Secretary and she may be contacted by telephone on **(0674) 72932**. Also most helpful is the professional **Kevin Stables**; he can be reached on **(0674) 72634**.

Being a public links there are few restrictions on the times visitors can play; indeed the only one as such is that visitors cannot play on Saturdays or tee off before 10.00am on Sundays. It should also be noted that visitors wishing to play the Medal Course are requested to produce a handicap certificate.

In 1992 a day ticket to play on the Medal Course was priced at £18 during the week and £25 at weekends with a single round costing £11 midweek and £16 at weekends. To play a round over the Broomfield Course the fee is £6.50 or £10 for midweek and weekend respectively, with a day ticket available for £10 (£15 at weekends). Those staying in the area might consider a weekly ticket; in 1992 these were priced at £60 for the Medal course and £40 for the Broomfield Course. Reductions of up to fifty per cent are usually available to junior golfers.

Apart from their length, the Medal course measures 6443 yards (par 71) and the Broomfield 4815 yards (par 66), the two courses differ in other respects. The Broomfield is laid out on the landward side of the Medal and is considerably flatter. With its many subtle – and many not-so-subtle – undulations the Medal is by far the more testing and it is not surprisingly over this links that the major Championships are held; these have included the Scottish Professional Championship, the Scottish Amateur Championship, and the British Boys Championship and Internationals.

For twelve of its eighteen holes, the Medal course follows closely the line of the dunes, with the **4th** and **6th** being especially memorable. However, some of the best holes appear at the end of the round: the **16th** (Gully) being a particularly long par three and the **17th** (Rashes) with its raised green, one of those par fours requiring, as a caddy once put it, three damned good shots to get up in two!

As the crow flies Montrose lies approximately midway between St Andrews and Aberdeen. For those of us without wings the A92 is likely to be of most assistance. Those travelling from the St Andrews region, or indeed from all points south, should head for Dundee. The A92 runs from Dundee to Aberdeen passing though the centre of Montrose. Montrose links lies to the north of the town, east off the A92 and is well signposted. Anyone approaching from the west, including Blairgowrie (in golf course terms a world away) can avoid Dundee by heading for Brechin and thereafter following the A935 into Montrose, passing Montrose Basin (where in winter you may sight a few rare pink-footed Arctic geese – quite possibly the only birdies you'll see all day).

As for a 19th hole, the catering requirements of visitors are more than adequately met by the Golf Clubs mentioned above, each having clubhouses adjacent to the links.

There are no airs and graces about Montrose; it is what might be described as a good honest links. But if you've come to Scotland to admire the golf, then Montrose is clearly one that shouldn't be missed.

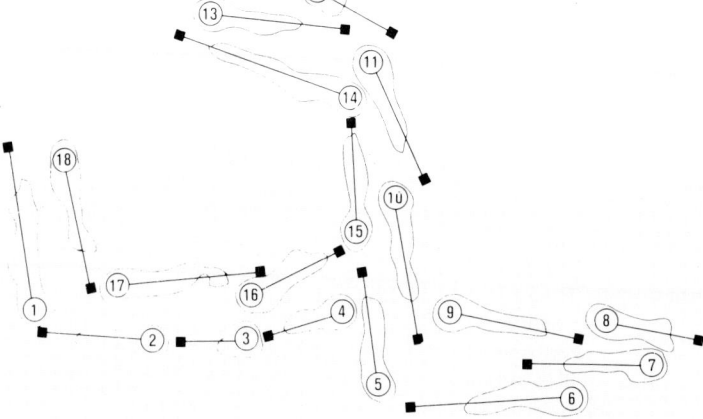

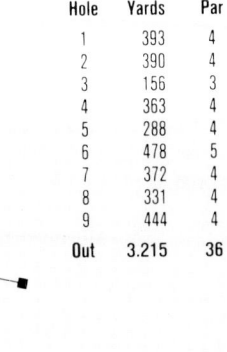

Medal Course

Hole	Yards	Par	Hole	Yards	Par
1	393	4	10	382	4
2	390	4	11	440	4
3	156	3	12	153	3
4	363	4	13	323	4
5	288	4	14	416	4
6	478	5	15	524	5
7	372	4	16	234	3
8	331	4	17	415	4
9	444	4	18	349	4
Out	3.215	36	In	3,236	35
			Out	3,215	36
			TOTALS	6,451	71

CARNOUSTIE
CHAMPIONSHIP GOLF

Walter Hagen – a shrewd judge you might think – once described Carnoustie as the greatest course in the British Isles. There are many who would agree with the great man, though doubtless the disciples of St. Andrews and several honourable gentlemen at Muirfield would beg to differ. Greatest or not, very few would dispute that when the winds blow – as they invariably do in these parts – Carnoustie is the toughest of all our Championship links.

In the days when the Campbells and the MacDonalds were busy slaughtering each other up in the Highlands, down at Carnoustie more civilised pursuits were taking place. Records suggest that golf was being played on the adjoining Barry Links, as early as the 16th century. The first official Club at Carnoustie – today there are six – was founded in 1842 and golf was played over a ten hole course laid out by **Allan Robertson**. Later, **'Old' Tom Morris** came on the scene and extended the links to a full 18 holes, but the present Championship course didn't really take shape until **James Braid** made several alterations in 1926. By 1931 Carnoustie was ready to stage its first **Open Championship**.

As previously mentioned there are presently six Clubs at Carnoustie and play is now over three 18 hole courses; the Championship, the Burnside and the Buddon. Administrative matters are in the hands of the **Carnoustie Golf Links Management Committee** and persons wishing to visit Carnoustie should direct correspondence to the Committee's Secretary, **Mr. E.J.C. Smith**. Their full address is **The Carnoustie Golf Links Management Committee, Links Parade, Carnoustie, Tayside, DD7 7JE**. Contact by telephone can be made on **(0241) 53789** and by fax on (0241) 52720. Starting times must be booked in advance.

In 1992, the green fees to play at Carnoustie were £31 for a single round on the Championship course with £37 securing a round over both the Championship and Burnside courses. Fees to play just the Burnside or Buddon courses are good value and it is also possible to obtain a three day and five day pass enabling two or three rounds over the Championship course. Details can be obtained by phoning the above number (caddies can also be arranged.)

The cluster of Clubs that go to make up Carnoustie's permanent golfing village provide all the ususal amenities for the visiting golfer – golf shops for clothing, equipment and club hire and of course a more than adequate 19th hole.

Travelling to Carnoustie shouldn't present too many problems. The Forth Road Bridge and the M90 link the Edinburgh region with Perth; Perth in turn is linked to Dundee by the A85 (dual carriageway all the way) and Dundee to Carnoustie by the A390. Those on golfing tours will quite likely be coming via St. Andrews: the A91 (A919) runs from St. Andrews towards Dundee; it picks up the A92 just before the Tay Road Bridge and on crossing the Bridge the A930 should immediately be joined. Approaching from northerly directions, the A92 runs from Aberdeen (and beyond) to within a couple of miles of Carnoustie at Muirdrum, while the A958 links the town with Forfar. Carnoustie can also be reached by train with connections from Perth, Dundee and Aberdeen.

It isn't only the wind of course that makes Carnoustie such a difficult test. When the Championship tees are in use the course stretches close to 7200 yards making it the longest of our Open Courses. From the Club medal tees, 6936 yards is still a formidable proposition.

Scotland is the land of Burns. It is also the land of burns – streams or little rivers anywhere else in the English-speaking world – and Carnoustie is famous for them. The ubiquitous **Barry Burn** and its wee brother **Jocky's Burn** traverse the fairways in the most unfriendly of places, often in front of greens and across the spot you'd ideally like to drive to. More than anything else though, Carnoustie is renowned for its incredibly tough finishing stretch. The **16th** is an exceptionally long short hole and **Jack Nicklaus** is said to have once needed a driver followed by an 8 iron to get up! The **17th** has the Barry Burn meandering across its fairway, making it a particularly difficult driving hole and at the **18th** the Burn crosses in front of the green necessitating one of the most exciting (or nerve-racking) closing shots in golf.

Each of the five Opens held at Carnoustie has produced great Champions: **Tommy Armour** (1931), **Henry Cotton** (1937), **Ben Hogan** (1953), **Gary Player** (1968) and **Tom Watson** (1975). Many consider Hogan's victory in 1953 – he won by four strokes with ever decreasing rounds of 73-71-70-68 – to be the greatest ever performance in a major Championship. There are also those who feel that his final round of 68 represents the true course record. The wind blew that day and Carnoustie's teeth were gnashing. Twenty two years later when **Jack Newton** scored his 65 Carnoustie was smiling. It was the only Open Hogan ever played in.

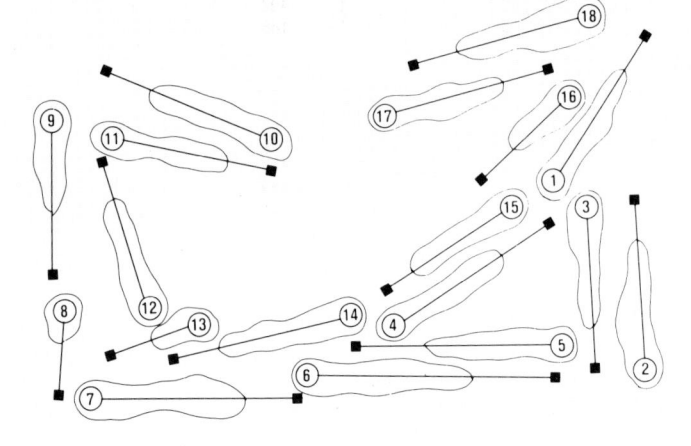

Championship Course

Hole	Yards	Par	Hole	Yards	Par
1	407	4	10	446	4
2	425	4	11	353	4
3	342	4	12	477	5
4	375	4	13	161	3
5	387	4	14	483	5
6	524	5	15	456	4
7	390	4	16	245	3
8	168	3	17	433	4
9	420	4	18	444	4
Out	3,438	36	In	3,498	36
			Out	3,438	36
			TOTALS	6,936	72

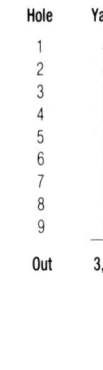

LETHAM GRANGE
CHAMPIONSHIP GOLF

There are 'dreamers' and there are 'doers'. Once in every blue moon – thank heavens – the two combine.

Soon after the late **Sir Henry Cotton** officially opened Letham Grange in 1987, **Malcolm Campbell**, the then editor of Golf Monthly bravely announced, "We now have the 'Augusta of Scotland'". In a generally critical article a second leading U.K. golf magazine later lambasted this judgement saying it was, "a bit like trying to sell blended whisky as a 12 year old malt". But then we are a nation of 'Knockers' aren't we? Of course Letham Grange isn't the equal of Augusta, where the azaleas and dogwoods run riot, but it is a wonderfully enjoyable place to play golf nonetheless and there is at least one parallel in the manner of its creation. Like Augusta, Letham Grange is the result of one man's dream. Down in Georgia the guiding force was a man named Jones; up in Angus it was a man called Smith. Letham Grange was **Ken Smith's** dream and aside from the quality of the end product I wouldn't be quick to criticise Letham Grange for the very fact that Ken Smith had the guts, vision and determination to do something about his dream.

It is an extraordinary place. Located inland, four miles north of Arbroath, and roughly midway between Montrose and Carnoustie, Letham Grange is were a typical and, until recently, 'oh so timeless' Scottish Country estate confronts 20th century 'hotel and country club golf' head on. In fact the Victorian mansion which presides over the heavily wooded and rolling estate had become derelict by the mid 1970s, before the golfing dream was conceived. This same mansion is now one of Scotland's most luxurious 19th hole retreats; moreover time no longer stands still at Letham Grange for since 1991 the estate has boasted two 18 hole courses – the slightly revised 1987 layout now being called the Old Course(!).

At 5528 yards, par 68, the New Course is more than 1000 yards shorter than its older sister (6614 yards, par 73) and there are none of the water hazards that make the Old Course at once potentially treacherous and positively spectacular. The green

fees at Letham Grange reflect this. In 1992 a round on the Old Course cost the visitor £17 midweek and £22 at the weekend; on the New Course the fees were £10 and £15 respectively. Tee reservations can be made by telephoning the club on **(0241) 89323**. **Heather MacDougall** is the Golf Secretary, she can be contacted via this number, while the professional, **David Scott** can be reached on **(0241) 89377**. All written correspondence should be addressed to **Letham Grange Hotel and Golf Courses, Colliston, by Arbroath, Angus, DD11 4RL**. The only specific restriction on visitors is before 10.30am on Tuesdays (both courses) and before 10.30am (Old Course) and 9.00am (New Course) at weekends. Bookings can normally be made for all other times.

When the **New Course** was constructed two holes from the original Letham Grange course were incorporated in the design, namely the old 9th and 10th. The **Old Course** has thus acquired two new holes and the other significant change to the design has been to reroute the course by starting from the former 7th tee. The 2nd on the Old Course is now the original 8th; the old 9th and 10th are now part of the New Course and so the 3rd is now the former 11th and the 4th the old 12th. The two new holes open the back nine and the last six holes comprise the former holes 1 – 6. Yes, it is a little confusing!

In a nutshell the changes mean that many of the most dramatic holes at Letham Grange must be confronted on the front nine of the Old Course. The **2nd**, **3rd** and **4th**, for instance, – a par three, par five and par four – are as memorable and as varied and challenging a sequence as the celebrated 10th, 11th and 12th at St Mellion. The pick of these is probably the two-shot 4th where the player drives from an elevated tee (usually with an iron), threading it along an ever-narrowing fairway and then fires an approach across the corner of an encroaching lake to a stage-like green. Another superb hole is the par three **9th**: here the green is once again the 'wrong side' of water and is set at such an angle that only the very bold, precisely struck tee shot will be rewarded. Not a hole for the nit-picking 'knockers'.

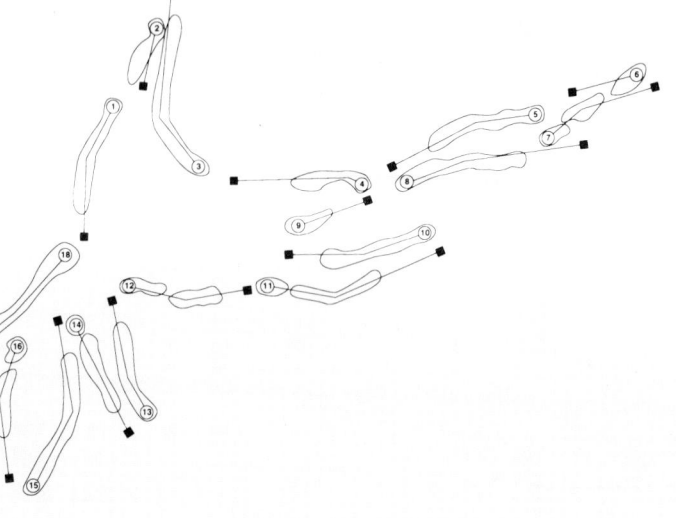

Letham Grange Old Course

Hole	Yards	Par	Hole	Yards	Par
1	402	4	10	406	4
2	166	3	11	511	5
3	550	5	12	379	4
4	381	4	13	342	4
5	435	4	14	334	4
6	184	3	15	476	5
7	342	4	16	398	4
8	485	5	17	154	3
9	189	3	18	480	5
Out	**3,134**	**35**	**In**	**3,480**	**38**
			Out	**3,134**	**35**
			TOTALS	**6,614**	**73**

LETHAM GRANGE HOTEL AND GOLF COURSES

In the heartland of golf lies the superb new Letham Grange Hotel and Golf Courses. The magnificent Victorian Mansion nestles with the panoramic Letham Grange Estate. The Mansion has been restored to its former glory as a top quality, 3 star hotel with 20 bedrooms, offering a style and standard of living which is both traditional and sumptuous.

36 Holes of magnificent golf! Widely acclaimed as one of the premier courses in Scotland, the Old Course provides a blend of tree lined parkland and open rolling fairways. With water playing a major role, the Course is both scenic and dramatic. The New Course, although slightly shorter - and without the water hazards, offers golfers a more relaxed and less arduous round. However, it can be deceptive!

For further information on special golfing breaks, or a day's golf

Letham Grange Hotel
Colliston
by Arbroath
DD11 4RL
Tel: (0241) 89 373
Fax: (0241) 89 414

285

THE MERRYBURN HOTEL

Situated at the Gateway to the Highlands makes Merryburn the ideal centre for an unrivalled golfing, fishing, walking, touring holiday. The beautiful surrounding countryside, especially Birnam Wood immortalised by Macbeth, walks along the River Tay and to the top of Birnam Hill with its incredible panoramic views over Perthshire. We are easily located just off the A9 - 12 miles north of Perth.

Merryburn is a small family run hotel with very pleasant staff. All bedrooms recently fully refurbished to a high standard having satellite TV, radio alarms, beverages and snacks. In the intimate atmosphere of our restaurant you will enjoy cuisine to satisfy the most discerning of palates. The finest of ingredients of which many are produced locally are cooked with the delicacy, skill and flair, complemented by our selection of wines. Scottish and modern music is often featured in our Lounge Bar or you might wish to meet the locals in our Cellar Bar.

With over 45 golf courses within 30 miles Merryburn is a golfers' paradise. Some well known courses within this are Gleneagles, Dunblane, Grangemouth, Carnoustie, King James, Murrayshall, Taymouth Castle.

<u>PERTHSHIRE HIGHLAND GOLF TICKET.</u> 5 days of golfing on 5 different courses with unlimited rounds. Hotel with full table d'hote dinner and breakfast the very best quality and service. We are able to offer this 5 day break at an unbelievable price - brochure available. Alternatively we can arrange courses of your choice. Salmon and trout fishing packages also available.

The Merryburn Hotel
Station Road
Birnam, Dunkeld,
Perthshire PH8 0DS
Tel/Fax: (0350) 727216

THE GLENFARG HOTEL - THE GOLFER'S HOTEL

Crieff * Balbirnie Park * CARNOUSTIE * Elie * Murrayshall * ST ANDREWS * Lundin Links * Downfield * ROSEMOUNT * Taymouth Castle * Scotscraig * GLENEAGLES * Letham Grange

Situated in the heart of Scotland's golfing country, the Glenfarg Hotel is the perfect setting for your golfing break. We will be happy to make all your golfing arrangements, from advising on choice of courses and green fees, to booking tee-times and lunches at the club.

All bedrooms en suite with tea/coffee-making and colour TV including satellite. The attractive candlelit restaurant offers an excellent choice of dishes, using the best of fresh local produce. Extensive wine list. Home-cooked bar meals. Only 40 minutes from Edinburgh.

The Glenfarg Hotel
Glenfarg
Perthshire PH2 9NU
Tel: (05773) 241

THE LANDS OF LOYAL HOTEL

Set on a hillside overlooking the Vale of Strathmore to the Sidlaw Hills beyond, are 10 acres of tiered and rambling gardens, at the heart of which lies the 'Lands of Loyal'.

This impressive Victorian Mansion was built in the 1830s, commissioned by Sir William Ogilvy, who, on his return from Waterloo, chose Loyal Hill as the site for this magnificent home.

The Lands of Loyal was subsequently owned by a succession of families until being converted into a Hotel in 1945.

It has since been very prominent in the area, holding fond memories for the oldest generations. It is also highly regarded as a second home to country sportsmen who have remained loyal for many years. More recently, an extensive refurbishment programme, carried out in the public rooms, has further enhanced the unique atmosphere of this much respected country house hotel.

A highly acclaimed restaurant in its own right, our style of cuisine is traditional and imaginative, making full use of local fish and game.

An extensive wine list, featuring several wines and madeiras,

some over 150 years old, is available to complement your meal.

The Lands of Loyal makes an ideal base for the ambitious golfer. Perthshire has 30 golf courses in total with remarkable variety. All courses are within an hour's drive of the hotel with some of the most famous and desirable spots only a few minutes away.

As fundamentally a sportsman's hotel, The Lands of Loyal appreciates the needs of the golfer. Very early breakfasts and unusually flexible dining arrangements, quality packed lunches etc., are offered courteously. Private rooms for parties can be requested in advance.

The Hotel management are delighted to arrange a complete itinerary for the golfer, whether an individual or a group. Tee times can be arranged and green fees paid. Any correspondence with golf clubs will gladly be undertaken by us.

The Lands of Loyal provides a complete and competitive golfing package. A full colour brochure and tariff is available on request.

Karl-Peter & Patricia Howell
The Lands of Loyal Hotel
Alyth
Perthshire
Scotland PH11 8JQ
Tel: (08283) 3151
Fax: (08283) 3313

CULCREUCH CASTLE

Culcreuch Castle, the home of the Barons of Culcreuch since 1699 and before this the ancestral fortalice of the Galbraiths and indeed Clan Castle of the Galbraith chiefs for over three centuries (1320 to 1630), has now been restored and converted by its present owners into a most comfortable family-run country house hotel, intimately blending the elegance of bygone days with modern comforts and personal service in an atmosphere of friendly informal hospitality. The eight individually decorated and furnished bedrooms all have en suite facilities, colour television and tea and coffee making facilities. Most command uninterrupted and quite unsurpassed views over the 1600 acre parkland grounds, described by the National Trust for Scotland as a 'gem of outstanding beauty', and beyond a kaleidoscope of spectacular scenery of hills, moorlands, lochs, burns and woods comprising the Endrick valley and the Campsie Fells above.

All the public rooms are decorated in period style and furnished with antiques giving the aura and grace of a bygone age. Log fires create warmth and intimacy and the candlelit evening meals in the panelled dining room make for most romantic occasions, well complemented by freshly prepared local produce and a carefully selected wine cellar.

The Loch Lomond, Stirling & Trossachs area offers the visitor a wide and varied range of country activities, including golf, fishing, shooting, water sports, nature study and bird watching, historical research, or simply walking and exploring in stunningly beautiful countryside. Whatever your interests, whatever the time of year, the wide open spaces, lack of crowds and the serene tranquility give to the area a special fascination, be it bathed in sunshine or feathered in frost.

With over 40 golf courses within a 25 mile radius of the Castle,

Culcreuch is a golfer's paradise. A special Golfing Brochure is available on request which gives details of the packages available at a large number of these venues listed below:

Gleneagles, Aberfoyle, Alloa, Alva, Airdrie, Balmore, Bearsden, Bishopbriggs, Bonnybridge, Braehead, Bridge of Allan, Buchanan Castle, Callander, Campsie, Cardross, Cawder, Clober, Dunblane, Dougalston, Douglas Park, Drumpellier, Dullater, Dumbarton, Erskine, Falkirk, Falkirk Tryst, Glenbervie, Grangemouth, Helensburgh, Kilsyth, Kirkintilloch, Lenzie, Lethamhill, Littlehill, Milngavie, Polmont, Stirling, Tillicoultry, Tulliallan, and Windyhill.

Whether for either business or pleasure, Culcreuch is a most convenient centrally positioned base for visiting Edinburgh (55 minutes by motorway), Glasgow (35 minutes) and Stirling (25 minutes). For business clients there is no comparable venue for entertaining and the Castle specialises in offering its unique facilities for small meetings.

From Autumn to Spring, reduced terms for off-season breaks are offered, together with House Parties over the Christmas and New Year Holidays' and during these cooler months the log fires offer a cheerful welcome on your return from a day out in the Trossachs.

The location of Culcreuch is rural but not isolated, and with the fresh air of the countryside, the space, grace, comfort, good wholesome food and that unique warmth of friendship and hospitality offered from a family run home from home, a stay here is most conducive to shedding the cares and pressures of modern day life and utterly relaxing.

We look forward to your company. — The Haslam Family

Culcreuch Castle
Fintry
Stirlingshire G63 OLW
Tel: (036 086) 228
Fax: (0532) 390093
Telex: 557299

TAYSIDE AND CENTRAL
COMPLETE GOLF

TAYSIDE

Aberfeldy G.C
(0887) 20535
Taybridge Road, Aberfeldy, Perthshire
10 miles from Ballinluig off the A827
(9) 2733 yards/***/F

Alyth G.C
(08283) 2268
Pitcrocknie, Alyth, Perthshire
Off the B954 road, off the A926
(18) 6226 yards/***/F

Arbroath G.C
(0241) 72666
Elliot, Arbroath, Angus
2 miles S. of Arbroath on A92
(18) 6078 yards/***/F

Auchterarder G.C
(0764) 62804
Orchil Road, Auchterarder, Perthshire
S.W of town, off the A9
(18) 5737 yards/***/F

Blair Atholl G.C
(079681) 274
Blair Atholl, Perthshire
6 miles N. of Pitochry on the A9
(9) 5710 yards/***/F

Blairgowrie G.C
(0250) 873116
Rosemount, Blairgowrie, Perthshire
Take A923 from Perth and turn off to
Rosemount
(18) 6588 yards/***/F/H
(18) 6895 yards/***/F/H

Brechin G.C
(03562) 2383
Trinity, by Brechin, Angus
In Trinity village, 1 mile N. of Brechin on B966
(18) 5267 yards/***/D

Caird Park G.C
(0382) 453606
Mains Loan, Dundee
N. of city, just off Kingsway
(18) 6303 yards/***/F

Callander G.C
(0877) 30090
Aveland Road, Callander, Perthshire
Signposted off the A84
(18) 5125 yards/***/D

Camperdown G.C
(0382) 623398
Camperdown Park, Dundee
In Coupar Angus Road, off Kingsway
(18) 6561 yards/***/E

Carnoustie
(0241) 53789
Links Parade, Carnoustie, Angus
12 miles E of Dundee, off the A630
(18) 6020 yards/***/F/H
(18) 5732 yards/***/F/H
(18) 6931 yards/***/F/H

Comrie G.C
(0764) 70544
c/o Sec, Donald C McGlashan
10 Polinard, Comrie, Perthshire
6 miles W. of Crieff on the A85
(9)5966/***/F

Craigie Hill G.C
(0783) 22644
Cherrybank, Perth
1 mile W. of Perth
(18) 5739 yards/***/E

Crieff G.C
(0764) 2397
Perth Road, Crieff, Perthshire
18 miles along the A85, Perth-Crieff Road
(18) 6402 yards/***/F
(9) 4772 yards/***/F

Dalmunzie Hotel & G.C
(025085) 226
Spittal of Glenshee, Blairgowrie, Perthshire
22 miles N. of Blairgowrie on the A93
(9) 2035/***/E

Downfield G.C
(0382) 825595
Turnberry Avenue, Dundee
Leave Dundee by Kingsway and take A923
(18) 6804 yards/***/F

Dunblane New G.C
(0786) 823711
Perth Road, Dunblane, Perthshire
6 miles N. of Stirling on A9
(18) 6876 yards/**/D

Dunkeld and Birnam G.C
(035 02) 524
Fungarth, Dunkeld, Perthshire
1 mile N. of Dunkeld off the A9
(9) 5264 yards/***/E

Dunning G.C
(076484) 398
Rollo Park, Dunning, Perth
9 miles S.W of Perth off the A9
(9) 4836 yards/***/F/H

Edzell G.C
(03564) 7283
High Street, Edzell, By Brechin, Angus
Leave the A94 for the B966 at by-pass
(18) 6299 yards/***/F

Forfar G.C
(0307) 62120
Cunninghill, Arbroath Road, By Forfar, Angus
1 mile from town on road to Angus
(18) 6255 yards/***/C

Gleneagles Hotel & G.C
(0764) 62231
Auchterarder, Perthshire
Take A9 from Perth S.W for 16 miles
(18) 6471 yards/*/F
(18) 5964 yards/*/F

Killin G.C
(056 72) 312
Killin, Perthshire
On outskirts of village
(9) 2508 yards/***/E/H

King James VI G.C
(0738) 32460
Moncreiffe Island, Perth
By footbridge over River Tay
(18) 6026 yards/***(not Sat)/D

Green Hotel G.C
(0577) 63467
Beeches Park, Kinross, Perthshire
17 miles S. of Perth
(18) 6111 yards/***/D

Kirriemuir G.C
(0575) 72729
Kirriemuir, Angus
1 mile N. of town centre
(18) 5591 yards/**/E

Letham Grange G.C
(024 189) 373
Letham Grange, Colliston, By Arbroath, Angus
Take the A933 for 4 miles
(18) 6789 yards/***/F/H

Milnathort G.C
(0577) 64069
South Street, Milnathort
2 miles N. of Kinross, off the M90
(9) 5411 yards/***/E

Monifieth Links G.C
(0382) 532767
Dundee, Angus
Just outside Monifieth on the A930
(18) 6657 yards/***(not Sat)/D/H
(18) 5123 yards/***(not Sat)/E/H

Montrose Links Trust
(0674)72932
Trail Drive, Montrose, Angus
1 mile from town centre off the A92
(18) 6451 yards/***/F/H
(18) 4815 yards/***/F/H

Murrayshall Hotel & G.C
(0738) 52784
Murrayshall, by Scone, Perthshire
On the A94 from Perth
(18) 6416 yards/***/F/H

Muthill G.C
(0764) 81523
Peat Road, Muthill, Crieff
Signposted off the A822
(9) 2371 yards/***/E

North Inch G.C
Near centre of Perth off the A9
(18) 4736 yards/***/E

Panmure G.C
(0241) 53120
Barry, Angus
Take A930 to Barry
(18) 6317 yards/***(not Sat)/D/H

Pitlochry G.C
(0796) 2796
Golf Course Road, Pitlochry
Half mile from Pitlochry on A9
(18) 5811 yards/***/F/H

St Fillans G.C
(0764) 85312
St Fillans, Perthshire
On A85 between Crieff and Lochearnhead
(9) 5268 yards/***/E

Strathtay G.C
(08874) 367
Tighanoisinn, Grandtully, Perthshire
4 miles W. of Ballinkrig
(9) 4980 yards/***/E

Taymouth Castle G.C
(088 73) 228
Kenmore, by Aberfeldy, Tayside
6 miles W. of Aberfeldy
(18) 6066 yards/***/D/H

CENTRAL

Aberfoyle G.C
(08772) 441
Braeval, Aberfoyle, Stirlingshire
1 mile from Aberfoyle on the A81
(18) 5205 yards/***/D

Alloa G.C
(0259) 722745
Schawpark, Sauchie, Clackmannanshire
On A908 between Alloa and Tillicoultry
(18) 6230 yards/***/E

Alva G.C
(0259) 60431
Beauclerc Street, Alva, Clackmannanshire
3 miles N. of Alloa on the A91
(9) 2407 yards/***/F

Bonnybridge G.C
Larbert Road, Bonnybridge, Stirlingshire
3 miles W. of Falkirk on the B816
(9) 6060 yards/*(with member only)/F

Brachead G.C
(0259) 722078
Cambus, By Alloa, Clackmannanshire
1 mile W. of Alloa on the A907
(18) 6013 yards/***/E/H

Bridge of Allan G.C
(0786) 832332
Sunlaw, Bridge of Allan, Stirling
Over the River Allan off Stirling Road
(9) 4932 yards/***(not Sat)/E

Dollar G.C
(02594) 2400
Brewlands House, Dollar, Clackmannanshire
(18) 5144 yards/**/F

Falkirk G.C
(0324) 611061
Stirling Road, Cumlins, Falkirk
2 miles W. of Falkirk centre on A9
(18) 6202 yards/**/F

Falkirk Tryst G.C
(0324) 562091
Burnhead Rd, Larbert
1/4 mile from Larbert Station
(18)6053 yards/***/D

Glenbervie G.C
(0324) 562605
Stirling Road, Larbert, Stirlingshire
1 mile N. of Larbert on the A9
(18) 6469 yards/**(by intro only)/C

Grangemouth Municipal G.C
(0324) 714355
Polmont Hill, Polmont, Falkirk, Stirlingshire
Leave M9 at junction 4 and follow signs to Hill
(18) 6314 yards/***/F/H

Muckhart G.C
(025 981) 423
Drumburn Road, Muckhart, Dollar,
Clackmannanshire
Signposted off the A91 and A823 S. of Muckhart
(18) 6115 yards/***/E

Polmont G.C
(0324) 711277
Maddiston, by Falkirk, Stirlingshire
4 miles S. of Falkirk
(9) 3044 yards/**/E

Stirling G.C
(0786) 64098
Queens Road, Stirling
Half mile W. of town centre on A811
(18) 5976 yards/**/D

Tillicoultry G.C
(0259) 50124
Alva Road, Tillicoultry
(9) 2528 yards/***/E

Tulliallan G.C
(0259) 30897
Alloa Road, Kincardine on Forth, By Alloa
2 miles N. of Kincardine Bridge on Alloa Road
(18) 5982 yards/***/F

GRAMPIAN & HIGHLAND

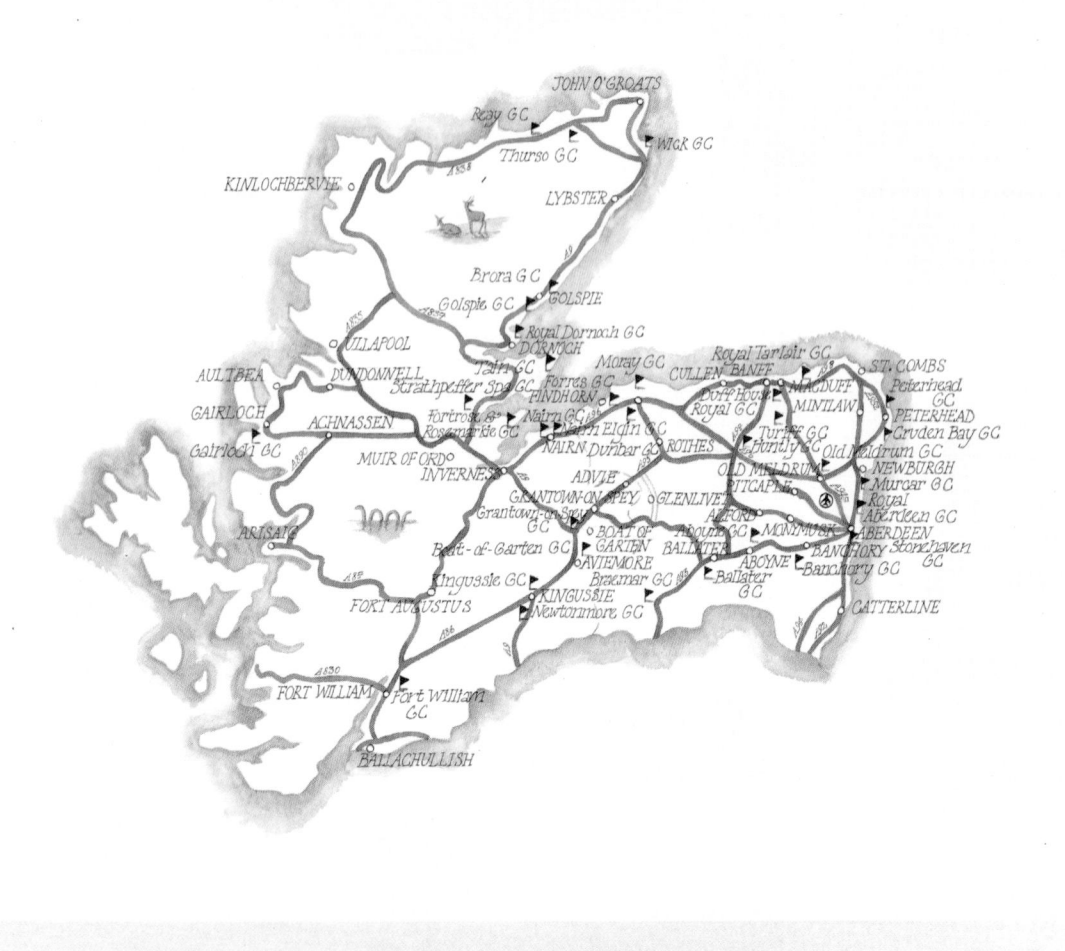

Bill Waugh **ROYAL DORNOCH** *Burlington Gallery*

GRAMPIAN & HIGHLAND
CHOICE GOLF

Mist-covered mountains and bottomless lochs, bagpipes, whisky and haggis. I doubt whether there is a more romantic place in the world than the Highlands of Scotland. I doubt also that there is a place quite so shatteringly beautiful.

For our purposes 'the Highlands' covers the administrative regions of Grampian and Highland. The latter extends from the Cairngorms northwards, encompassing the Great Glen and the Western Isles. Grampian covers a similarly vast area, the entirety of north eastern Scotland. The area was at one time covered by a dense forest of pine broken only by the soaring granite peaks of the Grampian mountain range. It was the home of the savage Caledonian tribe, a land where wolves hunted in packs. Nowadays very little of the forest remains. As for the wolves, most of them were killed by the Caledonians, but then unfortunately most of the Caledonians were killed by the Romans. No wonder they called life 'nasty, brutish and short'!

GRAMPIAN

Let us make a start in Grampian. Forgetting the wolves, the savages and the Romans, what we need is a good 18 holes – and, of course, a suitable 19th. Aberdeen is a fine place to begin. Balgownie and Murcar lie right on the town's doorstep and are unquestionably two of the finest courses in Scotland. Balgownie links is the home of the **Royal Aberdeen** Golf Club and is featured ahead but **Murcar** is certainly not over-shadowed and is a true Championship test. It is a classic Scottish links with plenty of sandhills and a meandering burn and is quite a bit more undulating than Balgownie.

If the above are the best two courses around Aberdeen, (there are dozens in the area) and they are to the north of the city perhaps the most spectacular is to the south at **Stonehaven**, laid out right alongside the lashing North Sea. And in total contrast to Stone-haven – and indeed to Aberdeen's great links layouts is the new 'American-styled' course at **Newmachar**, north west of the city.

There are even more hotels in Aberdeen than golf courses but a large number are modern and somewhat unattractive and many may prefer to stay outside the town. Anyway some of the best include The Holiday Inn (0224) 770011, The Skean Dhu Hotel (0224) 725252 and the strangely named Bucksburn Moat House (0224) 713911. Two other hotels strongly recommended by the golfing fraternity are The Atholl (0224) 23505 in Kings Gate and The New Marcliffe (0224) 321371 in Queens Road. Many of the city's innumerable guesthouses provide a more friendly ambience then their larger counterparts with Cedars Private Hotel (0224) 583225 a prominent example. An excellent seafood restaurant to visit is the Atlantis (0224) 591403 while Gerrard's (0224) 639500 is also highly thought of.

North of Aberdeen The Udny Arms (03586) 444 at Newburgh enjoys a splendid situation overlooking the Ythan Estuary and is a total contrast to the many modern hotels of Aberdeen. Due west of the latter another striking location is found at Kildrummy by Alford. Here The Kildrummy Castle (09755) 71288 is a first class establishment. To the north west, The Pittodrie House Hotel (0467) 861444 at Pitcaple enjoys glorious surroundings and in Old Meldrum one finds the similarly splendid Meldrum-House Hotel (06512) 2294 is convenient for Aberdeen but obviously also for the pleasant 18 hole **Old Meldrum** course.

Looking to play outside Aberdeen, the golfer is faced with two

equally appealing choices – one can either head north along the coast towards Cruden Bay, or alternatively head inland along the A93. The latter choice broadly involves following the path of the River Dee and will take the traveller through some truly magnificent scenery. The 18 hole courses at **Banchory, Aboyne, Ballater** and **Braemar** all lie along this road and not surprisingly boast spectacular settings.

There are several superb places in which to stay as you golf your way along the Dee. In Banchory, Raemoir House (03302) 48184 is outstanding and the Tor-na-Coille (03302) 2242 has excellent facilities, as does the Banchory Lodge Hotel (03302) 2625. Aboyne offers the Birse Lodge Hotel (03398) 86253 while the especially attractive town of Ballater boasts a number of fine establishments. Tullich Lodge (0338) 55406 is one of the leading mansion houses in Scotland but also note the Craigendarroch Hotel (03397) 55858 with its fine restaurant and Darroch Learg (03397) 55443. Should you time it right then Braemar boasts that magnificent spectacle, The Highland Games.

Journeying due northwards from Aberdeen, **Cruden Bay** is clearly the first stopping point. A truly splendid golf links this, situated some 23 miles north of Aberdeen on Scotland's Buchan Coast. It is detailed on a later page. The old fishing and whaling town of **Peterhead** has an interesting seaside course where sea winds can make scoring tricky.

From fishing port to Georgian elegance – The **Duff House Royal** Golf Club at Macduff is overlooked by an impressive baroque- style mansion. The course too has a touch of class being designed by Alister Mackenzie immediately prior to his constructing the legendary Augusta National course in America – note the many two-tiered greens. Although not far from the sea Duff House is very much a parkland type challenge. **Royal Tarlair** at Banff is well worth a visit and like Duff House is always beautifully maintained. To the south of Banff, along the A947, **Turriff** can also be recommended while even further inland (but a marvellous drive anyway) from the Banff/Macduff area on the A97, is the charming little course at **Huntly** and the very relaxing Castle Hotel (0466) 792696. West of Huntly lies the well run Craigellachie Hotel (0340) 881204. In Macduff, the Fire Arms Hotel (0261) 32408 is convenient and in Banff's High Street, The Country Hotel (02612) 5353 is one to note. Also to be found in Banff is the charming Carmelite House Hotel (0261) 22152, whilst nearby Cullen Bay accommodates the welcoming Cullen Bay Hotel (0542) 40432.

Crossing the salmon-filled River Spey at Fochabers the City of **Elgin** is soon reached. There aren't too many cathedrals in this part of the world but Elgin, the capital of Morayshire, has a beautiful one that dates from the 13th Century. It also possesses one of the finest inland golf courses in the north of Scotland. A mile or so south of the city and some distance away from the often fierce coastal winds, the course is sheltered by many pines and silver birch trees. Inevitably, it occupies a glorious setting with distant purple hills forming a spectacular horizon.

Inland from Elgin, a drive through the Glen of Rothes will lead the golfer to **Dufftown** where there is a pleasant and not too difficult course but if a coastal challenge is sought then Lossie-mouth is the place to head for. Here, the **Moray** Golf Club has two outstanding links courses, the 'Old Course' which is more than a hundred years old and the 'New Course', a little over ten years old. Whilst the fighter aircraft from nearby RAF

GRAMPIAN & HIGHLAND
CHOICE GOLF

Lossiemouth may occasionally irritate, it would be difficult to find a finer combination of superb natural golf and scenic splendour. Moray is another Club featured later in this section.

In Elgin, two recommended hotels, The Mansion House (0343) 48811 and The Eight Acres (0343) 3077 and in Rothes, The Rothes Glen (03403) 254 is superbly relaxing. Finally in Lossiemouth, ideal for golf at Moray is the adjacent Stotfield Hotel (0343) 812011.

HIGHLAND

In Scotland where there is land there is golf and although the Highland region may be a wild and somewhat remote part of the country it nonetheless has its share of golfing gems – and more than that, in the minds of many, it has in **Royal Dornoch** the finest of them all.

As well as its gems, the region has a number of golf's genuine outposts, none more so than the **Gairloch** Golf Club situated in the far west of Scotland with views across to the Isle of Skye. There are 9 holes at Gairloch, each wonderfully named. The 6th, however, baffles me – 'Westward Ho!' is its title?! The 9th though has more of a Celtic ring to it – 'Mo Dhachaidh'. There is no Sunday golf at Gairloch though visitors can play at all other times. Others in the 'lonely category' include **Fort Augustus** on the edge of Loch Ness and **Fort William**, a moorland course, laid out in the shadows of Ben Nevis. In addition the very intrepid golfer will find a number of courses to play in the Western Isles and the Hebrides although the scenery may cause many to lift their heads too quickly.

In the south of Highland, the area around Aviemore has become an increasingly popular holiday retreat, particularly for winter sports enthusiasts. However, whilst the skis must go on the roof, the golf clubs can fit in the boot, and there are five or six courses at hand each of which possesses a truly glorious setting. Picking two of the best, the **Kingussie** and **Boat of Garten** Golf Clubs lie either side of Aviemore close to the A9. Both have spectacular courses at which visitors are always made welcome. Neither is particularly long, though the hills at Kingussie and the narrow fairways and small greens at Boat of Garten can make scoring extremely difficult and you are more likely to see eagles than score one! At Boat of Garten you may also catch a glimpse of one of the famous ospreys.

Some thoughts for the 19th include in the Newtonmore-Kingussie area, The Highlander (05403) 341 and The Osprey (05402) 510, both are pleasant hotels and The Cross (05402) 762 is an outstanding restaurant in Kingussie. In Fort William one finds The Inverlochy Castle (0397) 2177, one of the country's finest hotels and restaurants, while two other gems are the remote Arisaig House (06875) 622 in Arisaig on the western coast and in Ballachulish, The Ballachulish Hotel (08552) 606 which enjoys a superb loch side setting. In Boat of Garten, The Boat (047983) 258 is exceptionally convenient overlooking the golf course (note the special 'golf weeks'). Both Seafield Lodge (0479) 2152 and The Grant Arms Hotel (0479) 2526 in Grantown-on-Spey are comfortable and good value, as is the Aultnagar Hotel (054) 982 245 in Lairg, whilst nearer the coast at Advie is the extremely gracious Tulchan Lodge (08075) 200.

Inverness, as the so-called 'Capital of the Highlands', is where many may choose to spend a day or two – the Loch Ness monster lives nearby and the famous fields of destruction at Culloden Moor are only a few miles to the east. Golfers may wish to note the city's 18 hole course situated just south of the town centre. However, many are likely to be drawn towards **Nairn** (16 miles away) where in addition to the magnificent championship links – see feature page – there is an excellent second course, **Nairn Dunbar**.

Both Inverness and Nairn have a number of good hotels. In the former, The Dunain Park Hotel (0463) 230512 and the 18th Century Kingsmills (0463) 237166 are ideal, and near to the famous battlefield is the impressive Culloden House Hotel (0463) 792181 where a portrait of the Bonnie Prince will welcome you. Relaxation and comfort can also be found at Glenruidh House (0463) 226499 and Ballifeary House Hotel (0463) 235572. The Golf View Hotel (0667) 52301 is situated right alongside the famous Nairn course but there are strong recommendations also for The Newton Hotel (0667) 53144, Lochloy House (0667) 55355, The Alton Burn Hotel (0667) 52051 and The Clifton Hotel (0667) 53119 also in Nairn.

On the Chanonry Peninsula, linked to Inverness by way of the Kessock Bridge, the A9 and the A832, is the flattish links course of **Fortrose and Rosemarkie** – surrounded by sea and well worth a visit. **Strathpeffer Spa**, a moorland course, is the prettiest of stepping stones for those heading north of Inverness along the A9 and Craigdarroch Lodge Hotel (0997) 421265 will provide comfortable respite. This road passes through **Tain**, home of the famous Glenmorangie whisky, and where there is another outstanding 18 holes – but by now most will be itching to reach Dornoch.

Royal Dornoch (see ahead) is ranked among the top 10 golf courses in Great Britain and Ireland (Golf World). For those wishing to reflect on their day's golf The Dornoch Castle (0862) 810216 is genuinely splendid. Other hotels to try are The Royal Golf Hotel (0862) 810283 and The Burghfield House (0862) 810212 and there are a number of more modest B&B type places.

Having played **Royal Dornoch**, many find it difficult to tear themselves away, but there are two excellent courses a short distance to the north, namely, **Golspie** and **Brora**. Both are testing links courses set in the most majestic surroundings with views to distant hills and along what is a truly spectacular coast. Brora (where the greens are reputed to be the equal of those at Royal Dornoch and are ringed by electric fences to keep the sheep out!) stretches out right alongside three miles of deserted sandy beach. Being so far north golf can be played at absurdly late hours and at both, the green fees are very inexpensive.

In Brora, The Royal Marine (0408) 21252 and The Links (0408) 21225 hotels are both strategically placed on the aptly named Golf Road, while another well titled hotel can be found at Golspie, The Golf Links Hotel (04083) 3408; all three are recommended.

Beyond Brora we really are getting remote! However, the A9 makes it all the way to John O'Groats. There are 18 hole courses at **Wick** and **Reay**, but the furthest north is **Thurso**, not too far from the Dounreay Power Station. I should imagine it gets pretty cold up there, but if you do make it, and are looking for fresh challenges then there is always the golf club in the Arctic – fittingly called the 'Polar Bear Club' – and which, I suppose it goes without saying, was founded by Scotsmen!

CRAIGELLACHIE HOTEL

One of the most beautiful villages in Moray, Craigellachie, lies at the confluence of the Fiddich and Spey rivers in a picturesque setting equal only to the sumptuous and elegant Victorian hotel itself. Only one hour's drive from the airports of Aberdeen and Inverness, the Craigellachie is a haven of highland hospitality set in a spectacular countryside - unspoilt, wild and beautiful and ideal for all kinds of modern sporting activities.

According to the season you can play tennis, ski, ride horseback or mountain bike along forest and mountain trails and fish for salmon or brown trout.

And then there's the golf. The Craigellachie offers a unique opportunity to enjoy a holiday in the land where golf was born, with a choice of links, moor or parkland courses all within a short drive of the hotel. whatever your handicap, there's a course her to challenge your skill. We can arrange golf club hire and private tuition by professionals at selected clubs.

After sampling the variety of outdoor pursuits or one of the many golf courses in this beautiful part of Scotland, it's always a pleasure to return to the Craigellachie and sit beside the glowing embers of a real log fire in the hall or one of the comfortable lounges. An equally warm welcome will await you in the Quaich cocktail bar and when it's time to dine, the Ben Aigan Restaurant offers a tempting menu in the hearty tradition of the finest Scottish cuisine. Here, you can savour the delights of our culinary excellence (which, according to season, feature prime local produce from sea and countryside) and then linger over coffee in the drawing room before retiring to the comfort and luxury of one of 30 splendidly appointed bedrooms. Each has its own en suite bath/shower, direct-dial telephone, radio remote-control colour television and special hospitality features. And for your further enjoyment you can make use of our library, billiards room, exercise room, sauna, solarium and rod room.

Here, at the Craigellachie, all the amenities of an international class hotel have been tastefully incorporated to retain all the original charm of a delightful Scottish country house.

Craigellachie Hotel
Craigellachie
Speyside
Banffshire AB38 9SR
Scotland
Tel: (0340) 881204
Fax: (0340) 881253

ROYAL ABERDEEN
CHAMPIONSHIP GOLF

Founded in **1780**, Royal Aberdeen is the sixth oldest Golf Club in the world. For the first thirty five years of its existence the Club was known as **The Society of Golfers at Aberdeen** with membership of the Society being determined by ballot. They were clearly a meticulous group of gentlemen for in **1783** they became the first to introduce the five minute limit on searching for golf balls. A sensible idea you may think, but one that has caused the modern day Aberdeen Golfer much distress – a subject to which I shall return in due course.

In 1815, on the eve of the Battle of Waterloo, the Society changed its name to the Aberdeen Golf Club and in 1903 the Royal prefix was bestowed on the Club. Originally the members played over a strip of common land between the Rivers Don and Dee but in the second half of the 19th century the Club acquired its own course at **Balgownie** on the northern side of the River Don. Today Balgownie Links is regarded as one of Scotland's greatest Championship courses.

Ron MacAskill is both the General Manager and PGA Professional at Royal Aberdeen and he may be contacted by telephone on **(0224) 70221** or **(0224) 702571**. All written correspondence should be addressed to him at **The Royal Aberdeen Golf Club, Balgownie, Bridge of Don, Aberdeen, AB2 8AT.**

Visitors are made extremely welcome at Royal Aberdeen and they may play at Balgownie on any day subject to making a tee reservation with the professional. The green fees for 1992 were set at £25 per round or £30 per day during the week with a £30 fee for a single round at the weekend. Travelling to Aberdeen is made fairly straightforward by the A92. From the south this road passes along the coast from Dundee via Arbroath, Montrose and Stonehaven to Aberdeen. It also connects the town to Fraserburgh in the north. Those approaching from the north west should find the A96 helpful (it in fact runs directly from Inverness.) Other roads which may prove of assistance are the A947 from Oldmeldrum and the A93 which links Aberdeen to Perth and passes through Blairgowrie. The links itself is situated 2 miles north of Aberdeen and can be sighted immediately to the right after crossing the River Don.

From its medal tees, Balgownie measures 6372 yards, par 70 (s.s.s. 71) with the forward tees reducing the length to 6104 yards, par 69. Although perhaps not overly long, the course is very exposed to the elements and the wind can often make a mockery of some of the distances. There is also a considerable spread of gorse and the rough can be very punishing. It should be added that there are no fewer than ninety-two bunkers – ten of which appear on the short par three 8th! Balgownie has the traditional out and back links layout, the front nine hugging the shore and the back nine returning on the landside towards the Clubhouse.

The outward nine is perhaps the more interesting of the two halves; the eminent golf writer **Sam McKinlay** was moved to say: 'There are few courses in these islands with a better, more testing, more picturesque outward nine than Balgownie'. However, the most difficult hole on the course is possibly the last hole, a lengthy par four, well bunkered and usually played into the teeth of the prevailing wind.

Golfers may also wish to investigate the Club's second course, the shorter **Silverburn Course** which measures 4066 yards, par 60.

Royal Aberdeen has played host to a number of major events including the British Youth's Championship, the Scottish Amateur Championship and the Northern Open Championship. In 1993, the British Seniors Championship will be played over the Balgownie links. Numerous exhibition matches have also taken place; participants have included **Tom Morris Junior, Harry Vardon, James Braid, John H. Taylor, Walter Hagen** and **Henry Cotton.**

I now return to the matter of the five minute rule. In the opening paragraph, I mentioned how in 1783 the Aberdeen Golfers had introduced the five minute limit on searching for lost balls. Well somebody somewhere it seems didn't approve and 200 years later a plague of crows was sent to deliver retribution. Throughout the long summers of 1983 and 1984 the crows determined that no one should search for his ball. They descended on the links stealing Titleists and Top-Flites, Pinnacles and Penfolds. Several Members had more than one ball stolen in a round. Numerous suggestions were put forward as to how to rid the links of this turbulent pest but alas to no avail. Even a crow trap was built but still they plundered. Then just as suddenly as they came, they left, never it is presumed to return. Sanity restored, Balgownie became once more one of Britain's friendliest links.

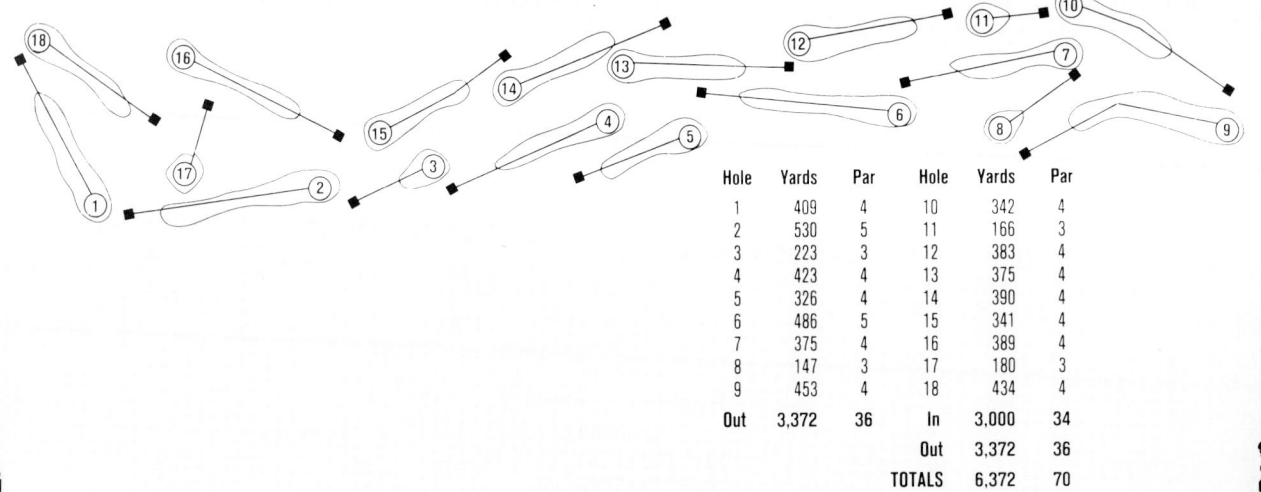

Hole	Yards	Par	Hole	Yards	Par
1	409	4	10	342	4
2	530	5	11	166	3
3	223	3	12	383	4
4	423	4	13	375	4
5	326	4	14	390	4
6	486	5	15	341	4
7	375	4	16	389	4
8	147	3	17	180	3
9	453	4	18	434	4
Out	3,372	36	In	3,000	34
			Out	3,372	36
			TOTALS	6,372	70

THE CASTLE HOTEL

The Castle Hotel is a magnificent eighteenth-century stone building, standing in its own grounds above the ruins of Huntly Castle, on the banks of the River Deveron. Sandston as it was originally known was built as a family home to the Dukes of Gordon.

Run by a keen hotel family, the Castle Hotel has recently been refurbished providing good comfortable accommodation with en suite facilities. Good traditional food using local fresh produce is served in our spacious Dining Room, complemented by a selection from the well stocked wine cellar.

Only forty minutes drive away from the Royal Aberdeen and Cruden Bay Golf courses (listed in the U.K. top fifty courses) the hotel is ideally situated for your Golfing holiday. Closer to home the Royal Tarlour, Duff House Royal and Elgin courses can be found. Huntly's own attractive and well laid out eighteen hole Golf course, Cooper Park, lies at the bottom of the hotel's drive adjacent to the River Deveron.

The town lies in Scotland's famous Castle Country and provides an abundance of leisure and sporting activities. Not to be missed are the many famous distilleries which make up the Whisky Trail.

Our aim is to make your stay an enjoyable and memorable one. We look forward to welcoming you to the Castle Hotel. Situated on the main A96 between Aberdeen (45 minutes away) and Inverness the hotel is easily reached by road, rail and air.

The Castle Hotel
Huntly
Aberdeenshire AB54 4SH
Tel: (0466) 792696
Fax: (0466) 792641

BANCHORY LODGE

The Banchory Lodge Hotel, enlarged and improved first by General William Burnett in the 18th century and then by the Jaffrays since 1966 combines Georgian charm with the distinctive leisured atmosphere of a country house.

There is ample opportunity for sport and relaxation, with local golf courses, tennis courts, putting and bowling, forest walks and nature trails nearby. Salmon fishing on the River Dee can be arranged through the hotel.

The public rooms, including the dining room, where cuisine of a very high standard is served, offer superb views of the River Dee. All the 24 bedrooms are individually furnished and have private bathrooms, colour television and tea-making equipment.

The traditional hospitality of the Lodge ensures an enjoyable and comfortable stay.

Banchory Lodge Hotel,
Banchory,
Banchory on Royal Deeside,
Aberdeen,
Scotland
Tel: (03302) 2625
Fax: (03302) 5019

CRUDEN BAY
CHAMPIONSHIP GOLF

One often reads of famous Golf Clubs having been founded in local hostelries; **Deal** (The Black Horse), **Crail** (The Golf Inn) and **Hoylake** (The Royal) to name but three; well the birth of **Cruden Bay** apparently took place during a meeting in the North of Scotland Bank – one presumes a much more sober affair! The precise date of the meeting was 16th June 1898 and in March the following year the Cruden Bay Hotel and Golf Course were opened.

The Hotel (alas long since demolished) and the 18 hole golf course were originally both owned by the Great North of Scotland Railway Company. Within a month of their opening the company staged a professional tournament which attracted many of the day's leading players including **Harry Vardon** (then Open Champion), **James Braid** and **Ben Sayers**. The event proved an outstanding success with Vardon taking the first prize of £30.

Today the Club's full address is the **Cruden Bay Golf Club, Aulton Road, Cruden Bay, Peterhead, Aberdeenshire AB42 7NN**. In addition to the 18 hole Championship Course there is also a well-kept 9 hole short course, the **St Olaf**.

The present Secretary (or Golf Manager) is **Mr Ian McPherson**. He may be contacted via the above address and by telephone on **(0779) 812285**. The Club's professional, **Robbie Stewart**, can be reached on **(0779) 812414**. Casual visitors are welcome at Cruden Bay, although not surprisingly certain restrictions apply during Saturdays and Sundays. It is generally advisable to telephone the Club at weekends to check whether the tees have been reserved for any competition or, as may be the case during holiday periods, a starting sheet system is being operated. Visitors should also note that they are not permitted to play the 18 hole course between 4.30 pm and 6.30 pm on Wednesdays and that at weekends, unless accompanied by a Member, handicap certificates must be provided. No specific restrictions relate to the St Olaf course.

In 1992 the green fee to play on the Championship course was priced at £18.50 for a weekday ticket, with £25.50 payable at weekends. A week's golf could be purchased for £76 and a full fortnight for £130. For juniors (under 18) the respective rates were £7.50, £10, £35 and £60. A day's golf on the St Olaf course could be obtained for £9.50 during the week and £13.50 at weekends (£5.50 and £7 for juniors).

Cruden Bay is situated on Scotland's Buchan Coast, some 23 miles north of Aberdeen and seven miles south of the old whaling port of Peterhead. The course itself has a dramatic setting with nearby **Slains Castle** providing a rather eerie backdrop. **Bram Stoker** who spent some time in these parts is reputed to have been inspired by the castle when writing his **Dracula** stories. Fortunately the rest of the surrounding countryside bears little resemblance to Transylvania and strangers should find travelling in the area a pleasant experience. The best route when journeying from the south is probably by way of the A92 coastal road which runs from Dundee via Montrose and through Aberdeen. One should leave the A92 near Newburgh and follow the A975 direct to Cruden Bay. The A92 approaches from the North via Fraserburgh and Peterhead.

Originally laid out by **Thomas Simpson**, Cruden Bay is very much a traditional Scottish links (there are a number of blind and semi-blind shots) of fairly medium length, being around the 6400 yards mark. Par is a fairly tight 70 (s.s.s. 71). From the ladies tees the course measures 5761 yards (par 74). A good old Scottish burn is a predominant feature of the course affecting several of the holes, there are a number of vast sand dunes and hills to be negotiated while the beach too (if one is a little wayward) can come into play around the **14th** and **15th**. As one might expect given its geography the wind is often a major factor and the golfer that can master the low run-up shot to the subtly contoured greens will be on to a winner. The views over the Bay of Cruden naturally add to the pleasure of the round, and it isn't difficult to comprehend why Golf World magazine ranks Cruden Bay amongst its top 50 courses in the British Isles.

The magnificently appointed Clubhouse has the kind of atmosphere one comes to expect in this part of the world – very friendly – and casual dress may be worn at all times. Meals are served throughout the day with lunches, high teas, dinners and some delightful steak suppers being offered in addition to bar snacks.

South of Hadrian's Wall, Cruden Bay is probably not as well known as it ought to be. The legions who arrange their golfing trips around the more traditional favourites often miss out on some of Scotland's finest courses. Cruden Bay should be included in anyone's itinerary – it is a genuinely spectacular course and perhaps of equal importance, a place where the warmest of welcomes can be guaranteed.

Hole	Yards	Par	Hole	Yards	Par
1	416	4	10	380	4
2	339	4	11	158	3
3	286	4	12	320	4
4	193	3	13	550	5
5	454	4	14	372	4
6	521	5	15	239	3
7	392	4	16	215	3
8	260	4	17	428	4
9	462	4	18	416	4
Out	3,323	36	In	3,078	34
			Out	3,323	36
			TOTALS	6,401	70

THE CULLEN BAY HOTEL

Set in its own grounds the Cullen Bay Hotel has magnificent views of Cullen Bay, with its long sweep of white sand, and Cullen Golf Course.

Within easy reach are numerous golf courses, and there are opportunities for bowling, fishing, pony-trekking, cycling and bird watching.

Other attractions close by include: the world's only Malt Whisky Trail; Scotland's Fishing Heritage Trail and the Castle Trail, taking in Fyvie, Cawdor and Brodie. There are many gardens and pretty villages to explore as well as coastal and woodland walks and places of interest such as Baxters of Speyside.

All 14 bedrooms have been upgraded and refurbished and now have en suite bathrooms with power showers, individually controlled central heating, remote control colour television, radio, direct-dial telephone, hairdrier and tea and coffee tray. The hotel's other facilities include the Cullen Bay Restaurant, overlooking the bay; the newly refurbished Verandah Restaurant and Bar with garden patio in the summer and log fire during the winter; a lounge with log fire; and a garden with children's play area. For conferences, dinner dances or weddings we can cater for up to one hundred and fifty guests in the Farskane Function Suite.

At the Cullen Bay you'll enjoy good food using local produce and can choose from an informal bar meal or high tea to a three course dinner from our a la carte menu. All this amidst a friendly atmosphere adds up to an unforgettable stay.

The Cullen Bay Hotel
Cullen
Buckie
Banffshire
AB56 2XA
Tel: (0542) 40432
Fax: (0542) 40900

SEAFIELD LODGE HOTEL

The town of Grantown was founded in 1765 by Sir James Grant and later evolved into a favourite Victorian Health Resort. Seafield Lodge itself was built in 1879 and first let to visitors back in 1881. Despite over a century of rich heritage, recent improvements provide the modern guest with every convenience; all rooms are en suite and include hairdryers, direct dial telephones, colour television and tea / coffee making facilities.

For the sportsman the surrounding area is ideal; nearby are many golf courses, including Grantown's 18-hole course set in breathtaking scenery. On the doorstep is one of the most famous salmon rivers in Scotland, The Spey, where the hotel can easily arrange fishing on literally miles of banks and tributaries as well as hundreds of lochs where wild brown trout are just waiting to be caught.

The mountains and hills that circle the area are tempting places for those looking for perfect peace and solitude; your only company the native stags, eagles and ospreys. In the winter months the same slopes offer marvellous skiing and tuition can be provided.

After such bracing activity the Seafield Restaurant is a welcome sight, with its wide range of local and continental dishes using the freshest ingredients, such as game, fresh salmon from the Spey and prime Aberdeen angus beef. Afterwards, the lodge bar with log fire and fine selection of 'wee drams' offers the perfect end to the perfect day.

Seafield Lodge Hotel
Woodside Avenue
Grantown-on-Spey
PH26 3JN
Tel: (0479) 2152
Fax: (0479) 2340

MORAY (LOSSIEMOUTH)
CHAMPIONSHIP GOLF

For a relatively small nation, the Scots have given the world much to savour; two of its greatest gifts are golf and whisky. The origins of each are shrouded in mystery, lost in the murky depths of time, yet both have never been more popular – especially it seems among the Americans and Japanese! There can surely be few better places to enjoy a combination of golf and whisky than in **Lossiemouth** in Morayshire. Within a short drive of some of the finest whisky distilleries in the world is one of the greatest links courses in Scotland. As the Moray Golf Club has its own ten year old single malt whisky, it would seem a perfect place in which to while away a few days – there is certainly an added allure here to a drink at the 19th!

I've no idea when whisky was first consumed in Morayshire but records indicate that golf was being played in the area from at least the late 16th century. In 1596, Walter Hay (presumably no relation to Walter Hagen) an Elgin goldsmith, found himself in hot water with the local authorities for 'playing at the boulis and golff on Sundaye'. The first Moray Golf Club at Lossiemouth was formed in 1875 but lapsed after some years and the present Club was founded in 1889. The initial 16 holes soon became 18 and as golf mushroomed in popularity, Lossiemouth became one of Scotland's most fashionable golfing resorts. Indeed, the popularity of Lossiemouth grew to such an extent that in 1905 an additional nine hole course was constructed to relieve the congestion on the Old Course. Bringing us up to the present, the late **Sir Henry Cotton** was called in as a golf architect in 1970 and a second 18 holes was opened for play in 1976.

The current Secretary at the Moray Golf Club is **James Hamilton** who may be contacted by telephone on **(034381) 2018.** All correspondence should be addressed to The Secretary, **The Moray Golf Club, Lossiemouth, Moray IV31 6QS. Alistair Thomson,** the club's helpful professional can be contacted on **(034381) 3330.** Visitors are welcome at Lossiemouth seven days a week but it is advisable to book by telephone to avoid disappointment in the summer months. The cost of a day's golf on the Old Course in 1992 was pitched at £18 on weekdays with £25 payable at weekends and on the New Course at £12 on weekdays and £18 at weekends. Again in 1992, weekly tickets were available on the Old for £60 (excellent value) and on the New for £45. Visitors may be required to produce handicap certificates.

Travelling to Lossiemouth is fairly straightforward. The main road from Aberdeen to Inverness is the A96 which passes through Elgin where the well-signposted A941 will take the motorist the five miles to Lossiemouth. We have already mentioned one of the pleasures of the 19th hole and, as one might imagine, the atmosphere in the clubhouse is decidedly relaxed and friendly. Casual dress may be worn at all times. Meals are served throughout the day but visitors are encouraged to make their arrangements with the catering manager before starting their round.

The **New Course** at Lossiemouth is now well established and, if a little less testing than the Old at 6,005 yards, par 69, is still a worthy challenge and a troublesome ditch comes into play at no fewer than five holes. However, after a day's golf at Lossiemouth, it is the **Old Course** that most first time visitors will relish a return to – if only to get even with it! Measuring 6,443 yards from the medal tees, with a demanding par of 71 (6,131 yards, par 75 for the ladies) it has many outstanding holes and like St Andrews it starts and finishes in the town.

The most celebrated sequence of holes on the Old Course at Lossiemouth comes towards the end of the round. The **14th,** appropriately called 'Sea' for it is played directly towards it, is a fine par four and is immediately followed by a most attractive par three. The best, however, is saved for the very end. The **18th,** a par four measuring 423 yards, has been described as 'the noblest finishing hole in Scotland'. With the gardens of the Stotfield houses on the right and several bunkers patrolling the left side of the fairway, the second shot has to be played to an elevated plateau green which sits in a natural amphitheatre in front of the handsome old clubhouse. The green is also beside the main street of the town and as a small critical crowd often gathers to watch players 'come home' there is no more appropriate place to register one's first birdie of the day!

Since 1912, the Scottish Ladies Amateur Championship has been played on four occasions at Lossiemouth, and the Club played host to both men's and ladies' Scottish Amateur Championships in 1989. The Northern Scottish Open was played at Moray in May 1991 for the eighth time, a fitting tribute to a golf course which is regarded as one of the finest tests on the Scottish Tartan Tour circuit.

Old Course

Hole	Yards	Par	Hole	Yards	Par
1	333	4	10	314	4
2	493	5	11	415	4
3	400	4	12	402	4
4	203	3	13	422	4
5	419	4	14	417	4
6	141	3	15	190	3
7	439	4	16	359	4
8	460	4	17	497	5
9	316	4	18	423	4
Out	**3,204**	**35**	**In**	**3,439**	**36**
			Out	**3,204**	**35**
			Totals	**6,643**	**71**

THE STOTFIELD HOTEL

The Stotfield Hotel is situated overlooking the superb championship Golf Course of the Moray Golf Club - a true links course. For the less accomplished golfer there is a second 18 hole course alongside of which is the sandy beach of the Moray Firth and in the distance lie the Sutherland Hills.

The Stotfield Hotel is privately owned by Mike and Patricia Warnes who, together with the assistance of their son Damon, enjoy an enviable reputation for personal supervision. The Hotel will celebrate its centenary very shortly and combines modern amenities with traditional charm. It has the comfortable and friendly atmosphere of a family run hotel, with 50 en suite bedrooms all equipped with colour television, direct dial telephone, alarm clock radio, and tea and coffee making facilities. The superior rooms which overlook the Golf Course also have trouser presses and hair dryers.

A high standard of service and cuisine is offered with menus ranging from 'sizzler' steaks served in the Firth Bar, table d'hote dinner and traditional Sunday lunch served in the main dining room, or for those wishing to enjoy a more specialised cuisine one may choose from the a la carte menu which is served in the sun lounge overlooking the sparkling water of the Moray Firth which reflects the magnificent Lossiemouth sunsets.

The head chef, Mr Derek Roy, places special emphasis on using fresh local produce of which salmon smoked in oak chippings from the Macallan Distillery, Seafood Crepes, Fillet de Boeuf Balmoral are amongst his specialities. To enhance the menus an extensive wine list is available which includes Organic wines. A new attraction for a relaxed style of eating is the 'Bourbon Street Bar and Grill', specialising in American style Barbecued cuisine with imported beers.

For those interested in the Whisky Trail one may commence at the Firth Bar with its cosy relaxing atmosphere, sampling the extensive range of 120 malt whiskies.

As well as the Moray Golf Club, the Stotfield Hotel is surrounded by numerous Golf Courses, many of them championship status and all within a short distance. Golf parties are catered for with specialised golfing packages available. Hotel guests playing the Moray Golf Course enjoy a 10% discount on green fees.

Your hosts, Mike, Patricia and Damon Warnes, together with their staff, will endeavour to make your Scottish Golfing Holiday a memorable one.

Stotfield Hotel
Stotfield Road
Lossiemouth
Moray IV31 6QS
Tel: (0343) 812011
Fax: (0343) 814820

NAIRN
CHAMPIONSHIP GOLF

A glorious setting, a superb Championship course and a warm welcome to visiting golfers – that, in a nutshell, is Nairn. In 1987 the Club celebrated its centenary and played host to both mens' and ladies' Scottish Amateur Championships; in 1994 the Club is due to stage the British Amateur.

Originally designed by **Archie Simpson**, and modified two years later by **'Old' Tom Morris**, the present layout owes much to the work of **James Braid**, arguably the greatest of all Scottish golf architects.

Nairn is very much a traditional links with the opening holes stretching out along the shoreline. At the 10th comes the inevitable about-turn, and the head for home. It is a fine test of golf and with the abundant heather, the great sea of gorse and the distant mountains providing a spectacular backdrop, this is a veritable haven.

Being so far north on the golfing map Nairn has probably not received the recognition it must surely deserve – at least in terms of attracting professional tournaments. Yet with an airport (Inverness) a mere 8 miles away and an adequate road and rail network Nairn ought not to be considered too remote in the way that Royal Dornoch traditionally is.

A refreshing atmosphere prevails throughout the Club. Visitors to the area are actively encouraged to play on the links and there is no requirement for a handicap certificate. Except during peak hours at weekends, visitors may play when they choose, though early starters should note that fourballs are not permitted before 9.30am.

For a genuine Championship course the green fees at Nairn are fairly reasonable. In 1992 the Club is charging £23 for a weekday round with £28 payable at weekends. For only £5 extra, a day ticket can be purchased, whilst junior golfers should find Nairn something of a golfing paradise – in 1992 their green fee is a mere £12.

The Club's Secretary is **Mr. Jim Somerville**; anyone wishing to arrange a Society game should contact him via **Nairn Golf Club, Seabank Road, Nairn, Highland IV12 4HB**. Tel. **(0667) 53208**. Both clubs and caddy carts can be hired from the professional, **Robin Fyfe**, tel. **(0667) 52787**.

Unless the long distance traveller has made use of Inverness airport (80 minutes flying time from London and 40 minutes from Glasgow) he is sure to have taken in some wonderfully spectacular scenery. Motoring from the south the A9 runs from Perth to Inverness via Pitlochry, Blair Atholl and Aviemore – over the mountains, through the valleys, beside forests and lochs – breathtaking stuff! The A96 links Inverness with Nairn, a journey of some 25 miles passing Culloden Forest – scene of that rather nasty skirmish. An alternative route from Glasgow is to follow the A82 which runs to the west of Loch Lomond, through Glencoe and along the shores of Loch Ness all the way to Inverness, an equally beautiful road. From the east, the A96 is the main Aberdeen to Inverness road, passing through Nairn. The golf course is located on the town's west shore.

From the medal tees the course measures 6452 yards and has a par of 71 (the Championship tees extend the course by a further 270 yards) whilst the ladies play over 5755 yards, par being 75. Nairn is certainly no monster and accuracy rather than length should determine the quality of scoring. The front nine is the shorter of the two although the prevailing south-westerly may well cause this to be the tougher half. Anyone suffering a bout of the dreaded sliced tee-shot is likely to find himself doing battle with the Moray Firth – the early holes really do run very close to the sea. The Scottish golf writer **Sam McKinlay** clearly relished the early challenge for he once said 'There is no more attractive **1st** tee in all Scotland.' (It's amazing what a good drive can inspire!)

Perhaps the best series of holes, however, are found on the back nine namely holes **12**, **13** and **14.** Anyone who can manage three pars here can call himself a golfer. Staying out of the gorse and avoiding the numerous well-positioned bunkers is undoubtedly the key to a good round, for with the magnificent, and not overly large greens, there is no excuse for poor putting at Nairn.

And so, as they say, to the nineteenth and at Nairn that means entering one of the newest and most relaxing clubhouses in Britain. During summer the Club hosts a number of open competitions and these are invariably well supported. It isn't difficult to imagine why. For those of us who enjoy our golf in pleasant and dramatic surroundings and who occasionally feel the urge to get away from it all, there can surely be no finer place to visit than Nairn.

Hole	Yards	Par	Hole	Yards	Par
1	400	4	10	500	5
2	474	4	11	161	3
3	377	4	12	445	4
4	145	3	13	430	4
5	378	4	14	206	3
6	183	3	15	309	4
7	494	5	16	418	4
8	330	4	17	361	4
9	325	4	18	500	5
Out	**3,106**	**35**	**In**	**3,330**	**36**
			Out	**3,106**	**35**
			TOTALS	**6,436**	**71**

CULLODEN HOUSE

Culloden House is a handsome Georgian mansion with a tradition of lavish hospitality stretching back hundreds of years. Among its famous visitors was Bonnie Prince Charlie who fought his last battles by the park walls. The house stands in forty acres of elegant lawns and parkland, enhanced by stately oaks and beech trees.

The resident proprietors, Ian and Marjory McKenzie, extend a warm welcome to all visitors to their hotel. Culloden House is decorated to the highest standard, particulary the comfortable drawing room, which is decorated with magnificent Adam-style plaster work.

Every bedroom is individually decorated and has redirect dial telephone, television, trouser press, bath and shower. Guests can chose from four-poster bedrooms, standard rooms, or rooms with a jacuzzi. The garden mansion also has non-smoking garden suites for those who wish. Dining is also a memorable experience at Culloden House; the emphasis in the Adam Dining room is on friendly and unobtrusive service, matched by the highest standards of cuisine. The wine cellars hold a superb range of wines from the great vineyards of the world, and there is a wide selection of aged malt whiskies.

Leisure facilities include a hard tennis court, sauna and solarium. There is much to visit in the area - golfing, fishing and shooting can be arranged and the Highlands, Loch Ness and Inverness are just waiting to be explored. Also nearby are Cawdor Castle, the Clava Cairns and Culloden Battlefield.

Situated three miles from the centre of Inverness, off the A96, Inverness - Nairn Road, Culloden House extends the best of Scottish hospitality to all its guests.

Culloden House
Inverness
Scotland
IV1 2NZ
Tel: (0463) 790461
Fax: (0463) 792181

ROYAL DORNOCH
CHAMPIONSHIP GOLF

Usually when a person describes his first visit to a golf course as 'the most fun I've had playing golf in my whole life,' very little is thought of it. However, when that person happens to be **Tom Watson**, five times Open Champion, one tends to sit up and take notice. Like **Ben Crenshaw** and **Greg Norman** who have also made the pilgrimage, Watson was enchanted by the 'Star of the North'.

There are two words that are normally associated with Royal Dornoch; one is 'greatness' and the other is 'remoteness'. Situated fifty miles north of Inverness, Dornoch enjoys a kind of splendid isolation. It is the course every golfer wants to play but the one that very few actually do.

So what is the charm of Dornoch? Firstly, there's the setting (this is when people forgive its remoteness!) Bordered by the Dornoch Firth and a glorious stretch of sand, distant hills with their ever-changing moods fill the horizon creating a feeling that one is playing on a stage. And then of course, there's the history: Royal Dornoch Golf Club dates from 1877 but mention is made of golf being played on the links at least as early as 1616. Writing in the 17th century **Sir Robert Gordon** wrote of Dornoch: 'About this town are the fairest and largest links on any part of Scotland, fit for Archery, Golfing, Ryding and all other exercises; they doe surpasse the fields of Montrose and St Andrews.' Finally, and most importantly, there's the very links itself described on more than one occasion as the most natural golf course in the world; to quote Tom Watson again, 'One of the great courses of the five continents.'

The Secretary at Royal Dornoch is **Mr. Ian Walker**, he may be contacted by telephone on **(0862) 810219** and by fax on (0862) 810729. All written correspondence should be addressed to **The Secretary, Royal Dornoch Golf Club, Golf Road, Dornoch IV25 3LW Sutherland**. **William Skinner** is the Club's professional; he may be reached on **(0862) 810902**.

Visitors are welcome at Royal Dornoch seven days a week. However, it is probably wise to telephone the Club prior to setting off to check if any tee reservations have been made – an ever-growing number of people are now making the trip and during the months of July and August the links can get busy. The cost of a day's golf in 1992 was priced at £45 (£55 at the weekend) with a single round fee (available on weekdays for those teeing

off after 11am) of £25. A weekly ticket is available, priced at £120 in 1992. There is now a second eighteen hole course at Dornoch, the **Struie** course measuring 5242 yards, par 68; a day ticket for this course could be purchased for £13 during the week (£7.50 per round) with £45 securing a full week's golf.

Travelling to Dornoch gets ever easier. The A9 runs from Perth to John O'Groats, Perth being linked to Edinburgh by the M90. There are regular flights from London and other parts of the country to Inverness Airport and the links itself has an adjacent landing strip for light aircraft; moreover there is now a road bridge over the Dornoch Firth and this reduces the motoring time from Inverness to 40 minutes. By today's standards Dornoch could probably be described as being of only medium length, the links measuring 6577 yards, par 70 (s.s.s. 72). However, the last thing in the world that Dornoch is, is an easy course. It has been said that the prevailing wind at Dornoch comes from every direction but even when the winds don't thunder in from across the Firth or down from the hills, the links can be the proverbial 'smiler with the knife'.

Although the club was founded in 1877, ten years later when **'Old' Tom Morris** was brought from St. Andrews to survey the links there was still only a rather crude nine hole layout. The master craftsman set to work and not only completely redesigned the nine but extended the course to a full eighteen holes. By using the natural contours of the terrain many magnificent plateau greens were created and despite major alterations made to the links by **John Sutherland** thirty years later, it is the plateau greens that remain the hallmark of Dornoch, the classic example perhaps being the celebrated **14th**, Foxy, a double dog-leg hole. **Donald Ross**, considered by many to be the greatest of all golf architects was for many years the professional and head green keeper at Dornoch and several of the great American courses he later designed incorporate many of Dornoch's features.

Today there are signs that Dornoch is at last shedding its remoteness tag. In 1985 the Club staged the **Amateur Championship** for the first time in its history – this being in the minds of many alarmingly overdue. It may be to indulge in pure fantasy but one cannot help wondering what it would be like if the hallowed links were ever visited by the greatest of all compliments.

Hole	Yards	Par	Hole	Yards	Par
1	336	4	10	148	3
2	179	3	11	445	4
3	414	4	12	504	5
4	418	4	13	168	3
5	361	4	14	448	4
6	165	3	15	322	4
7	465	4	16	405	4
8	437	4	17	406	4
9	499	5	18	457	4
Out	3,274	35	In	3,303	35
			Out	3,274	35
			TOTALS	6,577	70

CRAIGDARROCH LODGE HOTEL

In a glorious setting at the foot of the mountains midway between the two jewels of highland golf, Royal Dornoch and Nairn what better 19th than CRAIGDARROCH LODGE HOTEL.

After an exhilarating days golf played against an ever changing backdrop of mountain, loch, forest and seascapes come home to CRAIGDARROCH, relax and unwind with good food, good wines and good company.

Once the dower house of the clan McKenzie, CRAIGDARROCH is now a comfortable traditional country house hotel in 8 acres of lawns and woodland with plenty of space to practise your swing. Alternatively you can swim in our new indoor pool, try the sauna and solarium, or enjoy a game of croquet on the lawn. We can also arrange clayshooting, fishing, horse riding, and sailing for you, so there's plenty for the non golfer too.

We offer 3 and 7 night golf packages inclusive of green fees on a selection of 18 hole courses. Tee times are prearranged to avoid disappointment and green fees are paid. All you have to do is play. Alternatively we are happy to tailor a golf holiday to your exact requirements, any number of nights and any of the courses within reasonable travelling distance of the hotel from Golspie and Brora in the North to Boat of Garten in the South and from Gairloch in the West to Elgin in the East.

If your holiday dates are flexible you may be able to take advantage of the special FREE GOLF deals that we run from time to time.

Away from the courses you will something to see or do around every corner. Visit Macbeths castle at Cawdor. Learn how whisky is made and sample a dram at the local distillery. Bask in the sun on an uncrowded beach and swim in the clean warm waters of the Gulf Stream. Cruise around the Summer Isles, and photograph the seals or look for dolphins in the Moray Firth. Explore wild Strathconon and keep an eye on the skyline for eagles, or sit by the falls at Rogie to watch the salmon leap. Climb Ben Wyvis for a view from the North Sea to the Atlantic. Listen to the Strathpeffer pipe band and watch the Highland dancers in the village square on Saturdays.

For the best of golf holidays it has to be Scotland, the home of golf and for the best value in Scotland it has to be CRAIGDARROCH, so let Julia and Mark Garrison and their attentive staff provide for you a most memorable holiday.

Craigdarroch Lodge Hotel
Contin
Ross-shire
IV14 9EH
Tel: (0997) 421265

ALTON BURN HOTEL

Alton Burn Hotel is an imposing building, originally constructed as a Preparatory School in 1901. It stands in it's own grounds overlooking the 17th Tee of the Nairn Golf Club, with glorious views across the course, Moray Firth with the Sutherland Hills in the background. The hotel has been owned and run by the MacDonald family since 1956, and is geared to the needs of the golfer and families in particular.

There are 25 rooms all with Private facilities, Colour T.V., Radio, Baby Listening and Tea & Coffee Makers.

Recreational facilities abound and one can have a relaxing round of putting on the green, or an exacting game of Tennis, followed by a session on the Practice Golf Area, finished off by a swim in the Heated Out-door Swimming Pool. There is also a Games Room with Pool Table and Table Tennis.

Nairn has a very fine Indoor Deck Level Swimming Pool, and Squash can be arranged from the Hotel, for the very energetic guest.

There are many fine courses in the area, and one cannot fail to mention Nairn Dunbar Golf Course – very popular venue for this year's Northern Open and only 2 miles from the Hotel. Forres, Grantown on Spey, Boat of Garten, Elgin, Lossiemouth, Inverness and Dornoch are all within easy driving distance of the Hotel. Inverness Airport is 8 miles from the Hotel and with prior notice, transport to the Hotel is easily arranged. It is possible therefore to be on the Nairn Courses within 2 hours of leaving Heathrow or Gatwick.

The A9 North now makes Nairn very accessible by car, with Edinburgh and Glasgow a comfortable 3 hours driving time. Within the surrounding area Cawdor and Brodie Castles, Loch Ness and the elusive Monster, Culloden Battlefield, Clava Stones are just a few of things to see. If you feel you are 'Over-golfed,' the Whisky Trail is also easily found and never forgotten!

So if you want to get away from it all, and enjoy good golf, good food and good company, there can be no better choice than Alton Burn Hotel, where we can cater for groups of up to 40.

Alton Burn Hotel
Nairn
Scotland

Tel: (0667) 53325

304

GRAMPIAN AND HIGHLAND
COMPLETE GOLF

KEY

*** Visitors welcome at most times
** Visitors usually allowed on weekdays only
* Visitors not normally permitted (Mon, Wed) No visitors on specified days

APPROXIMATE GREEN FEES
A – £30 plus
B – £20 – £30
C – £15 – £25
D – £10 – £20
E – Under £10
F – Green fees on application

RESTRICTIONS
G – Guests only
H – Handicap certificate required
H(24) – Handicap of 24 or less required
L – Letter of introduction required
M – Visitor must be a member of another recognised club.

GRAMPIAN

Aboyne G.C
(03398) 86328
Formaston Park, Aboyne, Aberdeenshire
Signposted on the A93 from Aberdeen
(18) 5330 yards/***/F

Auchenblae G.C
(05612) 407
Auchenblae, Laurencekirk
5 miles N. of Laurencekirk
(9) 2174 yards/***/E

Auchmill G.C
(0224) 642121
Auchmill, Aberdeen
(9) 2538 yards/***/E

Ballater G.C
(03397) 55567
Ballater, Aberdeenshire
40 miles W. of Aberdeen on A93
(18) 5704 yards/***/D

Banchory G.C
(03302) 2365
Kinneskie, Banchory, Kincardineshire
18 miles W. of Aberdeen
(18) 5305 yards/***/F

Balnagask G.C
(0224) 876407
St Fitticks Road, Aberdeen
2 miles S.E of the city centre
(18) 5468 yards/***/E

Bon-Accord G.C
(0224) 633464
19 Golf Course Road, Aberdeen
Beside Pittodrie Stadium near the beach
(18) 6384 yards/***/F

Braemar G.C
(03397) 41618
Cluniebank, Braemar, Aberdeenshire
Half mile from the village centre
(18) 4916 yards/***/E

Buckpool G.C
(0542) 32236
Barhill Road, Buckie, Banffshire
At end of A98 to Buckpool
(18) 6259 yards/***/E

Caledonian G.C
(0224) 632 443
20 Golf Road, Aberdeen
Adjacent to the Pittodrie Stadium
(18) 6384 yards/***/F

Cruden Bay G.C
(0779) 812285
Aulton Road, Cruden Bay, Peterhead, Aberdeenshire
7 miles S. of Peterhead
(9) 4710 yards/***/E
(18) 6370 yards/***/F

Cullen G.C
(0542) 40585
The Links, Cullen, Buckie, Banffshire
W. of Cullen off the A98
(18) 4610 yards/***/E

Deeside G.C
(0224) 867697
Bieldside, Aberdeen
3 miles W. of Aberdeen on the A93
(18) 6332 yards/***/D/H or M or L

Duff House Royal G.C
(02612) 2062
Barnyards, Banff, Banffshire
2 minutes from town centre off A97 and A98
(18) 6161 yards/***/F/H

Elgin G.C
(0343) 54238
Hardhillock, Elgin, Morayshire
Signposted off the A91
(18) 6401 yards/***/D

Forres G.C
(0309) 72949
Muiryshade, Forres
1 mile S. from town centre
(18) 5615 yards/***/E/H

Fraserburgh G.C
(0346) 28287
Philorth, Fraserburgh, Aberdeenshire
1 mile S.E of Fraserburgh on the A92
(18) 6217 yards/***/E

Garmouth and Kingston G.C
(034 387) 388
Garmouth, Fochabers, Moray
(18) 5649 yards/***/E

Hazelhead G.C
(0224) 321830
Hazelhead Park, Aberdeen
4 miles W. of the city centre
(18) 5303 yards/***/E
(18) 5673 yards/***/E

Hopeman G.C
(0343) 830578
Hopeman, Moray
(18) 5439 yards/***/E

Huntly G.C
(0466) 2643
Cooper Park, Huntly, Aberdeenshire
Half mile from town centre on the A96
(18) 5399 yards/***/(not Wed or Thur)/F/H

Inverallochy G.C
(03465) 2324
Inverallochy, Nr Fraserburgh, Aberdeenshire
3 miles S. of Fraserburgh on the B9033
(18) 5137 yards/***/E

Inverurie G.C
(0467) 24080
Blackhall Road, Inverurie, Aberdeenshire
On the A96 Aberdeen-Inverness Road
(18) 5096 yards/***/E

Keith G.C
(05422) 2469
Fife Park, Keith, Banffshire
Half mile off the A96
(18) 5811 yards/***/F

Kings Links G.C
(0224) 632269
Golf Road, Kings Links, Aberdeen
E. of city, near Pittodrie Stadium
(18) 5838 metres/***/E

Kintore G.C
(0467) 32631
Balbithan Road, Kintore, Inverurie, Aberdeenshire
12 miles N.W. of Aberdeen off the A96
(9) 2650 yards/***/E

Macdonald G.C
(0358) 20576
Hospital Road, Ellon, Aberdeenshire
Leave Ellon on A948 for Auchnagatt
(18) 5986 yards/***/E

Moray G.C
(034 381) 2018
Stotfield Road, Lossiemouth, Moray
6 miles N. of Elgin off the A941
(18)6643 yards/***/F/H
(18)6005 yards/***/F/H

Murcar G.C
(0224) 704354
Bridge of Don, Aberdeen
3 miles N.E of Aberdeen on the A92
(18) 6240 yards/**/F

Newburgh-On-Ythan G.C
Newburgh, Aberdeenshire
14 miles N. of Aberdeen on the Peterhead Road
(9) 6404 yards/***(not Tues pm)/F

Nigg Bay G.C
(0224) 871286
St Fitticks Road, Balnagask, Aberdeen
S.E of the city centre
(18) 5984 yards/***/E

Peterhead G.C
(0779) 72149
Craigewan Links, Peterhead, Aberdeenshire
30 miles from Aberdeen, between A92 and A975
(18) 6182 yards/***/D
(9) 2950 yards/***/E

Royal Aberdeen G.C
(0224) 702571
Balgownie, Bridge of Don, Aberdeen
Over River Don, 2 miles N. of Aberdeen on A92
(18) 4033 yards/**/F/H
(18) 6372 yards/**/F/H

Royal Tarlair G.C
(0261) 32897
Buchan Street, Macduff
48 miles from Aberdeen on the A98
(18) 5866 yards/***/D

Spey Bay G.C
(0343) 820424
Spey Bay, Fochabers, Moray
Follow the B9104 Spey Bay road to the coast
(18) 6059 yards/***/F/H

Stonehaven G.C
(0569) 62124
Cowie, Stonehaven
N. of the town on the A92
(18) 5103 yards/***(not Sat/Sun am)/F

Strathlene G.C
(0542) 31798
Portessie, Buckie, Banffshire
Take A942 to Buckie and to Strathlene
(18) 6180 yards/***/E

Tarland G.C
(033981) 81413
Tarland, Aboyne, Aberdeenshire
3 miles W. of Aberdeen on the A93
(9) 5812 yards/***/E

Torphins G.C
(033982) 493
Golf Road, Torphins, Banchory, Aberdeenshire
6 miles W. of Banchory on A980
(9) 2330 yards/***/E

Turriff G.C
(0888) 62745
Rosehall, Turriff, Aberdeenshire
Signposted off the B9024
(18) 6105 yards/***/E

Westhill G.C
(0224) 740159
Westhill Heights, Westhill, Skene, Aberdeenshire
6 miles from Aberdeen on the A944
(18) 5866 yards/***(not Sat/Sun pm)/E/H

HIGHLAND

Abernethy G.C
(0479 82) 637
Nethybridge, Inverness-shire
N. of Nethybridge on the B970
(9) 2484 yards/***/F

Alness G.C
(0349) 883877
Ardross Road, Alness, Ross-shire
10 miles N.E. of Dingwall on the A9
(9) 4718 yards/***/E

J Hassall   'A DRIVE'   Burlington Gallery

THE BURGHFIELD HOUSE HOTEL

Originally the home of Lord Rothermere and now commended by the Scottish Tourist board, Burghfield House has been run by the Currie family as a hotel since 1946. This welcoming family atmosphere is well in evidence and the hotel is relaxed and friendly. Standing in over five acres of beautiful gardens it overlooks the city of Dornoch with its fascinating 13th century cathedral.

The elegant restaurant can seat 120 people, this is particularly useful as the hotel is renowned for its superb food and great pride is taken in the preparation and serving of the extensive menu which boasts classical dishes to mouth-watering Highland fare, which makes good use of the very best of the fresh, local produce including prime beef, game, salmon and shellfish. Vegetables and flowers are grown in the hotel's own greenhouses and gardens. There is an excellent wine list available to complement the menu.

For the serious golfer, the Burghfield is only a few minutes drive from the renowned Royal Dornoch Golf Course. Ranked as the 10th greatest course in the world by an international panel of golf architects, professionals and journalists, it is a wonderful course to play. It is also a fabulously historic course indeed golf has been played on these links since 1616. The 14th, Foxy, is considered by many to be the finest natural hole in the game. As one would expect, the hotel has had a long association with the course and can arrange bookings, tee-times etc. For a change of scenery the courses of Tain, Golspie and Brora are also close by.

For a break from the golf, this is an excellent centre for exploring the beauty of the North, with miles of sandy beaches nearby and a number of stunning lochs available for fishing.

All of the 38 bedrooms have private facilities and colour television; all have radio, direct-dial telephones, baby listening and tea/coffee making facilities.

Following extensive re-furbishment during 1991 the hotel boasts two lounges, two cocktail bars, a TV room, games room and more than enough space for energetic children and energetic golfers.

The Burghfield House Hotel
Dornoch
Sutherland
Scotland IV25 3HN
Tel: (0862) 810212

GRAMPIAN AND HIGHLAND
COMPLETE GOLF

Askernish G.C
Askernish, Lochboisdale, South Uist,
Western Isles
Take ferry from Oban to S.Uist
(9) 5114 yards/***/F

Boat of Garten G.C
(0479 83) 282
Boat of Garten, Inverness-shire
Take the A9 to the B970
(18) 5720 yards/***/E

Brora G.C
(0408) 21417
Golf Road, Brora, Sutherland
65 miles N. of Inverness on the A9
(18) 6110 yards/***/F

Carrbridge G.C
(047984) 674
Carrbridge, Inverness-shire
200 yards from the village on the A938
(9) 2623 yards/***/F

Fort Augustus G.C
(0320) 6460
Markethill, Fort Augustus, Inverness-shire
Entrance is just off the A82
(9) 5454 yards/***/E

Fortrose and Rosemarkie G.C
(0381) 20529
Ness Road East, Fortrose, Ross-shire
Take A9 from Inverness and follow signs to
Fortrose
(18) 5973 yards/***/F

Fort William G.C
(0397) 4464
North Road, Turlundy, Fort William
2 miles N. of Fort William off the A82
(18) 5686 yards/***/F

Gairloch G.C
(0455) 2407
Gairloch, Ross-shire
S. of the town, on the A832
(9) 2093 yards/***(not Sun)/E

Golspie G.C
(04083) 3266
Ferry Road, Golspie, Sutherland
Take A9 from Inverness to Golspie
(18) 5900 yards/***/F

Grantown-On-Spey G.C
(0479) 2079
Golf Course Road, Grantown-On-Spey
N. of town off the A939
(18) 5745 yards/***/E

Invergordon G.C
(0349) 852116
Cromlet Drive, Invergordon, Ross and
Cromarty
The club house is in King Geoge Street
(9) 6028 yards/***/E

Inverness G.C
(0463) 239882
Culcabock Road, Inverness
1 mile from town centre on S. of River Ness
(18) 6226 yards/***/D/H

Kingussie G.C
(054 02) 600
Gynack Road, Kingussie, Inverness-shire
Take A9 to village and follow signs
(18) 5504 yards/***/E

Lybster G.C
Main Street, Lybster, Caithness
13 miles S. of Wick on the A9
(9) 1898 yards/***/E

Muir of Ord G.C
(0463) 870825
Great Northern Road, Muir of Ord, Ross and
Cromarty
12 miles N. of Inverness on the A862
(18) 5129 yards/***/E

Nairn G.C
(0667) 53208
Seabank Road, Nairn
1 mile N. of the A96, near Nairn
(18) 6556 yards/***/F/H

Nairn Dunbar G.C
(0667) 52741
Lochloy Road, Nairn
Half mile E. of town on the A96
(18) 6431 yards/***/D

Newtonmore G.C
(05403) 328
Golf Course Road, Newtonmore, Inverness-
shire
Near centre of village off the A9
(18) 5890 yards/***/E

Reay G.C
(084 781) 288
By Thurso, Caithness
11 miles W. of Thurso towards Bettyhill
(18) 5865 yards/***/E

Royal Dornoch G.C
(0862) 810219
Golf Road, Dornoch, Sutherland
Take A949 for Dornoch and follow signs
(18) 6577 yards/***/F/H
(9)***/F

Sconser G.C
(0478) 2277
Sconser, Isle of Skye, Inverness-shire
Between Broadford and Portree on the
main road
(9) 4796 yards/***/E

Stornoway G.C
(0851) 2240
Castle Grounds, Stornoway, Isle of Lewis
Near town centre, in castle grounds
(18) 5119 yards/***(not Sun)/E/H

Strathpeffer Spa G.C
(0997) 21219
Strathpeffer, Ross-shire
5 miles W. of Dingwall on the A834
(18) 4792 yards/***/E

Tain G.C
(0862) 2314
Tain, Ross-shire
Half mile from town centre off A9 N.
(18) 6222 yards/***/F

Tarbat G.C
(086287) 236
Portmahomack, Ross-shire
7 miles E. of Tain on the B9165 off A9
(9) 2329 yards***(not Sun)/E

Thurso G.C
(0847) 63807
Newlands of Geise, Thurso, Caithness
2 miles S.W of Thurso station on B870
(18) 5818 yards/***/E

Torvean G.C
(0463) 237543
Glenurquhart Road, Inverness, Inverness-shire
1 mile W. of city on the A82
(18) 4308 yards/***/F

Wick G.C
(0955) 2726
Reiss, Wick, Caithness
3 miles N. of Wick on the A9
(18) 5976 yards/***/E

ORKNEY AND SHETLAND

Orkney G.C
(0856) 2457
Grainbank, St Ola, by Kirkwall, Orkney
Half mile W. of Kirkwall
(18) 5406 yards/***/E

Shetland G.C
(059584) 369
Dale, P.O Box 18, Lerwick, Shetland
3 miles N. of Lerwick on the main road
(18) 5776 yards/***/E

Stromness G.C
(0856) 850772
Ness, Stromness, Orkney
(18) 4600 yards/***/E

Shortspoon   IN THE BURN   Burlington Gallery

DUMFRIES, GALLOWAY AND BORDERS

BALCARY BAY HOTEL
Auchencairn, Nr. Castle Douglas, Tel: (055664) 217
Despite a rich history that was wrapped up with local smuggling practices, Balcary today concentrates on Scottish hospitality, modern facilities and traditional atmosphere. The presence of the Gulf Stream ensures a predominantly mild climate, enabling visitors to enjoy local golf and fishing.

COMLONGON CASTLE
Clarencefield, Dumfries, Tel: (038) 787 283
Cromlongon offers guests excellent hospitality in an awe-inspiring setting. Rooms are spacious and comfortable and fifty acres of grounds provide nature trails and woodland walks. Golf and fishing are also to be found nearby.

CORSEMALZIE HOUSE HOTEL
Port William, Newton Stewart, Wigtownshire, Tel: (098) 886254
This popular hotel is perfect for golfers, anglers and active tourists, with Culzean Castle not too far afield.

CREEBRIDGE HOUSE HOTEL
Newton Stewart, Wigtownshire, Tel: (0671) 2121
Built in 1760 and formerly owned by the Earl of Galloway, the hotel sits in three acres of gardens and woodlands and is now an eighteen bedroom Country House Hotel with accommodation of an extremely high standard. Excellent local fishing is on hand.

CRINGLETIE HOUSE HOTEL,
Peebles, Tel: (0672 13) 244
Cringletie is an elegant and distinguished mansion, that exudes the genteel atmosphere of a country house. At only twenty miles from Edinburgh, there is no shortage of things to do and places to see.

EAST BARCLOY
Colvend, Dalbeattie, Dumfries, Tel: (055663) 424
Guests are assured of a warm welcome, fantastic cooking and comfortable rooms at this highly recommended farmhouse cottage. Mr and Mrs Beckitt make friendly and attentive hosts.

HEATHERLIE HOUSE HOTEL
Heatherlie Park, Selkirk, Tel: (0750) 21200
Heatherlie is a privately owned and managed mansion house of great character, set in secluded wooded grounds that offer interesting walks. The hotel is noted for its relaxed, friendly atmosphere, for its excellent food prepared by Mrs Fleming and for an extensive wine list.

HOEBRIDGE INN
Gattonside, Melrose, Tel: (0896 82) 3082
This locally renowned restaurant comes highly recommended. Enjoy a freshly prepared meal of local game, fish, a vegetarian dish or one of many Italian specialities in a friendly informal atmosphere. Managed by Chef proprietor Carlo Campari and his wife Joy, the restaurant is only ten minutes from Melrose and Galashiels.

MENNOCKFOOT LODGE HOTEL
Mennock, By Sanquar, Dumfriesshire, Tel:(0659) 50382
For golfers and anglers, Mennockfoot Lodge is a splendid retreat. Fishing is to be had in abundance within twenty yards of the hotel, whilst the golf courses of Sanquar, Thornhill and many others await the enthusiast.

SELKIRK ARMS HOTEL
High Street, Kirkcudbright, Tel: (0557) 30402
Set in the pretty fishing town of Kirkubright, the hotel has sixteen bedrooms, all ensuite. A fine restaurant is justly proud of its dishes, made from fresh Galloway beef or locally caught fish, especially Dover Sole and Scallops.

SOLWAYSIDE HOUSE HOTEL AND RESTAURANT
Auchencairn, Castle Douglas, Tel: (055) 664 280
A comfortable, family run hotel offering good food and superb sea and country views. Amongst the many local attractions are Dundrennan Castle, Sweetheart Abbey and Threave Garden and Castle. Excellent local fishing is also available.

THE IMPERIAL HOTEL
35 King Street, Castle Douglas, Southerness, Tel: (0556) 2086
The Imperial enjoys a central, convenient location and makes a perfect holiday base. Golfers are particularly well catered for with Castle Douglas and the acclaimed Southerness little more than a well struck drive away.

FIFE

COTTAGE,
Blairburn, Culross, Tel: (0383) 880704
Centrally situated and convenient for Perth, Stirling, Glasgow and Edinburgh, this guesthouse is naturally popular with wayfarers travelling in various directions. A bedtime drink is one of many thoughtful extras.

DUNBOG,
Newburgh, Fife, KY14 6JF, Tel: (0337) 40455
Dunbog is a charming farm house situated in the gentle hills of Fife, close to the river Tay. Two comfortable twin bedrooms are both ensuite and evening meals can be arranged by appointment.

DYKES,
69 Pittenweem Road, Anstruther, Tel: (0333) 310537
Modern bungalow at town's edge, set in large garden with beautiful unimpeded views over local golf course to the sea and landward to the hills of Fife. St Andrews is only nine miles away and the picturesque East Neuk fishing villages and harbours are similarly close. Anstruther is the home of a fisheries' museum.

GREIGSTON FARM,
Peat Inn, Cupar, Tel: (033) 484284
This elderly stone house offers comfortable accommodation in an attractive environment – interior and exterior. Meals are most definitely edible, served by a friendly host.

RED HOUSE,
Freuchie, Falkland, Tel: (0337) 57555
The golfing kingdom of Fife is a golfer's paradise and The Red House will spare no effort to ensure a memorable stay. However the delights of Fife are far from limited to golf and guests will find a multitude of things to do and see.

RESCOBIE HOTEL,
Rescobie Hotel, Leslie, Fife, Tel: (0592) 742143
Ten comfortable and well appointed bedrooms make this hotel a perennial favourite. Every effort will be made to accommodate conferences and receptions with an added bonus of special 3 and 6 day sporting rates.

ROYAL HOTEL,
20 Rodger Street, Anstruther, Tel: (0333) 310581
The Royal attracts more than its fair share of local and visiting trade. all are attracted, no doubt, by tastefully furnished bedrooms and a splendid restaurant. Special golfing rates are available.

SCORES HOTEL,
St Andrews, Fife, Tel: (0334) 72451
The Scores is a traditional, 3-star, independently owned hotel with magnificent views over St Andrews Bay and the Royal and Ancient Clubhouse. First-time visitors are always delighted to discover that the first tee of the Old Course is practically opposite the hotel.

THE SPENDRIFT,
Pittenweem Road, Anstruther, Fife, Tel: (0333) 310573
Escape to a little piece of paradise in the heart of Fife. All bedrooms have private facilities, colour TV, hospitality tray and sea views. Golf and fishing opportunities abound, together with a wealth of local attractions.

GRAMPIAN AND HIGHLAND

ARISAIG HOUSE,
Beasdale, Arisaig, Inverness-shire, Tel: (068 75) 622
Arisaig House lies by the famous Road to the Isles to the west of Fort William. Built in 1864, the hotel offers elegant and high-standard accommodation amid beautiful gardens and spectacular scenery.

AUCHENDEAN LODGE,
Dulnain Bridge, Grantown-on-Spey, Morayshire, Tel: (047) 985 347
Situated high above the river Spey, eight comfortable bedrooms make this a perfect base for no less than ten golf courses within forty-five minutes drive. Auchendean Lodge also features log fires, award-winning food, forest and mountain views and excellent fishing.

CALEDONIAN THISTLE HOTEL,
Union Terrace, Aberdeen, Tel: (0224) 640233
This excellent city-centre hotel offers elegant accommodation and modern facilities. Aberdeen is a thriving city with a wealth of attractions. Local golfers and anglers are also superbly catered for.

COPTHORNE,
122 Huntly Street, Aberdeen, Tel: (0224) 630404
The Copthorne combines the facilities of a first-class international hotel with traditional Scottish hospitality. This elegant establishment, in association with Better Golf Scotland, can also offer the opportunity of sampling twelve local golf courses including the renowned Royal Aberdeen.

CORROUR HOUSE HOTEL,
Inverdruie, Aviemore, Inverness-shire, Tel: (0479) 810220
The many and varied attractions of Aviemore make this comfortable hotel perfect for a family holiday. A range of accommodation is available and discounts are available during the low season. There is naturally much to occupy keen golfers and fishermen.

CRAIGELLACHIE HOTEL,
Craigellachie, Aberlour, Banffshire, Tel: (0340) 881204
A wealth of sporting and leisure opportunities await visitors to this splendid hotel. As well as a gym, sauna and solarium, tennis, golf and fishing are all within easy reach. Nearby Balmoral is an additional attraction.

CRANNTARA GUESTHOUSE,
High Street, Grantown-on-Spey, Tel: (0479) 2197
This comfortable guesthouse offers friendly service and a wealth of local amenities. Golfers and fishermen are particularly well catered for with numerous local golf courses and trout/salmon fishing easily available. Excellent local produce is served in the Dining Room.

CULDUTHEL LODGE,
14 Culduthel Road, Inverness, Tel: (0463) 240089
Culduthel Lodge is a Georgian Mansion Hotel located in lively Inverness. All bedrooms are tastefully furnished and offer extensive views of the beautiful surroundings. Inverness golf club is within one mile and Royal Dornoch and Nairn are tantalisingly close.

DELNASHAUGH INN,
Ballindalloch, Banffshire, Tel: (08072) 255
This recently renovated and refurbished Old Drovers Inn is ideally placed between the rivers Avon and Spey. The hotel is personally run by proprietors Mr and Mrs D.M. Ogden who will be pleased to advise on local fishing, shooting, golf and malt whisky trails.

DUNAIN PARK HOTEL,
Dunain Park, Inverness, Tel: (0463) 230512
Twelve comfortable twin and double rooms in this elegant house are complemented by an award winning restaurant, indoor heated swimming pool, sauna and six acres of beautiful gardens. Excellent local fishing and golf are easy to find.

EIGHT ACRES HOTEL,
Sherrifmill, Elgin, Moray, Tel: (0343) 543077
This popular establishment is equipped to satisfy every holiday requirement. Weddings and conferences can also be arranged, with visitors able to enjoy the indoor pool, squash courts, sauna, gym and solarium.

GLENGARRY HOUSE HOTEL,
Invergarry, Inverness-shire, Tel: (08093) 254
A range of comfortable accommodation is available at this highly recommended hotel. All rooms are furnished to a high standard and offer relaxing comfort after a day's energetic golf, tennis or fishing.

HAUGH HOTEL,
Cromdale, Morayshire, PH26 3LW, Tel: (0479) 2583
This comfortable roadside hotel on the banks of the river Spey is an ideal base for a Highland holiday. This is an area famous for its fishing, malt whiskies and many local places of interest. Four good golf courses are within a short drive.

HOTEL SEAFORTH,
Dundee Road, Arbroath, Tel: (0241) 72232
This is an extremely comfortable and welcoming hotel and is convenient for the wealth of golf courses that characterize this area. The Elliot course is virtually on the hotel doorstep and famous Carnoustie is a mere six miles away. The hotel has an indoor leisure suite and a snooker room.

KILBRECK GUEST HOUSE,
410 Great Western Road, Aberdeen, Tel: (0224) 316115
Situated in a quiet, residential area in the west end of the city, Kilbreck offers comfort and service and is within easy reach of many places of interest such as Drum Castle, Crathes Castle, Fyvie Castle, Fraser Castle and Craigievar Castle.

KNOCKOMIE HOTEL,
Grantown Road, Forres, Moray, Tel: (0309) 673146
The challenging course at Forres is only a mile from this pleasant hotel, with the famous links at Lossiemouth not much further afield. Conferences and weddings can be catered for.

LINKS HOTEL,
1 Seafield Street, Nairn, Tel: (0667) 53321
The Links Hotel is conveniently located midway between the challenging links of Nairn and Nairn Dunbar with magnificent views of the Black Isle. Ten comfortable bedrooms are at the disposal of touring golfers and anybody also exploring the glorious Highlands of Scotland.

LOVAT ARMS HOTEL,
Beauly, Nr. Inverness, Tel: (0463) 782313
Good food and comfort are available in this elegant 'A' listed building. All rooms are ensuite with telephone, T.V. and tea/coffee maker. The Capital of the Highlands, Inverness, is only ten miles distant. Local golf and fishing is plentiful.

NETHER LOCHABER HOTEL,
Onich, Fort William, Inverness-shire, Tel: (085) 53235
This comfortable and cosy Highland inn is an ideal base from which to explore Lochaber, the Ardnamurchan Peninsula and Glencoe. Traditional home cooking goes hand-in-hand with homely service and accommodation.

POLMAILY HOUSE HOTEL,
Drumnadrochit, Inverness-shire, Tel: (045 62) 343
Polmaily House is a small, comfortable Country House Hotel situated on the slopes of Glen Urquhart. Great golf can be played at Dornoch and Nairn, fishing is available locally and Cawdor and Brodie are nearby stately homes.

SCOTLAND
GOURMET GOLF

ROSSLEA HALL HOTEL,
Ferry Road, Rhu, Helensburgh, Dunbartonshire, Tel: (0436) 820684
Full amenities and facilities are found at this highly recommended hotel. Conferences and weddings can be tailored to individual requirements, with local fishing and golf a bonus for the leisure enthusiast.

ROYAL HOTEL,
Fortrose, Tel: (0381) 20236
The Royal is the perfect location for a Highland golfing break with Fortrose, Rosemarkie and Nairn amongst others within easy reach. All rooms are well appointed and are complemented by good food and hospitality.

ROYAL HOTEL (CAITHNESS),
Trail Street, Thurso, Caithness, Tel: (0847) 63191/2
This is a large, 104 bedroom, family-run hotel. All rooms have private facilities, T.V. and tea and coffee making facilities. Three golf courses – Thurso, Reay and Wick are within easy reach and discounts can be arranged.

ST ANNS HOUSE HOTEL,
37 Harrowden Road, Inverness, Tel: (0463) 236157
A first class, family run establishment enjoying a reputation for friendliness and good service. All rooms have central heating and colour T.V.s. The town centre is only ten minutes walk away.

SUNNY BRAE GUESTHOUSE,
Marine Road, Nairn, Tel:(0667) 52309
This relaxing guesthouse is an ideal base for touring the North of Scotland, with golf at Nairn an additional attraction. Cawdor and Brodie are well worth an inspection. Clean, reasonably priced accommodation is provided.

THE STAGE HOUSE,
Glenfinnan, Inverness-shire, Tel: (0397) 83246
This beautiful old coaching inn dates back to 1658 and is situated in a picturesque glen at the head of Loch Shiel. The hotel owns fishing rights on Loch Shiel which is famous for salmon and sea trout.

LOTHIAN

HOPE COTTAGE,
Stenton, By Dunbar, Tel: (03685) 293
Hope Cottage provides travellers with a comfortable resting place. Situated in a conservation village between the Lammermuir Hills and the sea, Hope Cottage is ideally situated for golf, fishing and racing.

Robert Turnbull   CLEAR FAIRWAYS   Private Collection

SCOTLAND
GOURMET GOLF

MALLARD HOTEL,
East Links Road, Gullane, East Lothian, Tel: (0620) 843288
One of the area's most popular hotels, the Mallard is a popular haunt for both locals and visitors. Many notable golf courses are within easy reach, in particular Gullane's three courses and Muirfield.

OPEN ARMS HOTEL,
Dirleton, East Lothian, Tel: (0620) 85 241
This is a splendid hotel that offers the highest standard of accommodation, in a quiet, intimate atmosphere. Golf, fishing, racing and many places of interest are all within easy reach.

POINT GARRY HOTEL,
20 West Bay Road, North Berwick, Tel: (0620) 2380
The attractive resort of North Berwick is the location for this popular hotel. The acclaimed West Course is literally a few yards away and there are plenty of alternative courses and places of interest.

SIBBET HOUSE,
26 Northumberland Street, Edinburgh, Tel: 031-556 1078
Sibbet House was built in 1809 and is generously furnished with antiques and draperies. An elegant and comfortable Georgian family home, Sibbet offers well-appointed guest rooms with private facilities.

STUART HOUSE,
12 East Claremont Street, Edinburgh, Tel: 031-557 9030
Stuart House is a lovely Georgian-style Town House located in the refined elegance of New Town, Edinburgh. All bedrooms are ensuite and also feature direct-dial telephone, colour television and tea/coffee hospitality tray.

WOODLANDS,
55 Barnton Avenue, Davidson Mains, Edinburgh, Tel: 031-336 1685
Edinburgh is renowned for the number and quality of its golf courses and this comfortable Bed & Breakfast overlooks the eleventh tee of one of its finest, Royal Burgess. The equally challenging Bruntsfield course is also within close proximity.

STRATHCLYDE

ARDSHEAL HOUSE HOTEL,
Kentallen of Appin, Argyll, Tel: (063) 174 227
This historic Stewart Manor house, now a small country hotel, is set in nine hundred acres of the woods and meadows of the magnificent West Highlands. A shorefront location completes the idyllic picture.

ARDSHIEL HOTEL,
Kilkerren Road, Campbeltown, Tel: (0586) 552133
The spectacular links of Machrihanish is only three miles from this popular establishment. Anglers will find excellent sport at Lussa reservoir whilst Brodick Castle is one of several local places of historic interest.

ARGYLL ARMS HOTEL,
60 Main Street, Campbeltown, Tel: (0586) 553431
This town centre hotel is a popular meeting place amongst the local population and provides high-quality accommodation for visitors. A restaurant serves appetizing fare and snooker provides indoor relaxation.

BLACKWATERFOOT HOTEL,
Isle of Arran, Tel: (0770 86) 202,
A warm welcome is the order of the day at this friendly, family-run hotel in the glorious Isle of Arran. Good food is an additional bonus.

DRUIMNACROISH COUNTRY HOUSE HOTEL,
Druimnacroish, Isle of Mull, Argyll, Tel: (06884) 274
Druimnacroish is a small, exclusive Hotel, situated in the beautiful Bellart Glen. A Scottish country house atmosphere contributes to a uniquely personal service for guests. The hotel has its own stalking and can arrange fishing.

KIRKTON HOUSE,
Cardross, Dunbartonshire, Tel: (0389) 841 951
This comfortable guesthouse is within easy reach of the thriving city of Glasgow and its huge array of attractions. Pollok House and the fantastic Burrell collection will be of particular interest to many patrons.

MALIN COURT,
Turnberry, Ayrshire, Tel: (0655) 31457
There are few more inspiring sights in the world of golf than Turnberry and Malin Court has the good fortune to overlook the famous links. The quiet, ranch style building is tastefully furnished.

MARINE HIGHLAND HOTEL,
Troon, Ayrshire, KA10 6HE, Tel: (0292) 314444
Only 45 minutes from Glasgow and five minutes from Prestwick Airport, the Marine Highland is one of Scotland's finest hotels. Seventy two immaculately furnished bedrooms are complemented by a fine range of cuisine and breathtaking views across to the Isle of Arran.

RICHMOND HOTEL,
38 Park Circus, Ayr, Tel: (0292) 265153
Situated in a quiet conservation area minutes from the town centre, this friendly, family run guesthouse offers good food and comfortable, ensuite bedrooms. The racecourse and dozens of golf courses are within easy reach.

SAVOY PARK HOTEL,
16 Racecourse Road, Ayr, Tel: (0292) 266112
An elegant building and traditional furnishings are features of this comfortable, family run hotel. A high level of service and cuisine also ensures that guests return regularly, with the nearby racecourse a popular attraction.

SOUTH BEACH HOTEL,
South Beach, Troon, Tel: (0292) 312033
The popular seaside town of Troon is the setting for this well established hotel. Rooms are nicely furnished and include two luxury penthouse suites. Local places of interest include Burns Cottage and Blairquhan Castle.

ST NICHOLAS HOTEL,
41 Ayr Road, Prestwick, Tel: (0292) 79568
This well established hotel is within five miles of numerous well known golf courses. All bedrooms have colour TV, phones and en suite bathrooms. Meals are served from 1200-1400 and 1700-2100 hrs.

TAYSIDE AND CENTRAL

BHEINNE MHOR,
Perth Road, Birnam, Dunkeld, Tel: (0350) 727779
This charming, Victorian turreted house offers four comfortable guestrooms with modern amenities. Features include an attractive guest TV lounge and good home-cooking, together with a splendid setting in the heart of Perthshire.

CENTRAL HOTEL,
Church Street, Edzell, Tel: (0356) 648218
Twenty comfortable and well appointed rooms are at the disposal of guests in this highly recommended establishment. Edzell golf course is nearby, and the challenges of St Andrews and Carnoustie are well within reach.

CLAYMORE HOTEL,
Atholl Road, Pitlochry, Tel: (0796) 472888
This superbly situated, high class hotel is convenient for Pitlochry golf course and provides an ideal base for exploring the magnificent local countryside. Hospitality and cuisine are both first class.

CLUNIE GUESTHOUSE,

12 Pitcullen Crescent, Perth, Tel: (0738) 23625

This appealing guesthouse is conveniently situated for the many delights of the city of Perth. Seven comfortable bedrooms will ensure that guests depart refreshed and relaxed. Murrayshall restaurant and golf course are only minutes away.

COLLEARN HOUSE HOTEL,

Auchterarder, Perthshire, Tel: (0764) 63553

Golf, fishing and heritage devotees will find this relaxing guesthouse a perfect location. Gleneagles, the rivers Earn and Tay and Scone Palace are all worthy of exploration. Special three-day stays are available.

COSHIEVILLE HOTEL,

By Aberfeldy, Perthshire, Tel: (0887) 830319

The Coshieville is a small country inn with pleasant ensuite accommodation and a relaxed atmosphere. Traditional Scottish food is served by happy and attentive staff, guaranteeing guests an extremely agreeable stay.

FORTINGALL HOTEL,

By Aberfeldy, Perthshire, PH15 2NQ, Tel: (0887) 830367

Fortingall Hotel is a friendly family concern situated amongst some of Scotland's finest scenic and landscaped conservation areas. Accommodation is tastefully designed and leisure pursuits available include fishing and deer-stalking, there are also numerous golf courses nearby.

GAVELMORE HOUSE,

Gavelmore Street, Crieff, Perthshire, Tel: (0764) 2277

This comfortable Georgian house is located close to the centre of picturesque Crieff, near to the challenging 18-hole golf course. Numerous other courses, including Gleneagles are within reach and Perth also provides regular race meetings.

GRAIGOWER HOTEL,

134-136 Athull Road, Pitlochry, Perthshire, Tel: (0796) 472590

One of Scotland's prettiest and best-known towns, Pitlochry is a never-changing joy for tourists, and the Craigower Hotel makes an extremely convenient headquarters.

GUINACH HOUSE,

By the Birks, Aberfeldy, Tel: (0887) 820251

The agreeable combination of excellent accommodation and spectacular scenery can be discovered through a stay at this comfortable hotel. Golf, fishing and racing are all available in the vicinity and Scone Palace and Blair Castle are other notable attractions.

IONA GUEST HOUSE,

2 Pitcullen Crescent, Perth, Tel: (0738) 27261

A warm welcome awaits at this popular guesthouse. Rooms, many of which are ensuite, feature colour TV, hospitality trays and central heating. A residents lounge is available all day, and excellent evening meals will satisfy every palate.

LETTER FARM,

Loch of Lowes, By Dunkeld, Perthshire, Tel: (0350) 724254

Set in the heart of Perthshire's best fishing waters and ideally situated for several challenging golf courses, Scone Palace, Blair and Glamis Castles, Letter Farm offers quality accommodation in a tranquil location. Bird and wildlife enthusiasts will also find both in abundance.

THE NORTHERN HOTEL,

2-4 Clerk Street, Brechin, Scotland, DD9 6AE, Tel: (0356) 622156

This well-known and established hotel caters for the business and holiday traveller alike. Brechin is situated between Aberdeen and Dundee in the heart of golf-rich Angus and is also at the centre of some of the best fishing and shooting on the East Coast.

THE OLD BANK HOUSE,

Brown Street, Blairgowrie, Perthshire, Tel: (0250) 872902

Situated adjacent to Rosemount golf course, The Old Bank House has been tastefully converted, retaining the elegance of the Georgian era, whilst having a warm, relaxed atmosphere. The beautifully furnished bedrooms are all ensuite and the cuisine on offer is highly recommended.

TIGH-NA-CLOICH HOTEL,

Larchwood Road, Pitlochry, Tel: (0796) 472216

Hospitality, comfort, good food and beautiful views typify this small, highly-recommended Highland hotel. Bedrooms are thoughtfully and pleasantly furnished and the traditional Scottish dishes are prepared using the best of local produce.

Charles Crombie   RULE XVIII   Rosenstiel's

NORTHERN IRELAND

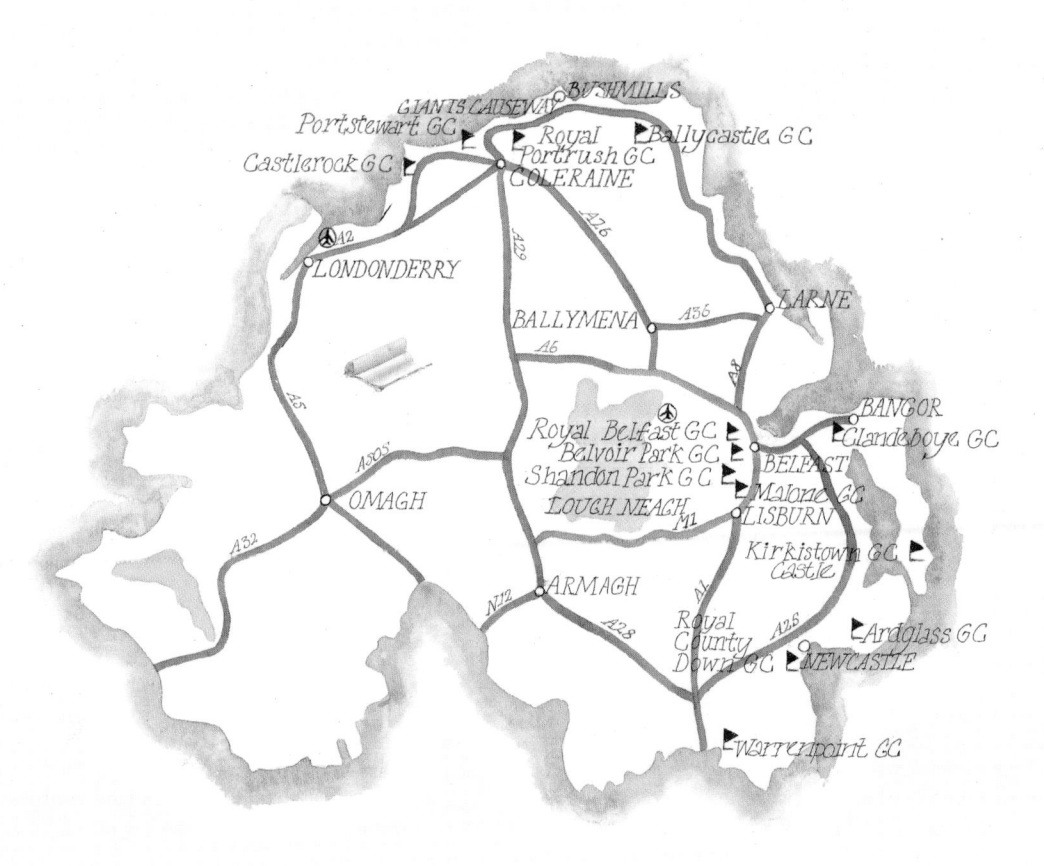

Douglas Adams   THE LINKS   Burlington Gallery

NORTHERN IRELAND
CHOICE GOLF

It is no secret that Northern Ireland has experienced a turbulent history; what is less widely known, however, is that it is a stunningly beautiful place. It is a land of forests and lakes, of mountains and glens. It boasts some of the most spectacular coastal scenery in the British Isles and where else can you view the handiwork of a giant? So much in a country no larger than Yorkshire.

The quality of golf is equally outstanding. There are approximately sixty courses in all, a large number of which are to be found close to the aforementioned coast enjoying some quite splendid isolation. Belfast, which is about the size of Bristol, has no shortage of good courses, and not just parkland types either, and then, of course, there are the two jewels in the crown – Portrush and Newcastle, or if you prefer, **Royal Portrush** and **Royal County Down**.

BELFAST AND COUNTY DOWN

Belfast is a likely starting point and getting there should be fairly straightforward. Approaching from Dublin it is a case of following the N1 and the A1, while from Britain car ferries run regularly from Stranraer and travelling by air is even simpler should you be thinking of hiring a car when you arrive.

Having declared nothing but your urge to break 80, resist at all costs the temptation to zoom off northwards to Portrush or southwards to Newcastle; Belfast offers much more than you probably imagine. The best known golf course immediately at hand is the appropriately named **Royal Belfast**. It is situated just outside the city on the north coast alongside Belfast Lough and is a classic example of well-manicured parkland golf. A number of holes here are very scenic, particularly around the turn and there is considerable challenge to combine with the charm. Royal Belfast is the oldest Golf Club in Ireland having been founded in 1881. It is therefore older than either Royal Lytham or Royal Birkdale just across the Irish Sea. The course is understandably very popular but with a little forward planning the visitor should be able to arrange a game. The Clubhouse by the way is a magnificent 19th century building.

Remaining in Belfast, **Malone** Golf Club at Dunmurry is one of the leading inland courses in all Ireland – a visit is therefore strongly recommended – and two 'Parks' are also decidedly worth inspecting. The first is Belvoir (pronounce it Beever) and the second is Shandon. **Belvoir Park** lies about five miles south of the city centre, **Shandon Park** just to the north; both are Championship courses. The former is definitely the pick of the two with its magnificent tree-lined fairways however, Shandon has the advantage of offering some interesting views over historical Stormont. **Clandeboye** Golf Club, not too far from Royal Belfast along the Bangor Road offers a different test of golf. Clandeboye is more wooded and 'heathy' with a considerable splash of gorse. There are two courses; the more difficult Dufferin and the Ava. Both are attractive and on the Dufferin course some very precise shots are called for.

To the south of Newtownards, **Scrabo** Golf Club is worth an inspection – its opening hole is reckoned to be the toughest in Ireland – and circling back towards Belfast, **Lisburn** is almost in the same league as Malone and Belvoir Park.

A good base is required. In Belfast itself, The Wellington Park Hotel (0232) 381111 offers comfortable rooms and a thriving night life, particularly at weekends. Alternatively, the Europa Hotel (0232) 327000 is both modern and very comfortable but the most popular choice for golfers will probably be the Culloden Hotel (02317) 5223 at Holywood (very convenient for Royal Belfast). The Culloden is an impressive looking building, a Baronial styled Victorian mansion. Its restaurant is particularly recommended. Another good eating place in Holywood is the Iona Restaurant (02317) 5655 and on the subject of sumptuous fare, Belfast offers The Strand (0232) 682266 and Restaurant 44 (0232) 244844. Belfast in fact is becoming renowned for its eating places and Roscoff (0232) 331532 and Manor House (0232) 238739 are two further places that offer particularly appealing fare. Whatever you do don't forget to sample one or two of the local pubs; in most the atmosphere is tremendous. For a really cosy inn, however, the best bet is to head east from Royal Belfast towards Bangor to Crawfordsburn where The Old Inn (0247) 853255 is a superb hostelry; full of character, its food is first class and there are some delightful bedrooms.

Relaxed, well fed, well lubricated and swing nicely grooved, the next golf course to play is **Kirkistown Castle**. It lies near the foot of the Ards Peninsula (once described somewhat alarmingly as the proboscis of Ulster!) Kirkistown is a real old-fashioned gem. James Braid assisted in the design of the course and is reputed to have commented wistfully 'If only I had this within 50 miles of London'. The town of Portaferry is no great distance away and the Portaferry Hotel (02477) 28231 is a marvellous place to spend the night. It is another of those cosy inns (note the splendid seafood here).

If you're not in a rush it is worth spending some time on the Ards Peninsula. It is a remote and very beautiful corner of Ireland and Lough Strangford is one giant bird sanctuary and wild life reserve. From Portaferry, a ferry can be taken to Strangford and from here a short drive will take you to **Ardglass** on the coast. Perched on craggy rocks the layout here is reminiscent of some of the better seaside courses in Cornwall. A perfect holiday course, we have featured Ardglass on a separate page ahead.

Beyond St John's Point and around Dundrum Bay, a journey of approximately twelve miles lies Newcastle, an attractive seaside town and where, as the famous song tells you, 'the mountains O'Mourne sweep down to the sea'. For golfers it is a paradise. **Royal County Down** Golf Club is quite simply one of the greatest courses in the world and it too is featured on a later page. For those lucky people who are able to enjoy a few days here, the Burrendale Hotel (03967) 22599 is very popular (and only about a five minute drive from the golf course). Equally recommended is The Slieve Donard Hotel (03967) 23681 which practically adjoins the famous links; in fact you'll be aiming a couple of drives at its spires. There are alas nowadays fewer and fewer hotels able to combine old-fashioned elegance with modern comforts and the Slieve Donard is an opulent and memorable example. Newcastle is a holiday town and good quality guesthouses and Bed and Breakfasts are plentiful. If one is staying in the area some sight seeing is strongly advised. To the south and west the mountain scenery is quite magnificent while the southern coastal road takes in some very different but beautiful views. It is an area where smuggling was once notorious and before reaching the border we recommend that you smuggle in a quick 18 holes at **Warrenpoint**, where Ronan Rafferty learnt to play.

NORTHERN IRELAND
CHOICE GOLF

THE CAUSEWAY COAST

Our journey now takes us back northwards, past Belfast to the Antrim coast. Here there is perhaps the most spectacular scenery of all and, equally important, yet more glorious golf.

Now, what kind of being can pick thorns out of his heels whilst running and can rip up a vast chunk of rock and hurl it fifty miles into the sea? Who on earth could perform such staggering feats? The answer is Finn McCool (who, alas is not eligible for Ryder Cup selection). Finn was the great Warrior Giant who commanded the armies of the King of all Ireland. He inhabited an Antrim headland, probably not far from Portrush in fact. Having fallen madly in love with a lady giant who lived on the Hebridian Island of Staffa, Finn began building a giant bridge to bring her across the water. Either Finn grew fickle or the lady blew him out but the bridge was never completed; still the Giants Causeway remains a great monument to one Finn McCool.

Royal Portrush is a monument to the Royal and Ancient game. Like County Down, Ardglass and Portstewart it is featured separately. However, don't limit your golf to Portrush, there are three other superb eighteen hole courses nearby. To the east of Portrush, **Ballycastle** has an attractive situation overlooking an inviting stretch of sand and, if it didn't look so cold, the sea would be equally inviting. It is nothing like as tough as Portrush, more of a holiday course really, but tremendously enjoyable all the same.

Midway between Ballycastle and Portrush there is a pleasant nine holes at Bushfoot in Portballintrae where the Bayview Hotel (02657) 31453 provides a comfortable base. One should visit the famous Bushmills Distillery nearby. It is the oldest distillery in the world and whiskey has been produced here since 1608 – just think what Finn might have done after a magnum of Black

Bush. Another popular place to stay is the excellent Bushmills Inn (02657) 32339 – ideal for those who wish to avoid both kinds of drinking and driving! Portrush's most celebrated eating place is Ramores on the quay, where there is a top class restaurant (0265) 824313 and a casual wine bar (0265) 823444. Those who have over-indulged and are seeking a comforting bed for the night should look (or stumble) no further than the excellent Magherabuoy House (0265) 823507. Last but most definitely not least is the Royal Court Hotel (0265) 822236, whose location and interior are equal to those of any in Northern Ireland.

Four miles west of Portrush and further along the coast is the fishing town of **Portstewart**. It has another very fine golf course. (See feature page) The Edgewater Hotel (026583) 3314 in town is convenient and adequate, although more stylish accommodation and good food can be found at Blackheath House (0265) 868433 at Gurvagh 5 miles from Coleraine, and only a mile out of Portstewart. Also convenient for Portrush and Portstewart, Maddybenny Farm (0265) 823394 is one of the finest guesthouses anywhere in Europe. Honestly!

One final course remains to be played on this splendid Causeway coast and that is **Castlerock**, just a few miles across the River Bann from Portstewart. The course has staged a number of important championships. Once again it is a classic links set amid towering sand dunes and there are many marvellous and far-reaching views.

There are many golfing delights in Northern Ireland that we have not explored, however should Castlerock be your last port of call you'll have no excuses for not leaving Ireland a very contented soul. What's more, if this has been a first visit to the country you'll probably have a very different view of the place from the one you had when you arrived. This really is a charming land.

Robert Guy **ON THE GREEN** *Burlington Gallery*

SLIEVE DONARD HOTEL

The Slieve Donard Hotel is located in Newcastle, Co Down, just 45 minutes south of Belfast.

Magnificently situated at the foot of the beautiful Mountains of Mourne, the Slieve Donard Hotel stands in 6 acres of private grounds which extend to an extensive golden strand. Originally a luxurious railway hotel, the Slieve Donard is now owned by the Hastings Hotels Group and offers Grade 'A' accommodation and excellent facilities. It is the most popular hotel in the province for a conference, wedding or holiday break.

Each of its 120 luxury bedrooms are beautifully appointed with all the modern facilities you would expect from a top international hotel.

The Slieve Donard Hotel is the first choice for golfers who play at the world famous Royal County Down Golf Club. It is only 2 minutes through a beautiful hedged, arched walk to the course. Other courses close at hand are Kilkeel, Ardglass and Warrenpoint. The Slieve Donard warmly welcomes all golfers and can arrange starting times with local courses, including Royal County Down.

Within the hotel, the Elysium Health and Leisure Club is a must for all visitors, with tennis, swimming in the luxurious indoor pool, putting on the lawn, or a relaxing sauna or jacuzzi. The Chaplin's Bar and the Percy French, an informal pub/restaurant in the grounds of the hotel, are also popular venues.

The Slieve Donard at Newcastle is truly one of Ireland's great holiday hotels. Newcastle is a splendid centre for golfers and also for fishermen. Newcastle is the gateway to the Mourne Mountains and Tollymore Forest Park, providing excellent walking on clearly marked trails. Pony-trekking is also popular. Everyone visiting the Slieve Donard is given a very warm welcome and customers often comment on the friendliness and efficiency of the service. The Oak Restaurant is renowned for its gourmet food and fine wines.

The Slieve Donard is a member of Hastings Hotels, the leading chain of hotels in Northern Ireland. This is a further guarantee of its excellence. Newcastle - 'Where the Mountains of Mourne sweep down to the sea' - Percy French.

Slieve Donard Hotel
Downs Road
Newcastle
Co. Down BT33 0AH
Tel: (03967) 23681
Fax: (03967) 24830

ROYAL COUNTY DOWN (NEWCASTLE)
CHAMPIONSHIP GOLF

Approximately thirty miles to the south of Belfast and beneath the spectacular gaze of the Mountains of Mourne there lies the most beautiful golf course in the world. A daring statement perhaps, but will anyone who has visited disagree?

Royal County Down is situated in Newcastle and the course stretches out along the shores of Dundrum Bay. It was laid out in 1889 by **'Old' Tom Morris** from St. Andrews, who for his labours we are told, was paid the princely sum of four pounds. In a way though, there was little that Old Tom had to do, for Royal County Down is also one of the world's most natural golfing links.

Within four years of the first ball being struck the course was considered good enough to stage the Irish Open Amateur Championship which was duly won by the greatest amateur of the day, **John Ball**. Before the 20th century had dawned, County Down was already being considered as the finest course in all Ireland and some were even extending the accolade further.

Beautiful and natural, what next? Degree of difficulty. 'It was in fact the sternest examination in golf I had ever taken', the words of the very knowledgeable and well travelled golf writer **Herbert Warren Wind**. From its Championship tees, County Down measures 6968 yards, par 71. The fairways are often desperately narrow, the greens small, slick and not at all easy to hold; there are a number of blind shots amid the dunes and the rough can be, as someone once put it, 'knee-high to a giant'. Imagine what it's like in a fierce wind! Royal County Down is one of the toughest courses in the world.

Those wishing to pay homage should telephone the Club well in advance of intended play. Visitors are certainly welcome, but the course can naturally only accommodate so many. Weekends are best avoided as indeed are Wednesdays, but Mondays, Tuesdays and Fridays are relatively easy for visitors; a letter of introduction from the golfer's home Club is helpful. The Secretary, **Mr Peter Rolph** can be approached by telephone on **(03967) 23314** while the address to write to is **Royal County Down Golf Club, Newcastle, Co. Down. BT33 0AN**. The Club's professional, **Kevan Whitson**, can be contacted on **(03967) 22419**. In 1992 the green fees were set at £35 per day during the week with £40 payable at the weekend.

Visitors looking for a more sedate challenge might wish to take note of the **No. 2 Course** at Royal County Down, which measures 4087 yards, par 65. This course is open to visiting golfers all week, with green fees currently set at £7 per day during the week and £9 at weekends.

The thirty mile journey from Belfast is via Ballynahinch along the A24 and the A2. The road is a good one and it should take less than an hour. From Dublin to the south the distance is about ninety miles and here the route to follow is the N1 to Newry and then again the A24, this time approaching Newcastle from the west. On a very clear day the Mountains of Mourne are just visible from Portmarnock's Championship links.

Unlike many of the great natural links courses, County Down doesn't have the traditional out and back type of layout; rather there are two distinct loops of nine. The outward loop, or half, is closer to the sea and hence is more sandy in nature and the dunes are consistently larger. You can hear the breaking of the waves as you play down the **1st** fairway and your first blind tee shot comes as early as the par four **2nd**. It is said that you can always spot the first time visitor to Newcastle for he walks up the 1st fairway backwards so enchanting is the view behind!

Among the finest holes on the front nine are the short **4th**; here the tee shot must carry over a vast sea of gorse directly towards the majestic peak of Slieve Donard, the dog-legged **5th**, and the **9th** where an uphill drive must be targeted at the red spire of the Slieve Donard Hotel and followed (assuming the drive has successfully flown the hill and descended into the valley below) by a long second shot to a well guarded plateau green – a particularly memorable hole to conclude what many people consider to be the finest nine holes in golf.

The back nine may not have so many great sandhills, but there is still a plentiful supply of heather and gorse. Of the better holes perhaps the **13th**, where the fairway curves its way through a beautiful heather lined valley and the very difficult **15th** stand out.

Given its rather remote situation and the lack of facilities or space to cope with a vast crowd of spectators the Open could never be staged at Royal County Down – sadly. The Amateur Championship has been played here though, **Michael Bonallack** completing a hat trick of victories in 1970. The Irish Amateur Championship visits County Down regularly and there have been some truly memorable finals. In 1933, **Eric Fiddian** playing against **Jack McLean**, holed in one at the **7th** in the morning round and then again at the **14th** in the afternoon. A magical moment in a magical setting – and I don't suppose Fiddian felt too sore when McLean eventually won the match.

Hole	Yards	Par	Hole	Yards	Par
1	500	5	10	200	3
2	374	4	11	429	4
3	473	4	12	476	5
4	217	3	13	422	4
5	418	4	14	213	3
6	368	4	15	445	4
7	129	3	16	265	4
8	428	4	17	376	4
9	431	4	18	528	5
Out	3.338	35	In	3.354	36
			Out	3.338	35
			TOTALS	6.692	71

THE MAGHERABUOY HOUSE HOTEL

On the Causeway Coast in Northern Ireland, stone walls blend into green fields and sweeping cliffs roll towards the sea. This is also natural golfing country, and it is difficult to find anywhere that surpasses this natural coastal setting or a hotel that offers such a delightful base for exploring surrounding golf courses. Stand on the steps of the Magherabuoy House Hotel and you can breathe in the fresh salt air of the Atlantic Ocean.

The Magherabuoy House Hotel incorporates the period home of the former Minister of Home Affairs and has been carefully restored and extended, providing modern comforts in a majestic setting. Opulence is the key note, the elegant reception area creating a warm, sophisticated atmosphere, reflecting the standard and quality of service throughout. There are 38 luxurious bedrooms, all with private bathrooms, colour T.V. and tea and coffee making facilities. Guests can enjoy delicious a la carte meals in the Lanyon Room after a day on the golf course.

The jewel in the crown is undoubtedly the famous fairways of the championship course of Royal Portrush. Barely five minutes from the hotel, the links of Portrush set a challenge to players of every standard. There are three excellent courses: the Dunluce Course on which the Championships are played; the Valley Course on which the Ladies mainly play and the nine hole pitch and putt course at the end of the links nearest the town known as the Skerries. Throughout the years more than forty national championships, British and Irish, have been decided on these links.

Exhilarating rounds of golf in a stunning setting are available at five other courses in the area. The recently improved Portstewart can offer a challenge almost on a par with Royal Portrush; and Rathmore, Castlerock, Bushfoot, and Ballycastle all provide varied and testing golf.

The Hotel is situated only an hour's drive from the airport and docks, and guests can be collected from the airport in the hotel's own courtesy transport. For a really unusual golfing holiday you can be assured of a warm welcome.

The Magherabuoy House Hotel
41 Magheraboy Road
Portrush BT56 8NX
Tel: (0265) 823507
Fax: (0265) 824687

ROYAL PORTRUSH
CHAMPIONSHIP GOLF

In May 1988, Royal Portrush celebrated its one hundredth birthday. One could say that this famous Club was born with a golfing silver spoon in its mouth. Within four years of its foundation, patronage was bestowed and there could never be a finer natural setting for a Championship links. The course is laid out amid huge sand dunes which occupy slightly elevated ground providing commanding views over the Atlantic. And what views! The Antrim coast is at its most spectacular between **The Giant's Causeway** and Portrush and overlooking the links are the proud ruins of a magnificent castle, **Dunluce**, from which the Championship Course takes its name. The first professional the Club employed was **Sandy Herd**, who went on to win the Open Championship in 1902, and as if by way of a final blessing, in **1951**, Portrush became the first (and to this day the only) Club in Ireland to stage **The Open Championship**.

There are in fact two Championship Courses at Portrush. When people talk of 'the Championship links' they are invariably referring to the **Dunluce** links, but there is also The **Valley** links which can stretch to 6278 yards and is used for many important events; somewhat surprisingly it has only twenty bunkers. Visitors are made very welcome at Portrush and can play either course on any day of the week except Wednesday afternoons; the Valley course is also closed to visitors on Sunday mornings. It is always wise to telephone the Club in advance as tees may have been reserved and Portrush is extremely popular in the summer.

In 1992 the green fees to play over the Dunluce links were set at £30 per round between Monday and Friday, £35 on weekends and Bank Holidays (when available) and £12 for the Valley course during the week (£16 at the weekend). Fees differ for those living outside Ireland, and are a little more expensive. On both courses, weekly tickets are available and are excellent value for those staying in the area. Golfing Societies are equally welcome, subject of course to prior arrangement with the Secretary, **Wilma Erskine**. She may be contacted by writing to the **Royal Portrush Golf Club, Portrush, Co. Antrim. BT56 8JQ.** Tel: **(0265) 822311** or fax. (0265) 823139.

The Golf Club lies about half a mile from Portrush town.

Portrush itself is easily accessible as it is linked by coastal road to Portstewart and Ballycastle and to Belfast by major road, a distance of approximately sixty miles. Londonderry is about thirty-five miles to the west. The Club is immediately off Bushmills Road and don't forget to visit the famous distillery when you're in the area – it's less than 10 minutes from the links and is guaranteed to do wonders for your golf!

Although the game has now been played at Portrush for a hundred years, the Dunluce links in fact bears little resemblance to the original Championship course. **Harry Colt** is responsible for the present layout and we all owe him a great debt. Work was carried out between 1929 and 1932 and on completion he is said to have considered it his masterpiece – and Harry Colt built many a great course. **Bernard Darwin** wrote in 'The Times' after viewing the links during the 1951 Open: 'It is truly magnificent and Mr. H.S. Colt, who designed it in its present form, has thereby built himself a monument more enduring than brass'.

Portrush's most celebrated holes are the **5th** and the **14th**. The 5th, **White Rocks,** is one of the most exhilarating two-shot holes in golf. From the tee, there is a splendid view of the Antrim Coast towards The White Rocks and The Giant's Causeway beyond. However spellbound, considerable care is required with both the drive and the approach. The hole is properly a dog-leg and although a brave drive can cut the angle, failure will result in a trip into the deep, deep rough; over-hit your second and you're in the Atlantic. The green here nearly fell into the sea some years ago but a retaining wall was built and it has been saved. The 14th is titled **Calamity Corner**, and not without good reason – a par three of over 200 yards in length, the direct line to the pin requires a very precise shot to carry an enormous ravine – mis-hit this one and you can be playing your next shot from at least fifty feet below the hole.

As with most of the great links courses, the greens at Portrush are very large and the bunkers often deep. The course poses a considerable challenge but it's a fair one nonetheless. In the 1951 Open only twice during the entire tournament did a player break 70. Silver spoon or not, you can be sure my good friend Finn McCool would have been mightily impressed.

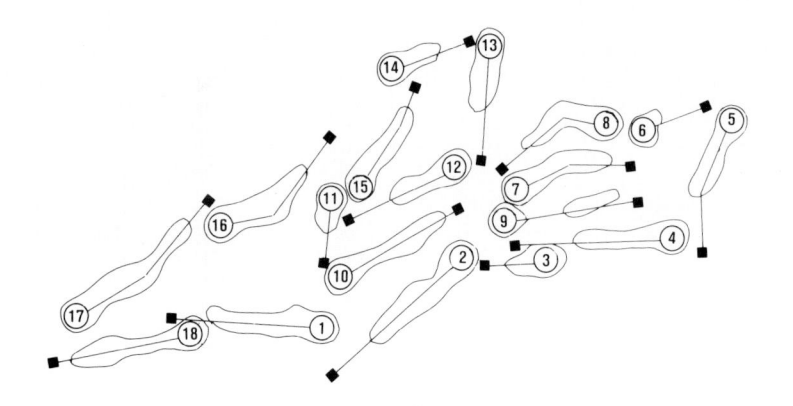

Hole	Yards	Par	Hole	Yards	Par
1	381	4	10	477	5
2	493	5	11	166	3
3	150	3	12	389	4
4	454	4	13	366	4
5	380	4	14	205	3
6	187	3	15	361	4
7	420	4	16	415	4
8	365	4	17	508	5
9	476	5	18	477	5
Out	3.306	36	In	3.364	37
			Out	3.306	36
			TOTALS	6.670	73

PORTSTEWART
CHAMPIONSHIP GOLF

The Causeway Coast of Northern Ireland – essentially the coast of Antrim with a bit of County Londonderry stuck on – has long been regarded as a fine place for a golfing break with three very good courses and one outstanding championship links to play. The last-mentioned is of course Royal Portrush, the only golf links in Ireland to have staged the Open Championship; the three supporting courses being Ballycastle, Portstewart and Castlerock. In the last few years all this has changed. It is not the opening of a new course (although some might describe it as such) but rather the extraordinary transformation of one of the supporting cast. Portstewart now ranks, or at least soon will rank among the greatest courses in Ireland. How come? Two words will suffice, Thistle Hollow.

Visitors to Portstewart have always marvelled at the magnificent 425 yard par four lst hole. The best opening hole in Ireland is the proud boast, and only the Members at Portrush seem to grumble loudly. Of course the difficulty of having such a spectacular starter is that the main course has got a lot to live up to. Although the following seventeen holes at Portstewart are considered well above average, they have not been able to sustain the sensation of wonder – that is until now. After playing the glorious lst, golfers used to gaze up into the nearby range of sand hills known as Thistle Hollow and ruminate on how fantastic it would be if only they could build some golf holes amidst those towering dunes. Well now they have, and that is why Portstewart is such a fantastic golf course.

One of the people best able to tell you how this came about – for he presided over much of it – is the Club's enthusiastic Secretary, **Michael Moss.** Visitors wishing to explore the awesome sand hills and the rest of the links are advised to contact the Club a little in advance. The full address is **Portstewart Golf Club, Strand Head, Portstewart, Co. Londonderry, BT55 7PG.** Mr Moss can also be contacted by telephone on **(026583) 2015**, while Portstewart's professional, **Alan Hunter** can be reached on **(026583) 2601.**

Although it is easy to get carried away with the major reshaping of the Championship course it should be pointed out that there are now 45 holes of golf to enjoy at Portstewart. The short 18 hole Town Course has been around for a little while but a new nine hole course, the 'Riverside 9' has evolved

following the aforementioned reshaping of the Championship links. Broadly speaking, what has happened is that much of the former back nine at Portstewart has become the Riverside 9 and the new holes have been 'inserted' to immediately follow the famous lst. This is only roughly what has happened for the 'new' 18th is still more or less the 'old' 18th – confused? The best bet is to pay a visit!

Portstewart welcomes visitors at most times, although a round on the Championship course is not normally possible on Saturdays and only limited times are available on Sundays. The green fee in 1992 for the Championship course was £20 during the week and £28 at the weekend. A full eighteen holes on the Riverside 9 is priced at £10 midweek and £15 at weekends, while at similar times the green fee for the Town Course is £6 and £9 respectively. There are no reduced rates for junior golfers.

Portstewart is situated right on the coast, some 4 miles from Coleraine and no greater a distance from Portrush which is to the east of Portstewart. The road that links each to the other is the A2. Belfast is approximately 65 miles away, though its airport is a little nearer and from which one doesn't have to journey through the capital to get to the Causeway Coast: the A26 is a very direct route. Londonderry is about 30 miles to the west and there is a second airport here.

So having played the splendid dog-leg **lst** with its superbly elevated tee (every bit as exhilarating as the 5th at Portrush) and amphitheatre-like green, instead of gazing up into the sand hills the golfer playing the Championship links must now get amongst them. The 'new' front nine holes at Portstewart are being compared with the back nine holes at Tralee Golf Club in County Kerry – and anyone who has played that exceptional links, designed by Arnold Palmer, will know that this is a mighty compliment. Not only are these new holes at Portstewart reckoned to be as similarly challenging and dramatic as Tralee, but also the views they afford are just as breathtaking. There is no better vantage point than on the **3rd**, a quite stunning par three hole. Two other outstanding new challenges at Portstewart are the long sweeping par five **4th** and the narrow dog-legged par four **8th**, where both fairways are bordered by towering dunes. The golfer may feel in a world of his own as he plays these holes but then that's Portstewart, a quite extraordinary golf course.

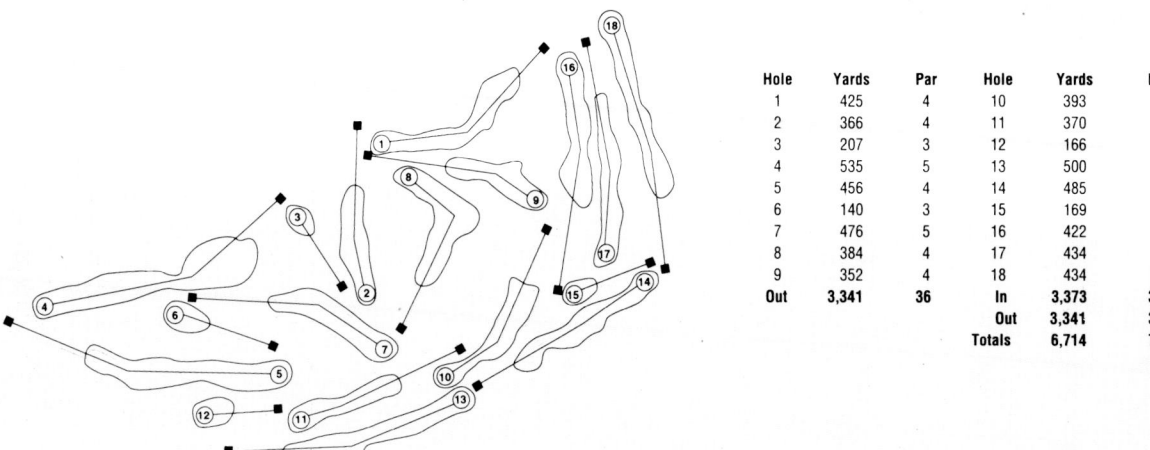

Hole	Yards	Par	Hole	Yards	Par
1	425	4	10	393	4
2	366	4	11	370	4
3	207	3	12	166	3
4	535	5	13	500	5
5	456	4	14	485	5
6	140	3	15	169	3
7	476	5	16	422	4
8	384	4	17	434	4
9	352	4	18	434	4
Out	**3,341**	**36**	**In**	**3,373**	**36**
			Out	**3,341**	**36**
			Totals	**6,714**	**72**

ARDGLASS
CHAMPIONSHIP GOLF

The golfer in a hurry – or the golfer without a soul – will travel to Portrush from Belfast by journeying inland, by driving through the heart of Northern Ireland after picking up the A26 at Ballymena; he or she, will bypass the Causeway Coast. That same person will head speedily for Newcastle, travelling due south via Ballynahinch. A bally idiot, you might think.

The route to Ardglass we recommend (for those travelling from Belfast, anyway) is a very leisurely trip around the Ards Peninsula and in this instance the first town to head for is Newtownards. Such a route will please the birdwatcher, for the road runs alongside Strangford Lough – one of the finest and largest bird sanctuaries in Europe, the country house enthusiast and historian, as the road passes near several magnificent houses (including Mount Stewart, famed for its wonderful gardens) as well as numerous castles, abbeys and monuments, and it will interest the golfer for a game could be sneaked in at Kirkistown Castle. On reaching Portaferry the traveller takes a quick ferry ride and then heads for Ardglass, just seven scenic miles away along the coast of Co. Down. The mountains of Mourne loom on the horizon and Newcastle is just 12 miles beyond Ardglass. Now we suggest that all and sundry make a decent length pit stop.

Ardglass is an historic little town. It has a great seafaring tradition and was once, though it's hard to believe now, the busiest port in Ulster. It is particularly famous for its collection of 14th to 16th century castles (there are about half a dozen of them in various states of ruin) and is apparently celebrated for its herrings, though I cannot recall ever having sampled any. Perhaps they are a speciality at the 19th hole of Ardglass Golf Club? 18 holes of golf here will certainly create an appetite, though my guess is that the first time visitor will be even more keen on getting back out and playing a second round on what is unquestionably one of the most spectacular courses in Ireland.

Let us not pretend that Ardglass is a Royal Co. Down or a Royal Portrush: we are talking about a sporting holiday course not an Open Championship type challenge. From its back tees the course measures 5515 metres (or a little under 6100 yards) and from the ladies tees, 4819 metres (c.5200 yards). What makes Ardglass so enjoyable is the dramatic layout of the course with several tees and greens overlooking the ocean; it has a really rugged feel and is part links part cliff top in nature. Much of the course is overrun with thick, wiry rough and vast swathes of heather.

Although the club was founded almost a century ago in 1896, it was not until 1971 that Ardglass could boast 18 holes. Today the club is run efficiently by the secretary, **Alan Cannon**, tel **(0396) 841219/841841** and the professional **Kevin Dorrian, (0396) 841022**. Visitors are welcomed by arrangement throughout the week, 1992 green fees being £13 midweek and £16 at the weekend. Weekly and fortnightly tickets are also available.

Essentially the course meanders its way out on to a headland and then meanders its way back. The front nine holes are the more memorable, especially the first five which all run right alongside the sea. The par three **2nd** is many people's favourite – and many people's undoing – with its tee shot needing to be fired across a rocky inlet: a real death or glory hole and somewhat reminiscent of the 3rd at Tralee. A second magnificent par three is tackled early on the back nine, the short, downhill **11th** which is at the far end of the course. Whilst it is the ball hit short and left that will find the Irish Sea on the 2nd, it is the overhit shot to the right that is similarly punished on the 11th. Often this latter hole is just the proverbial 'flick with a wedge' but when the wind is dead against it can be truly intimidating. Some pretty demanding shots are called for between the **12th** and **15th**, and the **17th**, yet another good par three, can be deceptively tricky, but the **18th** offers a good chance of a closing birdie. Then of course it is off to the 19th which, being Ardglass, is a converted ancient castle, and time to relax with a drink or two – unless, that is, you are a golfer in a hurry, or a golfer without a soul.

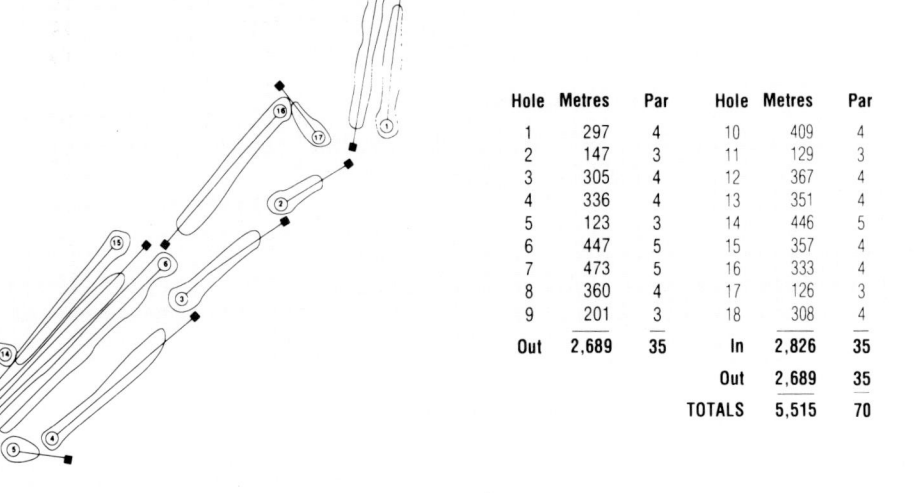

Hole	Metres	Par		Hole	Metres	Par
1	297	4		10	409	4
2	147	3		11	129	3
3	305	4		12	367	4
4	336	4		13	351	4
5	123	3		14	446	5
6	447	5		15	357	4
7	473	5		16	333	4
8	360	4		17	126	3
9	201	3		18	308	4
Out	**2,689**	**35**		**In**	**2,826**	**35**
				Out	**2,689**	**35**
				TOTALS	**5,515**	**70**

BLACKHEATH HOUSE

Blackheath House is a fine old Rectory built by Frederick Harvey, the Earl of Bristol in 1791 for the Parish of Aghadowey. It is a listed building with an interesting history set in two acres of landscaped gardens.

Once the home of Archbishop William Alexander, whose wife Cecil the poetess wrote 'There is a green hill far away' and 'All things bright and beautiful'.

In Winter, residents can enjoy a glass of hot punch in the drawing room by a welcoming fire and in the Summer can have a cool drink in the gardens.

Each of the spacious bedrooms is individually styled for comfort with bathrooms, colour television and tea/coffee making facilities.

Blackheath House is situated in the beautiful countryside of Aghadowey, once the centre of flax growing for the linen industry, whose rivers are famous for salmon and trout. Shooting and fishing can be arranged and there are excellent equestrian facilities nearby.

Aghadowey is only 7 miles from Coleraine and 11 miles from the Causeway Coast with its magnificent coastline, sandy beaches, picturesque seaside resorts and eight golf courses. We have special rates with local Golf Courses and can arrange sea fishing.

There are many interesting places to visit in the area including the Giants Causeway, Carrick-a-Rede Rope Bridge, Dunluce Castle and Old Bushmills Distillery - the home of the oldest whiskey in the world.

MACDUFF'S RESTAURANT - The Restaurant situated in the cellars of the house is renowned for its excellent food, friendly service and warm and intimate atmosphere.

Macduff's offers Country House cooking at its best using freshly grown produce, local game, salmon and seafood.

From an extensive and interesting wine list you can choose a wine from the original wine vault.

Blackheath House
112, Killeague Road
Blackhill
Coleraine
Co. Londonderry BT51 4HH
Tel: (0265) 868433

NORTHERN IRELAND
COMPLETE GOLF

CO ANTRIM

Ballycastle G.C
(02657) 62536
Cushendall Road, Ballycastle
40 miles W. of Larne on the A2
(18) 5882 yards/***/D/H

Ballyclare G.C
(09603) 22696
25 Springvale Road, Ballyclare
Travel N. from Belfast to A8 for Ballyclare
(18) 5840 yards/**(not Thur)/E/H

Ballymena G.C
(0266) 861207
128 Raceview Road, Broughshane, Ballymena
2 miles E. of town on the A42
(18) 5168 yards/***/E/H

Bushfoot G.C
(02657) 31317
50 Bushfoot Road, Portballintrac, Bushmills
Take A2 from Portrush to Bushmills
(9) 5572 yards/***/E(D at weekends)/H

Cairndhu G.C
(0574) 83324
192 Coast Road, Ballygally, Larne
4 miles N. of Larne on the A2
(18) 6112 yards/***(not Sat)/F

Carrickfergus G.C
(09603) 62203
North Road, Carrickfergus
9 miles N. of Belfast on the A2
(18) 5752 yards/***(not Sat)/D/H

Cushendall G.C
(02667) 71318
Shore Road, Cushendall, Ballymena
25 miles N. of Larne on the A2
(9) 4678 yards/***/E

Dunmurry G.C
(0232) 610834
91 Dunmurry Lane, Belfast
S.W from Belfast to Upper Malone Road(18)
5832 yards/**(not Tues/Thurs pm)/D/H

Greenisland G.C
(0232) 862236
156 Upper Road, Greenisland, Carrickfergus,
Belfast
9 miles N. of Belfast on the A2
(9) 5887 yards/***(not Sat)/E

Larne G.C
(09603) 82228
54 Ferris Bay Road, Islandmagee, Larne
Cross to Isle of Magee at Whitehaven off A2
(9) 6082 yards/***(not Sat)/E/H

Lisburn G.C
(0846) 677216
68 Eglantine Road, Lisburn
3 miles S of Lisburn on the A1
(18) 5708 yards/***/D

Masserene G.C
(08494) 28096
51 Lough Road, Antrim
1 mile S. of Antrim, towards airport
(18) 6614 yards/***(not Sat)/F

Royal Portrush G.C
(0265) 822314
Bushmills Road, Portrush
1 mile E. of Portrush on the A2
(18) 6273 yards/***/C/H
(18) 6784 yards/***/C/H

Whitehead G.C
(09603) 53631
McCraes Brae, Whitehead
Leave Belfast by A2 to Whitehead and follow
signs
(18) 6426 yards/***(not Sat)/E

CO ARMAGH

Ashfield G.C.
(0693) 861315
Freeduff, Cullyhana
(18) 5645 yards/***/E

County Armagh G.C
(0861) 522501
Newry Rd, Armagh
1 mile from Armagh, towards Newry
(18) 6184 yards/***/E

Craigavon Golf & Ski Centre
(0762) 6606Silverwood, Lurgan
2 miles from Belfast off M1
(18) 6496 yards/***/E

Lurgan G.C
(0762) 322087
Lurgan
Beside Lake Lurgan
(18) 6380 yards/***/B

Portadown G.C
(0762) 335356
Carrickblacker, Portadown
2 miles S of Portadown
(18) 6119 yards/***(Tues,Sat)/D

Trandragee G.C
(0762) 840727
Trandragee, Craigavon
5m from Portadown towards Newry
(18) 6084 yards/**/F

BELFAST

Balmoral G.C.
(0232) 381514
Lisburn Rd, Belfast
2 mile S of Belfast
(18) 6250 yards/***(Sat)/D

Belvoir Park G.C
(0232) 646714
Newtownbreda, Belfast
3 miles outside Belfast
(18) 6476 yards/***(Sat)C

Cliftonville G.C
(0232) 744158
Westland Rd, Belfast
2 mile from Belfast towards Antrim
(9) 6240 yards/***(Sat)/D

Fortwilliam G.C
(0232) 370770
Downview Ave, Belfast
3 miles N of Belfast
(18) 5642 yards/***(Sat)/D

The Knock G.C
(0232) 483251
Summerfield, Dundonald
4 miles E of Belfast
(18) 6292 metres/***(Sat)/D

Malone G.C
(0232) 612578
Upper Malone Rd, Dunmurry
4 miles from Belfast
(18) 6433 yards/***(Sat)Wedpm/F

Ormeau G.C
(0232) 641069
Ravenhill Road, Belfast
2 miles SE of Belfast
(9) 5306 yards/**/F

Shandon Park G.C
(0232) 794856
Shandon Park, Belfast
3 miles from Belfast towards Knock
(18) 6252 yards/***/C

CO DOWN

Ardglass G.C
(0396) 841219
Castle Place, Ardglass
7 miles S of Downpatrick
(18) 6000 yards/***/D

Banbridge G.C
(08206) 22342
Huntly Rd, Banbridge
(18) 5879 yards/***/E

Bangor G.C
(0247) 270922
Broadway, Bangor
(18) 6450 yards/**/C

Bright Castle G.C
(0396) 841319
Bright, Downpatrick
(18)7000 yards/***/E

Carnalea G.C
(0247) 270368
Carnalea
2 miles from Bangor
(18) 5513 yards/***/D

Clandeboye G.C
(0247) 271767
Conlig, Newtownards
Off A21 to Bangor
(18) 6650 yards/***(Sat)/B
(18) 5634 yards/***(Sat)/B

Donaghadee G.C
(0237) 883624
Warren Road, Donaghadee
6 miles from Bangor
(18) 6099 yards/***(Sat)/F

Downpatrick G.C
(0396) 612152
Saul Rd, Downpatrick
Nr A7
(18) 6196 yards/***/B

Helens Bay G.C
(0247) 852601
Helens Bay, Bangor
Off A2 E of Belfast
(9) 5638 yards/***(Sat)/F

Holywood G.C
(02317) 3135
Nuns Walk, Demense Rd, Holywood
6 miles E of Belfast
(18) 5885 yards/***(Sat)/D

Kilkeel G.C
(069) 3762296
Mourne Park, Ballyardle
3 miles S of Kilkeel
(9) 5623 metres/***(Tues,Sat)/E

Kirkistown Castle G.C
(02477) 71233
Cloughey, Newtownards
(18) 6157 yards/***/F

Mahee Island G.C
(0238) 541234
Comber
Mahee Island
(9) 5580 yards/***/D

Royal Belfast G.C
(03967) 23314
Holywood, Craigavad
(18) 6205 yards/***/C

Royal County Down G.C
(039) 6723314
Newcastle
(18) 6968 yards/A/Winter B
(18) 4100 yards/A/Winter B

Scrabo G.C
(0247) 812355
Scrabo Road, Newtownards
(18) 6000 yards/**(Wed)/D

The Spa G.C
(0238) 562365
Grove Rd, Ballynahinch
(9) 5770 yards/***(Sun)/E

Warrenpoint G.C
(069) 3772219
Lower Dromore Rd, Warrenpoint
5 miles S of Newry
(18) 6215 yards/***(Sun, Wed)/D

CO FERMANAGH

Enniskillen G.C
(0265) 848314
Enniskillen
1 miles NE of Enniskillen
(18) 5476 yards/***/D

CO LONDONDERRY

Castlerock G.C
(0265) 848314
Circular Rd, Castlerock
5 miles from Craigavern Bridge
(18) 6362 yards/**/F
(9) 4708 yards/**/F

City of Derry G.C
(0504) 46369
Prehan, Londonderry
(18) 6450 yards/***/D

Moyola Park G.C
(0648) 68392
Shanemullagh, Castledawson
(18) 6517 yards/***/D

Portstewart G.C
(0265) 832015
Strand Rd, Portstewart
5 miles W of Portrush
(18) 6800 yards
(18) + (9)***/C/***/E

CO TYRONE

Dungannon G.C
(08687) 22098
Mullaghmore, Dungannon
1 mile outside Dungannon
(18) 5914 yards/***/D

Fintona G.C
(0662) 841480
Fintona
10 miles S of Omagh
(9) 6250 yards/***/D

Killymoon G.C
(06487) 62254
Killymoon, Cookstown
(18) 6000 yards/***(Sat)/D

Newtownstewart G.C
(06626) 61466
Golf Course Rd, Newtownstewart
(18) 6100 yards/***/D

Omagh G.C
(0662) 3160
Dublin Rd, Omagh
(18) 5800/***/E

Strabane G.C
(0504) 882271
Ballycolman, Strabane
(18) 6100 yards/***/F

NORTHERN IRELAND

ARDSHANE COUNTRY HOUSE,
5 Bangor Road, Holywood, Tel: (023 17) 2044
Extensive restoration has transformed this former Edwardian gentleman's residence into an elegant hotel that has not lost touch with yesterday's values. An impressive restaurant offers la carte and table d'hote menus.

THE BEECHES,
10 Dunadry Road, Muckamore, Tel: (084 94) 33161
Situated near to the airport, this secluded detached guesthouse provides quiet rural accommodation in the peaceful locality of Dunadry. Local attractions include golf, fishing, bowling and Lough Negh.

CARRICK-DHU GUESTHOUSE,
6 Ballyreagh Road, Portrush, Tel: (0265) 823666
Portrush is one of Northern Ireland's most vibrant resorts and all types of visitor will enjoy its animated atmosphere. Carrick-Dhu is pleasantly situated in a residential area and is particularly noted for its cuisine.

DOWNHILL INN,
5 Mussenden Road, Castlerock, Tel: (0265) 848090
Impressively located overlooking the beach at Downhill, recent refurbishment has made this hotel even more tempting. The busy resort of Portrush is just four miles away.

ENNISKEEN HOUSE HOTEL,
98 Bryansford Road, Newcastle, Tel: (039 67) 22392
Splendid views across the Shimna Valley to the Mourne Mountains make this country house hotel an idyllic retreat. All bedrooms have ensuite facilities, colour TV and telephones.

GLEN HOUSE,
212 Crawfordsburn Road, Crawfordsburn, Tel: (0247) 852610
Quietly situated with character and charm within large grounds in the beautiful village of Crawfordsburn. Excellent for golf (4 golf courses within two miles), business and holidays. Rooms are all en-suite and private parking is provided.

GREENMOUNT LODGE,
58 Greenmount Road, Gortaclare, Omagh, Tel: (0662) 841325
Greenmount is a particularly popular establishment with touring holidaymakers, partly due to an enviable location. The varied attractions of Fermanagh Lakeland, Gortin Forest Park and Ulster History Park can all be reached with ease.

HALL CRAIG,
Springfield, Enniskillen, Tel: (036589) 330
Hall Craig enjoys an enviable location and is convenient for Belmore Forest, Lough Navar Forest, Lower Lough Erne and National Trust properties. Enniskillen is six miles away and Derrygonnelly some four miles.

LE MON HOUSE HOTEL,
41 Gransha Road, Castlereagh, Tel: (0232) 448631
Enjoying a countrified location only five miles from Belfast City Centre, Le Mon offers a host of modern comforts. Bedrooms are ensuite and are equipped with TV and telephone, whilst for the insatiably active, a health spa will prove invigorating and refreshing.

MADDYBENNY FARM,
Logestown, Portrush, Tel: (0265) 823394
This award winning guesthouse is justifiably the pride and joy of its friendly proprietor. Bedrooms are beautifully furnished but the real piece de resistence are the sumptuous breakfasts that often eliminate the need for lunch and tea!

TULLYHONA HOUSE,
Marble Arch Road, Florencecourt, Enniskillen, Tel: (036 582) 452
This acclaimed beef and sheep farm guesthouse is situated beside Florencecourt National Trust House and Marble Arch Caves. Game shooting, golf, fishing and lambing tours offer plenty to keep everyone occupied.

TWENTY ACRES,
46 Torr road, Ballyvoy, Ballycastle, Tel: (02657) 62629
This farm bungalow is pleasingly located on the scenic coast road to Murlough Bay, Torr Head and Cushendun. Two double rooms and two ground floor rooms are available from April to October.

WELLINGTON PARK HOTEL,
Belfast, Tel: (0232) 381111
One of the popular weekend spots for local revellers, the Wellington Park also offers fairly reasonably-priced accommodation and more than edible cuisine.

WINDERMERE HOUSE,
60 Wellington Park, Belfast, Tel: (0232) 662693
Belfast city centre offers a surprising amount, and this comfortable guesthouse is convenient for shops, theatres, cinemas and restaurants. In addition, the Ulster Museum and Botanic Gardens are only a ten minute walk away.

J.A.B.   ISOLATION   Burlington Gallery

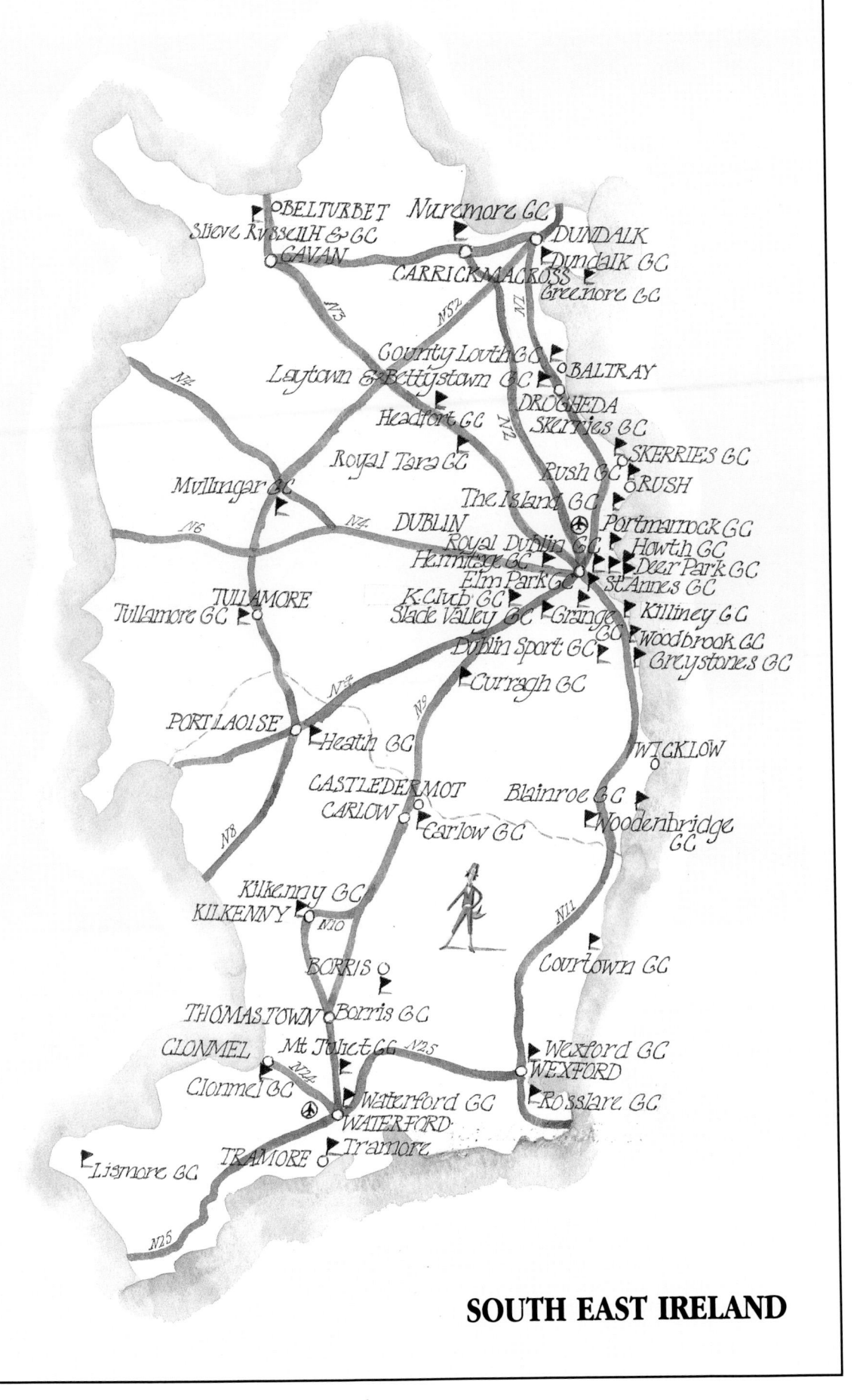

IRELAND - AN INTRODUCTION

This is a country of great natural beauty, a country where immense value is placed on the quality of life. Life in Ireland is to be enjoyed ... never wasted, if there is an opportunity to wring a memorable moment from it.

Ireland's rugged landscape, perched on the edge of the Atlantic Ocean, has presented a succession of great golf architects with unrivalled prospects for developing great golf holes. They have responded to the challenge magnificently and produced a treasury of great golf.

Men of stature – Tom Watson, Sam Snead, Tony Jacklin, Arnold Palmer, Severiano Ballesteros and Gary Player – have unhesitatingly spoken highly of Irish golf courses they have played. In fact, they admit to spending some of their happiest golfing hours here, and all have returned for more.

In Ireland, it is virtually impossible to distance oneself more than 20 miles away from a golf course. Every town or village of population more than 1,000 souls has a golf course of its very own.

The courses are relatively uncrowded. Visitors will have little difficulty in getting a game at any time. However, prudence does suggest making prior contact with your suggested ports of call, to ensure you are not clashing with visiting groups or other fixtures. Indeed, you just might be lucky to catch an open week. And do try to avoid the city courses at weekends when, quite understandably, the local members like to take their recreation.

To assist in planning your Irish golfing holiday, Bord Failte - the Irish Tourist Board has divided the country into six golfing regions and highlighted clubs that are most admirably equipped in terms of their golfing quality. Your choice of any of these golfing regions will give you a truly memorable golfing expe-

IRELAND - AN INTRODUCTION

rience. You'll have a different challenge each day; a variety of terrain from spectacular links or coastal layouts, to genteel parkland courses, and virtually all at championship standard clubs. Which means you get the full Irish golfing experience and all within easy reach of you selected accommodations. This way you spend your time golfing on quality courses, with the minimum travel and that is what these groups are all about.

The adventurous golfer can undertake the tournament circuit of the great links layouts that form a necklace round Ireland, each a gem. Places to visit under this heading include: Baltray, Portmarnock, Royal County Down, Royal Portrush, Royal Dublin, Waterville, Ballybunion, Lahinch and Rosses Point.

For those new to golf, we have a special tuition and improver groups to help you advance your game.

As if all of that is not enough, Irish golfers extend a warm

welcome to visitors wishing to play their courses. Not one of the golf clubs dotted around the Emerald Isle fails to welcome visitors, whether singly or in groups.

The Irish welcome is not just for on course use. Visitors are encouraged to make themselves 'at home' in the clubhouse, dining rooms and lounges. It is here the cultural exchange, or English - as spoken by the Irish - finds fertile groups and the friendship extended by Irish clubs comes in to its own.

Compared to many golf holiday destinations, Ireland is competitively priced - green fees range from about IR£8. Golf is playable year round, and is best April to September.

Getting to Ireland is no problem. There are direct flights to Dublin, Cork, Shannon, Knock, Galway, Farranfore, Waterford and Carrickfin, Co.Donegal and car ferry ports at Dublin, Dun Laoghaire, Rosslare and Cork.

DUBLIN & THE NORTH EAST
CHOICE GOLF

From the time you arrive in Ireland and crack your first drive straight down the middle, to the time you leave having holed that tricky putt on the final green (and then drained your last drop of Guinness at the 19th), you cannot fail to be impressed by the natural charm and helpfulness of the Irish people. Nowhere is it more immediately apparent than in Dublin – what a contrast to many of the world's capital cities! Nothing seems rushed and nothing seems too much trouble. You see, the welcome from these folk is quite simply second to none.

You may have come by rail and sea, car and car ferry or you may have flown – whichever way you'll be itching to play some golf. In Dublin, as indeed throughout Ireland, the only real problem is deciding where to start.

DUBLIN

Within ten miles of the city centre there are two great championship links and at least twenty other courses, the majority of which are of a very high standard. **Portmarnock** is the most celebrated, and indeed is one of the great golf links of the world. It is explored on a later page. **Royal Dublin** is said to be the only Championship course located within the boundaries of a capital city. It lies just to the north of Dublin's centre on Bull Island in the charmingly named area of Dollymount. It is generally considered less severe than Portmarnock, (although the wind can blow just as fiercely!) for it is not as long and the rough isn't quite so punishing. It makes an ideal place for us to crack that first one straight down the middle.

The two best known holes on the course are probably the 5th and the 18th. The former is one of the most frighteningly difficult holes to be found anywhere. There is a story that when Danny Kaye visited the course he took one look at the 5th and turned to his caddy to ask for a rifle! The 18th is a shortish par five, reachable with two good hits but only if the second is carried over a dog-leg out of bounds – an all or nothing finish. The Irish Open Championship has been played here on a number of occasions. In 1966 Christy O'Connor came to the 16th needing three birdies to tie Eric Brown – he finished eagle-birdie-eagle! Another memorable finish occurred in 1985 when Seve Ballesteros defeated Bernhard Langer in a thrilling play-off to win his second Irish title.

Portmarnock lies to the north of Royal Dublin, and a short distance to the north of Portmarnock on a tiny peninsula is **The Island** golf links. Until the mid 1970's the course could only be reached by rowing boat from the village of Malahide and the fare paid was included within the green fee. It is a delightful, old-fashioned type of course, not overly long, but deceptively tough with a number of blind holes – something of an Irish Prestwick perhaps.

In Malahide The Grand Hotel (01) 450633 provides a perfect place to base oneself when playing the Dublin courses. It is particularly handy for The Island and Portmarnock and is less expensive (and certainly more attractive) than the majority of the capital's more centrally located hotels. However, if one does wish to be more in the middle of things then among the better hotels in Dublin are The Shelbourne (01) 766471 (which is attractive), The Berkeley Court (01) 601711, The Burlington (01) 605222, Mont Clare (01) 616799 and Jury's (01) 605000. Also well worth noting is the Victor Hotel in Dun Laoghaire, (01) 2853555. In Howth, The King Sitric (01) 325235 is an

excellent seafood restaurant, and again particularly convenient for the courses to the north of Dublin. Good restaurants abound in the centre of Dublin and suggestions could include The Grey Door (01) 763286, Le Coq Hardi (01) 689070 and Locks (01) 543391. Visiting a Dublin bar is an experience in itself and ought not to be missed. Take your pick, but when you do venture in be prepared for a good sing-song.

If most of the celebrated golf courses are found to the north of Dublin there are many more to the south and west of the capital, indeed, the city is practically encircled by golf courses – what a marvellous prospect! Noted 18 hole courses worthy of mention here include; **Hermitage, Howth, Deer Park, The Grange,** the splendid new course at **St Margaret's** and **Slade Valley**; while a good 9 hole course not far from Dun Laoghaire is found at **Killiney**. Without question the most talked about course in the Dublin area is the new Palmer-designed course at the **Kildare Country Club** (01) 6273333 at Straffan (see ahead).

The leading club to the south of Dublin is **Woodbrook**. It too has played host to the Irish Open, in addition to many other important tournaments. Woodbrook offers a mixture of semi-links and parkland golf and although not the most challenging of courses is always immaculately kept. A few miles further down the coast and into County Wicklow is the pleasant course at **Greystones**, from the back nine of which there are some marvellous views of the Wicklow Mountains, and near the town of Wicklow, **Blainroe** Golf Club has a much improved – and pretty demanding – championship length layout. Finally there is a very scenic 9 hole course at **Woodenbridge**; it's a bit of a drive from Dublin, but well worth it.

Following a round at Woodbrook, the Parks (01) 2886177 restaurant in Blackrock Village is highly recommended and in Bray, not far from Greystones or Killiney an evening spent at The Tree of Idleness (01) 2863498 should be extremely relaxing. The Wicklow area is well served by Tinakilly House (0404) 69274 at Rathnew and by Rathsallagh House (045) 53112.

NORTH OF DUBLIN

Thirty miles north of Dublin in the charming village of Baltray near Drogheda is the **County Louth** Golf Club. In the opinion of many this is the most attractive links on the east coast. **Baltray**, as the course is known, enjoys a wonderfully remote setting, but while it may be a peaceful place the course will test your game to the full. Baltray is featured ahead. One needn't look far for a bed as the Club offers its own accommodation and fabulous food, (telephone 041 22329 for details) however, if there's no room at the 19th the best bet is The Neptune (041) 27107 in nearby Bettystown. The hotel is very close to the **Laytown and Bettystown** links which while not in the same class as Baltray certainly poses enough problems. It is the home club of the former Ryder Cup player Des Smyth. Those in search of a good restaurant at Dunderry should investigate the Dunderry Lodge (046) 31671 near Navan – it's reputed to be one of the best in Ireland.

Further north the course at **Dundalk** deserves inspection. Again it's not in the same league as Baltray, but then very few are. Still, it's definitely worth visiting if only for the tremendous scenery it offers. Although very much a parkland type challenge, the course is set out alongside the shores of Dundalk

Bay with the Mountains of Mourne and the Cooley Mountains providing a spectacular backdrop. The Ballymascanlon Hotel (042) 71124 in Dundalk is very good value if a night's stopover is required while for an outstanding restaurant try Quaglinos.

Dundalk in fact provides a fine base for playing our final recommendation in the north east, the course at **Greenore** where a more dramatic location couldn't be wished for. Laid out alongside Carlingford Lough, Greenore golfers have recently built three new holes which are destined to be the envy of every golf course in Ireland. You don't believe it? Then go and visit, you'll be made most welcome.

TRAVELLING INLAND

For those who enjoy horseracing as well as golf (this must include near enough every Irishman), a good route to take out of Dublin is the N7. Given a clear road The Curragh is little more than half an hour's drive away. This is the Epsom of Ireland. Golf has been played on the great stretch of heathland since the 1850's and the **Curragh** Golf Club was founded in 1883 making it the oldest Golf Club in the Republic. Rather like England's senior links, Westward Ho!, the fairways are shared with the local farmer's sheep. There's also a nearby army range – one presumes golf is rarely uneventful at the Curragh! It's actually a very good course and the green fees are typically modest.

Baberstown Castle (01) 288157 at Celbridge is an excellent place to head for after a day on the heath, especially if a game of golf has been combined with a day at the races. The Hotel Keadeen (045) 31666 at Newbridge is also strongly recommended and is in fact a little closer to the Curragh.

Venturing further inland, **Mullingar** in County Westmeath has long rivalled Carlow as Ireland's best inland course; it again is featured ahead. **Headfort** near Kells, and **Royal Tara** at Navan, both in County Meath are two of the regions better parkland courses, and in County Offaly, **Tullamore** is of a similar nature although it perhaps has a little more variety. All three enjoy delightful locations and welcome visitors at most times.

Finally, two hotel golf courses that are decidedly worth inspecting are at the **Nuremore** Hotel (042) 61438 near Carrickmacross, in Co. Monaghan and one of Ireland's newest gems, the spectacular **Slieve Russell** Hotel course (049) 26444 at Ballyconnell in Co. Cavan which opened in the second half of 1992.

H. Rountree "PORTMARNOCK" Sarah Baddiel's Book Gallery

PORTMARNOCK
CHAMPIONSHIP GOLF

One day in 1893, a Scot domiciled in Dublin named **W.C. Pickman** was riding his bicycle along the road from Baldoyle to Portmarnock when, so the story goes, looking across the estuary, it occurred to him that he was looking at magnificent golfing terrain ....

Portmarnock is located to the North of Dublin and lying on a peninsula is surrounded by water on three sides. It can be as tough a challenge as any in the world – more than 7,000 yards from the back tees with the rough often mercilessly punishing (knee-high in parts!) But Portmarnock, rather like Muirfield, offers a genuinely fair challenge. There are no blind shots, no hidden traps and the greens are among the finest in the world. As for that rough, well, as an obviously straight-hitter once remarked, you've no business being there in the first place and you cannot really argue with that! Portmarnock has its beauty too: to the South, the Hill of Howth and the great sweep of Dublin Bay and to the North West, Drogheda and the distant Mountains of Mourne. On a fine day, the links provides the player with a spectacular 360 degree vista; all in all it is a truly wonderful place to pursue the Royal and Ancient game.

The Secretary at Portmarnock is the very helpful **Mr. Wally Bornemann**. He may be contacted by writing to **The Secretary, Portmarnock Golf Club, Portmarnock, Co. Dublin** and by telephone on **(01) 323082** (the code is **(010 353 1)** from the U.K.) The Club's professional is **Joey Purcell,** he can be reached on **(01) 325157**.

Providing visitors possess a handicap of 24 or less they are very welcome to play the famous links; however, ladies cannot play at weekends or on Bank Holidays. It seems that half of Dublin wants to play Portmarnock (not to mention you and me) and the course can be extremely popular. The wisest move is to telephone the Club before you set off. The green fees as set in 1992 are, for gentlemen £35 midweek, £45 at the weekend, and for lady visitors, £15 midweek. As a bit of a tip, Mondays and Tuesdays are the quietest days. Golfing Societies are equally welcome subject to prior arrangement with the Secretary.

It is far easier to travel to Portmarnock than to many of the country's other great golfing attractions. The capital is very well served by international flights and Dublin's airport is only six miles from the links. From Britain, it is also worth noting that both B&I and Sealink sail regularly to Dublin. As mentioned, Portmarnock lies to the north of the capital, a distance of about eight miles. By road it's essentially a case of heading for Portmarnock village and then looking out for signs: from Dublin the course should be signposted off to the right, and from Malahide, look to your left.

The casual visitor will not have to attempt the full 7,000 yards plus, but he's still likely to be facing a good 6,600 yards so he'd better have his game in fine fettle! Happily there is a relatively gentle break-in with three holes measuring less than 400 yards. The course then changes direction and the **4th**, the stroke one hole confronts you. Normally, the wind will be with you, but don't bank on it! A number of second shots will be played to plateau greens which can be very difficult to hold and a good Irish pitch-and-run may be needed frequently. The most celebrated holes are probably the **14th** and the **15th**, the former has been described by **Henry Cotton** as one of the greatest par fours in golf and it's easy to see why. The hole is played towards the sea along a gently curving fairway; the narrow green sits on a plateau and is protected by two bunkers set into the rise of the green with many humps and hillocks surrounding the putting surface – nothing but a precise second shot will do. As for the 15th, **Ben Crenshaw** has called it, 'one of the greatest short holes on earth'. Out of bounds in the form of the beach lurks the length of the hole to the right. Even then there is no let up and the five-four-four finish is one of the toughest around.

The gentle wind down of course begins at the 19th. Portmarnock has a splendid Clubhouse, though not the original, which unfortunately burned down. The atmosphere is tremendous and some very good value snacks are offered daily with dinner also possible during the week.

The Club has staged many great Championships in the past including, somewhat surprisingly, the (British) **Amateur Championship** which was won – it goes without saying – by an Irishman. The **World Cup** was played at Portmarnock in 1960, **Palmer** and **Snead** winning for the United States, while winners of the Irish Open on this links have included Americans **Crenshaw** and **Hubert Green** and an illustrious quartet of European stars; **Ballesteros**, **Langer**, **Woosnam** and **Olazabal** – proving the old adage that a great course will always produce a great champion.

In 1991 Portmarnock successfully hosted the **Walker Cup** and there are many who consider it a travesty that the **Ryder Cup** matches will not be coming here in 1993.

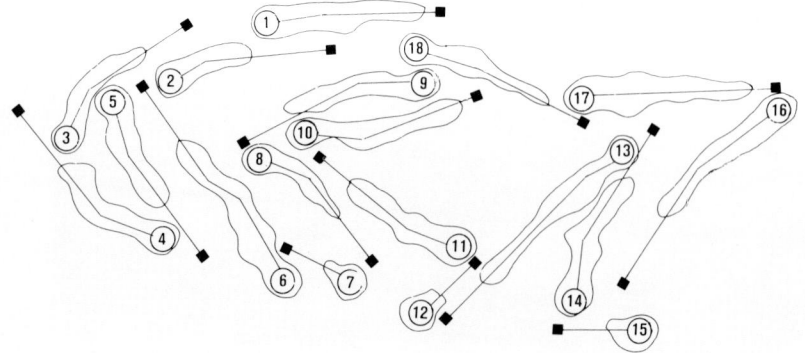

Hole	Yards	Par	Hole	Yards	Par
1	388	4	10	380	4
2	368	4	11	445	4
3	388	4	12	144	3
4	460	4	13	565	5
5	407	4	14	385	4
6	586	5	15	192	3
7	180	3	16	527	5
8	370	4	17	466	4
9	444	4	18	408	4
Out	**3,591**	**36**	**In**	**3,512**	**36**
			Out	**3,591**	**36**
			TOTALS	**7,103**	**72**

COUNTY LOUTH (BALTRAY)
CHAMPIONSHIP GOLF

Golfing visitors to the east coast of Ireland can almost be forgiven if having arrived in Dublin they fail to travel any real distance beyond the fair city. Dotted around the fringes of Ireland's capital are numerous first rate challenges, something like 20 courses within 10 miles (or half an hour's drive) of O'Connell Street (How many within thirty minutes of Piccadilly Circus?)

There is great variety too with classic links courses to the north, including world famous Portmarnock and Royal Dublin and some very pleasant, well manicured parkland courses to the south of the city; and the quality of golf isn't the only reason why so many decide not to venture away from Dublin – the city and its people have much to offer. But I did say at the beginning, 'can almost be forgiven', this is because one of the greatest courses in Ireland lies no more than 40 miles north of Dublin (and about an hour's drive) just beyond Drogheda in the small fishing village of Baltray. This is where County Louth Golf Club is situated, and a truly magnificent and totally natural golf links.

Baltray, as everyone calls it, is probably the least widely known of Ireland's great championship links; give the Club a major professional tournament and all this would probably change, but for the moment Baltray retains a fairly low profile, which doubtless suits many of the members! Not that they won't welcome you, mind you, for this must be one of the most friendly and informal Clubs around. A genuinely relaxed Saturday afternoon atmosphere prevails throughout the week.

One gentleman who helps maintain the marvellous mood is the secretary, **Michael Delany**; visitors wishing to arrange a game at Baltray should contact him in advance of intended play either by writing to him at **County Louth Golf Club, Baltray, Co. Louth** or by telephoning **(041) 22329** (010 353 41 22329 from Great Britain). Green fees are good value; in 1992 they were £24 during the week and £30 at the weekend with reduced rates for juniors. Club competitions may make it difficult to arrange a game for the weekend but usually the only other day to try to avoid is Tuesday. Golf Societies normally visit Baltray on Mondays and Thursdays. One other person you may wish to consult before striding out on to the links is the Club's affable professional **Paddy McGuirk,** tel. **(041) 22444.**

As already mentioned, Baltray is about an hour's drive from Dublin; it is less from the city's airport which is located 8 miles north of the capital. The road to pick up, both from Dublin and

the airport is the N1. It links the city with Drogheda (and indeed carries on towards Belfast) and is well signposted – if you follow the course of the River Boyne towards the Sea you cannot go far wrong, but make sure you journey north of the river.

We were about to stride out onto the links, and tackle all 6567 yards, par 73 from the medal tees (6783 yards, par 73 from the back markers). The first two holes tempt us to open the shoulders (after all the rough doesn't look too menacing), but on both holes a wayward drive can easily find a bunker, and this is the story all the way around. Architect **Tom Simpson** may have been presented with a wonderful piece of golfing terrain to work with when he designed the course in the 1930s, but he clearly put an enormous amount of thought into the positioning of bunkers and other hazards. The good shot at Baltray, however, is always rewarded, no more so than at the par five **3rd** where the second must be played blind over a rise in the fairway to a narrow green. The **4th** is only a drive and a pitch but it is a classic links hole with a tumbling, folding, dune lined fairway. The **5th** green is actually perched high in these dunes; it is a splendid short hole, one of Baltray's 'four little gems'.

For many the most exciting holes appear between the 12th and 16th at the far end of the links, the part closest to the Sea and where nature presents the dunes at their wildest. The **12th** fairway looks as if it has been carved out of the surrounding towering sandhills. The shot to the green has to be targeted through a gap in the dunes and only a perfect long iron will suffice; spray it to the left or right and disaster awaits. The **13th** is almost as difficult but the far reaching views from the elevated **14th** tee will placate most wounded souls. This is a beautiful and historic part of the world and as you smash your drive at the 14th (well it's almost reachable with a mighty blow) the broad estuary of the River Boyne, famed for its 17th century battle, stretches out ahead while over your shoulder are the far off romantic Mountains of Mourne. Another fine hole comes at the **16th** where the angled approach is played into an amphitheatre green. It is a superb dog-leg hole, and again one of several at Baltray. A new championship tee has added considerable teeth to the par five **18th**; however from the forward tees it still offers a real chance of a finishing birdie.

The way to celebrate such a feat at Baltray is with a drop of the famous black and white stuff, almost, but not quite obligatory. Good food and overnight accommodation in the Clubhouse can also be arranged. Like every good Irish Golf Club, Baltray has 19 splendid holes.

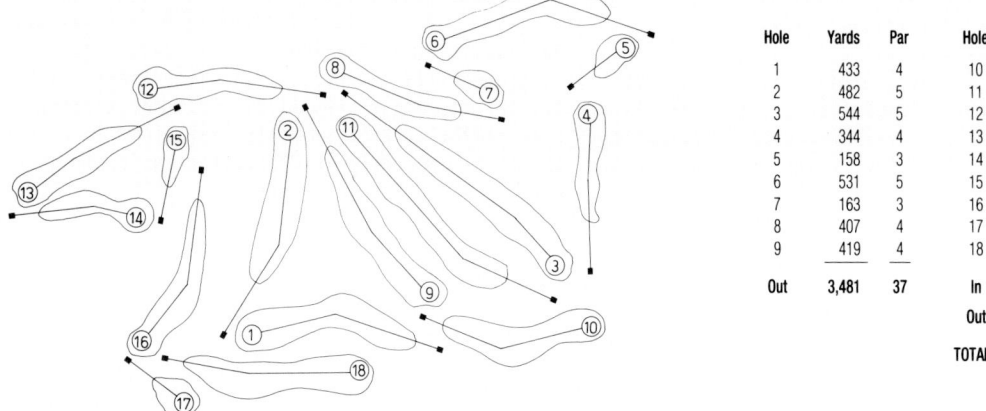

Hole	Yards	Par	Hole	Yards	Par
1	433	4	10	398	4
2	482	5	11	481	5
3	544	5	12	410	4
4	344	4	13	421	4
5	158	3	14	332	4
6	531	5	15	152	3
7	163	3	16	388	4
8	407	4	17	179	3
9	419	4	18	541	5
Out	3,481	37	In	3,302	36
			Out	3,481	37
			TOTALS	6,783	73

KILDARE HOTEL AND COUNTRY CLUB

The fifteenth of July 1991 saw the official opening of the Kildare Hotel and Country Club, widely acclaimed as Ireland's premier resort development and a five star complex to rival the very best that Europe can offer.

The Kildare Hotel and Country Club has been developed at a cost of £27.5 million by the Jefferson Smurfit Group plc. Ireland's first world class hotel and sporting facility encompasses an 18 hole championship golf course designed by Arnold Palmer, salmon and trout fishing, indoor and outdoor tennis, exercise, swimming and croquet.

The entire project was created in less than three years and involved the complete renovation of the existing Straffan House. A new wing was added in the style of the existing house, establishing in the process 45 bedroom hotel, whose exacting standards have few equals.

The bedrooms and suites are complemented by exquisitely appointed self-contained apartments and a magnificent three bedroomed lodge in the grounds. Meetings and private dining take place in the 'Tower' and 'River' rooms, where work can happily be combined with play by taking advantage of the wide range of leisure and recreational activities.

The Kildare Country Club, now fast becoming known simply as the 'K' Club, is a multi-facility sporting paradise. Members, hotel guests and visitors alike can enjoy the Championship golf course, river and lake fishing, indoor and outdoor fishing, squash, exercise rooms, swimming pool, beauty treatment room, sauna and solarium.

The golf course, designed by Arnold Palmer and his expert team, has already received excellent reviews and is scheduled to host many national and international tournaments. Covering 177 acres of prime Co. Kildare woodland, the course has a championship length of 6,456 metres and a testing par of 72 (four par fives, four par threes and ten par fours).

Among eighteen exquisitely and imaginatively sculpted holes, particularly outstanding memories could stem from the monster par five seventh, the water-clad eighth or the spectacular par three seventeenth. Every hole, however, has its own challenge and its own beauty. In the words of Arnold Palmer himself, reflecting proudly on his work whilst standing on the terrace of the elevated clubhouse sited behind the eighteenth green: "We could draw for 100 years and not come up with as good a vision".

The Kildare Hotel and Country Club
Straffan
Co. Kildare
Ireland
Tel: (010 353) 1 6273333
Fax: (010 353) 1 6273312

THE 'K' CLUB (STRAFFAN)
CHAMPIONSHIP GOLF

In timeless fashion, and without a care in the world the River Liffey meanders its way through the ancient Straffan Estate in Co. Kildare en route to Dublin and the Irish Sea. In 1988 the estate was acquired by Ireland's largest, and possibly most ambitious company, Jefferson Smurfit; undoubtedly the great attraction being the vast 19th century Straffan House, one of the most striking country houses in Ireland. Such a company, such an estate – a heady mix if ever there was one. For some time it had been the dream of company chairman **Dr Michael Smurfit** to develop a 'world class country club'. At Straffan he saw the potential for an extremely grand, even palatial 5 star hotel (the restored and extended Straffan House) and sufficient land to build a challenging championship length golf course, one good enough to host national and international tournaments. Thus the Kildare Country Club, or 'K' Club as everyone calls it, was born.

When it came to the design of the golf course the word 'challenging' was clearly given special emphasis, for though four leading golf architects submitted proposals for the 18 hole layout, it seems there was not much of a contest once **Arnold Palmer** and his team had presented their ideas. Palmer had already created one course in Ireland, the ultra-spectacular links at Tralee on the west coast, now was the opportunity to demonstrate his swashbuckling design theories on an inland site, just 25 miles south west of Dublin.

The new course, (which measures over 7,100 yards from its championship tees), was officially opened in July 1991 and has straightaway generated an enormous amount of interest. It has to be said that not all press coverage has been favourable, although the criticisms have not been directed at the quality or shape of the layout itself. The course at Straffan has suffered serious drainage problems and frankly it has not been the best place to visit after a prolonged spell of rain.

The owners are naturally determined to rectify the situation and by the time you read this they may have already done so! Drainage difficulties aside, tackle this course on a fine day and you are likely to be awestruck and amazed by some of the shots you are asked to take on: Straffan is no ordinary golf course.

First though, a couple of quick introductions. The Golf Secretary at the 'K' Club is the very personable **Eddie Fallon**, tel **(01) 6273987**, and the professional is **Ernie Jones** tel **(01) 6273111**, whom many may remember as the professional at Royal Co. Down. Visitors can make tee reservations by telephoning the hotel reception on **(01) 6270295**. All players must be golf club members and have a handicap; finally the green fee in 1992 was £70 with reduced rates available for groups of 15 and over.

Time then to 'attack' Arnie's golf course. A long straight drive at the **1st**, carrying the large fairway bunker should set up a relatively easy opening par five. The same, however, cannot be said of the **2nd** where two very precise shots are essential. The drive must be perfectly positioned for the approach is downhill to a smallish green guarded by trees on one side and water on the other. And so the gauntlet is laid down. There are two par threes in the first five holes, the **5th** being the more demanding but for most people the round really comes alive at the par five **7th**. From tee to green this is one long, dramatic, 'S shaped' voyage of discovery as the hole double dog-legs its way over sand, rough and water and in between a plethora of colourful trees and shrubs. The green occupies its own pretty little island and is sandwiched between two arms of the River Liffey. A quaint old iron bridge transports us to and from the island. Our friend the River Liffey is an inseparable companion for the entire length of the **8th** (a hooker's nightmare) and then comes the **9th**, a truly intimidating stroke one hole.

There is absolutely no let up on the back nine, indeed the drama most definitely increases. The **12th** is probably the best par three on the course, the tee shot here must be struck over a small lake to a superbly angled green – between the lake and green is a deep beach-like bunker where the sand literally runs into the water's edge. The downhill par five **13th** rivals the 18th as the most exhilarating hole: like the 7th it is a double dog-leg with a highly illusive and heavily contoured green. From the 15th to the end of the round a series of heroic shots alongside or across water are called for. Two daring water carries in fact confront us at the **16th** and a good drive at the last begs one final question: 'shall we risk all and go for the **18th** green in two – a real grandstand finish in front of the magnificent clubhouse? Well, what would Arnie do?

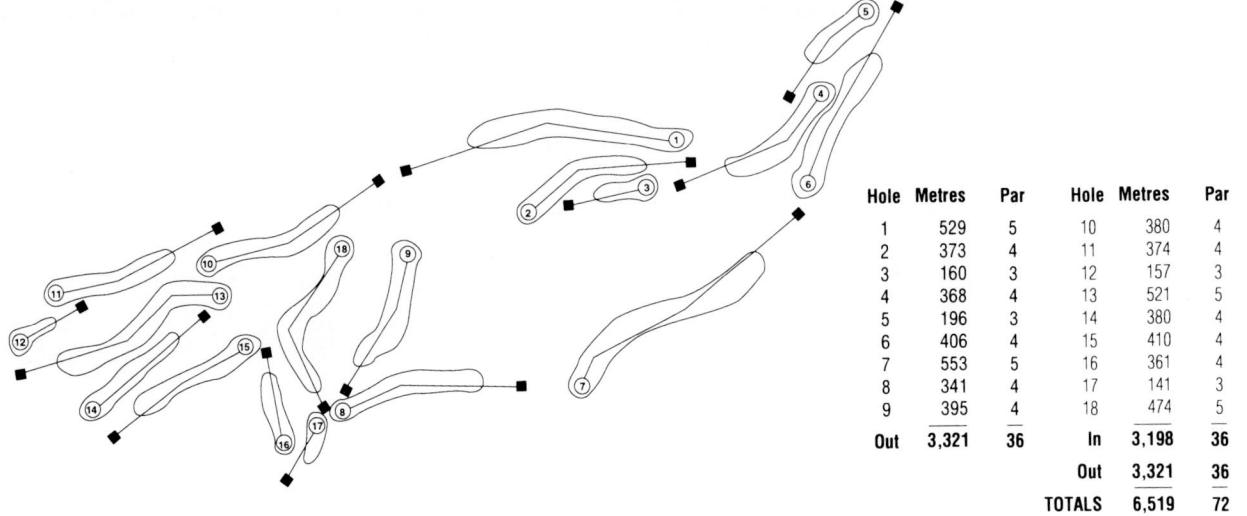

Hole	Metres	Par	Hole	Metres	Par
1	529	5	10	380	4
2	373	4	11	374	4
3	160	3	12	157	3
4	368	4	13	521	5
5	196	3	14	380	4
6	406	4	15	410	4
7	553	5	16	361	4
8	341	4	17	141	3
9	395	4	18	474	5
Out	**3,321**	**36**	**In**	**3,198**	**36**
			Out	**3,321**	**36**
			TOTALS	**6,519**	**72**

MOUNT JULIET
CHAMPIONSHIP GOLF

Joseph II of Austria (1741-1790) was an enlightened despot and a thoroughly miserable soul to boot. He wrote his own epitaph: 'Here lies a man who never succeeded in anything he attempted.' When, and let's hope it's a long, long way off, people begin to consider a fitting epitaph for **Jack William Nicklaus** someone should suggest, 'Here lies a man who succeeded in almost everything he attempted'.

Not content to go down in history as merely the greatest golfer who ever lived, the 'Golden Bear' (as if any other colour were appropriate) is determined to establish himself as the finest golf course designer the world has known. Jack's original career goal was to better Bobby Jones' record of 13 Major Championship victories: by 1986 he had totalled 20. Many believe that he would have won even more Major titles had he not devoted so much of his energy to designing championship courses. But then again, had he not done so there would of course be no Muirfield Village, no St Mellion, no Glen Abbey......and no Mount Juliet.

Nicklaus once said, 'Building a golf course is my total expression. My golf game can only go on so long. But what I have learned can be put into a piece of ground to last beyond me'. Mount Juliet estate is a heavenly piece of ground, in fact 1500 acres of subliminally beautiful Irish countryside, through which the River Nore flows and on which Jack Nicklaus has built a masterly 18 hole golf course. Situated approximately 75 miles south of Dublin (via the N7/N9) on the outskirts of Thomastown in Co. Kilkenny, Mount Juliet may just be the ultimate golfing oasis. The Mount Juliet Hotel, a splendidly refurbished 18th century mansion house and the golf course have only recently opened yet the reputation of both is already immense. Some people are predicting that Mount Juliet will become the Turnberry or Gleneagles of Ireland, but there appears to be none of their overt 'flashiness' or commercial brashness; everything about Mount Juliet seems very understated and the ambience is at once graceful and peaceful. In front of the great house, somewhere between the hotel reception (where you may be greeted by the soppiest of Irish Wolfhounds) and the 11th tee, is a veritable Garden of Eden. Amid the ancient oaks, beeches and lime trees a hundred colours dazzle the eye and Mount Juliet's famous strutting peacocks can simply vanish into the floral background. It is the perfect place for an early morning 'get your mind together' stroll before going out and tackling Jack's formidable but spectacular parkland layout.

Unlike Gleneagles, golf at Mount Juliet is not restricted to residents and Golf Club members, although hotel guests do pay reduced green fees. Advance bookings can be made for any day of the week by telephoning the Club on **(056) 24725**. Both the Director of Golf, **Katherine MacCann** and the professional, **Keith Mongan** can be contacted on this number. Handicap certificates are required and the green fees for 1992 were £55 (throughout the week). A special rate of £40 (£45 at weekends) is available for groups of 20 or more, while the residents' fee is £30.

The course officially opened on 14th July 1991 and a vast crowd were present to watch Nicklaus play a friendly match against Christy O'Connor. Naturally, the two golfing legends played from the championship tees – all 7103 yards (or 6493 metres) and neither could manage to better the par of 72. Although it is certainly a mighty challenge from those back markers each hole has four sets of tees so one needn't get too despondent! From the medal tees the course measures approximately 6650 yards and from the ladies tees, 5500 yards, par 73.

When writing the piece on East Sussex National (the only other 'new course' ranked among the 'Following the Fairways Top 20 Courses in the British Isles') I fantasised about a 'dream nine holes' made up entirely from some of the finest holes on East Sussex National's West Course. To that nine I'm now going to add the **2nd**, **3rd**, **5th**, **8th**, **10th**, **11th**, **13th**, **14th** and **18th** from the Mount Juliet Course. This collection will provide three exceptional short holes: the 3rd (which has a serious water carry), the 11th (over a plunging valley occupied by a cascading stream and rockery) and the 14th (with its marvellous backdrop of trees); three par fours: the 2nd (a beautifully shaped dog-leg), the 13th (a hint of Augusta's back nine) and the 18th (reminiscent of the closing hole at St Mellion); as well as three outstanding par fives, namely the 5th (whose 12 bunkers Nicklaus ignored in the aforementioned exhibition match when he eagled the hole after reaching the green with a driver and a six iron!), the huge 8th (a fabulous elevated tee here) and the 10th (where like the 5th a real sea of traps must be negotiated en route to a superbly angled green). A dream round for sure, but sweet dreams? Nightmares, I reckon!

Hole	Yards	Par	Hole	Yards	Par
1	363	4	10	546	3
2	415	4	11	168	5
3	184	3	12	417	4
4	403	4	13	436	4
5	534	5	14	197	4
6	229	3	15	371	4
7	417	4	16	433	3
8	577	5	17	515	5
9	424	4	18	474	4
Out	**3,546**	**36**	**In**	**3,557**	**36**
			Out	**3,546**	**36**
			TOTALS	**7,103**	**72**

RATHSALLAGH HOUSE

Converted from Queen Anne stables which burnt to the ground in 1798 this large comfortable farmhouse is situated in 500 acres of peaceful parkland surrounded by some of the most beautiful countryside of Eastern Ireland.

The addition of full modern amenities has done nothing to spoil the traditional splendour of the house where welcoming log fires combine with full central heating to ensure your comfort. The delightful bedrooms are individually decorated with care and attention; all are large and luxurious and offer en suite bathrooms with enormous bath towels.

The atmosphere is happy and relaxed in this hotel with its huge variety of diversions; choose from Tennis, Golf Driving Range, Golf Practice Holes, Putting, Archery, Croquet, Clay Pigeon Shooting with C.P.S.A Club Coach and snooker, or simply take a stroll around the award winning two-acre walled garden. Either way treat yourself to a sauna afterwards, then cool off with a dip in the indoor swimming pool.

For the racing enthusiast the hotel is ideally situated for the Irish National Stud, along with Curragh, Punchestown and Naas Racecourses, and Goffs Sales Paddock.

For a change deer-stalking can be arranged, while your host, Joe O'Flynn, is master of the local hunt and can arrange fox-hunting in season. Besides the outstanding natural beauty of the surrounding area there is also a variety of historic sites well worth a visit, not least of these being Glendalough and Russborough House.

At the end of such a day, the real log fire of the restaurant provides a pleasing welcome. The cooking is superb with the emphasis on fresh, local produce, while the too-tempting sweet trolley fairly groans with luscious offerings.

Naturally Rathsallagh is fully able to cater for business meetings and offers, amongst other things, a fully-quipped purpose-built Conference Room and Helipad.

Rathsallagh Country House and Restaurant
Dunlavin
Co. Wicklow
Ireland
Tel: (010 353 45) 53112
Fax: (010 353 45) 53343

MULLINGAR
CHAMPIONSHIP GOLF

'St. Patrick was a gentleman
Who through strategy and stealth
Drove all the snakes from Ireland,
Here's a toasting to his health;
But not too many toastings
Lest you lose yourself and then
Forget the good St Patrick
And see all those snakes again.'

So, reading between the lines, golfers who restrain themselves at the 19th hole have about as much chance of bumping into an Irish snake as they have of meeting the Man in the Moon. But just suppose we've been less than restrained....now, we will direct the Man in the Moon towards Connemara or the New Course at Ballybunion where he should feel very much at home and as for snakes we'll send them anywhere but Mullingar. Why? Well, Mullingar may not resemble The Seychelles but it must be about the nearest thing in Ireland to a golfing Garden of Eden.

'Sylvan' is an adjective commonly used to describe the setting at Mullingar and when one adds the indisputable quality of the golf course and the friendliness of the welcome to the equation it is easy to see why this has become one of Ireland's most popular Clubs to visit. Yet before the war the most accurate word to describe the Mullingar golfer might well have been 'pernickety', or 'restless' at best. This is because by the mid 1930s, less than 50 years after their Club's foundation the golfers were already searching for a fifth home. Pernicketiness obviously paid off though for when they 'discovered' the site at Belvedere to the south of Mullingar (off the N52), and close to the peace and beauty of Lough Ennell, they knew at once that they had struck gold. And of course the obvious person to design their new layout was James Braid, architect of the majestic King's Course at Gleneagles. Braid came, advised and left; the 18 hole course at Belvedere opened for play; the Mullingar golfer stopped being pernickety and the Club hasn't looked back since. In fact the course has attracted top class tournaments and generous praise in equal abundance.

Today the best interests of the Mullingar golfer, and all visitors to this wonderful 'out in the country' location, are in the capable hands of the Club's Manager, **Mr C. Mulligan**. He may be contacted by telephone on **(044) 48366**, while the professional, **John Burns** can be reached on **(044) 40085**. Visitors, preferably with official handicaps can make advance bookings, indeed this is recommended although there are no general tee restrictions. In 1992 the green fees were £15 on weekdays with £20 payable at weekends. As a rule the best days to arrange a game are Tuesdays, Thursdays and Fridays and unless one is an exceptionally good golfer (or avid spectator) the August Bank Holiday should be avoided: this is when the Club hosts the highly prestigious **Mullingar Scratch Cup**, an annual event first staged in 1963, and with an impressive list of winners including the likes of **Joe Carr, Peter Townsend, Des Smyth** and the course record holder (with an astonishing 63), **Philip Walton**.

From the Championship tees, Mullingar measures 6451 yards, par 72. Ballybunion was mentioned above and just as it is the massive dunes that fashion and frame the holes on this glorious seaside links, so it is the spectacular collection (and enormous variety) of trees that shape the rolling parkland fairways at Mullingar.

The most celebrated hole on the course is probably the **2nd**, a long and difficult par three where the pin sits on a small, slippery table of a green flanked either side by several magnetic little pot bunkers. None of the four par fives at Mullingar is especially frightening, indeed each represents an obvious birdie opportunity for the good, straight hitter but to my mind it is the par fours that are the real strength of Mullingar. Picking out five of these I would select the **7th** (the most testing two-shot hole of the round); the **8th** (a severe dog-leg right with an elevated tee and an uphill approach); the **10th** (again a downhill drive to a fairway bordered by some magnificent pine trees); the **11th** (shades of Wentworth here) and the **17th** (a sweeping dog-leg left to yet another raised and well guarded green).

The closing hole at Mullingar is one of those 'birdieable' par fives (providing you successfully carry the watery ditch that fronts the green) and the 19th is where first class sustenance can be found. Recently refurbished, the clubhouse is a fine place in which to relax, unwind and reflect on your visit to Jimmy Braid's Garden of Eden – just go easy on the toastings!

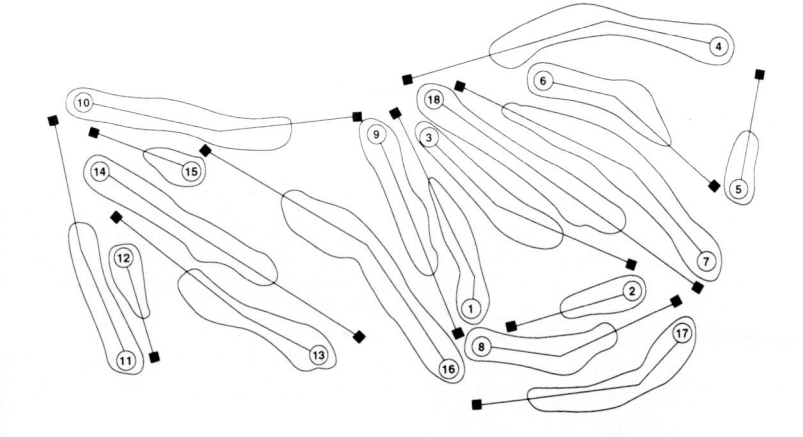

Hole	Yards	Par	Hole	Yards	Par
1	338	4	10	433	4
2	189	3	11	354	4
3	389	4	12	152	3
4	496	5	13	370	4
5	186	3	14	480	5
6	330	4	15	162	3
7	453	4	16	493	5
8	343	4	17	392	4
9	338	4	18	502	5
Out	**3,062**	**35**	**In**	**3,338**	**37**
			Out	**3,062**	**35**
			TOTALS	**6,400**	**72**

SLIEVE RUSSELL

The Slieve Russell Hotel Golf and Country Club opened it's doors on the 1st August 1990. The hotel is situated on 300 acres of parkland landscape and encompasses gardens and two natural lakes in the grounds covering 50 acres.

Each of the 150 bedrooms is furnished with impeccable taste and great attention has been given to guest comfort. The deluxe rooms offer the added luxury of an Airbath. The Suites are spacious and luxurious, many offer a fine view of the Golf Course.

There are two restaurants; the elegant Conall Cearnach Restaurant serves the finest of Irish Cuisine. The Brackley restaurant, the less formal of the two, specialises in traditional Irish and French dishes. Both restaurants offer a comprehensive Wine List to complement your menu choice.

Guests have a choice of three bars in which to enjoy a drink in relaxed surroundings. The Kells bar, the public bar, is decorated on the theme of the Book of Kells and features a handmade copy of that famous tome. The Pike bar, the residents bar, is the perfect place to idle way your time busily doing nothing or why not have your favourite tipple in the Conservatory.

The Slieve Russell is the perfect Conference Venue with meeting rooms suitable for 4-800. A comprehensive range of audio-visual equipment is available to conference groups.

Leisure facilities include Leisure Pool (20m), Saunas, Steamroom, Jacuzzi, Fitness Suite, Solarium, Tennis and Squash Courts, Health and Beauty Salon.

The 18-hole championship standard golf course opened in August 1992. The unique style of the course fits and complements the typical Cavan drumlin and valley landscape, with gently tumbling fairways and contoured greens.

The superb golf Clubhouse is an added bonus and includes a golf shop, restaurant and bar. An excellent feature is the marvellous view which extends over most of the course.

The Slieve Russell Hotel
Golf & Country Club
Ballyconnell
Co. Cavan
Tel: (010 353 49) 26444
Fax: (010 353 49) 26474

NUREMORE HOTEL

The Nuremore Hotel is located 50 miles north-west of Dublin, and is beautifully situated within 200 acres of woods and parkland in the rolling countryside of Co Monaghan.

Originally a Victorian country house, the Nuremore has, over the years, been skilfully converted and extended into a magnificent luxury hotel. Each of its 70 bedrooms has been individually designed and beautifully appointed.

The Nuremore offers its guests an unrivalled range of sports and leisure facilities, including an 18m swimming pool, whirlpool, steamroom, sauna, gymnasium, tennis courts, squash courts and an 18 hole championship-length golf course in the hotel grounds.

The golf course, with a total length of 6246 metres and a par of 73, nestles snugly among the drumlins and lakes for which this part of Ireland is justly famous. The course designer, Eddie Hackett, has managed to carve out of the Monaghan hillside a layout that will present a challenging test of golf for the low handicapper when played off the back tees, or a round of enjoyment for the average golfer, when played from the forward tees.

In addition to its own course, there are many excellent golf courses within easy reach of the Nuremore Hotel, including the championship courses at Baltray and Headfort, both within 30 minutes of the hotel, and Portmarnock, Royal Dublin and Royal Co Down, each no more than an hour and a half away.

For those who want to improve their game during their stay at the Nuremore, the course professional, Maurice Cassidy, is available to give tuition and golf clinics.

Situated just an hour and a half from Dublin, the Nuremore Hotel is an ideal venue for a relaxing break, and, as extensive conference facilities are provided, it is also ideal as a location for working breaks.

Nuremore Hotel
Carrickmacross
Co Monaghan
Ireland
Tel: (010 353 42) 61438
Fax: (010 353 42) 61853

SOUTH EAST IRELAND
CHOICE GOLF

Continuing to wander down through the counties of Ireland, County Laois is the next we come across. There's only one eighteen hole course, **The Heath** and no guesses as to the type of golf offered. The course is laid out on common land and rather like The Curragh, there's a fair chance that you'll spot more sheep than golfers. Stumbling into County Carlow we find probably the best inland course (aside from the new Mt. Juliet) in south east Ireland. **Carlow** is a superb course; well-bunkered and well-wooded, it presents a considerable test of golf but a very fair one nonetheless. Carlow is highlighted later in this chapter. There are a number of convenient hotels in Carlow itself but for a real treat stay in Castledermot at Kilkea Castle (0503) 45100, a converted 12th century castle. A very popular restaurant is also found in Castledermot, The Doyles School House (0503) 44282 (some accommodation also).

Kilkenny is one of those places that has to be visited. It's a town steeped in Irish history. In medieval times it housed the Irish Parliament, then there's the famous Kilkenny Castle and Kytelers Inn. The golf course is a bit of a youngster in comparison, but it's a fine parkland course, very typical of Ireland's better inland courses. The Newpark Hotel (056) 22122 is just one of several comfortable establishments in the town. Nearby, Thomastown is the setting for the magnificent new **Mt. Juliet** complex (056) 24455, featuring 18 spectacular holes designed by Jack Nicklaus, and a luxurious Country House Hotel (see ahead). One mile from Thomastown and adjacent to Jerpoint Abbey is the Abbey House (056) 24192 – a highly recommended guesthouse.

From Kilkenny it's a pleasant drive to **Borris** where there is an excellent 9 holer and it's certainly not a long way to Tipperary either. Visitors to the county with the famous name should slip a game in at **Clonmel**. This is a fairly isolated part of Ireland and you may just have the course to yourself on a quiet weekday. A good place to put the feet up after a game is the Hotel Minella (052) 22388 or alternatively, the Clonmel Arms Hotel (052) 212333. Not too far away in Cashel, (and be sure to visit the magnificent Rock), The Cashel Palace Hotel (062) 61411 and its restaurant, The Four Seasons are quite outstanding. Before heading down to the Waterford area a quick recommendation for the 18 hole course at **Courtown**, close to the north Wexford coast which boasts some fabulous beaches – in fact the golden sands stretch practically all the way south to Wexford town.

Waterford is our penultimate destination. The world famous Waterford Crystal factory is reason enough for stopping a while in this part of Ireland, but there are other sound reasons too. The first is **Waterford Castle**, the kind of place you dream about: an ivy-clad 12th century castle dominating a small island which can only be reached by ferry. Today, the castle is in fact one of Ireland's finest hotels (051) 78203, both sumptuous and intimate and also exceptionally welcoming. Moreover, the island isn't quite so small that the owners can't find space for a new 18 hole golf and country club! The course, designed by Ryder Cup golfer Des Smyth, opened in the summer of 1992. The other good reasons for visiting Waterford are **Tramore** Golf Club and **Waterford** Golf Club – both offer very good parkland golf. The former, just 15 minutes from Waterford, is a real test and is good enough to have staged the Irish Amateur Championship in 1987, the latter, however, is possibly more enjoyable having greater variety; especially on the back nine which features a magnificent downhill finishing hole: if ever there was a hole that tempted the golfer to open his shoulders and let rip, this is it – a good drive will run forever, a bad drive – well.... Anyway, read on as the course is described in greater detail on a later page.

We end our journey at **Rosslare** in the far south east corner of the country. Having started on a heath, we end on a links; Rosslare may not have the glamour of a Portmarnock or a Royal Dublin but for lovers of the traditional game – rolling sand dunes and a hammering wind – it will do perfectly.

Harry Elliot   ON THE FAIRWAY   Burlington Gallery

CARLOW
CHAMPIONSHIP GOLF

Like Scotland, Ireland is blessed with such a large number of outstanding links courses that overseas visitors tend to overlook its many inland treasures (each country having one great exception of course – Gleneagles in Scotland and Killarney in Ireland). In my view the links courses in Ireland represent the best collection in the world, but there is also much more to inland golf in the Emerald Isle than the twin gems of 'Heaven's Reflex'.

While it may be little known internationally, Carlow Golf Club has a proud reputation in Ireland. In 1978 it hosted the Irish Close Championship (normally the preserve of links courses) and in March 1992 a 24-strong panel of golfing experts ranked Carlow as the best inland course in Ireland after Killarney and the two new lavish developments at Mount Juliet and the Kildare Country Club. Strictly speaking, Carlow is a parkland type course and it certainly boasts a wealth of wonderfully mature trees, however, in places it has much more of a moorland, even heathland feel and the sub-soil is quite sandy. In fact Carlow has more than a hint of Yorkshire's Lindrick and Moortown about it – and it's just as good.

The course was designed by **Tom Simpson**, the architect who created the famous Old Course at Ballybunion and the magnificent links at Baltray, and opened in 1922; visitors have always been made very welcome. The current Secretary at Carlow is **Margaret Meaney** and she can be contacted by telephone on **(0503) 31695**. Advance bookings are recommended and although it is naturally much easier to arrange a game during the week, weekend golf is always a possibility. The 1992 green fees were set at £16 for Monday to Friday with £20 payable on Saturdays and Sundays. Weekly and fortnightly tickets can also be purchased; in 1992 these cost £60 and £100 respectively. Carlow's professional is **Andrew Gilbert** and he can be reached by telephone on **(0503) 41745**.

The county town of Carlow is located approximately 50 miles south of Dublin and the road linking each to the other is the N9. The same road joins Carlow with Thomastown (Mount Juliet), Kilkenny and Waterford to the south. The golf club is situated just to the north of the town, immediately off the Dublin Road.

From the championship tees Carlow is certainly no monster, measuring just under 6400 yards, (5844 metres) but it has a fairly tight par of 70 and is never 'torn apart'. The round commences with a pair of very contrasting par fours. The **1st** is one of Carlow's toughest, a lengthy dog-leg left to a heavily guarded green: only a long straight drive up the right hand side of the fairway will suffice; at the **2nd**, though, the sensible shot is to lay up with an iron off the tee, still leaving only a pitch to the green: a big smash with a driver might get you close to the green but it might also cause you to take a drop out of the water hazard. Probably the best two holes on the front nine are the stroke one **7th** where the fairway meanders around to the left yet tries to throw your ball off to the right – a marvellously sited green here – and the spectacular downhill **8th** where if you were prudent and held back on the 2nd tee no one could begrudge you now winding up and letting fly from this superbly elevated tee.

The real fun, however, is still to come. Carlow's back nine is exceptionally good and precision becomes the name of the game. A deft pitch is required over an attractive pond at the **10th** and disaster can befall the shot that misses the green at the **12th**: Carlow's rough is nothing if not punishing! A trio of par fours, the **14th, 15th** and **16th** guide you into deepest Co. Carlow; each is a really fine hole, the 16th which is played through a tunnel-like valley, perhaps being the most demanding two-shotter of the entire round, and is followed immediately by the most celebrated par three hole. I mentioned 'precision' earlier, well, tackling the **17th** at Carlow has been likened to threading a needle. How's your eyesight! The par five **18th** offers the chance of a closing birdie and a grandstand finish as it tumbles downhill all the way back to the clubhouse. A good ending to a memorable round.

Carlow is less than 25 miles from Mount Juliet. It offers a very different type of challenge from the new Nicklaus designed course, but if you happen to be in this delightful part of 'Middle Ireland' why not play the pair? You won't regret it, that's for certain.

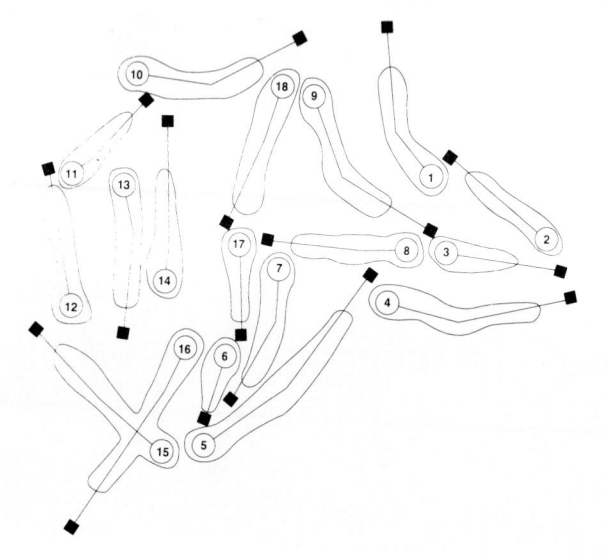

Hole	Metres	Par		Hole	Metres	Par
1	399	4		10	277	4
2	285	4		11	389	4
3	133	3		12	340	4
4	338	4		13	154	3
5	457	5		14	420	4
6	167	3		15	343	4
7	395	4		16	396	4
8	399	4		17	139	3
9	344	4		18	469	5
Out	**2,917**	**35**		**In**	**2,927**	**35**
				Out	**2,917**	**35**
				TOTALS	**5,844**	**70**

WATERFORD
CHAMPIONSHIP GOLF

Many of the greatest prizes in golf come from Waterford. What a dazzling place! Home of the most famous crystal in the world, Waterford is a town that people have long been drawn to. In the early days they were not always welcome. First it was the Vikings: a race not exactly renowned for their good manners. A few centuries later it was Cromwell's Round-heads, a particularly wretched bunch who apparently named the spectacular hill that overlooks the town and its splendid bay, Mount Misery. Crystal came to Waterford in 1783 about one hundred and thirty years after Cromwell's Roundheads, and then one hundred and thirty years after the Penrose Brothers founded their first glass manufacturing business, golf came to Mount Misery.

Waterford Golf Club was formed in March 1912, although the first nine hole course was not officially opened until June 1913. The architect of this layout was **Willie Park Jnr.** of Musselburgh, a former British Open Champion and son of Willie Park Snr., the first ever winner of that event in 1860. Park's course was revised and extended to 18 holes in 1934 by another great Scottish golfer and celebrated architect, **James Braid.**

Whatever the Roundheads thought of Mount Misery, it makes a fine setting for a golf course. Although only a few miles from the sea, Waterford is regarded as one of the finest inland courses in Ireland. Ninety per cent of the course couldn't be described as anything other than classic parkland but on the highest parts of the course – on the top of Mount Misery if you like – there is just a hint of a moorland type course, or even, if you really stretch your imagination, a Formby-like links.

Golfing visitors have always been welcome at Waterford. Subject to availability they may play on any day of the week; naturally it is easier to arrange a game during the week but the only specific tee reservation at weekends is on Saturday when the 1st tee is often reserved for societies between 10.30am and 12.30pm. The Club's Secretary, **John Colfer** can be contacted either by writing to: **Waterford Golf Club, Newrath, Waterford** or by telephone on **(051) 76748** (the code from the UK is 010 353 51). The professional, **Eamonn Condon** can be reached on **(051) 54256** and the Club's fax number is (051) 54257.

The green fees at Waterford for 1992 were set at £15 during the week with £18 payable at weekends and on Bank Holidays. There are no reduced rates for junior visitors. In terms of its location, Waterford the town is approximately

two and a half hours drive from Dublin (via the N9/N7); about one hour south of Kilkenny (N9/N10) and forty five minutes west of Wexford (N25). There is an airport at Waterford, served daily from the UK by Ryan Air from Stanstead. The Golf Club itself is to the north of Waterford, and from the town centre that means crossing the famous bridge then taking the dual carriageway towards Kilkenny, exiting left after about a mile and a half.

From the back tees, Waterford measures 5722 metres, or just under 6300 yards and has a fairly friendly par of 71. By no means is this Ireland's most difficult course but there is ample challenge nonetheless. The **1st** demands an uphill drive to a blind target and is quite a testing opener. Immediately apparent on reaching the green is the quality of the putting surfaces at Waterford – undoubtedly among the best in Ireland. There are three short holes on the front nine and the **3rd** and the **7th** both demand tricky downhill tee shots: the former requires little more than a deftly flighted pitching wedge but the green is surrounded by bunkers and can be very illusive; the 7th requires at least a medium iron and it is again very difficult to judge the distance accurately.

If the first nine holes are pleasant enough, the back nine at Waterford is quite something. The **11th, 12th** and **13th** make for a very attractive run of holes and the finish is quite spectacular with a superb par three (the **16th**) being followed by an almost driveable par four and then a magnificent downhill **18th**. The back tee for this classic closing hole couldn't have been better positioned. The 360 degree views over the surrounding countryside are quite awe-inspiring and the view down the narrow fairway is pretty invigorating too! In fact the fairway twists and turns downhill for almost the entire length of the hole. Ever hit a ball 350 yards? Here's your chance!

South east Ireland will never be as famous for its golf as the south west. Few, if any, areas of the world can compete with County Kerry and Ireland is always likely to be more famous for its links courses than for its inland tests, but there is still much to offer the golfer who journeys to this part of the world. Waterford is a fine course and not far away there is a good test at Tramore, while exciting things have been happening nearby at historic Waterford Castle and half an hour or so north of Waterford, Jack Nicklaus has built an outstanding Championship course at Mount Juliet. Waterford and its surrounds should force even the golfing misery to lick his lips with anticipation.

Hole	Metres	Par	Hole	Metres	Par
1	384	4	10	270	4
2	334	4	11	452	5
3	119	3	12	443	5
4	380	4	13	178	3
5	370	4	14	398	4
6	361	4	15	439	5
7	164	3	16	128	3
8	494	5	17	270	4
9	170	3	18	368	4
Out	**2,776**	**34**	**In**	**2,946**	**37**
			Out	**2,776**	**34**
			Totals	**5,722**	**71**

WATERFORD CASTLE

Waterford Castle's long history stretches back as far as the sixth century when the Island was occupied by a monastery. The strategic importance of the Island eventually drove the monks elsewhere.

However, it was during the Norman Invasion of Ireland in 1160 that Maurice Fitzgerald, cousin to Strongbow, the English Earl of Pembroke, landed on the Island and built the original castle.

It was from the Island that Edward, perhaps the most famous of the Fitzgeralds, completed his elegant translation of the Rubaiyat of Omar Khayyam.

The family's unbroken stewardship of the Castle, one of the longest recorded in Irish history, lasted until 1958 when Mary Fitzgerald married an Italian Prince and moved to Dublin, selling the Island as she left. The Island saw a number of owners until 1987, when Eddie Kearns moved in and restored this magnificent building to create the Hotel.

The Island's private ferry provides the only access to the Hotel. Once there, guests will find rooms of supreme elegance and luxury and enjoy exceptional cuisine in the oak-panelled majesty of the Great Dining Room.

The Castle boasts its own leisure club which offers tennis, an indoor heated swimming pool, gymnasium and sauna, while horse riding and clay pigeon shooting can also be arranged.

In April, Waterford Castle Golf Course will be ready for play. The Castle may be private, but it is not remote. Ryanair fly direct from Stansted to Waterford Airport, itself only ten minutes' drive from the Castle.

For tranquility and luxury inherited from the Island's monastic past, there is nothing quite like the Isle of Waterford Castle.

Waterford Castle - the Isle of the Castle
For further information and bookings, contact:
Geraldine Fitzgerald
Tel: (010 353 517) 8203
Fax: (010 353 517) 9316

NORTH WEST IRELAND

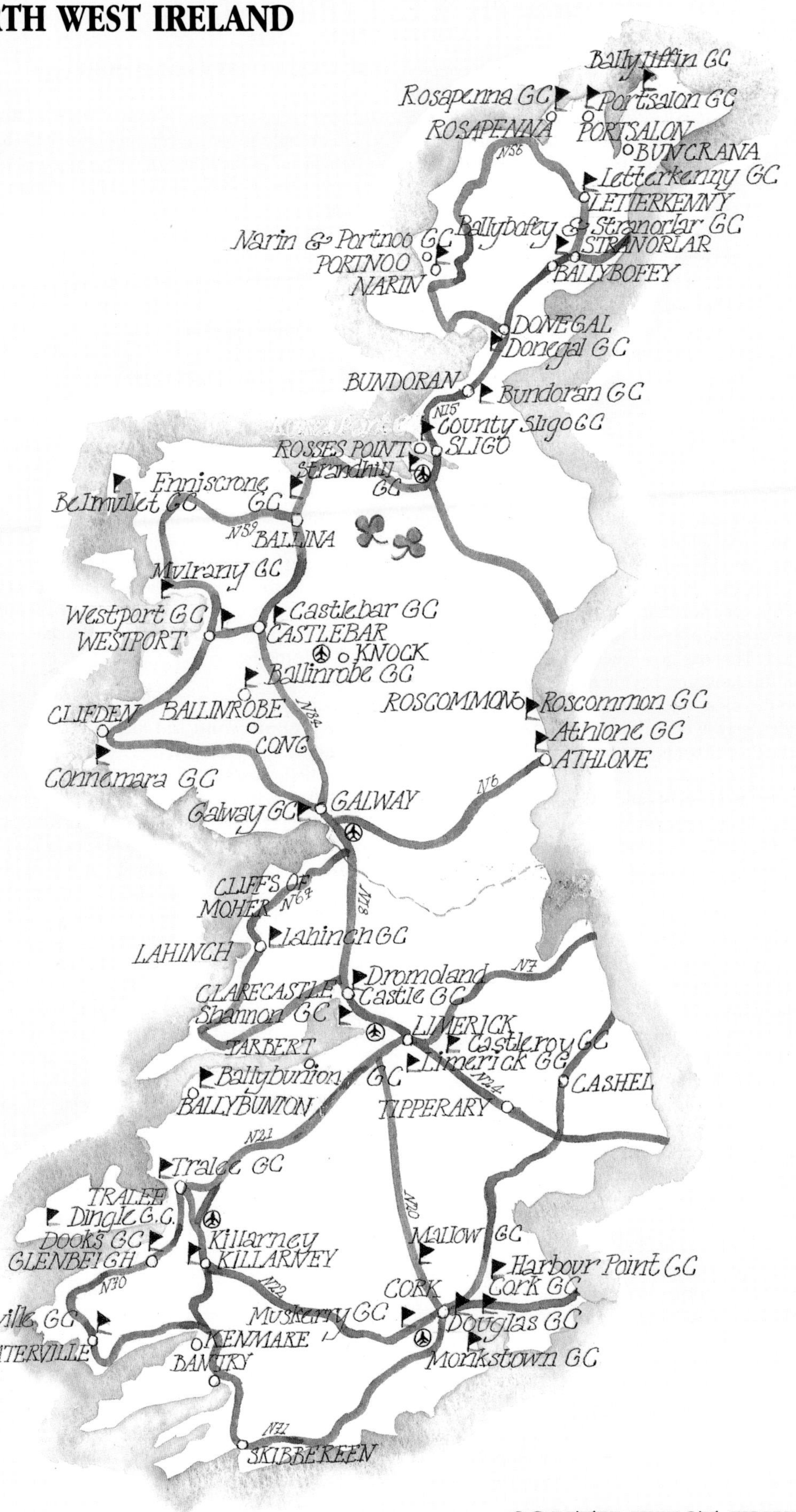
Ballyliffin GC
Rosapenna GC
Portsalon GC
ROSAPENNA
PORTSALON
BUNCRANA
N56
Letterkenny GC
LETTERKENNY
Ballybofey & Stranorlar GC
STRANORLAR
BALLYBOFEY
Narin & Portnoo GC
PORTNOO
NARIN
DONEGAL
Donegal GC
BUNDORAN
Bundoran GC
N15
County Sligo GC
ROSSES POINT
SLIGO
Strandhill GC
Enniscrone GC
Belmullet GC
N59
BALLINA
Mulrany GC
Westport GC
WESTPORT
Castlebar GC
CASTLEBAR
KNOCK
Ballinrobe GC
BALLINROBE
N84
ROSCOMMON
Roscommon GC
Athlone GC
ATHLONE
CLIFDEN
CONG
Connemara GC
Galway GC
GALWAY
N6
CLIFFS OF MOHER
N67
N18
Lahinch GC
LAHINCH
Dromoland Castle GC
CLARECASTLE
Shannon GC
N7
LIMERICK
Castletroy GC
TARBERT
Limerick GC
Ballybunion GC
N24
CASHEL
BALLYBUNION
TIPPERARY
N21
Tralee GC
TRALEE
Dingle G.C.
Dooks GC
Killarney
KILLARNEY
GLENBEIGH
N70
N20
Mallow GC
Harbour Point GC
CORK
Cork GC
N22
Muskerry GC
Douglas GC
Waterville GC
WATERVILLE
KENMARE
BANTRY
Monkstown GC
N71
SKIBBEREEN

SOUTH WEST IRELAND

NORTH WEST IRELAND
CHOICE GOLF

Without any shadow of doubt some of the greatest golf courses in the world are to be found in the south west of Ireland. But as any Irishman worth his Guinness will tell you, great golf in the west of Ireland certainly isn't confined to the south western corner – it starts from County Donegal downwards. Apart from its magnificent golf, the south west is renowned for its beautiful scenery: majestic Killarney, the glorious Ring of Kerry and the Dingle Peninsula; stunning for sure but further north can be equally spectacular. This is what W.M. Thackeray had to say of the area around Westport: 'It forms an event in one's life to have seen the place, so beautiful is it, and so unlike all other beauties that I know of'. Clearly inspired, he continued: 'But the Bay – and the Reek which sweeps down to the sea – and a hundred islands in it, were dressed up in gold and purple and crimson, with the whole cloudy West in a flame'. Marvellous! And have you ever been to Connemara?

DONEGAL

I don't suppose many golfers are likely to begin a tour in the very far north and head all the way downwards but we shall have a go all the same. (It is possible I suppose if one were approaching from the Causeway Coast?) Let us start at **Ballyliffin** on the very northern tip of Donegal. Now Ballyliffin is a course we overlooked in the early editions of Following The Fairways. This has now been rectified (see ahead); suffice to say at this juncture, having inspected the links we believe it to be the most underrated course in Ireland and suggest that golfers stay overnight in the nearby Strand Hotel (077) 76107 – the Proprietor is a club member!

Rosapenna is our next port of call. Like Ballyliffin it is somewhat isolated, but a fine eighteen hole course nonetheless. It was laid out in 1893 by Old Tom Morris and is part-links, part-inland in nature, although I understand that 9 new 'links holes' are presently being constructed. There are said to be more rabbits on this course than on any other – not a description of the members I might add! The place has a bleak beauty and the coast is very dramatic – note the spectacular nearby Atlantic Drive. The Rosapenna Golf Hotel (074) 55301 provides a comfortable and convenient base while those looking for really deluxe accommodation might consider Rathmullan House (074) 58188 in Rathmullan, a Georgian building with splendid gardens. Not far from Rosapenna there is a magnificently situated course at **Portsalon** and another delightfully old fashioned links at **Nairn and Portnoo.** Further inland, 18 holes can be played at **Letterkenny** and again at **Ballybofey & Stranorlar** where the Kee's Hotel (074) 31018 provides a perfect base for touring in Donegal.

Donegal town, famed for its tweeds and woollens, has one of the longest courses in Ireland measuring 7,200 yards (try playing it in a fierce wind!) The course is actually outside of the county town at **Murvagh.** A truly great course and again we explore it on a later page. There are a number of hotels in Donegal, but perhaps the best bet for golfers looking for a lively night is the Schooner Inn (073) 21671 on Upper Main Street. More sedate accommodation is to be found at Rossnowlagh, here the Sand House Hotel (072) 51777 enjoys superb views over Donegal Bay and there is a short nine hole golf course within the hotel grounds. A little south of Rossnowlagh is **Bundoran**, another tough, though fairly open links. Right in the middle of the course is the Great Northern Hotel which has 150 rooms.

THE WEST COAST 4 – AND MORE

Our next visit is a real gem. **County Sligo**, or **Rosses Point** as it is commonly known, is certainly among the top ten courses in Ireland and is the home of the prestigious West of Ireland Amateur Championship. Laid out right alongside the Atlantic coast it is a true links and can be greatly affected by the elements. This great course is tackled ahead. County Sligo and surrounds is another charming area of Ireland; it is the country of W.B. Yeats and the landscape is dominated by the formidable Ben Bulben mountain. An outstanding seafood restaurant is located in Rosses Point – The Moorings (098) 25874. The Sligo Park Hotel (071) 60291 and the Yeats Country Ryan Hotel (071) 77211 are both very convenient for the course while only a mile or so away on Rosses Point Road is the attractive Ballincar House Hotel (071) 45361. Just to the south of Sligo, Coopershill (071) 65108 is another fine hotel. Rosses Point is marketed alongside Enniscrone, Westport and Connemara as one of the West Coast 4 but there are many other fine golfing challenges in this part of Ireland and a recommended neighbour of Rosses Point is the links at **Strandhill**, adjacent to County Sligo airport. Furthermore, at **Belmulett** in the far northwest of Co.Mayo, a magnificent links course is being constructed at Carne Beach amid Ballybunion-like sand dunes! A fun place to stay in Belmulett is the Drom Caoin (097) 81195 guesthouse.

Perhaps the most underrated of the West Coast 4 is the delightful links at **Enniscrone,** laid out on the shores of Killala Bay; it is, to quote Peter Dobereiner, 'an undiscovered gem of a links.' The best place to stay nearby is the Downhill Hotel (096) 21033 in Ballina (the owner is a past Captain of the Golf Club!). A short drive from Ballina and we reach **Westport**, Thackeray's paradise. The town nestles in the shadows of the massive Croagh Patrick mountain. It was on its peak that St. Patrick is said to have fasted and prayed for 40 days. The golf course (from which there are many marvellous views of Croagh Patrick) is another on the grand scale – 7,000 yards when fully stretched. It's a relatively new course having been designed by Fred Hawtree in 1973. Although some holes run spectacularly along the shoreline, (note particularly the superb par five 15th which curves around Clew Bay) Westport is most definitely a parkland type course and is a very friendly Club. The Irish Amateur Championship has been played here twice in recent years. There is no shortage of good accommodation in Westport and many hotels offer golfing packages. One of the most comfortable hotels in town is the Hotel Westport (098) 25122 near Westport House, although the Newport Hotel (098) 41222 and the Castlecourt Hotel (098) 25444 are also popular with travel-weary golfers. Approximately twenty miles away at Cong stands the redoubtable **Ashford Castle** (092) 46003 a place fit for a king and possibly the finest hotel in Ireland. Its setting on the edge of Lough Corrib is quite breathtaking; it also has a pleasant 9 hole golf course within the hotel grounds.

Connemara is located about thirty miles south of Westport amid very rugged country. It is a wild, remote and incredibly beautiful part of the world. The course must be one of the toughest links that one is ever likely to meet; we visit it a few pages on. Despite the remoteness there are several first class establishments at hand. The best places for a night's stay are the Rock Glen Country House Hotel (095) 21035 and the Abbeyglen Castle Hotel (095) 21201. Both are in Clifden and both have very

good restaurants. Another of Ireland's leading country houses is to be found in Cashel, the Cashel House Hotel (095) 31001.

Galway is a delightful place to visit and the lively county town has a very enjoyable course overlooking Galway Bay. It was here that Christy O'Connor developed many of his skills. Galway has a number of centrally located hotels includ-ing The Great Southern Hotel (091) 64041 and Ardilaun House (091) 21433. In Spiddal the Bridge House (091) 83118 is a cosy inn in a charming little village. Somewhat further inland at Abbeytown in County Roscommon, the Abbey Hotel (0903) 26505 is a most pleasant retreat and a good base for visiting the courses at **Roscommon** and **Athlone**.

A. Weaver   PREPARING TO PUTT   Burlington Gallery

ASHFORD CASTLE

An historic Irish castle, dating back to the 13th century, Ashford is now one of the finest hotels in the world.

Enter the main reception hall and the feeling of genuine history is matched only by the warmth of the welcome. Solid oak beams and wood panelling reflect a more formal age, but the most modern facilities and comforts are reassuring signs that Ashford is very much a hotel of today. And it's that same sense of elegant luxury which has entitled Ashford to host former US Presidents, European royalty and international celebrities.

For the past three years, Ashford Castle has been nominated 'Best Hotel In Ireland' by Egon Ronay. Experience the finest food and wine in the George V dining room or in the Connaught Room gourmet restaurant where the most fastidious palate is treated to the exquisite delights of French cuisine.

Standing on the shore of Lough Corrib, Ireland's second-largest lake, it's no surprise that Ashford offers its guests some of the most sporting salmon, trout, pike and perch fishing in the West of Ireland. But if golfing is more your bag, the hotel grounds comfortably accommodate Ashford's own 9-hole golf course - and golf clubs are available. For variety and an even stiffer challenge two additional courses are less than fifty miles away. From November 1st, shots of a different kind abound as hunters go in search of duck and pheasant; with unlimited rough shooting.

With its spacious grounds offering their own calming air of quiet it's no surprise that Ashford is consistently chosen by national and international corporations and organisations for conferences and management get-togethers.

Seven centuries since the first brick was laid, the setting, atmosphere and discreet luxury have made Ashford Castle more than a unique hotel. It's an experience.

Ashford Castle
Cong
Co. Mayo
Ireland
Tel: (010 353 92) 46003
Fax: (010 353 92) 46260

NEWPORT HOUSE

Adjoining the town of Newport and overlooking the tidal river and quay the impressive country mansion of Newport House stands guard over the centuries of history that form the backbone to its grounds and the surrounding countryside. Once the home of a branch of the O'Donel family, descended from the famous fighting Earls of Tir Connell and cousins to 'Red Hugh' of Irish history, it is now a superb example of a lovingly maintained Georgian Mansion House.

Encircled by mountains, lakes and streams, Newport is within easy reach of some of Ireland's most beautiful rivers. Renowned as an angling centre, it holds private salmon and sea-trout fishing rights to 8 miles of the Newport River; and the prolific waters of the stunning Lough Beltra West are close by. Less than twenty minutes drive from the hotel are Lakes Mask and Corrib, while the nearby Loughs Feeagh and Furnace are the site of the Salmon Research Trust of Ireland.

The discerning golfer has the pleasure of the 18-hole championship course at Westport as well as the more relaxed 9-hole course near Mulrany.

Outdoor activities are numerous amidst the breath-taking scenery of County Mayo. Riding is easily arranged or try swimming and diving on wide and often empty beaches, while hang-gliding is a relatively new sport gaining popularity from the local Achill Cliffs. One of the best recreations though is simply walking across the ever changing panorama of mountain, forest and sea.

Warmth and friendliness fill this beautiful hotel in a country already famed for its hospitality. The house is furnished with a tasteful collection of fine antiques and paintings and the elegant bedrooms are individually decorated. Food is taken seriously, with much of the produce collected fresh from the fishery, gardens and farm. Home-smoked salmon and fresh sea-food are specialites, and all the dishes are complemented by a carefully chosen and extensive wine list.

Many of the staff have been long in the service of the estate, up to forty years in one case. Combine this with the solid background of the house and there is a rare feeling of continuity and maturity so rare in modern hotels today.

Newport House
Co. Mayo
Ireland
Tel: (010 353 98) 41222
Fax: (010 353 98) 41613

COUNTY SLIGO (ROSSES POINT)
CHAMPIONSHIP GOLF

Which is the best golf course in Ireland? Is it the Old Course at Ballybunion? Or perhaps Portmarnock near Dublin? Or what about the two 'Royal' courses north of the border, Portrush and County Down? These are the four courses which invariably receive the most nominations in the age-old favourite 19th hole debate. They are, if you like, the four with the biggest reputations; but there is another golf course that certainly deserves to be spoken of in the same breath and that is County Sligo, more commonly known as Rosses Point.

If we commit ourselves a little further, then of this magnificent five, Royal County Down at Newcastle has perhaps the strongest claim to possessing the finest front nine holes and Ballybunion the greatest back nine. But taking each of the eighteens as a balanced whole, Rosses Point must have a creditable claim. Don't just take my word for it either: **Peter Alliss** has been quoted as saying 'Rosses Point stands right at the very top of the list of Irish golf courses.' Another famous supporter of the west coast links which has hosted the **West of Ireland Amateur Championship** every year since 1923, is the great **Tom Watson.** If he were asked to name his three favourite links courses in Britain and Ireland (excluding those at which he won an Open Championship!) he would probably rattle off the names Ballybunion, Royal Dornoch and Rosses Point.

As well as having a glorious golf course, County Sligo Golf Club enjoys a glorious situation. The golf links (and the surrounding countryside) is dominated by the extraordinary mountain, Benbulben, which is a dead ringer for Cape Town's Table Mountain. Immediately adjacent to the links is a wonderfully sweeping bay with three beautiful beaches: little wonder that the scenery so intoxicated Ireland's greatest poet, **W. B. Yeats.**

Visiting golfers who wish to become similarly intoxicated by the golfing challenge are advised to contact the Club in advance. The Secretary, or Golf Manager at Rosses Point is **Ray Mullen**; he can be contacted by telephone on **(071) 77134** (from the UK the code is 010 353 71). There is no firm requirement that visitors produce handicap certificates but they must, however, be players of a 'reasonable standard'. The Club's professional, **Leslie Robinson** can be reached by telephone on **(071) 77171.** Finally, the green fees for 1992 were £20 per day (or round) during the week and, subject to availability, £30 per day at weekends.

Rosses Point is often tagged 'remote', not as remote as Waterville but more so than most of Ireland's finest golfing attractions. Naturally, it depends where one is coming from but there is an airport (County Sligo) just 20 minutes drive away at Strandhill. The town of Sligo is no more than 10 minutes away from the links (via the R291 road); Donegal is about one hour's drive north (N15) and Westport approximately an hour and a half to the south west (N17/N5/N60).

The **1st** at Rosses Point is a medium-length par four, fairly straight and gently uphill all the way to a well protected green. The **2nd**, is much more severely uphill and the approach shot, although likely to be no more than a short iron can be very difficult to judge. On reaching the green at the 2nd, one can feel on top of the world, almost literally, for the panoramic view from here is as vast as it is sensational. Benbulben is genuinely awe-inspiring, a geological freak which, if located in a more widely known part of the world would be universally acclaimed. From such dizzy heights the Atlantic looks positively inviting – so does the downhill drive at the **3rd**! This hole can be reached with two well struck shots but a series of fiendishly positioned bunkers await to punish the less accurate.

The **4th** is a fine par three where the green sits on a natural plateau and this is followed by another vertigo-inducing tee shot at the **5th**. The **6th** is perhaps the weakest hole on the course and the **7th** looks fairly straightforward for a stroke index one hole – that is until your second shot plummets into the brook in front of the green. The brook reappears on the **8th**, which is a magnificent and much photographed dog-leg. The front nine concludes with the excellent par three **9th** where the green is surrounded by bunkers.

The **10th** and **11th** offer the closest views of Benbulben and they are a very good pair of par fours. A fairly blind par five is followed by the difficult one-shot **13th**, where the tee looks down over the sea and sands. Then comes Tom Watson's favourite. The **14th** is a superb and extremely testing par four and when the wind is blowing can make even the 8th seem tame. If the wind is against on the 14th then it will be so again on the **15th**, which is bad news because the drive needs to be carried far over some very wild dunes close to the shore. The **16th** is the longest par three at Rosses Point and the **17th** calls for a long uphill second to an amphitheatre green. Then at long last, comes a fairly gentle hole! It is the last and if you play it on a fine summer's evening you may be lucky enough to see the sun setting behind the **18th** green: the perfect end to a perfect round.

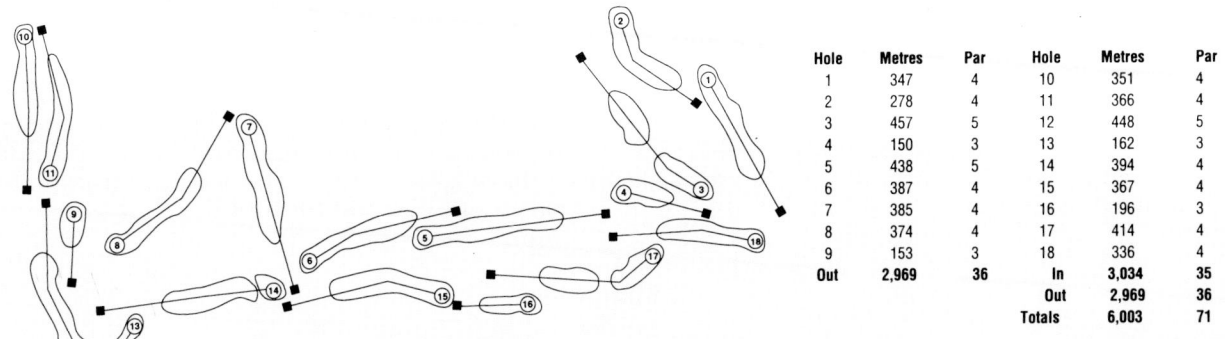

Hole	Metres	Par	Hole	Metres	Par
1	347	4	10	351	4
2	278	4	11	366	4
3	457	5	12	448	5
4	150	3	13	162	3
5	438	5	14	394	4
6	387	4	15	367	4
7	385	4	16	196	3
8	374	4	17	414	4
9	153	3	18	336	4
Out	**2,969**	**36**	**In**	**3,034**	**35**
			Out	**2,969**	**36**
			Totals	**6,003**	**71**

SLIGO PARK HOTEL

The Sligo Park Hotel, surrounded by four first class golf courses, is in an ideal situation for you to base your golf outing.

Many of our guests find the contrast between the courses a magnificent challenge. Bernhard Langer once said of Rosses Point, 'It was the first links course I ever saw as a young pro starting on the tour. I went to play one round and stayed two weeks.' Sligo's other golf links, Strandhill, offers a more rugged challenge where the magnificent Atlantic lashes its boundaries. This par 70 course with its magnificent sand dunes offers a completely different game than Rosses Point. An ideal course, it is suitable for beginners and experienced players. Visitors are made most welcome and are assured of a memorable game.

Enniscrone, set on the shores of Killala Bay, is a true adventure. This 6,610 yard links has all the hallmarks of a roller coaster. It is one of the best tests of the game to be found in Ireland. The terrain will sap all the energy a golfer is willing to give and leave him breathless in the beauty of its surroundings.

Just north of Sligo is one of Europe's longest courses. Donegal Golf Club at Murvagh is set on the rolling hills of Donegal. Renowned for its winding fairways and dense woodland, visiting golfers are always made welcome.

If it is golf you enjoy by day, good food and friendly service at night, then the Sligo Park Hotel is the place for you. The hotel also has one of the finest leisure centres in the country.

Sligo, the home of W.B. Yeats, is full of hidden delights. Golf is just one of them.

Sligo Park Hotel
Pearse Road
Sligo
Ireland
Tel: (010 353 71) 60291
Fax: (010 353 71) 69556

DOWNHILL HOTEL

Far away from polluted air and water is the Downhill Hotel adjacent to the River Moy which is famous for its salmon fishing, attached to Lough Conn and flowing into Killala Bay provides an area rich in fresh and sea water fishing, coarse angling also available. We are in a position to organise a boat for your day trip be it on the lake, estuary or river (advance booking necessary). For that perfect game angling holiday come to the Moy and stay at the Downhill Hotel in the West of Ireland.

This Grade A hotel offers excellent cuisine, personal and friendly service and fine facilities. Bedrooms are luxurious with TV/video, satellite TV, radio, telephone, tea/coffee making facilities and trouser press. The Downhill is situated in beautiful grounds and offers Frogs Pavilion Piano Bar, split level restaurant with extensive menu, swimming pool, sauna, jacuzzi, gymnasium, squash, snooker room, sunbed and craft shop. If you are unable to escape from work the Downhill offers excellent conference facilities and is equipped to meet the most exact requirements.

The Downhill Hotel is conveniently located from Knock Airport and Sligo Airport both 35 miles away. In addition to excellent game angling guests may enjoy golf on one of the three championship courses close by, Enniscrone, Rossespoint and Westport. For those in search of a more peaceful break, a walk on one of the many beautiful sandy beaches or perhaps a scenic tour.

Downhill Hotel Limited
Ballina, Co Mayo
Ireland
Tel: (010 353 96) 21033
Fax: (010 353 96) 21338

COOPERSHILL

Coopershill is a fine example of a Georgian family mansion. Home to seven generations of the O'Hara family since it was built in 1774, it combines the spaciousness and elegance of an earlier age with the comfort and amenities of today. Five of the seven bedrooms have four poster or canopy beds and all have their own private bathrooms. The rooms retain their original regal dimensions and much of the furniture dates from the time that the house was built.

Guests can relax in front of a log fire in the large and comfortable drawing room. Dinner by candlelight with family silverware and crystal glass, a wide choice of wines and the personal attention of the hosts all add to the special Coopershill atmosphere.

Standing in the centre of a 500 acre estate of farm and woodland, separation from the outside world seems complete. There are many delightful walks and wildlife is abundant and undisturbed.

We have five 18 hole links courses within an hours drive of

Coopershill; the up and coming Enniscrone course to the south, Bundoran and the Donegal course at Murvagh to the north, and the closest, Strandhill just 14 miles away. But perhaps the pick of them, the County Sligo Golf Club at Rosses Point, where the Home Internationals were played in 1991, is worth more than just one visit.

Long uncrowded beaches, spectacular mountains and hills for walking, lakes and megalithic monuments all add to make Sligo, which is Yeats' country, an ideal place to visit.

Coopershill is two miles from the village of Riverstown and 13 miles from Sligo town, signposted clearly from the Sligo to Dublin route N4.

We are served by two airports; Sligo Airport is 15 miles away with daily flights to Dublin; Knock Airport is 30 miles away with daily flights to Luton, North of London. Car hire is available at both Sligo and Knock.

Coopershill
Riverstown
Co. Sligo
Ireland
Tel: (010 353 71) 65108
Fax: (010 353 71) 65466

CONNEMARA
CHAMPIONSHIP GOLF

Not many people reading this book will have visited the Moon and, unless N.A.S.A. is keeping an extraordinary secret under wraps, only one man has ever played golf there: our friend from La Moye and Fulford, Admiral Alan Sheppard. I suspect the closest most of us are ever likely to get to experiencing golf in a lunar-like landscape is if we visit Connemara on the west coast of Ireland.

While much of County Kerry basks in picture-postcard prettiness, the countryside of Connemara boasts a truly rugged kind of splendour. Some of Connemara appears almost pre-historic. Great grey rocks are strewn all over a hilly, green landscape. Connemara National Park is surely where Finn McCool and his giant buddies staged an all-night rock throwing party but forgot to clear up afterwards. The village of **Ballyconneely** is about as far west as you can go in Connemara without slipping into the Atlantic and Ballyconneely is where Connemara Golf Club is found.

Before 1973 it used to be reckoned that the only people who ventured this far west were lost. This of course was in the days before golf came to Ballyconneely. Connemara's Championship golf links is worth discovering: it may not be in quite the same league as Rosses Point to the north or Ballybunion to the south (but then which courses are?) But it is a wonderful golfing experience.

Ballyconneely is situated 9 miles south of Clifden, (where trans-Atlantic aviators **Alcock** and **Brown** fell to earth) a journey of perhaps 15 to 20 minutes along a fairly deserted road. Clifden is joined to Galway by the N59, a distance of approximately 50 miles, roughly an hour and a quarter by car, a journey though that no one should rush. According to Thackeray this is one of the most beautiful districts that is ever the fortune of the traveller to examine. Thackeray was biased, but a thousand watercolours cannot lie. The N59 also links Clifden with Westport to the north east and the journey via Leenane, where 'The Field', which starred Richard Harris, was filmed is at least as dramatic.

Golfing visitors to Connemara are always made extremely welcome. Greatly responsible for the hospitable atmosphere at the Club is the Secretary/ Manager **Matt Killilea.** It is advisable to contact Mr Killilea in advance, tel **(095) 23502,** or fax (095) 23662 (from the UK the code is 010 353 95) to ensure that there aren't any tee reservations; moreover, during the summer months and at holiday weekends a starting sheet system is often operated. Subject to the above, and being able to provide proof of handicap there are no general restrictions on the times when visitors may play.

Green fees for 1992 were set at £16 between May and September, £14 for the months of March, April and October and £10 during the winter months. Junior visitors pay half the above rates.

Few clubhouses enjoy a better vantage point than the one at Connemara. Perched on high ground there are not only some magnificent views over the ocean (particularly splendid when the western sun dips into the sea on a summer's evening) but also across much of the course. It is a wonderful place in which to relax. But first we must tackle the course.

The first seven holes at Connemara are frankly nothing special – not bad, but nothing special. To say that the course steps up a gear at the 8th would be a gross understatement. Some of the holes between the 8th and 18th are as good as any one is likely to play, 'so good they are nearly ridiculous' reckoned Irish golf writer Pat Ruddy. The first seven holes are by no means easy but apart from the excellent dog-legged **1st** where from the tee the flag seems to be positioned somewhere in the middle of some particularly wild terrain, and the two short holes, the **3rd** and the **6th**, they are a bit of an up-and-down slog over what is easily the flattest part of the course.

The **8th** however is a fine par four; it is the stroke index one hole and the approach is a very testing one to a broad but plateau green. As for the **9th**, it is a real gem of a hole. Again a two-shotter, the player drives downhill from a magnificently placed high tee; over the players shoulder as he drives is a mountainous backdrop, the famous **Twelve Bens**, and stretching out ahead is the sea, the great Atlantic Ocean – the next terra firma being Long Island.

If the **9th** is a memorable hole, the par three **13th** is out of this world. This is where landscape is replaced by moonscape. As at the 9th, an exhilarating downhill tee shot is called for. From the back tees a long-iron shot will be needed as the carry is all of 200 yards. The **14th**, a par five, where you can really open the shoulders, and the **15th** which is a little reminiscent of the 14th at Portmarnock with its uphill second to a shelf-like green, are two more marvellous holes. Water can play the devil at the **16th** while the **17th** and **18th** are a pair of par fives that seem to stretch forever and a day.

If you've played Connemara from the back tees (well over 7,000 yards) the chances are youll be breathless by the finish. Breathless at Connemara – like being on the Moon.

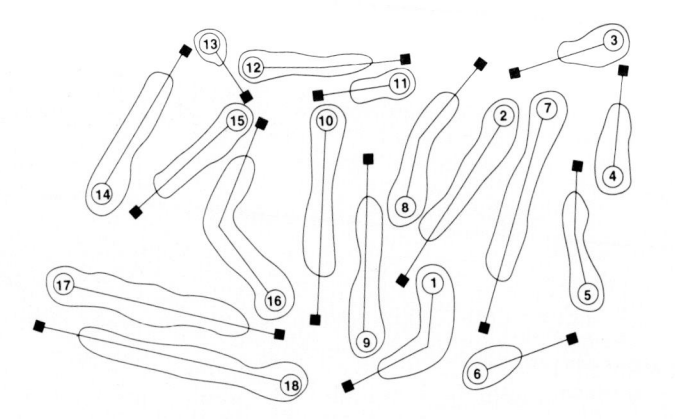

Hole	Metres	Par	Hole	Metres	Par
1	331	4	10	383	4
2	366	4	11	151	3
3	145	3	12	399	4
4	335	4	13	180	3
5	342	4	14	460	5
6	175	3	15	349	4
7	482	5	16	370	4
8	418	4	17	468	5
9	344	4	18	475	5
Out	**2,938**	**35**	**In**	**3,235**	**37**
			Out	2,938	35
			Totals	6,173	72

ROCK GLEN HOTEL

A converted shooting lodge first built in 1815, the Rock Glen is now a 29 bedroomed cosy first class Grade A Hotel, nestling in the heart of Connemara.

Lush pasture rolls from the door of this 18th century former shooting lodge and down to the shore of the narrow bay where Connemara's mountain range, the Twelve Bens, drift in and out of the clouds.

Family run, the Hotel is renowned for its exceptional cuisine. An extensive five course menu with a wide variety of meat, shellfish, salmon, trout and lobster, all fresh and available locally, is personally supervised by John Roche, the owner. There is a fine selection of wines to complement the fine food.

The bar is cosy where plump armchairs out-number bar stools and a turf fire glows all year round. Guests can enjoy a pleasant evening of musical entertainment with our resident pianist. Spontaneous sing-songs occur regularly, and you are invited to join in. Coffee is served in the drawing room where you can relax and enjoy the conversation and our cosy sun lounge can be a delight to all even on the dullest day.

AMENITIES

The superb full size snooker table is guaranteed to give pleas-

ure to all. Clay pigeon shooting can be arranged by request. The all-weather floodlit tennis court is in excellent condition and is free to residents. The bedrooms, 15 of which are on the ground floor, are all individually and comfortably decorated and have private bathroom, radio and television, trouser press, hairdryer, and direct dial telephone.

LOCAL AMENITIES

The hotel is ideally situated for the golf enthusiast. Connemara's 18 hole championship course is in a spectacular setting on the coast, with the Twelve Bens in the background. It is just a 15 minute drive from the Hotel. Lessons are available on request, golf clubs and caddy cars can be hired also at the club.

For the non-golfer the area is perfect for walking, hill climbing, river, lake and deep-sea fishing. Miles of sandy beaches for the swimmer and pony trekking (Clifden is famous for its Connemara ponies) can all be arranged at the reception desk.

John and Evangeline Roche, their family and staff look forward to welcoming you to the Rock Glen where you may recall the pleasures of a leisurely and more sedate way of life, then return home refreshed, rested and fit.

Rock Glen Country House Hotel
Clifden
County Galway
Ireland
Tel: (010 353 95) 21035
Fax: (010 353 95) 21737

DONEGAL (MURVAGH)
CHAMPIONSHIP GOLF

The Irish have an inborn wanderlust that is perhaps rivalled only by Australians and New Zealanders. This partly explains how, wherever you go in the world, you bump into an Irishman, sooner rather than later. And why sooner rather than later, you'll hear the phrase 'to be sure' or 'tis grand'. It also partly explains why the names of numerous relatively small towns in Ireland are famous the world over; places like Limerick, Blarney and Tipperary for example. Another place that just about everybody has heard of is Donegal – not for its rhymes, kisses or songs of course but for its tweed. Yet like Limerick, Blarney and Tipperary not all that many people born outside Ireland have visited Donegal. Every golfer however, given the chance, should visit the country's most north westerly county: there are many wonderful courses here and they are all wonderfully uncrowded. And every brave golfer should visit Donegal, the county town itself, and play its majestic links at nearby Murvagh.

Why only every brave golfer? This is because to get the most out of Murvagh you must enjoy a mighty challenge; it is the longest golf course in Ireland. A local joke is that if you are a short hitter you can spend a full day at Murvagh and not complete 18 holes. Donegal really is a tiger of a links: from the Championship tees it measures just over 7,300 yards (or 6,633 metres as the card will tell you.) In reality, most of us are never going to tackle the links from the tiger tees and while it is still a very long course from the tees of the day, real challenge becomes entwined with real pleasure.

Murvagh enjoys considerable seclusion. It is not exactly off the beaten track – Donegal is only 6 miles away – but quite a bit of the course is bordered by some fairly thick woodland and being situated on a peninsula, there is an added feeling of isolation. The other border of course is the great Atlantic Ocean.

Few golf clubs are as keen for visitors to come and experience the charms of their course as Donegal. The green fees in 1992 were a modest £12 during the week with £15 payable at weekends and on Bank Holidays. The Club operates a timesheet system on Saturdays and Sundays and it is only at the weekend when any restrictions are likely to apply. Donegal's Secretary, **John McBride** can be contacted on **(073) 34054** (or from the UK 010 353 73 34054) There is no professional at the Club but the Steward, **Eugene McLoughlin** is very helpful. Meals and snacks are available in the clubhouse throughout the day although players are requested to place an order for meals before teeing off. There are no formal dress requirements.

As already mentioned, Murvagh is approximately 6 miles from the centre of Donegal. The linking road is the N15 and the route off to the golf course is signposted. The town itself is about an hour's drive from the nearest airport which is at Sligo and again the route is the N15. Knock Airport is 80 miles away and Belfast 110 miles. Sligo Airport is obviously the most convenient and anyone playing golf at Donegal should try and include a game at County Sligo (or vice versa). Rosses Point and Murvagh – what a double for links enthusiasts!

Rather like at Rosses Point, the course opens with a fairly gentle hole. This time it is a par five and like every par five at Murvagh (there are four others) it is a dog-leg, but the approach to the green is not too demanding and the putting surface is fairly large. Things start to hot up at the **2nd.** This is a very tough par four that plays every bit of its 416 yards. Thick, tangling rough lines the left hand side of the fairway on this hole and there is an out of bounds on the right; as for the green, it sits on a natural shelf.

Neither the **3rd** or **4th** is an easy hole and the **5th** can be a horror. This is one of two really tremendous par threes at Donegal (the other is the 16th); here the tee shot must be struck perfectly to carry a ravine – miss-hit it slightly and you can be playing your second from sand thirty feet below the green. Beyond the green is the beach. A brilliant sequence of holes comes after the 5th. This is where the course runs close to Donegal Bay and the views (if you care to clamber up the sandhills) are tremendous.

Perhaps the most memorable holes on the back nine at Murvagh are the **10th, 11th** and **15th**, while the most demanding are the **12th** and **16th**. The former is once again a huge par five; from the back tees it would be a reasonable train journey and as on most three-shot holes the key is the second. If we are talking train distances then as par threes go the 16th must be the equivalent of the Trans-Siberian Express! One could sit behind this green all day and not see anyone reach the green with their tee shot. When the elements are stirred this is the kind of hole where, in days gone by, Jack Nicklaus would have peeled off his sweater and teed up with his driver. But then, Donegal is a place where another of those lovely Irish expressions 'good crack' takes on a new meaning.

Hole	Metres	Par	Hole	Metres	Par
1	478	5	10	320	4
2	379	4	11	340	4
3	173	3	12	503	5
4	380	4	13	145	3
5	170	3	14	479	5
6	473	5	15	370	4
7	352	4	16	209	3
8	499	5	17	323	4
9	306	4	18	344	4
Out	**3,210**	**37**	**In**	**3,033**	**36**
			Out	3,210	37
			Totals	6,243	73

DROMOLAND CASTLE
CHAMPIONSHIP GOLF

We all owe a great debt to televised pro-celebrity golf. Without it how familiar would we be with 'Braid's Brawest' and the glorious colours of the King's Course at Gleneagles? And how familiar would we be with 'Tappie Toorie', Ailsa Craig and the lighthouse at Turnberry? Without it, how many of us would have even heard of Dromoland Castle?

When it comes to discussing magical locations Dromoland Castle has a head start over most – it is situated in the west of Ireland. Located in Co. Clare, overlooking the Shannon estuary, it is roughly equidistant from Connemara and Westport to the north and the Dingle Peninsula and the Ring of Kerry to the south; the Cliffs of Moher and the extraordinary prehistoric scenery of the Burren Country are even closer at hand. Golf wise it is within striking distance of Lahinch, Tralee and Ballybunion, three of the greatest links courses in the world.

Yet for all the surrounding splendour, Dromoland Castle is a magical little kingdom of its own. Or that is what you can imagine the moment you drive through the castle gates and enter the beautifully wooded grounds of the estate. The castle itself (now of course a luxurious hotel) is quite majestic – as I suppose it should be, being the former ancestral home of the O'Briens, the direct descendants of Brian Boru, legendary 11th century High King of all Ireland. In front of the castle is a handsome lake, Dromoland Lough, and zig-zagging its way between the trees of the estate, occasionally glimpsing the lake and ocassionally glimpsing the castle are the emerald fairways of a challenging 18 hole golf course. All in all, Dromoland Castle isn't a bad place to while away a few days! But if you simply want to inspect the golf course then you don't have to be a resident or be accompanied by a club member; in fact visitors are not restricted in any way.

Golf Secretary, **John O'Halloran** and the professional **Philip Murphy** are the gentlemen most likely to welcome you. They may be contacted by telephone on **(061) 368144**. Tee times can be reserved and in 1992 the green fees were £18 on weekdays with £20 payable at weekends. The precise location of Dromoland Castle is immediately off the Limerick to Galway Road (the N7), 4 miles from Shannon (and its International Airport) at Newmarket on Fergus.

Prior to 1985 there was only a 9 hole course at Dromoland, and which, like the attractive 9 holer at Dromoland's sister castle, Ashford, was little more than a sporting, though enjoyable, 'holiday course'. Anyone who played Dromoland before 1985 but hasn't done so since and is contemplating a visit is in for a pleasant surprise – and perhaps one or two shocks as well! Measuring 5719 metres (or just under 6300 yards), par 71 from the back tees it is a good test of golf and the quality and condition of the course is ever improving, as of course the 1991 Pro-Celebrity Series bore witness to. Both team captains in that event, **Gary Player** and **Sandy Lyle**, were complimentary of the layout and clearly relished playing amidst surroundings that were not only extremely picturesque but marvellously relaxing too.

Apart from a fairly open area between the 4th and 6th holes most of the fairways are bordered by rich woodland, which in fact is becoming richer by the week thanks to a novel 'Plant a Family Tree' scheme operated by a company called **Forest Heritage Limited**. Fancy putting down some roots in the 'Kingdom of Dromoland'? (Telephone (061) 71144 for details). Among the most beautiful trees are a number of mature copper beaches – wonderful – unless of course you happen to land behind (or in) one of them.

If one were to single out special holes at Dromoland then on the front nine the **2nd**, **7th** and **8th** make for a splendid trio, comprising a spectacular dog-leg par five, a vertigo-inducing par three – a superb view of the castle and lake from this elevated tee – and a roller coaster of a par four where the fairway appears to tumble in every conceivable direction. On the back nine a new championship tee at the **10th** has made the drive an all-or-nothing shot across the edge of the lake – perfect for the likes of Sandy Lyle! The **15th** and **16th** are an entertaining pair of par fours and the two short holes are attractive, but perhaps the best two holes on the back nine are the **11th** and **18th**. The former dog-legs sharply right and takes you alongside Lough Dromoland and through an avenue of resplendent trees; at the 18th you aim your tee shot at the lake, after which the fairway dog-legs sharply to the left and back towards the castle. Just before you putt out on the final green take a deep breath and drink in the 360 degree views: magnificent towering trees, a peaceful lake, velvet fairways and, surveying all, Dromoland Castle. What more could you ask for!

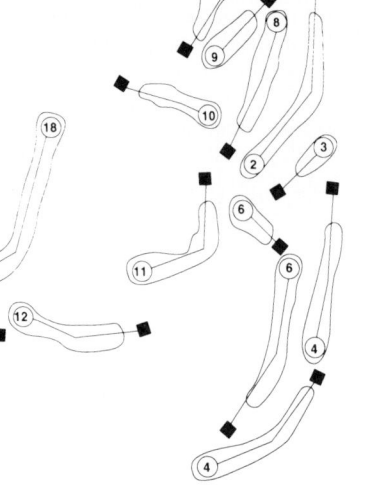

Hole	Metres	Par	Hole	Metres	Par
1	356	4	10	268	4
2	480	5	11	440	5
3	212	3	12	317	4
4	423	4	13	110	3
5	377	4	14	358	4
6	513	5	15	257	4
7	130	3	16	347	4
8	358	4	17	153	3
9	206	3	18	414	5
Out	3,055	35	In	2.664	36
			Out	3,055	35
			TOTALS	5,719	71

DROMOLAND CASTLE

Once the seat of the O'Brien clan, Dromoland Castle has all the imposing stature you'd expect of the Kings of Munster. It stands proud on its own lakeside setting - a location that instantly highlights it as a very exceptional hotel indeed.

The warm red carpet in the expansive reception hall reflects the warmth of the Dromoland welcome - a genuine attitude further supported by a subtle combination of informality and efficiency.

The numerous lounges are of truly regal proportions, extremely comfortable with exquisite decor. A cosy bar and a relaxing snooker room are two additional options to help pass the evening hours.

The magnificence of the hotel is more than equalled by the quality of the French and indigenous cuisine. In 1990, the Earl of Thomond Room restaurant won an Egon Ronay star as 'Best Hotel Restaurant' in Ireland. With its expansive views, it's an ideal setting to while away some delightful hours accompanied by the finest of wines from one of the most extensive cellars in the country.

Golfing guests can enjoy the challenge of the hotel's own 18-hole golf course and for an even greater challenge the championship courses of Lahinch and Ballybunion are nearby.

Anglers are catered for with trout in the hotel's own lake and salmon and trout in the nearby Shannon. An hour away, the more adventurous can tackle some deep-sea angling on the West coast. hunting of a different kind starts on November 1st, for snipe, pheasant and duck.

With Shannon international airport only 8 miles away, it's not surprising that Dromoland has proved a very popular location for international conferences and seminars. Its prestigious reputation adds a unique status to any such event or management think-tank.

If the O'Briens of old returned to day, they could only but be impressed. The manicured lawns...the calm elegance...the finest in food and facilities. It's true what they say - there is only one Dromoland.

Dromoland Castle
Newmarket-on-Fergus
Co. Clare
Ireland
Tel: (010 353 61) 368144
Fax: (010 353 61) 363355

BALLYLIFFIN
CHAMPIONSHIP GOLF

A time to be honest. Hands up who's heard of Ballyliffin? Not too many I would think. Until quite recently my hand would certainly have been in the air. And what is Ballyliffin? Not long ago I might have guessed at a trendy brand of mineral water. 'Ballyliffin' is the answer I received when I asked one of Britain's leading golf photographers, Matthew Harris to name the finest golf course he'd ever seen (and Matthew Harris has seen and photographed a lot of golf courses around the world.) I regret to say that I told him he must have meant Ballybunion and if so that I wasn't remotely surprised at his assessment. But he was insistent, so insistent that in March 1991 I found myself driving through the magnificent countryside of north west Ireland feeling like a golfing King Arthur in search of the Holy Grail.

Located in the far north of Donegal, Ballyliffin is Ireland's most northerly situated golf course. As I drove beyond the town of Donegal and continued northwards towards the Inishowen Peninsula, the scenery grew ever more enchanting but I still suspected that my photographer friend might have over imbibed the night before his visit to Ballyliffin, after all, the hospitality in these parts is legendary, if not to say intoxicating.

The setting is as stunning as it is remote. Located between dark, dramatic hills on the one side and a sweeping bay on the other this is a veritable haven. But what instantly hits you the moment you arrive at Ballyliffin is how natural a golf links this is. Golf has not been played here since the 16th century but you could easily imagine that it had. The sand dunes stretch as far as the eye can see. Amidst the dunes is the most perfect seaside grass and up, over, beside and around the dunes wend the fairways of Ballyliffin golf links. Stand on any tee of this course and the word to describe the fairway ahead is 'rippling'. The hole may dog-leg, it may climb or tumble downhill, but always it ripples. The instant impression of Ballyliffin is that it is a cross between Royal Dornoch and Ballybunion and if that to the reader sounds like absurd flattery then I simply say, go and pay a visit!

For many people, it is a bit of a trek to put it mildly. Ballyliffin is about a two hour drive from Donegal, the route being via Letterkenny and Buncrana (travelling initially along the N15 and the N56). Buncrana is the starting point for the Inishowen 100 mile scenic drive which, if not as famous as the Ring of Kerry arguably offers comparable beauty and the road to Ballyliffin will guide you through some of this splendour. The

nearest airport is just over the border at Derry, less than an hour away and not too far beyond Derry is the Causeway Coast and its much more famous golfing treasures.

Given the great distance that the traveller is probably coming from, it is always wise to telephone the Club before setting off. The Club's Secretary, **Karl O'Doherty** can be contacted on **(077) 76119** or **(077) 74417** and the address for correspondence is; **Ballyliffin Golf Club, Ballyliffin, Cardonagh, Co. Donegal.** The green fees at Ballyliffin are extremely good value. In 1992 they were £8 per round midweek and £12 per day at the weekend. Individual visitors are welcome on any day of the week although there are some restrictions at weekends due to Club competitions. The Clubhouse has no grandiose pretensions but is comfortable and friendly.

There is a beautiful feeling of symmetry to a game of golf at Ballyliffin. The front nine and back nine each comprise two par threes, two par fives and five par fours (making up the total yardage of 6,524 yards, par 72). Parallels between the two nines continue in that the **1st** and **10th** holes are remarkably similar, both mildly dog-leg to the right and are immediately followed by longer dog-legs to the left. Both nines possess something that is becoming a rarity on newly designed courses, a good short par four hole. On the first half, it is the **3rd,** with its ever narrowing fairway and where the tee shot must be targeted directly at the sea, and on the back nine it is the **14th** where the big hitter is teased into having a go for the green with his drive and of course is heavily punished if he fails to rise to the occasion. The **12th** is a long and testing par three but the most memorable is the **5th**, 'The Tank', where a long or medium iron must be struck perfectly to find an elevated plateau green surrounded by dunes.

If my theme of symmetry comes a little unstuck at the end of the two halves – the **9th** measures a mere 110 yards and the **18th**, 556 yards! – allow me to return to my rippling fairways and the **13th** which runs very close to the shore. This is a real gem of a hole, it might even rival the 11th at Waterville as the best par five in Ireland.......come to think of it, how many better par threes are there than the 5th at Ballyliffin? Surely it won't be long before Ballyliffin is being ranked among the great links courses of the world, but until then, Matthew and I will have to suffer incredulous looks whenever we rave over Ballyliffin, our 'Dornoch of Ireland'. But what a rippling yarn it is!

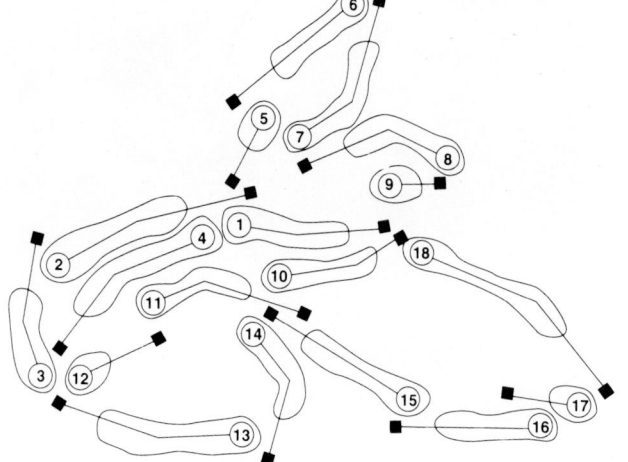

Hole	Yards	Par	Hole	Yards	Par
1	406	4	10	385	4
2	507	5	11	409	4
3	354	4	12	211	3
4	499	5	13	499	5
5	193	3	14	376	4
6	364	4	15	400	4
7	346	4	16	349	4
8	395	4	17	165	3
9	110	3	18	556	5
Out	**3,174**	**36**	**In**	**3,350**	**36**
			Out	3,174	36
			Totals	6,524	72

SOUTH WEST IRELAND
CHOICE GOLF

We begin our brief tour of south west Ireland in County Clare where **Lahinch** is found. The famous links is featured ahead but ideas for staying in the area must include the excellent Aberdeen Arms Hotel (065) 81100. In nearby Liscannor a visit to Joseph McHugh's pub is also recommended – not until you've played the course though! There is comfortable accommodation nearby in the popular Liscannor Bay Hotel. In Ennis, Mungovans (065) 24608 offers first rate accommodation. Slightly nearer Limerick in Newmarket-on-Fergus, Dromoland Castle (061) 71144 is for the true connoisseur. The person who stayed at Ashford Castle will probably be staying here; again the hotel has a golf course although Dromoland's course has recently been upgraded to championship standard – it is detailed on a later page. Surrounded by the Dromoland Castle course, the Clare Inn Hotel (0671) 71161 is very good value. Not far from Dromoland, **Shannon** Golf Club is also well worth a visit – friendly and a very good golf course. There are two fair courses either side of Limerick and a popular place to stay is the Dunraven Arms Hotel (061) 396209 in Adare and Jury's Hotel (061) 55266 in Limerick is also first rate, but many golfers will be itching to head-off to the delights of County Kerry.

KERRY'S GOLD

If we have crossed the Shannon via the Tarbert Ferry, **Ballybunion** is the first great Club we come across in County Kerry. Like Lahinch, Killarney, Waterville and Tralee it's featured ahead. Those wishing to stay in Ballybunion should note the large Ambassador Hotel (068) 27111 and the more cosy Marine Hotel (068) 27139 with its fine seafood restaurant. Glin Castle (068) 34364 is only a short drive from Ballybunion and has a spectacular setting. **Killarney** provides a more central base and as an enormously popular tourist destination has numerous hotels. Among the best are The Muckross Park Hotel (064) 31938, the Great Southern (064) 31262, the very attractive Cahernane (064) 31895, the renowned International (064) 31816 and the Castlerosse (064) 31144. Eating establishments are equally plentiful with Gabys (064) 32519, Foleys (064) 31217, and The Strawberry Tree (064) 32688) unlikely to disappoint anybody. To the south of Killarney, the Park Hotel Kenmare (064) 41200 is where our friends from Dromoland Castle will now be heading. Also in Kenmare, Sheen Falls Lodge (064) 41600 is extremely welcoming and good value. For an intimate and inexpensive stopover in Killarney, Kathleen's Country House Hotel is highly recommended (064) 32810 as is the friendly 19th Green guest-house (064) 32868 which is almost adjacent to the famous golf club. Whilst in the area, keep a close watch out for the excellent Towers Hotel (066) 68212 at Glenbeigh. Finally, no trip to the area would be complete without a visit to the Aghadoe Heights Hotel (064) 31766 where the lake and mountain views are quite simply out of this world.

Tralee is about 20 miles north west of Killarney. The links is actually some eight miles from the town itself; the journey takes a little longer than you expect but no golfer in the world could be disappointed when he reaches this course. Perhaps the best hotel for golfers in Tralee is the Mount Brandon Hotel (066) 23333.

There are very reasonable 18 hole courses at **Dingle** (Ballyferiter) and **Dooks** but **Waterville** is the other great course in County Kerry. Waterville is one of the longest courses in Europe, when played from the back tees. It has its charm as well though and it has been described as 'the beautiful monster'.

Suggestions for a 19th hole in Waterville include the convenient Waterville House (0667) 4102, The Waterville Lake Hotel (0667) 4133 and the Butler Arms Hotel (0667) 4144. (A quick note here for Shamrock Cottages (0749) 76715, a group which boasts a fine selection of cottages in the most scenic locations.)

CORK

Coming down from rather dizzy heights, County Cork deserves a brief inspection. In the city itself, the **Cork** Golf Club at Little Island is decidedly worth a visit. Approximately five miles east of the town centre the course overlooks Cork Harbour and is one of the top ten inland courses in Ireland. It was at Little Island that one of Ireland's legendary golfers Jimmy Bruen learnt to play. Other golfing challenges near to Ireland's second city include **Muskerry, Monkstown** and **Douglas**, plus a fine new 18 hole course, **Harbour Point,** which opened in 1991 and is not far from Cork Golf Club at Little Island. A delightful place to stay in Cork is the Arbutus Lodge Hotel (021) 501237 while just outside in Shanagarry is Ballymaloe House (021) 652531, where the restaurant is particularly outstanding. Cork also boasts the Silver Springs Hotel (021) 507533, which has numerous leisure facilities including its own nine-hole golf course. Not far away at **Mallow** we reach the end of this extraordinary (not to say exhausting!) golfing tour and the order of the day is an enjoyable round of golf followed by a relaxing stay at Longueville House (022) 47156. As everybody knows, Ireland is the land of 40 shades of green – after such a trip I think we are in need of 40 winks, and we'll certainly get them here.

Charles Crombie   THE ONLY WAY   Rosenstiel's

DUNRAVEN ARMS HOTEL

Dating back to the time of the Norman Conquest and nestling in the lush countryside of Ireland's Golden Vale, the little village of Adare is one of the prettiest in Ireland. It owes its story-book appearance to the 3rd Earl of Dunraven who, in the 1830s when other landlords were furiously replacing thatch with slate, thankfully went against the trend and re-built Adare with larger thatched houses. Today it remains a model village, surrounded by rich, quiet countryside, with a wide shady main street, ancient church, black and white timbered houses and fascinating ruins strewn along the banks of the River Maigue.

The Irish are a race well known for their unique welcome and for over 200 years now the Dunraven Arms Hotel has extended its hand from the heart of this rambling village. It is a hospitality that has not gone unnoticed; Princess Grace and Prince Rainier are just two of the guests from the hotel's past, drawn by the its justly acclaimed reputation for quiet relaxed comfort and service in the serenity of such traditional surroundings.

Since each guest to The Dunraven Arms is a special guest each of the 45 room has been individually decorated and furnished, incorporating many antiques into the taste and style. Naturally all have central heating, direct dial telephones, radio, television and private ensuite bathrooms, and most offer views of private gardens or look out over the charming village.

The Maigue Restaurant has received Bord Failte's 'Awards of Excellence'; acclamations richly deserved, with produce from the hotel's own gardens complementing succulent salmon and trout, tender beef and lamb, and ensuring cuisine of the highest quality.

For the golfer the Dunraven Arms is ideal; some of the region's, and indeed country's, best golf courses, Ballybunion, Lahinch, Tralee, Killarney, are all within easy driving distance of the village. This year is particularly exciting with the opening of Adare Manor's championship golf course; designed by Robert Trent-Jones it will be considered one of the top courses in the country and, needless to say, is awaiting a host of celebrities. This all new course will compliment the other local one which has been in existence since 1900. What used to be a compact but challenging 9 hole course has just been extended to 18. In a village the size of Adare, it must be unique to have two 18 hole courses; well worth a visit.

Of course a holiday cannot be all golf, and there are few countries in the world better for the lover of the outdoors than Ireland. Close by Adare is Bleech Lake with its stunning scenery and guaranteed good catch of trout and pike, while the waters of the West Coast are unpolluted and refreshingly underfished. For the equestrian enthusiast The Dunraven Arms is perfect; not only can the Clonshire Equestrian Centre offer trekking and tuition across its 120 acres of private parkland, but the hotel itself has long been established as the fox-hunting centre of Ireland. In addition the hotel would be only too happy to organise a shooting programme for guests who wish it. Of course, with Adare being recently named as one of Ireland's prime heritage towns a more sedentary day in its historical setting offers its own unique rewards.

With such an impressive backbone of tradition and experience The Dunraven Arms is confident that it can meet, not just the needs, but the wants of visitors looking for that elusive 'perfect escape'.

Dunraven Arms Hotel Ltd.
Adare
County Limerick
Ireland
Tel: (061) 396209
Fax: 353-61-396541 (Int'l)

BALLYBUNION
CHAMPIONSHIP GOLF

Ballybunion is a place of true pilgrimage. To golfers this is where gold has been struck, not once, but twice with two of the greatest golf courses in the world lying side by side. The **Old Course** at Ballybunion has long been regarded as the ultimate test in links golf. It lies in a very remote corner of County Kerry close to the Shannon estuary amid some of the largest sand hills in the British Isles. It has a very wild beauty; no course could be closer to the sea and a number of the holes run right along the cliff edges. It's incredibly spectacular stuff and when the wind lashes in from the Atlantic, it is not a place for faint hearts.

The Old Course was begun in 1896 although a full eighteen holes were not completed until thirty years later. The renowned American writer **Herbert Warren Wind** said of the creation: 'It is the finest sea-side course I have ever seen'. When **Tom Watson** first visited in 1981 (and he has returned many times since), he instantly supported Wind's contention and went on to tell the Members as much in a personal letter of thanks to the Club. What then of the **New Course**, constructed in the mid 1980s? Architect **Robert Trent Jones** had this to say: 'When I first saw the piece of land chosen for the new course at Ballybunion, I was thrilled beyond words. I said it was the finest piece of linksland I had ever seen. I feel totally confident that everyone who comes to play at Ballybunion will be as thrilled as I was by the unique majesty of this truly unforgettable course'.

Happily, Ballybunion isn't jealous of its treasures and visitors are always made to feel welcome. The Golf Manager at Ballybunion is **Jim Mckenna**. He can be contacted by telephone on **(068) 27146** or from the U.K. on (01035368) 27146. The professional at Ballybunion, **Ted Higgins**, can be reached on **(068) 27209**. A full day's green fee in 1992 was priced at £25 for members of other Irish golf clubs or £40 if not. This entitles the visitor to a round over both the Old and New – not of course compulsory, but if the body can take it, and it's likely to receive a fair battering en route, it would be a tragedy not to play the pair. A single round over the Old Course was priced at £30 in 1992 with £20 payable for 18 holes on the New.

Helped by the lavish praise of Messrs. Watson and Co. Bally-bunion has become a lot busier in recent years and visitors should book some time in advance of intended play. Week-days are naturally the easiest times for a visit and Sundays should be avoided if a game on the Old Course is sought.

The nearest airports to Ballybunion are at Shannon, a distance of approximately sixty miles to the north east, and the new Kerry Airport at Farranfore, some thirty miles due south. Cork's airport is about eighty miles to the south east. From either Cork or Shannon the journey can take about an hour and a half but there cannot be a soul on earth who didn't enjoy a trek through the south west of Ireland. From Shannon, travel via Limerick and from Cork via Mallow and Listowel; from Ballybunion town the course is about a mile's drive along the coast.

There is certainly no shortage of land at Ballybunion and both courses can be stretched to 7,000 yards – an alarming prospect! From the medal tees the two are of fairly similar length, the Old measuring 6503 yards, par 71, the New, 6477 yards, par 72. But don't be fooled by the scorecard, each can be a monster when the mood takes it.

The truly great holes on the Old Course begin at the **6th** which has a frighteningly narrow entrance to a plateau green. The **7th** fairway runs its entire length along the shore – one of the most spectacular par fours one is likely to play. The **8th** is a shortish downhill par three, but if you miss the green, you can be in serious trouble. And so it continues with the **11th** being perhaps the most famous hole on the course. The sight from the tee is intimidating to put it mildly; the Atlantic waves are beneath you to the right, with some enormous sand dunes to the left. The fairway drops in tiers until it finally culminates on a windswept plateau green overlooking the Ocean. It is unquestionably one of the greatest two-shot holes in the world.

The New Course is arguably more dramatic! The sand hills are even more massive, and some of the carries required from the tee are prodigious. Some people rate the course on a par with the Old. I wouldn't agree, although the front nine includes a tremendous series of holes between the **6th** and the **9th**.

The 19th at Ballybunion is a grand place for recuperation. It is conveniently situated midway between nature's two master-pieces. Nowhere are stories swapped so enthusiastically and perhaps nowhere will you hear so often the phrase, 'Just wait 'til next time!' Gold diggers them all.

Old Course

Hole	Yards	Par	Hole	Yards	Par
1	377	4	10	356	4
2	434	4	11	443	4
3	217	3	12	185	3
4	504	5	13	485	5
5	508	5	14	136	3
6	364	4	15	228	3
7	417	4	16	483	5
8	151	3	17	379	4
9	455	4	18	381	4
Out	**3.427**	**36**	**In**	**3.076**	**35**
			Out	**3.427**	**36**
			TOTALS	**6.503**	**71**

THE INTERNATIONAL HOTEL

The International Hotel is one of Killarney's most prominent and centrally situated hotels, convenient for touring, shopping and entertainment. Kerry airport is only 10 miles away.

This 90 bedroom first class hotel offers all rooms with private bath/shower en suite, centrally heated, telephone, TV, video and radio.

The Hotel has been recently modernised and improved without sacrificing its unique atmosphere and Irish charm. The Restaurant, Grill Bar and speciality Seafood Restaurant all offer very good food, using only the freshest local produce, superbly cooked and served in a truly relaxing atmosphere. The Bars and Lounges have an air of friendly informality, combined with efficient and personal service - the ideal rendezvous.

Its praise's sung by many travellers, the Lakeside Fells of Killarney. 'Beauty's Home' cast a spell on all those who visit the region and who often return year after year.

Killarney is the perfect place for a golfing holiday. It offers the visitor the finest facilities for golf with Killarney, the host of the 1991/92 Carroll's Irish Open and the Curtis Cup 1996, only five minutes from the Hotel. 'The beauty of the setting has few peers. All golfers should take a pilgrimage to his enchanting place'. The hotel offers concessionary green fees to the guest Monday to Friday.

Killarney also has excellent fishing in the lakes and rivers and pony trekking through the beautiful 25,000 acre National Park at Muckross.

There is so much to see and do in Killarney, and what better place to base yourself than the charming International Hotel, for a warm welcome and a truly relaxing stay and seven championship courses to choose from within 50 miles.

The International Hotel
Best Western
Killarney
Ireland
Tel: (010 353 64) 31816
Fax: (010 353 64) 31837

KILLARNEY
CHAMPIONSHIP GOLF

Killarney is often described as 'paradise on earth', and not merely by we blasphemous golfers. This is Ireland's most famous beauty spot; somehow the lakes here seem a deeper and clearer blue and the mountains a more delicate shade of purple. It is a place where even the most miserable of wretches would be forced to smile.

The two golf courses of the **Killarney Golf and Fishing Club** take full advantage of the majestic surroundings. A Gleneagles afloat perhaps? Not really. The golf at Killarney is parkland rather than heathland, but it can generate a similar degree of pleasure and, like Gleneagles, can be a welcome retreat from the tremendously testing links courses nearby. A place to sooth one's damaged pride.

Killarney has lived through a somewhat chequered history. Golf has been played here since the late 19th century. The first course was nothing grand, laid out in an old deer park owned by the Earl of Kenmare. However, in 1936 the Earl's very keen golfing heir, and a great character of his time, **Lord Castlerosse**, decided that Killarney deserved a course that would reflect the glorious setting. Eighteen holes were laid out by **Sir Guy Campbell** and the new course opened in 1939. Castlerosse, who had played a very active role in the design, was pleased with the creation but continued to suggest imaginative improvements, unfortunately, not all of which were carried through following his untimely death in 1943. In the 1970s a second eighteen holes were built and the two present courses, **Mahony's Point** and **Killeen** are each a combination of the old holes and the new. Basking beside the shores of Lough Leane and encircled by the splendour of the Macgillicuddy Reeks and the Carrauntoohill mountains, Killarney really is a golfer's dream.

The present Secretary at Killarney is the affable **Tom Prendergast**, who may be contacted by telephone on **(064) 31034** (from the U.K. (010 353 64) 31034). Any written correspondence should be addressed to **The Secretary, Killarney Golf and Fishing Club, O'Mahony's Point, Killarney, Co. Kerry, Ireland.** The Club's professional, **Tony Coveney** can be reached on **(064) 31615**. As seems to be the case with all of Ireland's great courses, visitors are warmly greeted – and they come from every foreseeable golfing country! There are no specific restrictions on playing during the week, although some do exist at the weekend. It's as well to telephone the Club before making any firm arrangements. The green fee at Killarney for 1992 was set at £22 per round, seven days per week. Handicap certificates are required for both courses. Good news for visiting golfers is that there are firm plans to construct a third 18 hole course in the not too distant future.

Killarney is the most accessible of Kerry's golfing delights, the town being linked to both Limerick (seventy miles) and Cork (sixty miles) by major road. The nearest airport is at **Farranfore** (Kerry Airport) which is served by both Aer Lingus and Ryan Air. The Golf Club lies about three miles west of the town off Killorglin Road and is well signposted. Those staying in the area might note that Killarney is the starting point of the famous one hundred mile Ring of Kerry road, which takes in surely some of the most marvellous scenery to be enjoyed anywhere in the world.

In such a setting, inspired golf is clearly on the cards (or so one hopes!) Mahony's Point is still probably the better known of the two courses, largely on account of its spectacular finishing holes, although in 1991 and 1992 it was the much improved Killeen Course which hosted the Carrolls **Irish Open,** and on both occasions victory went to **Nick Faldo**. The Killeen is in fact the longer of the two courses, measuring 6426 metres, par 73, compared with Mahony's Point, which measures 6138 metres, par 72. Among the better holes on the Killeen Course are the dog-legged **1st**, which follows the curve of Lough Leane's shore, the stunning par three **3rd**, also alongside the waters edge and the exacting **13th** – one of Castlerosse's favourites from the Campbell layout – a long par four which has a stream crossing the fairway to catch the mis-hit second.

Mahony's Point's celebrated finish begins at the par five **16th** where the course returns toward Lough Leane. The **18th** though is the hole that everyone remembers. It's a par three hole, which in itself is fairly unusual at the end of a round, and the tee shot is played directly across the edge of the lake, practically all carry. Rhododendron bushes and pine trees surround the green: very beautiful, yet potentially very treacherous. 'The best short hole in the world' enthused **Henry Longhurst**. He also suggested that it might be a fitting place to end one's days. I can think of many worse places than the 18th green on Mahony's Point, but to pass over the club's magnificent new 19th hole would be at best anti-social.

Mahony's Point Course

Hole	Metres	Par	Hole	Metres	Par
1	333	4	10	365	4
2	409	4	11	433	4
3	426	4	12	168	3
4	127	3	13	437	5
5	454	5	14	346	4
6	357	4	15	257	4
7	168	3	16	474	5
8	531	5	17	370	4
9	298	4	18	185	3
Out	3.103	36	In	3.035	36
			Out	3.103	36
			TOTALS	6.138	72

SHEEN FALLS LODGE

Discover the charming village of Kenmare along the coastal peninsula of Ireland's South West and you will come upon the luxurious Sheen Falls Lodge.

The Lodge nestles against a background of hazy mountain panoramas and overlooks the Falls of the Sheen River as they tumble dramatically into the Kenmare Estuary.

Sheen Falls Lodge is all you could possibly dream of in a gracious country hotel as it stands amid 300 acres of lawn, semi tropical gardens restored to their 17th century glory, green pastures and forests. Fishing rights on a 15 mile stretch of the Sheen River, famed for salmon and sea trout, are available in season to guests.

We invite you to golf on any of six golf courses within a 40 mile radius of the hotel, one of which is Killarney which hosted the 1991 Carrolls Irish Open. Alternatively Kenmare golf course only a short distance from the Lodge, offers a charming nine hole along the bay.

Other facilites include a conference centre, health and fitness centre, horseriding along wooded trails, tennis and croquet.

Sheen Falls Lodge
Kenmare
Co. Kerry
Ireland
Tel: 010 353 64 41600
Fax: 010 353 64 41386

ORANMORE LODGE

Built in 1850 as a wedding present, and originally known as Thornpark House, Oranmore was designed at a fashionable distance from the city of Galway at the land end of Galway Bay. The crest over the door bears the motto, 'comme de trouve' - 'as you find us'. This gracious old-world house holds to this, epitomising all that is best in traditional Irish hospitality.

As the hotel was not purpose built it retains its elegant atmosphere of country house living, with the emphasis throughout on excellence. With each of the ten rooms individually furnished, having their own style and character, the welcome is more akin to that of personal guest than a hotel customer. This attention to style and detail carries on into the spacious but still very homely and personal bar, and of course, into the host's pride, the beautiful dining-room. Here, with the Adam fireplace as focal point, you can enjoy haute cuisine with fresh seafood and locally grown vegetables a speciality, and of course, the best of famous Irish meat. All complemented by a carefully chosen wine list.

The local area offers breathtaking scenery, views which have inspired a great number of famous paintings. Much of the local population is Irish-speaking, adding a further charm for the visitor. The list of possibilities in the area is enormous. Fishing on Kilcolgan river and Lough Corrib, or sea-angling on Galway bay. The hotel is more than happy to arrange boats for guests. For the golfer, the 18-hole course at Salthill in Galway welcomes the new visitor. For the hunting enthusiast the famous Galway Blazers meet at Oranmore regularly and mounts can be hired. Shooting for Wild Geese, Duck and Snipe, and bathing in the refreshing sea. If racing is your sport the renowned Galway races are held regularly at nearby Ballybrit, and the fascinating International Oyster Festival is a must for any visitor to the area.

However you choose to spend your day, there can surely be no better base to return to than the beautiful Oranmore Lodge.

Brian O'Higgins
Oranmore Lodge Hotel
Oranmore
Co Galway
Ireland
Tel: (010 353 91) 94400

CARAGH LODGE

Caragh Lodge nestles on the shore of Caragh Lake in the heart of Kerry with superb views across the lake to the McGillicuddy Reeks – Ireland's highest mountain.

Only one mile from the famous 'Ring of Kerry' road and ten minutes drive from golden beaches it is the ideal centre for touring, golf or fishing holidays. Cork and Shannon Airports are only two hours away and Kerry Airport, with direct flights from London, 25 minutes drive.

Hospitality at Caragh Lodge is unsurpassed with your hostess, Mary Gaunt, attending to your every need. Mary personally supervises the kitchen in which Wild Salmon, Kerry Lamb and other fresh, local produce is prepared with the loving care of an expert cook.

The lounges, with their crackling log fires in the evening, are gracefully adored with antiques and rich furnishings and provide the perfect setting for a pre-dinner drink or a quiet evening with friends.

As the award winning gardens reach down to the lake shore, salmon and wild brown trout fishing are on the doorstep. Two boats are available for the use of guests and ghillies can be arranged. The two rivers flowing into and out of Caragh Lake also provide excellent salmon fishing and permits can be obtained through the Lodge.

Golf Courses in the vicinity include Ballybunion, Killarney, Waterville and Tralee, all within an hour's drive or Dooks Links course only ten minutes away. Mary Gaunt will be pleased to arrange tee-off times for guests.

Caragh Lodge
Caragh Lake
Co. Kerry
Tel: (010 353 66) 69115
Fax: (010 353 66) 69316

TRALEE
CHAMPIONSHIP GOLF

Like the Beatles, there will never be another **Arnold Palmer**. In his prime he attacked golf courses the way Errol Flynn attacked pirates. He led golf away from its stuffy, gin and tonic, plus fours image and took a vast army of hero-worshipping fans with him. When he stopped winning golf tournaments around the world, Palmer became involved in golf course design. Now let's face it, a man whose middle name is 'Charge' is unlikely to construct 'hum drum' golf courses. Hardly. The courses Arnold Palmer designs are the sort that any golfer with high blood pressure really ought to steer well clear of. Tralee's golf course, perched on the edge of the incomparably dramatic coast of County Kerry, is one that should carry such a health warning.

Tralee (the golf course is actually 8 miles west of the town at Barrow) understandably prides itself on being the first golf course that Arnold Palmer designed in Europe. Apparently, he had been looking to build across the water for some time but until the mid 1980s when he was approached by some remarkably astute Irish gentlemen he hadn't found a venue that suited. Doubtless the Irish chatted him up good and proper as only they can, but Palmer didn't need the Ancient Mariner's treatment. One look at the proposed site convinced him, 'I have never come across a piece of land so ideally suited for the building of a golf course', he declared.

For decades Tralee golfers had played on a rather ordinary 'town course.' When they discovered the tract of links land at Barrow they sensed they had discovered something very special – hence the bold approach to Palmer and the decision to 'quit town' and head for the coast.

The drive from Tralee to Barrow doesn't remotely hint at the pot of gold that awaits at the end of the long, winding road. The situation is sensational in the extreme and Palmer was the perfect choice to lay out a daring and heroic course alongside such a beautifully rugged coastal stretch; a seascape described by golf writer **Peter Dobereiner** as being 'in a different class even to California's Monterey Peninsula.'

The Secretary at Tralee is the affable **Mr Peter Colleran**; he can be contacted by telephone on **(066) 36379** or by fax: (066) 36008. The code from the UK is (010 353 66). The Club's full address is, **Tralee Golf Club, West Barrow, Ardfert, County Kerry**. Visitors wishing to test their skills at Tralee must be in possession of a current handicap (the doctor's certificate is optional) and advance booking with the club is

required. The best days to arrange a game at Tralee are Mondays, Tuesdays, Thursdays and Fridays when there are no general restrictions. On Wednesdays it is possible to tee off before 9.00 am or between 10.40 am and 12.30 pm. Weekend golf is possible between 11.00 am – 1.30 pm. Finally, the green fees in 1992 were set at £25 per round midweek, £30 at the weekend.

Measuring 6239 metres (about 6900 yards) from the Championship tees Tralee has the appearance of being two courses rather than one. The gentler outward half opens with an exacting par four where the second shot immediately guides you to the edge of the precipice; one of several greens overlooking the ocean and in this case, down over a vast, desolate beach that featured prominently in the film **Ryan's Daughter**. The **2nd** is a banana-shaped par five that follows the cliff edges – invigorating stuff! Then comes the classic short **3rd** across the rocks, a hole that American visitors frequently liken to the 7th at Pebble Beach. The view of the hole from the Championship tee is enough to make a brave man tremble. The **6th, 7th** and **8th** ('Palmer's Loop') offer more tremendous golf and provide views of a ruined 12th century castle and an old smugglers' haunt, but it is the back nine holes that leave most first-timers gasping.

After passing in front of the Clubhouse and playing the 10th the golfer then disappears into another world, a world of extraordinarily wild and massive dunes. This is where Palmer really went to town. In true Arnie fashion desperately daring carries are the order of the day. The par four **12th** is surely one of the most examining two shot holes in golf. Although downhill, it is invariably played into the teeth of the wind – and my how it can blow in these parts! The second must be fired over a huge ravine which continues around the left side of what is a painfully narrow table green. Barely do you have time to regain your breath when you must confront the par three **13th**, there the tee shot must carry an even deeper chasm! As you play these exhilarating holes all around are magnificent vistas of the Atlantic Ocean, the Dingle Peninsula and the great sweep of Kerryhead. The course doesn't let up and the downhill, par three **16th** (reminiscent of the 15th at Ballybunion Old), and the dog-legged **17th** (which is called 'Ryan's Daughter') are two more outstanding holes. On reaching the clubhouse which, like the one at Killarney, is new, pleasantly relaxing and extremely well-appointed, you feel that you've tackled more than just an extraordinary golf course – you may even feel you have challenged Palmer head to head. But that's Tralee – a unique golfing experience.

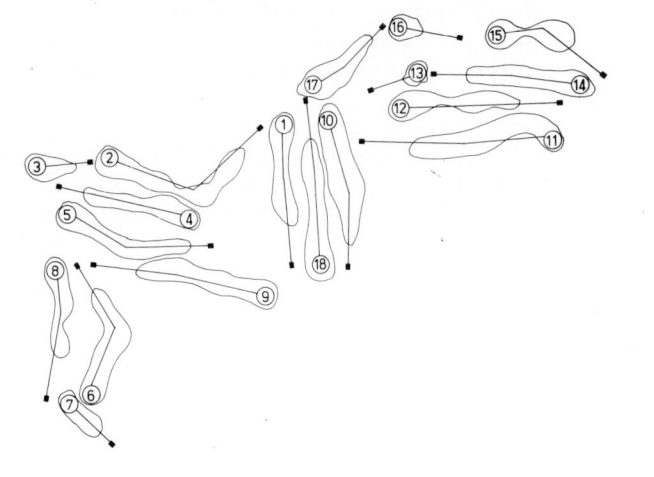

Hole	Metres	Par		Hole	Metres	Par
1	367	4		10	390	4
2	537	5		11	531	5
3	175	3		12	408	4
4	392	4		13	146	3
5	389	4		14	370	4
6	380	4		15	279	4
7	142	3		16	181	3
8	356	4		17	321	4
9	451	5		18	424	4
Out	3,189	36		In	3,050	35
				Out	3,189	36
				TOTALS	6,239	71

WATERVILLE HOUSE & GOLF LINKS

Geographically speaking, Waterville is something of an Irish Dornoch. No-one could pretend that it is anything but remote, but then who would really want it to be anything else? With remoteness comes the peace of a lost world; with remoteness comes charm.

Waterville sits at the far end of the Ring of Kerry; west of Waterville there is nothing for 2,000 miles, save the Atlantic Ocean, while completing the circle to the North, South and East are brooding mountains, majestic lakes, soft hills and babbling streams.

It may surprise some to learn that golf has been played at Waterville from at least as early as the 1870s; initially it was by those gallant and indominatable men who laid the trans-Atlantic cable, so bringing the New World close to the old. The land that these pioneering golfers played over was classic, sandy links terrain - greatly exposed to the elements, but neatly maintained by the local sheep.

Until the late 1960s Waterville was largely their own best-kept secret. About this time a second team of golfing pioneers led by the visionary Irish-American Jack Mulcahy determined that Waterville links should realise its full potential. 'Determined' is the word for in a few short years they, to adopt the words of leading Irish golf writer Pat Ruddy, 'transformed Waterville from a cosy localised scale to the pinnacles of world class'.

In the 20 years since 'modern' Waterville links opened for play it has been showered with praise; but there is also more to Waterville than spectacular golf. For one thing the 19th hole is one of the most comfortable clubhouses in Ireland and for lovers of golfing art and memorabilia it is a genuine treasure trove. And then there is Waterville House, the Irish residence of the owners of Waterville Links and a temporary home to guests who enjoy an intimate and timeless 'country house' ambience.

Built in the late 18th century and recently refurbished, Waterville House presides serenely on the shores of Ballinskelligs Bay. It has ten bedrooms all overlooking the pure waters of Butler's Pool (a favourite old fishing haunt of Charlie Chaplin) and the wider seascapes and landscapes of the Atlantic and the magnificent, untouched countryside. In addition to the warm hospitality and fine cuisine (note the hearty Irish breakfasts!) Waterville House offers its guests a heated pool, sauna, steam room, snooker and billiard room and golf practice facilities including a putting green.

Finally though, let us return to the nearby links and close with a few more choice words from Pat Ruddy, 'Waterville offers a person a splendid golfing challenge and a delicious taste of life as it must have been for primeval man - earth and clear sky, mountain and ocean and the ever present and teasing winds'.

Waterville House & Golf Links
Waterville
Co. Kerry
Ireland
Tel: (010 353 667) 4102
Fax: (010 353 667) 4482

WATERVILLE
CHAMPIONSHIP GOLF

How often have you read, or heard it said that 'Waterville is for the Big Man?' Given that Waterville is very much in the land of the Little People this sounds terribly exclusive. Wot, no Irishmen? Unlike Ballybunion, the name of the place sounds rather Anglo-French; the major influence however has undoubtedly been American. Modern Waterville in fact is very much the result of an American dream.

Oddly it was an American fisherman who first 'discovered' Waterville. Not your average fisherman of course but one **Charles Chaplin** who regularly came here after the War to escape the clutches of stardom. In Waterville he found total peace (as well as some marvellous fishing).

The man we have to thank for creating the golfing majesty that is Waterville Links is an Irish-American, **John A Mulcahy**. Like all the others who had explored this part of the world he fell in love with the area and like Castlerosse of Killarney fame he was both extremely wealthy and extremely crazy about golf. In the early seventies, Mulcahy talked to leading Irish course designer, Eddie Hackett........and the rest is history.

Immediately Mulcahy's Waterville opened for play, it was showered with the highest praise. Of course it helped that Mulcahy was able to bring his mates over from America, and that they happened to include people like **Sam Snead, Art Wall** and **Julius Boros,** but their enthusiasm for Waterville and the beauty of its situation was genuine. In any event people like **Henry Cotton, Tom Watson** and **Ray Floyd** have since been and marvelled at the creation, the last named in particular who thought it, 'the finest links I have ever played'.

Today, more and more people are 'discovering' Waterville, although at most times the links is still relatively and wonderfully uncrowded. The reason for this is its remoteness. Waterville is 50 miles from Killarney and the nearest airport is at Farranfore, by car a journey time of approximately one and a half hours. The international airports at Cork and Shannon are 100 and 110 miles away respectively. But what a journey it is! The direct route from all points is via Killarney, and Killarney is the starting point for the Ring of Kerry, one of the most scenic roads in the world. Whether the approach to Waterville is 'along the top' via Killorglin and Cahiraveen (this is the quicker but less dramatic route) or 'along the bottom' via Kenmare and Parknasilla, much of the Ring of Kerry will be taken in. Nobody in their right minds could arrive at Waterville uninspired and surely nobody will leave on anything less than a high.

The 1992 green fee at Waterville was £30 per round seven days per week. When available a second round cost an extra £10. Juniors pay half rates. Tee times can be guaranteed by making an advance booking with the Club, in this instance a 25 per cent deposit is payable one month in advance of the date of playing. The Secretary/Manager at Waterville is **Noel Cronin**, he can be contacted by telephone on either **(0667) 4545** or **(0667) 4102** and by fax on (0667) 4482. The Club's professional, **Liam Higgins** can be reached on **(0667) 4102.**

The danger of encouraging the description of a golf course as being 'for the big man' is that it risks putting off anyone who cannot thump a ball 300 yards. Naturally it is an advantage (though not necessarily on every hole) to be able to hit the ball like the professional, Liam Higgins, who once holed in one at the **16th** – all 352 yards of it!, but if you've got a twitchy short game, you are still going to be struggling, and besides, how often are you going to be asked to play Waterville from the Championship tees? From the forward and medal tees, Waterville is no more or less frightening than the other great links courses of Ireland and it is certainly as enjoyable.

Although there are some good holes on the front nine, notably the **3rd** and **4th**, it is the back nine at Waterville that everyone raves about. In golfing terms, this is life in the fast lane. The dunes are high and the fairways tumble; there are some spectacular carries and magnificent vantage points and three holes in particular that are simply world class; I refer to the 11th, 12th and 17th.

The **12th** and **17th** are both longish, short holes. On both the tee shots must be carried over a sea of dunes, and at the 12th, the 'Mass Hole', over a gaping gully as well. If the 12th tee is elevated then the 17th must be on a mini-mountain. In fact it is on 'Mulcahy's Peak', a purpose-built tower of a tee from which there is a superb view, not just down to the illusive green but across the entire links.

The **11th** 'Tranquillity' is rated by many to be the greatest par five in Ireland. The fairway winds its entire length beneath sand dunes that are reminiscent of Ballybunion or Birkdale. It is possible to reach the green in two, for the last sixty yards or so is downhill, but only if the drive has been perfectly positioned.

It's funny how the world not only turns but sometimes turns on its head. In the 19th century just about every self-respecting Irishman living in Co. Kerry wanted to explore America. Now every self-respecting American wants to explore Co. Kerry: to see the lovely Ring of Kerry and to play the glorious links of Kerry. But remember, Waterville isn't just for the Big Man, Waterville is for Everyman.

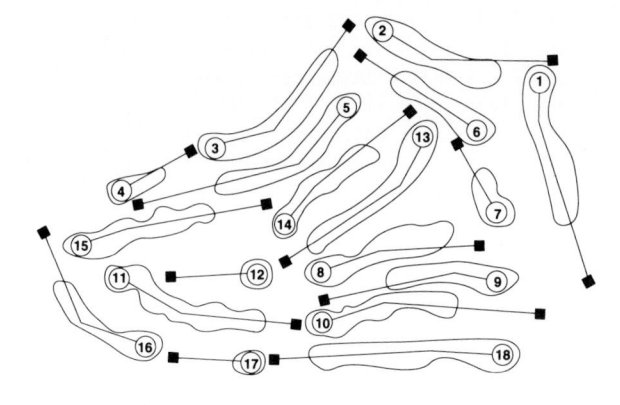

Hole	Yards	Par	Hole	Yards	Par
1	430	4	10	475	4
2	469	4	11	496	5
3	417	4	12	200	3
4	179	3	13	518	5
5	595	5	14	456	4
6	371	4	15	392	4
7	178	3	16	350	4
8	435	4	17	196	3
9	445	4	18	582	5
Out	**3,519**	**35**	**In**	**3,665**	**37**
			Out	**3,519**	**35**
			Totals	**7,184**	**72**

TOWERS HOTEL

The Towers is a family run, Grade A Hotel, situated on the famous ring of Kerry. The Hotel offers its visitors a friendly homely atmosphere and a genuine Irish hospitality.

Dining in our restaurant is a treat and is recognised as one of Ireland's most distinguished restaurants, offering the best in seafood and shellfish delicacies.

Residents at the Towers enjoy beautifully appointed bedrooms, with central heating, T.V., direct dial telephone and private bathroom. Old Bar with open turf fire and cocktail bar with baby grand piano.

For the golfer we are situated in one of the best spots in Ireland - Dooks 18 hole Golf Links is 3 miles away. There are championship courses at Waterville, Ballybunion and Killarney with the scenic Tralee and Dingle courses all within easy reach.

For the non-golfer the surrounding countryside provides a wealth of things to do and see, sightseeing, mountaineering, salmon and trout fishing - on rivers and lakes - boat and Ghillie can also be arranged. Ideal for a walk is a lovely uncrowded four mile long beach. Horse riding can be arranged, either trekking through 25,000 acres at the National Park at Killarney or a gallop on the beach at Rossbeigh.

Kerry Airport is only 30 minutes drive away, Cork or Shannon Airports are approximately 2 hours drive.

Towers Hotel
Glenbeigh
Co. Kerry
Ireland
Tel: (010 353 66) 68212
Fax: (010 353 66) 68260

LAHINCH
CHAMPIONSHIP GOLF

On the rugged coast of County Clare, two miles from the spectacular Cliffs of Moher lies the **'St. Andrews of Ireland'**.

In 1892, officers of the famous Black Watch Regiment stationed in Limerick discovered a vast wilderness of duneland. Being good Scotsmen, they knew at once that this was the perfect terrain for a golf links. On Good Friday 1893, Lahinch was duly founded. The obvious choice of person to design the course was **'Old' Tom Morris** of St. Andrews. Tom accepted but then other than laying out the tees and greens, he felt there was little he could do. He said: 'I consider the links is as fine a natural course as it has ever been my good fortune to play over'. More praise was to follow. In 1928, **Dr. Alister Mackenzie** was invited to make a number of adjustments to the links. On completion he suggested that 'Lahinch will make the finest and most popular course that I, or I believe anyone else, ever constructed'. Not perhaps the most modest statement ever made but coming from a man who had just designed Cypress Point and who was soon to create the legendary Augusta, it can hardly be taken lightly.

Visitors wishing to play at Lahinch will find the Club extremely welcoming. The only restrictions are as follows: Monday to Friday between 9am and 10am and 12.00 to 1.30pm and at Weekends between 8am and 11am and 12.30pm to 2pm. The present Secretary is **Mr. Alan Reardon**, who can be contacted by telephone on **(065) 81003** (from the U.K. (010 353 65) 81003. The club's full address is simply **Lahinch Golf Club, Lahinch, Co Clare.** The professional is **Robert McCavery** and he can be reached on **(065) 81408**.

Since Dr. Mackenzie's alterations, there have been two eighteen hole courses: the Championship **Old Course** and the shorter **Castle Course**, the latter having been extended from nine holes to eighteen in 1975. Green fees in 1992 to play on the Old Course were set at £25 per round between May and September with a reduced rate of £20 available for midweek golf between January and March and in November and December. A day's golf on the Castle Course was priced at £15 (all year round). Certain discounts are available to those staying in local hotels (contact the club for details). Golfing Societies are equally welcome and bookings can be made for any day other than Sunday.

Travellers coming from Britain (or indeed Europe and America) should find Lahinch more accessible than any of the great links of Co. Kerry; international flights to Shannon are frequent and Lahinch is located approximately thirty miles to the north west of the airport. On leaving Shannon, Ennis is the town to head for, and thereafter, Ennistimon, just two miles from Lahinch. The road passes through some marvellous countryside, and incidentally, do try to visit the Cliffs of Moher – in places they rise to a sheer drop of over six hundred feet, the highest in Europe. Golfers on a west of Ireland pilgrimage approaching from Ballybunion should cross the Shannon via the Tarbert Ferry. It leaves every 30 minutes – on the hour and at half past.

Lahinch is not as tough as a Portmarnock or a Waterville; it doesn't have the length for a start, but then it's anything but straightforward. The golfer who enjoys the challenge of Ballybunion will fall in love with Lahinch. The seascapes are just as dramatic and the fairways twist and tumble in a similar fashion. A premium is placed on accurate tee shots and the slightest straying will put you amongst the dunes. Many greens sit on natural plateaux and can be tricky to hold. It isn't easy to select the best holes, for so many are memorable, but perhaps the finest sequence is found between the **7th** and **10th** – four really tremendous par fours. The most famous holes however are undoubtedly the **5th** and **6th**, both of which Mackenzie was forbidden to touch. Having won four Open Championships at Prestwick, 'Old Tom' clearly relished the blind shot and this is what is called for at both the 5th (Klondyke) and the 6th (Dell). Not too many quibble with the 5th; it is a par five, although the blind second shot is over a prodigious sand hill and the green is a further two hundred yards on. The 6th however, is a par three! The green nestles between two steep sand dunes and all the player sees from the tee is a white marker-stone placed on the fronting hill to indicate the current pin position – 'hit and hope' perhaps, but charming all the same.

The Castle Course is literally over the road from the Old and occupies much more level ground. The fairways wind their way around the remains of **O'Brien's Castle**. It may be a little less challenging, but it's still a good honest links and is just as well maintained.

The Clubhouse at Lahinch is fairly small, but marvellously intimate and certainly an excellent place to adjourn to should the heavens open. And you'll have ample warning of the impending doom for legend has it that the goats that graze on the dunes will always make an early retreat towards the shelter of the 19th. A bit of Irish mist? Try telling that to the Members!

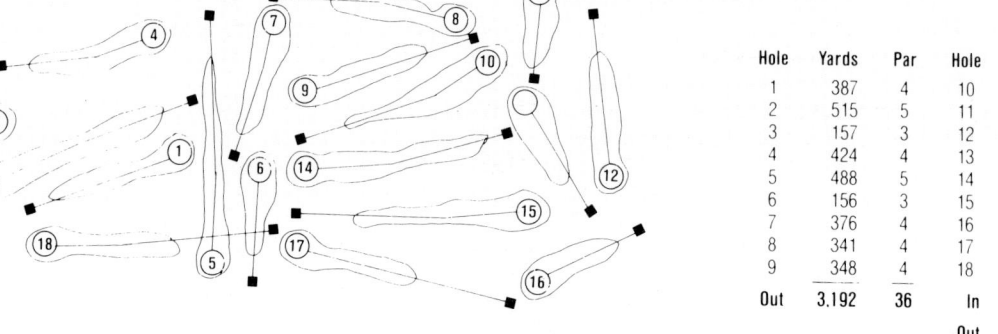

Hole	Yards	Par	Hole	Yards	Par
1	387	4	10	453	4
2	515	5	11	139	3
3	157	3	12	353	4
4	424	4	13	274	4
5	488	5	14	486	5
6	156	3	15	456	4
7	376	4	16	196	3
8	341	4	17	435	4
9	348	4	18	520	5
Out	3,192	36	In	3,312	36
			Out	3,192	36
			TOTALS	6,504	72

LONGUEVILLE HOUSE

Longueville is set in the centre of a 500 acre private wooded estate, overlooking one of the most beautiful river valleys in Ireland, the Blackwater - itself forming the Estate's southern boundary, famous as one of Ireland's foremost salmon and trout rivers.

Longueville is three miles on the Killarney road ex Mallow; Killarney itself in the heart of scenic Kerry being less than one hour away. Cork airport is 24 miles distant and Shannon airport is 54 miles away. Guests can make day trips to the Dingle and Beara Peninsulas. Blarney, Kinsale and the Vee Gap are all less than one hour's drive. For stay-at-homes, Longueville offers three miles of game fishing on the famous Blackwater river. There is horse-riding at nearby stables and golf at a dozen courses closeby including Premier Championship courses at Killarney, Ballybunion and Tralee.

A games room with full sized billiard table is in the basement. The estate is quiet and peaceful for walking or jogging with idyllic paths through wooded ways and water meadows.

Built in 1720, Longueville is the ancestral home of your hosts. Their aim is to maintain the friendly atmosphere of a home rather than a hotel. The centre block and two wings were added in 1800 and the Turner Curvilinear Conservatory was added in 1862.

Inside, Longueville offers many beautiful ceilings, doors and items of antique furniture in the public rooms and bedrooms - but in the latter, whether it be antique or otherwise, the acme of comfort is the bed. All bedrooms have en suite bathroom, colour television, radio and direct dial telephone.

The aim of Longueville's hosts is to have guests relax and feel completely at home in the comfort of their beautiful house, a classic Georgian country house. Central to all this is the kitchen, the heart of Longueville, over which the O'Callaghans' son William, a French-trained chef, presides. In here three lovingly prepared meals a day are made, using only the fresh produce of the estate's river, farm and gardens.

To match the superb food, Longueville's cellar includes over 150 wines, both from the Old and New World. The family's interest in wine has led them to plant their own three acre vineyard - unique in Ireland - produced in years of favourable climate.

Longueville House & Presidents' Restaurant
Mallow
Co Cork
Republic of Ireland
Tel: (010 353 22) 47156/47306
Fax: (010 353 22) 47459

IRELAND
COMPLETE GOLF

WEST OF IRELAND

CO CLARE

Dromoland Castle G.C
(061) 368144
Newmarket on Fergus
E. of Ennis on the N18 towards Shannon
(18) 6300 yards/***/D

Ennis G.C
(065) 24074
Drumbiggle, Ennis
1 mile W. of Ennis
(18) 5890 yards/***(not Sun)/D

Kilkee G.C
(048) 341
East End, Kilkee
Just out of Kilkee on Georges Head
(9) 6185 yards/***/D

Kilrush G.C
(065) 51138
Parknamoney, Kilrush
N.E of town on the R483
(9) 2739 yards/***/E

Lahinch G.C
(065) 81003
Lahinch
Take the R85 from Ennis
(18) 6702 yards/***/C
(18) 5265 yards/***/D (C at weekends)

Shannon G.C
(061) 61020
Shannon airport, Shannon
N. of Limerick on the N18
(18) 6854 yards/**/D

Spanish Point G.C
(065) 84198
Spanish Point, Miltown Malbay
2 miles from Mitown Malbay, near power station
(9) 6171 metres/**/E/H

CO CORK

Bandon G.C
(023) 4111
Castlebernard, Bandon
Through Bandon on the river side
(18) 5496 yards/***/E

Bantry Park G.C
(027) 50579
Donemark, Bantry
Outside Bantry near the Reendonegan lake
(9) ***/E

Cork G.C
(021) 353451
Little Island
Take N25 E. from Cork, then the R623
(18) 6635 yards/**(not Thurs)/D

Charleville G.C
(063) 81257
Ardmore, Charleville
25 miles S. of Limerick on the N20
(18) 6380 yards/**/E

Cobh G.C
(021) 812399
Ballywilliam, Cobh
15 miles from Cork on the N25 and R625 to Cobh
(9) 4338 yards/***(not weekends am)E

Doneraile G.C
(022) 24137
Doneraile
Take the V R522 to Doneraile, off the N20 from Cork
(9) 5528 yards/***/E

Douglas G.C
(021) 895297
Marylborough Hill, Douglas
Half mile from the bridge at Douglas on the R609
(18) 6179 yards/**/D

Dunmore G.C
(023) 33352
Clonakilty
S. of the town on the headland of Duneen Bay
(9) 4464 yards/***/E

East Cork G.C
(021) 631687
Goatacrue, Midleton
Take N25 E. out of Cork, left at roundabout
(18) 5207 yards/**/F/H

Fermoy G.C
(025) 31472
2 miles N. of town off the N8
(18) 5550 yards//**(not Mon/Wed pm)/E

Glengarriff G.C
(027) 63150
Glengarriff
Take N71 S. from Kilarny to harbour area
(9) 4328 yards/***/E

Kanturk G.C
(029) 50534
Fairy Hill, Kanturk
On the N579 Cork-Kanturk road
(9) 5527 yards/***/E

Kinsale G.C
(021) 772197
Ringenane, Belgooly
8 miles S. of Cork on the R600
(9) 5332 yards/**/E

Macroom G.C
(022) 41072
Lackaduve, Macroom
W from Cork on the N22
(9) 5439 yards/***/E

Mallow G.C
(022) 21145
Ballyellis, Mallow
E. of the town at the Mallow Bridge
(18) 6559 yards/**(not Tues)/F

Mahon G.C
(021) 362480
Cloverhill, Blackrock
Left off the R609 Douglas road
(18) 4818 yards/***/E

Mitchelstown G.C
(025) 24072
Mitchelstown
At junction of N8 and N73, N. of Cork
(9) 5057 yards/***/E

Monkstown G.C
(021) 841225
Parkgariffe, Monkstown
S. of Cork on the R610
(18) 6170 yards/**(not Tues/Wed)/D

Muskerry G.C
(021) 385104
Carrigrohane
W. out of Cork on R617 to Blarney village
(18) 5786 yards/**(not Wed/Thurs)/D

Skibbereen G.C
(028) 21227
Skibbereen
Out of town on R595 to Baltimore
(9) 5774 yards/***/E

Youghal G.C
(024) 92787
Knockaverry, Youghal
Take N25 from Cork to Youghal
(18) 6223 yards/**/D

CO DONEGAL

Ballybofey & Stranorlar G.C
(0704) 31093
Ballybofey
Signposted on the Donegal-Strabanne road
(18) 5913 yards/***(not Wed/Thurs/Fri)/E

Ballyliffin G.C
(077) 76119
Ballyliffin
(18) 6524 yards/***/E

Buncrana G.C
(077) ?
Buncrana
take the R238 N. from the N13
(9) 2020 yards/***/F

Bundoran G.C
(072) 41302
Bundoran
Take the N15 coastal road to Bundoran
(18) 6328 metres/***/F

Donegal G.C
(073) 345054
Murvagh
S. of Donegal, off the N15 to Sligo
(18) 7271 yards/***/E

Dunfanaghy G.C
(074) 36208
Dunfanaghy
Quarter mile off main road, E. of village
(18) 5066 yards/***/E

Greencastle G.C
(077) 81013
Greencastle, via Lifford
Behind the lighthouse, just out of town
(9) 5386 yards/**/E

Gweedore G.C
(075) 31140
Derrybeg, Gweedore
Leave the N56 coast road for R257 to Derrybeg
(18) 6230 yards/***/E

Letterkenny G.C
(074) 21150
Barnhill, Letterkenny
On the R245 outside of town on the lough
(18) 6299 yards/***(not Tues/Wed)/F

Nairn and Portnoo G.C
(075) 45107
Portnoo
Take the N56 to rdara, then R261 to Portnoo
(18) 5950 yards/***(not Sun)/E

North West G.C
(074) 61027
Lisfannon, Fahon, Lifford
2 miles S. of Buncrana on the R238
(18) 6203 yards/**(not Wed)/E

Otway G.C
(074) 58319
Rathmullen
Out of town, beside the lough
(9) 4134 yards/***/F

Portsalon G.C
(074) 59102
Portsalon
Take R245 N. to Millford, then R246 to town
(18) 5844 yards/**/E

Rosapenna G.C
(074) 55301
Downies
On the R248 to Downies and Rosapenna
(18) 6254 yards/***/E

CO GALWAY

Athenry G.C
(091) 94466
Derrydonnel, Oranmore
Leave N6 E. of Galway for the R348 to Athenry
(18) 6000 yards/***(not Sun)/E

Ballinasloe G.C
(0905) 42126
Ballinasloe, Rosgloss
2 miles S. of town on the R335
(18) 5800 yards/***/E

Connemara G.C
(095) 23502
Ballyconneely
Out of town on the cliff tops at Slyne Head
7107 yards/***/F

Galway G.C
(091) 22169
Blackrock, Salthill, Galway
2 miles W. of Galway centre
(18) 6376 yards/**(not Tues)/D

Gort G.C
(091) 31336
Laughtry, Shaughnessy, Gort
Take N18 S. from Galway to Gort
(9) 4976 yards/***/E

Loughrea G.C
(091) 41049
Loughrea
N. of town on the N6
99) 5578 yards/***/E

Mountbellow G.C
(0905) 79259
Shankhill, Mountbellow
Leave N17 from Galway for N63 for Mountbellow
(9) 5564 yards/***/E

Oughterard G.C
(091) 82131
Oughterard
15 miles W. of Galway on the N59
(18) 6150 yards/***/E

Tuam G.C
(093) 24354
Barnacurragh, Tuam
Half mile form town on the Athenry road
(18) 6321 yards/**/E

Portumna G.C
(0509) 41059
Portumna
Half mile W. of Portumna on the R352
(9) 5776 yards/***/F

CO KERRY

Ballybunion G.C
(068) 27146
Sandhill Road, Ballybunion
1 mile out of town on the dunes
18) 6542 yards/***/A/H/L
(18) 6477 yards/***/A/H/L

Ceann Sibeal G.C
(066) 56255
Ballyferriter
(18) 6222 yards/***/E

Dooks G.C
(066) 67370
Dooks, Killorglin
8 miles W. of Killorglin
(18) 6021 yards/***/E

Kenmare G.C
(064) 41291
Kenmare, Killarney
Take N71 S. from Killarney to Kenmare
(9) 2410 yards/***/E

Killarney G.C
(064) 31034
O'Mahony's Point, Killarney
3 miles W. of the town on the R562
7027 yards/**/B/H
6764 yards/**/B/H

Tralee G.C
(066) 36379
West Barrow, Ardfert
Take N22 N from Killarney to N21 and Tralee
(18) 6900 yards/***(not weekend am)/B

Waterville G.C
(0667) 4102
Waterville
1 mile out of Waterville
(18) 7184 yards/***/B

CO LEITRIM

Ballinamore G.C
(078) 44346
Crevy, Ballinamore
Take R209 from Carrick to Ballinamore
(9) 5680 yards/***/F

Carrick On Shannon G.C
(078) 67015
Woodbrook, Carrick on Shannon
Right before town on the N4
(9) 3922 yards/***/F

CO LIMERICK

Adare Manor G.C
(061) 86204
Adare
N. from Limerick on the N20 to Adare
(9) 5700 yards/**/D

Castleroy G.C
(061) 335261
Castletroy, Limerick
3 miles out of town on the N7
(18) 6340 yards/**/D

Limerick G.C
(061) 44083
Ballyclough, Limerick
S. out of Limerick on the Cork road
(18) 5767 yards/**(not Tues)/D

Newcastle West G.C
(069) 62015
Newcastle West
1 mile from Limerick on the Cork road
(9) 5482 yards/***/F

CO MAYO

Achill Island G.C
(098) 45197
Keel, Achill
Follow R319 over Achill Sound to Keel
(9) 5550 yards/***/E

Ballina G.C
(096) 21050
Mossgrove, Shanaghy, Ballina
E of the town on the R294
(9) 5702 yards/***/E

Ballinrobe G.C
(092) 41448
Coolnaha, Ballyhaunis
Out f town on the N83 Sligo road
(9) 5790 yards/***(not Sun)/E

Belmullet G.C
(097) 81266
Belmullet, Ballina
Take N59 from Ballina to Belmullet
(9) 2829 yards/***/E

Castlebar G.C
(094) 21649
Rocklands, Castlebar
S. of the town on the N84
(18) 6109 yards/**/E

Claremorris G.C
(094) 71527
Rushbrook, Castlemaggaret, Claremorris
S. of town on the N17 to Tuam
(9) 6454 yards/***/E

Mulrany G.C
(098) 36107
Mulrany, Westport
N. on the N50 from Westport to Mulrany
(9) 6380 yards/***/E

Swinford G.C
(094) 51378
Brabazon Park, Swinford
Out of town on the R320
(9) 5230 yards/***/D

Westport G.C
(098) 25113
Carrowholly, Westport
2 miles N. of town, past Westport Quay
(18) 6950 yards/***(not Sun)/C

CO ROSCOMMON

Ballaghaderreen G.C
(0907) 60295
Ballaghaderreen
On the R293, left out of town
(9) 5686 yards/***/E

Boyle G.C
(079) 62594
Roscommon Road, Boyle
On the N61 road to Roscommon
(9) 4957 yards/***/E

Castlerea G.C
(0907) 20068
Clonallis, Castlerea
N. of the town on the N61
(9) 5466 yards/***(not Sun)/E

Roscommon G.C
(0903) 6382
Mote Park, Roscommon
S. of the town next to the railway
(9)6215 yards/***/F

CO SLIGO

Ballymote G.C
(071) 3460
Carrigans, Ballymote
On the R293 before town
(9) 5032 yards/***/E

County Sligo G.C
(071) 77134
Rosses Point
N. of town on the R291 to Rosses Point
(18) 6631 yards/***(not Tues)/C

Enniscrone G.C
(096) 36297
Enniscrone (Inniscrone)
On the R297 near Bartragh Island
(18) 6610 yards/***/D

Strandhill G.C
(071) 68188
Strandhill
Signposted on road W. from Sligo to Strandhill
(18) 5937 yards/***/D

EAST OF IRELAND

CO CARLOW

Borris G.C
(0503) 73143
Deer Park, Borris
Take N9 S. from Carlow and onto R705
(9) 6026 yards/***/E

Carlow G.C
(0503) 31695
Deerpark, Dublin Road, Carlow
1 mile from the station on the N9
(18) 6347 yards/***/D

CO CAVAN

Belturbet G.C
(049) 22287
Erne Hill, Belturbet
5 miles N. of Cavan on the N3
(9) 5180 yards/***/E

County Cavan G.C
(049) 31283
Arnmore House, Drumellis, Cavan
1 mile from Cavan on the N198
(18) 5119 metres/***(not Sun)/E

Virginia G.C
(049) 44103
Virginia
50 miles N. of Dublin on the N3 to Cavan
(9) 4520 yards/***/F

CO DUBLIN

Balbriggan G.C
(01) 412173
Blackhall, Balbriggan
On the N1 just outside town
(18) 5717 yards/***(not Tues)/E

Ballinascorney G.C
(01) 512516
Ballinascorney
W. of Dublin on the N81
(18) 5322 yards/***/F

Beaverstown G.C
(01) 436439
15 miles N. of Dublin towards airport
(18) 6400 yards/***/F

Beech Park G.C
(01) 580522
Johnstown, Rathcoole
7 miles from Rathcoole on the Kitteel road
(18) 6250 yards/***/E

Castle G.C
(01) 904207
Woodside Drive, Rathfarnham, Dublin 14
S. of city on the N81
(18) 6240 yards/**(not Tues)/D

Carrickmines G.C
(01) 895676
Carrickmines, Dublin
7 miles S. of Dublin on the R117
(18) 6044 yards/**/F

Clontarf G.C
(01) 311305
Donnycarney House, Malahide Road, Dublin 3
N.E of Dublin on the Malahide Road
(18) 5447 yards/**(not Mon/Wed)/D

Corballis G.C
(01) 450583
Donabate
Take N1 from Dublin, then R126 to Donabate
(18) 4971 yards/***/E

Deer Park Hotel G.C
(01) 322624
Howth
Take Howth road for 8 miles out of Dublin
(18) 6647 yards/**/D

Donabate G.C
(01) 436346
Donabate
Leave N1 from Dublin for R126 for Donabate
(18) 6187 yards/**(not Wed)/D

Dun Laoghaire G.C
(01) 803916
Eglinton Park, Dun Laoghaire
Follow railway along coast road, take
York road
(18) 5463 yards/***(not Wed/Thurs pm
or Sat)/D

Edmondstown G.C
(01) 932461
Edmondstwn, Rathfarnham, Dublin 16
Take N18 from Dublin to Rathfarnham
(18) 5663 yards/**/D

Elm Park G.C
(01) 693438
Nutley House, Donnybrook, Dublin 4
Close to the University and Hospital
(18) 5485 yards/**/D

Forest Little G.C
(01) 401183
Forest Little, Cloghran
N. of Dublin on the N1
(18) 5852 yards/**(not Tues/Fri am)//D

Foxrock G.C
(01) 895668
Torquay Rd, Foxrock
On the right past the castle at Dalkey Point
(9) 5699 yards/**/F

Grange G.C
(01) 932832
Grange Road, Rathfarnham, Dublin 16
S. out of city centre, take N81 to Rathfarnham
(18) 6200 yards/**(not Tues/Wed pm)/F

Hermitage G.C
(01) 268491
Lucan
2 miles short of Lucan on the N4
(18) 6034 yards/**(not Tues/Wed)/C

Howth G.C
(01) 323055
Ten miles from Dublin, follow coast road
(18) 5573 yards/**/D

Island G.C
(01) 436462
Corballis, Donabate
N. from Dublin on N1, onto R126 to Donabate
(18) 6320 yards/**(not Wed/Thurs)/D

Killiney G.C
(01) 851983
Killiney
3 miles past Dun Laoghaire on the N11
(9) 6201 yards/***/D

Kilternan Hotel G.C
(01) 955559
S.E from Dublin on the Enniskerry Road
(18) 5413 yards/*(with member only)/E

Malahide G.C
(01) 461642
Coast Road, Malahide
N. from Dublin on the N1, take R106
to Malahide
(18) 6500 yards/***/C

Milltown G.C
(01) 976090
Lower Churchtown Road, Dublin 14
3 miles S. of the city centre
(18) 5669 yards/***(not Tues/Wed pm)/D

Lucan G.C
(01) 282106
Celbridge Road, Lucan
W. on N4 through Lucan, onto R403
(9) 6281 yards/**(not pm)/D

Newlands G.C
(01) 592903
Clondalkin, Dublin 22
Near junction of N7 and R113
(18) 6184 yards/**(not Tues/Wed)/D

Portmarnock G.C
(01) 323082
Portmarnock
leave Dublin on R107 coast road
(18)7079 yards/***(by arrangement)/F

Rathfarnham G.C
(01) 931201
Newtown, Rathfarnham, Dublin 16
2 miles S. of Rathfarnham on the N81
(9) 5787 yards/**(not Tues)/E

Rush G.C
(01) 437548
Rush
N. on the N1, onto R127 and then Rush
(9) 5598 yards/**(not Wed/Thurs)/E

Royal Dublin G.C
(01) 336346
Bull Island, Dollymount, Dublin 3
N.E from city on coast road towards
Bull Island
(18) 6929 yards/**(not Wed)/B/H

St Annes G.C
(01) 332979
Bull Island, Clontarf, Dublin 5
N.E from Dublin on coast road towards
Bull Island
(9) 5813 yards/*/D

Skerries G.C
(01) 491567
Hackestown, Skerries
N. on the N1, take R127 right to Skerries
(18) 5852 yards/**(not Tues/Wed)/D

Slade Valley G.C
(01) 582207
Lynch Park, Brittas
Take N81 S.W for 9 miles from Dublin
(18) 5337 yards/**(not Wed)/F

Stackstown G.C
(01) 942338
Kellystown Road, Rathfarnham, Dublin 16
Take N81 through Terenure to Rathfarnham
(18) 5952 yards/**/E

Sutton G.C
(01) 323013
Cush Point, Barrow Road, Sutton, Dublin 13
Take coast road N.E from Dublin towards
Howth
(9) 5522 yards/***(not Tues/Sat)/F

CO KILDARE

Naas G.C
(045) 97509
Kardiffstown, Salins, Naas
Leave Dublin on the N7, take R407 for Salins
(18) 6233 yards/***/D

Kildare Country Club ('K' Club)
(01) 6273987
Straffan
(18) 7000 yards/***/A

Knockanally G.C
(045) 69322
Donadea, N. Kildare
3 miles past Kilcock on the R407
(18) 6484 yards/***/E

Four Lakes G.C
(045) 66003
17 miles out of Dublin on the N7
(18) ***/E

Curragh G.C
(045) 41238
Curragh
Take N7 to Kildare, then R413 to Curragh
(18) 6565 yards/**(am only, not Tues)/D

Cill Dara G.C
(045) 21433
Kildare Town
N. of Kildare on the R415
(9) 6196 yards/***/E

Bodenstown G.C
(045) 97096
Bodenstown, Sallins
N. of Naas on the R407
(18) 7031 yards/**/F
(18) **/E

Athy G.C
(0507) 31729
Geraldine, Athy
2 miles before Athy on N78 from Kilcullen
(9) 6158 yards/***(not Sun)/F

CO KILKENNY

Callan G.C
(052) 25136
Geraldine, Callan, Co Kilkenny
1 mile from town on the N76
(9) 5844 yards/***/E

Castlecomer G.C
(056) 41139
Drungoole, Castlecomer
To th right of the town on the N78
(9) 6985 yards/***/E

Kilkenny G.C
(056) 22125
Glendine, Kilkenny
2 miles N. of Kilkenny on the N77
(18) 6374 yards/***/D

Mt Juliet G.C.
(056) 24725
Thomastown
5 miles from Thomastown
(18) 7100 yards/***/A

CO LAOIS

Abbeyleix G.C
(0502) 31450
Abbeyleix
Take N8 S. from Portlaoise
(9) 5680 yards/***/E

Heath G.C
(0502) 26533
The Heath, Portlaoise
On the N7 at the R419 turn-off
(18) 6247 yards/**/F

CO LONGFORD

County Longford G.C
(043) 46310
Dublin Road, Longford
E. of the town on the N4
(18) 5912 yards/***/F

CO LOUTH

Ardee G.C
(041) 53227
Town Parks, Ardee
On the N2, quarter mile N. of town
(18) 5833 yards/**/E

County Louth G.C
(041) 22329
Baltray, Drogheda
On the N1 coastal road
(18) 6798 yards/***(by arrangement)/F

Dundalk G.C
(042) 21731
Blackrock, Dundalk
Take the R172 from Dundalk to Blackrock
(18) 6115 yards/***(not Tues/Sun)/D

Greenore G.C
(042) 73212
Greenore, Dundalk
On the R73 from Dundalk
(18) 5614 yards/***/E

CO MEATH

Black Bush G.C.
(01) 250021
Thomastown, Dunshaughlin
1/2 mile E of Dunshaughlin off N
(18) 7000 yards /***/F
(9) 2800/***/F

Headfort G.C
(046) 40146
Kells
(18) 6372 yards/**(not Tues)/D

Laytown and Bettystown G.C
(041) 27170
Bettystown, Drogheda
On the N1 coastal road from Drogheda
on the R150
(18) 6254 yards/**/D

Royal Tara G.C
(046) 25244
Bellinter, Navan
Take N3 N.W from Dublin towards Navan
(18) 6300 yards/**(not Tues/Wed)/D

Trim G.C
(046) 31463
Newtonmuynagh, Trim
S.W of the town off the R160
(9) 6266 yards/**/E

CO MONAGHAN

Castleblayney G.C
(042) 40197
Castleblayney
Take N2 from Monaghan to Castleblayney
(9)2678 yards/***/E

Clones G.C
(049) 52354
Hilton Park, Scotshouse, Clones
S. on the N54 towards Scotshouse
(9) 5570 yards/***/E

Nuremore G.C
(042) 61438
Carrickmacross
Take 2 from Monaghan to Carrickmacross
(9) 6700 yards/***/E

Rossmore G.C
(047) 81316
Rossmore Park, Monaghan
S. of the city on the B189
(9) 5859 yards/**/E

CO OFFALY

Birr G.C
(0509) 20082
Glenns, Birr
N. of Birr on the R439
(18) 6216 yards/***/E

Edenberry G.C
(0405) 31072
Boherberry, Edenberry
Off the R402 just before town
(9) 5791 yards/***/E

Tullamore G.C
(0506) 21439
Brookfield, Tullamore
Outside of town on the R421 Birr road
(18) 6314 yards/***/D

CO TIPPERARY

Cahir Park G.C
(052) 41474
Kilcommon, Cahir
S. of the town on the R668
(9) 6262 yards/***/E

Carrick On Suir G.C
(051) 40047
Garravoone, Carrick On Suir
S. of the town off the R676
(9) 5948 yards/***(not Sun)/E

Clonmel G.C
(052) 21138
Lyteanearla, Mountain Road, Clonmel
S. of the town on the R678
(18) 6330 yards/**/D

Nenagh G.C
(067) 31476
Beechwood, Nenagh
4 miles S. of the town off the R491
(18) 5483 yards/**(not Thurs or Wed pm)/E

Roscrea G.C
(0505) 21130
Derry Vale, Dublin Road, Roscrea
Take N7 from Dublin to Roscrea
(9) 6059 yards/***/E

Templemore G.C
(0504) 31522
Manna, South Templemore
S. of the town off the N62
(9) 5442 yards/***/E

Thurles G.C
(0504) 21983
Turtulla, Thurles
S. of the town off the N62
(18) 6300 yards/**(not Tues)/F

Tipperary G.C
(062) 51119
Rathanny, Tipperary
S. of the town off the R664
(9) 60774 yards/***/E

CO WATERFORD

Dungarvan G.C
(058) 41605
Ballinacourty, Dungarvan
Out on the point off the R675 from town
(9) 5721 yards/**/E

Lismore G.C
(084) 54026
Lismore, Ballyin
Take N72 from Dungarvan to Lismore
(9) 5600 yards/***/E

Tramore G.C
(051) 81247
Newtown Hill, Tramore
Through the town off the R675
(18) 6660 yards/***(by arrangement)/D

Waterford G.C
(051) 76748
Newrath, Waterford
S. of Kilkenny on the N10/N9
(18) 6237 yards/***/D

CO WESTMEATH

Athlone G.C
(0902) 92073
Hodson Bay, Athlone
N. of the town off the N61
(18) 6000 yards/**/F

Moate G.C
(0902) 81271
Moate
8 miles E. of Athlone on the N6
(9) 5348 yards/***/F

Mullingar G.C
(044) 48366
Belvedere, Mullingar
3 miles S.W of town off the N52
(18) 6370 yards/**/D

CO WEXFORD

Courtown G.C
(055) 25166
Kiltennel, Gorey
At Courtown on the R742 E. of Gorey
(18) 6435 yards/***(not Wed)/D

Enniscorthy G.C
(054) 33191
Knockmarshal, Enniscorthy
2 miles from town on the New Ross Road
(9) 6368 yards/**/E

New Ross G.C
(051) 21433
Tinneanny, New Ross
W. of the town on the R704
(9) 6133 yards/***(not Sun)/E

Rosslare G.C
(053) 32203
Rosslare
Out of Wexford on coast at Rosslare Point
(18) 6485 yards/***/F/H

CO WICKLOW

Arklow G.C
(0402) 32492
Abbeylands
On S. of town off the N11
(18) 5770 yards/**/E

Baltinglass GC
(0508) 81350
Baltinglass
W. of the town off the R747
(9) 6070 yards***F

Blainroe G.C
(0404) 68168
Blainroe
3 miles from Wicklow on the N11
(18) 6681 yards/***(by arrangement)/D

Bray G.C
(01) 862484
Ravenswell Road, Bray
N. of the town off the N11
(9) 5230 yards/**/E

Delgany G.C
(01) 2874536
Delgany
Just off the R762 after Bray
(18) 6000 yards/***/C

European Club
(01) 2808459
Brittas Bay
(18) 7150 yards/**/F

Greystones G.C
(01) 876624
Greystones
Take coast road R761 fom Bray to Greystones
(18) 5227 yards/(Mon and Fri only)/D

Wicklow G.C
(0404) 67379
Dunbar Road, Wicklow
S. off Wicklow off the R750
(9) 5536 yards/*(intro only)/F

Woodbrook G.C
(01) 2824799
Bray
S. of Dublin on the N11
(18) 6541 yards/**(not Tues/Wed)/F

Woodenbridge G.C
(0402) 35202
Woodenbrige, Avoca
W. of the town off the R752
(9) 6104 yards/***(not Sat)/F

Roy Perry SEVEN IRON Rosenstiel's

ELEGANT IRELAND

Glin Castle

The Irish have always had a reputation for providing a memorable welcome; as far back as 1683 Tadhg Rody described them as 'very much addicted to hospitality'. Imagine the delight of experiencing, not only the warmth and friendship of that period, but indeed, the very same houses it was extended from.

Elegant Ireland is literally the key to the history of one of the world's most fascinating countries. Through this most prestigious of tour operators it is possible to discover at first hand the wonders that lie behind the doors of some of the most beautifully preserved country houses, mansions and castles. By special arrangements they have made it possible for the discerning guest to live in such places, either by renting the entire property, or as part of a party of select house guests.

This is the 'Unknown Ireland' - that Ireland that many have heard of, yet few have seen. Visitors are taken away from the beaten tourist tracks and familiar well-trodden sights to an altogether different world of custom-made itineraries, gaining admission into private places not normally open to the visitor, and provided with accomodation in historic castles, gracious mansions and spreading country estates; the homes of writers, academics, lords and ladies. For example, take some time to live the prominent history of Glin Castle, home to the Knight of Glin since the twelfth century; or choose to be the personal guest of the Earl of Inchiquin, direct descendant of the eleventh century King Brian Boru.

Naturally the standard of living and comfort they offer embrace a dimension which can only be experienced to be appreciated. Decorations are family heirlooms, now valuable antiques, paintings, furniture with a personal history, and the collections of books that symbolise this country of folklore and legend, storytellers and poets.

Birr Castle

ELEGANT IRELAND

Thomond House

Ross Castle

The history of the country embraces anyone who sets foot on it, but it is only certain visitors who may gain the insight of the expert guides - doubling as chauffeurs - the carefully arranged tours, the specialist lectures, and of course, access to houses, gardens and art collections not available to the general public. Unique, special-interest tours can be arranged; architecture, gardens, history, literature, folklore and modern Ireland are just a few of the more popular. Naturally, everything is organised for you, all you have to do is arrive, leisurely unpack and change before a pre-dinner drink with your amiable and talkative host.

Lisnavagh

It would be a crime in such a country not to sample the many sporting delights for which it is so justly famous. Elegant Ireland can arrange specialised packages for the country sportsman, or indeed combine a business and sporting break for the corporate market. For the golfer, Ireland is a paradise. There are more courses per square mile here than anywhere else in the world, as such it is virtually impossible to get more than 25 miles from one. The play is year round, and the breath-taking scenery of rolling Atlantic coastline, or the wide open lakes and rivers of the inland courses can only enhance your game. Relax while we arrange bookings and tee-off times to suit your schedule. For the fisherman Ireland boasts some of Europe's cleanest water, spread over 14,000km of rivers feeding over 4000 lakes. Almost every stream has a resident stock of brown trout, while the salmon you catch are wild from the Atlantic. As for the sailor, the famous American writer Don Steel puts it in perspective: 'This place is astonishing. Despite its long sailing tradition, it's still the new European cruising ground, uncrowded, unspoilt and welcoming, with great sailing off a wonderful coast.' Indeed, with almost 6,000 km of coastline to be challenged, not to mention the choice of inland waters, sailing in Ireland is a truly memorable experience. If shooting is your game, then again Ireland has a quite incredible selection, from driven pheasant, duck, snipe and woodcock, rough and walk-up shooting with ghillie and dog, to pigeon shooting and hunting fallow deer. Some of the properties you may stay in have their own sporting facilities on private estates, or if not, they are easily arranged locally.

Whether it be a dinner for six or a week-end for sixty, a private party in some of the most magnificent surroundings in the world, or a murder mystery week-end in the country, the choice is entirely yours. One thing is certain though, whatever you choose and wherever you decide to go, everything we do for you will be conducted with care and attention to detail and the backdrop of literally thousands of years of the vibrant magic and history that is Ireland.

Elegant Ireland
15 Harcourt Street
Dublin 2
Ireland
Tel: (01) 751632/751665
Fax: (01) 751012

IRELAND
GOURMET GOLF

CO CARLOW

BELMONT HOTEL,
Kilkenny Road, Carlow, Co. Carlow, Tel: (0503) 42002
Only three miles from Carlow, the Belmont is a popular establishment and possesses ten comfortable, ensuite bedrooms. The cuisine is worth a visit in its own right.

GARRYHILL,
Bagenalstown, Co. Carlow, Tel: (0503) 57652
A quaint farmhouse occupying a peaceful woodland setting, Garryhill is available for self-catering holidays. Mountain views provide many exhilarating walks.

CO CLARE

GREENBRIER INN,
Lahinch, Co. Clare, Tel: (065) 81242
The world-famous links of Lahinch is within a driver distance of the Greenbrier. Rooms with ensuite facilities will be very welcome after a day on the punishing links.

HALPINS HOTEL,
2 Erin Street, Kilkee, Co. Clare, Tel: (065) 56032
A family-run seaside hotel, Halpin's is constantly seeking to promote personal attention, combined with a relaxing ambience. Entertainment is regularly provided.

SHEEDYS SPA VIEW HOTEL,
Lisdoonvarna, Co. Clare, Tel: (065) 74026
This superb hotel offers sterling accommodation at moderate prices. Both hotel and restaurant are award winning and highly recommended, ensuring the regular return of many guests. For the more energetic, a tennis court is provided.

BUNRATTY LODGE,
Bunratty, Tel: (061) 72402
Bunratty Lodge is an elegant neo-Georgian house that can be reached by the road that cuts between Bunratty Castle and Durty Nelly's. All six rooms have private facilities, orthopaedic beds and colour TV.

SANCTA MARIA HOTEL,
Lahinch, Co. Clare, Tel: (065) 81041
The Sancta Maria possesses an enviable reputation for cuisine that is prepared using only the finest and freshest foods. That is only half the story however, and accommodation is of an equally high calibre.

CO CORK

ARBUTUS LODGE,
Montenotte, Cork, Co. Cork, Tel: (021) 501237
This highly-recommended hotel occupies a splendid setting, overlooking the city of Cork. The hotel is enhanced by an acclaimed restaurant.

MOUNT CARMEL,
Ballyvergan, Cork Road, Co. Cork, Tel: (024) 92542
Seaside and countryside can both be explored in abundance from this popular retreat. Bedrooms are spacious and even include electric blankets, just in case the climate does not live up to its warm reputation.

HILLSIDE,
Cahirkeem, Eyeries, Bantry, Tel: (027) 74005
Hillside is a thirty acre working farm, and visitors are more than welcome to join in with milking and walking cattle etc. Disabled guests can be specially catered for.

KILLEENLEIGH,
Glandore, Co. Cork, Tel: (028) 33103
Killeenleigh is an eighteenth century farmhouse that has been converted into a friendly country home. The picturesque and bustling harbour of Glandore is close by and birdwatchers and artists will also find plenty to keep them occupied.

CO DONEGAL

DERRYBEG HOTEL,
Cotteen, Derrybeg, Co. Donegal, Tel: (075) 31005
This is a family-run hotel and the difference is revealed in friendly service, warm hospitality and home cooking that will surely bring you back for a second visit (and helping!).

MANOR HOUSE,
Rosnowlagh, Co. Donegal, Tel: (072) 51477
Romantically situated between Swan Lake and the Atlantic, Manor House is an immaculate and engaging guesthouse. Bedrooms are spotlessly clean and all have ensuite facilities.

CO DUBLIN

THE DUNES HOTEL,
Donabate, Co. Dublin, Tel: (01) 436111
Only six miles from Dublin Airport, the Dunes is a haven for golf enthusiasts with four courses – the Island, Beaverstown, Donabate and Corballis – all ready to welcome visitors.

ELEGANT IRELAND,
15 Harcourt Street, Dublin 2, Tel: (01) 751632/751665
Elegant Ireland is an incoming Tour Operator that can offer a wide range of services to interested clients. In addition to securing all travel and accommodation arrangements, possibilities include Garden Tours, Stately Home Tours, Art Tours and Golf Tours – a comprehensive service indeed.

LANSDOWNE HOTEL
27 Pembroke Road, Dublin 4, Tel: (01) 682522
Georgian Dublin is a splendid sight and the Lansdowne Hotel is set right in its heart. A wealth of amenities are within easy reach including the Royal Dublin Society, Lansdowne Rugby Club and a multiplicity of shops.

MONT CLARE HOTEL,
Merrion Square, Dublin 2, Tel: (01) 616799
Close to Trinity College, in the very heart of Dublin City, Mont Clare Hotel is within walking distance of Grafton Street, DART, Dail Eireann Art Gallery and Museum. Needless to say, there are also plenty of distinguished bars in the vicinity.

SEA VIEW GUESTHOUSE,
Strand Road, Portmarnock, Co. Dublin, Tel: (01) 462242
Overlooking Dublin Bay, this warm, friendly guesthouse is an ideal base for Dublin Airport, Malahide Castle and the Dublin Mountains. A hair salon and sun bed in the hotel mean that good weather is not even a necessity!

CO GALWAY

ARD EINNE,
Cill Einne, Aran Islands, Inishmore, Co. Galway, Tel: (099) 61126
Some of Ireland's wildest and most spectacular scenery can be absorbed from this relaxing guesthouse. Bicycle and walking tours can be arranged for those who wish to take advantage of this glorious countryside.

IRELAND
GOURMET GOLF

ROCKLAND HOTEL,
The Promenade, Salthill, Co. Galway, Tel: (091) 22111
Fourteen sumptuous bedrooms feature ensuite facilities, direct dial telephone, satellite TV and coffee/tea making facilities. As if all that wasn't sufficient, the beach is only a few hundred yards away.

ERRISEASK HOUSE HOTEL,
Ballyconneely, Connemara, Co. Galway, Tel: (095) 23553
Breathtaking scenery and private beaches prove sufficeient to attract discerning holidaymakers to a beautiful corner of Ireland. The renowned Connemara golf course is but a few miles away.

CO KERRY

LINDEN HOUSE,
New Road, Killarney, Co. Kerry, Tel: (064) 31379
Set in a residential area away from the thronging town centre, Linden House is a family run guesthouse, renowned for its excellent and nutritious cuisine prepared by the owner/chef.

ST MARTINS,
Oakpark Road, Tralee, Co. Kerry, Tel: (066) 25004
As well as offering comfortable accommodation, St Martin's is conveniently situated for the bus/rail station and sports centre. The Championship golf course is also within easy reach.

EAGLE LODGE,
Ballybunion, Tel: (068) 27224
Eagle Lodge offers a great deal more than the average guesthouse. All bedrooms have private bathrooms and are centrally heated. The restaurant is renowned for its cuisine with a range of Table d'Hote and A la carte menus

HILLCREST,
Mountway, Ballyheigue, Tel: (066) 33306
Ballyheigue is a renowned family resort, whose shoreline and countryside provide walks and exploration for the energetic visitor. Hillcrest is a spacious bungalow that is convenient for all local amenities.

DOYLE'S SEAFOOD BAR AND TOWNHOUSE,
John Street, Dingle, Tel: (0660) 51174
Eight generously sized bedrooms await the lucky visitor at this popular townhouse. Moreover, every bedroom comes complete with private bathroom, direct-dial telephone and television.

CO KILDARE

HARBOUR VIEW,
The Harbour, Naas, Co. Kildare, Tel: (045) 79145
Service with a genuine smile are impressive trademarks of this family run guesthouse. Punchestown, the Curragh and Mondello are within easy reach.

CO. KILKENNY

NEWPARK HOTEL,
Castlecomer Road, Kilkenny, Co. Kilkenny, Tel: (056) 22122
The new and majestic Mt. Juliet complex is only a short drive from this popular hotel. The Newpark itself has more than enough to keep visitors happy, including an impressive leisure centre.

CO LAOIS

PARK HOUSE,
Stradbally, Portlaoise, Co. Laois, Tel: (0502) 25147
This award winning farmhouse accommodation, only an hour's drive from Dublin is actually a working tillage farm. Fresh farm produce is used to prepare meals that have to be seen to be believed.

CO LEITRIM

GORTMOR,
Lismakeegan, Carrick-on-Shannon, Co. Leitrim, Tel: (078) 20489
Only two miles from the main Dublin road, Gortmor House makes a convenient base for the many pleasures of Co. Leitrim. The standard of cooking is unlikely to hasten your departure!

RIVERSDALE,
Ballinamore, Co. Leitrim, Tel: (078) 44122
A glance at a reasonable tariff does not anticipate quite excellent facilities, including squash and sauna. The surrounding countryside is worthy of exploring and exploring.

CO LIMERICK

TUOGH-VILLA,
Askeaton Road, Adare, Tel: (061) 396432
This pleasant bungalow enjoys a peaceful setting, only a mile from the beautiful village of Adare. Golf, fishing and Curraghchase Forest Park figure among the nearby attractions.

FOUR SEASONS,
Ballyneety, Limerick, Tel: (061) 351365
This friendly, family run guesthouse will find favour with all the family – features include a children's playground, tea/coffee making facilities, board games and a free baby-sitting service. Lough Gur, the Hunt Museum and Bunratty Folk Park will provide endless hours of amusement.

WOODFIELD HOUSE HOTEL,
Ennis Road, Limerick, Tel: (061) 53023
Only a mile from Limerick City, Woodfield House Hotel is a family run establishment that has recently undergone extensive refurbishment. An excellent Steak House, lounge bars, sun lounges and a beer garden all ensure ample refreshment.

CO LOUTH

ORLEY HOUSE,
25 Brayanstown, Drogheda, Co. Louth, Tel: (041) 36019
A wide variety of local amenities can be found close to this splendid guesthouse. The bus/rail station, beach, golf, fishing and horse riding are among many attractions sure to keep everyone happy.

CO MAYO

MASK VIEW,
Treen, Tourmakeady, Co. Mayo, Tel: (092) 44021
With Lough Mask as an imposing and spectacular backdrop, Mask View provides modest, tasteful bedrooms and typically warm Irish hospitality.

SEASIDE HOUSE,
Dooega, Achill Island, Co. Mayo, Tel: (098) 45116
Only a short walk from the beach, this popular guesthouse is also convenient for sea angling and a nearby Art Gallery. Family holidays are a particular speciality.

TRAVELLERS FRIEND HOTEL,
Westport Road, Castlebar, Co. Mayo, Tel: (094) 23111
The name of this hotel is quite indicative of the atmosphere that prevails inside. Excellent restaurants and bars complement the historic John Moore Lounge and open fire foyer.

CO MEATH

HAMWOOD,
Dunboyne, Co. Meath, Tel (01) 255210
Hamwood was built in 1760 and has been lived in by the Hamilton family ever since. It is a very pleasant and comfortable house for guests and possesses beautiful gardens. Racing, golf and fishing are all nearby attractions.

CO SLIGO

TARA,
Ballina Road, Enniscrone, Co. Sligo, Tel: (096) 36398
The acclaimed championship golf course of Enniscrone ensures that this guesthouse receives plenty of attention. Organic produce and wonderful home cooking are two other reasons for recommending it.

CO TIPPERARY

BALLYCORMAC HOUSE,
Aglish, Borrisokane, Co. Tipperary, Tel: (067) 21129
Mouth watering Cordon Bleu food is served here using home-grown organic vegetables. All of the well-appointed bedrooms are ensuite.

BANSHA CASTLE,
Bansha, Co. Tipperary, Tel: (062) 54187
Dating from the nineteenth century and with a secluded woodland setting, Bansha House provides excellent accommodation at reasonable rates. Golf, fishing and walking are popular pursuits available in the locality.

CURRAGHBAWN HOUSE,
Lake Drive, Newtown, Nenagh, Tel: (067) 23226
A spacious residence set in a rural location, Curraghbawn House can provide visitors with a whole array of facilities and amenities. Fishing, golf, windsurfing, shooting and clay pigeon shooting can all be arranged with the minimum of fuss.

THE LOOKOUT,
Lake Drive, Portroe, Tel: (067) 23324
The magnificent setting of Lough Derg makes this comfortable guesthouse an attractive base for the glorious surrounding countryside. A relaxed and friendly atmosphere adds to the aura of well being.

CO WATERFORD

BYRON LODGE,
Ardmore, Co. Waterford, Tel: (024) 94157
Overlooking an immaculate beach, Byron Lodge offers open fires and superb seafood. Local places of interest include the fishing village of Ardmore and a Monastic Settlement Round Tower.

HANORAS COTTAGE,
Nire Valley, Ballymacarberry, Co. Waterford, Tel: (052) 36134
This converted ancestral cottage is beautifully set among woods and mountain splendour. Golf, walking, riding and fishing are all available locally.

HAVEN HOTEL,
Dunmore East, Co. Waterford, Tel: (051) 83150
Family owned and run, Haven Hotel is set in attractive woodland and overlooks the cliffs and sea beyond. Squash, tennis, golf and windsurfing are available locally.

CO WESTMEATH

GLENMORE HOUSE
Dublin Road, Mullingar, Tel: (044) 48905
A perfect 19th hole for the scenic parkland golf Course at Mullingar. Glenmore is a beautifully furnished Georgian guesthouse set in 4 acres of lawns and woodlands. What's more the owners are a real golfing family!

CO WEXFORD

WOODLANDS HOUSE,
Killinierin, Gorey, Co. Wexford, Tel: (0402) 37125
Accommodation and cuisine can both be highly recommended at this pleasant farmhouse. A resident pony will keep the children amused; if not, the beach is only ten minutes away.

CRANE FARM,
Ferns, Tel: (054) 33476
All the facilities that guests expect of high calibre farmhouse accommodation are present at Crane Farm. In addition, Co. Wexford is absolutely steeped in history, not least of which Crane Farm itself, landing site of the first plane to cross the Irish sea, in 1912.

DEVEREUX HOTEL,
Wexford Road, Rosslare Harbour, Co. Wexford, Tel: (053) 33216
The proximity of this hotel to Rosslare Ferry Port makes it an ideal first or last stop in Ireland. The steak and seafood delights of the Le Coquille Restaurant will make it all the more difficult to leave.

CO WICKLOW

ABHAINN MOR HOUSE,
Corballis, Rathdrum, Co. Wicklow, Tel: (0404) 46330
This acclaimed and highly popular establishment provides ensuite bedrooms and extensive conveniences. A tennis court offers an outdoor alternative to the local beaches.

BALLYKNOCKEN HOUSE,
Glenealy, Ashford, Co. Wicklow, Tel: (0404) 44627
Ballyknocken House offers bedrooms that are tastefully and elegantly furnished. Mount Usher Gardens, providing a wealth of colour, are only three miles distant.

FOLLOWING THE FAIRWAYS
COLLECTION OF LIMITED EDITION PRINTS

Please note the illustrations are for guidance only.
Sizes are not to a uniform scale throughout the list.
Sizes quoted are paper sizes unless otherwise quoted.
All prints are limited editions unless othewise quoted.

GLENEAGLES   28″ × 21¾ ″

ST. ANDREWS   28″ × 21¾ ″

TURNBERRY   28″ × 21¾ ″

ROYAL TROON   28″ × 21¾ ″

These limited editon prints by Robert Turnbull are available as a set of four.

WHAT SHALL I TAKE FOR THIS?   16″ × 12″

RULE XIII   12″ × 16″

THE ONLY WAY   16″ × 12″

RULE XVIII   12″ × 16″

RULE XXIII   12″ × 16″

Prints by Charles Crombie   **Rules by Charles Crombie**

THE FIRST, KING'S COURSE
by Robert Wade   19″ × 27″

SEVEN IRON by Roy Perry   20″ × 30″

THE CADDIE
by Robert Wade   19″ × 27″

TO HALVE THE MATCH by Roy Perry 20″ × 30″

THE LUCKY DOG by Victor Venner   12″ × 16″

BALLESTEROS' HOLE, THE BELFRY
by Bill Waugh   10 ¾″ × 16″

ADRESSING THE BALL by Victor Venner   12″ × 16″

AUGUSTA NATIONAL,16th HOLE
by Bill Waugh   16 ¼″ × 24 ¼″

ORDER FORM

	Edition	Price (£)	Qty.	Cost
Turnberry	500	75		
St. Andrews	500	75		
Gleneagles	500	75		
Royal Troon	500	75		
Set of 4	N/A	275		
What shall I take for this?	N/A	10		
The Only Way	N/A	10		
Rule XIII	N/A	10		
Rule XVIII	N/A	10		
Rule XXIII	N/A	10		
The First, Kings Course	600	70		
The Caddie	600	70		
The Lucky Dog	N/A	13		
Addressing the Ball	N/A	13		
Seven Iron	N/A	15		
To Halve the Match	N/A	15		
Ballesteros Hole, The Belfry	N/A	on application		
Augusta National, 16th Hole	850	124		
Postage and Packing				£5.00
			TOTAL	

All prints are individually signed, limited editions unless otherwise stated.

I enclose a cheque for the sum of £.............................. payable to Kensington West Productions

Please debit my: Access / Visa / Amex / Diners Card by the sum of £.....................................

No. ☐☐☐☐☐☐☐☐☐☐☐☐

Name ....

Address ....

Tel. No. .... Signature ....

All orders should be sent to:
Kensington West Productions Ltd., 338 Old York Road, Wandsworth, London SW18 1SS.
Alternatively, telephone your order on 081-877 9394

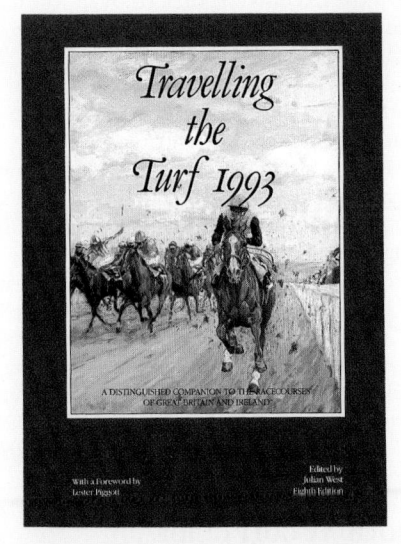

THE KENSINGTON WEST COLLECTION

Kensington West Productions Ltd publish a range of fine sporting and leisure publications, designed to suit the interest and pocket of every leisure enthusiast. Each book is lavishly illustrated and contains extensive and up-to-date information on a range of activities, together with invaluable advice on nearby places of repute (and occasionally of ill-repute!) to eat and stay. Each edition makes a beautiful addition to any library and will provide endless informative pleasure as both a guidebook and an enjoyable reading experience. They also make superb presents. Make your selection from the following titles.

TRAVELLING THE TURF (eighth edition).

The complete guide to the racecourses of Great Britain and Ireland. Travelling the Turf incorporates colour maps, extensive illustrations, many previously unpublished racing scenes with illuminating and witty analysis of every aspect of the racing scene. Comprehensive features on hotels, restaurants, pubs and Bed & Breakfasts are backed up with points and places of interest for the non-racegoer. A powerful resume of the worlds most stylish sport. With a foreword by the sports renowned figure **Lester Piggott**.

FOLLOWING THE FAIRWAYS (sixth edition)

The complete guide to the golf courses of Great Britain and Ireland. Following the Fairways contains an exhaustive directory of over 2,000 golf courses and in-depth features on one hundred of the nations most celebrated tests. The guide is superbly illustrated throughout with many rare examples of golfing art and contemporary golfing landscapes. Some 2,000 practical ideas for places to stay and entertainment off the course make this book a priceless guide for every golfer. An authoritative guide to the worlds fastest growing leisure pursuit. With a foreword by one of the games most respected personalities, **Peter Alliss**.

FISHING FORAYS (second edition)

This latest addition to the Kensington collection embraces in-depth appraisals of famous beats, maps of lochs, lakes and rivers with helpful tips for beginners to the sport on where to fish. Contacts on particular waters make the book a first class investment and provide a short cut to finding how, when and where to fish the celebrated rivers of Britain and Ireland. The usual comprehensive guide to where to stay and eat out combines to make Fishing Forays a treasured addition to any

fisherman's library. An engaging summary of one of the worlds most exclusive sports. A jovial foreword by **Chris Tarrant** adds to the originality and vitality of this distinguished guide.

THE HERITAGE OF GREAT BRITAIN AND IRELAND (second edition)

The cream of Britain and Ireland's stately homes, gardens, castles and country houses make this a lavish and not to be missed publication. Over one hundred of our most regal buildings are described in an informative, graphic and lively style, complemented by illustrations and photographs of a variety of paintings and memorabilia from the houses themselves. Additional coverage is given to over 1000 alternative historical sites, with essential recommendations of where to stay and eat out nearby. A beautifully illustrated and practical guide to one of the worlds most enviable collections. A delightfully written foreword by **Magnus Magnusson** adds further weight to this treasured tome.

THE HOLIDAY GOLF GUIDE

Of the plethora of books offering advice on where to golf throughout the world, the Holiday Golf Guide is undoubtedly the most authoritative and the most colourfully presented. An almost unbelievable amount of information is packed into this comprehensive handbook, and lavish photography is sure to make many of the destinations an irresistible attraction. Golfing information is backed up with all manner of enticements for non-golfing companions. The best guide to the best courses all over the world.

THE KENSINGTON COLLECTION (first edition)

As people continue to demand more for their money so hoteliers have created all manner of short breaks to catch the imagination. The Kensington Collection has been produced to reflect this demand. It earmarks all manner of information from prices to what activities each hotel has to offer. Whether you enjoy a stroll in the country or a ride in a hot air balloon, you'll find something to enjoy. Clearly laid out and thoroughly researched the book provides you with umpteen ideas to get away from it all or have a hell of a good time! Midweek breaks and bargain short holidays are listed with authoritative articles on a range of fascinating and original ideas for how to get that little bit more for your money.

ORDER FORM

	Softback	Hardback	Quantity	Value
Travelling the Turf 1993	14.95 1 871 349 01 X	15.95 1 871 349 06 0		
Following the Fairways 1993	14.95 1 871 349 11 7	15.95 1 871 349 16 8		
Fishing Forays 1993	14.95 1 871 349 21 4	15.95 1 871 349 26 5		
The Heritage of Great Britain and Ireland 1993	14.95 1 871 349 31 1	15.95 1 871 349 36 2		
The Kensington Collection 1993	12.95 1 871 349 41 9	14.95 1 871 349 46 X		
The Holiday Golf Guide	12.95 1 871 349 45 1	—		

Please send your order to: Kensington West Productions Ltd., 338 Old York Road, Wandsworth, London SW18 1SS, Tel: 081 877 9394 Fax: 081 870 4270
Cheque (payable to KWP Ltd.) / Access / Visa / AMEX / Diners

Card no. _____ Expiry date _____

Name: _____ Address: _____